About the Editor

Nicolás Kanellos has been professor at the University of Houston since 1980. He is founding publisher of the noted Hispanic literary journal, *The Americas Review* (formerly *Revista Chicano-Riqueña*) and the nation's oldest and esteemed Hispanic publishing house, Arte Público Press.

Recognized for his scholarly achievements, Dr. Kanellos is the recipient of a 1990 American Book Award, a 1989 award from the Texas Association of Chicanos in Higher Education, the 1988 Hispanic Heritage Award for Literature presented by the White House, as well as various fellowships and other recognitions. His monograph, *A History of Hispanic Theater in the United States: Origins to 1940* (1990), received three book awards, including that of the Southwest Council on Latin American Studies.

Among his other books are the *Biographical Dictionary of Hispanic Literature of the United States* (1989), *Mexican American Theater Legacy and Reality* (1987), and *Chronology of Hispanic-American History from Pre-Columbian Times to the Present* (1995).

Dr. Kanellos is the director of a major national research program, Recovering the Hispanic Literary Heritage of the United States, whose objective is to identify, preserve, study, and make accessible tens of thousands of literary documents of those regions that have become the United States from the colonial period to 1960. In 1994, President Bill Clinton appointed Dr. Kanellos to the National Council for the Humanities.

THE HISPANIC
AMERICAN
ALMANAC

Advisors

Dr. Edna Acosta-Belén, *Director, Center for Caribbean and Latin American Studies, University of Albany*

Dr. Rodolfo Cortina, *Director. Bibliographic Database, Recovering the U.S. Hispanic Literary Heritage Project, and Professor of Spanish, Florida International University*

Dr. Rodolfo de la Garza, *Professor of Political Science, University of Texas at Austin*

Dr. Ricardo Fernández, *President, Lehman College, City University of New York*

Dr. Arturo Madrid, *Director, Tomás Rivera Center, Claremont, California*

Dr. Michael Olivas, *Associate Dean of Law and Director of the Institute for Higher Education Law and Governance, University of Houston*

Contributors

Robert R. Alvarez, *Department of Anthropology, Arizona State University*

Ramiro Burr, *Music Critic, Houston Chronicle*

Gilbert Paul Carrasco, *School of Law, Villanova University*

Lynn E. Cortina, *Coordinator, Recovering the U.S. Hispanic Literary Heritage Project*

José Fernández, *Department of Foreign Language, University of Central Florida*

Gary D. Keller, *Bilingual Review Press, Arizona State University*

Thomas Leonard, *Department of History, Philosophy, and Religious Studies, University of North Florida*

John M. Lipski, *Department of Modern Languages, University of Florida*

Tatcho Mindiola, *Mexican American Studies Program, University of Houston*

Silvia Novo Pena, *Department of English and Foreign Languages, Texas Southern University*

Manuel Peña, *Foreign Languages, California State University, Fresno*

Jacinto Quirarte, *College of Fine and Applied Arts, University of Texas, San Antonio*

F. Arturo Rosales, *Department of History, Arizona State University*

Guadalupe San Miguel, *History Department, University of Houston*

Federico Subervi, *Department of Radio-Television-Film, University of Texas, Austin*

Dennis Valdez, *Chicano Studies Program, University of Minnesota*

Jude Valdez, *College of Business, University of Texas, San Antonio*

Reference Library of

HISPANIC AMERICA

THE HISPANIC AMERICAN ALMANAC

VOLUME

II

Nicholás Kanellos,

editor

**Distributed by
Afro American Press
African American Publications
and Proteus Enterprises**

Nicolás Kanellos, *Editor*

The Reference Library of Hispanic America/edited by Nicolás Kanellos
ISBN 0-7876-1549-8

This book is printed on acid-free paper that meets the minimum requirements of American National Standard for Information Sciences-Permanence Paper for Printed Library Materials, ANSI Z39.48-1984

Printed in the United States of America

10 9 8 7 6 5 4 3 2

Ofrezco esta labor a mi hijo adorado, Miguel José Pérez Kanellos, con la esperanza de que él, su generación y las que siguen puedan tener plena consciencia de su historia, sus artes, sus tradiciones y acceso a información básica acerca de su gente. Que el pueblo hispano y, particularmente los estudiantes, jamás vuelvan a carecer de básicos recursos informativos en sus bibliotecas y en sus escuelas. Que el pueblo americano en general tenga también acceso y plena conciencia de una parte importante—la contribución hispana—de la identidad nacional estadounidense y la abrace como suya.

I offer this labor of love to my adored son, Miguel José Pérez Kanellos, in hope that he, his generation, and those that follow will be able to possess a complete awareness of their history, arts, and traditions, and have access to basic information about their people. May Hispanic Americans of the United States, and especially Hispanic students, never again be impoverished of basic informational resources in their libraries and schools. May the American people in general have access to and a full awareness of an important part—the Hispanic contribution—of the national identity of the United States and embrace it as theirs.

N.K.

Contents

Volume 1

Acknowledgments xiii
Preface xv
Introduction xvii
Chronology xix

1 • A Historical Overview 1
Spanish Legacy 1
The Indigenous Caribbean Populations 4
The Indigenous Mexican Population 7
The Spaniards in the Valley of Mexico 11
Movement to the North 12
Anglo Encroachment into the
  Mexican North 19
Mexicans Under U.S. Rule 23
Africa and the Making of Society in
  Cuba and Puerto Rico 25
Independence of Cuba and Puerto Rico 28
Early Mexican Immigration to the
  United States 30
The Mexican Revolution and Immigration
  to the United States 34
The "Mexico Lindo" Generation 36
Depression, Repatriation, and Acculturation . . 38
World War II and the Mexican American
  Generation 39
From Chicanos to Hispanics 39
Migration to the United States from
  Puerto Rico 40
Early Settlement of Puerto Ricans in
  the United States 42
The Great Migration 43
Early Cuban Immigration to the
  United States 45
The Revolution of Fidel Castro and
  Cuban Immigration 46
Hispanic Identity in the United States 51

2 • Spanish Explorers and Colonizers 53
Native American Cultures 53
The Age of Exploration: The Caribbean,
  Mexico, and Florida 57

Spanish Expeditions to Florida 59
Spanish Exploration and Colonization
  of the Southwest 69
Spanish Explorations to California 73

3 • Significant Documents 77
Cessation of Louisiana 77
Cessation of Louisiana: Financial
  Arrangement 79
The Monroe Doctrine 80
Peace, Friendship, Limits, and Settlement:
  Treaty of Guadalupe Hidalgo 1848 86
Boundaries: Gadsden Treaty 1853 94
Our America by José Marti 96
Treaty of Peace (Treaty of Paris) 1898 100
Relations with Cuba 103
The "Hay-Herran" Treaty, January 1903 105
The "Hay-Bunau-Varilla Convention,"
  November 1903 111
Treaty of Relations between the
  United States and Cuba, 1934 116
Constitutional Convention of Puerto Rico . . . 117
Resolutions Approved by the Constitutional
  Convention Relating to the Constitution of
  the Commonwealth of Puerto Rico 130
The North American Free Trade
  Agreement (NAFTA) 131

4 • Historic Landmarks 133
Alabama 133
Arizona 133
California 134
Florida 140
Georgia 140
Louisiana 140
New Mexico 141
Panama Canal Zone 143
Puerto Rico 143
Texas 143
Virgin Islands 147

5 • Relations with Spain and Spanish
America 149

x • Contents

Policy Foundations 149
Developing a Relationship: The Nineteenth
   Century 153
A Period of U.S. Dominance: 1903–1954 . . 159
Suppressing Communism: U.S.-Latin
   American Relations Since 1954 165

6 • Hispanics and Race **176**
Racial Ideas among the Spaniards 176
European Americans and the Racialization
   of Hispanics 179
The Hispanic "Race" Today: Self-Perceptions
   and Anglo Impressions 183

7 • Population Growth and Distribution . . . **185**
Census Bureau Statistics and the
   Hispanic Population 185
Demographics 187
Hispanic Diversity 191

8 • Language **195**
Variations of Spanish Spoken 195
English Usage Among Hispanics 202
Spanish in Business, the Media, and
   in Other Social Environments 203
Bilingualism and Code-Switching 206

9 • The Family **213**
The Institutions of the Hispanic Family 215
Puerto Ricans: Born in the United States 219
Dominicans 222
Cubans 225
Mexican Americans 228

10 • Women **235**
Hispanic Women in Society 235
Women Making History 238
Women Inscribe Their Identity 240
Selected Outstanding Hispanic Women 245

Appendix: Illustrations. A-1
Glossary A-9
General Bibliography A-13
Index A-17

Volume 2

Acknowledgments xiii
Preface xv
Introduction xvii
Chronology xix

11 • Religion **253**
The Beginnings 253
Instruments of Religious Conversion 254
Our Lady of Guadalupe and the Saints 256

Florida 258
New Mexico 259
Texas 260
Arizona 261
California 262
The Anglo Conquest 262
Developing a Pastoral Approach 263
A Search for Parity 264
Protestantism and Hispanics 264
Popular Religiosity 266
Beyond Orthodoxy 270

12 • Military **273**
U.S. Revolutionary War 273
Mexican War for Independence from
   Spain 274
Mexican-American War 274
U.S. Civil War 274
World War I 275
World War II 275
Conflicts in Korea and Vietnam 276
Outstanding Hispanics in the Military 277

13 • Law and Politics **285**
Origins of Hispanics in the United States . . . 285
The Development of U.S.
   Immigration Law 287
The Current Debate Over U.S.
   Immigration Law 289
The Legalization Program 290
Employment Discrimination 291
Police Brutality 291
Federal Legislation Affecting Hispanic
   Americans 292
Important Cases Affecting Hispanic
   Americans 293
Hispanics in the Legal Profession 294
Hispanics in the U.S. Judiciary 301
Presidential Appointment of Hispanics
   to the Courts 304
Hispanics in the Political Process 312
Hispanic Voting and the Voting Rights
   Act of 1965 312
Congressional Hispanic Caucus 314
Hispanics in Congress 314
Selected Prominent Hispanic Federal
   Officials 326
Prominent Hispanic Politicians in
   State Government 333
Prominent Hispanic Metropolitan Leaders . . 335
Legal and Political Organizations 337

14 • Business **343**
The Cattle and Livestock Industry 344
Early Merchants and Entrepreneurs 346
Twentieth-Century Immigration and
   Hispanic Business 348

Contents • xi

Hispanic-Owned Businesses Today 349
Hispanics in the Corporate World 357
Prominent Hispanics in Business 359

15 • Labor and Employment **365**
Hispanics in Organized Labor 369
Immigration and Migration 372
Hispanic Employment in Industry 377
Federal Employment Programs and Laws . . . 379
Youth Employment 386
Women's Employment 386
Government Programs 387
Income, Poverty, and Unemployment 388

16 • Education **391**
Education of Hispanics in the
    Spanish Period, 1540–1821 392
Education of Hispanics in the
    Mexican Period, 1821–1848 394
Education of Hispanics: The American
    Period in the Nineteenth Century,
    1850–1900 396
Education of Hispanics in the
    Twentieth Century 402

17 • Scholarship **413**

18 • Science **431**
A General Overview 431
Prominent Hispanic Scientists 434

19 • Literature **455**
The Colonial Period 455
The Nineteenth Century 455
The Early Twentieth Century 458
World War II to the Present 465
Outstanding Hispanic Literary Figures 484

Appendix: Illustrations A-1
Glossary A-9
General Bibliography A-13
Index A-17

Volume 3

Acknowledgments xiii
Preface xv
Introduction xvii
Chronology xix

20 • Art **507**
The Sources of Hispanic Art 507
Exploration, Settlement, and History
    of Hispanics in the United States 508
New Spaniards and Mexicans:
    1599 to 1848 508

Hispanics and Mexican Americans: 1848
    to the Present 515

Hispanic American Artists: 1920s
    through the 1950s 520
Hispanic American Artists: 1960s
    and 1970s 524
Hispanic American Artists: 1970s
    to the Present 527
Chicano Murals 537

21 • Theater **549**
Hispanic Theater in the United States:
    Origins to 1940 549
Post World War II to the Present 564
Outstanding Figures in Hispanic Theater . . . 573

22 • Film **587**
Depiction of Minority Groups in
    Early American Film 587
Conglomeration of the Film Industry and
    the Production Code 591
First Decades: The Bandido, Buffoon,
    Dark Lady, Caballero, and Gangster 593
Hispanics in Film during the 1930s
    and the Era of Social Consciousness 596
Decline of the Production Code, Emergence
    of the Civil Rights Movement, and
    New Developments in Film: 1960s and
    1970s 601
Hollywood Films Since 1980 608
The Emergence of U.S. Hispanic Films 612
Hispanics in Film: Future Directions 623
Outstanding Hispanics in the
    Film Industry 624

23 • Music **643**
The Corrido and Canción-Corrido 646
Música Norteña
    (The Mexican-Texan Conjunto) 651
The Mexican American Orquesta 654
Salsa 660
Latin Jazz/Rock 665
Musica Tropical 665
The Contemporary Music Scene 666
Selected Discography 669

24 • Media **671**
Treatment of Hispanics in Mainstream
    Media 671
Newspapers 671
Film 674
Television 676
Advertising 680
Hispanic-Oriented Print Media 681
Hispanic-Oriented Electronic Media 691

25 • Sports **721**
    Baseball 722
    Rodeo 725
    Other Sports 726
    Prominent Hispanic Athletes 726

26 • Organizations **747**

27 • Prominent Hispanics **757**

Appendix: Illustrations. A-1
Glossary A-9
General Bibliography A-13
Index A-17

Acknowledgments

My most sincere thanks to all the scholars who have contributed to this volume, for indulging me in my obsession and for producing such wonderfully researched and written chapters, despite the pressure I exerted on you for making deadlines and supplying illustrations and other materials. My thanks as well to my editors at Gale Research, especially Christine Nasso, Christine Hammes, and Rebecca Nelson, whose guiding hand was always characterized by a gentle touch, whose advice was always offered with compassion and understanding. I feel very fortunate to have become part of the Gale family.

Thanks also to my scholarly advisors, especially Dr. Michael Olivas, who assisted me greatly in contact contributors for this volume. My deepest appreciation and thanks to my assistant, Hilda Hinojosa, who helped organize, type, and maintain oral and written communications with the contributing scholars and with my editors. This, the largest project of my career as a scholar, was brought to press with her able, efficient, and enthusiastic support.

And from my wife, Cristelia Pérez, and my son Miguel, I beg their forgiveness for the months that I spent communicating more with my computer screen than with them. Without Crissy's love, support, and understanding, this project would never have gotten off the ground, much less seen the light of day. Thank you; I love you.

Nicolás Kanellos

Preface

Reference Library of Hispanic America is the research product of a national team of outstanding scholars who unanimously have invested their time, energy, and genius to create the first, one-stop source for information about a broad range of important aspects of Hispanic life and culture in the United States. In their labors for *Reference Library of Hispanic America,* as well as in their day-to-day academic work, these scholars have actively engaged in the difficult task of working with original documentary sources, oral interviews, and field work to create a written record of Hispanic life where none existed before. These scholars are among the first in U.S. academic history to research, analyze, and preserve much of the information offered here. The scholars, and this work, are dedicated to filling an informational void relating to the history and culture of Hispanics of the United States—a void that has existed for too long in libraries and classrooms.

Prior to this publication, the scant information that has been available has quite often resulted from prejudice, propaganda, and folklore (quite often created to support the political and economic exploitation of Hispanics) covering a people conquered through war or imported for their labor, but who were never fully incorporated into the national psyche, the national identity, or the national storehouse of educational, economic, and political opportunities.

The vast majority of Hispanics in the United States are working-class citizens. Even those Hispanics in the professional class often share working-class backgrounds. The majority of Hispanics in the United States are *mestizos*—the product of mixed races and cultures, for the American Indian and African heritages have blended in every aspect of everyday life to produce today's Hispanic peoples of the Americas. The Spanish language, which introduced and reinforced a common culture and religion for these peoples for centuries, serves as a unifying factor for Hispanics, regardless of whether or not the individual speaks Spanish in daily life. These central factors—social class, ethnicity, linguistic-cultural background—unify the people and the information presented in *Reference Library of Hispanic America,* while also representing the tremendous diversity in racial, ethnic, geographic, and historical backgrounds that exist among Hispanics today.

The final result of this endeavor, we hope, is an easy-to-use compendium that presents an up-to-date overview of each subject, summarizing the known data and presenting new, original research. Moreover, *Reference Library of Hispanic America* has been written in a language and style that make it accessible to students and lay people. Illustrations—photographs, drawings, maps, and tables—bring the data to life. For further reading, subject-specific bibliographies (at the end of each chapter) as well as a general bibliography (on pages A-13 through A-15 of each volume) provide ready reference to other important sources. A complete index (on pages A-17 through A-37 of each volume) assists the reader in locating specific information. A glossary of Spanish terms (on pages A-9 through A-12 of each volume) has also been included to facilitate the reading of *Reference Library of Hispanic America.*

Nicolás Kanellos
University of Houston

of each subject, summarizing the known data and presenting new, original research. Moreover, the *Almanac* has been written in a language and style that make it accessible to students and lay people. Illustrations—photographs, drawings, maps, and tables—bring the data to life. For further reading, subject-specific bibliographies as well as a general bibliography provide ready reference to other important sources. A complete index assists the reader in locating specific information. A glossary of Spanish terms has also been included to facilitate the reading of the *Almanac*.

Nicolás Kanellos
University of Houston

Introduction

The Hispanic Population

With a Hispanic population of more than 22 million, the United States is among the largest Spanish-speaking countries in the world. According to the U.S. Census Bureau, the number of Hispanics in this country grew by 53 percent from 1980 to 1990. It is projected that by the year 2000, there will be almost 33 million Hispanics living in the United States.

Reference Library of Hispanic America, based on *The Hispanic American Almanac*, is a one-stop source for information on people of the United States whose ancestors, or they themselves, originated in Spain, the Spanish-speaking countries of South and Central America, Mexico, Puerto Rico, or Cuba.

While the Spanish language is a unifying factor among Hispanics, the diversity that exists within the Hispanic community continues to profoundly influence the collective American experience.

Scope and Contents

Reference Library of Hispanic America covers the range of Hispanic civilization and culture in the United States—providing a Chronology and Historical Overview, presenting the facts and figures in such chapters as Law and Politics, and Population Growth and Distribution, and discussing the arts, including Theater, Music, and Film.

Twenty-seven subject chapters were written by scholars in the field of Hispanic studies. These experts have drawn upon the body of their works and new research to compile their chapters, ending each with a list of references that can be used for further research into any of the subjects covered in *Reference Library of Hispanic America*. A bibliography at the back of *Reference Library of Hispanic America* provides sources for general information on Hispanics.

Concise biographical profiles in many chapters highlight Hispanics who have excelled in their fields of endeavor.

More than 450 illustrations, including photographs, drawings, tables, and figures, punctuate the discussion in each chapter.

The keyword index provides quick access to the contents of *Reference Library of Hispanic America* .

A glossary of Spanish terms facilitates the reading of the material.

Suggestions Are Welcome

The managing editor and publisher of *Reference Library of Hispanic America* appreciate all suggestions for additions and changes that will make future editions of this book as useful as possible. Please send comments to:

Reference Library of Hispanic America
Gale Research
835 Penobscot Building
Detroit, MI 48226

Chronology

50,00–10,000 B.C. Asian peoples migrate to North and South America and continue through 14,000 B.C.

c. 1000 B.C. Celts move into the Iberian Peninsula.

c. 500 B.C. Carthagenians establish themselves on the south coast of Spain.

200 B.C. The Iberian Peninsula becomes part of the Roman Empire.

350–850 A.D. Teotihuacan civilization flourishes in the central plateau of Mexico.

500 A.D. Vandals and Goths invade and conquer the peoples of the Iberian Peninsula.

700–900 A.D. Nahua peoples gain ascendancy in Mexico's central plateau.

711 A.D. The Moors invade and conquer the Visigothic kingdoms of the Iberian peninsula.

718–1492. The Reconquest of the Iberian peninsula takes place. Queen Isabella and King Ferdinand unify Spain through their marriage in 1469, and culminate the reconquest by defeating the last Moorish stronghold—Granada.

1000. Mayan civilization flourishes in the Yucatán peninsula and Guatemala.

1492. The Native American population of the Western Hemisphere may have reached between 35 to 45 million.

August 3, 1492. Christopher Columbus sails from the Spanish port of Palos de Moguer with three ships: the *Pinta,* the *Niña,* and the *Santa María,* his flagship.

October 12, 1492. The Spaniards land on an island called San Salvador—either present-day Watling Island or Samana Cay in the eastern Bahamas.

October 27, 1492. Columbus and his crews land on the northeastern shore of Cuba. Convinced that it is either Cipango or Cathay (in Asia), Columbus sends representatives to the Great Khan and his gold-domed cities, only to find impoverished Arawak living in bohíos.

November 1493. On his second voyage, Columbus discovers the Virgin Islands and Puerto Rico.

1494. After establishing Isabela on La Española (Hispaniola), the first permanent European settlement in the New World, Columbus sets sail and encounters Jamaica in the summer of 1494.

1508. Juan Ponce de León sails in a small caravel for Puerto Rico, where he establishes friendly relations with the native chieftain, Agueibana, who presents him with gold.

1509. Ponce de León is appointed governor of Puerto Rico.

1510. Diego Velázquez de Cuéllar departs with more than 300 men to conquer Cuba, and lands at Puerto Escondido. He is successful in defeating Arawak chieftain Hatuey's guerrilla raids.

1511. Velázquez is commissioned governor of Cuba. That same year the Cuban Indians are subjected to the *encomienda.*

1512. The Jeronymite Fathers in La Española decide to save the decimated Arawak population by gathering them into missions. Soon, missions spread like wildfire throughout the Spanish Empire.

1512. The Laws of Burgos. Promulgated by the Crown, the regulations are in response to the extremely harsh treatment that desperate colonists in the Caribbean imposed on natives through the deplorable *encomienda* system.

1513. Juan Ponce de León lands on the shores of Florida, exploring most of the coastal regions and some of the interior. At the time, there were an estimated 100,000 Native Americans living there.

September 27, 1514. Ponce de León is granted a patent, empowering him to colonize the island of Bimini and the island of Florida.

1515. Diego Velázquez becomes a virtual feudal lord of Cuba, and establishes what are to become Cuba's two largest cities, Santiago and Havana. He also directs the explorations of the Mexican Gulf Coast by Francisco Hernández de Córdoba and his nephew Juan de Grijalva. These expeditions betray the existence of civilizations in the interior of Mexico.

1518. Hernán Cortés sets out from Cuba to explore the mainland of Mexico in order to confirm reports of the existence of large, native civilizations in the interior.

1519. Alonso Alvarez de Pineda claims Texas for Spain.

1519. Hernán Cortés lands on the coast of Veracruz, Mexico.

1520. Explorer Alvarez de Pineda settles the question of Florida's geography: He proves it is not an island, but part of a vast continent.

1520s. Continuing their maritime adventures, the Spanish explorers cruise along the northern shore of the Gulf of Mexico, seeing Alabama, Mississippi, and Texas, and also sailing up the Atlantic coast to the Carolinas.

July 1, 1520. Under the leadership of Cuitlahuac, Moctezuma's brother, the Aztecs force the Spaniards out of Veracruz, just a year after the Spaniards had come into the city. The Spaniards called this *La noche triste* (The Sad Night). Moctezuma was stoned to death by his own people during this debacle.

1521. Cortés and his fellow Spaniards level the Aztec empire's city of Tenochtitlán, and begin building Mexico City on the same site.

1524. King Charles establishes the Council of the Indies, designed to oversee the administration of the colonies of the New World.

1536. Álvar Núñez Cabeza de Vaca returns to Mexico, indirectly involving Spain in exploring and colonizing what becomes the American Southwest: In Mexico City rumors were that Cabeza de Vaca and his companions had discovered cities laden with gold and silver, reviving the legend of the Seven Cities, which dated from the Moorish invasion of the Iberian Peninsula.

1537. Álvar Núñez Cabeza de Vaca returns to Spain and spends some three years writing *La relación,* an account of his wanderings in the North American continent. Published in 1542, *La relación* is a document of inestimable value because of the many first descriptions about the flora, fauna, and inhabitants of what was to become part of the United States.

May 18, 1539. From Havana, Cuba, Hernando de Soto sets sail for Florida; he eventually reaches as far north as present-day Georgia and South Carolina. His expedition later crosses the Great Smoky Mountains into Tennessee. From the mountains, the expedition heads southwest through present-day Georgia and Alabama.

1540. There are an estimated 66 Pueblo villages in the area of New Mexico, growing such crops as corn, beans, squash, and cotton.

April 23, 1541. Coronado sets out to reach Quivira—thought to be the legendary Cities of Gold—near present-day Great Bend, Kansas.

1542. The New Laws are proclaimed. They are designed to end Spain's feudal *encomienda.*

July 1542. Francisco Vásquez de Coronado returns to Mexico City with fewer than 100 of the 300 Spaniards that once formed part of his company.

September 28, 1542. Juan Rodríguez de Cabrillo, a Portuguese sailor commissioned by the viceroy to sail north of Mexico's west coast in search of treasures, enters what he describes as an excellent port—present-day San Diego, California.

1563. Saint Augustine, Florida, the earliest settlement in North America, is founded. It remains a possession of Spain until 1819.

1573. The Franciscan order arrives in Florida to establish missions, which a century later would extend along the east coast of North America, from Saint Augustine, Florida, to North Carolina. The Franciscans also establish a string of missions from Saint Augustine westward to present-day Tallahassee.

1580s. Diseases have all but wiped out the Indians of Puerto Rico. The flourishing of sugar production would now have to await the importation of large numbers of African slaves.

1598. Portuguese sailor Juan de Oñate begins the colonization of New Mexico.

1610. Santa Fe, New Mexico is founded.

1680. A Pueblo Indian named Popé leads a rebellion that forces the Spaniards and Christianized Indians out of northern New Mexico southward toward El Paso, Texas; they found Ysleta just north of El Paso.

1689. In part due to the need to provide foodstuffs and livestock to the rich mining regions in southern Mexico, the first royal *mercedes* (land grants) are granted to Spaniards in the fertile valleys of Monclova, in northern Mexico, just south of the present border.

May 1690. The first permanent Spanish settlement in Texas, San Francisco de los Tejas, near the Neches River, is established.

1691. Father Eusebio Kino, an untiring Jesuit missionary, makes the first inroads into Arizona. By 1700, Kino establishes a mission at San Xavier del Bac, near present-day Tucson; he later establishes other missions in Arizona: Nuestra Señora de los Dolores, Santa Gertrudis de Saric, San José de Imuris, Nuestra Señora de los Remedios, and San Cayetano de Tumacácori.

1693. Despite the fact that Texas is made a separate Spanish province with Don Domingo de Terán as its governor, the Spanish Crown orders its abandonment. Fear of Indian uprisings is the reason given by the Spanish authorities.

1716. Concerns about possible French encroachment prompt the Spaniards to reoccupy Texas in 1716 by establishing a series of missions, serving to both ward off the French and convert the natives to Catholicism. Of these missions, San Antonio, founded in 1718, is the most important and most prosperous.

1718. The San Antonio de Béjar and de Valero churches are built where the city of San Antonio is located today.

1760. After the Seven Years' War, which united France and Spain against Britain, France cedes claims to all lands west of the Mississippi in order not to give them to the victorious British. Overnight, New Spain's territory expands dramatically.

September 17, 1766. The presidio of San Francisco is founded, becoming Spain's northernmost frontier outpost.

1767. King Charles III expels the Jesuits from the Spanish Empire. This event opens the door for the Franciscan conquest of California. This conquest would never have been accomplished without Fray Junípero de Serra.

July 3, 1769. Fray Junípero de Serra establishes the first mission of Alta California in what would become San Diego. Serra eventually founded ten missions, traveled more than 10,000 miles, and converted close to 6,800 natives.

1770–1790. At least 50,000 African slaves are brought to Cuba to work in sugar production.

1774. Pedro de Garcés, a Spanish Franciscan missionary, founds the first overland route to California.

1776. In the American Revolution, because of their alliance with France, the Spaniards are able to obtain lands all the way to Florida.

1776. Anglo-Americans declare their independence from England, and 34 years later Hispanics proclaim their independence from Spain. The thirteen former British colonies come to be known as the United States of America in 1781, and the newly independent people of New Spain name their nation the Republic of Mexico.

1783. Spain regains Florida. In July 1821, the sun finally sets on Spanish Florida when the peninsula is purchased by the United States for $5 million.

1790s–1820s. The Apache threat subsides because of successful military tactics and negotiations on the part of local Spanish leaders, and Hispanic settlements begin to thrive in Pimería Alta (California). At one point as many as 1,000 Hispanics live in the Santa Cruz Valley.

1798. The Alien Act of 1798 grants the U.S. president the authority to expel any alien deemed dangerous. Opposed by President Thomas Jefferson, the Alien Act expires under its own terms in 1800.

1798. The Naturalization Act of 1798 raises the number of years, from 5 to 14, an immigrant has to live in the United States before becoming eligible for citizenship.

1800. Large, sprawling haciendas with huge herds of cattle and sheep characterize the economy and society of northeast New Spain.

1803. A powerful France under Napoleon Bonaparte acquires from Spain the Louisiana Territory, which was ceded during the Seven Years' War in the previous century. Napoleon, vying for dominance in Europe and in need of quick revenue, sells the vast territory to the United States, thus expanding the borders of the infant nation to connect directly with New Spain.

1804. To the consternation of Spain, President Thomas Jefferson funds the historical expedition of Lewis and Clark. Spain is obviously worried that the exploration is a prelude to the settlement of the territory by Anglos.

1810. In Mexico, Father Miguel Hidalgo y Castilla leads the revolt against Spain.

September 16, 1810. With the insurrection of Father Miguel Hidalgo y Castilla, the Spaniards withdraw their troops from the frontier presidios.

1819. When Andrew Jackson leads a U.S. military force into Florida, capturing two Spanish forts, Spain sells Florida to the United States for $5 million under the Onís Treaty.

1820. James Long leads a revolt, ostensibly as part of the Texas independence movement against the Spanish, but obviously he is acting as a filibusterer for his countrymen. Spain finally enters into deliberations with Moses Austin, a Catholic from Missouri, to settle Anglo-Catholic families in Texas.

1821. Mexico acquires its independence from Spain. By this time permanent colonies exist in coastal California, southern Arizona, south Texas, and in most of New Mexico and southern Colorado. The imprint of evolving Mexican culture is stamped on today's Southwest. Soon after Mexico gains independence, Anglo-American settlers begin to move into the Mexican territories of the present-day U.S. Southwest, especially Texas.

1823. Erasmo Seguín, a delegate to the national congress from Texas, persuades a willing U.S. Congress to pass a colonization act designed to bring even more Anglo settlers to Texas. Between 1824 and 1830, thousands of Anglo families enter east Texas, acquiring hundreds of thousands of free acres and buying land much cheaper than they could have in the United States. By 1830, Texas has 18,000 Anglo inhabitants and their African slaves, who number more than 2,000.

1823. Fray Junípero de Serra's death does not stop missionary activity in California. His fellow Franciscans establish another 12 missions. The famous mission trail of California includes the missions San Diego de Alcalá (1769), San Carlos de Monterey (1770), San Antonio de Padua (1771), San Gabriel Arcángel (1771), San Luis Obispo de Tolosa (1772), San Francisco de Asís (1776), San Juan Capistrano (1776), Santa Clara de Asís (1777), San Buenaventura (1782), Santa Bárbara (1786), La Purísima Concepción (1787), Santa Cruz (1791), San José de Guadalupe (1797), San Juan Bautista (1797), San Miguel Arcángel (1797), San Fernando Rey (1797), San Luis Rey (1798), Santa Inés (1804), San Rafael Arcángel (1817), and San Francisco Solano (1823).

1829. Slavery in Mexico is abolished by the new republican government that emerges after independence.

1836. The Anglo settlers declare the Republic of Texas independent of Mexico.

1836. The Texas constitution stipulates that all residents living in Texas at the time of the rebellion will acquire all the rights of citizens of the new republic, but if they had been disloyal, these rights are forfeited. Numerically superior Anglos force Mexicans off their property, and many cross the border to Mexico.

1840. To meet the wage-labor demands, 125,000 Chinese are brought to Cuba between 1840 and 1870 to work as cane cutters, build railroads in rural areas, and serve as domestics in the cities. Also, the influx of European immigrants, primarily from Spain, increases during that period. Newly arrived Spaniards become concentrated in the retail trades and operate small general stores called *bodegas*.

1845. Texas is officially annexed to the United States.

1846. The United States invades Mexico under the banner of Manifest Destiny. The Treaty of Guadalupe Hidalgo ends the Mexican War that same year. Under the treaty, half the land area of Mexico, including Texas, California, most of Arizona and New Mexico, and parts of Colorado, Utah, and Nevada, is ceded to the United States. The treaty gives Mexican nationals one year to choose U.S. or Mexican citizenship. Approximately 75,000 Hispanic people choose to remain in the United States and become citizens by conquest.

1848. The gold rush lures a flood of Anglo settlers to California, which becomes a state in 1850. Settlement in Arizona and New Mexico occurs at a slower pace, and they both become states in 1912.

1850. The Foreign Miners Tax, which levies a charge for anyone who is not a U.S. citizen, is enacted.

1851. Congress passes the California Land Act of 1851 to facilitate legalization of land belonging to Californios prior to the U.S. takeover.

1853. General Santa Anna returns to power as president of Mexico and, through the Gadsden Treaty, sells to the United States the region from Yuma (Arizona) along the Gila River to the Mesilla Valley (New Mexico).

1855. Vagrancy laws and so-called "greaser laws" prohibiting bear-baiting, bullfights, and cockfights are passed, clearly aimed at prohibiting the presence and customs of Californios.

1855. The Supreme Court rules that the Treaty of Guadalupe Hidalgo did not apply to Texas.

1857. Anglo businessmen attempt to run off Mexican teamsters in south Texas, violating the guarantees offered by the Treaty of Guadalupe Hidalgo.

1862. Homestead Act is passed in Congress, allowing squatters in the West to settle and claim vacant lands, often those owned by Mexicans.

April 27, 1867. Spanish troops stationed in Puerto Rico mutiny, and are executed by the colonial governor.

1868. Cubans leave for Europe and the United States in sizable numbers during Cuba's first major attempt at independence.

1868. Fourteenth Amendment to the U.S. Constitution is adopted, declaring all people of Hispanic origin born in the United States U.S. citizens.

September 17, 1868. A decree in Puerto Rico frees all children born of slaves after this date. In 1870, all slaves who are state property are freed, as are various other classes of slaves.

September 23, 1868. El Grito de Lares, the shout for Puerto Rican independence, takes place, with its disorganized insurrectionists easily defeated by the Spanish.

October 1868. Cuban rebels led by Carlos Manuel de Céspedes declare independence at Yara, in the eastern portion of the island.

1872. Puerto Rican representatives in Spain win equal civil rights for the colony.

1873. Slavery is finally abolished in Puerto Rico.

1875. The U.S. Supreme Court in *Henderson v. Mayor of New York* rules that power to regulate immigration is held solely by the federal government.

1878. The Ten Years' War, in which Spanish attempts to evict rebels from the eastern half of Cuba were unsuccessful, comes to an end with the signing of the Pact of El Zajón. The document promises amnesty for the insurgents and home rule, and provides freedom for the slaves that fought on the side of the rebels.

1880s. In Cuba, slavery is abolished by Spain in a gradual program that takes eight years. The influx of new European immigrants has made Cuba more heterogeneous, leading to the social diversity that is still apparent today.

1880s. Mexican immigration to the United States is stimulated by the advent of the railroad.

1892. The Partido Revolucionario Cubano is created to organize the Cuban and Puerto Rican independence movement.

1894. The Alianza Hispano Americana is founded in Tucson, Arizona, and quickly spreads throughout the Southwest.

1895. José Martí and his Cuban Revolutionary Party (PRC) open the final battle for independence.

1896. A Revolutionary Junta is formed in New York to lead the Puerto Rican independence movement.

1897. Spain grants Cuba and Puerto Rico autonomy and home rule.

April 1898. The USS *Maine* mysteriously explodes in Havana Harbor. And on April 28, President William McKinley declares war against Spain.

May 1888. The U.S. military invades San Juan in pursuit of Spaniards, and is welcomed by the cheering crowds, longing for independence.

December 10, 1898. Spain signs the Treaty of Paris, transferring Cuba, Puerto Rico, and the Philippines to the United States.

1900s. Brutality against Mexican Americans in the Southwest territories is commonplace. Lynching s and murders of Mexican Americans become so common in California and Texas that, in 1912, the Mexican ambassador formally protests the mistreatment and cites several brutal incidents that had recently taken place.

1900. The Foraker Act establishes a civilian government in Puerto Rico under U.S. dominance. The law allows for islanders to elect their own House of Representatives, but does not allow Puerto Rico a vote in Washington.

1901. The Federación Libre de los Trabajadores (Workers Labor Federation)—or FLT— becomes affiliated with the American Federation of Labor, which breaks from its policy of excluding non-whites.

1902. The Reclamation Act is passed, dispossessing many Hispanic Americans of their land.

1902. Cuba declares its independence from the United States.

1910. The Mexican Revolution begins, with hundreds of thousands of people fleeing north from Mexico and settling in the Southwest.

1911. In Mexico, the long dictatorship of Porfirio Díaz comes to an end when he is forced to resign in a revolt led by Francisco Madero.

1913. Victoriano Huerta deposes Francisco Madero, becoming provisional president of Mexico.

1914. President Woodrow Wilson orders the invasion of Veracruz in an effort to depose Victoriano Huerta, who soon resigns.

1917. During World War I, "temporary" Mexican farm workers, railroad laborers, and miners are permitted to enter the United States to work.

1917. The Jones Act is passed, extending U.S. citizenship to all Puerto Ricans and creating two Puerto Rican houses of legislature whose representatives are elected by the people. English is decreed the official language of Puerto Rico.

February 1917. Congress passes the Immigration Act of 1917, imposing a literacy requirement on all immigrants, aimed at curbing the influx from southern and eastern Europe, but ultimately inhibiting immigration from Mexico.

May 1917. The Selective Service Act becomes law, obligating non-citizen Mexicans in the United States to register with their local draft boards, even though they are not eligible for the draft.

1921. Limits on the number of immigrants allowed to enter the United States during a single year are imposed for the first time in the country's history.

1921. As the first of two national origin quota acts designed to curtail immigration from eastern and southern Europe and Asia is passed, Mexico and Puerto Rico become major sources of workers.

1921. A depression in Mexico causes severe destitution among Mexicans who suddenly find themselves unemployed.

1925. The Border Patrol is created by Congress.

July 1926. Rioting Puerto Ricans in Harlem are attacked by non-Hispanics as the number of Puerto Ricans becomes larger in Manhattan neighborhoods (by 1930 they number 53,000).

1929. With the onset of the Great Depression, Mexican immigration to the United States virtually ceases and return migration increases sharply.

1929. The League of United Latin American Citizens is founded in Texas by frustrated Mexican Americans who find that opportunities for them in the United States are limited.

1930s–1940s. With the onset of the Great Depression, many Mexican workers are displaced by the dominant southern whites and blacks of the migrant agricultural labor force.

1930. The United States controls 44 percent of the cultivated land in Puerto Rico; U.S. capitalists control 60 percent of the banks and public services, and all of the maritime lines.

1930. Within the next four years, approximately 20 percent of the Puerto Ricans living in the United States will return to the island.

1933. The Roosevelt Administration reverses the policy of English as the official language in Puerto Rico.

1933. Mexican farm workers strike the Central Valley, California, cotton industry, supported by several groups of independent Mexican union organizers and radicals.

1933. Cuban dictator Gerardo Machado is overthrown.

September 1933. Fulgencio Batista leads a barracks revolt to overthrow Cuban provisional President Carlos Manuel de Céspedes y Quesada, becoming the dictator of the Cuban provisional government.

1934. The Platt Amendment is annulled.

1938. Young Mexican and Mexican American pecan shellers strike in San Antonio.

1940s–1950s. Unionization among Hispanic workers increases rapidly, as Hispanic workers and union sympathizers struggle for reform.

1940. The independent union Confederación de Trabajadores Generales is formed and soon replaces the Federación Libre de los Trabajadores (FLT) as the major labor organization in Puerto Rico.

1940. Fulgencio Batista is elected president of Cuba.

1941. The Fair Employment Practices Act is passed, eliminating discrimination in employment.

1941. With the U.S. declaration of war in 1941, Hispanics throughout the country enthusiastically respond to the war effort.

1943. Prompted by the labor shortage of World War II, the U.S. government makes an agreement with the Mexican government to supply temporary workers, known as *braceros,* for American agricultural work.

1943. The so-called "Zoot Suit" riots take place in southern California.

1944. Fulgencio Batista retires as president of Cuba.

1944. Operation Bootstrap, a program initiated by the Puerto Rican government to meet U.S. labor demands of World War II and encourage industrialization on the island, stimulates a major wave of migration of workers to the United States.

1946. The first Puerto Rican governor, Jesús T. Piñero, is appointed by President Harry Truman.

1947. More than 20 airlines provide service between San Juan and Miami, and San Juan and New York.

1947. The American G.I. Forum is organized by Mexican American veterans in response to a Three Rivers, Texas, funeral home's denial to bury a Mexican American killed in the Pacific during World War II.

1950s. Throughout the early 1960s, segregation is abolished in Texas, Arizona, and other regions, largely through the efforts of the League of United Latin American Citizens (LULAC) and the Alianza Hispano Americana.

1950s. Immigration from Mexico doubles from 5.9 percent to 11.9 percent, and in the 1960s rises to 13.3 percent of the total number of immigrants to the United States.

1950s–1960s. Black workers continue to be the most numerous migrants along the eastern seaboard states, while Mexican and Mexican-American workers soon dominate the migrant paths between Texas and the Great Lakes, the Rocky Mountain region, and the area from California to the Pacific Northwest.

1950s–1960s. As more and more Puerto Ricans commit to remaining on the U.S. mainland, they encounter a great deal of rejection, but at the same time demonstrate a growing concern for social and economic mobility. Their early employment pattern consists of menial jobs in the service sector and in light factory work—in essence low-paying jobs.

1950. Despite the resurgence of Mexican immigration and the persistence of Mexican cultural modes, Mexican Americans cannot help but become Americanized in the milieu of the 1950s and 1960s, when more and more acquire educations in Anglo systems, live in integrated suburbs, and are subjected to Anglo-American mass media—especially television.

July 3, 1950. The U.S. Congress upgrades Puerto Rico's political status from protectorate to commonwealth.

1951. The Bracero Program is formalized as the Mexican Farm Labor Supply Program and the Mexican Labor Agreement, and will bring an annual average of 350,000 Mexican workers to the United States until its end in 1964.

1952. Congress passes the Immigration and Nationality Act of 1952, also known as the McCarran-Walter Act, reaffirming the basic features of the 1924 quota law by maintaining a restrictive limit on immigration from particular countries. Immigration from the Western Hemisphere remains exempt, except that applicants must clear a long list of barriers devised to exclude homosexuals, communists, and others.

1952. Fulgencio Batista seizes power of Cuba again, this time as dictator, taking Cuba to new lows of repression and corruption.

1954. In the landmark case of *Hernandez v. Texas* the nation's highest court acknowledges that Hispanic Americans are not being treated as "whites." The Supreme Court recognizes Hispanics as a separate class of people suffering profound discrimination, paving the way for Hispanic Americans to use legal means to attack all types of discrimination throughout the United States. It is also the first U.S. Supreme Court case to be argued and briefed by Mexican American attorneys.

1958–1958. Operation Wetback deports 3.8 million persons of Mexican descent. Only a small fraction of that amount are allowed deportation hearings. Thousands of more legitimate U.S. citizens of Mexican descent are also arrested and detained.

1959. The Cuban Revolution succeeds in overthrowing the repressive regime of Batista; Fidel Castro takes power. The vast majority of Cuban Americans immigrate to the United States after this date: between 1959 and 1962, 25,000 Cubans are "paroled" to the United States using a special immigration rule. Large-scale Cuban immigration to the United States occurs much more quickly than that from either Puerto Rico or Mexico, with more than one million Cubans entering the country since 1959.

1959. Most of the two million Puerto Ricans who have trekked to the U.S. mainland in this century are World War II or postwar-era entries. Unlike the immigrant experience of Mexicans, or Cubans before 1959, the majority of Puerto Rican immigrants entered the United States with little or no red tape.

1960s. A third phase of labor migration to the United States begins when the established patterns of movement from Mexico and Puerto Rico to the United States are modified, and migration from other countries increases. The Bracero Program ends in 1964, and, after a brief decline in immigration, workers from Mexico increasingly arrive to work under the auspices of the H-2 Program of the Immigration and Nationality Act of 1952, as well as for family unification purposes, or as undocumented workers.

1960s–1970s. The migrant agricultural work force is changing rapidly. With the rise of the black power and Chicano movements, the appearance of modest protective legislation, and the increasingly successful unionization efforts of farm workers, employers seek to recruit and hire foreign workers to replace the citizens.

1961. Aspira (Aspire) is founded to promote the education of Hispanic youth by raising public and private sector funds. Aspira acquires a national following, serving Puerto Ricans wherever they live in large numbers.

April 1961. Anti-Communist Cuban exiles who are trained and armed by the United States, attempt a foray into Cuba that is doomed from the beginning. The failure of the infamous Bay of Pigs invasion embitters thousands of exiled Cubans, while strengthening Castro's position at home. Many observers throughout the world criticize the Kennedy administration for the attempt to overthrow a legitimately based government.

1962. The United Farm Workers Organizing Committee in California, begun as an independent organization, is led by César Chávez. In 1965 it organizes its successful Delano grape strike and first national boycott. It becomes part of the AFL-CIO in 1966. Today the union is known as the United Farmworkers of America.

October 1962. President Kennedy redeems himself from the Bay of Pigs disgrace by blocking a Soviet plan to establish missile bases in Cuba. Soviet Premier Khrushchev agrees to withdraw the missiles with the proviso that the United States declare publicly that it will not invade Cuba.

1964. Congress enacts the first comprehensive civil rights law since the Reconstruction period when it passes the Civil Rights Act of 1964. One result of the act is the establishment of affirmative action programs. Title VII of the Act prohibits discrimination on the basis of gender, creed, race, or ethnic background, "to achieve equality of employment opportunities and remove barriers that have operated in the past." Discrimination is prohibited in advertising, recruitment, hiring, job classification, promotion, discharge, wages and salaries, and other terms and conditions of employment. Title VII also establishes the Equal Employment Opportunity Commission (EEOC) as a monitoring device to prevent job discrimination.

1964. The Economic Opportunity Act (EOA) is the centerpiece of President Lyndon B. Johnson's War on Poverty. The EOA also creates the Office of Economic Opportunity (OEO) to administer a number of programs on behalf of the nation's poor. These include the Job Corps, the Community Action Program (CAP), and the Volunteers in Service to America (VISTA).

1965. The experienced *braceros* (manual laborers) inspire other Mexicans to immigrate to the United States. Many of these contract laborers work primarily in agricultural communities and in railroad camps until the program ends in 1965.

1965. A border industrialization program, the *maquiladora* (assembly plant), is initiated. Mexico hopes to raise the standard of living in its northern border region, while the United States hopes to avoid the possible negative political and economic consequences of leaving hundreds of thousands of Mexican workers stranded without employment as the Bracero Program is ended.

1965. Although the single aim of the Voting Rights Act of 1965 is African American enfranchisement in the South, obstacles to registration and voting are faced by all minorities. The act's potential as a tool for Hispanic Americans, however, is not fully realized for nearly a decade.

1965. For the first time, the United States enacts a law placing a cap on immigration from the Western Hemisphere, becoming effective in 1968.

1965. Fidel Castro announces that Cubans can leave the island nation if they have relatives in the United

States. He stipulates, however, that Cubans already in Florida have to come and get their relatives. Nautical crafts of all types systematically leave Miami, returning laden with anxious Cubans eager to rejoin their families on the mainland.

1965. A major revision of immigration law results when Congress amends the Immigration and Nationality Act of 1952. The national origin quota system is abolished.

Late 1960s–early 1970s. Intellectual foment and rebellion reign in the United States. Caught up in the mood, young Mexican Americans throughout the country seek a new identity while struggling for the same civil rights objectives of previous generations. This struggle becomes known as the Chicano Movement. The word "Chicano" is elevated from its pejorative usage in the 1920s when it denoted lower-class Mexican immigrants, and from its slang usage of the 1940s and 1950s, to substitute for "Mexicano."

1966. Hundreds of Chicago Puerto Rican youths go on a rampage, breaking windows and burning down many of the businesses in their neighborhoods. Ostensibly, the riots are in response to an incident of police brutality, but the underlying causes are broader, linked to the urban blight that characterizes their life in Chicago.

1966. A program is initiated to airlift Cubans to the United States. More than 250,000 Cubans are airlifted to the United States before the program is halted by Castro in 1973. About 10 percent of the island's population immigrates to the United States between 1966 and 1973.

1968. Chicano student organizations spring up throughout the nation, as do barrio groups such as the Brown Berets. Thousands of young Chicanos pledge their loyalty and time to such groups as the United Farmworkers Organizing Committee, which, under César Chávez, has been a great inspiration for Chicanos throughout the nation. An offshoot of both the farm worker and the student movements, is La Raza Unida party in Texas, an organization formed in 1968 to obtain control of community governments where Chicanos are the majority.

1969. After the establishment of the Central American Common Market in the 1960s leads to economic growth and improved conditions in the region, the border war between Honduras and El Salvador brings its collapse and a rapid decline of economic conditions in Central America.

1970s. Immigration and Naturalization Service (INS) Commissioner Leonard Chapman seeks to increase funding and expand the power of his organization, claiming that there are as many as 12 million undocumented workers in the country. Other observers most commonly place the number in the range of 3.5 million to 5 million people.

1970s–early 1980s. The rise in politically motivated violence in Central America spurs a massive increase in undocumented immigration to the United States.

1970. At this time 82 percent of the Hispanic population of the nation lives in nine states, with the proportion rising to 86 percent in 1990. The major recipients of Hispanic immigrants are California, Texas, and New York, and to a lesser degree Florida, Illinois, and New Jersey.

1970. A Chicano Moratorium to the Vietnam War is organized in Los Angeles. Journalist Rubén Salazar is accidentally killed by police.

1970. The struggle over affirmative action continues when opponents coin the term "reverse discrimination," suggesting that white males are victims of discrimination as a result of affirmative action on behalf of women, blacks, Hispanics, and other under-represented groups.

1970. Brutality against Mexican Americans continues. In *López v. Harlow*, a case filed in an attempt to bring the violence under control, a police officer shoots and kills López, a Mexican American, allegedly in self-defense, because he thought López was about to throw a dish at him.

1970. The amendments constituting the landmark Voting Rights Act of 1970 add a provision that is designed to guard against inventive new barriers to political participation. It requires federal approval of all changes in voting procedures in certain jurisdictions, primarily southern states. This act prevents minority votes from being diluted in gerrymandered districts or through at-large elections.

1971. La Raza Unida Party wins the city elections in Crystal City, Texas.

1972. Ramona Acosta Bañuelos becomes the first Hispanic treasurer of the United States.

1973. The right of the Puerto Rican people to decide their own future as a nation is approved by the United Nations. In 1978, the United Nations recognizes Puerto Rico as a colony of the United States.

1973. An employment discrimination case, *Espinoza v. Farah Manufacturing Company*, argues discrimination toward an employee, Espinoza, on the basis of his citizenship status under the Civil Rights Act. However, the Supreme Court holds that there is nothing in Title VII, the equal employment opportunities provisions of the Civil Rights Act of 1964, that makes it illegal to discriminate on the basis of citizenship or alienage.

1973. The Labor Council of Latin American Advancement (LCLAA) forms to promote the interests of Hispanics within organized labor.

1974. Congress passes the Equal Educational Opportunity Act to create equality in public schools by making bilingual education available to Hispanic youth. According to the framers of the act, equal education means more than equal facilities and equal access to teachers. Students who have trouble with the English language must be given programs to help them learn English.

1975. The Voting Rights Act Amendments of 1975 extend the provisions of the original Voting Rights Act of 1965 and makes permanent the national ban on literacy tests. Critical for Hispanic Americans, the amendments make bilingual ballots a requirement in certain areas.

1977. The Immigration and Naturalization Service (INS) apprehends more than one million undocumented workers each year.

1977. A group of young Cuban exiles called the Antonio Maceo Brigade travels to Cuba to participate in service work and to achieve a degree of rapprochement with the Cuban government.

1978. The median income of Hispanic families below the poverty level falls from $7,238 in 1978 to $6,557 in 1987, controlling for inflation.

1978–1988. Hispanic female participation in the work force more than doubles, from 1.7 million to 3.6 million. In 1988, 56.6 percent of Hispanic women are in the work force, compared with 66.2 percent of white women and 63.8 percent of blacks.

1978–1988. The proportion of Hispanic children living in poverty rises more than 45 percent, and by 1989, 38 percent of Hispanic children are living in poverty.

1979. Political upheaval and civil wars in Nicaragua, El Salvador, and Guatemala contribute to large migrations of refugees to the United States.

1980s. Japanese industrialists take advantage of the maquiladoras by sending greater amounts of raw materials to Mexico where they are finished and shipped duty-free to the United States.

1980s. The rates of immigration approach the levels of the early 1900s: legal immigration during the first decade of the century reached 8.8 million, while during the 1980s, 6.3 million immigrants are granted permanent residence. The immigrants are overwhelmingly young and in search of employment, and Hispanic immigrants continue to account for more than 40 percent of the total.

1980s. Programs to apprehend undocumented immigrants are implemented, and reports of violations of civil rights are reported.

1980. A flotilla converges at Cuba's Mariel Harbor to pick up refugees. By year end, more than 125,000 "Marielitos" migrate to the United States. Castro charges that the exiles he allowed to return on visits had contaminated Cubans with the glitter of consumerism.

1980. The Refugee Act of 1980 removes the ideological definition of refugee as one who flees from a Communist regime, thus allowing thousands to enter the United States as refugees.

April 1980. A bus carrying a load of discontented Cubans crashes through the gates of the Peruvian embassy in Havana and the passengers receive political asylum from Peru. Castro begins to revise his policy of gradually allowing Cubans to leave.

1980–1988. The Reagan administration maintains that affirmative action programs entail quotas, constituting a form of reverse discrimination.

1980–1988. The number of Hispanics in the work force increases by 48 percent, representing 20 percent of U.S. employment growth.

1986. After more than a decade of debate, Congress enacts The Immigration Reform and Control Act (IRCA), creating an alien legalization program: legal status is given to applicants who held illegal status in the United States from before January 1, 1982, until the time of application. The program brings legal status to a large number of undocumented Hispanics.

1987. At this time, 70.1 percent of Hispanic female-headed households with children are living in poverty.

1988. President Ronald Reagan appoints the first Hispanic Secretary of Education: Dr. Lauro F. Cavazos.

1989. Median family income for white families is $35,210; for blacks, $20,210; and for Hispanics,

$23,450. Per capita income is $14,060 for whites, $8,750 for blacks, and $8,390 for Hispanics.

1989. Immigration from the Americas rises from 44.3 percent in 1964 to 61.4 percent. Of the major countries, Mexico accounts for 37.1 percent of total documented immigration to the United States, the next highest number of immigrants being from El Salvador, 5.3 percent.

1990. President George Bush appoints the first woman and first Hispanic surgeon general of the United States: Antonia C. Novello.

1990. The erosion of past civil rights legislation by the Supreme Court during the Reagan and Bush administrations results in efforts by representatives of civil rights, black, and Hispanic organizations to initiate a push for a new Civil Rights Act. A series of compromises produces a watered-down Civil Rights Act in 1991.

1991. The proposed North American Free Trade Agreement between Mexico, the United States, and Canada expands even further the maquiladora concept, offering potentially greater tax abatements for U.S. businesses.

1991. Erosion of past civil rights legislation by the Supreme Court during the Reagan and Bush administrations results in efforts by representatives of civil rights, black, and Hispanic organizations to initiate a push for a new Civil Rights Act in 1990 to return to previous standards. A series of compromises produces a watered-down Civil Rights Act in 1991.

1991. Despite the U.S. Congress' refusal to consider the statehood of Puerto Rico, a referendum is held on the island, clearly showing that the population is in favor of statehood.

March 1991. Unemployment among Hispanics in the United States reaches 10.3 percent, roughly double the rate for whites.

March 1991. A jury exonerates Los Angeles police of the brutal beating of African American Rodney King, which was captured on videotape. African Americans in central Los Angeles are joined by many Latinos in protesting the verdict by rioting for a number of days. The volatile reaction of the minority community leads the country to reassess social and economic policy, as well as police training as it affects minorities.

February 1992. The Farabundo Martí National Liberation Front (FMLN) ends its guerrilla movement by signing a peace treaty with the government of El Salvador. One of the bloodiest civil wars, one that had killed some 75,000 people, finally comes to an end. In exchange for the FMLN laying down its weapons and becoming a legal political party, the government agrees to sweeping changes in the military, including the retirement of more than a hundred officers believed responsible for widespread human rights abuses. El Salvador was a key battleground for the Cold War during the 1980s, with the United States pouring in more than $6 billion in economic and military aid to defeat the FMLN. With the fall of Communist states in Europe, the end of the Cold War brings considerable peace benefits to Central America.

October 23, 1992. President George Bush signs the Cuban Democracy Act, also known as the Torricelli Bill, which bans trade with Cuba by U.S. subsidiary companies in third countries and prohibits ships docking in U.S. ports if they have visited Cuba. The Torricelli Bill is heaving backed by Cuban Americans, and Bush makes a point of signing it in Miami. The passage and signing of the bill illustrate the power of U.S. ethnic groups in creating legislation and affecting foreign policy. Upon passage of the Cuban Democracy Act, the United States is condemned by the United Nations General Assembly for maintaining is 30-year embargo of Cuba; the vote is 59 to 3, with 71 countries abstaining. Even most of the United States' allies either vote to end the embargo or they abstain.

1993. President Bill Clinton names Federico Peña to the position of Secretary of Transportation; he is the first Hispanic to hold that post.

1993. President Bill Clinton names Henry Cisneros to the cabinet position of Secretary of Housing and Urban Development (HUD); he is the first Hispanic to hold that post.

1993. President Bill Clinton appoints Norma Contú, the former director of the Mexican American Legal Defense and Education Fund, to the position of Assistant Secretary for Civil Rights, Department of Education. The president also appoints 25 Hispanics to positions that need confirmation by the Senate, including Nicolás Kanellos to the National Council for the Humanities.

January 1, 1994. The North American Free Trade Agreement (NAFTA) takes effect to eliminate all tariffs between trading partners Canada, Mexico, and the United States within fifteen years from this date. The measure is a first step toward integrating the economies of the three countries and possibly toward the creation in the future of an American common market that will include the whole hemisphere. Regarding Mexico and the United States, on this date 53.8 percent of U.S. imports from Mexico became duty free, while 31 percent of imports from the United States, excluding those imported by maquiladoras, became duty free. The most immediately affected industries are energy, automobiles, textiles, agriculture, electricity, banks and insurance, bus and trucking services, ports, railroads, and telecommunications. NAFTA passage is opposed in the United States by labor unions, which fear the continuing loss of jobs to Mexico, and domestic industries artificially protected by tariffs, such as textiles. In Mexico, revolutionary outbreaks by Mayan peasant farmers in Chiapas are timed to coincide with the beginning of NAFTA, and, in fact, they start shortly after 12:00 a.m. New Year's Day. As many as one thousand Mayan guerrillas, baptizing themselves the Zapatista National Liberation Army (in honor of the revolutionary general Emiliano Zapata), with some of them uniformed and well armed, take over the important southern city of San Cristobal de las Casas, as well as the towns of Ocosingo, Las Margaritas, and others. This leads to bloody confrontations with and repression by the Mexican Army until a cease-fire is accepted by both sides on January 12, with an agreement to dialogue on the problems of the Mayas in Chiapas. The Mayas of southern Mexico, who have suffered poverty and dispossession of their communal lands for years, are now faced with the prospect of imported corn displacing their main farm product and dietary staple. All of this crystallizes in an environment of increasing indigenous overpopulation, poverty, and exploitation as Mexico bows to the demands of foreign debtors, the constraints of the International Monetary Fund to control inflation, and recent devaluations of the peso.

With the economic policy of President Carlos Salinas de Gortari straining to bring Mexico into the "first world," the gap between the select few who are rich, and getting richer under new economic programs, and the poor in Mexico is accentuated. After a cease-fire is established, the government and Mayan rebels sign a tentative 32-point accord on March 2, calling for a new local government designed to serve Indian communities and a redrawn Chiapas state legislature to increase Indian representation; it also calls for the government to build roads, improve schools, upgrade health services, and extend electricity and water to remote areas in Chiapas, the poorest state in the Mexican republic. The government agrees to grant rebels amnesty, to outlaw discrimination against Indians, and to enact laws that would allow officials to confiscate large landholdings in Chiapas and divide them among the peasants. The government also promises to help retrain farmers harmed by NAFTA. In the months following the cease-fire, Mayan farmers proceed t seize some 75,000 acres of ranch lands, claiming that the lands had been stolen from them as far back as 1819. An agrarian court in 1989 had ruled in favor of the Mayas, but the government has done nothing to enforce the ruling.

President Carlos Salinas de Gortari announces, however, that redistribution of farmland is no longer an option in Mexico. Thus, the issue of land remains on the table in the continuing negotiations with the Mayas.

March 23, 1994. Luis Donaldo Colosio, presidential candidate for Mexico's Institutional Revolutionary Party (PRI), is assassinated in Tijuana, Mexico, while campaigning. The conspiracy to assassinate the candidate handpicked by President Carlos Salinas de Gortari is assumed to be political in nature and provokes insecurity in Mexico's trading partners through the North American Free Trade Agreement. On March 24, acting unilaterally, the United States extends a $6 billion line of credit to Mexico. This is followed later by both NAFTA partners, the United States and Canada, moving rapidly to create a multibillion-dollar fund to stabilize Mexico's currency and protect it from onslaughts from global speculation. The centerpiece of the fund is a $6.7 billion line of credit for the Central Bank of Mexico. All three parties to the treaty see their economies as interdependent. Critics charge that the United States has repeatedly shored up and supported the PRI with loans and lines of credit during elections and political transitions to ensure stability. Had it not been for the loans in 1988, they charge, the Party of the Democratic Revolution candidate, Cuauhtémoc Cárdenas, would have defeated Carlos Salinas de Gortari in what was a close election.

November 8, 1994. Californians pass Proposition 187 with 59 percent of the vote. The initiative bans undocumented immigrants from receiving public education and public benefits such as welfare and subsidized health care, except in emergency circumstances; makes it a felony to manufacture, distribute, sell, or use false citizenship or residence documents; and requires teachers, doctors, and other city, county, and state officials to report suspected and apparent illegal aliens to the California attorney general and the Immigration and Naturalization Service (INS). Governor Pete Wilson issues an executive order for state officials to begin following the initiative by cutting off government services to undocumented pregnant women and nursing home patients. On November 9, 1994, eight lawsuits are filed in state and federal courts protesting the measure. On November 16, 1994, Judge William Matthew Byrne, Jr., of the Federal Court in Los Angeles, temporarily blocks California state officials from enforcing the proposition. Mark Slavkin, president of the Los Angeles Unified School District Board, and other officials are threatened with recall efforts for proposing Proposition 187. Similar proposals are being considered on the federal level to severely limit or ban undocumented immigrants from receiving public benefits and attending public schools. Hispanics and other minorities perceive the initiate as an anti-immigrant sentiment stemming from a weak economy.

November 16, 1994. In Los Angeles, California, Federal District Court Judge William Matthew Byrne, Jr., temporarily blocks the enforcement of Proposition 187, stating that it raises serious constitutional questions. Judge Byrne exempts the provisions that increase penalties for manufacturing or using false immigration documents.

January 1995. Signatures are collected to put an initiative on the 1996 ballot that states: "Neither the State of California nor any of its political subdivision or agents shall use race, sex, color, ethnicity or national origin as a criterion for either discriminating against or granting preferential treatment to any individual or group in the operation of the State's system of public employment, public education or public contracting." The initiative is labeled Son of 187—a reference to Proposition 187, the immigration-control measure passed by Californians on November 8, 1994.

February 21, 1995. President Bill Clinton is successful in arranging for an international loan-guarantee package of $53 billion, with $20 million from the United States, to prop up the devalued peso and restore confidence in the Mexican economy. On December 20, 1994, after the PRI ruling party's victory at the polls, outgoing President Carlos Salinas de Gortari allows the peso to float against the dollar, thus revealing the extent of weakness in the economy that has been covered up during negotiations and implementation of the North American Free Trade Agreement (NAFTA). With additional stress to the economy and international investor confidence in Mexico brought on by the assassination of a presidential candidate during the elections and the armed insurrection by Maya Indians in Chiapas, the peso plunges, losing one-third of its value. During January and February, a monetary and investment crisis takes hold of the economy, and the Mexican stock market, *Bolsa,* loses 40 percent of its value. After Clinton is unsuccessful in moving Congress to help abate Mexico's monetary crisis, which also affects the U.S. economy, Clinton taps sources not needing congressional approval to put together the $20 billion package. Clinton goes on to appeal to the International Monetary Fund, Canada, and various European and South American countries to come to the aid of Mexico. As soon as the loan package is announced, both the peso and Mexican stocks stabilize, and the Mexican nation prepares for some of the strictest austerity policies in its history, including placing oil revenues as collateral for the U.S. loans. In the wake of much higher prices for even the most basic of staples, and rising unemployment in Mexico, the United States is bracing for another large wave of immigrant Mexican labor.

11

Religion

✳ The Beginnings ✳ Instruments of Religious Conversion ✳ Our Lady of Guadalupe and the Saints
✳ Florida ✳ New Mexico ✳ Texas ✳ Arizona ✳ California ✳ The Anglo Conquest
✳ Developing a Pastoral Approach ✳ A Search for Parity ✳ Protestantism and Hispanics
✳ Popular Religiosity ✳ Beyond Orthodoxy

Hispanics are an eminently religious people. Throughout the centuries, regardless of the accessibility of priests or places of worship, or the availability of religious instruction, they have maintained their faith through the nurturing of their families and villages. Often misunderstood and chastised as ignorant, retrograde, or pagan, they have clung to the symbols of a deep spirituality received from their elders. Religious expression is apparent in the exchanges of everyday life—in the readiness with which Hispanics add the expressions Gracias a Dios *(Thanks be to God) or* Si Dios quiere *(God willing) and the ever-present invocations to God, the Virgin, and the saints. That the manner of religious expression for U.S. Hispanics is fundamentally Christian and Catholic is natural; Catholicism is still the religion of choice of Hispanics everywhere. The most recent surveys reveal that 75 percent of U.S. Hispanics consider themselves Catholic, 19 percent Protestant, and 5 percent "other" (Jewish, Jehovah's Witnesses, Mormon, to name a few).*

Hispanics brought Christianity to present-day Florida and the Southwest 250 years before the Pilgrims landed at Plymouth Rock. This period of Christianity on U.S. soil is largely ignored by mainstream church historians. A 1989 five-volume work on this subject commissioned by the U.S. Conference of Catholic Bishops devotes only nine pages to Hispanics. It places them exclusively in the context of an "immigrant" church. As Moisés Sandoval explains in On the Move, *a history of the Hispanic church in the United States, "There is great ignorance about Hispanics in the Church, extending not only to their past and current religious contributions but even to their very existence." Hispanic religious contributions are* worthy of examination, however, if prejudice is to be dispelled.

✳ THE BEGINNINGS

Catholicism, the religious affiliation of the majority of U.S. Hispanics, came to the New World with Christopher Columbus in 1492. The Spanish conquerors, imbued with the religious ardor of their day, were not content with seizing and claiming kingdoms and treasures in the name of the Spanish sovereigns; they also wanted to win over the inhabitants of the newly discovered territories to Christianity. This was a natural development, for Spain had just fought for seven centuries a religious crusade against the Moors on its own soil. Throughout the first two centuries of European presence in the Americas, Spain was the most zealous daughter of the Roman church.

Uniformity of religious belief, in this case Catholicism, was one of the main pillars on which the Spanish Empire rested. At the time of the discovery of the Americas, Spain was preoccupied with uniting into one nation and under one monarch the various medieval kingdoms into which the Iberian Peninsula was divided. Roughly 20 years before, through the marriage of Isabella of Castile and Ferdinand of Aragon, all but the southern, Muslim-occupied territories came under the royal couple's joint reign. Religious diversity, which provided for the more or less peaceful, if not totally tolerant, coexistence of Christians, Muslims, and Jews, seemed ill-advised to the monarchs; they were already having a difficult enough time coping with the behind-the-scenes machinations of noblemen who resented surrendering their prerogatives as feudal overlords to a centralized government.

The significance of the year 1492 goes far beyond the fateful encounter with the Americas; it constitutes the boundary between religious plurality and uniformity for Spain. Following that date, Spain tolerated no religion other than Catholicism on its soil or in the vast lands it set forth to bring beneath its imperial mantle. In January 1492, Isabella and Ferdinand captured Granada, the last Moorish stronghold in Iberia. This put an end to the 700-year-long Reconquest, which had begun shortly after 711 when the Moors invaded all but the extreme northern regions of Spain. In April, the monarchs gave notice to the Jews that they had until July to repudiate their faith or leave Spain. An estimated 140,000 chose the road to exile. Thenceforth, only the Cross would follow the sword of the Spanish soldiers, both to the European battlefields, where the Spanish Hapsburg kings fought their religious wars against Protestants, and to the remote jungles and deserts of the newly discovered regions of the Americas and Asia.

Father Virgilio Elizondo pointed out in his book *Galilean Journey* (1985) that in matters of religion the attitudes of the Spanish conquistador and his English counterpart were worlds apart. Early in the period of conquest and discovery, theologians like Father Francisco Vitoria, a Spanish Dominican, settled the question as to whether Indians were human. Indians, they determined, were made in God's image and likeness and were endowed with an immortal soul. Converting them to Christianity became a sacred mandate for the Spaniards. According to Elizondo, the Spanish conquerors were not concerned about their own personal salvation, of which they felt assured. Whenever they sought royal permission and support for their enterprises, they listed the evangelization of the native populations as a goal. In Bernal Díaz del Castillo's account of Hernán Cortés' conquest of Mexico, he states that after each village and town surrendered to the conquistadors, the Spaniards immediately took time to destroy the pagan idols and temples and in their place erected crosses and shrines in honor of the Virgin Mary. To Cortés and most Spaniards of his day, the conquest was not merely a political and economic enterprise but a religious crusade.

Their English counterparts, on the other hand, coming from the austerity of Protestant Europe, were obsessed with achieving their own salvation and gave no thought to the spiritual well-being of the American native. From their standpoint, the natives were less than human, unworthy of the Christian promise, children of the Devil. They were not to be evangelized, but rather destroyed; thus, the expression popular during the conquest of the American Far West, "The only good Indian is a dead Indian."

✳ INSTRUMENTS OF RELIGIOUS CONVERSION

Conversion of the Indians facilitated interbreeding of the Spanish and the Indians. The Spaniards, Virgilio Elizondo explained in *Galilean Journey: The Mexican American Promise* (1985), contrary to the early English colonists, considered sexual relations with the native women as something natural. The conquistadors took them as mistresses, concubines, and wives and accepted both their legitimate and illegitimate children, producing almost from the outset a generation of Christian mestizos.

On a less fortunate note, converting the Indians mandated the development of systems and strategies that would render them receptive to Christian teachings or force them into accepting them. In the name of evangelization, the unscrupulous or overzealous committed abuses never intended by either the Crown or the church. From the first, the Indians were exploited, enslaved or forced into some sort of servitude. The church consistently censured these excesses; the Spanish Crown attempted to prevent and remedy them, as the passing of the *Leyes de Indias* (Laws of the Indies) makes evident. This body of laws, among other things, recognized the natives as subjects of the Crown and forbade their forced conversion and enslavement. Unfortunately, the Spanish monarchs and their courts were an ocean away, and more often than not the letter of the law was executed rather than its intent.

The first approach to the orderly evangelization of the natives, the *encomienda,* further opened the door to the inhumane excesses that would characterize the colonization of the New World. The encomienda entrusted a group of Indians to a colonist, known as the *encomendero* (trustee), who was responsible for providing for the material needs and religious instruction of his charges. In exchange for his paternalism, the encomendero was entitled to work the Indians. The provisions of the laws that set down in detail the responsibilities of the encomendero and regulated the conditions under which the Indians would labor were largely ignored. The *repartimiento,* a variation of the encomienda, offered no relief to the sufferings of the newly conquered peoples. It merely placed colonial authorities instead of individuals in charge of the natives. The latter, when not forced to work in Crown-owned mines, farms, or other projects, were apportioned out to private citizens as laborers.

tives. The vulnerability of the unarmed, nonthreatening padre was often his greatest strength. Missionaries could succeed where the conquistadors failed. Such was the case in the Sonora region of northern Mexico (southern Arizona today) and in the peninsula of Baja California, where the hostility of the natives prevented the soldiers from making inroads. After several failed attempts, the Mexican viceroy entrusted the Jesuits with this conquest, which they performed successfully with no other weapon than the Cross.

The mission, in most cases, served as a center for religious instruction and a beachhead from which the padre could set out to scout for other promising mission sites, where another beachhead in the evangelization process could be established. Missions, therefore, as was the case in Florida and the Southwest, tended to stretch out over a territory much like the links of a chain. This arrangement, in turn, facilitated the logistics of supplying and defending them. The Texas and California missions established by the Franciscan friars were rather ambitious institutions. Some were villages unto themselves. The Indians learned Christian doctrine and a variety of skills—farming, animal husbandry,

The Franciscan methold of teaching the Indians by pictures. (From an engraving based on Fray Diego Valdés, O.F.M., in his *Rhetorica Christiana,* Rome, 1579.)

In either case, whether as part of an encomienda or a repartimiento, the Indians were brutalized, starved, and often worked to death. Whole populations were wiped out in the West Indies, where the encomiendas and the repartimientos were first imposed. Preeminent among the voices that rose to the defense of human rights for the Indians was Father Bartolomé de las Casas (1474–1566), a Spanish-born Dominican priest and historian. To his protests and pleas can be attributed the above-mentioned Laws of the Indies enacted by the Crown.

A vastly more humane instrument of evangelization, and the one most widely utilized in the Spanish territories now encompassed by the United States, was the mission, a temporary institution established and run by priests who resided among or in proximity to native populations. The missionary usually came right on the heels of the conquistador and built his rudimentary chapel and convent at a reasonable distance from the military garrison, once the area was somewhat pacified. Instead of force, it was the missionary's works of mercy and his teachings that often brought about the evangelization of the na-

Bartolemé de las Casas (1474–1566).

San Juan Capistrano Mission in San Antonio, Texas. (Photograph by Silvia Novo Pena.)

weaving, metalwork, leather craft, carpentry, and masonry—aimed at bringing about economic self-sufficiency to populations that once depended on collecting, hunting, or fishing for their sustenance. These missions became very wealthy, supplying not merely their own residents but the garrisons and townships in the immediate area.

The missions were secularized during the first part of the nineteenth century, either for political reasons or because their original aims had been achieved. By this time and because in most cases their residents had fused with the people of the surrounding townships and farms, missions became the nuclei for modern-day parishes. It is not uncommon for the descendants of the first Indian neophytes baptized within mission walls to still flock to the same old church buildings generation after generation.

In light of this, the assertion that missions and missionaries served the purposes of the empire cannot be denied. The missions contributed to the pacification of the Indians, and in so doing facilitated the process of colonization. They fostered the development of townships in their immediate vicinity. Furthermore, by Christianizing and Hispanicizing the Indians, the missionaries transformed entire populations into loyal subjects of the Spanish kings and obedient children of the Roman church.

One of the services offered by the church, which served to both Christianize and Hispanicize the native and mestizo populations, was formal education. In townships and missions, the clergy was expected to establish schools, both for boys and girls, to teach the children to read and write and learn the catechism. The curriculum sometimes included Indian languages. As early as 1534, archbishop of Mexico Juan de Zumárraga had a school built at Tlatelolco, the first in the Americas. Countless Indian children spent their mornings reading, writing, and singing and their afternoons involved in religious instruction. Zumárraga, an indefatigable worker for the education of the Indians, published numerous books on the subject, paying special attention to the education of girls.

✳ OUR LADY OF GUADALUPE AND THE SAINTS

The spiritual conquest of Mexico served as the first chapter in the spiritual conquest of the Hispanic territories now encompassed by the United States, Florida and Louisiana being the exceptions. As Carey McWilliams aptly underscores in his book *North from Mexico* (1968), the Spanish-speaking colonists who settled Texas and the Southwest were, but for rare exceptions, mestizos, second generation and beyond, born of Spanish fathers and Mexican Indian mothers; the balance was constituted by Christianized Mexican Indians (the ductile Tlaxcalans, in particular), blacks, and mulattoes. The Catholic religiosity of the Mexican mestizo would come to predominate in this area even after the final invasion of northern Mexico by the United States in 1846. This religiosity continues to be reaffirmed by the various waves of Mexican immigrants that have entered the United States since the late nineteenth century.

A providential event that contributed to the conversion of the native population of Mexico and Central America to Roman Catholicism was the alleged miraculous apparition of the Virgin Mary in Tepeyac in the environs of Moctezuma's vanquished capital of Tenochtitlán shortly after the conquest of the Aztec Empire by Hernán Cortés in 1521. In the early morning hours of December 9, 1531, Juan Diego, a converted Indian, was on his way to mass when he was surprised by the sound of beautiful singing voices coming from a hill. As he approached the site, he saw a woman enveloped by a brilliant aura. She identified herself as the Virgin Mary. In the course of several apparitions, she requested that Juan Diego inform Archbishop Zumárraga of what he had seen and heard and that she wished for a temple to be built on the hill at Tepeyac so that she could communicate all her love and compassion, help and defend all the inhabitants of the land, and remedy their misery, pain, and suffering. The archbishop refused to believe Juan Diego's story. Finally, so that he could prove his veracity, the Virgin performed a miracle. She instructed Diego to gather roses from a bush that would not normally bloom that time of year and take them to the archbishop. When the humble messenger unfolded his cloak before Zumárraga, so as to put before him the roses the Lady was sending, the image of the Virgin Mary appeared imprinted on the cloth.

Detractors have claimed that the clergy perpetrated a hoax on the credulous natives in order to speed up their conversion. It was too much of a coincidence that the apparition took place on a site dedi-

The image of Our Lady of Guadalupe on tour from Mexico at Our Lady of Guadalupe Church in Houston, Texas, 1992. (Photograph by Curtis Dowell.)

cated to the cult of the Aztec mother goddess Tonantzin. The image, however, displayed to this day in the basilica of Our Lady of Guadalupe in Mexico City, has not disintegrated in over four centuries, even though it is imprinted on a highly perishable cloth made of agave fibers. Furthermore, scientific testing has failed to explain the origin of the image or its durability.

News of the miracle spread throughout the colony, bringing about mass conversions. To the natives, the fact that the Virgin had chosen to appear before one of the oppressed and the vanquished, that she had adopted the physical appearance of a brown woman, and that she communicated in Nahuatl, the language of the Indians, established a bond between them and Christianity. The fact that her body blocked the face of the sun, the focal point of the native religions, established the precedence of the new faith brought by the Spaniards over the old faith of the Aztec.

Noted Mexican writer Carlos Fuentes observed in a 1992 presentation at the University of Houston that mestizo artisans invariably portrayed Christ as a broken, bleeding god suffering on the Cross. The Virgin of Guadalupe, on the other hand, appears surrounded by flowers, rays of sunlight, and all of nature triumphant. As he explained it, the first Indian converts identified the death of their old gods with Christ. He was a god who was willing to be destroyed to save his people. The Virgin, on the other hand, surrounded by all the symbols of a joyous nature, brought the hope for a new beginning.

The colorful liturgy of Catholicism and its doctrine of the veneration of saints further paved the way for native conversions. The Mexican Indians were accustomed to paying tribute to a wide variety of deities. Each clan, each site, each day, week, and month was the purvey of a god or goddess whose favor was sought to ensure the happy outcome of events. They felt quite at home with the feast days assigned by the church calendar to holy men and women of the past, who were also named patrons for townships and villages, professions and trades and protectors for individuals. By the same token, elaborate priestly vestments, music, incense, candles, ornate sacred vessels, and other external aspects of the Catholic church must have appeared to the Indians as echoes of their past devotions.

✳ FLORIDA

The first chapter of the Christian saga in present-day Florida began shortly after the Easter season— la Pascua Florida—of 1513 with the arrival of Juan Ponce de León. Although no priest is known to have accompanied this expedition, the customs of the day presupposed that there was an act of thanksgiving to God for the safe arrival of the conquistadors. Ponce de León returned in 1526 as military escort for a contingent of secular and regular priests. He was commissioned by the Crown to establish mission posts for the dual purpose of affirming Spain's presence in the newly discovered territories and spreading the gospel. Finding armed resistance from the Indians of the Gulf Coast area where they landed, the Spaniards retreated to Cuba, Ponce de León dying en route from wounds he sustained.

After several failed attempts, Spain abandoned all efforts to colonize Florida until 1564, when a handful of French soldiers, some of them Protestant Huguenots, founded Fort Caroline on the Saint John's River near present-day Saint Augustine. Pedro Menéndez de Avilés, a man known for his zeal and cruelty, was dispatched by the government to protect its claims against the intruders and to destroy the fort. Carried away by the religious fanaticism typical of the day, Menéndez ordered the non-Catholic French soldiers put to the sword even after they had surrendered. Three years later, the Spanish garrison that held the little fort, by then renamed San Mateo, was subjected to the same fate at the hands of the Frenchman Dominique Gourges.

The establishment of Saint Augustine in 1565 by Menéndez was pivotal to the evangelization efforts. Using Saint Augustine as a base, the handful of diocesan priests who first accompanied Menéndez— Jesuits from the order's province of Andalusia after 1566 and Franciscans after 1587—sailed north along the Atlantic coast, establishing and operating missions among the Indians. The diocesan priests also ministered to the white settlers in garrisons and outposts. Time and conditions permitting, they also saw to the spiritual welfare of neighboring Indian tribes. By 1647, a chain of missions and forts spanned from Saint Augustine in the south to Fort San Felipe on Parris Island, South Carolina.

Beginning in 1607, the Franciscans, with Father Francisco Prieto in the role of pioneer, ventured into northwestern Florida to do missionary work among the Apalache Indians. Their dedication bore fruit, and by 1655 the friars could claim 26,000 converts. Their missions in the Gulf and northwestern areas of Florida stretched from the Suwannee River in the south to the Apalachicola River in the northwest.

The state of the church in Florida in 1674 was recorded by Bishop Gabriel Díaz Vara Calderón of Santiago de Cuba, who, at the insistence of Queen Mariana, made an episcopal visit there. Upon his return, after confirming 13,152 Christianized Indians and Spaniards and traveling hundreds of leagues to visit every one of the 36 missions in the province, Bishop Calderón gave a detailed account of his observations in a letter to the pious Spanish queen. His assessment was that despite the hardships and the indifference and sometimes cruelty of the civil authorities, the missionaries had succeeded. The missions, although poor, served as firm bulwarks of the faith upon which the empire rested.

Less than 50 years later, beginning with the outbreak in 1702 of the War of Spanish Succession, which pitted France and Spain against England, the network of Florida missions was laid to waste. When in 1763, at the end of the war, Spain ceded Florida to France according to the terms of the Treaty of Paris, only two parish churches and a handful of mission buildings still stood.

✳ NEW MEXICO

As in Florida, the early expeditions or *entradas* into New Mexico from Mexico were of little consequence to the efforts of evangelization. From 1536, when Álvar Núñez Cabeza de Vaca, after years of captivity among the Karankawa Indians of Texas, heard of the big Zuni pueblos of New Mexico and mistook them for the legendary Seven Cities of Gold, until 1598, when Juan de Oñate led his group of settlers northward along the banks of the Rio Grande, New Mexico remained virtually unaffected by religious campaigns elsewhere. Heroes, cowards, martyrs, and scoundrels crossed from Mexico into the northern frontier, with or without permission from the Crown, leaving behind nothing but their failed hopes, a few relics, the carcasses of their beasts, their fallen comrades, and their rusting swords.

The course of religious history took a turn with Oñate's entrada of 1598. Oñate, a silver miner and the wealthiest man in Mexico, like Ponce de León in Florida, had a mandate from the Crown to Christianize the native people of New Mexico, among which his settlers were to dwell. Consequently, he took—in addition to his 83 oxcarts of goods, 7,000 head of stock, and 400 soldiers—a handful of priests and a plan that called for the creation of seven mission districts, each to be headed by a Franciscan friar. By 1630, 25 missions had been founded among the various settled tribes known collectively as the Pueblos.

As would be the case wherever sword and Cross ventured jointly, a conflict soon developed between the priests and the civil and military authorities. Abuse and exploitation of the natives were the order of the day. The military, sent to establish an orderly government among the Indians, stole from them, did them all sorts of violence, and raped the women.

The Pueblos were an agricultural people. They raised corn, beans, and a variety of foodstuffs. As the newcomers saw their own supplies dwindle, they robbed the Pueblos of their stores. Oñate, an irascible man who had little patience with either the settlers or the Pueblos, ordered the removal of grain from the Indians, even when it meant destroying villages and injuring the defenders.

The clergy protested. They described the excesses and the sufferings of the Pueblos at the hands of the Hispanic contingent in official reports to the civil and ecclesiastic authorities in Mexico. Fray Francisco de Zamora, to give an example, wrote that the depredations of the Hispanics against the Pueblos were a discredit to Christian teaching. He said that the natives were "stabbed and knifed when things were taken from them" and that the women were often raped by the soldiers. Echoing the feelings of other friars, he recommended that New Mexico be abandoned, so that the Pueblos might live in peace and the Word of God not be further dishonored.

Needless to say, Oñate's supporters countered these reports to the authorities with accusations of sloth on the part of the clergy and recommendations that the colony not be abandoned. They made these arguments hypocritically in the name of Christian evangelization. A later report to the viceroy that the conversion of 7,000 Indians had been accomplished was instrumental in saving the colony, pointing to the fact that religious accomplishments were vital to determining the success or failure of the colonizing enterprise. The viceroy made provisions to ensure against any further injustices and ill treatment of the natives. These included replacing Oñate as governor with Pedro de Peralta in 1609 and limiting the largest military garrison to 50 married soldiers.

The Pueblos were not willing converts to Christianity. They had their own cults to ancestors and to various natural forces that had to be propitiated to ensure abundant crops. They worshiped the sun and the mother earth and believed in life after death. Their ceremonial life was rich and colorful. To give in to the missionaries, as they saw it, could result in famine and many other calamities. Conversions were seldom totally sincere, and apostasy was quite common. Those who were outwardly Christianized more than likely practiced the old rituals secretly. For these infractions they were routinely punished by the friars. The troublemakers were sold into slavery along with Apache caught raiding the settlements. The yearly trade caravan from Santa Fe to Mexico City led them tethered like cattle, a human chain of captives to be sold in the marketplace along with the buffalo hides and wool of the New Mexican Hispanos.

The excesses of the civilian population and the unbending zeal of the Franciscan friars brought about the Pueblo Revolt of 1680. Fanning the fires of religious discontent, Popé, a Pueblo chieftain from Taos, organized the villages against the Hispanics. An initial bloody rampage forced 1,500 settlers and Christianized Indians to retreat South to Isleta, near present-day El Paso. Upriver, Popé and his men ransacked the churches of the hated religion, burning vestments, defacing statues, and destroying sacred vessels and ornaments. Furthermore, in an effort to remove all traces of Christianity, they rubbed themselves with a solution made out of yucca to erase the waters of baptism from their bodies.

The Cross and the sword, however, did not concede defeat. On September 13, 1893, a well-armed detachment of soldiers headed by Diego de Vargas, a deeply religious man, arrived outside Santa Fe after an almost bloodless campaign to retake New Mexico. Popé, seen as the devil incarnate, was dead. Under his reign the Pueblos had suffered almost as much as under the Hispanics. The Pueblo delegation that had met with Vargas initially argued that if it surrendered, their people would be subjected to forced labor, put to work in encomiendas as slaves, and be made to rebuild the churches. Vargas assured them that the people who had abused them would not return. He further gave them one hour to abjure their pagan beliefs, to pledge their allegiance to the Spanish king, and to be willing to adopt Christianity. The alternative was destruction. The Pueblos acceded. On December 16, a vanguard of soldiers and priests, which was part of a long column of more than 800 colonists and 18 supply wagons, arrived at the outskirts of Santa Fe. The priests entered the city singing hymns while the sullen Indians watched. Christianity was permanently implanted on New Mexican soil, even though it would never succeed in eradicating the ancient Pueblo beliefs.

✳ TEXAS

Altogether, 20 expeditions are known to have entered Texas before the threat of French encroachment forced the Spanish Crown to think of making good its territorial claims over the region.

In 1685, Robert Cavalier, sieur de la Salle, established Fort Saint Louis on Matagorda Bay. The Spanish, having word of this development ordered the colony found and destroyed. Four consecutive expeditions by Alonso de León searched the upper Gulf Coast of Texas before the ruins of the French fort were found. In the course of the fourth expedition, a Franciscan from the College of Querétaro, Father Damián Massenet, was invited by an Indian chief whom he met near the Guadalupe River to visit his people. He indicated that they dwelled further east. The Indian's invitation, according to some accounts, came from the tradition among his people of a lady in blue who had appeared to their ancestors and had recommended they go seek priests that would bring the true faith to them.

The story of the lady in blue first surfaced among the Jumano Indians near Isleta. In 1639, 50 Jumanos appeared before missionaries in Isleta, requesting instruction in the Christian faith so that they could eventually be baptized. After some investigation, it was determined that the lady in blue was Sor María de Jesús, a cloistered nun who had never gone beyond the confines of her convent in Agreda, Spain. A mystic, she was so well known for her piety that on occasion King Philip IV visited and consulted her. Sor María is said to have experienced in her mystical trances the phenomenon of bilocation, whereby she found herself in the New World teaching religion to the Indians.

Father Massenet was enthusiastic in responding to the Indian chief. For years the competing Franciscan colleges of Querétaro and Zacatecas, in Mexico, had sought the opportunity of opening Texas as a new mission field, but the Crown had only lent a deaf ear to their pleas. No missions had been allowed north of the Rio Grande. The implications of La Salle's failed expedition changed the political picture. The expedition pointed to the fact that the French, who already had claimed the valley of the Mississippi River, were harboring imperial designs for Texas. Consequently, in 1690 Alonso de León was sent at the head of a fifth expedition into Texas. He was accompanied by Father Massenet and three other Franciscans sent to establish missions in the easternmost region of Texas and evangelize the Hasinai Indians (incorrectly labeled "Tejas" by the first explorers). The underlying purpose was to buttress Spanish claims to the territory. The Franciscans founded two missions: San Francisco de los Tejas and El Santísimo Nombre de María. The missions were short-lived. Constant bickering between the friars and the military authorities over the treatment of the Indians, poor crops, the inability to make a settled people out of the nomadic eastern Texas tribes, and the easing of tensions with France brought about their closing in 1593.

In 1714, a French trader, Louis Juchereau de St. Denis, appeared at the San Juan Bautista mission on the southern bank of the Rio Grande. That a foreigner could openly enter Mexico through the back door instilled fear in the Spanish authorities. Once again they decided to establish missions along the eastern Texas border as a buffer against the

French. "By this means similar incursions will be prevented and, what is more important, these Indians will obtain instruction in our Holy Catholic Faith and the spiritual welfare of their souls," the viceroy wrote in 1715, outlining the plan for resettlement of eastern Texas.

The following year, Captain Domingo Ramón, commandant of the San Juan Bautista presidio, led the expedition aimed at founding the new missions. Altogether, 25 soldiers and their families, 11 Franciscans, from both the Colleges of Querétaro and Zacatecas, and 1,000 head of cattle traveled to eastern Texas. Among the missionaries was a leading figure who would come to be known as the Father of Texas Missions, Fray Antonio Margil de Jesús. Already 60 years of age when he joined the expedition, Margil had previously established missions in Guatemala, founded the Franciscan College of Zacatecas, and helped establish its rival institution in Querétaro. Years later, Margil would be the founder of Mission San José y San Miguel de Aguayo in San Antonio, Texas, which is reputedly the best example of Spanish missionary architecture in the United States. In a flurry of activity fired by evangelical zeal, Margil and his brethren built six missions among the Hasinai between July 1716 and the early part of 1717. Once the task was completed, it became evident that the logistics of supplying eastern Texas called for the establishment of another outpost midway between the Rio Grande and this distant frontier.

A proposal made by Father Antonio de Olivares, who had long strived to establish a mission on the San Antonio River, paved the way for the new foundation. Over 20 years before, Father Olivares swam across the Rio Grande into Texas and ambled north to the site occupied today by the city of San Antonio. The good friar was overcome with excitement by the sight of thousands of Indians congregated on the banks of San Pedro Springs. Having assumed these to be permanent Indian settlements, Fray Olivares set off on a campaign to establish missions in their midst, projecting a plentiful harvest of converts to the faith. He returned years later with Captain Diego Ramón on a journey of exploration geared to whetting the appetite of the Crown on behalf of his missionary project. In the course of this expedition, the river was given the name San Antonio de Padua. In December 1716, Olivares' proposal was approved with additions that provided for a presidio and a township to house the relatives of the garrison soldiers. In 1718, Mission San Antonio de Valero, the fateful Alamo of Texas revolutionary history, was founded, together with the presidio and the township.

The height of missionary activity in Texas followed the inspection tour of the royal visitor the Marquis de Aguayo in 1720. After assessing the situation in Texas, Aguayo granted permission to build Mission San José in San Antonio and the Presidio La Bahía near the mouth of the San Antonio River on Matagorda Bay. From San José, missionaries would subsequently set off to evangelize the Lipan Apache Indians, who eventually made peace with the Hispanic population. In the environs of La Bahía, missions were founded to attempt the conversion of the Karankawa and the Apache.

Missions in Texas were never truly successful. The Apache, for instance, are said to have assisted in the building process to please the friars, but they were never willing to give up their nomadic life and their horse-thieving ways. Time and again they made promises of settling down "next season" or "after the hunt," but they never remained for long. Like migratory birds, their sojourns were brief. As to the other Indians, mission life was never too attractive. At its peak, Mission San José had no more than 1,400 native dwellers. Their lack of success notwithstanding, some of the missions became wealthy in terms of arable lands and herds, awakening the greed of the authorities. By the time of Mexican independence in 1821, they all had been secularized, their lands and herds had been forfeited, and their buildings had fallen into disrepair. The settled areas of Texas at the time, however—Nacogdoches, San Antonio, and La Bahía (Goliad)—owed their existence to the efforts of the old friars.

✳ ARIZONA

The name of Jesuit Father Eusebio Kino, a German-educated Italian, pervades the history of evangelization in southern Arizona. Kino, a cartographer, among other things, had labored in the missions of Baja California, which he succeeded in proving was a peninsula rather than an island.

In 1687, he was sent to the northern Sonoran Desert to work in the conversion of the region known as Pimería Alta. In the course of the next 24 years, until his death in 1711, Kino established 29 missions, using the Mission Nuestra Señora de los Dolores in Sonora as his base of operations. Three of these missions—Guevavi, Tumacacori, and San Xavier de Bac—were located within the borders of the modern state of Arizona.

Kino was first and foremost a diplomat. He succeeded where others failed in winning the goodwill of Indian chieftains. Kino's mediation succeeded in bringing peace to the region in 1695, when war broke out among the Indian tribes divided over the issue of loyalty to the Spanish newcomers. As a missionary, Kino developed in the people a desire for conversion.

In the course of developing a mission, and before settling down to the task of religious instruction, he routinely introduced cattle ranching to the Indians. Then, after convincing the chieftains of the advantages of Christianity, he would have them travel to the Jesuit superior to request missionaries for their people. Unfortunately, there were never enough missionaries to satisfy the demands. The Hispanic settlers, on the other hand, were always eager to dismantle the missions. They wanted control of the herds and wanted Indian labor in the form of repartimientos to support work in the mines.

A second Pima uprising in 1751 and the expulsion of the Jesuits from all Spanish territories left little of Father Kino's work intact. The Franciscans who were entrusted with the Arizona missions were largely confined to Tumacacori and San Xavier. The Pimas for the most part returned to their ancient pagan ways.

✳ CALIFORNIA

The last mission territory to be opened in the northern frontier of Mexico was California. On July 1, 1769, more than 200 years after the Portuguese Juan Rodríguez Cabrillo, sailing under the flag of Spain, first discovered it, Franciscan Father Junípero Serra celebrated a solemn mass of thanksgiving on the shores of the Bay of San Diego. Months before, four expeditions, two by sea and two by land, had left Baja California for San Diego for the purpose of initiating the missionary process.

The original force behind this effort was Don José de Gálvez, visitor general for King Charles III, a man as visionary and driven by faith as Fray Junípero. As part of his duties, Gálvez visited in 1767 a handful of desolate missions in the rugged peninsula of Baja California. Built by the Jesuits, upon their expulsion these missions were entrusted to the Franciscans. Gálvez had a plan for Father Serra. Worried about the activities of Russian fur trappers who traveled into North America through the Bering Straits, the Spanish Crown began to look with interest at long-neglected California. Gálvez's proposal to Serra, the president of the Baja California missions, was a plan to establish a series of missions along the coast of northern California.

Junípero Serra (1713–1784) was born on the island of Mallorca, off the southern coast of Spain. Shunning the opportunity for further training as a theologian, for which he was eminently qualified, he offered himself for mission work and was sent to Mexico in 1747. From that date forward, Serra tirelessly traveled through Mexico giving himself completely to the task of evangelization and, as a result,

putting his health at serious risk. Needless to say, José Gálvez's mission plan was earmarked for the indefatigable padre, and during the late spring of 1769, the visitor general and Serra, undertaking the task of stevedores, personally packed and loaded on board a ship bound for San Diego chalices, vestments, altar cloths, and other items for the churches soon to be built in the northern California frontier.

July 16, 1769, marks the foundation of the first California mission, San Diego de Alcalá, on a hill overlooking the beautiful bay of the same name; and 54 years later, in 1823, the last of a chain of 21 missions, San Francisco Solano, was established north of the city of San Francisco. The missions were joined by the Camino Real, or Royal Road. They achieved, as nowhere else, great prosperity, with some of the missions owning over a dozen cattle ranches. Vineyards, orchards, vast fields of grain dotted the landscape surrounding the mission buildings.

Within their confines life was orderly, the ringing of bells dividing the day into work, rest, instructional, and devotional periods. Artisans and craftsmen brought from Mexico taught the residents a wealth of skills. Additionally, the missions operated schools and hospitals. The role that the missions played in the development of California cannot be overexaggerated. The development of a population from the fusion of the Hispanic mestizo settlers that came from Mexico and the native populations, the founding of townships and villages, and the emergence of a prosperous agricultural and cattle industry are primarily owed to the missions.

✳ THE ANGLO CONQUEST

By the time of the Treaty of Guadalupe Hidalgo in 1848, the mission system had disappeared, but the faith was kept alive by the people. Secular priests belonging to the northern dioceses of Mexico ministered to the needs of the faithful as well as they could, considering the vast distances they had to travel and the sparseness of their numbers. In distant villages and ranches, months and years would pass without a visit from a priest. In northern New Mexico, the Brotherhood of the Penitente s (Fraternidad Piadosa de Nuestro Padre Jesús Nazareno—the Pious Fraternity of Our Father Jesús the Nazarene) filled in the spiritual vacuum. These penitential organizations, which, according to some historians, have their roots in the Third Order of St. Francis, a lay arm of the Franciscans, practiced scourging and a rigorous piety centered on the sufferings of Christ. In the absence of clergy, they organized liturgies for the different feasts in the church calendar and taught religion to the young.

Although originally Rome had intended for the bishops of northern Mexico to continue administering the affairs of the church in what had now become the southwestern frontier of the United States, the North American bishops protested, voicing the displeasure of their government and probably their own jealousy. Political expediency forced the Vatican to bow before the pressures of the new rulers and appoint foreign bishops to each newly erected diocese or vicariate. The effects of this decision are still felt in our day. Texas, which fell under the diocese of Coahuila, was made a missionary vicariate under Rome in 1841. In 1847, the diocese of Galveston (now Galveston-Houston) was erected by the Vatican. It encompassed the entire state and its first bishop was Jean Marie Odin, a native of Lyon, France. The spiritual needs of the thousands of European Catholic immigrants that poured into Texas became the primary concern of the local church. Neglect of the Hispanic faithful became the norm.

The fate of the church in Texas was repeated in New Mexico, Arizona, Colorado, and California. Vicariates and dioceses were erected in all conquered territories, and with rare exceptions non-Hispanic bishops were appointed to head them. The new bishops and vicars, in turn, brought in almost exclusively European priests and congregations of religious men and women. The disdain that the newcomers felt toward the native population was reflected in the myth that its clergy were worthless and lazy. Underlying this assumption was the fear of the authorities that Hispanic priests were by virtue of their place in the community natural leaders who could induce their flocks to rebellion. Their fears materialized in the person of Father Antonio José Martínez of Taos, New Mexico.

Father Martínez (1793–1868), a native of Río Arriba County, New Mexico, was ordained to the priesthood after being widowed and fathering a daughter. His defense of the rights of Hispanic clergy before the unreasonable demands of French-born bishop Jean Baptiste Lamy of Santa Fe and his resistance to the suppression of the Penitente brotherhood led to his excommunication. Lamy's attitude toward the Hispanic faithful was typical of the church leaders sent to the conquered territories at the bequest of the U.S. bishops. The religious traditions of the people were shunned. The beautiful old adobe churches were allowed to decay. Plaster religious images replaced the colorful hand-carved cottonwood santos. Popular Hispanic religiosity was attacked as superstitious or pagan. To be Catholic you first had to be American, you had to pray in English, you had to give up your traditional religious practices.

By the end of the nineteenth century, Father Moisés Sandoval states, Hispanic Americans in the Southwest had no institutional voice in the church. The native Hispanic priests who had been their spokesmen in mid-century had all been purged or had died of old age. The Hispanic laity returned to their homespun religious traditions, which had served them well throughout the centuries.

Ironically enough, during this same period a Hispanic priest was working on behalf of the destitute Irish Catholic immigrants who were arriving in droves to this country. Cuban-born Father Félix Varela (1778–1853) was a political exile living in New York when Catholicism was the faith of a minority. The plight of the poor Irish, who would become the backbone of the church in the United States, was a catalyst that drove this intellectual into active social ministry. His acts of charity on behalf of the Irish and the sensitive and intelligent manner in which he defended and promoted Catholicism—he established the second Catholic newspaper in the United States—have served to bolster the cause for his canonization.

✳ DEVELOPING A PASTORAL APPROACH

Although the original attitude of the English-speaking conquerors of the Mexican Southwest was that Hispanics would eventually disappear, migrations from Mexico, Cuba, and Puerto Rico in the latter part of the nineteenth century and the early years of the twentieth mandated a new approach on the part of the church. The church now saw herself as an instrument in the process of integrating Hispanics into the mainstream. For this purpose, national parishes were established for Hispanics, an approach utilized with other ethnic groups, such as the Polish, the Italians, and the Germans. Contrary to other nationalities, however, native Hispanic priests who could supply leadership and role models for their own people were seldom available. One of the salient reasons for this absence was the failure by church authorities to promote vocations among Hispanics, who, because of prevalent social and economic conditions, could seldom meet the educational standards required by seminaries and novitiates. The gap was filled by Spanish-speaking priests of other national origins. In Texas, two religious orders, the Oblates of Mary Immaculate and the Claretians, were invited in by the different bishops specifically to minister to Hispanics.

In the meantime, Hispanics grew in number and began to settle in areas other than the Southwest. Waves of migration came from Mexico and, after 1917, when its people were granted U.S. citizenship, from Puerto Rico. By the 1920s, it was evident that more than a diocesan approach was needed to serve this population. In 1923, the U.S. bishops established an immigration office in El Paso, Texas, aimed at ministering to the large number of Mexicans fleeing the revolution, which had begun in 1910. In 1944, Archbishop Robert E. Lucey of San Antonio held a seminar for the Spanish-speaking to discuss the needs of the Hispanic faithful. In 1945, the Bishops Committee for the Spanish-speaking was created to establish programs, both of a social and a pastoral nature, in Texas, California, Colorado, and Santa Fe. One of its goals was to put an end to prejudice and discrimination against Hispanics in the church. The catalyst for these measures was the increasing proselytism of Hispanics by Protestant churches.

✳ A SEARCH FOR PARITY

Although in the 1950s and 1960s the number of Hispanic priests and nuns increased, they were often not allowed to work with their own people. Archbishop Patrick Flores, the highest-ranking Hispanic in the U.S. Catholic church today, likes to recall how as a young priest assigned to a predominantly Hispanic parish in Houston, Texas, he was forbidden by his pastor the use of Spanish except in the confessional.

The reforms imposed on the church by the Second Vatican Council in the early 1960s, particularly those calling for the use of the vernacular rather than Latin in the celebration of the Mass, and the activism among minority groups in the period that followed brought to a head the silent struggle of Hispanic Catholics. Demands that the Mass and the sacraments be offered in Spanish mounted. In 1967, Henry Casso of San Antonio was named executive director of the Bishops Committee for the Spanish-speaking, a position occupied by Anglos from its inception. In 1969, Hispanic priests organized Priests Associated for Religious, Educational and Social Rights (PADRES), and in 1971 Hispanic sisters followed suit with the creation of Las Hermanas, an organization representing 20 religious orders. The same year saw the creation in San Antonio of the Mexican American Cultural Center (MACC), a Hispanic pastoral institute aimed at training clergy and lay leaders to serve the spiritual needs of Hispanics. The moving force behind MACC was Father Virgilio Elizondo, a native of San Antonio and a leading Hispanic theologian. Hispanic offices at the regional and diocesan level were also established about this time. Finally, in 1974, the U.S. bishops, at the instance of PADRES, created the Secretariat for Hispanic Affairs as a permanent office within the U.S. Catholic Conference. The secretariat is charged with assisting and advising the bishops.

Three Encuentros, or national meetings, of delegates representing Hispanic Catholics from throughout the land have been held in the nation's capital, in 1972, 1977, and 1985. The Encuentros served to voice the needs and expectations of Hispanic Catholics and were instrumental in promulgating the U.S. bishops' pastoral letter, "The Hispanic Presence: Challenge and Commitment" (1983), and a national plan for Hispanic ministry approved by the bishops in 1987.

The first Hispanic to be ordained bishop was Patrick Flores, the son of poor migrant workers from Ganado, Texas. Flores was ordained on May 5, 1970, and named auxiliary bishop of San Antonio and later installed as bishop of El Paso, Texas. With his appointment in 1979 to the archdiocese of San Antonio, which heads the ecclesiastical province of Texas, he became the first Hispanic to be installed as an archbishop in this country. Since 1971, the Vatican has appointed more Hispanics as auxiliary bishops, but only infrequently as full bishops to U.S. dioceses. Their numbers, however, fail to reflect demographic reality. Although population projections indicate that by the year 2000 the majority of U.S. Catholics will be Hispanic, as of 1992 only 19 out of more than 360 bishops and only one out of some 45 archbishops in the United States were Hispanic—of these, two were Cubans, two Puerto Ricans, one Ecuadorian, one Venezuelan, two Spaniards, and two Mexicans. The balance were U.S.-born Hispanics.

In 1991, the Missionary Catechists of Divine Providence, the only religious order of Mexican American women, was granted total independence by the Vatican. Having begun as an organization for lay catechists in Houston, Texas, in the 1930s, the missionary catechists are dedicated to foment leadership among Hispanics in different dioceses of the Southwest.

✳ PROTESTANTISM AND HISPANICS

Latin America was missionary territory for the nineteenth-century U.S. Protestant churches. As the Latin American nations gained their independence from Catholic Spain, Protestant England's traditional foe, English-speaking missionaries, aware of the anticlericalism present in the independence movements south of the border decided that the time had come for the spiritual conquest of the region. Proselytism of Hispanics born in the United States was now a goal of the Protestant ministers who traveled south to the lands newly conquered from Mexico. Those who converted were valuable as Spanish-speaking leaders who could be sent to the promising mission fields of Mexico. A case in point was Alejo Hernández, a former Catholic priest who had converted to the Methodist faith and was ordained deacon in Corpus Christi, Texas, in 1871. Shortly after his ordination, he had to abandon the work he had begun in Texas among his own people to become a missionary in Mexico City. As in the case of the Catholic church after the U.S. takeover of Texas and the Southwest, the Protestant churches assumed that the native Hispanic population would disappear in time. Ministering to U.S. Hispanics also helped Anglo missionaries to learn the ways and the language of the people south of the border, whose conversion was their ultimate goal.

The level of preparation for Hispanic ministers was lower than that of their Anglo counterparts. A system of patronage developed in Texas and the Southwest whereby Hispanic congregations and ministers were made to depend upon their more enlightened and wealthier Anglo counterparts. According to Methodist Church Historian Edwin E. Sylvester, the essential patterns and structures of Hispanic American Protestantism in this region were fixed in the second half of the nineteenth century. Anglos controlled the churches and their institutions. Hispanic churches were not encouraged to develop self-determination, but to assimilate and accommodate to the customs and the institutional interests of the conquering culture. Hispanic leaders were trained out of expediency rather than out of respect for the values that their culture could bring to the churches.

In 1898, after the end of the Spanish-American War, Protestant missionaries descended upon Cuba and Puerto Rico, where they achieved a modicum of success. Some were born in Cuba or Puerto Rico and had converted as exiles in the United States. Catholicism was seen by many as the faith of the old oppressive order and Protestantism as a more enlightened faith.

Conversion, however, implied relinquishing traditional values. Cuban-born Protestant theologian and church historian Justo González explains in his book *Mañana* (1990) that for Hispanics to become Protestant entailed a surrender of their identity similar to that expected of Hispanic Catholics in the United States. Becoming Protestant required Americanization, partly because Catholicism was so ingrained in Hispanic culture. As González points out, when these Cuban and Puerto Rican Protestants migrated to the United States, they had a sense of alienation from both the Anglos and their own compatriots.

The seeds planted during the first part of the twentieth century began to root and by the 1930s a Spanish-speaking Protestant clergy was emerging. For Methodists and Presbyterians, a big stumbling block, then as now, was the integration of Hispanics into national conferences of their respective churches. Hispanics, wishing to preserve their cultural and linguistic identities, often fear being absorbed by the non-Hispanic majority in the conferences. One of the most successful of the mainstream Hispanic churches has been the Rio Grande Conference, which includes Hispanic Methodists in Texas and New Mexico. Its roots date back to the early 1930s when Alfredo Náñez, the first Hispanic to receive his B.D. degree from Southern Methodist University, and Francisco Ramos were selected as presiding elders of the Texas American Conference. In 1939, it became the Rio Grande Conference, a powerful group of churches that has chosen, in spite all pressures, to remain independent. Under similar historical circumstances, the Latin American Conference of Southern California opted to merge with the Anglo conferences, a move that has resulted in declining membership. The less structured nature of the Southern Baptists and the Pentecostals, whereby each congregation retains partial or total autonomy, has contributed to their increasing Hispanic membership, the only mainstream churches to experience such growth.

Pentecostalism, a brand of evangelical Christianity that is sweeping Central and South America, is growing in leaps and bounds among U.S. Hispanics. Its popularity seems to rest in the small-community atmosphere of the individual churches, which allows Hispanics a feeling of belonging. More particularly, because Pentecotalism does not dismantle for Hispanics the building blocks of their religious expression, Hispanic converts to Pentecostalism find in their new church room to express their religiosity. According to a study done in Chile by Lalive d'Epinay, although Pentecostalism disallows Catholic traditions such as processions and other external religious manifestations, it provides the convert with a highly emotional form of worship. The place that the saints and the Virgin occupied as protectors, intercessors, and healers of suffering humanity is now replaced with the healing powers of the Holy Spirit. Catholic clerical authority finds its counterpart in the authority that those who have received the baptism of the Holy Spirit acquire. Interestingly enough, the charismatic renewal movement in the Roman Catholic church, which like the Pentecostals stresses the worship of the third person of the Trinity (God the Holy Spirit), is most popular among Hispanics.

During the period of brown power activism in the 1960s, Hispanic Protestants tended to remain on the sidelines. But it must be noted that two of the early leaders of the Chicano movement were Reies Tijerina, a Pentecostal minister who fought for the rights of New Mexicans to their ancestral land grants, and Rudolfo "Corky" González, a Presbyterian leader. González, a former boxer who had served time for his political involvement in the struggle for Mexican American rights, was an early Chicano literary figure, having authored the important epic poem "Yo soy Joaquin."

✳ POPULAR RELIGIOSITY

Hispanics who lived in the territories occupied by the United States in the nineteenth century and those who migrated from Mexico and the other Spanish American countries have succeeded in preserving the religious traditions of their forefathers. Perhaps because of the almost universal scarcity of priests in the Spanish-speaking Americas, the family and the home have always been at the center of Hispanic religiosity. This religiosity is not necessarily derived from the teachings of childhood catechisms nor the homilies of parish priests. It is formed by assimilating and adapting the private religious practices that individuals observe within their extended family, which includes not only relatives, but friends and neighbors as well.

The religious instruction of the children, rosaries, novenas, *promesas* or *mandas* (the practice of making sacrificial offerings for some specific purpose), and the wearing of scapulars and medals occur or are promoted in the home usually at the behest of the grandmother or some other elderly female figure. For Hispanics, religion is often the concern of the women, who must look out for the spiritual well-being and even the salvation of their menfolks. In this context, it should be noted that in some cultures, particularly among Hispanics of Mexican origin, the *quinceañera* (fifteenth birthday) celebration, which marks the coming of age of the young girls, involves a mass or prayer service with a sermon that usually reminds the young woman of her future responsibilities as a Christian wife and mother.

Within the Hispanic household it is not unusual to find a place that functions as an altar. In creating the altar, the Hispanic woman tries to gather within the confines of her private domain symbols of the spiritual forces on which she depends for assistance in fulfilling her primary responsibility as caretaker of a family. The home altar might be nothing more than a religious picture before which candles are lit in a wordless form of prayer; it can be a statuette of a saint, of Christ or the Virgin on a table or a television set accompanied by a vase filled with flowers; or it can be elaborate, attempting to approximate an altar within a church, with a profusion of religious images, hand-embroidered cloths, candles, incense, holy water, and other objects of the Roman Catholic worship.

Veneration of the Virgin Mary in her different aspects is foremost for most Hispanic groups: Our Lady of Guadalupe and Our Lady of San Juan de los Lagos for the Mexicans, Our Lady of Providencia for the Puerto Ricans, La Caridadholid del Cobre for the Cubans, and Altagracia for the Dominicans, to name a few. Veneration of Our Lady of Sorrows (Dolores) is prevalent among all groups, particularly among women, who as mothers identify with the Virgin suffering for her son. The degree of identification with this aspect of the Virgin is manifest in a tradition observed by some Mexican Americans that involves visitation of a local image of the Virgin on Good Friday to offer condolences for the death of Christ. Another tradition that reveals the intimacy of the people with their celestial Mother is observed on February 2, the feast of the Purification of Mary. For Mexican Americans this is the day when the Holy Infant first sits up—"El Asentamiento del Niño." A *madrina* (godmother) is selected for the

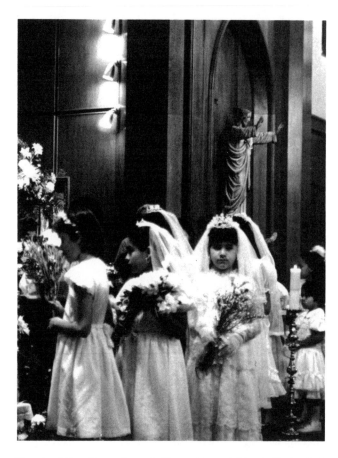

Feast of the Crowning of Mary, Sacred Heart Cathedral, Houston, 1987. (Photograph by Curtis Dowell.)

Annual mass on the feast day of Our Lady of Guadalupe, Houston, Texas.

Child. She thus strengthens her bonds through god-parenting with Our Lady. The madrina, often a young girl, dresses a doll-like image of the Infant with new clothes and helps him sit up. This feast concludes for the Mexicans the Christmas season, which begins with the apparition of Our Lady of Guadalupe on December 12.

The special meaning of the Virgin for Hispanics cannot be stressed enough. For the males she is the understanding mother who forgives and intercedes for her errant sons; for the women she sympathizes with the earthly travails of a mother, sister, or daughter. Even Protestants are not immune to the appeal of this veneration. Justo González, the Protestant historian, recounts how in his seminary days some of the students, wanting to ingratiate themselves with their teacher, began to mock the cult of Our Lady of Guadalupe. The old professor, a Mexican, stopped them with the admonition that they were free to tear down Roman Catholic dogma, but they should be careful of being disrespectful toward "mi virgencita" (my little Virgin).

Adoration of particular images of Christ is traditional among certain national groups: for Guatemalans there is El Cristo Negro de Esquipulas (The Black Christ of Esquipulas); for Colombians, El Señor de los Milagros (The Lord of Miracles); and for Salvadorans, Cristo El Salvador (Christ the Savior). Additionally, the cult of the Sacred Heart of Jesus, representing the suffering aspect of Christ's human love for people, is universally popular. As noted previously, these cults invariably center on a bleeding, wounded representation of Jesus. It is not unusual for theologians or priests to bemoan Hispanics' stress on the dead rather than on the resurrected Christ.

Hispanics worship Jesus as a child, frequently under the name El Santo Niño de Atocha (The Holy Child of Atocha). This traditional cult dates back to the time of the Reconquest of Spain, when allegedly a child brought a basket of bread to Christian captives held in a Moslem prison. The child revealed himself to them as Jesus, who had come to bring them the bread of Holy Communion. Theorists claim that the fear of the early explorers and settlers of falling captive to the Indians is responsible for the popularity of the Niño de Atocha in the Americas. Similar reasons are adduced for the popularity of El Niño Perdido (Jesus lost and found in the temple by his parents).

According to Father Virgilio Elizondo, in a 1990 speech at Peabody University, the most popular saint among U.S. Hispanics is Martin of Porres, a seventeenth-century Dominican lay brother who was the illegitimate son of a black woman and a Spaniard. Martin chose to perform the most menial tasks at his convent and to personally feed and heal the poor.

The veneration of different Franciscan saints was propagated by the early missionaries, a great many of whom were members of the Franciscan order. Saint Francis of Assisi, founder of this order, and his close friend Saint Anthony of Padua have been popular since colonial days. Veneration of Saint Joseph dates back to the days of exploration and colonization, because he is the patron saint of expeditions. The same can be said about Saint Christopher, protector of travelers. Among Cuban Americans, the veneration of Saint Lazarus and Saint Barbara are very popular and more than likely related to the phenomenon of religious syncretism evident in Santería. *Velorios de santos*, celebrations on the eve of either saint's feast day, are often held in the homes of devotees.

Processions, pilgrimages, and other external manifestations are an important element of religious expression for Hispanics. In the United States, the feast of the patron saint of a national group or a town still calls for a solemn mass followed by different forms of merriment. Processions sometimes are held, but seldom do they go beyond the grounds of the church. Exceptions to this rule are the processions of Our Lady of Guadalupe in the Southwest and of La Caridad del Cobre in the Miami area.

Pilgrimages to the shrine of Our Lady of Guadalupe in Mexico City are routinely organized wherever large groups of Mexican Americans reside. Of great interest are the pilgrimages to the shrine of Our Lady of San Juan de los Lagos in Jalisco, Mexico, which dates back to colonial times and is popular among people in northern Mexico and the U.S. Southwest. The subject of this veneration is an image of the Immaculate Conception that since the early 1600s has been said to possess healing powers. Today a large shrine to the Virgin in the Texas border town of San Juan attracts many pilgrimages from within the United States. The shrine to La Caridad del Cobre facing Biscayne Bay in Coral Ga-

The celebration of the feast day of Our Lady of Caridad del Cobre, the patron of Cubans, in Houston, 1986. (Photograph by Curtis Dowell.)

A Christmas *posada* sponsored by the Club Sembradores de la Amistad in Houston, 1988. (Photograph by Curtis Dowell.)

bles, Florida, built with funds collected among Cuban exiles in the 1960s, attracts Cuban American pilgrims from throughout the United States.

An integral part of many pilgrimages is the fulfilling of vows made by the faithful. This may involve making the final part of the journey on one's knees. Among Mexican Americans and some Central Americans, the tradition of the ex voto (gifts presented to a saint as a show of gratitude for a favor conceded) still remains. Colonial ex votos were often primitive drawings on tin or wood depicting the miracle performed by the saint and often included a written explanation. Modern ex votos can be photographs, bridal wreaths, baby shoes, letters of gratitude, and, in many cases, the traditional *milagrito* (a charm made out of tin, gold, or silver and shaped in the form of an arm, a leg, a baby, or a house, for instance). More graphic ex votos are crutches, leg braces, eyeglasses, and other devices that through supernatural intercession the presenter was able to discard. Both the magnificent shrine in San Juan, Texas, and the quaint Sanctuary of Chimayo in Chimayo, New Mexico, where the soil behind the chapel is said to have curative powers, are excellent examples of churches where this practice flourishes.

Mexican Americans have preserved to this day the traditional *posada,* a novena that ends on Christmas eve and dates back to colonial days. For nine nights a different neighborhood family serves as host for the posada. The "pilgrims," reenacting Mary and Joseph's search for lodging, knock at the designated home, singing a traditional hymn and asking for shelter, but are refused repeatedly. Finally, an innkeeper allows them into a home, a rosary is said, and refreshments are served. The *Pastorela*, a folk play dating to the colonial period that reenacts the adoration of the shepherds, is still presented in some Mexican American communities during this season.

In northern New Mexico, despite periods of persecution, the *penitentes* continue to observe their Holy Week traditions. The brothers, all laymen, gather in the "moradas," or secret meeting places. They still practice some sort of corporal punishment, if not the extreme forms of flagellation and crucifixion observed up through the nineteenth century. After commemoration of the death of Christ on Good Friday, "tinieblas" is observed. In the completely dark morada, fearful sounds meant to instill in the faithful a contemplation of the horrors of hell are made with traditional wood and metal noisemakers.

Mexican Americans as a whole reflect, less severely perhaps, the spirit of the penitentes. Without question, Ash Wednesday draws the biggest crowds of faithful to Catholic churches in Mexican American neighborhoods. According to Virgilio Elizondo's, 1990 speech at Peabody University, this penitential tendency reveals the feelings of inferiority of the Indian and the mestizo before the Spanish conquistador. At the opposite end of the spectrum is December 12, the feast of Our Lady of Guadalupe, which also draws multitudes to the churches. The faithful come to this feast to rejoice in their new hope, according to Elizondo. Symbols of this joy and this hope are the flowers with which they shower the Virgin and the traditional singing of "Las Mañanitas" (Morning Songs) by mariachi groups at the break of dawn.

✳ BEYOND ORTHODOXY

Despite all precautions by church authorities, pagan or non-Christian cults have always coexisted with orthodox practices. Herb shops known as "yerberías" by Mexican Americans and "botánicas" by people of Hispanic-Caribbean descent offer not only medicinal plants but also a variety of products used or recommended by spiritualists and faith healers.

Yerberos are herb specialists who know the medicinal qualities of plants and utilize them to cure physical ailments. They claim that the roots, leaves, and seeds of many herbs can offset snakebite, infertility, arthritis, kidney stones, and any other conceivable illness.

The *curandero* is also a folk healer, but one who can cure ailments of a physical and a spiritual nature. He can also remedy just about any human condition by utilizing the forces of good and evil. To bring about the desired results, the *curandero* uses, among other things, medicinal plants, eggs, candles, spells, perfumes, prayers, incense, holy water, and religious images. The curandero can, to name a few gifts, remove a spell that renders a person physically ill, make an unfaithful husband return to his wife, cure a child of "ojo" (the effects of someone's covetousness) or "susto" (fright), help someone have good luck in business or gambling, prevent or terminate pregnancies, and prepare amulets, oils, ointments, and charms. A curandero who does evil is technically a witch, a *brujo* or *bruja*. He uses the tools of his trade to do harm to others. Most curanderos, however, practice both white and black magic.

Spiritism and spiritualism sometimes coexist with curanderismo. Spiritism is a pseudoscience developed in Europe in the last century by Alan Kardec. By the 1860s it had reached Latin America. Spiritists invoke the spirits of the dead through me-

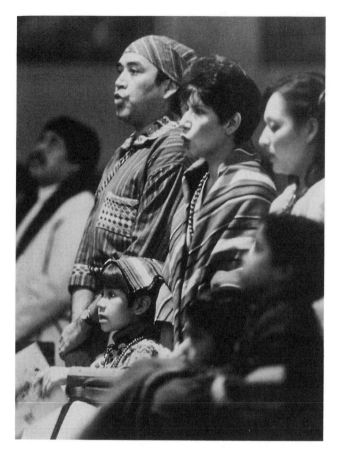

Diversity in Hispanic evangelism. (Photograph by Curtis Dowell.)

diums. They seek through these communications to give guidance, advice, and revelations of a supernatural nature. Spiritists may pride themselves in having access to the spirits of famous persons, such as Napoleon, Moctezuma, or Cleopatra, or they may "work" through ordinary spirits—a black slave, a great-grandmother, a fisherman. The services performed by a spirit relate to characteristics it allegedly had while alive. In this context it should be noted that Pancho Villa, the Mexican bandit and revolutionary, is a favorite among U.S. Hispanic spiritists. Villa, who was known for his hot temper, is called upon to chase away all evil spirits.

Spiritualism is a cult developed in Mexico, also during the nineteenth century. Spiritualists, unlike spiritists, are usually practicing Catholics. They consider themselves vehicles or "cajas" (boxes) for great religious figures and utilize these powers to heal. Among Mexican Americans, spiritualists often serve as channels for two late spiritualists: Don Pedrito Jaramillo, a curandero from Falfurrias, Texas, and the Niño Fidencio, from a village outside Monterrey, Nuevo León, Mexico. Today there is a popular movement of canonization of these healers by the Catholic church. Others have created separate cults. In the case of Fidencio, his devotees display images of Our Lady of Guadalupe and the Sacred Heart of Jesus bearing the healer's face where the face of Mary or Jesus would normally appear.

Santeros and *babalaos* are the curanderos and brujos of Caribbean Hispanics. They are the spiritual healers, advisers, and witches of the cults brought from the western coast of Africa by the Yoruba slaves, who were imported in large numbers to Cuba and Puerto Rico during the last century. Today Miami, Tampa, New York, and San Juan, Puerto Rico, are centers of this religious cult. Santería in the United States has spread beyond the Cuban and Puerto Rican communities to people of other national origins. It is already influencing and being influenced by Mexican American curanderismo. Santería merges elements from different Yoruba cults and Catholicism. African slaves, often forced to accept baptism by their masters, continued to worship their African gods under the external cult of the Christian saints. A less complex form of Santería is practiced by people from the Dominican Republic. This cult is a modified form of the Haitian voodoo.

A Catholic charismatic prayer meeting.

Santería is a cult of the *orishas* (deities), who control the forces of nature. The most popular of these gods are portrayed on candles and icons labeled Las Siete Potencias (the Seven Powerful Spirits). Ruling over all of these spiritual forces is Olofin, God the Creator. His son, Obatala, takes the form of Our Lady of Mercy, although he is also worshiped in his male aspect as Christ, and in some Mexican American areas as Our Lady of San Juan. Obatala is vengeful, powerful, and indifferent, and his devotees wear white. Chango, the god of war, snakes, storms, and thunder, takes the form of Saint Barbara. Her color is red, the color of blood. Babalu-aye, the god of healing, is Saint Lazarus, portrayed as a leper on crutches, often accompanied by two dogs. Ogun is John the Baptist, a wild man of the forest who controls things made out of iron. Ochun, Our Lady of la Caridad del Cobre, is the goddess of love. Yemaya rules the waters. She is Our Lady of Regla. Orula, St. Francis of Assisi, can see the future.

The babalaos are the diviners of Ifa, a system they learn after many years of study. Their powers come from the god Orula. They use the so called Rosary of Ifa (16 cowrie shells, mango seeds, or pieces of coconut shell) to determine which god or orisha is affecting a person's life. The babalao casts the shells or seeds and determines which of the possible 16 x 16 patterns they follow. Each pattern asks for a verse the babalao recites by rote and then interprets for the client. The babalao further determines what sacrifice must be offered to the orisha to appease him or win his favor and performs it. The client must pay him for both the divination and the sacrifice. The sacrifice varies. Different gods like different gifts in terms of food, perfumes, ornaments, and so forth. Before reaching most of these gods, however, one must appeal to Elegua, who under the guise of Saint Christopher, rules road crossings. Some of the saints demand animal sacrifices. In the case of Obatala, for example, because his favorite color is white, it must be a white hen or dove.

Santeros are the devotees of the different gods. After rigorous initiation, they become the son or daughter of the orisha and are endowed with special faculties. The orisha lives in a container within the santero's house (in the United States it is usually an expensive soup tureen in the orisha's favorite color). The santero wears the orisha's color, builds him elaborate altars, and celebrates his feast day with great fanfare and at great expense. The priests and priestesses of Santería are charged with directing the liturgy.

There are three "reglas," or ways to practice Santería. The one described above is the regla of Obatala, the most widespread. The regla Lucumi is similar to the regla Obatala, although there is less syncretism between African and Christian saints. The third way is the regla Mayombera or Palo Mayombé, which intermingles Congolese rites with spiritism or the cult of the dead. It is similar to Haitian voodoo in that it works more with the *ngangas* (the spirits of the dead) than with the orishas or deities. The practitioners (*mayomberos*) are feared as powerful magicians. They can exorcise evil spirits, cast spells, and make amulets. A client may chose to consult a babalao to determine the nature of his problem and go to a mayombero for the cure or solution.

A cult incorrectly connected with Santería is Nañiguismo. Nañigos are members of the Sociedad Abakúa, a secret society that combines religious elements of the Carabalí (Efik people from the coast of Calabar in southern Nigeria) and Freemasonry. Nañiguismo has its roots in the early days of slavery. Encouraged by the church, slaves grouped themselves into cabildos (religious brotherhoods dedicated to promoting the veneration of a saint). The cabildos helped slaves from the same African nations to maintain their ties unbeknownst to their white masters. The Sociedad Abakúa developed from a cabildo formed by the Carabalí. Nañiguismo, as it is commonly known, has survived to this date, thanks to its elaborate secret rules and rituals.

References

Bolton, Herbert Eugene. *Rim of Christendom: A Biography of Fray Eusebio Kino*. Tucson: University of Arizona Press, 1984.

Castañeda, Carlos. *Our Catholic Heritage in Texas*, seven volumes. Austin: Von Boeckmann-Jones, 1936–41.

Diaz Del Castillo, Bernal. *La verdadera historia de la conquista de la Nueva España*. México City: Porrúa, 1966.

Elizondo, Virgilio. *Galilean Journey: The Mexican American Promise*. Maryknoll, New York: Orbis Books, 1985.

Gannon, Michael V. *The Cross in the Sand: The Early Catholic Church in Florida, 1513–1870*. Gainesville: University Presses of Florida, 1983.

González, Justo. *Mañana: Christian Theology from a Hispanic Perspective*. Nashville: Abingdon Press, 1990.

Goodpasture, H. McKennie. *Cross and Sword: An Eyewitness History of Christianity in Latin America*. Maryknoll, New York: Orbis Books, 1989.

Kessell, John L. *Kiva, Cross and Crown: The Pecos Indians and New Mexico, 1540–1840*. Albuquerque: University of New Mexico Press, 1987.

McWilliams, Carey. *North From Mexico: The Spanish-Speaking People of the United States*. Westport, Connecticut: Greenwood Press, 1968.

Macklin, June, and Margarite B. Melville, eds. "All the Good and Bad in this World." In *Twice a Minority: Mexican American Women*. St. Louis: Mosby, 1980: 127–148.

Mirandé, Alfredo. *The Chicano Experience: An Alternative Perspective*. Notre Dame: University of Notre Dame Press, 1985.

Palou, Fr. Francisco. *Vida de Fr. Junípero Serra y Misiones de la California Septentrional*. Mexico City: Editorial Porrúa, 1975.

Pena, Silvia Novo, and Robert Flores, eds. *Interiors: Secular Aspects of Religion*. Houston: Houston Public Libraries, 1982.

Pollak-Eltz. *Cultos afroamericanos*. Caracas: Universidad Católica Andrés Bello, 1977.

Sandoval, Moisés. *On the Move: A History of the Hispanic Church in the United States*. Maryknoll, New York: Orbis Books, 1990.

Steele, Thomas J. *Santos and Saints: The Religious Folk Art of Hispanic New Mexico*. Santa Fe, New Mexico: Ancient City Press, 1974.

Terrell, John Upton. *Pueblos, Gods and Spaniards*. New York: Dial Press, 1973.

Silvia Novo Pena

⑫

Military

✳ U.S. Revolutionary War ✳ Mexican War for Independence from Spain ✳ Mexican-American War
✳ U.S. Civil War ✳ World War I ✳ World War II ✳ Conflicts in Korea and Vietnam
✳ Outstanding Hispanics in the Military

The history of Hispanics in military service in North America begins before the founding of the 13 British colonies. It includes service under at least five flags: those of the King of Spain, the Republic of Mexico, the Republic of Texas, the Confederacy and the United States of America—not to mention the Hispanics that lived in the southern portions of what would become the United States under British and French rule. The exploration and colonization of the areas of today's United States that were once New Spain and later Mexico—much of the Southeast, Southwest and West (See chapter on Spanish Explorers and Colonizers)—was accomplished by soldiers in the service of Spain. Although many of the first explorers of the Floridas and the Atlantic and Gulf coasts were military men from Spain, later exploration and especially colonization was effected over a period of three centuries by people born in the Americas, many of whom already were the product of mixed racial heritage, such as mestizos and mulattoes, as well as full-blooded American Indians and Africans who had been Hispanicized. The Spanish pattern of settling the frontier was to establish a military fort, or presidio *alongside a mission for evangelizing and acculturating the natives, as well as to lay out towns as population centers for the agricultural exploitation of the surrounding fields. This basic pattern not only led to extensive military presence throughout the Southwest and Southeast, but also to the development of a racially mixed population, including the ranks of the military.*

There were other Spanish traditions and practices, moreover, that also led to racial and ethnic diversity in the military. The Spanish attitude about race was quite distinct from that of the British. Since the Roman domination of the Iberian Peninsula, slavery was seen as the result of spoils of war—not as an elaborate ideology of inferiority of the enslaved. Under Spanish law and practice, slaves had certain rights, and Spanish culture and the Catholic church were more disposed to releasing slaves than was British culture and Protestant religions. Slaves were seen as people who should share in the salvation of the Christian religion. They could have the opportunity to earn their freedom, progress independently in trades and professions, and, while still being slaves, even move up in the ranks of the military. By the year 1600, there already existed a black Spanish militia in Florida. Many of the colonists of Florida were free black craftsmen and black soldiers in the Spanish army. The black militia comprised both free and enslaved blacks serving as soldiers and officers. In fact, by 1738, the first black commander of a Spanish regiment had been named in lands that would become part of the United States. He was a runaway slave by the name of Francisco Menéndez. Originally a Mandingo from West Africa, Menéndez escaped from English slavery in the Carolinas. After assisting Yamassee Indians in battle, they helped him to reach the Spanish sanctuary for runaway slaves in St. Augustine, Florida. He was betrayed by an Indian and sold into Spanish slavery as a soldier. He became an officer while still a slave, and in 1738 was freed and made commander of the all-black regiment of soldiers at Fort Mose, just north of St. Augustine. Captain Menéndez held the position until 1763, when Florida became a British colony and the inhabitants of Ft. Mose were evacuated to Cuba.

✳ U.S. REVOLUTIONARY WAR

During the Revolutionary War, the Spanish army assisted the cause of U.S. independence from England by engaging in direct combat with the British in the South and especially in the Gulf of Mexico, cutting off supply lines and otherwise harassing the "Redcoats." One of the most outstanding and effective supporters of the revolutionary effort was governor of Louisiana Bernardo de Gálvez, who engaged British forces repeatedly for three years along the Gulf of Mexico, destroying their forts, capturing Mobile and Pensacola, and generally rendering great support to the Continental Army. Gálvez's victory at Pensacola, in particular, made the American victory at Yorktown possible. (In 1980, the U.S. government commemorated the Hispanic contribution to the American War of Independence by issuing a stamp recognizing General Bernardo de Gálvez's 1780 victory at the Battle of Mobile.)

One of the first, if not the first, Hispanic Revolutionary War hero was Jorge Farragut, a seaman born on the Spanish island of Minorca who joined the South Carolina Navy as a lieutenant and fought at the battle of Savannah (1779) and at the second defense of Charleston (1780), where he was captured. After being freed, Farragut joined the Continental Army and earned the rank of major. He stayed in the newly independent United States, married and fathered a son who would become the first admiral of the United States Navy—David Farragut.

✳ MEXICAN WAR FOR INDEPENDENCE FROM SPAIN

Hispanics not only played a role in the American Revolution, but Hispanics from the Southwest also participated in the war to free Mexico from Spain. In fact, in 1811, a captain in the militia in Texas, Juan Bautista Casas, became the first martyr for Mexican independence from areas that would become the United States. Casas led a local revolt in San Antonio, Texas, against the Spanish governor, Colonel Manuel de Salcedo. Casas seized the governor and officials, proclaiming support for Mexico's revolution and declaring himself the governor of Mexican Texas. Casas was captured and executed by Spanish soldiers and his head was exhibited at the central plaza as a warning to other sympathizers of the revolution led by Miguel Hidalgo (See Historical Overview chapter). In 1812, Bernardo Gutiérrez de Lara became the first hero from the area in the struggle for Mexican independence. In June, Gutiérrez de Lara led his men in taking the towns of Nacogdoches and Salcedo from the royalist garrison. Gutiérrez also sent emissaries to other parts of Texas and to the Rio Grande Valley to spread the word of the revolution.

✳ MEXICAN-AMERICAN WAR

Later, in 1836, when Texas sought its independence from Mexico, numerous Hispanic soldiers distinguished themselves in battles against the central government in Mexico, with Lorenzo de Zavala and Juan N. Seguín emerging as leaders; later the former was elected vice president of the Texas Republic and the latter mayor of San Antonio. Mexico lost Texas and, in the 1846–1848 war, the rest of what would become the Southwest and West of the United States, with Hispanics often ambivalent or engaged in fighting with relatives and friends. Some of the Mexican commanders of forces in California and New Mexico, despite their defeat, often made a successful transition to American rule, and served in the territorial and state governments and their militia.

✳ U.S. CIVIL WAR

Soon after the Mexican War, the United States engaged in its own Civil War. This again had the effect of dividing the Hispanics of the Southwest, with some from Texas, such as Santos Benavides (who rose to become the highest ranking Hispanic in the Confederate Army), distinguishing themselves in service to the Confederacy, while others, especially in New Mexico and California, served the cause of the Union. In 1863, the U.S. government authorized the formation of the first Hispanic battalion during the Civil War. The First Battalion of Native Cavalry was formed to take advantage of the extraordinary horsemanship of the Mexican American Californians, under the command of Major Salvador Vallejo. Some 469 Mexican Americans served in the four companies of the battalion throughout California and Arizona. Also for the Union, four independent militia companies were formed in New Mexico, known by their commanders' names (Gonzales, Martínez, Tafolla, and Perea). Hispanics served significantly in southern battalions in Alabama, Florida, Louisiana, and South Carolina for the Confederacy. Because the noteworthy horsemanship of Hispanics during the Civil War had become legendary, Teddy Roosevelt later recruited many of his Rough Riders for the Spanish-American War from Hispanics in New Mexico and Texas.

In 1864, Diego Archuleta (1814–1884) became the first Hispanic Brigadier General of the United States, commanding the New Mexican militia during the Civil War. Archuleta was born into a prominent New Mexican family and was educated in Durango, Mexico. From 1843 to 1845, he served in the Mexican National Congress as a delegate from New Mexico. After conquest of New Mexico by the United States, Archuleta took part in two unsuccessful rebellions in 1846 and 1847. After the Mexican-American War, Archuleta took the oath of allegiance to the United States, served in the state assembly and became a brigadier general for the Union. In 1857, he was appointed a U.S. Indian agent, a position to which he was reappointed by President Abraham Lincoln after the Civil War.

During the Civil War, Hispanics also emerged in the intelligence service for the first time. The first Hispanic spy for the United States was Captain Román Antonio Baca, an officer in the New Mexico Volunteers—a unit that was incorporated into the Union forces during the Civil War. The first Hispanic female spy in U.S. history was the Cuban-born woman who disguised herself as a Confederate soldier and served as Lieutenant Harry Buford. Loretta Janet Vásquez left her married, domestic life in San Antonio, Texas, without her husband's knowledge, and fought at such battles as Bull Run, Ball's Bluff, and Fort Donelson. After her female identity had been detected twice and she was discharged, she began her life as a spy working in male and female guise.

During the Civil War, the long tradition of extraordinary valor of Hispanics in combat for the United States began. In 1865, the first Hispanic Medal of Honor winner in history was awarded to Philip Bazaar, a seaman born in Chile, South America, who on January 15, 1865, courageously engaged in an assault on a fort from a six-man boat. It was during the Civil War, too, that the first Admiral of the United States Navy, David, G. Farragut (1801–1872), the son of a Spanish immigrant, was commissioned, on July 26, 1866. Farragut was appointed a midshipman at the age of nine. As a commander during the Civil War, Farragut was engaged in numerous battles, including the capture of New Orleans, Vicksburg, and Mobile. It was after the tremendous victory that he had led at Mobile Bay (where he is reported to have said, "Damn the torpedoes! Full speed ahead!") that he was commissioned an admiral. In today's Navy, the guided missile destroyer USS *Farragut, DDG-37,* bears his name.

✳ WORLD WAR I

Hispanics have fought bravely in every war in which the United States was engaged. As mentioned above, their service was distinguished in the Spanish-American War, despite the popular press questioning their loyalty to the United States because of confronting an Hispanic enemy. During World War I, Hispanics again rendered extraordinary service; but at least one Hispanic soldier who deserved the Medal of Honor was denied the nation's highest award. Private Marcelino Serna was awarded the Distin-guished Service Cross for single-handedly capturing 24 German soldiers on September 12, 1918. The Albuquerque native was not recommended for a Medal of Honor because he was only a "buck" private and could not read and write English well enough to sign reports.

✳ WORLD WAR II

It was during World War II, however, that Hispanic soldiers as a group made military history. Hispanics enlisted in force, perhaps as means of proving their Americanism; for to that date, many in the United States persisted in looking upon Hispanics as foreigners. So many Hispanics enlisted and were drafted, in fact, that entire neighborhoods were depopulated of their young men. In Silvis, Illinois, just west of Chicago, eight young Mexican American men on one short street gave up their lives for their country in World War II. A total of 84 men from this street saw action in World War II, the Korean war and the Vietnam war. This street reportedly contributed more men to service, 57, during World War II and the Korean war, than any place of comparable size in the United States. The street, which was once Second Street, was renamed Hero Street.

During World War II, Mexican American soldiers, in particular, won proportionately more Medals of Honor and other recognition for valor than any other ethnic group—far exceeding their percentage of the population of the armed services or Hispanic population of the United States. The first Hispanic Medal of Honor winner of World War II was Private José P. Martínez, who took part in the American invasion of the Aleutian Islands in May 1943. The Taos, New Mexico, native led his out-numbered platoon in fighting Japanese soldiers in their trenches, and was finally mortally wounded in his valiant attacks. A Disabled American Veterans chapter in Colorado and an American Legion Post in California are named in his honor. Another Mexican American made national news and passed into folklore and popular culture for his valor in action. He was Guy Gabaldón (1927–), a Mexican American born in Los Angeles who was adopted by a Japanese American family. His heroism was demonstrated at the battle for Saipan Island, and later became the subject of a Hollywood film: *From Hell to Eternity.* In 1970, Gabaldón returned his Navy Cross and Purple Heart to the government in protest of discrimination against minorities in the United States.

The story of Hispanic valor in American wars, and particularly World War II (when Mexican American youth, for example, were being used as scapegoats by the press and subjected to street violence at the hands of soldiers and sailors in southern California) had been a well-kept secret. And even when the documentation was finally available, there was very little support for publicizing it. Raúl Morín (1913–1967), a Mexican American veteran and commercial artist from Lockhart, Texas, researched and wrote *Among the Valiant,* the first book to document the heroism and valor of Mexican Americans in the armed services during World War II. However, Morín was denied publication of the book for ten years until the American G.I. Forum, a civil rights organization made up of Mexican American veterans, backed its publication and distribution in 1963. After the book's successful publication, Morín remained active in Mexican American and Democratic political organization and in veterans affairs. In 1968, a veterans' memorial in East Los Angeles was officially named Raúl Morín Memorial Square.

World War II was a watershed in Mexican American history. After so many young men from the barrios across the Southwest had fought so bravely on foreign soil for *their* country, they believed they had earned the right to enjoy the full benefits of American citizenship. The veterans returned to the Southwest, many of them furthering their education under the G.I. Bill, and pursued the American Dream. They were now unwilling to tolerate discrimination, the way many of their parents were forced to as immigrants. More than ever before in history, thus, Mexican Americans founded and supported a wide range of civil rights and political organizations, and it was the World War II veterans that took the lead. One of the sparks that ignited the post-war Mexican American civil rights movement was the refusal of authorities in Three Rivers, Texas, to allow the burial in the city cemetery of Private Félix Longoria, who had lost his life in the Pacific. This outrageous case of segregation became notorious among Mexican American veterans, whose American G.I. Forum, a nascent political action group formed by veteran Dr. Héctor García Pérez, protested to Congressman Lyndon Baines Johnson. The congressman, who later as president would further the cause of civil rights for Hispanics, had Longoria's remains flown to Washington, D.C., and buried at Arlington National Cemetery. The American G.I. Forum grew into one of the largest civil rights organizations in U.S. Hispanic history; it is still very active today.

✳ CONFLICTS IN KOREA AND VIETNAM

As mentioned above, the Korean war saw continued Hispanic valor and leadership, with Hispanics becoming more represented among the ranks of offi-

cers and even the prestigious and previously segregated Air Corps. The Korean war saw the emergence of the first Hispanic "ace": Colonel Manuel J. Fernández Jr., who from September 1952 to May 1953 flew 125 combat missions in an F-86, engaging Communist MIG aircraft. On his fifth victory, he became an "ace" and ended the war with 14.5 "kills" to his credit. His 14.5 air victories placed him sixtieth among the top U.S. Air Force aces of the two world wars and the Korean conflict combined. During the Vietnam war, another pilot, Lieutenant Junior Grade Everett Alvarez Jr. became the longest held POW in U.S. history. He was also the first U.S. serviceman shot down over North Vietnam. The Salinas, California, native was captured after his plane was shot down over the Gulf of Tonkin, North Vietnam, and remained imprisoned for eight and a half years. He was repatriated by the North Vietnamese in February 1973. In 1981, President Ronald Reagan appointed war hero Everett Alvarez the first Hispanic deputy director of the Veterans Administration. The previous year, the president had appointed him deputy director of the Peace Corps.

Beginning during the Korean conflict, and continuing to the present, more and more Hispanics were promoted to officer rank in the armed services. It was not until the mid-1970s, however, that the military academies began graduating Hispanic officers regularly. Currently, there are many Hispanic officers commanding soldiers of all ethnic backgrounds; and there are Hispanics represented at the highest ranks among generals and admirals. In 1964, Horacio Rivero became the first Hispanic four-star admiral in the Navy. The native of Puerto Rico graduated from the United States Naval Academy, saw action, and was decorated in World War II. He later rose to Commander of Allied Forces in Southern Europe for NATO. In 1976, Richard E. Cavazos became the first Hispanic general in the United States Army. A Texas native, Cavazos distinguished himself as a commander in Vietnam and later served extensively in the Pentagon and as a commander at Fort McPherson, Georgia. In 1979 also, Hispanics saw one of their own named to the highest armed service position ever: Edward Hidalgo became the first Hispanic to serve a Secretary of the Navy. His two-year stint followed a career in which he had served as special assistant to the Secretary of the Navy, special assistant for economic affairs to the Director of the U.S. Information Agency and General Counsel, and congressional liaison for the Agency. From 1977 to 1979, he served as assistant secretary of the Navy. Hidalgo was born in Mexico City and immigrated to the United States as a child.

Santos Benavides.

✳ OUTSTANDING HISPANICS IN THE MILITARY

Roy P. Benavides (1935–)

Born on May 8, 1935, in Cuero, Texas, Benavides was educated in southeastern Texas and received his B.A. degree in 1981 from Wharton County Junior College. He served as a Green Beret in the U.S. Army from 1952 to 1976, when he retired as a master sergeant. One of the country's most decorated soldiers of the Vietnam War, his medals include the Congressional Medal of Honor, the Purple Heart with an Oak Leaf Cluster, the Defense Meritorious Service Medal, and the Army Commendation Medal. His valor and life story have been celebrated in books and in the founding of the Roy P. Benavides Airborne Museum. Benavides, with coauthor Oscar Griffin, published his autobiography, *The Three Wars of Roy Benavides*, in 1986.

Santos Benavides (1823–?)

Born on November 1, 1823, in Laredo, Texas, Benavides became the patriarch of a family that would render military service and even service in the Texas Rangers for generations. As a young man he partici-pated in Mexican civil war battles in the Rio Grande Valley. In 1856, he became mayor of Laredo and a leading financial figure. When the Civil War broke out, he rose rapidly to the rank of colonel, thus becoming the highest rankling Hispanic officer in the Confederacy. He commanded his own regiment, known as the "Benavides Regiment"; it was the only sizable force defending Texas from the Union. And he used that force to drive Union forces back from Brownsville, Texas. After the war, he and his brothers, who fought alongside him, returned to civilian life.

Robert Léon Cárdenas (1920–)

Air Force Brigadier General Robert León Cárdenas was born in Mérida, Yucatán, Mexico, on March 10, 1920. He received his early education in San Diego and his B.S. degree in Mechanical Engineering from the University of New Mexico in 1955. Cárdenas served in the Army from 1941 until 1989. Among his many military awards are the Air Medal with four oak leaf clusters, Joint Service Commendation Medal, Air Force Outstanding Unit Award with two oak leaf clusters, Legion of Merit with oak leaf cluster, Distinguished Flying Cross, the Purple Heart, and others. He also received the Spanish

Robert Léon Cárdenas.

Grand Cross of the Order of Aeronautical Merit. Since his retirement in 1989, Cárdenas has served as a member of the California Veterans Board.

Richard E. Cavazos (1929–)

Richard E. Cavazos became the first Hispanic general in the United States Army in 1976. A Texas native, Cavazos distinguished himself as a commander in Vietnam and later served extensively in the Pentagon and as a commander at Fort McPherson, Georgia. Born in Kingsville, Texas, on January 31, 1929, he received a Bachelor of Science degree in Geology at Texas Tech University and was commissioned a second Lieutenant in 1951. During his 30 years of military service, he attended various military training schools and commanded forces in Vietnam as well as served in the Pentagon. In 1976, he became commanding general of the 9th Infantry Division and Post Commander of Fort Lewis, Washington. From 1982 to 1984, General Cavazos was Commander of the United States Armed Forces Command, Fort McPherson, Georgia. Under his command, combat troops were deployed to Grenada. He retired in June, 1984. During his career, he re-

Richard E. Cavazos.

ceived the Distinguished Service Cross with oak leaf cluster, the Silver Star with oak leaf cluster, the Defense Superior Service Medal, the Legion of Merit with oak leaf cluster, the Distinguished Flying Cross, the Purple Heart, and many others.

Pedro A. del Valle (1893–)

The first Hispanic to rise to the rank of general in the United States Marine Corps was Pedro A. del Valle, who was born on August 28, 1893, in San Juan, Puerto Rico. Del Valle graduated from the U.S. Naval Academy in 1915 and served on the USS *Texas* during World War I. During his career at a variety of duty posts in the U.S. and abroad, including service in Nicaragua and Cuba, Del Valle rose up through the ranks. During World War II, he served as Commanding Officer, 11th Marines (Artillery), and assisted in the seizure and defense of Guadalcanal, for which he was awarded the Legion of Merit. From May to July, 1943, he served as Commander of Marine forces, less aviation, on Guadalcanal, Tulagi, Russel and Florida Islands. In 1944, he served as Commanding General, Third Corps Artillery, Third Amphibious Corps. He participated in the Guam operation and was awarded the Gold Star. He received a Distinguished Service Medal for his command in the Okinawa operation in 1945. After the war, Del Valle served as Inspector as General and later as Director of Personnel for the Marine Corps. He retired in 1948; whereupon he was advanced to lieutenant general on the retired list.

Francisco de Miranda (1756–1816)

Francisco de Miranda was a Venezuelan officer who served under Bernardo de Gálvez in the gulf campaigns in support of the American Revolution. Educated and trained as an officer in Spain, he served as a captain under Gálvez in the campaign which returned the lower Mississippi River to Spanish control. He later participated in the siege and capture of Pensacola. From Cuba, he was instrumental in obtaining supplies for the French Admiral de Grasse, who sailed to the Chesapeake Bay to assist in the American capture of Yorktown. After participating in the American Revolution and becoming inspired by all of those ideas of "liberty, fraternity, equality," Miranda founded the American Lodge in London in 1797, whose membership swore allegiance to democracy and was to work for the independence of the Spanish American colonies. In 1806, Miranda tried to liberate Venezuela by embarking from New York with a group of 200 soldiers. When they disembarked in Coro, Venezuela, they did not find the necessary support and the mission failed. Miranda returned to England, and from there pre-

Francisco de Miranda.

pared the liberation of his country with Simón Bolívar. When Miranda returned to Venezuela in 1810, he was arrested and sent to Spain, where he died in a Cádiz jail on July, 14, 1816.

Luis R. Esteves (1893-1958)

Luis R. Esteves was the first Puerto Rican to graduate from the United States Military Academy at West Point, in 1915. Born in 1893 in Aguadilla, Puerto Rico, before the American occupation, he obtained his elementary and secondary education under American military rule of the island and, without his parents' knowledge, took the test and was admitted to West Point. After graduating, he rose through the ranks to become a Brigadier General in 1937. During World War I, he served in Puerto Rico training officers for service—the draft laws had recently been applied to Puerto Rico, and he served as instructor and commander of three officer training camps which produced the officers who led more than 20,000 men from the island. In 1919, he organized the first Puerto Rican National Guard, commanding its first battalion and its first regiment. In 1937, Esteves was made Adjutant General, a posi-

tion he held until his retirement in 1957. General Quesada died on March 12, 1958.

David G. Farragut (1801-1872)

The most distinguished Hispanic soldier in the Union forces during the Civil War was David G. Farragut, who became the first Admiral of the United States Navy. Born in Campbell's Station, Tennessee, on July 5, 1801, the son of an Hispanic immigrant, Jorge Farragut, who had distinguished himself in the American Revolution and the War of 1812, David G. Farragut was appointed a midshipman in the U.S. Navy at the age of nine. At the age of 13, he served aboard the USS *Essex* during the War of 1812. During the Mexican War, he commanded a sloop-of-war, the Saratoga, but saw no action. In 1854, Farragut established the Mare Island Navy Yard near San Francisco. During the Civil War, he took New Orleans after a furious battle in 1862, and then proceeded up the Mississippi River to capture Vicksburg and, through attacks on Port Hudson, was able to break the Confederate supply routes. Farragut returned to Gulf action and, in 1864, despite heavy defense from forts, torpedoes and iron-clads, Farragut took Mobile, Alabama. It was at this battle

Luis R. Esteves.

David G. Farragut.

that he was reported to have uttered the famous phrase, "Damn the torpedoes! Full speed ahead!" Farragut was commissioned Admiral of the Navy on July 26, 1866, and took command of the European Squadron.

Héctor García Pérez (1914–)

Héctor García Pérez, the Mexican American civil rights leader, was born on January 17, 1914, in Llera, Tamaulipas, Mexico. Educated in the United States, after his parents immigrated to Texas, he received his B.A. in 1936 and his M.D. in 1940, both from the University of Texas. During World War II he served with distinction in the Army Medical Corps, earning the Bronze Star and six Battle Stars. At the end of the war, he opened a medical practice in Corpus Christi and, outraged at the refusal of local authorities to bury a Mexican American veteran in a local city cemetery, he organized the American G.I. Forum, which is still one of the largest and most influential Hispanic civil rights organizations. García became the most effective Hispanic veteran in working for the peacetime advancement of his people. Besides becoming active in a wide variety of

civil rights organizations, García also became active in the Democratic Party and was appointed to the Democratic National Committee in 1954. In the 1960 presidential campaign, García became the national coordinator of the Viva Kennedy Clubs, and he was later appointed to various national positions by presidents Kennedy and Johnson. In 1967, President Johnson named García alternate delegate to the United Nations with the rank of ambassador, and he also appointed him the first Mexican American member of the United States Commission on Civil Rights. In 1965, the president of Panama awarded García the Order of Vasco Núñez de Balboa in recognition of his services to humanity. In 1984, he was awarded the United States of America Medal of Freedom.

Diego E. Hernández (1934–)

Vice Admiral Diego E. Hernández was born in San Juan, Puerto Rico, on March 25, 1934. He graduated from the Illinois Institute of Technology in with a B.S. in 1955 and also received an M.S. in International Affairs in 1969 from George Washington University; that same year he also attended the U.S. Naval War College. Among his important command

Diego E. Hernández.

Edward Hidalgo.

as an air combat intelligence officer on the carrier USS *Enterprise,* and later served as Special Assistant to the Secretary of the Navy. From 1946 to 1965, he developed his private law practice in Mexico City, but then in 1965 was named Special Assistant to the Secretary of the Navy. He later took on positions at the U.S. Information Agency, and was back as an Assistant to the Secretary of the Navy when he, himself, was named Secretary in 1979.

Benjamin F. Montoya (1935-)

Rear Admiral Benjamin F. Montoya was born in Indio, California, on May 24, 1935. He graduated with a B.S. degree in Naval Science from the U.S. Naval Academy in 1958; he also received a B.S. degree in Civil Engineering from Rensselaer Polytech in 1960 and an M.S. degree in Environmental Engineering from Georgia Institute of Technology in 1968. He received his law degree from Georgetown University in 1981. Montoya served as a rear admiral from 1958 to 1989, whereupon he retired from the service and became the manager of the Sacramento division of the Pacific Gas and Electric Company. Since 1991, he has served as senior vice president and general manager of Gas Supply for the same

posts was that of Commanding Officer on the aircraft carrier USS *John F. Kennedy* from 1980 to 1981, after which he served as chief of staff of the Naval Air Forces Atlantic Fleet until 1982. From 1986 to 1989, he served as deputy commander-in-chief, U.S. Space Command. Hernández became a vice admiral in 1955. Among his decorations are the Distinguished Service Medal with Gold Star, the Distinguished Flying Cross, the Purple Heart and numerous others. He also holds decorations from abroad: The Venezuelan Naval Order of Merit and the Peruvian Cross of Naval Merit.

Edward Hidalgo (1912–

In 1979, Edward Hidalgo became the first Hispanic to serve as Secretary of the Navy. Born in Mexico City on October 12, 1912, he came with his family to the United States as a child. He graduated from Holy Cross College in 1933 and from Columbia Law School in 1936. In 1959, he also received a degree in Civil Law from the University of Mexico. From 1942 to 1943, Hidalgo was assigned to the State Department as a legal advisor to the U.S. Ambassador in Montevideo, Uruguay. From 1943 to 1945, he served

Benjamin F. Montoya.

Horacio Rivera.

company. Among his military honors are the following: Legion of Merit, Meritorious Service Medal, Bronze Star with Combat V, the Navy Commendation Medal and the Vietnam Service Medal with three bronze stars. In 1989, he was named Hispanic Engineer of the Year.

Horacio Rivera (1910–)

Horacio Rivera became the first Hispanic to rise to the rank of four-star admiral in modern times (Farragut has the distinction of being the first U.S. admiral). Born in Ponce, Puerto Rico, on May 16, 1910, Rivero graduated from the United States Naval Academy in 1931, and began serving on a variety of cruisers and battleships. During World War II, he saw considerable action in the Pacific, and participated in the Iwo Jima and Okinawa campaigns and the first carrier raids on Tokyo. He was awarded the Legion of Merit for saving his ship and preventing loss of life during a fierce typhoon in 1945. In 1955, he was promoted to Rear Admiral and to Vice Admiral in 1962. In 1964, he was promoted to Admiral and became Vice Chief of Naval Operations. In 1968, he commanded NATO forces as Commander in Chief of

Allied Forces, Southern Europe. He retired in 1972 and was later named ambassador to Spain.

Carmelita Schemmenti (1936–)

Carmelita Schemmenti is the first Hispanic female general in the armed services. Born in Albuquerque, New Mexico, on December 16, 1936, she received a Nursing degree from the Regina School of Nursing in Albuquerque and a B.S. in Nursing from the University of Pittsburgh; she also received a Master of Public Health degree from the University of North Carolina. Today she is a Brigadier General in the United States Air Force and has won numerous awards, including the Legion of Merit, the Air Force Commendation Medal, the Air Force Outstanding Unit Award, the National Defense Service Medal and others.

Juan N. Seguín (1806–1890)

One of the founders of the Republic of Texas, Juan N. Seguín was born into a prominent family of French extraction in San Antonio, Texas. At the age of 18, he was elected mayor of San Antonio. One of the developers of a nationalist spirit in Texas, Seguín led Texans in opposition to the centrist

Carmelita Schemmenti.

Juan N. Seguín.

government of Antonio López de Santa Anna in the
1830s. In the struggle for independence from Mexico,
Seguín served as a captain in the Texas cavalry,
eventually achieving the rank of lieutenant colonel.
He fought with distinction at the Battle of San Antonio in 1835 and at the Battle of San Jacinto in 1836.
He was among the defenders of the Alamo, but
averted his demise because he was sent for reen-
forcement. After the war, Seguín returned to San
Antonio, where he commanded the military post
there and served as mayor. In 1838, he was elected to
the Texas senate, and in 1840 again to the mayoralty
if San Antonio. He was active in defending Tejanos
against profiteering Anglos that were rushing into
the state to make their fortune at all costs. Unjustly
accused of favoring invading Mexican forces and be-
traying the Santa Fe Expedition to foment revolt in
New Mexico against Mexico, Anglos forced Seguín to
resign as mayor in April, 1842. He moved with his
family across the Río Grande into Mexico in fear of
reprisals. In Mexico, he was jailed and forced to
serve in the Mexican army, including in battle
against the United States during the Mexican War.
In 1848, he once again moved to Texas, only to
return to live out his days in Nuevo Laredo, Mexico,
from 1867 until his death in 1890.

References

Gleiter, Jan, and Kathleen Thompson. *David Farragut.*
    Milwuakee, WI: Raintree Publications, 1989.

Gómez-Quiñones, Juan. *Roots of Chicano Politics, 1600–
    1940.* Albuquerque: University of New Mexico Press,
    1994.

Henderson, Ann L., and Gary R. Mormino, eds. *Spanish
    Pathways in Florida.* Sarasota, FL: Pineapple Press,
    1991.

Hispanics in U.S. History. 2 vols. Englewood Cliffs, NJ:
    Globe Book Company, 1989.

Kanellos, Nicolás. *Hispanic Firsts.* Detroit: Gale Inc.,
    forthcoming.

Kanellos, Nicolás, with Cristelia Pérez. *Chronology of His-
    panic American History.* Detroit: Gale Inc., 1995.

Meier, Matt S., and Feliciano Rivera. *Dictionary of Mexi-
    can American History,* Westport, CN: Greenwood Press,
    1981.

Office of the Secretary of Defense, *Hispanics in America's
    Defense.* Washington, DC: U.S. Printing Office, 1990.

Nicolás Kanellos

13

Law and Politics

✳ Origins of Hispanics in the United States ✳ The Development of U.S. Immigration Law
✳ The Current Debate over U.S. Immigration Law ✳ The Legalization Program
✳ Employment Discrimination ✳ Police Brutality ✳ Federal Legislation Affecting Hispanic Americans
✳ Important Cases Affecting Hispanic Americans ✳ Hispanics in the Legal Profession
✳ Hispanics in the U.S. Judiciary ✳ Presidential Appointment of Hispanics to the Courts
✳ Hispanics in the Political Process ✳ Hispanic Voting and the Voting Rights Act of 1965
✳ Congressional Hispanic Caucus ✳ Hispanics in Congress
✳ Selected Prominent Hispanic Federal Officials ✳ Prominent Hispanic Politicians in State Government
✳ Prominent Hispanic Metropolitan Leaders ✳ Legal and Political Organizations

The Hispanic experience is unique in U.S. history. U.S. Hispanics are at once the oldest and the newest immigrants to the United States. In a nation of immigrants from all over the world, Hispanic immigrants have endured a long history of obstacles.

To understand the problems facing many Hispanics, how those problems arose and why they still exist today, we must first examine the Hispanic American experience in history. Unique historical milestones have colored the collective experience of Hispanics and have influenced American attitudes and decisions throughout the past. Unlike any other ethnic group in the United States, Hispanics are the only people to become citizens by conquest, with the exception of certain Native Americans.

✳ ORIGINS OF HISPANICS IN THE UNITED STATES

From the landing of Christopher Columbus on October 12, 1492, until the early nineteenth century, the entire Spanish-speaking world was controlled by Spain. The Spanish settled in North America long before the American Revolution, with the earliest settlement established at Saint Augustine, Florida, in 1563. Spanish settlers then began immigrating to the Southwest and founded El Paso, Texas, in 1598 and Santa Fe, New Mexico, in 1609. By 1760, there were an estimated 20,000 settlers in New Mexico and 2,500 in Texas. In 1769, the mission at San Diego, California, was established and the colonization of California began.

In 1810 in Mexico, Father Miguel Hidalgo y Castilla led the revolt against Spain, and Mexico gained its independence in 1821. Soon after Mexico became independent, Anglo-American settlers began to move into the Mexican territories of the present-day U.S. Southwest, especially Texas. In 1836, the Anglo settlers declared the Republic of Texas independent of Mexico. In 1846, the United States invaded Mexico under the banner of Manifest Destiny. The treaty of Guadalupe Hidalgo ended the Mexican War that same year. Under the treaty, half the land area of Mexico, including Texas, California, most of Arizona and New Mexico, and parts of Colorado, Utah, and Nevada, was ceded to the United States. The treaty gave Mexican nationals one year to choose U.S. or Mexican citizenship; 75,000 Hispanic people chose to remain in the United States and become citizens by conquest. James Gadsden was later sent to Mexico to complete the U.S. acquisition of the Southwest and negotiated the purchase of an additional 45,532 square miles, which became parts of Arizona and New Mexico. As more Anglos settled in the newly acquired lands, the new Hispanic Americans gradually became a minority population in the Southwest. The 1848 gold rush lured a flood of Anglo settlers to California, which became a state in 1850. Settlement in Arizona and New Mexico occurred at a slower pace, and they both became states in 1912.

The Treaty of Guadalupe Hidalgo guaranteed the property rights of the new Hispanic American landowners by reaffirming land grants that had been made by Spain and Mexico prior to 1846. However, the treaty did not explicitly protect the language or cultural rights of these new U.S. citizens. Over the next 50 years, most Southwestern states enacted language laws inhibiting Hispanic participation in voting, judicial processes, and education. More devastating, the Reclamation Act of 1902 dispossessed many of these same Hispanic Americans of their land. Only in New Mexico were the civil rights of the descendants of the original Spanish-speaking settlers protected.

Such conditions of discrimination discouraged immigration to the United States for most of the late nineteenth century, even though the United States had no immigration statutes relating to the admission of foreign nationals until 1875. In fact, entering the country without a visa was not a punishable offense until 1929. However, in the 1890s there was a demand for low-wage laborers to construct American railroads, and Mexican immigration was encouraged, especially after 1882, when Congress passed the Chinese Exclusion Act of 1882, which virtually ended immigration from China to the United States.

By 1910, conditions in Mexico deteriorated under the considerable political repression of the dictatorship of President Porfirio Díaz, who ruled Mexico for 34 years, from 1876 to 1910. Dispossession of property, widespread poverty, and runaway inflation forced many Mexicans to join forces in revolt. After the Mexican Revolution began in 1910, hundreds of thousands of people fled north from Mexico and settled in the Southwest. Between 1910 and 1930, about 10 percent of the entire population of Mexico immigrated to the United States, including 685,000 legal immigrants. They were welcomed during this period because of the labor needs of the expanding U.S. economy. Special rules were developed in 1917, during World War I, to permit "temporary" Mexican farm workers, railroad laborers, and miners to enter the United States to work. By the late 1920s, as much as 80 percent of the farm workers in southern California were of Mexican descent.

The Great Depression of the 1930s brought rapid change to Mexican immigration. From 1929 to 1934, more than 400,000 persons were "repatriated" to Mexico without any formal deportation proceedings. Thousands of U.S. citizens were illegally deported because they were of Mexican descent.

During World War II, the United States again needed workers and immigration was encouraged. In 1942, an arrangement was made with the Mexican government to supply temporary workers, known as "braceros," for American agriculture. Formalized by legislation in 1951, the Bracero Program brought an annual average of 350,000 Mexican workers to the United States until its end in 1964.

Mexican Americans again faced economic difficulties and discrimination because of competition for jobs during the late 1950s. This led to Operation Wetback, in which 3.8 million persons of Mexican descent were deported between 1954 and 1958. Only a small fraction of that amount were allowed deportation hearings prior to being deported. Thousands more legitimate U.S. citizens of Mexican descent were also arrested and detained.

In 1965, the United States enacted a law placing a cap on immigration from the Western Hemisphere for the first time, which became effective in 1968. Immediate family members of U.S. citizens were not subject to the cap and could legally immigrate. Legal immigration from Mexico averaged about 60,000 persons per year from 1971 to 1980. A substantial number of undocumented persons entered the United States from Mexico during those years, and that number has increased dramatically since. Estimates of the number of undocumented immigrants in the United States often range from three to five million people. In the early 1980s, programs to apprehend undocumented immigrants were again implemented, and once more there were reports of violations of civil rights of U.S. citizens and lawful permanent residents of Mexican descent.

Mexican Americans are only a part of the entire U.S. Hispanic population. Many other Spanish-speaking peoples became U.S. citizens under different circumstances. For example, Florida, Puerto Rico, and Cuba were possessions of Spain until the nineteenth century. Florida was claimed for Spain after its discovery by Juan Ponce de León in 1513. Saint Augustine in Florida was the earliest settlement established in North America, founded in 1563. It remained a possession of Spain until 1819. After Andrew Jackson led a U.S. military force into Florida, capturing two Spanish forts, Spain sold Florida to the United States for $5 million under the Onís Treaty.

Puerto Ricans, like the first Mexican Americans, became U.S. citizens through conquest. In 1898, following the brief Spanish-American War, Puerto Rico became a U.S. possession through the Treaty of Paris. Many Puerto Ricans assumed that annexation meant that all Puerto Ricans were U.S. citizens, thus entitling them to all the rights and privileges of citizenship. However, that was not the case. Many Puerto Ricans were denied the right to vote, and many were prevented from moving to the U.S. mainland.

Nearly 20 years later, the Jones Act of 1917 finally resolved this problem, making all Puerto Ricans U.S. citizens. Since then, Puerto Ricans have had the unrestricted right to travel between the island and the mainland. By the early 1920s, there were a significant number of Puerto Rican communities in U.S. cities, most notably New York.

Cuba also became a U.S. possession in 1898 through the Treaty of Paris, which ended 387 years of Spanish rule. However, Cuba was a possession only for a brief time and became independent in 1902. In the late nineteenth century, a small number of Cubans migrated to the United States, mainly to Florida and New York. By 1930, only about 20,000 Cubans lived in the United States, and by 1950, only about 35,000.

The vast majority of Cuban Americans immigrated to the United States after 1959, when Fidel Castro took power in Cuba. Between 1959 and 1962, 25,000 Cubans were "paroled" to the United States using a special immigration rule. The immigration laws did not provide for special refugee status without proof of physical persecution until 1965. In 1966, a program was initiated to airlift Cubans to the United States, but it was halted by Castro in 1973. Over 250,000 Cubans were airlifted to the United States during that period. About 10 percent of the island's population immigrated to the United States between 1966 and 1973.

Throughout the remainder of the 1970s, many Cubans immigrated to the United States by routes through other Latin American countries. In 1980, a boatlift of Cubans from Mariel Harbor was permitted by Castro, and about 130,000 refugees arrived in the United States. Controversy surrounded this boat-lift because a small percentage of the refugees were from Cuban prisons and institutions for the mentally ill.

Today, about one million Cuban Americans live in the United States, with the majority residing in Florida, although there are increasing numbers in California, Illinois, Massachusetts, New York, and New Jersey. While many early Cuban refugees expected to return to Cuba, the continuation of the Communist regime under Castro has led many to conclude that they will not be able to return. They have become naturalized citizens at a much higher rate than any other Hispanic immigrant group.

At different times in U.S. history, waves of immigrants have arrived from other Latin American countries, such as Nicaragua, Colombia, the Dominican Republic, Guatemala, Honduras, and El Salvador, as well as many others. More than half of these immigrants have come to the United States since 1970. Often they have entered the United States through Mexico. Some have entered legally under established immigration quotas, others have come as students or tourists and stayed in this country after their temporary legal status expired. Many immigrants from the Caribbean and Central and South America have come through circuitous and difficult routes to escape civil war, poverty, and repression.

More recent Central American immigration can be traced largely to economic and political conditions in the source countries, especially during the past two decades. During the 1960s, the establishment of the Central American Common Market led to economic growth and improved conditions in the region. In 1969, however, the border war between Honduras and El Salvador led to the collapse of the common market and the rapid decline of economic conditions in Central America.

Since 1979, political upheaval and civil wars in Nicaragua, El Salvador, and Guatemala have contributed to large migrations of refugees to the United States. The number of Central and South Americans in the United States in 1950 was about 57,000. Estimates in 1985 ranged from 1.4 million to 1.7 million, but these figures may be low because of difficulties in accurately counting large numbers of undocumented emigrants from Central and South America.

✳ THE DEVELOPMENT OF U.S. IMMIGRATION LAW

Americans have always taken pride in their immigrant heritage but ironically have feared new immigration at the same time. Since the United States declared its independence from Great Britain in 1776, protectionism has had its place in the population's subconscious. In later years it was often used as justification for restricting immigration.

Article I of the U.S. Constitution entrusted Congress with the power to regulate immigration and "to establish an uniform Rule of Naturalization." During the first 100 years following the American Revolution, the United States had an open-door policy with regard to immigration, which meant that immigrants from any country in the world were allowed to enter the United States unimpeded.

The first legislation to limit immigration to the United States came during the administration of President John Adams; it did not, however, limit the numbers or the origin of immigrants. The Naturalization Act of 1798 raised the number of years an immigrant had to live in the United States to be eligible for citizenship from five years to 14. The Alien Act of 1798 granted the president the authority to expel any alien he deemed dangerous. Opposed by President Thomas Jefferson, the Alien Act expired under its own terms in 1800, during his presidency.

Although the United States had a neutral immigration policy with few restrictions, some state legislatures enacted laws restricting immigration, most notably denying entry to Catholic immigrants in the early 1800s owing to fear of being dominated by the pope. These fears were used in 1854 by the American party, better known as the Know-Nothing party, which mounted successful local campaigns by denouncing immigration of Catholics and other groups. The Know-Nothing party won 40 seats in the Congress that year. In 1856 the party launched a national campaign and nominated former president Millard Fillmore for the presidency. Fillmore suffered defeat and won only 8 of 296 electoral votes.

In 1875, the U.S. Supreme Court in *Henderson v. Mayor of New York,* 92 U.S. 259, ruled that all power to regulate immigration was held solely by the federal government and struck down state restrictions as unconstitutional. However, Congress passed the first major federal immigration restrictions during the ensuing years.

The first statutes aimed at excluding certain persons from immigrating to the United States denied admission to convicts and prostitutes. In 1882, the first general federal immigration law was enacted, which included an entry tax of 50 cents per person and denied entry to the United States to "idiots, lunatics, convicts and persons likely to become public charges." But the first major legislation to reverse the century-old tradition of free and open immigration to the United States was the Chinese Exclusion Act of 1882. By its terms, the Exclusion Act put an end to Chinese immigration to the United States for ten years; later laws extended the ban indefinitely and prohibited the naturalization of Chinese persons already in the United States. It was not repealed until 1943.

The first literacy test law to restrict immigration was enacted in 1917, over the veto of President Woodrow Wilson. The literacy test acted to limit immigration from areas outside northern Europe, requiring literacy in some language for immigrants over age 16. Ironically, that same year the Jones Act of 1917 was passed, which extended U.S. citizenship to all Puerto Ricans.

By 1920, Congress had passed about a dozen major immigration laws that restricted certain kinds of individuals from immigrating to the United States, such as criminals, persons with chronic diseases, and persons with unacceptable moral or political beliefs. In 1921, limits on the number of immigrants allowed to enter the United States during a single year were imposed for the first time in the

country's history. This legislation limited immigration from Europe to 3 percent of each European nationality present in the United States in 1910, a sharp reduction from previous immigration levels. The National Origins Quota Law of 1924 restricted the immigration of southern and eastern Europeans even more, and immigration from Asia was banned.

Immigration from Latin American countries was exempt from the quota restrictions that Congress created for two reasons. The first, and most important, was that farmers and manufacturers in the southwestern states had become dependent on cheap, plentiful labor from Mexico. The second reason was that the United States was attempting to emerge as a leader of cooperative spirit among its neighbors in the Western Hemisphere under the banner of Pan-Americanism. Even without the quota restrictions, immigration from Latin America, excluding Mexico, remained low from the 1930s through the 1950s.

Following World War II, President Harry Truman allowed large numbers of displaced persons from Europe to enter the United States far in excess of the countries' quotas. In response to Truman's action, Congress passed the Immigration and Nationality Act of 1952, also known as the McCarran-Walter Act. The act reaffirmed the basic features of the 1924 quota law (the Immigration Act of 1924) by maintaining a restrictive limit on immigration from particular countries. Immigration from Asia was legalized, but only at very low levels. England, Ireland, and Germany represented two-thirds of the yearly quota for the entire world. Immigration from the Western Hemisphere remained exempt, except that applicants had to clear a long list of barriers devised to exclude homosexuals, Communists, and others.

Immigration from Latin America increased following the enactment of the McCarran-Walter Act. During the 1950s, immigration from Mexico doubled from 5.9 percent to 11.9 percent, and in the 1960s it rose to 13.3 percent of the total number of immigrants to the United States. Immigration from Cuba during this same period was 7.75 percent of the total. The total number of immigrants from Latin American countries during this time, including Mexico and Cuba, was 39 percent of all immigrants entering the United States

In 1965, a major revision of immigration law resulted when Congress amended the Immigration and Nationality Act of 1952. The national origin quota system was abolished. A complex seven-category preference system for granting visas was created in its place. The 1965 amendments gave preference to family reunification. Spouses, parents, and children of U.S. citizens were given preference in awarding visas and were not bound by a quota. The amendments maintained limits on immigration through the seven-category preference system, providing for immigration from each country of no more than 20,000 immigrants per year. Race or national origin was no longer a consideration. More important, the 1965 amendments imposed a quota ceiling on immigration from countries in the Western Hemisphere as well. This marked the first time in U.S. history that such a numerical restriction was placed on immigration from these countries.

Amendments to the law passed in 1978 removed the ceilings for each hemisphere and established a worldwide competition for 290,000 visas granted each year. Every country in the world was subject to the seven-category preference system and to the 20,000-per-year limit. The 1965 and 1978 amendments led to a dramatic shift in immigration. No longer were Europeans, formerly favored by law, the largest group of immigrants. They now represented only 13 percent of the total. Asians benefited most, representing 21 percent of the total number of immigrants entering the United States per year. Immigration from Latin American countries and the Caribbean remained at about 40 percent of the total.

The Immigration Act of 1990 continues to permit immigration of immediate relatives of U.S. citizens without numerical limitation but sets a "pierceable" overall cap on worldwide immigration of 700,000 for fiscal years 1992 through 1994, and of 675,000 for fiscal year 1995. The seven-category preference system has been replaced by one based on family relationships, employment, and diversity. The per-country limit is 25,000.

The 1970s and early 1980s brought a different kind of immigration problem to the attention of the American public. The rise in politically motivated violence in Central America spurred a massive increase in undocumented immigration to the United States. The flight of "boat people" from Indochina following the Vietnam War created an enormous refugee settlement challenge for the United States. In a six-month period alone in 1980, some 125,000 Cubans arrived in Florida in an uncontrolled sea migration to the United States. At about the same time, over 10,000 Haitians fled the repressive regime of dictator Jean Claude Duvalier and sailed to the United States in overcrowded fishing boats.

These immigrants, or more appropriately, refugees, created a problem for U.S. immigration authorities. They were not eligible to enter the United States under established quotas without visas, nor could many of them meet the requirements to enter the United States under an exemption to the quota system as "refugees." Previous U.S. law provided for the admission of persons fleeing persecution or having a well-founded fear of persecution from Middle Eastern Communist-dominated countries. This was advantageous to the Cubans fleeing Communist dictator Fidel Castro and the Vietnamese fleeing the Communist regime in Vietnam but was no help to the thousands of Central Americans who were fleeing political violence. The Refugee Act of 1980 removed the ideological definition of refugee as one who flees from a Communist regime, thus allowing thousands to enter the United States as refugees who otherwise would have been excluded.

✳ THE CURRENT DEBATE OVER U.S. IMMIGRATION LAW

The high level of illegal immigration from Mexico and other Latin American countries has fueled continuing debate about U.S. immigration policies. Beginning in the early 1970s, Congress, along with Presidents Nixon and Ford, assembled high-level commissions to study the problem, with no tangible results.

President Jimmy Carter appointed the bipartisan Select Commission on Immigration and Refugee Policy to forge a consensus in Congress and to propose solutions. The commission went through hundreds of reports on trends in immigration and their effects on the nation and held a long series of hearings throughout the country. The commission's final report was issued in 1981 and is entitled *U.S. Immigration Policy in the National Interest*. The report states, "The United States is disturbed by immigration. The very fact that so many come outside of the law or abuse their nonimmigrant visas is troubling in a nation which prides itself on respect for law generally, and for its legal immigration system specifically."

Once separated from the fear and deception of racist sentiments, the current immigration policy debate involves three key issues: control of U.S. borders, economic interests of the United States, and enforcement of U.S. immigration law. There is genuine concern over the nation's ability to humanely control immigration at its borders. As the number of undocumented immigrants apprehended at the U.S.-Mexican border rises, so does concern over regaining control of the rate of immigration. There is also illegal immigration from the north, but the numbers are smaller, and there is a higher proportion of native English-speakers who look American in appearance.

If the United States is to maintain an immigration policy consistent with the American notion of an open society, while at the same time limiting immigration to serve the national interest, most national policymakers believe that immigration must be controlled. But border enforcement must also be equitable and must maintain an open society. Limits imposed because of color, race, nationality, or religion are not fair. Moreover, those who are admitted must be allowed the full rights of participation in U.S. society.

The U.S. economy is a key force behind illegal immigration as well as a major cause for American concern about it. In much of Mexico, especially in rural areas, finding employment is extremely difficult, and a job pays only a small fraction of the minimum wage in the United States. Similar economic pressures encourage immigration from other countries, but illegal immigration is most practical for Mexicans and Central Americans, who can reach the United States by land. In southwestern states, certain U.S. industries depend on undocumented laborers, who work hard for very low pay and who seldom complain. Thus, illegal immigration is welcomed by many employers. As history demonstrates, the United States typically welcomes immigrants in times of economic growth and labor shortages, and repels them during economic hard times.

The economic effects of illegal immigration are intensely argued today. Some argue that undocumented laborers steal jobs from American workers and that undocumented aliens abuse the welfare and social services system. However, others argue and several studies demonstrate that undocumented laborers actually create jobs and thereby bolster the national economy. Furthermore, the data show that undocumented aliens rarely use any form of public assistance and, for the most part, are ineligible for government assistance because of their immigration status. Immigration policy should take into account the economic impact on the national economy, but it must first carefully examine labor needs and the actual effects of illegal immigration.

Enforcement of U.S. immigration law is a key issue in the immigration debate. Once policy is set and law is enacted, it should be enforced fairly. Our immigration laws should reestablish and maintain a consistent, practicable and humane rule of law.

✳ THE LEGALIZATION PROGRAM

The Immigration Reform and Control Act of 1986 created a major alien legalization program. Under the act, legal status was given to applicants who had held illegal status in the United States from before January 1, 1982, until the time of application. The act also offered legal status to Special Agricultural Workers (SAW) who could prove they had spent at least 90 days during a qualifying period doing agricultural work in specific crops. The Immigration and Naturalization Service (INS) accepted legalization applications between May 5, 1987, and May 4, 1988, and SAW applications from June 1, 1987, to November 30, 1988.

It is estimated that approximately three to five million undocumented immigrants lived in the United States at the time the legalization program began. On a case-by-case basis, the program has allowed those undocumented immigrants who could demonstrate continuous residence in the United States since 1982 and who would otherwise be admissible as immigrants to become legal residents. The program dealt with a complex statute and was often the subject of intense controversy, particularly over who was eligible and what documentation was needed. Disputes with the INS over the regulations led many applicants to the courtroom, where the INS usually lost.

Despite these problems, the program was successful and brought major benefits to a large number of Hispanics. More than three million applicants applied for legal status under the program, and over 90 percent of such applicants received at least temporary legal status. The largest number of applicants, about 69 percent, was from Mexico. Approximately 11 percent were from Central America, 2 percent from Caribbean countries, and about 1.5 percent from South America. The remaining applicants were from various countries around the world.

Among the most obvious and immediate benefits is the ability of applicants to cross borders legally. Additionally, the massive number of applicants has been vital in unscrambling close to two million Social Security accounts that were incorrect or fraudulent. Applicants who had acquired a false or incorrect Social Security card had the opportunity to correct their Social Security account. One subtle change has been in the behavior of the newly legalized. Many are showing an increased willingness to use public health facilities and to assert legal rights they always had but were afraid to invoke for fear that it would lead to questions about their immigration status. Many have left the very worst jobs and are now able to seek higher-paying employment.

The legalization program might not have been without its difficulties, but the program has made a necessary difference for a powerless class of individuals. It has improved the lives of millions of Hispanics and provided them with the opportunity to obtain full U.S. citizenship.

✳ EMPLOYMENT DISCRIMINATION

As demonstrated by the history of U.S. immigration law, employment has always been closely related to patterns of immigration by Hispanics. Mexican American workers suffered widespread abuses after the Southwest was ceded to the United States by Mexico. Mexican American workers endured various forms of mistreatment, including intolerable working conditions, substandard pay, and extended work hours.

Following the conquest of the Southwest, Hispanic Americans, deprived of virtually any means of building a decent economic base, were forced to work in the employ of newly arrived Anglo-Americans. During the 1800s, many Mexican Americans worked 12-hour days, six days a week, in mines, yet they were paid only half the wages paid to white miners. Mexican American workers were denigrated and were always the most poorly paid.

Mexican American farm workers in Texas were described as subhuman by historian Pauline Kibbe in 1946. She referred to this population of laborers as "but a species of farm implement that comes mysteriously into being coincident with the maturing of the cotton, that requires no upkeep or special consideration during the period of usefulness, needs no protection from the elements, and when the crop has been harvested, vanishes into the limbo of forgotten things, until the next harvest season rolls around."

Hispanic American citizens historically have always faced employment discrimination on the basis of their national origin. Such discrimination is comparable to that experienced by members of other minority groups. It was not until the landmark case of *Hernández v. Texas* (1954) that the nation's highest court acknowledged that Hispanic Americans were not being treated as "whites." The Supreme Court recognized Hispanics as a separate class of people suffering profound discrimination. The 1954 decision paved the way for Hispanic Americans to use legal means to attack all types of discrimination throughout the United States.

Among the most important legislation enacted to end employment discrimination against all minorities was the Civil Rights Act of 1964, which made it illegal for an employer to discriminate on the basis of race, color, religion, sex, or national origin. The statute was designed to protect Hispanic Americans and other minorities. It is still often used to challenge unlawful denial of jobs to Hispanic Americans.

Today, the law of employment discrimination is complex, and there are many relevant federal statutes. An important development regarding employment discrimination against immigrants was the enactment of antidiscrimination provisions in the Immigration Reform and Control Act of 1986. As noted earlier, the immigration laws were amended in 1986, making it unlawful for employers to hire undocumented persons. However, Congress believed, when passing this legislation, that the threat of sanctions created the risk that employers might refuse to hire or might discriminate against persons who appear to be foreign, have foreign-sounding names, or speak in a foreign language or with a foreign accent. Consequently, Congress included the antidiscrimination provisions in the act as a counterbalance to employer sanctions. These provisions created a new legal tool for Hispanic Americans who have experienced discrimination on the basis of national origin. The law states that it is an unfair immigration-related employment practice to discriminate in hiring, recruitment, or discharge because of a person's national origin or citizenship status. Protection against discrimination arising from citizenship status extends to all citizens, as well as to other classifications of immigrants who are legally in the United States.

✳ POLICE BRUTALITY

In the 1800s, brutality against Mexican Americans in the Southwest territories was commonplace. In fact, lynchings and murders of Mexican Americans became so common in California and Texas that, in 1912, the Mexican ambassador formally protested the mistreatment of Mexicans and cited several brutal incidents that had recently taken place.

The prevailing conditions in the 1920s along the Texas-Mexico border were intolerable. Texas Rangers killed Mexicans along the border without fear of penalty. No jury along the border would ever convict a white man for shooting a Mexican. Abuse of Mexican Americans by rangers and police continued unchecked in the 1930s.

In 1943, *Time* magazine reported that 200 navy men, angered by scuffles with Hispanic youth, commandeered taxicabs and began attacking Mexican Americans in East Los Angeles. The Los Angeles police followed the caravan of navy men and watched them beat the Hispanics and did nothing to stop them. Mexican American boys were dragged from movie theaters, stripped of their clothing, beaten, and left naked in the streets. Police did nothing to stop the attacks.

Courts of law were rarely a source of justice for Mexican American victims of such abuse. In 1947, for example, a 19-year-old Mexican American was convicted of murder in Hudspeth County, Texas. He was blind and mentally retarded, and had retaliated to an attack on his elderly father. He was not proved to have the legally necessary intent to kill to justify first-degree murder, but an all-white jury found him guilty of first-degree murder anyway. He was sentenced to death. The ruling was appealed on the grounds that some Mexican Americans should have been on the jury because the population of Hudspeth County was 50 percent Hispanic. The appellate court held that the Fourteenth Amendment, which prohibits discrimination on the basis of race or color, did not protect Mexican Americans, and the young man was executed.

As late as 1970, brutality against Mexican Americans continued. In *López v. Harlow,* a case filed in an attempt to bring the violence under control, a police officer shot and killed López, a Mexican American, allegedly in self-defense, because he thought López was about to throw a dish at him.

Since the 1970s, Hispanics have come forward in greater numbers and have documented abuses by police, abuses that include unreasonable seizures, physical brutality, and incarceration without cause. Ammunition against police abuse is growing, but the fight on this issue is destined to be a long one.

✳ FEDERAL LEGISLATION AFFECTING HISPANIC AMERICANS

Reclamation Act of 1902

From a Hispanic perspective, the Reclamation Act of 1902 is among the most devastating pieces of legislation in history. This law dispossessed Hispanic Americans of their land in the Southwestern territories 50 years after the Treaty of Guadalupe Hidalgo ceded these lands to the United States in 1846. Only in New Mexico were the civil rights of the descendants of the original Spanish-speaking settlers protected.

Jones Act of 1917

The Jones Act of 1917 gave residents of Puerto Rico full U.S. citizenship. Puerto Rico had been annexed by the United States in 1898 following the Spanish-American War. With the enactment of this law, Puerto Ricans were granted the unrestricted right to travel between the island and the U.S. mainland.

Civil Rights Act of 1964

Among the most important laws enacted to end discrimination against all minorities, the Civil Rights Act of 1964 made it illegal to discriminate on the basis of race, color, religion, sex, or national origin. The statute was designed to protect Hispanic Americans and other minorities, and it is often used to challenge unlawful denial of jobs for Hispanic Americans.

Immigration and Nationality Act of 1965

In 1965, Congress, for the first time in history, placed a limitation on the number of persons allowed to immigrate to the United States from Western Hemisphere countries, which had always been exempt from quotas until the enactment of this law. The abolition of the national origins system brought greater equality to the American immigration system.

Voting Rights Act of 1965

Although the single aim of the Voting Rights Act of 1965 was African American enfranchisement in the South, obstacles to registration and voting faced by all minorities were affected. Its potential as a tool for Hispanic Americans, however, was not fully realized for nearly a decade.

Voting Rights Act of 1970

The 1970 amendments constituting the landmark Voting Rights Act of 1970 added a provision that was designed to guard against inventive new barriers to political participation. It requires federal approval of all changes in voting procedures in certain jurisdictions, primarily southern states. This act prevents minority votes from being diluted in gerrymandered districts or through at-large elections.

Equal Educational Opportunity Act of 1974

Congress passed the Equal Educational Opportunity Act of 1974 to create equality in public schools by making bilingual education available to Hispanic youth. According to the framers of the act, equal education means more than equal facilities and equal access to teachers. Students who have trouble with the English language must be given programs to help them overcome their difficulties with English.

Voting Rights Act Amendments of 1975

The Voting Rights Act Amendments of 1975 extended the provisions of the original Voting Rights Act Voting Rights Act of 1965 and made permanent the national ban on literacy tests. Critical for Hispanic Americans, the amendments made bilingual ballots a requirement in certain areas.

Refugee Act of 1980

Under previous U.S. law, persons fleeing persecution or having a well-founded fear of persecution in Middle Eastern or Commmunist-dominated countries could be admitted to the United States despite any applicable restrictions. This was advantageous to Cubans fleeing Communist dictator Fidel Castro and the Vietnamese fleeing the Communist regime in Vietnam, but it was no help to the thousands of Central Americans who were fleeing political violence. The Refugee Act of 1980 removed the ideological definition of refugee as one who flees from a Communist regime, thus allowing thousands who otherwise would have been excluded to enter the United States as refugees.

Voting Rights Act Amendments of 1982

The Voting Rights Act Amendments of 1982 prohibit any voting law or practice created by a state or political subdivision that "results" in denial of the right of any citizen of the United States to vote on account of race, color, or language minority status. This amendment also eliminates the need to prove that the state or political subdivision created a voting law with the "intention" of discriminating against minority voters.

Immigration Reform and Control Act of 1986

The Immigration Reform and Control Act of 1986 created a major alien legalization program. Lawful resident status was extended to applicants who had held illegal status in the United States from before 1982 until the time of application. The Immigration and Naturalization Service (INS) accepted applications for one year, from May 1987 until May 1988. The program was successful and brought legal status to a large number of undocumented Hispanics. More than three million applicants applied for lawful residence under the program, and over 90 percent of them received at least temporary legal resident status.

Additionally, the act made it unlawful for employers to hire undocumented workers. However, because of the threat that sanctions might deter employers from hiring or cause them to discriminate against persons appearing to be foreign, Congress included antidiscrimination provisions in the Immigration Reform and Control Act.

Immigration Act of 1990

The Immigration Act of 1990 continued to permit immigration of immediate relatives of U.S. citizens without numerical limitation but set a "pierceable" overall cap on worldwide immigration to the United States of 700,000 for fiscal years 1992 through 1994, and 675,000 for fiscal year 1995. The seven-category preference system has been replaced by allocation of visas based on family relationships, employment, and diversity. The per-country limit is now 25,000.

✴ IMPORTANT CASES AFFECTING HISPANIC AMERICANS

Hernández v. Texas
347 U.S. 475 (1954)

A crucial case argued in 1954, *Hernandez v. Texas* was the first Mexican American discrimination case to reach the nation's highest court. It was also the first U.S. Supreme Court case to be argued and briefed by Mexican American attorneys. The case was brought by lawyers Carlos Cadena and Gus García. It was an important victory.

The defendant, Pete Hernández, had been tried and convicted for murder in Jackson County, Texas. Jackson County was 14 percent Hispanic, but the jury panel that found Hernández guilty did not include any Hispanics. In fact, no Spanish-surnamed person had served on any jury of any sort in Jackson County for 25 years prior to the trial.

Chief Justice Earl Warren, speaking for the Supreme Court, held that the Texas court was in error by "limiting the scope of the equal protection clause to the white and negro classes" and that Mexican Americans were entitled to the protection of the Fourteenth Amendment of the U.S. Constitution. The Court had acknowledged that Mexican Americans were not being treated as "whites" in the Southwest. Mexican Americans were recognized as a separate class of people who were suffering profound discrimination. The 1954 decision paved the way for Hispanic Americans to use legal means to attack discrimination throughout the country.

Allen v. State Board of Elections
393 U.S. 544 (1969)

In *Allen v. State Board of Elections,* the U.S. Supreme Court extended federal authority to object to discriminatory alterations in voting districts, the introduction of at-large voting, and other such changes, in addition to reaffirming the original power to object to discriminatory innovations involving registration and voting.

Graham v. Richardson
403 U.S. 365 (1971)

Graham v. Richardson was a decision involving application of the equal protection clause of the U.S. Constitution to state welfare laws discriminating against aliens in Arizona and Pennsylvania. The Supreme Court held that provisions of state welfare laws conditioning benefits on citizenship and imposing durational residency requirements on aliens violated the equal protection clause.

San Antonio Independent School District v. Rodríguez
411 U.S. 1 (1973)

A suit brought on behalf of poor schoolchildren, *San Antonio Independent School District v. Rodríguez,* challenged the Texas system of financing its school system based on local property taxation. The Supreme Court held that the system did not violate the constitutional right of the children to equal protection under the Fourteenth Amendment. By a five-to-four majority, the Court ruled that education is not a fundamental right and poverty is not a reason to hold otherwise.

Espinoza v. Farah Manufacturing Company
411 U.S. 86 (1973)

An employment discrimination case, *Espinoza v. Farah Manufacturing Company* was brought against Farah for discrimination toward an employee, Espinoza, on the basis of his citizenship status under the Civil Rights Act. However, the Supreme Court held that there was nothing in Title VII, the equal employment opportunities provisions of the Civil Rights Act of 1964, that makes it illegal to discriminate on the basis of citizenship or alienage.

Lau v. Nichols
414 U.S. 563 (1974)

Lau v. Nichols was brought before the Supreme Court by students who did not speak English. The Court held that the California school system's failure to provide English-language instruction to the students denied meaningful opportunity to participate in public educational programs and was in violation of Title VI of the Civil Rights Act of 1964.

Matthews v. Díaz
426 U.S. 67 (1976)

Resident alien Díaz, age 65, brought suit challenging the constitutionality of the Social Security Act provision requiring resident aliens to have resided in the United States for five years before they are eligible for Medicare. The U.S. district court in Florida held that it was an unconstitutional requirement, but the Supreme Court reversed, holding that Congress may condition aliens' eligibility for participation in Medicare, or any other federal program, on citizenship or continuous residence in the United States.

Plyler v. Doe
457 U.S. 202 (1982)

Plyler v. Doe was brought on behalf of Mexican children who had entered the United States illegally and resided in Texas. The suit challenged a Texas statute excluding the children from attending public schools. The Supreme Court struck down the Texas statute as unconstitutional and in violation of the equal protection clause, which provides that no state shall deny to any person the equal protection of the laws.

League of United Latin American Citizens v. Pasadena Independent School District
662 F. Supp. 443 (S.D. Tex. 1987)

In the *League of United Latin American Citizens v. Pasadena Independent School District,* the League of United Latin American Citizens (LULAC), on behalf of undocumented aliens who were terminated from their employment as Pasadena school district custodial workers because they provided false Social Security numbers, brought suit against the school district. The U.S. District Court for the Southern District of Texas held that the aliens were entitled to their jobs because the termination violated the anti-discrimination provision of the Immigration Reform and Control Act of 1986.

Hernández v. New York
111 S. Ct. 1859 (1991)

In *Hernández v. New York,* Hernández appealed a conviction by a New York State court on the basis that the prosecutor had discriminated against him by dismissing two prospective Spanish-speaking jurors. The prosecutor argued that he doubted the jurors' ability to defer to the official translation of anticipated Spanish-language testimony. The Supreme Court held that the state trial court was justified in concluding that the prosecutor did not discriminate on the basis of race.

✳ HISPANICS IN THE LEGAL PROFESSION

As early as the 1730s, with the formation of the Society of Gentlemen Practisers in the Courts of Law and Equity, attorneys have established organizations for the purpose of improving standards in the American legal profession. Historically, however, such professional have established an elite class of lawyers who are able to maintain control over the legal profession and its development. These lawyers came to represent the bar and established the rules and guidelines affecting the entire legal community.

In particular, they were able to limit participation by defining the qualifications for admission to the bar, thereby maintaining the status quo. The early legal profession was designed to promote certain political views and to resist change. Such standards were effectively, if not intentionally, racist and served to restrict access to the powerful bar. The American Bar Association, established in 1878, itself has recognized its unenviable history of inaction in reaching out to minorities.

Adoption of the Fourteenth Amendment to the U.S. Constitution in 1868 marked a turning point. This constitutional amendment, along with civil rights legislation, helped the United States move toward equality. The road was difficult, and even after a century had passed, discrimination and inequality still existed.

Congress enacted the first comprehensive civil rights law since the Reconstruction period when it passed the Civil Rights Act of 1964. One result of the act was the establishment of affirmative action programs. During the early years of affirmative action, equal opportunity plans were an effective way of ending employment discrimination. The U.S. Supreme Court supported this view, in many cases striking down employment and hiring practices that discriminated on the basis of race, color, gender, or national origin. As a result, civil rights legislation and affirmative action programs were pivotal in providing minorities with equal opportunities in professions from which they were previously barred.

Despite these legislative advances, Hispanic Americans continue to be underrepresented in the legal profession, especially in the nation's largest law firms. To increase Hispanic representation, large law firms must recognize that a greater, more concerted effort is needed to assist Hispanic Americans in getting through the subtle acculturation process found within law firms.

The number of Hispanic attorneys working for U.S. corporations is 50 percent greater than the number of Hispanic attorneys in the nation's largest law firms. A survey conducted by the *National Law Journal* reported that Hispanics represent 1.2 percent of all the attorneys in the 251 largest law firms in the United States. In large part, the reason for underrepresentation of Hispanic Americans in the legal profession, especially in large law firms, is that Hispanics are not attending law schools in numbers proportionate to the Hispanic population in the United States.

Hispanics and Legal Education

Despite many advances, Hispanic American representation in the legal profession, as in most prestigious fields, is still not proportionate to the number of Hispanics in the general population. The low number of Hispanics admitted to U.S. law schools is the major barrier.

The American Bar Association (ABA) reported that Hispanic American enrollment in ABA-approved law schools was 1.5 percent of all law students in 1975. About ten years later, the ABA reported that the number had increased slightly to 2 percent. Although this is an improvement, it is far from representative of the Hispanic presence in the general population. Hispanic American law school enrollment is also adversely affected by a high attrition rate, much higher than that of law students overall. Even more devastating is the high dropout rate among Hispanic youth in high school and college; almost half of all Hispanic college students drop out during their first two years, which has prevented large numbers of them from reaching law school or other professional schools.

Another commonly noted problem of Hispanic students is a deficiency in academic background. This often requires a long academic adjustment period, private tutoring, or some other form of academic support to assist the student in completing law school. This may often be the case for Hispanic students who speak Spanish as their native language. Many Hispanic students also experience pressure from peers who attempt to dissuade them from pursuing higher education. These academic problems are often accompanied by financial difficulties. Unfortunately, many, if not most, law schools do little to accommodate Hispanic students' needs.

Obstacles to financing the high costs of a legal education may be a significant reason for the high number of law school dropouts. Many of the resources that helped Hispanic Americans to attain higher education in the 1970s are becoming more and more scarce. Financial aid has been decreasing because of government cutbacks, and the political climate has become less receptive to affirmative action and other programs that had previously facilitated the higher education of Hispanics and other minorities.

Hispanic Americans who do graduate from law school may face additional obstacles before entering law firms. Perhaps the most significant one is the bar examination, which all attorneys must pass to practice law. The bar is a hurdle for all would-be attorneys, but is a more significant impediment for Hispanics. In California, which has a large Hispanic population, scores for the California Bar Examination in July 1985 showed that while 61.5 percent of whites passed, only 33.5 percent of Hispanics did. Whether the bar examination is discriminatory against minorities is a volatile issue that is hotly debated.

Hispanics in Large Law Firms

As attorneys, Hispanics face formidable obstacles in joining law firms. According to a survey conducted by Stanford Law School in 1987, Hispanic American

TRENDS IN LAW SCHOOL ENROLLMENT

J.D. Enrollment
1981-82 to 1990-91

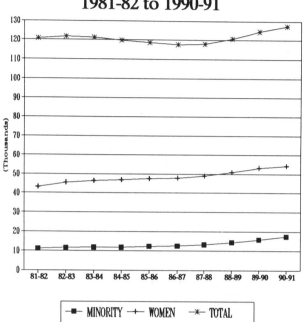

J.D. Enrollment
Women and Minorities
1981-82 to 1990-91

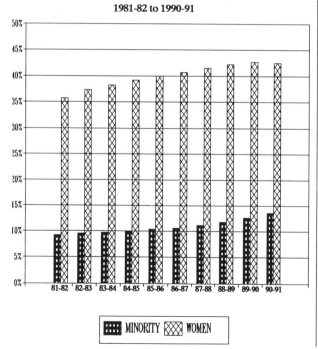

MINORITY ENROLLMENT COMPOSITION
1981-82

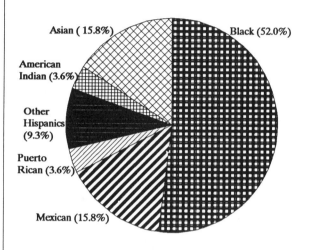

MINORITY ENROLLMENT COMPOSITION
1990-91

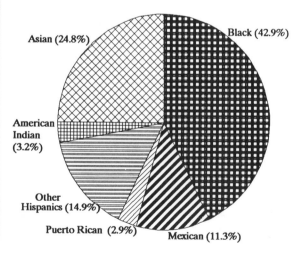

Four charts on law school enrollment. (*Consultant's Digest,* May 1991.)

graduates reported they felt they had to overcome barriers when joining law firms that nonminorities do not face. At the interviewing stage of the hiring process, Hispanics must confront the preconceptions many interviewers will have of them, preconceptions that large law firm interviewers may not even be aware of. Hispanic students are often stereotyped as being oriented more to public service careers than to careers with large law firms. In the past, Hispanic law school graduates have generally gravitated toward government jobs, poverty law, or legal services. This phenomenon is largely the result of greater opportunity in those types of law practice. Today, however, many Hispanics are pursuing careers in large law firms more aggressively.

Overcoming preconceptions about the kind of law Hispanics want to practice is not the only problem facing Hispanic American law graduates. Although major law firms are gradually opening up opportunities for minorities, they usually hire only attorneys, including minorities, with outstanding academic records who have attended top law schools.

The problems Hispanics face in getting jobs at the country's major law firms do not end with the first job after law school. Having been barred from entry-level positions at large law firms, Hispanics are effectively prevented from joining firms later as lateral hires, because few Hispanics have substantial legal experience in corporate law or in other fields of law in which many large firms specialize. As long as Hispanics have difficulty joining these firms at entry level, the number gaining experience at large law firms will continue to be minimal. Because the firms tend not to hire lawyers without that required experience, Hispanic representation in large law firms is not likely to be improved through lateral hiring.

Increasingly, however, Hispanic attorneys are overcoming the entry barriers and joining large law firms. Even for some of these attorneys, disadvantages may appear within the law firm in the form of additional barriers or added pressures. Breaking the racial barriers of a firm by being the first or only Hispanic attorney is not an easy task. Culture shock for Hispanics entering corporate law firms may not be an uncommon experience. A feeling of isolation may result and is often enhanced by the lack of Hispanic mentors within the law firm. Mentors serve as role models and advisers, and many attorneys think not having a minority mentor hurts their progress within the firm.

Hispanics in the Public Interest

A great number of Hispanic attorneys have chosen a career in the public interest. Many serve at government posts or with nonprofit legal organizations established to aid underprivileged and disenfranchised clients. Many attorneys who enter service in the public interest do so because they have a desire to aid other Hispanic Americans with legal, social, and cultural problems.

In public interest service, Hispanic attorneys have the opportunity to make gains for not only themselves and their community but also all Americans. They take pride in the victories made in the struggle for equal rights at a time when the tide is running against civil rights efforts of minorities. Public interest firms often act as watchdogs that monitor government action to see that public resources are effectively channeled into the Hispanic community. By monitoring these agencies, they can ensure that programs they devise realistically account for the needs of Hispanics. However, public interest firms and organizations are plagued by insufficient funding and staff. Despite these limitations, those people who join the public interest have achieved a great deal in this country.

Issues often monitored by public interest groups include immigration, employment, education, housing, voter registration and elections, public funding, discrimination, and civil rights. In the past two decades, there has been dramatic growth in the number of public interest organizations specifically created to assist Hispanics with legal problems and to advocate political involvement. Some of the most well known and effective national public interest groups in the United States include local offices funded by the Legal Services Corporation; Migrant Legal Action Program; Mexican American Legal Defense and Educational Fund; Puerto Rican Legal Defense and Education Fund; and the National Immigration Law Center.

Selected Prominent Hispanic Attorneys and Law Professors

Michael J. Aguirre (1949-)

Civil Litigation Attorney

Born in San Diego, California, on September 12, 1949, Aguirre was educated in California, earned a bachelor of science degree at Arizona State University in 1971, a law degree from the University of California, Berkeley, in 1974 and a master of public administration degree from Harvard University in 1989. He has worked as deputy legislative counsel for the California legislature, 1974–1975; as assistant U.S. attorney, 1975–76; assistant counsel for the U.S. Senate Subcommittee on Investigations, 1976–77; and as special reports legal counsel for the C.B.S. network, 1977. Since that time he has worked in private practice.

In 1980, he became the president of his own law

Michael J. Aguirre.

firm, Aguirre and Meyer, A.P.C., which specializes in civil litigation. He has also been an adjunct professor and lectured in law at the University of California, San Diego, and at the University of Southern California. Aguirre is active in the community and has also been the author of various laws passed by the California legislature. His awards include the Wille Velásquez Community Service Award, given by the Chicano Federation in San Diego in 1989. In 1987, he was voted the most distinguished name in the San Diego legal community by the readership of the *San Diego Daily Transcript*.

James E. Blancarte (1953–)

Litigation Attorney

Blancarte was born in 1953 in Pomona, California, and graduated from Pomona College. He received his law degree from the University of California School of Law and was admitted to the bar in 1979. Blancarte's current areas of practice are litigation and entertainment and business law. Blancarte was president of the Mexican American Bar Association of Los Angeles in 1983 and was president of the western region of the Hispanic National Bar Associ-

ation in 1988. He is currently a partner with the firm of Mitchell, Silberberg & Knupp in Los Angeles.

Wilfredo Caraballo (1947–)

Public Advocate / Public Defender, State of New Jersey

Caraballo was born in Yabucoa, Puerto Rico, and grew up in a tough neighborhood in New York City. He attended St. Joseph's University and went on to New York University Law School, receiving his law degree in 1974. He then worked the streets of New York City as a community activist and a legal aid lawyer. Caraballo was also active in the Puerto Rican Legal Defense and Education Fund. In 1975, he joined Seton Hall Law School in Newark, New Jersey, as a clinical professor. During his 15 years at Seton Hall, Caraballo specialized in teaching contract, commercial, and bankruptcy law. He was a visiting professor at New York University, the City University of New York, and Pace College law schools. In 1982 he was named associate dean of Seton Hall Law School. Caraballo took a leave of absence from his post as associate dean in 1990. Governor James Florio appointed Caraballo to the Office of Public Advocate and Public Defender in 1990, a cabinet post he served until 1992.

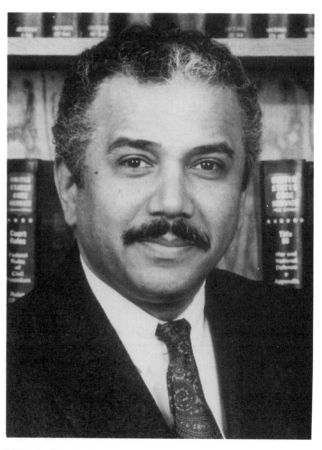

Wilfredo Caraballo.

Daniel P. García (1947-)

Attorney

García was born in Los Angeles. He attended Loyola University, where he received a degree in business in 1970, and went on to the University of Southern California, earning his M.B.A. in 1971. García then attended U.C.L.A. School of Law and was awarded a law degree in 1974, at which time he joined the prestigious firm of Munger, Tolles & Olson in Los Angeles and became a partner. Since 1991, he has served as an attorney for Warner Brothers in Burbank, California. He is a member of the board of the Mexican American Legal Defense and Education Fund and has been active in Los Angeles politics. García was a member of the Los Angeles Planning Commission from 1976 to 1988 and was its president from 1978 to 1988. He has served as president of the Mexican American Bar Association.

Antonia Hernández

President and General Counsel, Mexican American Legal Defense and Educational Fund (MALDEF)

Born in Coahuila, Mexico, Hernández earned her B.A. at U.C.L.A. in 1968, a teaching credential at the university's School of Education, and her law degree at the U.C.L.A. School of Law in 1974. Hernández began her legal career as a staff attorney with the Los Angeles Center for Law and Justice that same year. In 1977, she became the directing attorney for the Legal Aid Foundation office in Lincoln Heights. An expert in civil rights and immigration issues, Hernández worked with Senator Edward M. Kennedy and the U.S. Senate Committee on the Judiciary in 1979 and 1980. She was also the Southwest regional political coordinator of the Kennedy for President campaign in 1980. Active in community affairs, she presently serves on the board of directors of several organizations, including the National Hispanic Leadership Conference, the Latino Museum of History, Art & Culture, and the Independent Sector.

Hernández has been the president and general counsel of MALDEF since 1985, served as its vice president from 1984 to 1985, as employment program director from 1983 to 1984, and as an associate counsel from 1981 to 1983. As president of MALDEF, she directs all litigation and advocacy programs, manages a $4.5 million budget and a 65-person staff, and is responsible for the organization's long-range plans and goals. In 1992 after the Los Angeles riots, Hernández was appointed by Mayor Tom Bradley to the Rebuild L.A. Commission.

Antonia Hernández.

Gerald P. López (1948-)

Law Professor

López attended the University of Southern California and received his law degree from Harvard Law School in 1974. He then served as law clerk to U.S. District Court Judge Edward Schwartz from 1974 to 1975 in San Diego. López has taught at California Western School of Law, U.C.L.A. Law School, and Harvard Law School. He has been a professor at Stanford School of Law since 1985.

Vilma Socorro Martínez (1943-)

Former General Counsel, Mexican American Legal Defense and Educational Fund (MALDEF)

Martínez is a partner in the firm of Munger, Tolles & Olson in Los Angeles. Born in San Antonio, Texas, in 1943, she attended the University of Texas and went on to Columbia University Law School, where she received her law degree in 1967. As general counsel of MALDEF from 1973 to 1982, Martínez was an influential advocate during the congressional hearings for the Voting Rights Act of 1975, which opened the door to greater access to political participation by Hispanics. Martínez also served as a consultant to the U.S. Commission on Civil Rights from 1969 to 1973. In the 1990s, Martínez returned to MALDEF, this time as a member of its board of directors. In 1978 and 1992, Martínez received the medal of excellence from the Columbia Law School as a major figure in civil rights.

Miguel Angel Méndez-Longoria (1942–)

Professor

Méndez-Longoria attended Texas Southmost College and received his law degree from George Washington University Law School in 1968. He was admitted to the Texas bar that same year. He served as a law clerk for the U.S. Court of Claims in Washington, D.C., from 1968 to 1969. He then was legal assistant to U.S. Senator Alan Cranston (D-California) from 1969 to 1971. He was a staff attorney for the Mexican American Legal Defense and Educational Fund (MALDEF) in San Francisco from 1971 to 1972 and was deputy director of California Rural Legal Assistance in San Francisco from 1972 to 1974. From 1975 to 1976, he served as deputy public defender for Monterey County, California. Since 1976, Méndez-Longoria has taught law at the University of Santa Clara Law School, University of California at Berkeley Law School (Boalt Hall), Vermont Law School, University of San Diego Law School, and Stanford University Law School, where he has been a professor since 1984.

Mario G. Obledo (1932–)

Cofounder, Hispanic National Bar Association (HNBA) and Mexican American Legal Defense and Educational Fund (MALDEF); Past President, League of United Latin American Citizens (LULAC)

Born in San Antonio, Texas, Obledo attended the University of Texas, where he was awarded a degree in pharmacy. After serving in the Korean war, he returned to Texas and received his law degree from St. Mary's University Law School in 1961. Obledo has been active in Hispanic affairs for over 30 years. In LULAC he has held local, district, state, and national offices, including the presidency. He was also active in the Southwest Voter Registration Project. Obledo has been active in government and is a former Secretary of the California Health and Welfare Agency, where he was instrumental in bringing thousands of Hispanics into state government. Obledo was also assistant attorney general for the state of Texas and has lectured at Harvard Law School. Currently, Obledo is chairman of the National Rainbow Coalition. He has offices in Austin,

Mario G. Obledo.

Texas, Sacramento, California, and Washington, D.C., where he remains active in national politics.

Michael A. Olivas (1951–)

Professor

Olivas attended Pontifical College in Columbus, Ohio, where he was awarded a B.A. degree in 1972 and an M.A. degree in 1974. He then went on to Ohio State University to receive his Ph.D. degree in 1977. Olivas received his law degree from Georgetown University Law School in 1981. He served as director of resources for the League of United Latin American Citizens (LULAC) Education Resource Center in Washington, D.C., from 1979 to 1982. In 1982, he began teaching law at the University of Houston Law School. He is director of the Institute for Higher Education Law and Governance there and was named associate dean in 1990.

Andrea S. Ordin (1940–)

Former U.S. Attorney, District of California

Ordin was born in 1940 and attended the University of California, where she received her B.A. degree in 1962 and her law degree in 1965. She served as deputy attorney general for California from 1965–72; she then worked as legal counsel for Fair Employment Practices Commission, 1972–73; she served as assistant district attorney for Los Angeles County, 1973–77, and U.S. attorney for the central district of California, Los Angeles, 1977–81; she taught as an adjunct professor at U.C.L.A. law school in 1982; between 1983–90, she was chief assistant attorney general, Los Angeles; and since 1993, she has been a partner in the firm of Morgan, Lewis & Bockius in Los Angeles.

Leo M. Romero (1943–)

Dean, University of New Mexico Law School

Romero is the only Hispanic dean in the United States. He attended Oberlin College and received his J.D. degree from Washington University Law School in St. Louis, Missouri, and his LL.M. degree from Georgetown University Law School in Washington, D.C. Romero was associate editor of the *Washington University Law Quarterly,* and was editor-in-chief of the *Urban Law Review* at Washington University. Romero has taught law at Dickinson University Law School, the University of Oregon Law School, and the University of New Mexico Law School. He became associate dean at the University of New Mexico Law School in 1989 and was named dean in 1991.

Gerald Torres (1952–)

Professor

Torres was born in Victorville, California, in 1952. He attended Stanford University, where he received his B.A. in 1974. He received his J.D. degree from Yale Law School in 1977 and his LL.M. degree from the University of Michigan Law School in 1980. He was admitted to the bar in 1978. Torres was staff attorney for the Children's Defense Fund in Washington, D.C., from 1977 to 1978. He began teaching law in 1980 and has taught at the University of Pittsburgh Law School, the University of Minnesota Law School, and Harvard Law School. He now teaches jurisprudence, environmental law, property law, and agricultural law, at the University of Texas School of Law. Since 1993, he has served as head of the U.S. Justice Department's Environmental Division.

Abelardo López Valdez (1942–)

Attorney, Former Presidential Aide, and Governmental Official

Valdez was born in Floresville, Texas, and attended Texas A & M University. He received a J.D. degree from Baylor University Law School and an LL.M. degree from Harvard Law School. He was admitted to the bar in 1970. Valdez served as an aide to President Lyndon Johnson from 1965 to 1967. He was an attorney for the Overseas Private Investment Corporation from 1971 to 1973 and was general counsel for the Inter-American Foundation from 1973 to 1975. Under President Carter, Valdez was assistant administrator of the Latin American and Caribbean region for the U.S. Agency for International Development from 1977 to 1979. He served as U.S. ambassador and chief of protocol for the White House from 1979 to 1981. In 1981, Valdez joined the law firm of Laxalt, Washington, Perito and Dubuc in Washington, D.C., where he is a partner. Valdez specializes in administrative, regulatory, and international law.

✵ HISPANICS IN THE U.S. JUDICIARY

The U.S. federal court system was created by the Constitution of the United States. Article III of the Constitution states that the "judicial Power of the United States, shall be vested in one supreme Court" and authorizes the Congress to create lower federal courts, which the first Congress did in 1789. Congress created federal trial courts, which are known as district courts and, later, intermediate appellate courts, which are called circuit courts. Article II provided that all federal judges, including Supreme Court justices, are to be appointed by the president and confirmed by the U.S. Senate. Article III provides that federal judges hold their offices for life terms. The American judiciary has great independence, yet its judges are carefully selected through the process of presidential nomination and Senate confirmation.

Almost all of the nation's judicial business was handled by state courts in the early years of the country, partly because there were few federal judges and their jurisdiction was limited. Each state system differed, but nearly all had lower courts to hear trials and appellate courts to hear appeals. Even today, most of the nation's judicial business is handled by state rather than federal courts.

The federal government expanded significantly after the Civil War ended in 1865, and the federal courts grew along with it. In 1891, Congress created the tier of regional appellate courts called courts of appeals, to which appeals of the decisions of the federal trial courts could be taken. These appellate courts, more commonly known as circuit courts, were so named from the days when a judge used to ride a "circuit" on horseback.

The growth of the federal courts was gradual but accelerated after 1958, when the number of cases filed in federal court increased at a rapid pace. Between 1958 and 1988 Congress responded by doubling the number of judges serving in the district courts and courts of appeals. Additionally, Congress created a host of diverse judicial adjuncts, such as magistrates and administrative law judges, to which some of the caseload is delegated.

The Supreme Court, the nation's highest court, consists of the chief justice and eight associate justices. The Supreme Court has original jurisdiction in all cases involving "ambassadors, other public Ministers and Consuls" and those arising from disputes between the states. The Supreme Court can also hear appeals of decisions of the courts of appeals, the intermediate court, and the final decisions of the highest courts of each state if they involve federal questions. The Supreme Court may choose which cases it wants to hear and generally limits its review to cases involving national questions or to issues on which different courts of appeals have reached conflicting results.

There are currently 13 courts of appeals, or circuit courts. The United States is divided into 12 geographical circuits. In addition to these, there is a U.S. Court of Appeals for the Federal Circuit, a specialized court that hears appeals from the Court of Claims and the Court of Customs and Patent Appeals. Each circuit court of appeals is headed by a chief judge and has between six and 26 judges. They usually sit in three-judge panels to review decisions of lower courts, but occasionally meet in greater numbers in important cases. In rare cases, all the judges of the circuit will preside *en banc* to hear an appeal.

U.S. district courts have been established in every state, the District of Columbia, and the U.S. territories. Each state has at least one U.S. district court, and states with large populations are divided into two or more subdistricts. For example, the heavily populated states of California, New York, and Texas are each divided into four subdistricts, while the states of Alaska, Arizona, Montana, and New Mexico each contain one district despite their enormous size.

Hispanic Judges in Federal Courts

Almost all Hispanic judges currently sitting on the bench at all levels of the judiciary received their appointments in the last three decades. Hispanics now sit on both the U.S. district courts and the U.S. courts of appeals. However, no Hispanic has yet sat on the U.S. Supreme Court.

In 1985, the Fund for Modern Courts conducted a study identifying minority judges in all 50 states, excluding Puerto Rico and the District of Columbia. According to that study, there was a total of 24 Hispanic judges in the federal courts at all levels, representing 3.2 percent of the 753 federal judges nation-wide. Two of the 24 Hispanic judges were court of appeals judges and 22 were district court judges.

According to the *Directory of Hispanic Judges of the United States,* there were 85 Hispanic members of federal tribunals in 1991, but this includes judges in the District of Columbia and Puerto Rico as well as U.S. magistrates and administrative law judges.

Today seven Hispanic judges sit on the court of appeals, the second-highest federal court in the united States. Arthur L. Alarcón and Ferdinand Fernández sit on the Ninth Circuit for California, Arizona, Nevada, Washington, Oregon, Idaho, Montana, Alaska, Hawaii, Guam and the Northern Mariana Islands. Fortunato P. Benavides, Emilio M. Garza, and Reynaldo G. Garza sit on the Fifth Circuit for Texas, Louisiana and Mississippi. Carlos Lucero sits on the Tenth Circuit for Colorado and New Mexico.

There are 27 Hispanic judges who have been appointed to U.S. district courts across the country. They sit on district courts in Arizona, California, Connecticut, Florida, Illinois, Indiana, Michigan, Missouri, New Jersey, New Mexico, New York, Pennsylvania, Rhode Island, Texas, Washington, D.C., and Puerto Rico.

Additionally, eight Hispanic judges serve as U.S. magistrates, four serve on the U.S. Bankruptcy Court, and 43 currently serve as administrative law judges for various federal agencies, such as the Executive Office for Immigration Review (special inquiry officers), the Social Security Administration, and the Federal Communications Commission (FCC).

Hispanic Judges in State Courts

Currently 90 percent of the nation's judicial business is handled by state rather than federal courts. Each state system differs, but nearly all have trial courts, intermediate courts, and a court of last resort. Those states that mirror the federal three-tier court system generally have district or superior courts in each county, intermediate courts of appeals to review decisions of the trial courts, and state supreme courts, which provide the ultimate review of decisions of the lower courts.

Hispanic Americans have made the greatest inroads at the state, county, and municipal court levels, where hundreds have been appointed or elected to these courts. Hispanic judges have served on state courts throughout the history of the United States, but almost always at the lowest levels. In recent years this trend has changed, as large numbers of Hispanics have been both appointed and elected to all levels of state courts.

In its 1985 study, the Fund for Modern Courts found that there were approximately 163 Hispanic state court judges across the country, representing 1.3 percent of the 12,093 full-time judges of state courts. In 1992, the Hispanic National Bar Association found that over 600 Hispanic Americans are judges on state tribunals of all kinds, including state supreme courts, state appeals courts, and state trial courts.

The growing number of Hispanic judges can be attributed to the increasing Hispanic population as well as to favorable legislation such as the Civil Rights Act of 1964 and the Voting Rights Act of 1965, which have enabled Hispanics to become full participants in the U.S. political and judicial process.

Today, Hispanics serve on some of the highest state courts in the nation. Five Hispanics are state supreme court justices, in Colorado, Michigan, New Mexico, and Texas. There are 14 Hispanics serving

TABLE 13.1
HISPANIC JUDGES IN STATE COURTS

COURT	HIGHEST (A)	INTERM. (B)	TRIAL (C)	MUNICIPAL (D)	MAGISTRATE/JOP (E)	OTHER (F)
AL	0	0	1	0	0	0
AK	0	0	1	0	0	0
AZ	0	2	42	18	19	0
CA	0	3	86	41	0	9
CO	1	1	14	3	0	1
DC	0	0	3	0	0	0
FL	0	0	25	0	0	0
HI	0	0	1	0	0	0
IL	0	0	16	0	0	0
IN	0	0	2	0	0	0
KS	0	0	1	0	0	0
LA	0	0	4	0	0	0
MD	0	0	1	0	0	0
MI	1	0	2	0	0	1
MN	0	0	2	0	0	0
MO	0	0	1	0	0	0
MT	0	0	1	0	1	0
NV	0	0	7	0	2	0
NJ	0	0	13	5	0	0
NM	1	4	86	35	18	1
NY	0	1	25	11	0	0
OH	0	0	2	0	0	0
OR	0	0	1	0	0	0
PA	0	0	2	0	0	0
TX	2	3	280	93	114	0
UT	0	0	1	0	0	0
VA	0	0	1	0	0	0
WA	0	0	4	0	0	0
TOTAL	5	14	625	206	154	12

Source: Hispanic National Bar Association Nationwide Summary of Hispanics in the State Judiciary (1992). This summary excludes judges sitting in Puerto Rico courts.

A. Judges in state courts of last resort; in most states, such courts are called supreme courts

B. State appellate or intermediate court judges

C. State judges in trial courts of general jurisdiction

D. Municipal or metropolitan court judges

E. Local magistrates, or justices of the peace

as state appeals court judges in the states of Arizona, California, Colorado, New Mexico, New York, and Texas.

Most dramatic are the large numbers of Hispanic Americans serving in lower state courts—625 Hispanics serve on various state trial courts. Table 13.1 lists the number of Hispanic judges in each state.

Critics of the process of selecting judges charge that the system is subject to a wide range of problems and abuses, including discrimination against minorities. The appointment process, critics charge, is also subject to political interference from special interest groups, influence peddling, and highly inflammatory campaigning by opposition groups. The nominee's qualifications are rarely the test of whether he or she should be a judge. For example, a 1988 analysis of U.S. Supreme Court appointments published in *Texas Lawyer* found that of 27 failed nominations to the Court, only five were denied because of qualifications or ethical concerns. Political concerns were the primary reasons the other nominees were not confirmed.

Discrimination is a serious problem in the appointive system. The Mexican American Legal Defense and Educational Fund (MALDEF) recently concluded that the appointive system is discriminatory. According to MALDEF, approximately 97 percent of all individuals making judicial appointments are white, which consequently tends to limit the opportunities for minority nominees. (MALDEF states that the elective system is of the greatest benefit to Hispanics and other minorities.) Instead of taking politics out of the system, the appointive process takes the voter out of the system.

Fortunately, today the majority of states select judges through the election process. Eight states choose all their judges in partisan elections; 12 use nonpartisan elections. One state, Virginia, uses legislative election exclusively to select its judges. Another 13 states have variable procedures, appointing judges to certain courts and electing them to others.

The elective franchise is a fundamental and cherished right for all Americans. Advocates of the election process state that judicial officeholders should be held accountable to voters in the same manner as legislators. Proponents of an appointive system often state that areas of the country with small Hispanic populations would be better served by the appointment process. Election advocates charge that the underlying assumption of those who promote an appointive system is that the voters cannot be trusted to select good judges. Regardless of which method is used, if the courts of the United States are to reflect the population they serve, Hispanic lawyers must be included in greater numbers among those who become members of the judiciary.

✳ PRESIDENTIAL APPOINTMENT OF HISPANICS TO THE COURTS

The president appoints federal judges, with the advice and consent of the U.S. Senate. The presidential appointment process has had varied success in elevating Hispanics to the federal courts during the last three decades. The most significant progress for Hispanic Americans was seen during the administration of President Jimmy Carter.

Presidents generally receive district court recommendations for nominations from the senior home-state senator of the president's party, or if there is no such senator, from the state's governor, senior member of Congress of the president's party, or party leader. President Lyndon B. Johnson, whose presidency was from 1963 to 1968, appointed three Hispanic Americans to the district court. President Richard M. Nixon appointed two Hispanics to the court during his presidency, from 1968 to 1974. President Gerald R. Ford appointed one Hispanic American to the district court during his brief presidency, from 1974 to 1977.

The years of the presidency of Jimmy Carter, from 1977 to 1981, were years of change in the judicial selection process. Carter issued an executive order creating a U.S. Circuit Judge Nomination Commission in 1977, modeled after the merit selection system he established while governor of Georgia. The president's order resulted in the appointment of 16 Hispanic Americans to federal courts, nearly thrice the total appointed by Presidents Johnson, Nixon, and Ford combined, and more than all previous presidents of the United States combined throughout the history of the country. Of these, 14 were appointed to the district court and two to the court of appeals.

President Ronald Reagan did not continue the nomination commission begun by President Carter and reverted to the old system used by earlier presidents. During the Reagan years, from 1981 to 1989, ten Hispanic Americans were appointed to the district court and one to the court of appeals. President George Bush did not change the old system used by President Reagan.

From the time Bush became president in 1989 through December of 1991, he had appointed only two Hispanic Americans to the district court and two to the court of appeals. After Supreme Court Justice Thurgood Marshall announced his retirement in mid-1981, there was intense speculation that Bush might nominate the first Hispanic to the Supreme Court. Speculation ended when he nominated Judge Clarence Thomas, an African American, to the Court.

Prominent Hispanics at the Federal and State Judicial Levels

Raymond L. Acosta (1925–)

Acosta was born in New York City and grew up in Teaneck, New Jersey. After graduating from high school in 1943, Acosta joined the U.S. Navy during World War II and took part in the Normandy invasion. He returned to New Jersey after the war and graduated from Princeton University in 1948. Acosta received his law degree in 1951 from Rutgers University Law School in Newark, New Jersey. From 1951 to 1954, he was in private practice in Hackensack, New Jersey, and worked for the Federal Bureau of Investigation in Washington, D.C., from 1954 to 1958. In 1958, he moved to Puerto Rico to serve as assistant U.S. attorney there. From 1962 to 1980, he was in the private sector, practicing law in San Juan, Puerto Rico, with the firm of Igaravídez and Acosta, and held posts with various real estate and banking interests. From 1980 to 1982, Acosta was the U.S. attorney for Puerto Rico. In 1982, President Reagan appointed Acosta to the U.S. District Court for the District of Puerto Rico.

Arthur L. Alarcón.

Raymond L. Acosta.

Robert P. Aguilar (1931–)

Former judge of the U.S. District Court for the Northern District of California, Aguilar attended the University of California, Berkeley, where he received his B.A. degree in 1954. He then went on to receive his law degree from the University of California Hastings College of Law. He practiced law with the firms of Mezzetti and Aguilar, Aguilar & Aguilar, and Aguilar & Edwards from 1960 to 1979. In 1979 Aguilar was appointed a California Superior Court judge for Santa Clara County. He was later appointed to the U.S. District Court for the Northern District of California by President Jimmy Carter in 1980, where he remained until his resignation in 1991.

Arthur L. Alarcón (1925–)

Alarcón received his B.A. degree in 1949 and his LL.B. degree in 1951, both from the University of Southern California. President Carter appointed him to the U.S. Court of Appeals for the Ninth Circuit in 1979.

John Argüelles (1927-)

Former supreme court justice for the state of California, Argüelles was born in Los Angeles, California, to Arturo Argüelles, a Mexican American who graduated from Columbia University with an accounting degree, and Eva Powers, the daughter of an Oklahoma judge. Argüelles was educated in public schools in Los Angeles and went on to U.C.L.A. where he received a degree in economics in 1950. He continued his education at the U.C.L.A. law school and received his degree in 1954. Argüelles practiced law in East Los Angeles and Montebello, California, from 1955 to 1963. During that time, he was president of the local bar association and was elected to the Montebello City Council with the largest vote in that city's history. In 1963 Governor Edmund G. Brown, Sr., appointed Argüelles municipal court judge for the East Los Angeles Municipal Court. He was then elevated to the Los Angeles Superior Court by Governor Ronald Reagan in 1969. Argüelles was appointed to the California Court of Appeal for the Second District in 1984 by Governor George Deukmejian. Three years later, Deukmejian named Argüelles to the California Supreme Court, where he served until his retirement in 1989. At the end of 1989, Argüelles joined the law firm of Gibson, Dunn & Crutcher.

Joseph Francis Baca (1936-)

Baca was born in Albuquerque, New Mexico, to Mexican American parents. He graduated from the University of New Mexico in 1960 with a degree in education and studied law at George Washington University in Washington, D.C., receiving his degree in 1964. Baca served as assistant district attorney in Santa Fe from 1965 to 1966, then as special assistant to the attorney general of New Mexico from 1966 to 1972. He also established a private law practice in Albuquerque during this time. In 1972 Baca was appointed by Governor Bruce King to fill a vacancy in the New Mexico District Court for the Second District in Albuquerque. Baca was elected to six-year terms in 1972, 1978, and 1984. In 1988, Baca was elected to an eight-year term as justice of the New Mexico Supreme Court. In 1989, Baca was named Judge of the Year by the People's Commission for Criminal Justice.

Juan C. Burciaga (1929-)

Burciaga attended the U.S. Military Academy at West Point, where he received his B.S. degree in 1952. He then served in the U.S. Air Force from 1952 to 1960. He received his law degree from the University of New Mexico School of Law in 1963. Burciaga was in private practice from 1964 to 1979 with the firm of Ussery, Burciaga & Parrish. In 1979, President Jimmy Carter appointed Burciaga to the U.S. District Court for the District of New Mexico. Burciaga became chief judge of that court.

José A. Cabranés (1940-)

Born in Mayagüez, Puerto Rico, Cabranés is the first native Puerto Rican appointed to the federal court within the continental United States. Cabranés moved with his family to New York from Puerto Rico when he was only five. After attending public schools in the Bronx and Flushing, Queens, he graduated from Columbia College in 1961. He received his law degree from Yale University Law School in 1965, and an LL.M. degree in international law from the University of Cambridge in Cambridge, England, in 1967. Cabranés served as general counsel of Yale University from 1975 to 1979. Previously he had practiced law at the firm of Casey, Lane & Mittendorf in New York City from 1967 to 1971; taught law at Rutgers University School of Law in New Jersey from 1971 to 1973; and served as special counsel to the governor of Puerto Rico and as administrator, Office of the Commonwealth of Puerto Rico, Washington, D.C.

Cabranés also served in the administration of President Jimmy Carter as a member of the President's Commission on Mental Health from 1977 to 1978; as a member of the U.S. delegation to the Belgrade Conference on Security and Cooperation in Europe from 1977 to 1978; and as consultant to U.S. Secretary of State Cyrus Vance in 1978. In 1979, Carter appointed Cabranés to the U.S. District Court for the District of Connecticut; he served as chief judge from 1992 to 1994, when he was named judge of the U.S. Court of Appeals. In December 1988 U.S. Supreme Court Chief Justice William H. Rehnquist named Judge Cabranés as one of five federal judges for the 15-member Federal Courts Study Committee, created by an act of Congress "to examine problems facing the federal courts and develop a long-range plan for the future of the federal judiciary."

Santiago E. Campos (1926-)

Campos served in the U.S. Navy during World War II. He attended Central College in Fayette, Missouri, and received his law degree from the University of New Mexico in 1953. Campos was assistant attorney general for the state of New Mexico from 1954 to 1957 and from 1971 to 1978 he was a New Mexico district judge. President Carter appointed Judge Campos to the U.S. District Court for the District of New Mexico in 1978; he became a senior judge in 1992.

John M. Cannella (1908-)

Cannella is a Colombian American who played professional football for the New York Giants from 1933 to 1935. He attended Fordham University, where he received his B.A. degree in 1930 and his law degree in 1933. Cannella was assistant U.S. attorney for the Southern District of New York from 1940 to 1942. In 1963 President Kennedy appointed him to the U.S. District Court for the southern district of New York.

Carmen C. Cerezo (1940-)

Cerezo attended the University of Puerto Rico, where he received his B.A. degree in 1963 and his LL.B. degree in 1966. He was a judge on the Puerto Rico Court of Inter Appeals from 1976 to 1980, and was on the Superior Court of Puerto Rico from 1972 to 1976. President Carter appointed Judge Cerezo to the U.S. District Court for the District of Puerto Rico in 1980; and in 1993, he became chief judge.

James DeAnda (1925-)

Born in Houston in 1925, DeAnda received his B.A. degree from Texas A & M University and his J.D. degree from the University of Texas in 1950. He was in private practice from 1951 until 1979. In 1979, Judge DeAnda was appointed to the U.S. District Court for the Southern District of Texas where he subsequently became chief judge.

Ferdinand Francis Fernández (1937-)

Fernández attended the University of Southern California and was awarded his B.A. degree in 1958 and his J.D. degree in 1962. He was in private practice from 1964 to 1980 with the law firm of Allard, Shelton & O'Connor in Pomona, California. Fernández was on the U.S. District Court for the Central District of California from 1985 to 1989. In 1989, Fernández was appointed to the U.S. Court of Appeals for the Ninth Circuit by President Bush. Fernández was reportedly considered as a potential replacement for retiring U.S. Supreme Court Justice Thurgood Marshall.

José Antonio Fuste (1943-)

Fuste attended the University of Puerto Rico, where he received his B.A. degree in 1965 and his LL.B. degree in 1968. He was in private practice from 1968 to 1985 with the law firm of Jiménez and Fuste. Fuste was appointed to the U.S. District Court for the District of Puerto Rico by President Reagan in 1985. President Bush appointed Gaitán to the U.S. District Court for the Western District of Missouri in 1991.

Fernando J. Gaitán, Jr.

President Bush appointed Gaitán to the U.S. District Court for the Western District of Missouri in 1991.

Edward J. García (1928-)

García attended the Sacramento City College and graduated in 1951. He received his law degree from the McGeorge School of Law in 1958. García was deputy district attorney for Sacramento County from 1959 to 1964, supervising deputy district attorney from 1964 to 1969, and chief deputy district attorney from 1969 to 1972. He was a Sacramento Municipal Court judge from 1972 until 1984. President Reagan appointed Judge García to the U.S. District Court for the Eastern District of California in 1984.

Hipolito Frank García (1925-)

García served in the U.S. Army during World War II. He then attended St. Mary's University, where he received his B.A. degree in 1949 and his LL.B. degree in 1951. He was a Texas county court judge from 1964 to 1980. In 1980 President Carter appointed García to the U.S. District Court for the Western District of Texas.

Ferdinand Francis Fernández.

Emilio M. Garza (1947–)

Garza attended the University of Notre Dame and was awarded his B.A. degree in 1969 and M.A. degree in 1970. He received his law degree from the University of Texas in 1976. He was in private practice from 1976 to 1987 with the law firm of Clemens, Spencer, Welmaker & Finck. Garza was a judge for the U.S. District Court for the Western District of Texas from 1988 to 1991. President Bush appointed Judge Garza to the U.S. Court of Appeals for the Fifth Circuit in 1991.

Reynaldo G. Garza (1915–)

Garza was born in Brownsville, Texas, in 1915. His parents were both born in Mexico and had immigrated to the United States in 1901. Garza attended the University of Texas, where he received his law degree in 1939. He practiced law in Brownsville as a solo practitioner until he joined the air force during World War II. After the war, he resumed his private practice until 1950, when he joined the firm of Sharpe, Cunningham & Garza.

President Kennedy in 1961 appointed Garza to the U.S. District Court for the Southern District of Texas; in 1974 he became chief judge of that court. In 1979, Garza was appointed to the U.S. Court of Appeals for the Fifth Circuit by President Jimmy Carter. In 1987, U.S. Supreme Court Chief Justice William H. Rehnquist appointed Garza to the Temporary Emergency Court of Appeals of the United States. He was later named by Rehnquist as chief judge of that court.

Garza has often been recognized for his active role in education, community affairs, and the law. He was honored when a small law school opened its doors in Edinburg, Texas, and was named the Reynaldo G. Garza School of Law. Pope Pius XII twice decorated Garza for his work with the Knights of Columbus, conferring on him the Medal Pro Ecclesia et Pontifice in 1953 and recognizing him as a Knight of the Order of St. Gregory the Great in 1954. Garza received the American Association of Community and Junior Colleges Alumnus of the Year Award in 1984, and in 1989 he was given the Distinguished Alumnus Award of the University of Texas.

President Carter offered the position of attorney general of the United States to Judge Garza. Garza declined the cabinet post because he would have had to resign from his position as a federal judge, which is a lifetime appointment. Today, Judge Garza is on reduced duty and close to retirement.

Gilberto Gierbolini (1926–)

Gierbolini attended the University of Puerto Rico, where he received his B.A. degree in 1951 and his LL.B. degree in 1961. He was a captain in the U.S. Army and served during the Korean War from 1951 to 1957. Gierbolini served as assistant U.S. attorney for Puerto Rico from 1961 to 1966, as a superior court judge from 1966 to 1969, as assistant secretary of justice for Puerto Rico from 1969 to 1972, and as solicitor general of Puerto Rico from 1970 to 1972. Gierbolini was in the private practice of law between 1972 and 1980. In 1980, President Carter appointed Judge Gierbolini to the U.S. District Court for the District of Puerto Rico.

Ricardo H. Hinojosa (1950–)

Hinojosa attended the University of Texas, where he received his B.A. degree in 1972. He received his law degree from Harvard University Law School in 1975 and was in private practice as a partner in the law firm of Ewers & Toothaker in McAllen, Texas, from 1976 until 1983. From 1975 to 1976, Hinojosa served on the Texas Supreme Court. In 1983, Hinojosa was appointed by President Reagan to the U.S. District Court for the Southern District of Texas.

Ricardo H. Hinojosa.

Héctor M. Laffitte (1934–)

Héctor M. Laffitte was born in Ponce, Puerto Rico. Laffitte received his B.A. from the Interamerican University in 1955, his law degree from the University of Puerto Rico in 1958, and his LL.M. degree from Georgetown University in 1960. He was the Civil Rights Commissioner for the commonwealth of Puerto Rico from 1969 to 1972. He was in private practice from 1972 to 1983 with the firm of Laffitte, Domínguez and Totti. President Reagan appointed Laffitte to the U.S. District Court for the District of Puerto Rico in 1983.

George La Plata (1924–)

La Plata was born in 1924 in Detroit to Mexican American parents. He attended Wayne State University, where he received his B.A. degree in 1951. He received his law degree from the Detroit College of Law in 1956. La Plata also served in the U.S. Marine Corps during World War II, reaching the rank of colonel. La Plata, in conjunction with George Menéndez, adviser to the Republic of Mexico, helped pioneer the representation of migrant workers in Michigan, Ohio, and Indiana during the 1950s. From 1956 to 1979, La Plata was in private practice. He served as a Michigan county judge from 1979 to 1985, making him the first Hispanic judge in Michigan history. President Reagan appointed Judge La Plata to the U.S. District Court for the Eastern District of Michigan in 1985. He remains active in providing pro bono services to Hispanics in his community.

Rudolpho Lozano (1942–)

Lozano attended Indiana University, where he received his B.A. degree in 1963 and his law degree in 1966. He was in private practice with the law firm of Spangler, Jennings, Spangler, & Dougherty in Merrillville, Indiana, from 1966 to 1988. In 1988 President Reagan appointed Lozano to the U.S. District Court for the Northern District of Indiana.

Alfredo C. Márquez (1922–)

Márquez served in World War II as an ensign in the U.S. Navy. After the war, he attended the University of Arizona, where he received his B.S. degree in 1948 and his law degree in 1950. Márquez served as assistant attorney general for the state of Arizona from 1951 to 1952, as prosecutor for the city of Tucson and assistant county attorney for Pima County from 1953 to 1954, and as an aide to Congressman Stewart Udall (D-AZ) in 1955. Márquez was in private practice with the firm of Mesch, Márquez and Rothschild from 1957 until 1980. Márquez was appointed by President Carter in 1980 to the U.S. District Court for the District of Arizona.

Harold R. Medina, Sr. (1888–1991)

Former U.S. circuit court judge, Harold Medina was born in Brooklyn, New York, on February 16, 1888, of Mexican American and Dutch American parents. His father, Joaquín Medina, came to the United States as a refugee from a bitter civil and race war in the Yucatan Peninsula. Harold Medina attended Princeton University, where he graduated with honors in 1909. He went on to Columbia University Law School and received his law degree in 1912. Medina began practicing law and also lectured at Columbia Law School at the invitation of Dean Harlan Fiske Stone. In 1918, Medina formed his own law firm and specialized in appeals. The most famous case argued by Medina was the Cramer treason case during World War II. Anthony Cramer, of Brooklyn, was accused of helping two Nazi spies who had landed from a submarine. Medina initially lost the case in the lower courts but won it on appeal to the U.S. Supreme Court. After World War II ended, Medina was appointed to the U.S. District Court for the District of New York by President Harry Truman. In 1951 President Truman appointed Medina to the U.S. Court of Appeals for the Second Circuit.

Harold R. Medina, Sr.

Federico A. Moreno, Sr. (1952–)

Moreno was born in Caracas, Venezuela, and immigrated to the United States with his family in 1963. In 1974, Moreno graduated from the University of Notre Dame, where he received his B.A. degree in government. He worked as a janitor and in restaurants to pay his way through college. After graduating, he taught at the Atlantic Community College in Mays Landing, New Jersey, and at Stockton State College in Pomona, New Jersey, in 1975 and 1976. In 1978, Moreno received his law degree from the University of Miami School of Law. Moreno was an associate with the law firm of Rollins, Peeples & Meadows in 1978 and 1979, and served as an assistant federal public defender from 1979 to 1981. He was a partner in the law firm of Thornton, Rothman & Moreno from 1982 to 1986. He served as Dade County judge in 1986 and 1987. Moreno was a Florida Circuit Court judge from 1987 until 1990. President Bush appointed Moreno to the U.S. District Court for the Southern District of Florida in 1990.

Philip Newman (1916–)

The first Mexican-born U.S. judge, Newman was born in Mexico City to a German American father and a Mexican mother. His family fled Mexico in the 1920s during the Mexican civil war and settled in California. Arriving destitute in the United States, Newman's father put himself through law school at night and became an attorney. Newman also became an attorney in 1941. He won landmark cases protecting the rights of individuals against unwarranted searches and seizures and leading to changes in immigration law. He was also the founder of the Community Services Organization in Los Angeles. In 1964, Newman was appointed by Governor Edmund G. Brown to a Los Angeles municipal judgeship, where he remained until his retirement in 1982.

Juan M. Pérez-Giménez (1941–)

Pérez-Giménez received his B.A. degree in 1963 and his LL.B. degree in 1968 from the University of Puerto Rico; his M.B.A. degree was conferred by George Washington University in 1965. He was an assistant U.S. attorney for Puerto Rico from 1971 to 1975. President Carter appointed Pérez-Giménez to the U.S. District Court for the District of Puerto Rico in 1979.

Jaime Pieras, Jr. (1924–)

Pieras served in the U.S. Army during World War II. He received his B.A. degree from Catholic University in 1945 and his J.D. degree from Georgetown University in 1948. Pieras was in private practice from 1949 until 1982. In 1982, Pieras was appointed to the U.S. District Court for the District of Puerto Rico by President Reagan.

Edward C. Prado (1947–)

Prado attended the University of Texas, where he received his B.A. degree in 1969 and his J.D. degree in 1972. In 1984, President Reagan appointed Prado to the U.S. District Court for the Western District of Texas.

Raul Anthony Ramírez (1944–)

After receiving his law degree from the University of the Pacific, McGeorge School of Law, Ramírez went into private practice. He served as a municipal court judge in Sacramento from 1977 until 1980. In 1980, he was appointed by President Carter to the U.S. District Court for the Eastern District of California. Since 1990, he has been a senior partner in the firm of Orrick, Herrington & Sutcliffe in Sacramento.

Manuel L. Real (1924–)

Real's parents immigrated to the United States from Spain. His mother was born in 1924 in Albunol, Granada, Spain, and his father was born in Sierra de Yegas, Malaga, Spain. Real was educated in California and received his B.S. degree from the University of California in 1944 and his LL.B. degree from Loyola University in 1951. Real also served as assistant U.S. attorney from 1952 to 1955 for the Southern District of California. He was in private practice from 1955 to 1964 in San Pedro, California, and was assistant U.S. attorney for the Southern District of California from 1964 to 1966. In 1966, Real was appointed to the U.S. District Court for the Central District of California by President Johnson. He was named chief judge of that court in 1982.

Cruz Reynoso (1931–)

A former state supreme court justice for California, Reynoso was born on May 2, 1931, to farm worker parents in the small town of Brea, California, where he was raised and received his early education. He attended Fullerton Junior College and Pomona College, where he earned his B.A. degree in 1953. From 1953 to 1955, he served in the U.S. Army. After his discharge, Reynoso began studying law at the University of California, Berkeley, and was awarded his degree in 1958. That same year he began a private law practice in El Centro, California. During the 1960s, Reynoso acted as assistant chief of the Division of Fair Employment Practices for California. From 1967 to 1968, he was associate general

Cruz Reynoso.

troit in 1924. She attended Wayne State University, where she received both her B.A. degree in politics and her law degree. She went into private practice in 1950 and established the firm of Riley and Roumell in 1968. Riley sat on the Michigan Court of Appeals from 1976 until 1982, when she was elevated to the Michigan Supreme Court as an associate justice. Riley was named chief justice in 1987 and remains in that position.

Joseph H. Rodríguez (1930–)

Rodriguez received his B.A. degree from LaSalle University in 1955 and his J.D. degree from Rutgers University in 1958. He was in private practice from 1959 to 1982 with the firm of Brown, Connery, Kulp, Wille, Purcell, & Greene and was also an instructor at Rutgers University School of Law from 1972 to 1982. In 1982, Rodriguez was appointed New Jersey public advocate, a state cabinet position, and served until 1985. He litigated landmark cases in the areas of education and housing. President Reagan appointed Rodriguez to the U.S. District Court for the District of New Jersey in 1985. Rodriguez is active in community affairs.

counsel to the Equal Employment Opportunity Commission in Washington, D.C., returning to California to become the first deputy director and then director of California Rural Legal Assistance. In 1972, he accepted a position at the University of New Mexico Law School, where he served for four years.

In 1976, Reynoso was appointed to the California Court of Appeals in Sacramento as an associate justice. Governor Jerry Brown then appointed him to the California Supreme Court in 1982. Reynoso became the first Hispanic on the court and served until 1986. In 1987, he entered private practice with the firm of O'Donnell & Gordon in Los Angeles and subsequently was of counsel to Kaye, Scholer, Fierman, Hays & Handler in Sacramento. Reynoso has been honored with appointments to four presidential commissions, including the Select Commission on Immigration and Refugee Policy and the UN Commission on Human Rights. He was appointed to the law faculty of the University of California, Los Angeles, in 1990.

Dorothy Comstock Riley (1924–)

Supreme court justice for the state of Michigan, Dorothy Riley was born to Hispanic parents in De-

Dorothy Comstock Riley.

Luis D. Rovirá (1923-)

Supreme court justice for the state of Colorado, Rovirá was born in San Juan, Puerto Rico. His family moved to Colorado, where he was educated. Rovirá attended the University of Colorado and received both B.A. and law degrees. He was in private practice with the firm of Rovirá, DeMuth & Eiberger until 1976. In 1976, Rovirá was appointed to the Colorado District Court for the second district. In 1979, he was elevated to the Colorado Supreme Court as an associate justice and became chief justice in 1990.

Ernest C. Torres (1941-)

Torres graduated from Dartmouth College in 1963 and received his law degree from Duke University School of Law in 1968. He was in private practice from 1968 to 1974. In 1975, Torres was elected to the Rhode Island House of Representatives, where he served until 1980. After leaving the state house, he went into private practice. Torres was appointed by President Reagan in 1988 to the U.S. District Court for the District of Rhode Island.

Juan R. Torruella (1933-)

Torruella received his B.A. degree from the University of Pennsylvania in 1954 and his LL.B. degree from Boston University in 1957. He was appointed by President Ford to the U.S. District Court for the District of Puerto Rico in 1974 and was chief judge of that court from 1982 to 1984. In 1984, President Reagan appointed Torruella to the U.S. Court of Appeals for the First Circuit.

Filemón B. Vela (1935-)

Vela graduated from the University of Texas and received a J.D. degree from St. Mary's University in 1962. He was in private practice from 1962 to 1975 and also served as an attorney for the Mexican American Legal Defense and Educational Fund (MALDEF) from 1962 to 1975. He was a Texas district court judge from 1975 to 1980. President Carter appointed Vela to the U.S. District Court for the Southern District of Texas in 1980.

✱ HISPANICS IN THE POLITICAL PROCESS

Widespread political activity at the national level by Hispanic Americans has been intermittent since the first Hispanic was elected to Congress. Joseph Marion Hernández was elected to Congress representing Florida in 1822 as a member of the Whig party. No other Hispanic held national office for 30 years. A total of 11 Hispanics were elected to the U.S. Congress in the entire nineteenth century, all from New Mexico, except for one from California and Congressman Hernández from Florida. From the turn of the century until the 1950s, there were a total of 15, five from New Mexico, two from Louisiana, and eight resident commissioners from Puerto Rico, which became a U.S. possession in 1898. Since the 1960s, the number of Hispanic Americans elected to Congress has been steadily increasing. In 1996, there were 17 Hispanics serving in Congress, representing constituents from Arizona, California, Florida, Illinois, New Jersey, New Mexico, New York and Texas. All are congressmen and women; none are senators. In addition, there are three non-voting representatives from Puerto Rico, Guam, and the U.S. Virgin Islands.

For a century, the majority of Hispanic Americans holding political office at the local level was limited to southwestern states, southern Florida, and New York City. Since the 1960s, growth in the population of Hispanics and favorable civil rights legislation, such as the Voting Rights Act of 1965, have combined to create opportunity for Hispanic candidates to win public office in other areas of the country. Hispanic Americans have made the greatest inroads at the municipal level. In 1991, Hispanics held elected office at the local level in 35 of the 50 states.

Harry P. Pachón, national director of the National Association of Latino Elected and Appointed Officials (NALEO), stated that in 1990 NALEO identified "4,004 Hispanic Americans holding publicly elected offices throughout the country." Pachón stated that "although this number is only a small fraction of the nation's 504,404 elected officials, less than one percent, the number of Hispanic elected officials for various states is quite large."

In the past 30 years, Hispanic Americans have become one of the largest and fastest-growing groups of elected officials in the United States. Congressman Bill Richardson (D-New Mexico) states, "National candidates and both major political parties are undertaking major campaigns to woo Hispanic American support. We are recognized as the nation's fastest growing minority group and are being courted as such. This attention will only increase our political strength."

✱ HISPANIC VOTING AND THE VOTING RIGHTS ACT OF 1965

The primary aim of the Voting Rights Act of 1965 was African American enfranchisement in the South. Specifically, obstacles to registration and voting faced by African Americans were the major concern of those who framed the statute in the 1960s. Its potential as a tool for Hispanic Americans was not fully realized until the act was extended and amended in 1970.

The 1970 amendments to this landmark legislation added a provision that was designed to guard against inventive new barriers to political participation by requiring federal approval of all changes in voting procedure in certain jurisdictions, primarily southern states. Disgruntled officials in Mississippi and other southern states embarked on schemes to dilute African American voter impact in elections by eliminating single-member districts and creating at-large voting.

The U.S. Supreme Court responded, in *Allen v. State Board of Elections,* 393 U.S. 544 (1969), by extending federal authority to object to proposed discriminatory alterations in voting districts, the introduction of at-large voting, and other such changes, in addition to reaffirming the original power to object to discriminatory innovations involving registration and voting.

Until 1980, the U.S. Census Bureau had historically classified Hispanic Americans as "white," with the single exception of the 1930 census, and many argued that to extend coverage of the Voting Rights Act to a class of people who considered themselves white was unjustifiable. The Fifteenth Amendment rights secured by the statute protected against denial of the right to vote only on account of "race, color or previous condition of servitude." If Hispanic Americans were white, they were ineligible for the special protection of the Voting Rights Act.

During congressional hearings to extend the Voting Rights Act in 1975, J. Stanley Pottinger, assistant attorney general of the U.S. Justice Department's Civil Rights Division, saw the labeling problem as inconsequential and told Congress that the Justice Department's practice "has been to treat Indians, Puerto Ricans, and Mexican Americans as racial groups." His argument hardly settled the matter for everyone, but Congress agreed to amend the act to include "language minorities," which specifically included Spanish-speakers.

Vilma S. Martínez, president of the Mexican American Legal Defense and Educational Fund (MALDEF), testified before Congress in 1975 about voting districts in Texas where assistance to non-English-speaking voters was being denied. She testified further that Texas had been gerrymandering voting districts to give unfair advantage to English-speaking residents. State action creating at-large voting, annexations to voting districts, and redistricting plans fragmented Hispanic voting strength. Additionally, majority vote requirements, numbered posts, and other confusing procedural rules diminished the likelihood that a Hispanic American would gain an elected office.

Congress acted decisively. The Voting Rights Act Amendments of 1975, which extended the provisions of the Voting Rights Act of 1965, made permanent the national ban on literacy tests. The amendments condemned any action by states, which was no longer limited to southern states, to realign voting districts to dilute the impact of minority voters who resided within the district. Any redistricting plan would have to be approved by the federal government.

In 1980, the U.S. Supreme Court, in *City of Mobile v. Bolden,* 446 U.S. 55, rejected a challenge to at-large elections in Mobile, Alabama, because the Court was not convinced that the city had acted with the purpose of discriminating against minority voters. The Court, in its sharply divided decision, found that the city had not violated the Voting Rights Act.

Congress reacted to the Supreme Court decision with the important Voting Rights Act Amendments of 1982. The amendments, under Section 2, prohibit any voting law or practice created by a state or political subdivision that "results" in denial of the right of any citizen of the United States to vote on account of race, color, or language-minority status. The amendments eliminated the need to prove that the state or political subdivision created a voting law with the "intention" of discriminating against minority voters.

In one of the first cases to be tried under Section 2 of the 1982 amendments, *Velásquez v. City of Abilene,* 725 F.2d 1017 (5th Cir. 1983), prominent judge Reynaldo G. Garza delivered the opinion of the U.S. Court of Appeals for the Fifth Circuit. Garza stated for the court that the intention of Congress was clear in cases of vote dilution, referring to the 1982 amendments. Garza stated that the city of Abilene's use of at-large voting, bloc voting, and other voting mechanisms resulted in vote dilution and had a discriminatory effect on Hispanic American voters in the city.

A year later, the Fifth Circuit Court made a similar ruling in *Jones v. City of Lubbock,* 727 F.2d 364 (5th Cir. 1984). The city of Lubbock, Texas, a medium-sized city with a diverse population, had a clear white majority. Under an at-large voting scheme, the majority uniformly elected an all-white city council. The court found that the voting method used by the city polarized voting between the white majority and minority voters, and the result was discrimination against minority voters.

In the last decade, holdouts of racially discriminatory electoral patterns have been coming under intense pressure from the courts to end discrimination against minority voters. The success in the courts has contributed to the growing numbers of Hispanic Americans holding elected offices across the United States. In 1991, for the first time in history, the city of Abilene had two Hispanics on its city council; the city of Lubbock had one Hispanic on its city council, as well as a Hispanic county commissioner.

✳ CONGRESSIONAL HISPANIC CAUCUS

The Congressional Hispanic Caucus, organized in December 1976, is a bipartisan group of 12 members of Congress of Hispanic descent. The caucus is dedicated to voicing and advancing, through the legislative process, issues affecting Hispanic Americans in the United States and its territories.

Organized as a legislative service organization under the rules of Congress, the caucus is composed solely of members of the U.S. Congress. Under these rules, associate membership is offered to dues-paying members of Congress who are not of Hispanic descent. With its associate members, caucus membership represents 20 states, Puerto Rico, Guam, and the U.S. Virgin Islands.

Although every issue that affects the quality of life of all U.S. citizens is a Congressional Hispanic Caucus concern, there are national and international issues that have a particular impact on the Hispanic community. The caucus monitors legislative action as well as policies and practices of the executive and judicial branches of government that affect these issues.

In 1995, Congress abolished funding for the minority caucuses. The overwhelmingly conservative Congress eliminated its funding for what the Republics saw as the opposition; the majority of minority congressmen and senators are Democratic and liberal.

✳ HISPANICS IN CONGRESS

The growing Hispanic population remains significantly underrepresented in the U.S. Congress today. Hispanic American voting levels have traditionally fallen well below the national average. In spite of favorable legislation, advocates actively seeking to increase Hispanic American voter registration still cite poverty, inadequate education, language barriers, and alienage as critical obstacles that have discouraged voting. Despite these problems, Hispanic Americans have been going to the polls in increasing numbers. This is evident at the national level, where, in 1991, 13 Hispanic Americans were serving in the U.S. House of Representatives.

Of the 20 Hispanic representatives currently hold-ing office, 17 have full voting privileges and represent districts in the states of Arizona, California, Florida, Illinois, New Jersey, New Mexico, New York, and Texas. The three nonvoting members are resident commissioners of Puerto Rico, Guam and the U.S. Virgin Islands. Of the 17 congressmen, 14 are Democrats. Three congressmen are Republicans: Henry Bonilla of Texas, and the two Florida congressmen, Lincoln Díaz-Balart, and Ileana Ros-Lehtinen.

No Hispanic American candidate has been elected to the U.S. Senate since 1970, when New Mexico Democrat Joseph Manuel Montoya won his second and last election. Senator Montoya served in the Senate from 1964 to 1977. The only other Hispanic American to be elected to the Senate was New Mexico Democrat Dennis Chávez, who served with great distinction from 1935 to 1962. Both Senators Chávez and Montoya served as members of the U.S. House of Representatives prior to being elected to the Senate.

Xavier Becerra (1958–)
(D-California)

Born on January 26, 1958, in Sacramento, California, Becerra received his B.A. from Stanford University in 1980 and his law degree from Stanford in 1984. He served as deputy attorney general in the California Department of Justice from 1987 to 1990, when he was elected to the state legislature. In 1994, Becerra was elected to represent Los Angeles' Thirtieth Congressional District; he is currently in his second term.

Henry Bonilla
(R-Texas)

Born in Calvert, Texas, Bonilla received his B.A. degree from the University of Texas in 1968 and his law degree from Texas in 1971. After working in private practice since graduation, he served as the state director of the League of United Latin American Citizens (LULAC) from 1977 to 1979. From 1979 to 1980, he served as president of LULAC and then from 1980 to 1985 as its general counsel. From 1985 to the president, he has been the chairman of the Mexican American Democrats of Texas. Bonilla is in his second term of serving the Twenty-third District of Texas, which covers San Antonio.

E. (Kika) de la Garza (1927–)
(D-Texas)

De la Garza was born on September 22, 1927, in the Mexican border town of Mercedes, Texas. He comes from a family with roots in the Rio Grande Valley that go back to the 1700's. After graduating from high school, de la Garza, by struggle and perseverance, obtained his education at Edinburg Junior

College and St. Mary's University in San Antonio. His education was interrupted by the Korean War, in which he served as an artillery officer from 1950 to 1952. He then earned his B.A. degree from St. Mary's in 1952 and later received his law degree from St. Mary's Law School.

With heavily Mexican American Hidalgo County as his base of support, de la Garza was elected to the Texas House of Representatives in 1952. He was reelected for another five terms. De la Garza was first elected to Congress in 1964 as a Democrat from the Rio Grande Valley's Fifteenth District. His election was a milestone for Texas Mexican Americans.

De la Garza is chairman of the House Agriculture Committee and an ex officio member of all its subcommittees. He is also a member and former chairman of the Congressional Hispanic Caucus. He is an active member of the League of United Latin American Citizens (LULAC) and a host of other organizations. In 1978 Mexican President José López Portillo awarded de la Garza Mexico's highest award to a foreigner, the order of the Aztec Eagle.

Lincoln Díaz-Balart (1961–)

(R-Florida)

Díaz-Balart was born on August 25, 1961, in Havana, Cuba. He received his B.A. from the New College University of Southern Florida in 1976 and his law degree from Case Western Reserve University in 1969. After entering the private practice of law, Díaz-Balart served as a state representative from 1986 to 1989 and as a state senator from 1989 until his election to the U.S. Congress in 1992. He represents the Twenty-first Congressional District of Miami.

Henry Barbosa González (1916–)

(D-Texas)

González was born on May 3, 1916, in San Antonio, Texas, to Mexican refugees. He grew up in a family that stressed education and intellectual pursuits. González received his early education in San Antonio public schools. He went on to attend San Antonio Junior College and the University of Texas at Austin, where he received his bachelor's degree. He then attended St. Mary's University Law School, where he received his law degree in 1943. After graduation, González worked at a variety of jobs, including teaching and social services. In 1950, González entered the political arena and ran for San Antonio City Council. He lost narrowly, but won in his second bid three years later. González fought for a city ordinance ending segregation in city facilities. In 1956, he was elected to the Texas Senate. González was the first Mexican American Texas state senator in

Henry Barbosa González.

110 years. He attracted national attention as an outspoken advocate of equal rights for minorities and as an opponent of racist legislation.

In 1960 González was elected to Congress for the first time, as a Democrat representing the Twentieth District of Texas. He has been overwhelmingly reelected to Congress for each subsequent term. Congressman González is currently the chairman of the influential House Banking, Finance and Urban Affairs Committee and is also chairman of the Housing and Community Development Subcommittee. The first Texan of Mexican descent to serve in the U.S. House of Representatives, he has fervently defended civil rights, distinguishing himself nationally as a liberal Democrat during the 1960s and 1970s. He was chairman of the Viva Kennedy campaign in 1960 and the Viva Johnson campaign in 1964. In 1964, he contributed significantly to the termination of the infamous Mexican Bracero Program.

Luis Gutiérrez (1953–)

(D-Illinois)

Gutiérrez was born in Chicago on December 10, 1953. He received his B.A. from Northeastern Illinois University in 1976 and worked as a teacher in the Chicago public schools until 1984, when he became an administrative assistant to the mayor of Chicago. In 1986, Gutiérrez became an alderman for the Twenty-sixth Ward, and in 1992 he was elected to Congress to represent Chicago's Fourth Congressional District.

Matthew G. Martínez (1929–)

(D-California)

Martínez was born on February 14, 1929, and resides in Monterey Park, California. Martínez attended the Los Angeles Trade Technical School and was involved in small business prior to his election to the U.S. Congress. He is also a veteran of the U.S. Marine Corps. Martínez was Mayor of Monterey Park, California, in 1974–75. He was a member of the California legislature from 1980 to 1982. Martínez was first elected to Congress as a Democrat in 1981, representing the Thirtieth District of California. He is a member of the important House Education and Labor Committee and is chairman of its Human Resources Subcommittee. Martínez is also a member of the House Government Operations Committee and the House Select Committee on Children,

Matthew G. Martínez.

Youth, and Families. In January 1991, Congressman Martínez was elected vice-chairman of the Congressional Hispanic Caucus.

Robert Menéndez (1954–)

(D-New Jersey)

Menéndez was born on January 1, 1954, in New York City to Cuban immigrant parents. He received his B.A. from St. Peter College in New Jersey in 1976 and his law degree from Rutgers University in 1979. While still in school, Menéndez served on the union City Board of Education, from 1974 to 1978. In 1978, Menéndez was elected to the New Jersey State Assembly. In 1986, he was elected mayor of Union City, the largest concentration of Cubans outside of Florida. In 1992, Menéndez was elected to represent the New Jersey's Thirteenth Congressional District. Menéndez, as one of the youngest Hispanic politicians on record, received many awards over his career, including being selected as a U.S. Delegate to Central America by the American Council of young political Leaders in 1988. He has also received special recognition in 1987 and 1988 from the U.S. Conference on Mayors.

Solomon P. Ortiz (1937–)

(D-Texas)

Ortiz was born on June 3, 1937, in Robstown, Texas. He attended Del Mar College in Texas. Ortiz was first elected to office in 1964 as Nueces County Constable. Four years later he was elected Nueces County Commissioner and was reelected to that post in 1972. In 1976, Ortiz was elected Nueces County Sheriff and was reelected in 1980. In 1982, Ortiz first ran for national office as a Democrat for a seat in the Ninety-eighth Congress. He was elected and has been reelected to each subsequent session to date. Congressman Ortiz is a member of the Congressional Hispanic Caucus and was elected chairman of the caucus in January 1991. He sits on the powerful House Armed Services Committee, the Merchant Marine and Fisheries Committee, and the Select Committee on Narcotics Abuse and Control.

Ed López Pastor (1943–)

(D-Arizona)

Pastor was born on June 28, 1943, in Claypool, Arizona. He graduated from Arizona State University with a B.A. in Chemistry in 1966. After working as a chemistry teacher in the Phoenix schools, he returned to his alma mater and received a degree in law in 1974. After receiving his law degree, he worked as the Director of Affirmative Action in the Office of the Governor of Arizona until 1977. He was

Solomon P. Ortiz.

member of the House leadership and serves as majority whip at-large. He is a member of the House Energy and Commerce Committee, the House Interior and Insular Affairs Committee, the House Select Committee on Aging, and the House Select Committee on Intelligence.

Ileana Ros-Lehtinen (1952–)

(R-Florida)

Ros-Lehtinen was born on July 15, 1952, and resides in Miami, Florida. She attended Florida International University, where she received both a bachelor's and a master's degree. After graduating from college, Ros-Lehtinen taught at a private school in Miami that she owned and operated. In 1982, she was elected as a Republican to the Florida legislature, and in 1986, she was elected to the Florida state senate, where she served until 1989. Congresswoman Ros-Lehtinen was elected in 1989 as a Republican to the U.S. Congress for the Eighteenth District in Florida. She is a member of the critical House Foreign Affairs Committee and the House Government Operations Committee and serves as the ranking minority member of the House Employ-

elected to the board of Maricopa County Supervisors in 1977 and served in that position until his election to Congress in 1992 to represent the Second District of Arizona. Pastor has served on national boards, including the National Council of La Raza from 1979 to 1991, the National Association of Counties from 1980 to 1991 and the National Association of Latino Elected and Appointed Officials.

William B. Richardson (1947–)

(D-New Mexico)

Richardson was born on November 15, 1947, and lives in Santa Fe, New Mexico. Richardson attended Tufts University and received a master's degree from the Fletcher School of Law and Diplomacy. Richardson was first elected to Congress in 1982 to represent New Mexico's newly created Third Congressional District, one of the largest in square miles and one of the most ethnically diverse in the country: 40 percent Anglo, 40 percent Hispanic, and 20 percent native American. He won reelection with over 70 percent of the vote in 1986 and 1988. Congressman Richardson rose relatively quickly to become a

William B. Richardson.

Ileana Ros-Lehtinen.

ment and Housing Subcommittee. Ros-Lehtinen has also been elected twice to the post of secretary-treasurer of the Congressional Hispanic Caucus, of which she is the only woman and the only Cuban American member.

Lucille Roybal-Allard (1941–)

(D-California)

Roybal-Allard was born in Los Angeles on June 12, 1941, the daughter of retired Congressman Edward Roybal and Lucille Roybal. Roybal-Allard received her education at California State University in Los Angeles and became the director of the National Association of Hispanic CPAs in Washington, D.C. From 1987 to 1992, she served in the California State Assembly, representing a Los Angeles district. When her father retired from his congressional office, she ran in his place and was elected to represent Los Angeles' Thirty-third District. She is now in her second term. Roybal-Allard has developed a record of special attention to dealing with assaults on women and domestic violence; for her involvement in these issues, she has won various awards.

José E. Serrano (1943–)

(D-New York)

Serrano was born in Mayagüez, Puerto Rico, on October 24, 1943. His family moved to the South Bronx in 1950. Serrano attended public schools and went to the City University of New York. He was a New York state assemblyman from 1974 until he was elected to Congress as a Democrat in 1990. He represents the Eighteenth District in New York. Congressman Serrano is a member of the influential House Education and Labor Committee and the House Small Business Committee. He is also a member of the Congressional Hispanic Caucus.

Frank Tejeda (1945–)

(D-Texas)

Tejeda was born on October 2, 1945. He received a master's degree in public affairs from Harvard University, and a law degree from the University of California-Berkeley. After law school, he worked in private practice until he was elected to the Texas legislature, where he served as a representative from 1977 to 1987. In 1987, Tejeda was elected to the Texas State Senate and held that seat until he was

José E. Serrano.

Frank Tejeda.

elected in to San Antonio's Twenty-eighth District Congressional seat in 1992. Tejeda was so popular that he ran unopposed for the congressional seat.

Esteban Edward Torres (1930–)

(D-California)

Torres was born on January 27, 1930, in Miami, Arizona, where his Mexican-born father was a miner. When his father was deported in 1936 as a result of his union-organizing activities, the family moved to East Los Angeles, where Torres received his early education. After graduating from high school in 1949, he joined the army and served during the Korean War. After being discharged in 1954, Torres took a job on an assembly line at Chrysler and attended California State University at night, receiving his B.A. degree in 1963. Torres was a supporter of the United Auto Workers Union. In 1974, Torres narrowly lost his first bid for the Democratic nomination for the U.S. House of Representatives. In 1977, President Jimmy Carter appointed Torres as the U.S. representative to UNESCO, with diplomatic rank. President Carter also appointed Torres as his special assistant for programs and policies concerning Mexican Ameri-

cans. After President Reagan took office in 1981, Torres returned to California. The next year, he was elected to Congress as a Democrat representing the Thirty-fourth District in California. He is a member of the House Banking, Finance and Urban Affairs Committee and is chairman of its Consumer Affairs Subcommittee. Torres is also a member of the House Small Business Committee and a member of the Congressional Hispanic Caucus.

Nydia Margarita Velásquez (1953–)

(D-New York)

Velásquez was born on March 23, 1953, in a working-class family in rural Yabucoa, Puerto Rico. An outstanding student who was the first in her family to graduate from high school, she began her studies at the University of Puerto Rico at age 16. Velásquez graduated from the university magna cum laude with a degree in Political Science in 1974 and began teaching in the public schools. She earned her M.A, from New York University in 1976 and then returned to the University of Puerto Rico in Humacao to teach Political Science. In 1981, she left Puerto Rico and became and adjunct professor of Puerto Rican Studies at Hunter College in New York. In

Esteban Edward Torres.

TABLE 13.2 HOUSE OF REPRESENTATIVES

NAME	PARTY AND STATE	YEARS SERVED
Joseph Marion Hernández	W-Florida	1822-1823
Jose Manuel Gallegos	D-New Mexico	1871-1873
Miguel Antonio Otero, Sr.	D-New Mexico	1856-1861
Francisco Perea	R-New Mexico	1863-1865
Jose Francisco Chaves	R-New Mexico	1865-1867
Trinidad Romero	R-New Mexico	1877-1879
Mariano Sabino Otero	R-New Mexico	1879-1881
Romualdo Pacheco	R-California	1879-1883
Tranquillino Luna	R-New Mexico	1881-1884
Francisco Manzanares	D-New Mexico	1884-1885
Pedro Perea	R-New Mexico	1899-1901
Julio Larringa	U-Puerto Rico*	1905-1911
Luis Muñoz Rivera	U-Puerto Rico*	1911-1916
Ládislas Lázaro	D-Louisiana	1913-1927
Benigno Cárdenas Hernández	R-New Mexico	1919-1921
Felix Córdova Dávila	U-Puerto Rico*	1917-1932
Nestor Montoya	R-New Mexico	1921-1923
Dennis Chávez	D-New Mexico	1931-1935
Joachim Octave Fernández	D-Louisiana	1931-1941
José Lorenzo Pesquera	NP-Puerto Rico*	1932-1933
Santiago Iglesias	C-Puerto Rico*	1933-1939
Bolívar Pagán	C-Puerto Rico*	1939-1945
Antonio Manuel Fernández	D-New Mexico	1943-1956
Jesús T. Piñero	PD-Puerto Rico*	1945-1948
Antonio Fernós-Isern	PD-Puerto Rico*	1949-1965
Joseph Manuel Montoya	D-New Mexico	1957-1964
Henry B. González	D-Texas	1961-present
Edward R. Roybal	D-California	1962-1992
E. (Kika) de la Garza	D-Texas	1965-present
Santiago Polanco-Abreu	PD-Puerto Rico*	1965-1969
Manuel Luján, Jr.	R-New Mexico	1969-1988
Jorge Luis Córdova	NP-Puerto Rico*	1969-1973
Herman Badillo	D-New York	1971-1977
Ron de Lugo	D-Virgin Islands	1981-present
Jaime Benítez	PD-Puerto Rico*	1973-1977
Baltasar Corrada	NP-Puerto Rico*	1977-1984
Robert García	D-New York	1978-1989
Matthew G. Martínez	D-California	1982-present
Solomon P. Ortiz	D-Texas	1983-present
William B. Richardson	D-New Mexico	1983-present
Esteban Edward Torres	D-California	1983-present
Ben Blaz	R-Guam*	1985-1992
Albert G. Bustamante	D-Texas	1985-1992
Jaime B. Fuster	D-Puerto Rico*	1985-1992
Ileana Ros-Lehtinen	R-Florida	1989-present
Ed Pastor	D-Arizona	1991-present
José E. Serrano	D-New York	1991-present
Xavier Becerra	D-California	1993-present
Henry Bonilla	R-Texas	1993-present
Lincoln Diaz-Balart	R-Florida	1993-present
Luis Gutierrez	D-Illinois	1993-present
Robert Menendez	D-New Jersey	1993-present
Lucille Roybal-Allard	D-California	1993-present
Carlos Romero-Barcelo	D/NP-Puerto Rico*	1993-present
Frank Tejeda	D-Texas	1993-present
Robert A. Underwood	D-Guam*	1993-present
Nydia M. Velazquez	D-New York	1993-present
SENATE		
Dennis Chávez	D-New Mexico	1935-1962
Joseph Montoya	D-New Mexico	1964-1977

Source: Congressional Hispanic Caucus. *Nonvoting member of Congress.
Party Affiliation: D = Democrat; R = Republican; C = Congress; PD = Popular Democratico; NP = Nuevo Progresista; U = Unida; W = Whig.

1983, Velásquez served as special assistant to Congressman Edolphus Town, a Democrat from Brooklyn, and in 1984 was appointed to the New York City Council to fill a vacancy, where she served until 1986. In 1989, she was appointed by the governor of Puerto Rico as Secretary for the Department of Puerto Rican Community Affairs in the United States, with offices in New York and other regions. In this position, she initiated voter-registration drives that resulted in the registration of more than 200,000 Puerto Ricans in the Northeast and Midwest. Velásquez was elected to represent Brooklyn's Twelfth District in 1992 in a very close run-off election. She became only the second Latina in history to serve in the U.S. Congress.

Selected Prominent Hispanic Former Members of Congress, 1822–1996

Herman Badillo (1929–)

The first Puerto Rican ever elected as a voting Member of Congress, Badillo was born in Caguas, Puerto Rico, on August 21, 1929. Orphaned at age five, he was eventually sent to the United States in 1940 to live with relatives in New York City. He attended the City College of New York, where he graduated with honors, then attended the Brooklyn Law School at night. In 1961, Badillo entered politics, narrowly losing a race for the state assembly. After serving in several local appointed positions, he ran unsuccessfully for mayor of New York. Badillo gained popularity as a result of his strong showing in the mayoral election and later won election to Congress in 1970. Badillo served as a U.S. congressman from New York for four terms, representing the Twenty-first District. After serving in Congress for seven years, Badillo resigned in 1978 to accept an appointment as deputy mayor of New York City under Mayor Edward Koch. Badillo went into the practice of law in New York after leaving the deputy mayor's office. In 1986, he ran for the post of New York state comptroller. He lost the statewide race, but carried 61 percent of the New York City vote. Many in the New York Hispanic community suggest that Badillo may again run for mayor.

José Francisco Chaves (1833–1904)

Chaves was born in 1883 in what is today Bernalillo County, near Albuquerque, New Mexico. His father, Mariano Chaves, was an important political figure in the Mexican government in the late 1830s. After his early education in New Mexico and Chihuahua, Chaves was sent to school in St. Louis by his father so that he might better cope with the westward flood tide of American frontierspeople. After

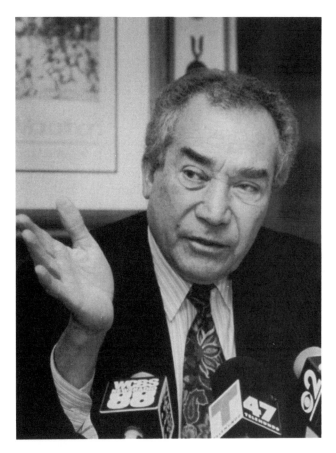

Herman Badillo.

returning to New Mexico during the U.S. war with Mexico, Chaves went to New York to complete his education. When his father died, Chaves returned to New Mexico to manage the family ranch. During the 1850s, he was involved in various Indian campaigns to preserve cattle ranges. His participation in the Indian campaigns proved useful in the Civil War, in which he reached the rank of lieutenant colonel in the New Mexico infantry. After the war, Chaves studied law and entered the New Mexico political arena. He was elected New Mexico territorial delegate in several bitter, brawling campaigns and served three terms between 1865 and 1871 as a Republican. In 1875, he was elected to the New Mexico territorial legislature and reelected until his death 30 years later. Chaves was a dynamic political leader, fighting the Sante Fe Ring and strongly supporting New Mexico Governor Miguel Otero, Jr. On the night of November 26, 1904, Chaves was assassinated by an unknown assailant at Pinos Wells, New Mexico. The murder was rumored to be politically motivated and connected with his opposition to the infamous Santa Fe Ring. Despite a $2,500 reward offered by the legislature, his murderer was never identified.

Dennis Chávez (1888–1962)

Chávez was a member of the U.S. House of Representatives and the first Hispanic U.S. senator. Chávez was born the third of eight children in 1888 in a village west of Albuquerque, New Mexico, to a poor family. The family moved to Albuquerque seven years later and Chávez attended school there, but his family's poverty forced him to drop out of school in the eighth grade to work delivering groceries for the next five years. He continued to educate himself in the evenings at the public library.

From 1906 to 1915, he worked for the Albuquerque city engineering department. In 1912, Chávez worked as a Spanish interpreter for the successful Democratic candidate for the U.S. Senate, Andrieus Jones. Jones obtained a clerkship in the Senate for Chávez, who entered law school at Georgetown University in Washington, D.C. In 1920, Chávez was awarded a law degree. Chávez then returned to New Mexico, where he began a successful law practice and ran for public office in the classic pattern of American political advancement. As Chávez rose in Democratic party ranks, he successfully ran for a seat in the New Mexico legislature. In 1930, Chávez defeated the incumbent Republican and won a seat

Dennis Chávez.

in the U.S. House of Representatives. He was reelected to the House in 1932.

In the 1934 elections, Chávez ran for the U.S. Senate seat held by the powerful Republican Bronson Cutting and was defeated by a narrow margin. Chávez challenged the validity of Cutting's reelection, charging vote fraud, and took the challenge to the floor of the U.S. Senate. While the challenge was pending, Cutting was killed in an airplane crash. Chávez was appointed by the governor of New Mexico to the U.S. Senate. Chávez was reelected easily in the 1936 elections.

As a Democratic senator, Chávez was a staunch supporter of President Roosevelt's New Deal. As chairman of the Public Works Committee, Chávez obtained federal funding for irrigation and flood control projects in New Mexico. As a Western isolationist, he opposed U.S. entry into World War II and argued that the country should follow a policy of strict neutrality. Serious attempts to unseat him at home were halted by the loyalty of New Mexico supporters who sustained him politically.

During the years after the war, Chávez did some of his best work in the Senate. Perhaps his greatest contribution to Hispanic Americans, and to the nation, was his support of education and civil rights. Chávez drafted a bill to create the federal Fair Employment Practices Commission and fought tirelessly for its enactment. In all, Senator Chávez was elected to the Senate five times. A champion of civil rights and full equality for all Americans to the last, the long and distinguished national career of this son of New Mexico was ended by a heart attack in mid-November 1962.

José Manuel Gallegos (1815–1875)

Gallegos was a territorial delegate to the U.S. Congress for New Mexico. He was born in 1815 in northwest New Mexico in present-day Rio Arriba County, in the town of Abiquiu, was raised in a prominent family, and was educated in Taos. Gallegos later went to the College of Durango, Mexico to study for the priesthood. Upon graduation in 1840, he was ordained a priest. He first went to southwestern New Mexico to work among the people of San Juan, and later to Albuquerque and Santa Fe.

While in Santa Fe, Gallegos began to get involved with politics. In 1843, he was elected to the New Mexico provincial legislature on the eve of the American conquest and served until 1846 in that assembly. After New Mexico became part of the United States by the Treaty of Guadalupe Hidalgo, he was elected to the first territorial council in 1851.

In 1853, Gallegos was elected territorial delegate to the U.S. Congress as a Democrat. He lost his bid at reelection in 1855 to Miguel Otero, Sr., in a hotly disputed campaign. He returned to service in the territorial legislature in 1860 and was named Speaker of the House. He again made a bid for territorial delegate two years later but lost.

Meanwhile, the Civil War broke out, and Gallegos, a staunch Unionist, was imprisoned in 1862 by invading Texan Confederate forces. At the end of the war, he was appointed territorial treasurer, an office he served from 1865 to 1866. At the end of his term, he again won election to the territorial legislature. In 1870, Gallegos again ran for territorial delegate to the U.S. Congress and won. His bid for reelection two years later was unsuccessful. He returned to Santa Fe and after a short illness died in April 1875.

Benigno Cárdenas Hernández (1862–954)

Benigno Hernández was born in 1862 in Taos, New Mexico, during the Civil War and was educated there in public schools. He began his business career as a store clerk in the 1880s. Ten years later he began a stock-raising business and in 1896 opened his own general store in Lumberton in Rio Arriba County.

Hernández entered politics in 1900 and served as Rio Arriba County's probate clerk, recorder, sheriff, treasurer, and tax collector over the following ten years. Very active in Republican politics, Hernández was elected to the U.S. House of Representatives in 1914 and was reelected in 1918. His bid for a third term was unsuccessful.

After the end of his second term in 1921, President Warren G. Harding appointed Hernández collector of Internal Revenue for the state of New Mexico. Hernández held that post until 1933, when President Franklin D. Roosevelt took office. He was then age 71. He later served on the Selective Service Board of New Mexico during World War II. In the 1950s, Hernández moved to Los Angeles, where he died at age 92 in 1954.

Joseph M. Montoya (1915–1978)

Joseph Montoya was born on September 24, 1915, in the small village of Pena Blanca, New Mexico, where his father was county sheriff. Montoya's parents were descendants of eighteenth-century Spanish immigrants to New Mexico. After graduating from high school in 1931, he attended Regis College in Denver, Colorado. In 1934, he entered Georgetown University Law School in Washington, D.C.

In 1936, during his second year of law school, Montoya was elected as a Democrat to the New Mexico House of Representatives at age 21, the youngest representative in the state's history. Two years later, he received his LL.B. degree from Georgetown University

Joseph M. Montoya.

and was reelected to the state legislature. In 1940, Montoya was elected to the state senate; at age 25, he was the youngest senator in the state's history. He served a total of 12 years in the state legislature. He then served four terms as lieutenant governor of New Mexico, from 1946 to 1950 and from 1954 to 1957.

In 1957, at age 42, Montoya was elected as a Democrat to the first of four consecutive terms in the U.S. House of Representatives. He established a reputation as a hardworking legislator and loyal party man. He followed a moderate political course and was regularly returned to Congress with well over 60 percent of the vote.

When Senator Dennis Chavez (D-NM) died in 1962 leaving a Senate seat vacant, Montoya won election to the Senate. He also won a second term to the Senate in 1970. One of the most influential senators in Washington, he was a member of the Appropriations Committee and the Public Works Committee. However, in the early 1970s Montoya's popularity at home waned, and he was defeated in his bid for reelection in 1976 by former astronaut Harrison Schmitt. Montoya's health declined rapidly following the 1976 election. After undergoing surgery for cancer, he died of complications on June 5, 1978.

Nestor Montoya (1862–923)

Montoya was born in Albuquerque, New Mexico, on April 14, 1862. He was educated in Albuquerque public schools and then graduated from St. Michael's College in Santa Fe. After college, he worked in the Santa Fe post office and the U.S. Treasury office there. In 1889, Montoya founded *La voz del pueblo,* a Spanish-language newspaper. Montoya founded a second paper in 1900 called *La bandera americana.*

In addition to his journalistic activities, Montoya was also involved in New Mexico politics. In 1892, he was elected to the New Mexico territorial legislature's lower house and was repeatedly reelected, serving until 1903. The following year Montoya was elected to the legislature's upper house and in 1910 was elected delegate to the New Mexico Constitutional Convention. He worked hard for the rights of Hispanics at the convention and gained the respect of many across the state. In 1920, Montoya was elected as New Mexico's representative to the U.S. Congress. He died in 1923 before his term ended.

Mariano S. Otero (1844–1904)

Otero was born in the tiny town of Peralta, New Mexico, on August 29, 1844, during the last years of Mexican control. As a member of the powerful Otero clan, he attended local parochial and private schools and later studied at Saint Louis University in Missouri. After college, Otero became a banker.

In the early 1870s, he was appointed probate judge of Bernalillo County. In 1874, he turned down the Democratic nomination for congressional delegate. In 1878, however, he accepted the Republican nomination for congressional delegate and won. He declined to run for reelection in 1882 and returned to his banking business. Between 1884 and 1886, Otero twice ran for Congress but was defeated. In the 1890s, Otero moved to Albuquerque to continue his banking activities. He died there in 1904 at age 59.

Miguel A. Otero, Sr. (1829–1882)

Born in Valencia, New Mexico, on June 21, 1829, Otero was the son of Vicente Otero, an important local leader during both the Spanish and Mexican eras. After completing his early education in Valencia, Otero was sent to Missouri in 1841 to attend St. Louis University. Six years later, he went to Pingree's College in New York. He later taught there and then began the study of law. In 1851, he returned to St. Louis, where he continued his legal studies and was admitted to the bar.

Returning to New Mexico in 1852 to practice law in Albuquerque, Otero became private secretary to territorial Governor William C. Lane and immediately plunged into politics. That same year, Otero was elected to the territorial legislature. Two years later, he was appointed New Mexico attorney general. Otero's political experience and broad family connections (his older brother Antonio Jose Otero was chief justice at the time) worked to his advantage, and in 1855 he was nominated by the Democratic party for the office of territorial delegate to Congress. Otero won the election and went on to win reelection to Congress, serving a total of six terms.

In Congress, Otero's efforts ensured that the transcontinental railroad would cross through New Mexico, giving great promise to the state's future. By doing so, he aligned himself with other southern states that favored a southern route for the railroad. As a result of Otero's influence, New Mexico legislated a slave code in 1859. The following year he supported a compromise to avoid civil war by extending slavery to the territories south of the thirty-sixth parallel, including New Mexico. The outbreak of the Civil War greatly reduced Otero's political influence. He did not support the Confederacy, but he did support a separate confederation of western states.

President Lincoln offered the post of minister to Spain to Otero, but he declined it in favor of the nomination of secretary of the Territory of New Mexico. The U.S. Senate did not confirm him because of his political views.

After the Civil War ended, Otero pursued banking and land business interests with the coming of the railroad. He founded and was the first president of the San Miguel National Bank. He was also part of the business group that purchased the immense Maxwell Land Grant in 1870. He was a director of the Maxwell Land Grant and Railroad Company and was also a director of the Atchison, Topeka, and Santa Fe Railroad. The first terminal of the Santa Fe Railroad was named Otero in his honor. In 1880, despite his failing health, Otero made a last bid for territorial delegate to Congress but was defeated. His health continued to deteriorate rapidly, and he died in 1882 at the age of 53.

Romauldo Pacheco (1831–1899)

Pacheco was born in Santa Barbara, California, on October 31, 1831. He was the son of an aide to the Mexican governor of California, Manuel Victoria. Pacheco's father was killed in battle shortly after his birth. His mother remarried and Pacheco's stepfather sent him to Honolulu to be educated at an English missionary school. When he returned to California at age 15, Pacheco began working on his stepfather's ships.

After the U.S. takeover of California, Pacheco left the sea to manage the family's large estate and began to show an interest in politics. During the 1850s,

Pacheco was successively elected county judge and state senator as a Democrat. Having switched from the Democratic party to the Union party (and later to the Republican party) at the outbreak of the Civil War, Pacheco was reelected to the state senate, and from 1863 to 1867 he served as state treasurer. In 1871 he was elected lieutenant governor and became governor of California in 1875 when then-Governor Newton Booth was appointed to the U.S. Senate. In the next election he failed to secure the Republican nomination for Governor.

In 1876, Pacheco was elected to the U.S. House of Representatives, and was reelected in 1879 and 1881. He was not known as an aggressive congressman, but he did serve on the influential Public Expenditures Committee and the Committee on Private Land Claims. In 1883, he did not seek reelection and returned to his family business interests in California. In 1890, he was named minister plenipotentiary to Central America by President Benjamin Harrison. He remained at that post until Democratic President Grover Cleveland took office in 1893. Pacheco then returned to his California home and died in 1899.

Francisco Perea (1830–1913)

Perea was born in 1830 in the small New Mexico town of Los Padillas, near Albuquerque, to Juan Perea and Josefa Chavez, descendants of two important families. Having completed his early education in Los Padillas and Santa Fe, he was sent to study with the Jesuits at St. Louis University in Missouri from 1843 to 1845. After the U.S. takeover of New Mexico, he went to New York and studied at the Bank Street Academy between 1847 and 1849.

In 1850, Perea returned to New Mexico to engage in stock trading. He became a commercial success by transporting sheep to California to sell to miners. His family connections and his commercial success helped him in 1858 to be elected to the New Mexico territorial legislature's upper house. After the Civil War broke out, he was twice reelected as an active supporter of the North.

Perea was also active in the military and formed "Perea's Battalion," which he commanded as lieutenant colonel. The battalion took part in the defeat of Confederate invaders of New Mexico at Glorieta Pass in 1862. After the victory at Glorieta Pass, Perea was elected to the U.S. Congress as territorial delegate for New Mexico. His bid for reelection two years later was unsuccessful. He returned to New Mexico and opened a resort hotel at Jemez Springs that he owned and operated until 1905. Perea then moved to Albuquerque, where he remained until his death in 1913.

Pedro Perea (1852–906)

Perea was born April 22, 1852 in the central New Mexico town of Bernalillo in Sandoval County. After his early education there, he was sent to Saint Michael's College in Santa Fe, then to Georgetown University in Washington, D.C. In 1871 he graduated from Saint Louis University in Missouri.

Like many sons of prominent New Mexican families of the era, he returned to New Mexico to engage in stock raising and business. From 1890 to 1894, he was president of the First National Bank of Santa Fe. He also began to take an interest in New Mexico politics at this time. Between 1889 and 1897, he served three terms in the New Mexico territorial legislature's upper house as a Republican. In 1898, he was elected territorial delegate to the U.S. Congress. He chose not to run for reelection and returned to New Mexico at the end of his term in 1900 to resume his banking activities. Perea died in 1906.

Edward R. Roybal (1916–)

Roybal was born on February 10, 1916, in Albuquerque, New Mexico, into a middle-class Mexican American family. When he was four, his family moved to the Boyle Heights area of Los Angeles.

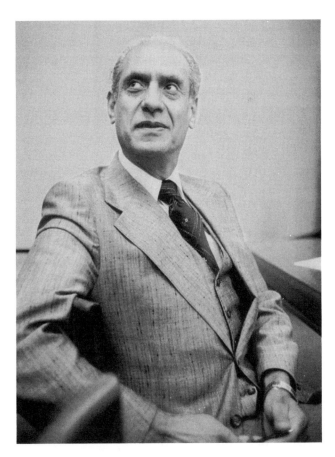

Edward R. Roybal.

Roybal began his education there in public schools. He graduated from high school in 1934 during the depths of the Great Depression and began working for the Civilian Conservation Corps. Later he continued his education at the University of California and Southwestern University. Roybal took a position as a health care educator beginning in the late 1930s. He served in World War II during 1944 and 1945, and returned to Los Angeles to continue to work in health care.

Following World War II, a group of concerned Mexican Americans formed a group to elect a Mexican American to the Los Angeles City Council, and Roybal was their choice for candidate. In 1947, he ran and was defeated. Instead of giving up, Roybal and the group intensified their efforts to get out the vote in East Los Angeles, and in his second bid for city council in 1949, Roybal was elected. He was the first Mexican American on the council since 1881. Roybal was reelected several times and served on the council for 13 years.

Roybal was first elected to Congress in 1962 as a Democrat from the Twenty-fifth District of California. He is a member of the powerful House Appropriations Committee and is chairman of the House Select Committee on Aging. Roybal is also a member and former chairman of the Congressional Hispanic Caucus. During his three decades in Congress, Roybal has worked for social and economic reforms. In 1967, he introduced legislation that became the first federal bilingual education act. In 1982, as chairman of the Congressional Hispanic Caucus, he led the opposition to employer sanctions for hiring the undocumented, which ultimately was enacted as the Immigration Reform and Control Act of 1986. Throughout his tenure, Congressman Roybal has consistently advocated greater citizen participation in party politics and in the federal and local government. In 1991, Edward Roybal retired from Congress. His daughter Lucille Roybal-Allard was elected to the seat that he had occupied for three decades.

✳ SELECTED PROMINENT HISPANIC FEDERAL OFFICIALS

Henry G. Cisneros (1947–)

Former Mayor of San Antonio, Texas, Cisneros was born in a west-side Mexican barrio of San Antonio in 1947 to a civil servant. He was educated in the city's parochial schools and attended Texas A&M University, where he received a B.A. degree and a master's degree in urban planning in 1970.

In 1971, Cisneros moved to Washington, D.C., where he worked for the National League of Cities

Henry G. Cisneros, Secretary of Housing and Urban Development (HUD).

and began full-time graduate studies in public administration at George Washington University. During 1971, at age 22, Cisneros became the youngest White House fellow in U.S. history. When his fellowship ended, he earned a second master's degree, in public administration, at Harvard University. He then went on to complete his work at George Washington University and received a Ph.D. degree in public administration. He then returned to San Antonio and taught government at the University of Texas.

Cisneros ran for the city council on the Good Government League ticket in 1975 and won. He gained a reputation as a bright, young politician, and in 1977 he was reelected in a landslide. In 1981, Cisneros ran for mayor of San Antonio, the ninth-largest city in the United States and won 62 percent of the vote. In 1983, he was reelected with 94 percent of the vote, again reelected in 1985 with 72 percent, and reelected in 1987 with twice as many votes as his closest opponent.

Controversy struck Cisneros' career in 1988. His public announcement of an extramarital affair indirectly led to his resignation as mayor. He reunited with his wife and ended the affair, but began making support payments to his former mistress. In July of 1994—about one year after being appointed secretary of Housing and Urban Development (HUD) by newly elected President Bill Clinton—Cisneros' former mistress sued him for discontinuing the payments. He claimed that his $148,400 annual salary as HUD secretary was so much less than what he had made as a private sector consultant and speaker that he could not afford to continue paying them. The resultant fall-out led to further investigation of his financial reports used during his cabinet background check. The Clinton administration continued to support Cisneros in fending off accusations of wrongdoing.

Tirso del Junco (1935-)

A member of the board of governors of the U.S. Postal Service in Washington, D.C., del Junco was born in Havana, Cuba, received a medical degree in 1949 from the Havana School of Medicine, and became a U.S. citizen in 1963. He is a member of the board of regents of the University of California and was a delegate to the Republican National Conventions for the past six presidential elections. In 1983 he was a U.S. delegate to the Twenty-second conference of UNESCO in Paris. Del Junco is the founder and former chairman of the Los Angeles National Bank and is a member of the Queen of Angels Hospital Clinic and Research Foundation. Del Junco was a captain in the U.S. Army and chief of surgery at the Camp Howland Army Hospital from 1955 to 1957. In 1948, del Junco was a member of the Cuban Olympic team and participated in the crew competition.

Cari M. Domínguez (1949-)

Director of the Office of Federal Contract Compliance Programs, U.S. Department of Labor, Domínguez was born in Havana, Cuba. Her family immigrated to the United States and she was raised in Takoma Park, Maryland. She holds a bachelor's degree and a master's degree from American University in Washington, D.C. In 1974, Domínguez joined the Office of Federal Contract Compliance Programs, where she held a variety of positions until 1983. In 1984, she left the Department of Labor and began working for the Bank of America in San Francisco, where she served as corporate manager of equal opportunity programs. In 1986, she was promoted to vice president and director of executive programs, in charge of executive compensation and benefits programs, succession planning, development, and staffing services. In 1989, President Bush appointed Domínguez director of the Office of Federal Contract Compliance Programs of the U.S. Department of Labor. As director, she is responsible for the enforcement of federal mandates prohibiting discrimination and requiring affirmative action in the employment and advancement of the disabled, women, minorities, and veterans.

Antonia Coello Novello (1944-)

Novello was born in Fajardo, Puerto Rico, on August 23, 1944. She received a B.A. degree in 1965 and an M.D. degree in 1970 from the University of Puerto Rico. Novello was awarded her master's degree in public health from Johns Hopkins University in 1982. Novello joined the U.S. Public Health Service in 1978 after working in the private practice of pediatrics and nephrology. She served in various capacities at the National Institutes of Health (NIH) beginning in 1978, including serving as deputy director of the National Institute of Child Health and Human Development. In 1990, President Bush appointed Novello as the fourteenth surgeon general. Among her duties as surgeon general, she was responsible for recommending precautions necessary to protect public health and safety. In 1992, President Bill Clinton reappointed Novello. Since 1993, she has

Antonia Coello Novello, Surgeon General, U.S. Public Health Service.

been a special representative for health and nutrition for U.N.I.C.E.F. in New York City.

Federico Fabian Peña (1947–)

Peña is a noted Hispanic American public official who served two terms in the Colorado General Assembly and two as mayor of Denver, Colorado. In 1992, he became U.S. Secretary of Transportation under President Bill Clinton. In this capacity, he has been responsible for several notable and controversial rulings and decisions. Peña was part of the "new generation" of socially-conscious Democrats who joined the administrative branch of the Federal Government after President Clinton's election.

Born on March 15, 1947, in Laredo, Texas, and raised in Brownsville, Peña was the third of six children, the final three being triplets. He attended St. Joseph's Academy, a local Catholic high school, from which he graduated with honors in 1965. After graduation, he entered the University of Texas at Austin. He graduated in 1969 and promptly enrolled in the University of Texas School of Law. In 1972, the year he received his Juris Doctor, Peña moved to Denver, Colorado where his brother Alfredo was already practicing law. From 1972 to 1974, he worked as a

Federico Fabian Peña, U.S. Secretary of Transportation.

staff lawyer for the Mexican American Legal Defense and Educational Fund, where he litigated police brutality and voting rights issues. He later became a legal adviser for the Chicano Education Project, where for four years he worked for bilingual education in the public schools and better school funding in Hispanic neighborhoods. In 1973, the brothers Alfredo and Federico opened their own law office.

In 1978, Peña successfully ran for a seat in the Colorado General Assembly. He held the position for two terms, during which he served on the House judiciary, legal services, rules, and finance committees. During his first term he was named outstanding House Democratic freshman by the Colorado social action committee. Peña was elected mayor of Denver in 1983 by a narrow margin. His first term was tempestuousand by the end of his first term, Peña's popularity in the polls was extremely low; however, with his strong base of support in the black and Hispanic communities, he was able to eke out a victory by a two-percent margin.

During his second term, Peña's public works program began to make progress. Construction on Denver International Airport began on 53 square miles of prairie 20 miles out of town, and Peña's renewed efforts for a new convention center found success. He also fought for and won a public bond issue which raised $330 million for various infrastructure repairs and new public works. Buoyed by his successes and an improvement in the general economy, Peña's popularity improved. However, he did not seek a third term, citing a desire to spend more time with his family. In May of 1988, he married Ellen Hart, a world-class distance runner and fellow attorney whom he had met four years earlier. They eventually had two daughters, Nelia Joan and Cristina Lucila.

After leaving office, he founded the financial management firm Peña Investment Advisors, which became known for hiring top-notch Hispanic legal talent and was also involved in a legal consultancy. He also served on a Colorado state panel that drew up a long-term statewide transportation plan with emphasis on mass transit and bicycles. In 1992, after Clinton won the presidential election, Peña joined his "transition team" for transportation issues, and was later nominated to be Clinton's Secretary of Transportation. Clinton was reportedly impressed by Peña's success with the Denver International Airport and his suitably liberal theories of transportation policy had become well-known. Clinton had also promised an ethnically diverse cabinet and Peña was by this time one of the most prominent Hispanic Democrats in the country.

Selected Prominent Hispanic Former Federal Officials

Everett Alvarez, Jr. (1937–)

Former deputy administrator of the U.S. Veterans Administration, Alvarez was born in Salinas, California, of farm worker parents from Mexico. His parents emphasized hard work and education as the way to succeed. Alvarez was awarded an engineering degree from the University of Santa Clara in 1960. Alvarez was a navy pilot during the Vietnam War and was shot down over the Gulf of Tonkin. He was held prisoner by the Vietcong for over eight years. After his release in 1973, Alvarez went back to school and received a law degree from George Washington University and practiced law as a patent attorney. In 1981, President Reagan appointed Alvarez deputy director of the Peace Corps. In 1982, the president appointed Alvarez deputy administrator of the Veterans Administration.

Diego Archuleta (1814–1884

U.S. Indian agent under President Abraham Lincoln, Archuleta was born of a prominent family in 1814 in the Rio Arriba country of New Mexico during the Mexican war for independence and was educated at the Seminary at Durango, Mexico. In 1840, he returned to New Mexico and from 1843 to 1845 served as representative from New Mexico at the National Congress in Mexico City. When American forces invaded New Mexico in 1846, Archuleta gave no resistance to General Stephen Kearny's army. Disappointed at not being made part of the new American government in New Mexico, Archuleta took a leading role in two unsuccessful Taos rebellions in 1846 and 1847. After his passions had cooled, Archuleta took the oath of allegiance to the United States and sought to use American institutions to his advantage. During the 1850s, he was repeatedly elected to the New Mexico state assembly, and in 1857 he was named U.S. Indian agent to the Utes and Apache, in which capacity he served until the Civil War broke out. He became a brigadier general in the New Mexico militia during the war and was reappointed U.S. Indian agent by President Abraham Lincoln. After the war, Archuleta returned to service in the New Mexico state assembly, where he served until his death in 1884.

Romana Acosta Bañuelos (1925–)

The first Mexican American and the sixth woman to hold the post of treasurer of the United States, Bañuelos was born in Miami, Arizona, in 1925 of undocumented Mexican parents. During the Great Depression, she was forced at age 6 to accompany

Everett Alvarez, Jr.

her parents when they were repatriated to Mexico in 1931. She grew up in Mexico and at age 19 moved back to the United States and settled in Los Angeles.

In 1949, she started a small tortilla factory with $400. Over the following 20 years, she developed it into a $12-million-a-year business, Romana's Mexican Food Products, employing hundreds of workers and producing dozens of food items. She also helped to establish the Pan American National Bank in Los Angeles, of which she was a director and chairwoman. In 1971, President Nixon appointed Bañuelos treasurer of the United States. She served as treasurer from December 1971 until February 1974. While retaining some interest in politics, she has since devoted herself principally to her business activities.

Arturo Morales Carrión (1913–1989)

Former deputy assistant secretary of state under President John F. Kennedy, and the first Puerto Rican to be appointed to such a high State Department position, Carrión was born in Havana, Cuba, on November 16, 1913. He earned a B.A. degree from the University of Puerto Rico in 1935, an M.A. degree from the University of Texas in 1936, and a Ph.D. degree from Columbia University in 1950. Carrión taught at the University of Puerto Rico and became chairman of the history department. He then went into politics and served as undersecretary of Puerto Rico's State Department, in charge of external affairs.

He joined the Kennedy administration in 1961 as deputy assistant secretary of state for inter-American affairs. He remained at that post until the assassination of President Kennedy in 1963. Carrión was a member of the Kennedy administration's Latin American Study Group, which warned of a Communist threat to Latin America. After leaving the State Department, Carrión became special assistant to the secretary general of the Organization of American States. He later returned to Puerto Rico to become president of the University of Puerto Rico. Carrión died in San Juan in 1989 at age 75.

Fernando E. Cabeza de Baca (1937–)

Former special assistant to President Gerald Ford and a direct descendant of the famous Spanish explorer Alvar Núñez Cabeza de Baca (often spelled "Vaca"), Cabeza de Baca was born in 1937 in Albu-

Romana Acosta Bañuelos.

querque, New Mexico. He received his early education in New Mexico, and at the end of the 1950s he received a degree in public administration from the University of New Mexico in Albuquerque. He also studied at the University of New Mexico School of Law. During the Vietnam War, he served in the U.S. Army and returned from the war disabled and decorated. In the late 1960s and early 1970s, Cabeza de Baca held high-ranking positions with the New Mexico Department of Transportation, the Civil Service Commission, and the Department of Health, Education and Welfare. He then became chairman of the Federal Regional Council for the Western United States.

In 1974, President Gerald Ford appointed Cabeza de Baca as special assistant to the president. In this role, at age 37, he became both the youngest and the highest-ranking federal executive of Hispanic descent. He returned to New Mexico to pursue business activities after Ford left the presidency in 1976. He remains deeply involved in veterans affairs and is active in the New Mexico Republican party.

Leonel J. Castillo (1939–)

Former director of the U.S. Immigration and Naturalization Service (INS), Castillo was born in 1939 in Victoria, Texas, where he grew up and attended school. He graduated from St. Mary's University in San Antonio, Texas, in 1961. Castillo joined the Peace Corps after graduation and served in the Philippines from 1961 to 1965. Upon his return to the United States, he attended the University of Pittsburgh, where he received his master's degree in social work in 1967. Castillo then returned to Texas and lived in Houston, where he took an active role in local politics. In 1970, he won a surprise victory in his election as Houston city comptroller against a 25-year incumbent. In 1974, he was named treasurer of the Texas Democratic party. President Jimmy Carter appointed Castillo to head the INS in 1977. After 30 months of trying to modernize the INS, to reduce violence on the border, and to emphasize service rather than enforcement, he resigned in 1979. Castillo then returned to Houston to head Castillo Enterprises.

Lauro F. Cavazos (1927–)

Born on January 4, 1927, on the King Ranch in Texas, Cavazos was an outstanding student who eventually earned a bachelor's (1949) and master's degree (1952) in zoology at Texas Tech University and a Ph.D. in physiology (1954) from Iowa State University. Cavazos became an outstanding professor of anatomy and an educational administrator. She rose through the ranks of academic administra-

Lauro F. Cavazos.

tion at the Medical College of Virginia, became dean of Tufts University's School of Medicine, and—at Texas Tech—was named the first Hispanic president of a major research university.

Cavazos only held that position for a short while before President Reagan appointed her as the first Hispanic U.S. secretary of education in 1988. After succeeding Reagan as President in 1989, George Bush reappointed Cavazos. She was instrumental in persuading President Bush to sign the executive order creating the President's Council on Educational Excellence for Hispanic Americans and her leadership and sensitivity raised the awareness of Congress regarding the educational needs of Hispanics in the United States. Secretary Cavazos resigned in December 1990 because of political differences with the Bush administration. (Lamar Alexander was appointed to replace her.) Cavazos' honors include the Medal of Honor from UCLA and the President's Medal from the City College of New York in 1989; election to the Hispanic Hall of Fame in 1987; the Outstanding Leadership Award in Education from President Reagan in 1984; and 11 honorary degrees.

Jimmy Gurulé

U.S. assistant attorney general, Gurulé grew up in Utah. He received both his bachelor's degree and his law degree from the University of Utah. Prior to joining the Department of Justice, Gurulé was an associate professor of law at the University of Notre Dame Law School. He is a former president of the Hispanic National Bar Association. Gurulé was appointed assistant attorney general by President George Bush and was sworn in on August 3, 1990. He is the highest-ranking Hispanic in the history of the Department of Justice. As assistant attorney general for the Office of Justice Programs, Gurulé is responsible for coordinating policy, management, and priorities within the Office of Justice Programs in Washington, D.C., and its five program bureaus and field offices. He works to form partnerships among federal, state, and local government officials to improve administration of justice, combat violent crime and drug abuse, meet the needs of crime victims, and find innovative ways to address problems such as narcotics trafficking, gang-related crime, white-collar crime, and corruption. Gurulé was awarded the Attorney General's Distinguished Service Award in 1990 for his excellence as an assistant U.S. attorney in prosecuting the killers of Drug Enforcement Administration Special Agent Enrique Camarena, who had been working in Guadalajara, Mexico.

Edward Hidalgo (1912–)

Former secretary of the navy, Hidalgo was born in Mexico City in 1912. His family immigrated to the United States. in 1918 and he was naturalized in 1936. He holds law degrees from both countries, a J.D. degree from Columbia University, which he received in 1936, and a similar degree from the University of Mexico, which was conferred in 1959. During World War II, Hidalgo was special assistant to Secretary of the Navy James Forrestal in 1945–46 and was a member of the Eberstadt Commission on the Unification of the Military Services in 1945. After the war, he returned to private practice as an attorney. In 1965, Hidalgo was named special assistant to Secretary of the Navy Paul Nitze. From 1977 to 1979 he served as assistant secretary of the navy. Hidalgo was appointed secretary of the navy by President Jimmy Carter in 1979 and remained there until 1981.

Manuel Luján, Jr. (1928–)

Born on May 12, 1928, in San Ildefonso, New Mexico, Luján grew up in Santa Fe, and earned his B.A. degree from the College of Santa Fe. After college, Luján was a partner in a family insurance and real estate business. Luján served as a Republican congressman and represented the First District of New

Mexico in the U.S. House of Representatives from 1969 to 1989. In Congress, Luján was the ranking minority member of the House Interior Committee. In 1989, President Bush appointed Luján as the forty-sixth Secretary of the Department of the Interior. As secretary, Luján asserted that the United States can have both the resource development needed for economic security and the environmental protection required to ensure quality of life. He implemented a "no net loss of wetlands" goal through actions to enlarge the Everglades National Park in Florida and a proposal to repair environmental damage at Kesterson Reservoir in California.

Robert Martínez (1934–)

Former director of the Office of National Drug Control Policy, Martínez was born in Tampa, Florida, on December 25, 1934. He received his bachelor's degree in education from the University of Tampa in 1957 and a master's degree in labor and industrial relations from the University of Illinois in 1964. Martínez went into business following college and owned and operated a restaurant in Tampa until 1983. He became involved in local politics in the late 1970s and was elected to two terms as a Republican mayor of Tampa from 1979 to 1987.

In 1988, Martínez was elected governor of Florida and served one term. During his tenure as governor, President Reagan named Martínez to the White House Conference on a Drug-Free America. Martínez was appointed by President Bush as director of the Office of National Drug Control Policy from 1991 to 1993. As director, he was responsible for developing a national strategy to combat illicit drugs. He was charged by law to coordinate and oversee both the international and domestic anti-drug abuse functions of all executive branch agencies, and to ensure that such functions sustain and complement state and local anti-drug abuse efforts. He is currently president of Bob Martinez & Co.

Katherine Davalos Ortega (1934–)

Former treasurer of the United States, Ortega was born in 1934 in rural south-central New Mexico. She received her early education in Tularosa, New Mexico. From her early years, she excelled in mathematics and accounting. After high school, Ortega worked at the Otero County Bank for two years until she saved enough money to go to college. She graduated with honors from Eastern New Mexico State University at Portales in 1957, with a B.A. in business and economics. After college, she began her own accounting firm in New Mexico. In 1969, she moved to Los Angeles, California to work as a tax supervisor with Peat, Marwick, Mitchell and Co. and later

Katherine Davalos Ortega.

became a vice president of the Pan American National Bank (1972). She then became the first woman president of a California bank when she was named president of the Santa Ana State Bank in 1975.

In 1978, she returned to New Mexico with her family and became active in the Republican party. Ortega served as a commissioner of the Copyright Royalty Tribunal (1982–83) and as a member of the President's Advisory Commission on Small and Minority Business. In 1983, President Reagan appointed Ortega as U.S. treasurer. She remained at that post throughout his presidency. (Upon his election, President George Bush replaced Ortega with another notable banking executive, Catalina Villalpando.) In 1989, the secretary of the treasury presented Ortega with the department's highest award, the Alexander Hamilton Award for outstanding service. Ortega then returned to New Mexico where she is still active in business and politics.

Catalina Vásquez Villalpando (1940–)

Born on April 1, 1940, in San Marcos, Texas, Catalina Villalpando attended various universities but never obtained a degree. She became the director of the Community Services Administration in 1969, an office she held until 1979. From there, she became a vice president of the Mid-South Oil Company in Dallas, and then a senior vice president of Communications International in Dallas where she directed all public relations and marketing for the company's northeast region.

Villalpando also has been active in the Republican party. She served as liaison director for the Republican party of Texas, vice president of the Republican National Assembly of Texas, and in 1983 special assistant to President Ronald Reagan. Villalpando's hard work paid off in 1988 when President George Bush appointed her as the thirty-ninth treasurer of the United States. As treasurer, Villalpando oversaw the operation of the U.S. Mint, the Bureau of Engraving and Printing, and the U.S. Savings Bond Division. She also advised the secretary of the treasury on matters relating to coinage, currency, and production of other negotiable instruments.

✳ PROMINENT HISPANIC POLITICIANS IN STATE GOVERNMENT

Toney Anaya (1941–)

Former Democratic governor of New Mexico from 1983 to 1986, Anaya was one of ten children born to

Jerry Apodaca

New Mexican parents in Moriarty, New Mexico, in 1941. He spent his childhood in an adobe house with a dirt floor and no electricity or plumbing. Although his parents had no more than a couple of years of schooling, they encouraged their children to get a good education. Anaya attended the New Mexico Highlands University, on a Sears Foundation scholarship. Anaya moved to Washington, D.C., where he graduated from Georgetown University. In 1967, he received his law degree from American University. While he was attending American University, he worked for Senator Dennis Chavez, and following graduation worked for Senator Joseph Montoya. In 1970, Anaya returned to New Mexico. He ran for attorney general of New Mexico in 1974 and won, serving until 1978. Anaya then ran for the Senate, but lost a close election to incumbent Pete Domenici. In 1982, Anaya was elected governor of New Mexico, where he served until 1986.

Jerry Apodaca (1934–)

Former governor of New Mexico, Apodaca was born and raised in his hometown of Las Cruces, New Mexico, where his family had lived for over 100

Toney Anaya.

years. He graduated from the University of New Mexico in 1957 and worked as a teacher and businessman. In 1966, Apodaca entered politics and was elected to the New Mexico state senate as a Democrat. After eight years in the state legislature, Apodaca, at age 40, was elected in 1974 as the first Hispanic governor of New Mexico in over 50 years (Governor Octaviano Larrazolo had served from 1918 to 1920). After Apodaca's term as governor ended, President Carter appointed him as chairman of the President's Council on Physical Fitness and Sports. Apodaca has since resumed his business interests and is currently on the board of directors of the Philip Morris Company.

Polly Baca-Barragán (1943–)

Baca-Barragán was born in La Salle, a small town near Greeley, Colorado, in 1943. She received a degree in political science form Colorado State University and later worked as an editor for two union publications. During the 1960s, Baca-Barragán was active in the Democratic party and worked on the presidential campaigns of President John F. Kennedy, President Lyndon B. Johnson, and Senator Robert F. Kennedy. From 1971 to 1972 she was Director of Spanish Speaking Affairs for the Democratic National Committee. In 1974, she was elected to the Colorado House of Representatives and in 1978 to the state senate. She was the first Hispanic woman to be elected to those offices. Baca-Barragán was re-elected to Colorado's state senate in 1982. She remains active in politics working on behalf of Mexican Americans and dealing with housing issues. Baca-Barragán served as Special Assistant to President Bill Clinton and Director of the U.S. Office of Consumer Affairs until November 1995, when she was named as the new regional administrator for the General Services Administration in Denver.

Casimiro Barela (1847–1920)

A delegate to the Colorado State Constitutional Convention and a Colorado state senator, Barela was born in Embudo, New Mexico, in 1847, and was educated in Mora by Archbishop Jean B. Salpointe. Barela's family moved to Colorado in 1867, where they raised cattle. In 1869, Barela was elected justice of the peace and over the next six years held several elected posts, including county assessor and sheriff. In 1875, Barela was elected as a delegate to the state constitutional convention, in which he took a leadership role. He secured a provision in the constitution protecting the civil rights of Spanish-speaking citizens as well as publication of laws in both Spanish and English, but this provision was limited to 25 years. Barela was elected to the first

Colorado senate in 1876 and served until 1916. He was twice elected president of the Colorado senate. He died around 1920.

Stephanie Gonzales (1950–)

Secretary of state for New Mexico, Gonzales was born in Santa Fe, New Mexico, in 1950. She is a graduate of Loretto Academy for Girls in Santa Fe. From 1987 to 1990, Gonzales was the deputy secretary of state under then-secretary Rebecca Vigil-Giron. In 1990, Gonzales, a Democrat, was elected secretary of state of New Mexico.

Art Torres (1941–)

State senator for California, Torres was born and raised in East Los Angeles in 1941. He received his B.A. degree from the University of California, Santa Cruz, and a J.D. degree from the University of California, Davis, Law School. He later served as a John F. Kennedy teaching fellow at Harvard University. In 1976, Torres was first elected to the California Senate and has been reelected for each subsequent term. As state senator, Torres has worked to improve education at all levels, particularly through legislation to prevent attrition of high school students. Torres was

Art Torres.

recently elected to the Council on Foreign Relations of New York. He also participates on the National Commission on International Migration and Economic Development, which recommends to Congress and the president the economic policies the United States should implement in Latin America.

✳ PROMINENT HISPANIC METROPOLITAN LEADERS

Ygnacio D. Garza (1953–)

Garza, son of U.S. Federal Court of Appeals Judge Reynaldo G. Garza, was elected mayor of the city of Brownsville in 1987 and served in that capacity until 1991. By law, the mayor of Brownsville is nonpartisan, and Garza is not affiliated with any political party. Brownsville's population is 85 percent Hispanic, and Garza believes that Hispanics are adequately represented in this border town: the mayor, all the city council members, and the majority of the school board members are Hispanic. However, Garza believes that the Hispanic population is not adequately represented nationally, and that the United States still has a long way to go in equalizing the balance of political power.

Ana Sol Gutiérrez (1942–)

A member of the Montgomery County, Maryland, Board of Education and the first Hispanic to be elected to any office in Maryland history, Gutiérrez was born in El Salvador in 1942. Her father, Jorge Sol Castellanos, was El Salvador's first finance minister. Her family moved to Montgomery County, Maryland, in 1945. She attended the University of Geneva in Switzerland and lived in South America briefly following graduation. She earned a B.S. in 1964 from Pennsylvania State University, and her M.S. in 1975 from American University. She was a professor at the Universidad Simon Bolivar in Venezuela (1975–78), and at the University of San Andres in Bolivia (1978–80). She joined Wang Laboratories in 1981, leaving in 1982 to join Computer Sciences Corporation. From 1986 to 1988, she was a senior associate at Booz, Allen & Hamilton; from 1988 to 1992, she was senior engineer for Loral Aero Systems; she then returned to Computer Sciences Corporation, where she was a senior consulting engineer from 1992 to 1994. She returned to Maryland and became active in local politics. Since 1994, she has been the deputy administrator and research and special programs administrator at the U.S. Department of Transportation.

In 1990, Gutierrez ran successfully for a seat on the Board of Education of Montgomery County, one of Maryland's most affluent counties. Gutierrez was

Ygnacio D. Garza, Former Mayor, Brownsville, Texas.

named by U.S. Senator Barbara Mikulski (D-Maryland) to serve on the senator's Academic Review Board, which advises her on national and state educational issues. Many in the Hispanic community regard Gutierrez as someone to watch and a possible contender for a seat in the U.S. Congress.

Gloria Molina (1948–)

County supervisor of Los Angeles, Molina was born in Los Angeles on May 13, 1948, to Mexican parents who had immigrated to the United States the year before. She grew up and received her early education in the small town of Pico Rivera, California, and then attended East Los Angeles College. In 1967, an accident suffered by her father forced her to become the full-time provider for the family at age 19. Her job as a legal assistant did not prevent her from continuing her education, and she received a bachelor's degree from California State University in Los Angeles. Taking a vigorous role in community affairs, Molina served on the board of United Way of Los Angeles and was active in the Latin American Law Enforcement Association. In 1973, she was the founding president of the Comision Femenil de Los

Gloria Molina, Los Angeles County Supervisor.

Manuel Requena (1802–1876)

Mayor of Los Angeles in 1856, Requena was born in 1802 and raised in Mexico and moved to Los Angeles in 1834. Active in the shipping business, he quickly became an important business and political figure. Avoiding conflict when U.S. forces invaded California during the Mexican-American War, Requena was elected to the Los Angeles City Council in 1850 as a member of the Democratic party. He was reelected to four more terms, serving most of the time as president of the council. In 1852, he was elected to the first Los Angeles County Board of Supervisors. Losing his 1855 bid for reelection to the city council, he ran again in 1856 and was reelected to a sixth term, and was again elected president. When the Los Angeles mayor resigned that year, Manuel Requena became mayor until an election was held 11 days later. He thus was briefly the only Mexican American to serve as mayor of Los Angeles during the American period.

Prior to the Civil War, Requena switched from the Democratic to the Republican party and openly supported the candidacy of Abraham Lincoln. At the time, Los Angeles was heavily Democratic and Re-

Angeles and served as national president from 1974 to 1976. She is also a founding member of Hispanic American Democrats, the National Association of Latino Elected and Appointed Officials, and Centro de Ninos.

Molina was first elected to office in 1982 as state assemblywoman for the Fifty-sixth District of California. In 1987, she was elected to the Los Angeles City Council, on which she served as councilwoman of the First District until 1991. In 1991, she was elected to the Los Angeles County Board of Supervisors. Molina is the first Hispanic American in history elected to the California state legislature, the Los Angeles City Council, and the Los Angeles County Board of Supervisors. Prior to being elected to public office, Molina served in the Carter White House as a deputy for presidential personnel. After leaving the White House, she served as deputy director for the U.S. Department of Health and Human Services in San Francisco. With a reputation for candor and independence, Molina is known for her strong, issue-oriented style and her commitment to community empowerment.

Louis E. Saavedra, Former Mayor of Albuquerque, New Mexico.

Xavier L. Suárez, Former Mayor of Miami, Florida.

quena did not win election to the city council again until 1864, when he was elected to a seventh term; subsequently he was reelected to an eighth term. During the 1860s, he continued his business interests, served on the school board, and founded an orphanage. He died in 1876.

Louis E. Saavedra (1933-)

Former mayor of Albuquerque, New Mexico, Saavedra was born in Socorro, New Mexico, in 1933. Saavedra's family has lived within 30 miles of Albuquerque since the 1600s. Saavedra received a B.A. degree and an M.A. degree from Eastern New Mexico University in Portales. Saavedra is the former president of the Albuquerque Technical Vocational Institute, a community college with an enrollment of 15,000. He has held high-ranking positions with the institute since 1965. Saavedra also served on the Albuquerque City Commission between 1967 and 1974. From 1973 to 1974, he was chairman of the city commission. In 1989, Louis Saavedra was elected mayor of Albuquerque, a post he held until 1994. Saavedra has been active in Latin American politics and has worked in 11 Latin American countries and seven countries in the West Indies.

Xavier L. Suárez (1949-)

Former mayor of Miami, Florida, Suárez attended Villanova University, studying engineering, and graduated first in his class. Suárez went on to Harvard Law School and the John F. Kennedy School of Government at Harvard, where he obtained the joint degrees of J.D. and master of public policy in 1975. He also holds an honorary law degree from Villanova University School of Law. After graduation, Suárez moved to Miami and began to practice law with the firm of Shutts & Bowen. In 1985, Suárez was elected mayor of Miami, and was reelected to second and third terms in 1987 and 1989. President Bush appointed Suárez to the board of directors of the Legal Services Corporation. Since 1993, he has been a partner in the firm of Shutts & Bowen in Miami.

✳ LEGAL AND POLITICAL ORGANIZATIONS

Selected Public Interest Law Organizations

Cuban American Legal Defense and Education Fund (CALDEF)

2119 South Webster Street
Fort Wayne, IN 46804
(219) 745–5421
Chairperson: Graciela Beecher.

The Cuban American Legal Defense and Education Fund (CALDEF) was established in 1980 and is a national nonprofit organization funded by corporate and public contributions. CALDEF was created to assist Cuban Americans and other Hispanics in gaining equal treatment and equal opportunity in the fields of education, employment, housing, politics, and justice. CALDEF strives to end negative stereotyping of Hispanics and to educate the American public about the problems faced by Hispanics.

The Hispanic National Bar Association (HNBA)

One Farragut Square South
1634 Eye Street, NW, Suite 901
Washington, DC 20006
(303) 771–6200

The Hispanic National Bar Association (HNBA) was originally established in 1972 as La Raza National Lawyers Association and is a professional association dedicated to the advancement of Hispanic Americans in the legal profession. Its membership includes Hispanic attorneys, judges, and law professors from around the United States. Members of the HNBA have joined together to open doors for Hispanic attorneys in the legal profession so that future lawyers may have greater opportunities. The HNBA also has been actively involved in providing testimony to congressional committees and national commissions, in litigation pertaining to issues of concern to the Hispanic community, and in advocacy regarding legislation and executive nominations. In addition, the HNBA created a Law Student Division to unite Hispanics in law schools across the country. The Law Student Division has affiliate memberships from more than 85 law schools and individual membership has risen from 40 to over 300. Both the HNBA and the Law Student Division sponsor an annual convention open to all members. It has become a forum for Hispanics in the legal profession to discuss barriers openly and to propose solutions.

Legal Services Corporation

400 Virginia Avenue, SW
Washington, DC 20024–2751
(202) 863–1820

The Legal Services Corporation Act created the Legal Services Corporation (LSC) in 1974. The LSC currently funds 16 national support centers providing a variety of services that promote representation of the poor on issues of substantial complexity as well as thousands of local offices throughout the country that represent indigents in a wide variety of civil legal matters.

In 1989, the LSC funded representation in 232,198 cases involving Hispanic clients. That represents 16.88 percent of the total number of clients assisted by offices funded by the LSC.

Mexican American Legal Defense and Educational Fund (MALDEF)

634 South Spring Street, Eleventh Floor
Los Angeles, CA 90014
(213) 629–2512
President: Antonia Hernández
Vice President for Legal Affairs: E. Richard Larson.

The Mexican American Legal Defense and Educational Fund (MALDEF) was established in 1968, and over the past 20 years has been at the forefront of promoting and protecting the civil rights of Hispanic Americans throughout the United States. MALDEF recognized the need for removing barriers preventing Hispanic Americans from fully participating in American society. Those efforts have allowed the organization to work within the legal system to create beneficial solutions through class action litigation, community education, and leadership training.

With a national office in Los Angeles and regional offices in Chicago, San Antonio, San Francisco, and Washington, D.C., MALDEF concentrates on building awareness among Hispanic Americans regarding their heritage and issues affecting their lives. MALDEF's specific program areas are education, employment, political access, immigration, and leadership. MALDEF also administers the Law School Scholarship Program for Mexican Americans. The Mexican American Legal Defense and Education Fund (MALDEF) currently has six affiliate offices, in San Francisco, Los Angeles, Sacramento, San Antonio, Chicago, and Washington, D.C. MALDEF is in the forefront of protecting Mexican American civil rights. It has been responsible for civil rights class-action litigation affecting Hispanics. Litigation departments are maintained in the areas of education, employment, immigration, and voting rights. It maintains a law school scholarship and other programs to assist students in entering the legal profession. MALDEF publishes two tri-quarterly newsletters, *Leadership Program Newsletter* and *MALDEF Newsletter*.

Migrant Legal Action Program, Inc. (MLAP)

2001 S Street, NW, Suite 310
Washington, DC 20009
(202) 462–7744
Chairperson: Gail McCarthy
President: Roger C. Rosenthal

The Migrant Legal Action Program (MLAP) was established in 1970 to protect and further the rights and interests of migrant and seasonal farm workers, the poorest group of working people in America. MLAP is not a membership organization and is funded by the Legal Services Corporation (LSC). MLAP provides assistance to migrant legal services programs funded by LSC, as well as to basic LSC-funded field programs and private practitioners in their representation of eligible clients. There are about 70 migrant attorney field offices and many private attorneys and groups for which MLAP provides services. Such services include resource materials, policy development, litigation support, public education and training on farm worker housing, labor conditions, and education.

National Immigration Law Center

1102 Crenshaw Boulevard, Suite 101215
Los Angeles, CA 90019
(213) 487–2531
Directing Attorney: Charles H. Wheeler
Senior Attorneys: Susan Drake, and Linton Joaquín.

The National Immigration Law Center (NILC), also known as the National Center for Immigrants' Rights, provides backup assistance to legal services programs and other nonprofit agencies on issues involving immigration law and aliens' rights. NILC specializes in areas relating to visa processing, legalization, defenses to deportation, and aliens' eligibility for public benefit programs. Other areas of litigation include constitutional challenges to actions of the Immigration and Naturalization Service (INS) and specific responses to INS unlawful conduct.

Puerto Rican Legal Defense and Education Fund (PRLDEF)

99 Hudson Street, Fourteenth Floor
New York, NY 10013
(212) 219–3360
President: Rubén Franco

The Puerto Rican Legal Defense and Education Fund (PRLDEF) was established in 1972. It was created to protect and further the legal rights of Puerto Ricans and other Hispanics. PRLDEF is a nonprofit organization that challenges discrimination in housing, education, employment, health, and political participation. PRLDEF maintains a placement service for Hispanic lawyers and offers advice and financial assistance to Hispanics considering entering the legal field.

Other National Hispanic American Political Organizations

Democratic National Committee Hispanic Caucus

430 South Capitol Street, SE
Washington, DC 20003
(202) 863–8000

Hispanic Elected Local Officials Caucus

1301 Pennsylvania Avenue, NW
Washington, DC 20004
(202) 626–3000

Hispanic Political Action Committee

246 O'Connor Street
Providence, RI 02905
(401) 941–6831

League of United Latin American Citizens (LULAC)

400 First Street, NW
Washington, DC 29001
(202)628–8516

Mexican American Democrats of Texas (MAD)

02 Stokes Building
Austin, TX 78701
(512) 585–4509

Mexican American Political Association (MAPA)

Box 32352
Los Angeles, CA 90032
(213) 225–8249

Mexican American Women's National Association (MANA)

1101 Seventeenth Street, NW, Suite 803
Washington, DC 20036
(202) 833–0060

National Association of Cuban American Women (NACAW)

2119 South Webster Street
Fort Wayne, IN 46802
(219) 745–5421

National Association of Latino Elected and Appointed Officials (NALEO)

708 G Street, SE
Washington, DC 20003
(202) 546–2536

National Conference of Puerto Rican Women (NACOPRW)

5 Thomas Circle, NW
Washington, DC 20005
(202) 387–4716

National Hispanic Democrats, Inc.

11011 Fourteenth Street, NW
Washington, DC 20005
(202) 371–1555

National Hispanic Leadership Conference (NHLC)

2590 Morgan Avenue
Corpus Christi, TX 78405
(512) 882–8284

National Latinas Caucus (NLC)

853 Broadway, Fifth Floor
New York, NY 10003
(212) 673–7320

National Puerto Rican Coalition, Inc. (NPRC)

1700 K Street, NW, Suite 500
Washington, DC 20006
(703) 223–3915

National Puerto Rican Forum

31 East Thirty-second Street, Fourth Floor
New York, NY 10016
(212) 685–2311

Republican National Hispanic Assembly of the U.S. (RNHA)

440 First Street, NW, Suite 414
Washington, DC 20001
(202) 662–1355

Southwest Voter Registration Education Project

403 East Commerce Street
San Antonio, TX 78205
(512) 222–0224

Directory of State-Level Advocacy Programs

Arizona Association of Chicanos for Higher Education (AACHE)

P.O. Box 24261
Tempe, AZ 85285
(602) 423–6163

Cafe de California (Chicano Advocates for Employment)

1012 J Street, Second Floor
Sacramento, CA 95814
(916) 448–9016

Colorado Institute for Hispanic Education and Economic Development

1006 Eleventh Street
Box 220
Denver, CO 80204
(303) 556–4436

Comite Hispano de Virginia

6031 Leesburg Pike
Falls Church, VA 22041
(703) 671–5666

Connecticut Association for United Spanish Action (CAUSA)

580 Main Street
Hartford, CT 06120
(203) 549–4046

District of Columbia Commission on Latino Community Development (CLCD)

1801 Belmont Road, NW
Washington, DC 20009
(202) 673–6772

Florida Commission on Hispanic Affairs

Office of the Governor
The Capitol
Tallahassee, FL 32399–0001
(904) 579–9000

Hispanic Women's Council of California

5803 East Beverly Boulevard
Los Angeles, CA 90022
(213) 725–1657

Iowa Spanish-Speaking Peoples Commission

Lucas State Office Building
Des Moines, IA 50319
(515) 281–4080

Kansas Advisory Committee on Hispanic Affairs (KACHA)

1309 Southwest Topeka Boulevard
Topeka, KS 66612–1894
(913) 296–3465

Maryland Commission on Hispanic Affairs

11 West Saratoga Street, Room 254
Baltimore, MD 21201
(301) 333–2532

Spanish-Speaking Community of Maryland, Inc.

7411 Riggs Road, Suite 222
Hyattsville, MD 20783
(301) 587–7217

Michigan Commission on Spanish-Speaking Affairs

P.O. Box 30026
Lansing, MI 48909
(517) 373–8339

Minnesota Spanish-Speaking Affairs Council

506 Rice Street
Saint Paul, MN 55103
(612) 296–9587

Nebraska Mexican American Commission

P.O. Box 94965
Lincoln, NE 68509–4965
(402) 471–2791

Nevada Association of Latin Americans

23 North Maryland Parkway
Las Vegas, NV 89101–3134
(702) 382–6252

Nevada Hispanic Services, Inc.

190 East Liberty Street
P.O. Box 11735
Reno, NV 89501
(702) 786–6003

New Jersey Office of Hispanic Affairs

Department of Community Affairs
101 South Broad Street
Trenton, NJ 08625
(609) 984–3223

New York State Governor's Office for Hispanic Affairs

2 World Trade Center, Suite 5777
New York, NY 10047
(212) 587–2266

Ohio Commission on Spanish-Speaking Affairs

77 South High Street, Eighteenth Floor
Columbus, OH 43266
(614) 466–8333

Oregon Commission on Hispanic Affairs

695 Summer Street, NE
Salem, OR 97310
(503) 373–7397

Oregon Council for Hispanic Advancement

520 Southwest Sixth Avenue, Suite 711729
Portland, OR 97204
(503) 228–4131

Pennsylvania Governor's Advisory Commission on Latino Affairs

Forum Building, Room 379–80
Harrisburg, PA 17120
(717) 783–3877

Puerto Rican Congress of New Jersey

515 South Broad Street
Trenton, NJ 08611
(609) 989–8888

Texas Association of Mexican American Chambers of Commerce (TAMACC)

823 Congress Avenue, Suite 1414
Austin, TX 78701
(512) 447–9821

Utah Governor's Office on Hispanic Affairs

Department of Community Development, Room 6234 Salt Lake City, UT 84114
(801) 538–3045

Washington Commission on Hispanic Affairs

1515 South Cherry Street
Olympia, WA 98504
(206) 753–3159

Wisconsin Governor's Council on Hispanic Affairs

819 North Sixth Street, Room 270
Milwaukee, WI 53203
(414) 227–4344

References

Alpert, Thomas M. "The Inherent Power of the Courts to Regulate the Practice of LawAn Historical Analysis." *Buffalo Law Review,* 32, 1983: 525.

Aranda, Benjamin III. *Directory of Hispanic Judges of the United States,* (Unpublished, 1991).

Boswell, Richard A., with Gilbert P. Carrasco. *Immigration and Nationality Law,* second edition. Durham: Carolina Academic Press, 1992.

Brunelli, Richard. "Study on the Task Force on Minorities in the Legal Profession of the American Bar Association." *Chicago Daily Law Bulletin,* 132, No. 7, November 1986: 1.

Camarillo, Albert. *Latinos in the United States.* Santa Barbara, California: ABC-CLIO, 1986.

Davila, Lind E., "The Underrepresentation of Hispanic Attorneys in Corporate Law Firms." *Stanford Law Review,* 39, July 1987: 1403.

Fund for Modern Courts. *The Success of Women and Minorities in Achieving Judicial Office: The Selection Process.* New York: Fund for Modern Courts, 1985.

Garcia, Bernardo M. "The Hispanic Lawyer: Equal Access to the Legal Profession." Hispanic National Bar Association-Law Student Division (HNBA-LSD) *Legal Briefs,* 1, No. 3, 1991.

Kurzban, Ira J. *Immigration Law Sourcebook,* second edition. Washington, D.C.: American Immigration Law Foundation, 1991.

League of United Latin American Citizens. "Immigration in the United States from Latin America, Past and Present," Washington, D.C., 1, No. 4, July 1986.

MacLachlen, Claudia, and Rita Henley Jensen. "Progress Glacial for Women, Minorities; But the Recession Hits White Male Associates the Hardest." *National Law Journal,* January 27, 1992.

Martinez, John. "Fighting Minority Underrepresentation in Law." Hispanic National Bar Association-Law Student Division (HNBA-LSD) *Legal Briefs,* 1, No. 3, 1991.

Meier, Matt S. *Mexican-American Biographies,* Westport, Connecticut: Greenwood Press, 1988.

Oliveira, Annette. *MALDEF: Diez Anos.* San Francisco: Mexican-American Legal Defense and Educational Fund, 1978.

Pachon, Harry P. *1990 National Roster of Hispanic Elected Officials.* Washington, D.C: NALEO Educational Fund, 1990.

Powers, William B., and Susan A. Weimer. "Trends in Law School Enrollment." *Consultant's Digest,* 1, No. 1, May 1991.

Roberts, Maurice A., and Stephen Yale-Loehr. *Understanding the 1986 Immigration Law.* Washington, D.C.: Federal Publications, 1987.

Select Commission on Immigration and Refugee Policy. *U.S. Immigration Policy and the National Interest.* 1981.

Silas, Faye A. "Minority Judges: More Appointed Than Elected." *American Bar Association Journal,* 72, March 1986: 19.

Spears, Franklin S. "Selection of Appellate Judges." *Baylor Law Review,* 40, 1988: 501.

Thernstrom, Abigail M. *Whose Votes Count?* Cambridge: Harvard University Press, 1987.

U.S. Bureau of the Census, *Statistical Abstract of the United States: 1991,* 111th edition. Washington, D.C.: U.S. Government Printing Office, 1991.

Wagman, Robert. *World Almanac of U.S. Politics.* New York: Pharos Books, 1991.

West, *Almanac of the Federal Judiciary.* St. Paul, Minnesota: West Publishing, 1991.

West, *Association of American Law Schools Directory of Law Teachers.* St. Paul, Minnesota: West Publishing, 1991.

Gilbert Paul Carrasco

14

Business

✳ The Cattle and Livestock Industry ✳ Early Merchants and Entrepreneurs
✳ Twentieth-Century Immigration and Hispanic Business ✳ Hispanic-Owned Businesses Today
✳ Hispanics in the Corporate World ✳ Prominent Hispanics in Business

The conquest and colonization of the Americas by the Spanish was a business enterprise as well as a religious and political one of conquering souls for the Catholic Church and enhancing the power of the Spanish throne. Much of the impetus behind the explorations was the charting of lands and human populations that could be exploited for the benefit of the Spanish royalty and the bourgeoisie. The individuals who became involved in the development of the lands and enterprises that enhanced the king's fortune would also share in that wealth through a variety of means: land grants, percentages of extracted mineral resources, government positions, etc. The colonization and settlement of the new lands followed patterns to convert those lands into religious and economic units that would bring prosperity to the colonists and the crown. The pattern of settlement on the frontier followed this sequence: the establishment first of a presidio or fort, a mission, and then a town. The fort, of course, was for protection against hostile Indians, but the mission was for evangelizing and acculturating the Indians, and teaching them the trades that would become important for the economic development of the area. Among the first prosperous businesses in what would become the western United States were the missions themselves, which developed trade in cattle and their by-products, such as hides and tallow. The third element in the pattern of colonization was the establishment of towns near the missions and presidios. The Spanish and mestizo settlers that established the towns in what would be the Floridas and the Southwest of the United States were principally farmers and ranchers, many of whom lived in town and traveled daily to their fields in the surrounding areas. Some of these settlers and their descendants on initial land grants developed the first prosperous businesses in the Floridas and

northern New Spain (what later became the U.S. Southwest). As with the missions, cattle and sheep brought the first private commercial success, creating a basis for inter-regional as well as international trade.

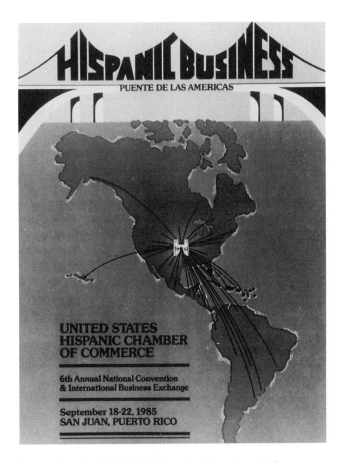

Poster for the 1985 U.S. Hispanic Chamber of Commerce convention showing U.S. Hispanic business people as the bridge for commerce in the Americas.

343

✳ THE CATTLE AND LIVESTOCK INDUSTRY

As early as 1565, stock raising and ranching became established under the Spanish around St. Augustine and Tallahassee, Florida. Most of the cattle were raised for local consumption, but there was enough surplus to make cattle the basis of trade and, in fact, smuggling to Cuba began to be instituted. By the mid-seventeenth century, Florida was home to the first cattle baron. In 1663, Florida-born Tomás Menéndez Márquez inherited his father's cattle ranch in central Florida and built it up over the years into the largest ranch and provider of hides, dried meat, and tallow to the Spanish colonies in Florida and for export through shipping to Havana via the Florida port of San Martín. Menéndez Márquez owned his own frigate, with which he brought some of his own goods to market in Havana and returned with extensive trade items to be sold in Florida; his business interests expanded into areas far beyond ranching, including the importation of Cuban rum. His fortunes increased further when, in 1684, he was appointed royal *contador*, or accountant/treasurer, for Florida. His La Chua Ranch became the largest cattle ranch on lands that would become the United States, extending from the St. Johns River westward to the Gulf and from Lake George northward to the Santa Fe River. Within its boundaries were what are today Ocala, Payne's Prairie, Alachua, Palatka, and Gainesville. The ranch produced more than one-third of Florida cattle and horses in the late seventeenth century. La Chua Ranch met its end when James Moore with Carolinians and Creek Indians invaded the Florida peninsula and overran La Chua in 1702, causing the ranch hands to flee and the cattle to become feral. Despite the early success of Menéndez Márquez, ranching did not flourish in Florida as it would in California and Texas. By 1800 the tax rolls showed only 34 ranches with some 15,000 to 20,000 cattle.

The first area in what would be the Southwest of the United States into which ranching was introduced was New Mexico. By 1598, the lead Spanish colonizer and future governor of the Province of New Mexico, Juan de Oñate, introduced livestock breeding to what became the American Southwest. He established a livestock industry that would supply the burgeoning silver mining industry in northern New Spain, especially around Zacatecas and Guanajuato. There was an intense demand for cattle, horses, and mules, as well as tallow for candles, hides for water and ore bags, clothing, harnesses, hinges, and numerous other items. From New Mexico and western Texas, cattle and livestock ranching spread into the Great Plains, and became the basis of much of the livestock industry of today.

Spain had one of the oldest sheep cultures in the Old World, and it introduced the *churro* sheep, a small, lean animal that gave coarse wool and could endure long marches and all types of weather. The *churro* became so acclimated to New Mexico and the Southwest that it became the basis for the large sheep industry that would develop over the centuries. Much later, about 1876, fine merino sheep were brought by Anglos from the eastern seaboard and crossed with the *churros* to produce a hybrid animal with a better quality wool while being ideally acclimated to the environment. By 1880, the Southwest was producing four million pounds of wool per year. In New Mexico, as elsewhere in the Southwest and the rest of Spanish America, it was the Hispanicized Indians who became the cowboys and shepherds over the centuries, especially since much of ranching originated in and around the missions. The Spaniards also taught the Indians to weave wool, and they became the manpower, especially Navajo women in the early nineteenth century, in the textile industry in New Mexico. The land grants to individuals, along with grazing rights, also facilitated the development of large cattle and sheep ranching. Mexican homesteads in the Southwest consisted of 4,470 acres, 28 times the size of an Anglo-American homestead in the Ohio Valley. The Spanish and Mexican land-use system was much better adapted to an arid environment, and facilitated the growth of the cattle industry on the open range within that environment. All of this was a particular inheritance from the Spaniards and Mexicans for Anglos when they came into the Southwest.

In 1687, Father Eusebio Kino established the mission of Nuestra Señora de los Dolores in Arizona, through which he introduced livestock to the Pimería Alta region of southern Arizona and northern Sonora. At this and at least 20 other locations in Arizona, Kino introduced and promoted livestock tending as essential in converting and feeding the Pima Indians. Franciscan missionaries continued to spread ranching and livestock tending throughout missions in Arizona, New Mexico and California. Under the Spanish and the Mexicans, ranching grew into an important and lucrative business, especially in California.

cattle ranching had been first introduced to California by Franciscan missionary, Father Junípero Serra, with the founding of the mission at San Diego in 1769. He proceeded to establish missions and their reliance on livestock tending, ranching and farming all along the California coast. In 1775 and 1776, Juan Bautista de Anza brought settlers and trailed livestock to northern California, from Arizona to Monterey and San Francisco. By 1810, Hispanic ranchers in California began shipping hides, tallow and dried beef to South America, thus providing impetus for expansion of the cattle business. The hide and tallow trade also expanded beginning in 1822, when the Boston markets opened to the Californios; thus the trade with markets back East far antedates the expansion of the United States into California. Hispanic ranchers and missions began exporting hides and tallow after a deal was struck between a British company and Father President Mariano Payeras of La Purísima Concepción Mission to make contracts with individual missions for their hides and tallow. (In the Franciscan missions of California—as well as those of Arizona, New Mexico and Texas—Indians herded and slaughtered the cattle, prepared the meat and by-products.) Demand in New England and England for these products became so intense that by the 1830s they became California's principal exports. It is estimated that Boston traders alone may have handled some six million hides and 7,000 tons of tallow from 1826 to 1848.

Under the Mexican Republic, founded in 1821, many more land grants were issued for California lands than under Spanish rule; many of these grants became the basis of an ever-expanding ranching industry. More than 400 land grants were issued between 1833 and 1846 for tracts of land ranging from 4,000 to 100,000 acres. By the time of the U.S. takeover, there were more than eight million acres held by some 800 ranchers. Under the United States, the ranching way of life soon succumbed. Most of the large tracts of land fell into the hands of speculators, land plungers, and railroad right-of-way, and prepared the way for the concentration of large land holdings in the hands of few owners who would become the builders of California's giant agribusiness. By 1889, one-sixth of the farms in the state produced more than two-thirds of the crops.

In 1690, an expedition headed by Captain Alonso de León brought livestock to the first Spanish mission in east Texas—San Francisco de los Tejas. This was the beginning of the cattle industry in east Texas, as this and other missions continued to be stocked as well as to raise their own livestock. By 1800, cattle ranching had spread along the Neches and Trinity Rivers. Then in 1721, the Marquis of San Miguel de Aguayo laid the ground for ranching along the northern Rio Grande River when he brought 400 sheep and 300 cattle into south Texas from Nuevo León. About 1722, he also introduced large numbers of horses, mules, cattle and sheep to be ranched at the missions in the San Antonio area. In 1748, José Escandón brought 4,000 colonists into the area, and the expanded population base made livestock-raising even more important. In 1757, one José de la Tienda reported more than 80,000 head of cattle, horses, and mules, and more than 300,000 sheep and goats in the area. In 1760, Captain Blas María de la Garza Falcón obtained a grant to 975,000 acres of land in Texas, which he called Rancho Real de Santa Petronila, which in time would become the largest cattle ranch in the United States: the King Ranch. By 1781, nearly all available land grants in South Texas had been assigned and nearly all of the lands were in use as ranches.

Cattle became such an important cash industry that smuggling to English, American and French territories soon became lucrative. It became so lucrative, in fact, that in 1750 the Spanish governor of Texas attempted to in vain to license and regulate the illegal trade in cattle between Spanish Texas and French Louisiana—these were the first cattle drives on record. Vaqueros, Hispanic cowboys, had been illegally driving cattle from Texas to market in French Louisiana for decades. When Spain acquired Louisiana in 1763, this trade was no longer illegal; however, when the Louisiana Territory passed to the United States in 1803, cattle driving from Texas to Louisiana once again constituted a lucrative smuggling trade. By the late eighteenth century, some 15,000 to 20,000 head of cattle moved eastward to Louisiana each year. By the early 1800s, illegal horse and mule trading also became a lucrative business, and Anglo settlers in the Mississippi Valley provided an expanded market for all Texas livestock.

By 1800, the first major livestock economies were flourishing in Texas: horse ranching in Nacogdoches, cattle and horse ranching along the Rio Grande Valley and around San Antonio south the La Bahía. Cattle ran free on the open range and were herded and driven to market and slaughter. The Anglo immigrants who settled in Texas considered these cattle "wild" and simply appropriated them, although they belonged to the Hispanic ranchers and were tended by vaqueros. They considered the cattle to be open game; they did not create a cattle industry, but simply took it over.

In 1830, the first Longhorn cattle appeared, resulting from the cross-breeding of the Spanish Retinto and animals brought to Texas by Anglo settlers. Immune to tick fever and accustomed to the tough brush country of South Texas, the Longhorn became the basis for the western livestock industry. After the Civil War, cattle ranching became especially important to the nation; Texas cowboys drove some ten million heads of Longhorn north to railheads and markets. Over time, the Longhorn was replaced by many other breeds, but in the initial stages of this important industry, it became the mainstay. Along with the trade in beef, an industry in hides, tallow and other by-products flourished in coastal "factories" of Texas.

Even under American rule and with intense competition from Anglo settlers and entrepreneurs, some Hispanic cattlemen were able to flourish. Bernabé Robles was the first Hispanic to become a millionaire ranching king by taking advantage of the Homestead Act. He and his brother, Jesús, applied for and received two homesteads in southern Arizona and opened a stage station there in 1882; then he founded what became the famous Three Points Ranch there. He expanded his holdings and eventually controlled more than one million acres between Florence and the Mexican border. Bernabé Robles was one of the largest and most successful cattlemen in Arizona. In 1918, he invested the profits from ranching in urban real estate in the Tucson area. Part of the inheritance he left his children was made up of 65 parcels of the most valuable Tucson properties. In Arizona, a small farm land grant in Tubac, received from Spain in 1789 by Toribio Otero, became the basis generations later for the making of "the cattle king of Tubac," his great grandson Sabino Otero. Building on this initial inherited ranch, Sabino Otero developed the largest ranching operation in southern Arizona during the 1870s and 1880s.

Besides forming the foundation on which today's cattle and livestock industries are based, the Spanish-Mexican ranching culture was also essential in bringing cattle ranching into areas outside of the Southwest. In 1832, King Kamehameha III of Hawaii arranged for Mexican *vaqueros* to come to Hawaii from California to teach ranching skills to the Hawaiians; thus the cattle industry was born in the Hawaiian Islands. Cattle had actually been introduced by George Vancouver in 1793, and horses by Richard J. Cleveland in 1803, but the cattle had been allowed to run wild and only in the 1820s had they begun to be hunted for their hides, tallow, and meat. The Hawaiian word for cowboy, *pianolo*, derives from *español*. Many of the techniques and traditions of the Hawaiian industry are owed to the Hispanic cowboy. In 1837, Philip Edwards drove cattle from California north to Oregon, thus opening up the Northwest for ranching, with the help of California *vaqueros*. And ranchers in Oregon established the tradition of employing Mexican American cowboys in the late nineteenth and early twentieth centuries; they came to comprise up to half of the cowhands. In 1869, again, six Mexican American cowboys led by Juan Redón drove 3,000 head of cattle for John Devine, who established the largest ranch in Oregon. Redón stayed on to work as Devine's foreman. And, of course, it is well known that cattle drives north from Texas began in the 1860s, with Mexican cowboys leading the way in introducing cattle ranching into the Great Plains.

✱ EARLY MERCHANTS AND ENTREPRENEURS

Of course, shipping, handling and selling provisions in the frontier settlements were essential businesses. Many Hispanic entrepreneurs were responsible for opening trade routes, establishing trading posts and the first stores in the Floridas and what became the Southwest of the United States. The first successful, large merchant and entrepreneur to be born in a mainland area that would become part of the United States was Francsico Javier Sánchez (1736–1807). He became the owner of vast cattle ranches in Florida that stocked the Spanish and British military and governments in Florida, as well as the civilian population of St. Augustine; he also became the owner and operator of stores, plantations and ships, and engaged in the slave trade—despite his having been married to a mulatto and cared for his mulatto offspring. While some Spanish and mestizo entrepreneurs became wealthy from the slave trade, Spain became the first European colonial power to outlaw the slave trade in all of its colonies to the north of the Equator, and signed a treaty with England providing for the suppressing of the slave trade. This included the selling of slaves in areas that eventually became part of the United States. In 1829, the new Republic of Mexico abolished slavery; this abolition also affected the Mexican lands to the north, which would eventually become part of the United States. From the very early explorations to the colonization and settlement of the Spanish territories in what became the United States, free Africans were represented as both settlers and soldiers; they also became cowboys on the sprawling ranches from Texas to California. In fact, some of the Spanish colonies and later Mexico, including Texas and the territories west, served as safe harbors for runaway slaves, who as free men intermarried with the creoles and mestizos, and engaged in agriculture and the trades.

In the sprawling expanses of what became the Southwest and the West of the United States, communications and transportation were essential businesses. One of the first industries to unite suppliers and markets, rural producers and ports was the freighting industry. Developed by Hispanics largely following routes used by Indians for centuries, numerous freighting companies were in place in Texas, New Mexico, Arizona, and California by the time of incorporation into the United States. So lucrative and competitive were the routes that soon Anglo-American newcomers sought to take them over.

Mexican teamsters, in particular, had controlled the important route from El Paso to San Antonio, Texas, since colonial times. Freighting on this route became the target of so much Anglo violence on Mexicans in 1857 that it became known as the Cart War, and necessitated the intervention of Texas Rangers to bring the peace. Amid this excessively competitive environment, nevertheless, some Mexican American entrepreneurs prevailed. Such was the case of Joaquín Quiroga, who in 1856 laid the foundations for the lucrative freighting business in Arizona by carrying the first load of goods from Yuma to Tucson in his 14-mule pack train. In the next decades, Mexican entrepreneurs would become the major owners of freighting companies, linking the California coast with the Arizona and New Mexico territories, Baja California and northern Mexico. They even reached as far east as Missouri. By 1875, Arizonan Estevan Ochoa (1831–1888) developed his freight business into the largest Hispanic-owned company in Tucson, second only in the overall community to E. N. Fish & Company, handling some $300,000 in transactions per year. By 1880, his Tully, Ochoa & Company was the largest taxpayer in Pima County. Expanding from the long-distance hauling of freight by mule train, he and his partner, Pickney Randolph Tully, went into the mercantile business with stores that depended on the freight hauling. Thus he and his partners were among the first businessmen on the frontier to implement vertical integration. They also invested in mining and raising sheep. At the beginning of the 1880s, they were grazing 15,000 sheep and operating a wool factory; a settlement, started at a camp where they raised sheep, eventually became the town of Ochoaville, founded in his honor. Ochoa is credited with having introduced to Tucson and surroundings a number of industrial technologies for turning out woolen blankets that had been developed in factories back East. Estevan Ochoa even became the first Arizona pioneer to plant cotton for commercial purposes. He investigated its potential by first planting an acre of Pima cotton and then sending samples back East.

There were numerous other industries related to transportation, freighting and horse culture, which had deep roots in Hispanic tradition. Such was the case of the carriage industry. In 1889, Mexican immigrant Federico Ronstadt founded a carriage business that became the largest carriage builders in Tucson, Arizona, and the region, including Sonora, Mexico. At its height, Ronstadt's wagon shop and hardware store employed 65 people who, besides repairing vehicles of all kinds, manufactured wagons, buggies, harnesses and saddles. Ronstadt executed most of the iron forging himself; he became known as one of the finest wagon and carriage maker in the Southwest. Ronstadt's business territory extended from California to Sonora, Mexico, where he had agents in Cananea, Nogales, Hermosillo, and Guaymas. By 1910, approximately one-third of his business was effected south of the border. Ronstadt also marketed nationally known brands of wagons and farm machinery.

As can be seen, the freight hauling business by mule and wagon train was very significant, and it led to the development of other businesses. Freighting only subsided with the introduction of the railroads, and then some of these same entrepreneurs made the transition to hauling freight and people by wagon and stage coach to secondary and outlying communities. While Hispanics had followed trails blazed and used by Indians for centuries, the Hispanics pioneered most of the freighting techniques and opened most of the trails that would later be used for trade and communications during the territorial and early statehood periods. In fact, some of today's major highways run along those routes pioneered for trade by Hispanics and Mexicans.

Fortunes were indeed to be made on the frontier, whether under the flags of the United States, Spain or Mexico. As the population increased, so did settlement and urban density, especially in the commercial centers. Among the commercial developers of cities and towns in the Southwest and West, Hispanics were also represented. One of the many was Leopoldo Carrillo, the first Hispanic urban real estate mogul in Tucson—and possibly the entire Southwest—under U.S. rule. Carrillo, who the 1870 census showed to be the wealthiest man in Tucson, owned rental homes, commercial properties and farm land; he also owned and operated ice cream parlors, saloons and even Tucson's first bowling alley. By 1881, he owned nearly 100 houses in Tucson, making him one of the largest landlords.

In another part of the country, a different immigration experience led to the development of an entire industry and the creation of some of the most extensive fortunes of Hispanics in the United States. During the 1880s, a whole Hispanic industry began its transplant to United States soil, when Cuban cigar factory owners decided to transplant their holdings to swamp lands outside of Tampa, Florida. The wars of Cuban independence against Spain, the high import taxes levied on cigars by the United States and the continuous unrest of organized labor in Cuba, led Vicente Martínez Ybor and other entrepreneurs to found Ybor City, construct factories and import Cuban and Spanish craftsmen to take advantage of the beneficial, excise-tax-free conditions offered in the United States. In 1880, the population of Tampa was only 721; a decade later the combined population of Tampa and Ybor City was 5,500, and that number tripled by 1900. The first of the entrepreneurs to establish their cigar factories, Vicente Martínez Ybor and Ignacio Haya, hoped to attract a docile work force, for which they built from scratch a company town, complete with mutual aid societies, theaters, schools and other amenities. The industry in Ybor City grew to ten factories by 1895 and became the principal cigar producing area in the United States, when smoking cigars was at its highest peak. The factories produced well into the 1950s some of the most beloved brands of cigars for the U.S. smoking public.

✳ TWENTIETH-CENTURY IMMIGRATION AND HISPANIC BUSINESS

Hispanic immigration to the United States during the twentieth century has been so high that it irrevocably changed the character of Hispanic communities throughout the United States. Made up predominantly of economic refugees responding to factors both pulling them to the United States and pushing them from their home countries, Hispanic culture in the United States has been overwhelmingly working-class. Shortages of labor during times of economic expansion and/or efforts to supply war efforts, as well as the need to fill jobs that other Americans considered too menial, low-paying or low in prestige, are among the pull factors that caused Hispanic workers to not only cross borders but to be contracted in their homelands to come labor in the United States. The most important push factors were depressed economies and little opportunity for advancement and better pay back home, as well as the chaos and danger brought on by revolutions and civil wars. Most of these wage laborers never had any other American work experience or economic opportunity than being exploited in factories and fields in the United States. Beginning in the post-World War II period, however, their children did gain better access to the American Dream.

It was and has been to the present the Hispanic political refugees who have come to the United States and created their version of the American Dream. Many of the Hispanics fleeing revolutions and civil wars in Mexico, Cuba, Spain and Central America came to the United States with a strong educational background, middle-to-upper-class culture and sensibility, as well as financial resources and business know-how. Their resources and expertise stood them well in re-creating their professional lives, investments and businesses in a foreign country. But what was most attractive to many of them was providing goods and services to their own cul-

tural community in exile. They spoke the language, knew the culture intimately and could provide the goods and services that their fellow refugees needed and were used to. Thus, from the beginning of the outpouring from the Mexican Revolution to the most recent waves of immigration from Cuba and Central America, businesses were developed primarily within the immigrant communities. The immigrant entrepreneurs provided for all aspects of the immigrants' lives—literally from birthing to funeral services—in the Spanish language according to their familiar customs and rituals, albeit often for a higher price. Small businesses provided everything from the humble tortilla made in local factories and bakeries to such mundane needs as money orders and translated documents quite often through store fronts in the barrios. To this date, the majority of Hispanic businesses in the United States are small businesses, quite often run by families. Beside the furniture stores, used car lots, record shops, working-class restaurants, etc., immigrant entrepreneurs have also provided for the cultural and intellectual needs of the community, first through theaters and vaudeville houses, later through movie houses and radio and television stations and networks (see the chapter on Media). Some of the greatest fortunes of Hispanic immigrant entrepreneurs have been made by providing media to the Spanish-speaking communities. Such businessmen as Ignacio Lozano founded newspapers, like his San Antonio daily *La prensa* in the teens, and went on to diversify their investments. Lozano, for example, mastered the schedules of the railroads so that his San Antonio newspaper could be shipped by rail as far as the west coast and up into the Midwest, thus becoming the closest thing to a national Spanish-language daily in the United States from the 1920s to the 1950s. So successful was he that in 1926, he also founded the Los Angeles daily *La opinión*, which is still published today (See the chapter on Media). Lozano and his family interests grew to control newspapers, a book publishing company, book stores and real estate. In all of his enterprises, Lozano and his editors promoted the concept of a Mexican exile culture that, in preparation for the day the Mexican exiles could return to Mexico, required the expatriates to preserve their language, religion and customs by shunning Anglo-American culture and Protestantism. While furthering nationalism and Mexican-Catholic identity, the ideology of exile was also good for business because it helped to isolate and solidify the Mexican immigrant and Mexican American markets and limited competition from Anglo businesses.

The market for the typical foods, kitchen implements and utensils has always been a mainstay of

Hispanic immigrant communities. It is through maintaining foodways that much culture is preserved and furthered. The story of such perennial Hispanic brand names as Goya, La Preferida, Old El Paso and others is the tale of how particular Hispanic entrepreneurs were able to standardize the delivery systems across borders and states for Cuban, Puerto Rican and Mexican foods. In particular, a modern success story is that of Joseph A. Unanue, who took a small family concern and built it into one of the largest food processing and distribution companies in the United States: Goya Foods. Related to the need to purchase the foodstuffs to maintain the cultural diet at home was also the need to feed the working man who was in the United States without his family, which in the early waves of immigration was the majority of Hispanics; thus thousands of Mexican and other Hispanic restaurants were founded in barrios and still proliferate today. From the 1950s to the 1970s, some of these restaurants were successful in establishing a following outside of the barrios and helped Mexican food, in particular, grow into the favorite ethnic food in the United States. In most Southwestern cities, some of these restaurants grew into chains and even began to market their own brand names through supermarkets. Such names as El Chico, El Toro, Ninfa's, Monterrey House, Cuéllars, etc., have become household names in these cities.

As the Hispanic population has grown in size, so has the buying power of Hispanics, and no longer has the Hispanic market remained the sole province of Hispanic small business owners. In fact, the so-called "Decade of the Hispanic," the 1980s, was basically a public relations ploy to attract attention from the media and major U.S. corporations for investing in marketing to the Hispanic community and for hiring Hispanic expertise at various levels, both within the corporations themselves and as consultants and public relations firms. Thus, beginning in the 1980s, a new type of Hispanic entrepreneur appeared, one who specialized in gaining access for American businesses to the Hispanic market, immigrant or otherwise. The Hispanic public relations firms and consultants began devising strategies for tapping into the Hispanic market that heretofore had been ceded without competition to the Hispanic immigrant and U.S. Hispanic entrepreneurs. Part of the rationale for the need of these specialized firms was that Hispanic consumers spoke mainly Spanish and were too foreign to be reached by the mainstream corporations. Hispanic public relations firms multiplied and numerous individual experts came on the scene to assist a diversity of corporate giants, such as AT&T, and local enterprises, such as department stores and supermarkets to get into the Hispanic market. Out of the intense

competition, such firms as San Antonio's Sosa and Associates developed to serve such national accounts as American Airlines, Anheuser-Bush, Burger King and Coca-Cola.

✳ HISPANIC-OWNED BUSINESSES TODAY

Hispanic-owned businesses form a dynamic and complex sector of commerce in the United States. During the 1980s, Hispanic-owned businesses made impressive and important advances. In 1977, there were approximately 219,000 Hispanic-owned businesses, according to the U.S. Census Bureau. By 1982, slightly more than 248,000 Hispanic-owned businesses were thriving, a 13 percent increase. By 1987, some 422,000 Hispanic-owned businesses were performing, an increase of 70 percent. By comparison, the number of nonminority businesses grew only 18 percent from 1977 to 1982 and 14 percent from 1982 to 1987. Table 14.1 charts the growth of Hispanic-owned and non-minority-owned businesses for the three census periods.

TABLE 14.1
HISPANIC AND NONMINORITY BUSINESSES

YEAR	HISPANIC	NONMINORITY
1977	219,355	10,210,000
1982	248,141	12,059,950
1987	422,373	13,695,480

Sources: United States Bureau of the Census, 1980, 5; 1986, 4; 1991, 1.

Mexican Americans own 54 percent of all Hispanic businesses, while Cuban Americans own 15 percent and Puerto Ricans, 7 percent. Figure 14.1 provides information on business ownership by Hispanic origin.

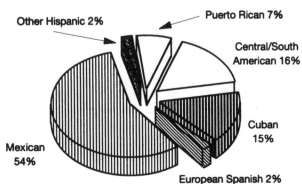

Figure 14.1
Origin of U.S. Hispanic Business Owners

Other Hispanic 2%
Puerto Rican 7%
Central/South American 16%
Cuban 15%
European Spanish 2%
Mexican 54%

TABLE 14.2

NUMBER OF BUSINESSES, SALES VOLUME, NUMBER OF EMPLOYEES, AND PAYROLL BY HISPANIC ORIGIN OF OWNERS

HISPANIC ORIGIN	ALL BUSINESSES		BUSINESSES WITH PAID EMPLOYEES			
	FIRMS	SALES (THOUSAND $)	FIRMS	EMPLOYEES	ANNUAL PAYROLL (THOUSAND $)	SALES (THOUSAND $)
Mexican	229,706	11,835,080	49,078	148,008	1,687,401	8,403,796
Puerto Rican	27,697	1,447,680	4,629	13,231	179,379	903,848
Cuban	61,470	5,481,974	10,768	47,266	638,459	4,227,065
Other Central or South American	66,356	3,202,238	10,793	27,386	343,039	2,031,768
European Spanish	24,755	2,054,537	5,299	21,196	293,976	1,628,133
Other Hispanic	12,389	710,091	2,341	7,759	101,088	534,822
Total	422,373	24,731,600	82,908	264,846	3,243,342	17,729,432

Source: United States Bureau of the Census, 1991, 12.

Many Hispanic businesses have no employees and are staffed by a single individual who is typically the owner. Approximately 83,000 of the 422,000 Hispanic-owned companies have one or more employees. Nationally, these businesses employ close to 265,000 individuals, have an annual payroll of $3.2 billion, and have sales in excess of $17 billion. But for the most part, Hispanic-owned businesses are small. Hispanic businesses that have employees other than the owner total 82,908. Fully 72 percent of these businesses had one to four employees in 1990. In addition, 17 percent had five to nine employees, and .2 percent had 100 employees or more. In terms of sales generated by Hispanic businesses, 70 percent of them generated less than $25,000 in annual sales (see Table 14.5). This would lead one to conclude that there is a large proportion of Hispanic businesses that are part-time operations. This conclusion is supported by evidence that 55 percent of all Hispanic business owners spend fewer than 40 hours per week working with their businesses (see Table 14.4). *Hispanic Business* magazine in an August 1993 study compared the 100 fastest growing Hispanic companies with the *Inc.* magazine's 500 fastest growing companies and found that Hispanic companies tend to employ more people. The average staff of the 100 fastest growing was 203, compared with 145 for the *Inc.* 500.

The majority of Hispanic-owned companies are concentrated in services and retail trade, an inheritance for many of them of having started off by serving the immigrant market in the barrio. Services and retail made up 60 percent of all Hispanic businesses and accounted for 55 percent of gross sales. Table 14.3 presents the number of companies and volume of sales for Hispanic businesses by industry category.

Hispanic-owned businesses exist in virtually every state; however, 78 percent of Hispanic companies, with 80 percent of the gross sales, are concentrated in California, Texas, Florida, New York and New Mexico. Most of the Hispanic businesses of these states are located in large urban areas. Table 14.4 shows the ten metropolitan statistical areas (MSAs) with the largest number of Hispanic companies and their sales. These ten MSAs account for

TABLE 14.3

HISPANIC BUSINESSES BY MAJOR INDUSTRY CATEGORY

INDUSTRY CATEGORY	NUMBER OF COMPANIES	SALES (MILLION $)
Agricultural services	16,365	694
Mining	829	29
Construction	55,516	3,438
Manufacturing	11,090	1,449
Transportation and public utilities	26,955	1,380
Wholesale trade	10,154	2,445
Retail trade	69,911	7,643
Finance, insurance, and real estate	22,106	864
Services	184,372	6,031
Industries not Classified	25,075	758
Total	422,373	24,731

Source: United States Bureau of the Census, 1991.

TABLE 14.4
NUMBER AND SALES VOLUME OF HISPANIC BUSINESSES IN THE TEN LARGEST MSAs* VS. THOSE IN THE ENTIRE STATE

MSA	MSA		STATE	
	BUSINESSES	SALES (THOUSAND $)	BUSINESSES	SALES (THOUSAND $)
Los Angeles-Long Beach, CA	56,679	3,346,076	132,212	8,119,853
Miami-Hialeah, FL	47,725	3,771,247	64,413	4,949,151
New York, NY	23,014	1,239,513	28,254	1,555,801
Houston, TX	15,967	584,356	94,754	4,108,076
San Antonio, TX	15,241	657,174	94,754	4,108,076
San Diego, CA	10,373	559,444	132,212	8,119,853
Riverside-San Bernardino, CA	10,195	576,537	132,212	8,119,853
Anaheim-Santa Ana, CA	9,683	650,604	132,212	8,119,853
El Paso, TX	8,214	450,840	94,754	4,108,076
Chicago, IL	7,848	506,393	9,636	588,646

*MSA = Metropolitan Statistical Area.
Source: United States Bureau of the Census, 1991, 4.

close to 50 percent of the gross sales. But the greatest concentration of the 100 Fastest Growing Hispanic Companies are located in California and Florida, according to an August 1993 study conducted by *Hispanic Business* magazine.

The number of large-size Hispanic-owned companies is increasing. *Hispanic Business* monitors the 500 largest Hispanic companies in the nation; the 1994 list (Table 14.6a) demonstrates the diversity of large Hispanic companies. Table 14.6b lists the fastest-growing Hispanic companies, as compiled by *Hispanic Business*.

Hispanic business owners tend to be dynamic individuals who in some ways are very much like their nonminority counterparts and in other ways quite different. Hispanic business owners are likely to be younger than their nonminority counterparts. In Table 14.7 the owner's age for both groups is compared. In all, 80 percent of all Hispanic business owners are married, while 79 percent of nonminority business owners are married. The *Hispanic Business* study of the 100 fastest growing Hispanic firms also found that the companies were more likely to be owned by women (12 percent) than the non-Hispanic fastest-growing companies. Hispanic business owners have less formal education than the nonminority owners: approximately 7 percent of the Hispanic group possess an undergraduate degree, compared with 15 percent of the nonminority group. On the other hand, 27 percent of all Hispanic business owners possess a high school diploma or equivalent, as opposed to 32 percent of their nonminority counterparts. In Table 14.8, the formal education of Hispanic business owners is compared with their nonminority counterparts. Generally, a larger percentage of Hispanic business owners are first-time entrepreneurs, compared with their

nonminority counterparts. Approximately 15 percent of Hispanic business owners have previously owned a business, while 21 percent of their nonminority counterparts have. In addition, 28 percent of Hispanic business owners have close relatives who own a business, while 40 percent of nonminority business owners do. Hispanic business owners as a group also possess less managerial experience prior to establishing their businesses than their nonminority counterparts; approximately 10 percent have ten or more years as managers before starting a business, while 21 percent of their nonminority counterparts possess such experience. Finally, 30 percent of Hispanic businesses were established prior to 1976, compared with 42 percent of the nonminority businesses. These data confirm that Hispanic business owners as a group tend to have less business experience and tend to be more recent entrants into the world of business than their nonminority counterparts. Variations between Hispanic and nonminority business owners across several dimensions are shown in Table 14.9.

TABLE 14.5
SALES VOLUME OF HISPANIC BUSINESSES

PERCENTAGE OF BUSINESSES	SALES ($)
34	Less than 5,000
35	5,000–24,999
20	25,000–99,999
7	100,000–249,999
3	250,000–999,999
1	1,000,000 or more

Source: United States Bureau of the Census, 1987, 140.

TABLE 14.6a
THE THIRTY LARGEST HISPANIC BUSINESSES

RANK	COMPANY AND LOCATION	CHIEF EXECUTIVE	TYPE OF BUSINESS	NUMBER OF EMPLOYEES	YEAR STARTED	SALES ($ MILLIONS)
1	**Goya Foods,** Secaucus, NJ	Joseph A. Unanue	Hispanic Food Mfg./Mktg.	1,600	1936	453.00
2	**Burt on Broadway Auto. Grp.** Englewood, CO	Lloyd G. Chavez	Automotive Sales & Svc.	600	1939	422.76
3	**Sedano's Supermarkets** Miami, FL	Manuel A. Herren	Supermarket Chain	1,500	1962	224.56
4	**Galeana's Van Dyke Dodge Inc.** Warren, MI	Frank Galeana	Automotive Sales & Svc.	334	1977	186.30
5	**Cal-State Lumber Sales Inc.** San Diego, CA	Benjamin Acevedo	Wood Products Sales	98	1984	169.64
6	**Ancira Enterprises Inc.** San Antonio, TX	Ernesto Ancira Jr.	Automotive Sales & Svc.	300	1983	168.00
7	**International Bancshares Corp.** Laredo, TX	Dennis E. Nixon	Financial Svcs.	650	1979	160.70
8	**Handy Andy Supermarkets** San Antonio, TX	A. (Jimmy) Jimenez	Supermarket Chain	1,705	1983	148.00
9	**Frank Parra Autoplex** Irving, TX	Tim & Mike Parra	Automotive Sales & Svc.	284	1971	146.62
10	**Normac Foods Inc.** Oklahoma City, OK	John C. Lopez	Meat Products Mfg.	255	1970	142.77
11	**Lloyd A. Wise Inc.** Oakland, CA	A.A. Batarse Jr.	Automotive Sales & Svc.	291	1914	137.21
12	**Infotec Development Inc.** Santa Ana, CA	J. Fernando Niebla	Aerospace Engr./Systems Devel.	600	1978	126.03
13	**CTA Inc.** Rockville, MD	C.E. (Tom) Velez	Aerospace/Defense Systems	1,280	1979	115.94
14	**Capital Bancorp** Miami, FL	Abel Holtz	Financial Svcs.	632	1974	114.17
15	**COLSA Corp.** Huntsville, AL	Francisco J. Collazo	Engineering Svcs.	700	1980	112.00
16	**Troy Ford** Troy, MI	Irma B. Elder	Automotive Sales & Svc.	115	1967	111.09
17	**CareFlorida Inc.** Miami, FL	Paul L. Cejas	Health Care Svcs.	194	1986	110.60
18	**Gaseteria Oil Corp.** Brooklyn, NY	Oscar Porcelli	Gasoline Stations	450	1972	108.00
19	**Eagle Brands Inc.** Miami, FL	Carlos M. de la Cruz Sr.	Beer Dist.	200	1984	97.95
20	**Precision Trading Corp.** Miami, FL	Israel Lapciuc	Consumer Electronics	35	1979	96.00
21	**Condal Distributors Inc.** Bronx, NY	Nelson Fernandez	Food Dist.	250	1968	95.00
22	**TELACU Industries** City of Commerce, CA	David C. Lizarraga	Economic Devel./Financial Svcs.	600	1968	93.00
23	**Rosendin Electric Inc.** San Jose, CA	Raymond J. Rosendin	Electrical Contracting	650	1919	91.00
24	**Mexican Indust. in Michigan Inc.** Detroit, MI	Henry J. Aguirre	Automotive Trim Mfg.	800	1979	87.50
25	**Vincam Group Inc.** Miami, FL	Carlos A. Saladrigas	Employee Leasing	6,500	1985	85.30
26	**Ruiz Food Products Inc.** Dinuba, CA	Frederick R. Ruiz	Mexican Food Mfg.	1,123	1964	83.26
27	**United Poultry/Belca Foodservice** Atlanta, GA	Alfredo Caceres	Foodservice Dist./Export	108	1976	78.22
28	**Pan American Hospital** Miami, FL	Carolina Calderin	Health Care Svcs.	600	1963	76.00
29	**H & H Meat Products Co. Inc.** dba H & H Foods, Mercedes, TX	Liborio E. Hinojosa	Meat Packing/Dist.	310	1947	68.79
30	**Advanced Sciences Inc.** Albuquerque, NM	Ed L. Romero	Environ. Engineering Svcs.	492	1977	66.59

Source: *Hispanic Business,* January 1994.

Table 14.6b
The Fastest Growing Hispanic-Owned Companies

Rank	Company and Location	Type of Business	Number of Employees	Year Started	Sales ($ Millions)	Compound Growth Rate 1988–1992
1	Superior Tomato and Avocado Co. Inc. San Antonio, TX	Fresh Vegetables & Fruit Dist.	175	1988	30.10	250.25
2	Shadrock Petroleum Products Inc. San Antonio, TX	Petroleum/Natural Gas Products Dist.	9	1946	41.69	243.31
3	Research Management Consultants Inc. Camarillo, CA	Environ. Engineering Svcs./Info. Syst.	188	1987	16.00	216.70
4	Stature Construction Co. Houston, TX	General Contracting	8	1987	11.45	178.87
5	HJ Ford Associates Inc. Arlington, VA	Systems Engineering/Integ.	105	1981	9.21	152.95
6	PCI International Lafayette, LA	Food Ingredient/Coconut Export	5	1981	4.54	134.44
7	Trandes Corporation Lanham, MD	Transport. Engr./Logistics/Mgmt.	180	1980	11.17	132.00
8	O.I.V. Systems Inc. San Antonio, TX	Computer Programming	76	1988	7.65	127.94
9	Oasis Technology Inc. Camarillo, CA	Computer Software/System Design	5	1979	4.78	124.52
10	Cal-State Lumber Sales Inc. San Diego, CA	Wood Products Sales	98	1984	169.64	121.88
11	Compu-Centro USA Inc. El Paso, TX	Computer Sales/Svc./Training/Net.	39	1986	8.03	118.85
12	MVM Inc. Falls Church, VA	Investigation/Security Svcs.	1,152	1979	24.45	117.43
13	Compatible Micro Solutions Inc. dba CMS, El Paso, TX	Computer Sales/Syst. Integ.	23	1987	3.29	111.01
14	HBLF Jacksonville, FL	Translations/Typesetting/Printing	76	1986	2.72	105.36
15	Certified Abatement Systems Inc. Houston, TX	Asbestos & Lead Abatement	50	1987	5.00	101.03
16	Perii Systems Inc. Ho-Ho-Kus, NJ	Systems Engineering/Integ.	30	1987	2.18	99.66
17	Scientech Inc. Idaho Falls, ID	Environ. Safety/Waste Mgmt.	257	1983	20.43	89.64
18	Sani Serv Inc. Indianapolis, IN	Ice Cream/Yogurt Machine Mfg.	96	1977	28.00	88.88
19	Maria Elena Toraño and Assos. (META) Miami, Fl	Mgmt. Consulting Svcs.	228	1980	15.45	88.84
20	Operational Technologies Corp. San Antonio, TX	Environ. Engineering Svcs.	156	1986	6.96	88.61
21	Vincam Group Inc. Miami, FL	Employee Leasing	6,500	1985	85.30	87.51
22	Tru & Associates Inc. Vista, CA	Petrol./Lubricant/Coal Prod. Dist.	3	1983	5.20	86.06
23	Montoya & Sons Construction Co. Inc. Schiller Park, IL	General Contracting	55	1986	10.31	84.28
24	Shifa Services Inc. Hackensack, NJ	Janitorial Svcs./Plant Maintenance	800	1980	13.80	84.15
25	C.P.F. Corporation Washington, DC	Janitorial/Painting Svcs.	417	1984	5.10	81.81
26	Copier Depot Inc. Miami, FL	Copier Equipment and Sales	23	1972	3.80	80.25
27	Film Roman N. Hollywood, CA	TV/Theater Anim. Entertain. Dist.	210	1984	25.00	77.83
28	Pinto Brothers Construction Inc. Chicago, IL	General Contracting/Painting	100	1987	7.20	73.21
29	JC's Mid America Building Services Inc. Carol Stream, IL	Janitorial/Painting Svcs.	480	1979	10.40	71.58
30	Comprehensive Technologies Internatl. Inc. Chantilly, VA	Software Develop./Systems Integ.	490	1980	39.23	70.57

Source: *Hispanic Business*, January 1994.

Figure 14.2
Sources of Start-up Capital for Hispanic and Nonminority Business Owners

Hispanic

Nonminority

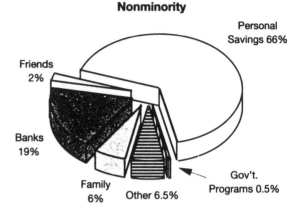

TABLE 14.7
HISPANIC AND NONMINORITY BUSINESS OWNERS BY AGE

	UNDER 25	25–34	35–44	45–54	55–64	OVER 65
Hispanic business owners	4%	22%	28%	24%	14%	4%
Nonminority business owners	3%	20%	25%	22%	18%	9%

Source: United States Bureau of the Census, 1987, 10.
Note: 4 percent of Hispanic business owners and 3 percent of nonminority business owners did not report age.

Other interesting similarities exist between the groups. Slightly over 76 percent of Hispanic business owners used $10,000 or less in capital to start or acquire their businesses, while 72 percent of nonminority businesses required $10,000 or less. Start-up capital requirements for Hispanic and nonminority businesses are illustrated in Table 14.10.

The sources of start-up capital for Hispanic and nonminority business owners are varied. The major portion for both groups has come from personal savings. However, 19 percent of nonminority business owners borrowed the capital from commercial banks, while 15 percent of Hispanic business owners did so. Approximately 8 percent of nonminority business owners obtained capital from family and friends, compared with 13 percent of Hispanic business owners. Sources of start-up capital for Hispanic and nonminority business owners are illustrated in Figure 14.2.

Some indication of business productivity can be obtained by examining net profit or loss of Hispanic businesses and comparing them to nonminority businesses. More than 4 percent of Hispanic-owned businesses generated net profits of $50,000 or more, compared with 6 percent for nonminority businesses. Approximately 14 percent of Hispanic businesses reported a loss, while 16 percent of nonminority businesses did. In terms of productivity when measured by profit or loss, it can be concluded that minority businesses are as productive as nonminority ones. Profit and loss for Hispanic and nonminority businesses are compared in Table 14.11

TABLE 14.8
HISPANIC AND NONMINORITY BUSINESS OWNERS BY YEARS OF EDUCATION

	LESS THAN 9 YEARS	9–11 YEARS	HIGH SCHOOL DIPLOMA	1–3 YEARS OF COLLEGE	COLLEGE DEGREE	MORE THAN 5 YEARS OF COLLEGE
Hispanic business owners	19%	11%	27%	20%	7%	12%
Nonminority business owners	5%	8%	32%	20%	15%	18%

Source: United States Bureau of the Census, 1987, 18.
Note: 4 percent of Hispanic business owners and 2 percent of nonminority business owners did not report education.

The dominant form of Hispanic-owned business is the sole proprietorship; this is also the dominant form of all U.S. businesses. The majority of Hispanic companies—94 percent—are sole proprietorships, compared to 92 percent for nonminority businesses, according to the Bureau of the Census. Hispanic-owned corporations, on the other hand, account for 2 percent of the total number of Hispanic companies, while 3 percent of nonminority firms are corporations. Approximately 4 percent of Hispanic businesses are partnerships, compared with 5 percent of nonminority businesses.

Hispanic-owned businesses tend to differ from their nonminority counterparts in at least one area; they tend to hire other Hispanics or minorities. Approximately 67 percent of Hispanic businesses report that their work force consists of 75 to 100 percent minority employees. This contrasts with the 14 percent of nonminority businesses that reported their work force to consist of 75 to 100 percent minority employees. The percentage of minority employees in both Hispanic and nonminority businesses is summarized in Table 14.12.

No clear and consistent information is available, but what little research does exist indicates that Hispanic-owned businesses fail at a rate slightly higher than those of similar nonminority firms. There is some evidence that minority firms are burdened by higher debt structure, resulting in more problems, especially during recessions or tight money periods.

TABLE 14.9
HISPANIC AND NONMINORITY BUSINESS OWNERS ACROSS FOUR CHARACTERISTICS

	HISPANIC BUSINESS OWNERS (%)	NONMINORITY BUSINESS OWNERS (%)
College education	7	15
First-time entrepreneur	85	79
Management experience of 10 years or more	10	21
45 years of age or older	42	49

Source: United States Bureau of the Census, 1987, 10, 18, 37, 74.

TABLE 14.10
START-UP CAPITAL REQUIRED FOR HISPANIC AND NONMINORITY BUSINESS OWNERS

	NONE	$1–4,999	$5,000–9,999	$10,000–24,999	$25,000–49,999	$50,000–99,999	$100,000–249,000	$250,000 OR MORE
Hispanic Businesses	27%	37%	12%	11%	4%	2%	6%	4%
Nonminority Businesses	27%	34%	10%	11%	6%	3%	2%	6%

Source: United States Bureau of the Census, 1987, 82.
Note: 6 percent of Hispanic business owners and 6.4 percent of nonminority business owners did not respond.

TABLE 14.11
PROFIT AND LOSS FOR HISPANIC AND NONMINORITY BUSINESSES

	PROFIT									
	LESS THAN $5,000	$5,000–9,999	$10,000–19,999	$20,000–24,999	$25,000–29,999	$30,000–49,999	$50,000–74,999	$75,000–99,999	$100,000–249,000	$250,000 or More
Hispanic	26%	14%	12%	4%	2%	4%	2%	1%	1%	0.5%
Nonminority	27%	11%	11%	4%	3%	5%	2%	1%	2%	1%

	LOSS			
	LESS THAN $5,000	$5,000–9,999	$10,000–24,999	$25,000 OR MORE
Hispanic-Owned Businesses	11%	2%	1%	0.6%
Nonminority-Owned Businesses	12%	2%	1%	1%

Source: United States Bureau of the Census, 1987, 114.
Note: 18.9 percent of Hispanic businesses and 17 percent of nonminority businesses did not respond.

TABLE 14.12
MINORITY EMPLOYEES IN HISPANIC AND NONMINORITY BUSINESSES

	NO MINORITY EMPLOYEES	1–9%	10–24%	25–49%	50–74%	75–100%
Hispanic Businesses	11	2	4	5	11	67
Nonminority Businesses	65	6	6	5	4	14

Source: United States Bureau of the Census, 1987, 130.

✱ HISPANICS IN THE CORPORATE WORLD

With higher college graduation rates and the implementation of Affirmative Action programs since the 1970s, more and more Hispanics are succeeding in entering corporate management, but as yet there are very few of them at the highest managerial levels and in the board rooms. In its January/February 1996 issue, *Hispanic Business* magazine reported on the 20 largest companies for employment of Hispanic managers, illustrated by Table 14.13.

Hispanics that are in the corporate world, like women in the corporate world, have hit a "glass ceiling," an invisible barrier that has to date stopped their advancement up the corporate ladder. While a Hispanic, Roberto C. Goizueta, is the President and CEO of one of the world's largest corporations, *Hispanic Business* magazine has shown that in 1995 its Corporate Elite directory included only 217 executives at 118 *Fortune* 1,000 companies. Hispanics remain far below parity with their 10 percent of the

TABLE 14.13
RANKING THE 20 LARGEST CORPORATIONS
ANALYSIS OF EMPLOYMENT REPORTS FOR 18 OF THE 20 LARGEST U.S. COMPANIES
AS LISTED BY *FORTUNE* MAGAZINE.

RANK OVERALL	COMPANY	RANK BY PERCENT OF HISPANICS IN WORK FORCE	RANK BY PERCENT OF OFFICIALS/ MANAGERS WHO ARE HISPANIC	RANK BY PERCENT OF PROFESSIONALS WHO ARE HISPANIC	RANK BY PERCENT OF HISPANIC EMPLOYEES WHO ARE OFFICIALS/ MANAGERS	RANK BY PERCENT OF HISPANIC EMPLOYEES WHO ARE PROFESSIONALS	TOTAL SCORE
1	Citicorp	2	1	1	3	7*	14
2	Exxon	8	5	7	4	5	29
3	Texaco	9	9	3	8	3	32
4	Mobil	7	7*	5	9	6	34
5	Chevron	5	6	6	7	11	35
6	AT&T	10	7*	8	1	10	36
7*	IBM	11*	11	10	6	1	39*
7*	Sears	3	3	2	13	18	39*
9	PepsiCo	1	2	4	18	16	41
10	Philip Morris	6	10	9	14	14	53
11*	General Electric	14	13*	12	11	4	54*
11*	Prudential	11*	12	11	5	15	54*
13	Procter & Gamble	17*	13*	13*	2	12	57
14*	Du Pont	17*	16	13*	10	2	58*
14*	Kmart	4	4	18	15	17	58*
16	Ford	15*	17	17	12	7*	68
17	Chrysler	15*	18	13*	16	9	71
18	General Motors	13	13*	16	17	13	72

*Indicates tie in vertical column. Note: Total score is based on sum of rankings in five categories; each category carries equal weight. Wal-Mart Stores Inc. and State Farm Mutual Automobile Insurance Company did not release employment reports to HISPANIC BUSINESS. The top three companies in each category are denoted by special type.
Hispanic Business, January–February, 1996.

U.S. population. The Hispanic percent of the 15,000 senior executives at these 1,000 corporations is thus only 1.4 percent. White males hold 95 percent of these senior positions, while white females hold 2 percent and all minorities account for only 3 percent. Among the diverse industries in the *Fortune* 1,000, pharmaceuticals has the highest representations of Hispanic senior executives; this lead is followed by telecommunications. Other companies employing above the average of Hispanic senior executives are beverages, entertainment, toys/sports, and soaps and cosmetics. Table 14.14 shows the corporations with the most Hispanic senior executives.

In the rarified air of the corporate board room, Hispanics have barely arrived. According to the January/February 1996 issue of *Hispanic Business*, there are only 62 Hispanics serving on the boards of a total of 85 *Fortune* 1,000 corporations and their divisions or subsidiaries. Anheuser-Bush Companies Inc. is the corporation with the most Hispanics on its board: five. The following corporations have three Hispanics on their boards: Barnet Bank of South Florida, Sun Trust Banks of Atlanta, and Miami and the Public Services Company of New Mexico. Utility and finance companies are the industrial sectors that have companies with two Hispanic board members, most of these located in New Mexico and California. Three Hispanic individuals serve on the most boards, each with five directorships, according to the *Hispanic Business* survey: Katherine Ortega, the former Treasurer of the United States; Armando Codina, chairman of Codina Group Inc. in Miami, and Roberto C. Goizueta, CEO of the Coca-Cola Co.

Despite the relative absence of Hispanics from most of the major board rooms in the United States, Hispanic businessmen and corporate executives have made some major advances in the corporate world in the last two decades. Included among those historical landmarks in Hispanic business history are the following: In 1977, Carlos José Arboleya became the first Cuban president and CEO of a major bank in the United States—Barnet Banks of Miami. Thanks to Arboleya and other Cuban American businessmen and bankers, Miami has become a major banking center for Latin America. In 1979, Humberto Cabañas became the first Hispanic CEO of a major corporation in the hospitality industry when he assumed the position of CEO and founding president of Benchmark Hospitality Group in the Woodlands, Texas. He was also the first U.S. Hispanic president of the International Association of Conference Centers, from which he received a distinguished service award in 1988. In 1980, Frank Lorenzo became the first U.S. Hispanic to serve as the

TABLE 14.14
TOP COMPANIES OF THE CORPORATE ELITE

COMPANY	NUMBER OF EXECUTIVES
American Telephone & Telegraph (AT&T)	9
Xerox Corp.	8
Dole Food Co. Inc.	7
CoreStates Financial Corp.	5
SBC Communications Inc.	5
Turner Broadcasting System Inc.	5
Viacom International Inc.	5
Colgate-Palmolive Co.	4
Gannett Co. Inc.	4
Mattel Inc.	4
Motorola Inc.	4
Philip Morris Cos. Inc.	4
US WEST Inc.	4
Chrysler Corp.	4
Dayton Hudson Corp.	3
Dial Corp.	3
International Business Machines (IBM)	3
Johnson & Johnson	3
Knight-Ridder Inc.	3
McDonald's Corp.	3
Northrop Grumman Corp.	3
PepsiCo Inc.	3
Principal Financial Group	3
Schering-Plough Corp.	3
WMX Technologies Inc.	3

Note: No other company placed more than two executives on this year's list.
Hispanic Business, January–February, 1996.

president of a major national and international airline, Continental Airlines, headquartered in Houston, Texas. From 1986 to 1990, Lorenzo served as chairman and CEO of Continental Airlines. A graduate of the Harvard M.B.A. program, Lorenzo served as president and chairman of the board of Texas International Airlines (TII), from 1972 to 1980; TII became the holding company for Continental Airlines. In 1981, Roberto C. Goizueta became the first U.S. Hispanic to lead one of the largest corporations in the world, Coca-Cola, when he became the company's CEO and chairman of the board. One of the highest paid CEOs, if not the highest, in the United States, the Cuban-born Goizueta started out as a Coca-Cola bottler in Miami, after receiving his B.S. degree in engineering from Yale University in 1953. In 1989, Edgar J. Milán became the first New York Puerto Rican to serve as controller and vice president of one of the largest U.S. corporations, Tenneco Inc. Raised in New York City, where he received a degree in accounting from Hunter College, Milán rose in the ranks of the oil industry, serving in the United States, Canada, England, Peru, and Nicaragua. In 1990, Sosa and Associates, the San Antonio advertising agency founded and headed by Lionel Sosa, became the first Hispanic concern to be named Agency of the Year and the Hottest Agency in the Southwest by *Adweek* magazine. In 1989, Sosa and Associates had billings of $54.8 million. There is certainly room for more of these success stories of Hispanics in the world of business.

✳ PROMINENT HISPANICS IN BUSINESS

Deborah Aguiar-Vélez (1955-)

Born on December 18, 1955, in New York City, Aguiar received a B.S. degree in chemical engineering from the University of Puerto Rico in 1977 and a certificate from the University of Virginia Entrepreneurial Executive Institute in 1989. In her early career, she was a systems analyst for Exxon and then worked in the small-business division of the New Jersey Department of Commerce. After that she founded and was president of her own business, Sistemas Corporation. Her honors include selection in 1990 as the Outstanding Women Entrepreneur Advocate by American Women in Economic Development and selection for Coca-Cola commercials as a Hispanic woman entrepreneurial role model. Aguiar has served on the boards of the Hispanic Women's Task Force, the Hispanic Leadership Opportunity Program, and the New Jersey Women's Business Advisory Council, which she chaired from 1987 to 1988.

Linda Alvarado (1951-)

Raised in Albuquerque, New Mexico, Alvarado was a good student and an outstanding athlete in basketball, volleyball and soft ball in both high school and college. After graduating from Pomona College in California, she became a contract administrator for a California development company and learned all aspects of the construction business. After some formal education in blue printing and other skills necessary for construction, she and a partner founded the Martínez Alvarado Construction Management Corporation in 1974. In 1976, she bought out her partner and became the sole general contractor under the title of Alvarado Construction Inc. The company experienced great success in constructing high rise office structures, commercial buildings, airport hangars and a convention center. In 1993, Alvarado became a partner in the Colorado Rockies franchise, a new major league baseball team. As such, she became the first Hispanic team owner in the history of baseball in the United States, a sport that has always been important to Hispanics. In addition to running her construction business and helping to administer the baseball franchise, Alvarado is a member of the board of directors of several *Fortune* 500 corporations.

Gabriel Eloy Aguirre (1935-)

Born on January 12, 1935, in Akron, Ohio, Aguirre worked for SaniServ in Indianapolis in the service and sales divisions from 1957 to 1977; in 1977, he became the owner of the company. For his outstanding success with the company, he was named the 1987 Minority Entrepreneur of the Year by the president of the United States. Aguirre has been very active in the community, serving on numerous boards and as president of school boards and police commissions. Since 1988, he has been a member of the board of the U.S. Senate Task Force on Hispanic Affairs.

Carlos José Arboleya (1929-)

Born on February 1, 1929, in Havana, Cuba, Arboleya is a graduate of the University of Havana who developed his early career in banking as the Havana manager of the First National City Bank of New York. After the Cuban Revolution of 1959, he immigrated to the United States and worked at a number

Gabriel Eloy Aguirre.

Carlos José Arboleya.

of banks in Miami, moving up the ranks from clerk to bank administrator. By 1966, he was executive vice president of the Fidelity National Bank of South Miami; by 1973, the co-owner, president, and director of the Flagler Bank; and by 1977, president and CEO of the Barnett Banks of Miami. Since 1983, he has been vice chairman of the Barnett Bank of South Florida. Arboleya has remained active in the profession and the community, serving as vice president of the American Institute of Banking and on the boards of such organizations as the Inter-American Affairs Action Committee, the National Advisory Council for Economic Opportunity, the American Arbitration Association, and the Cuban American Foundation. Among his many honors are the American Academy of Achievement Gold Plate Award in 1974, the Horatio Alger Award of the American Schools and Colleges Association in 1976, and the American Red Cross Man of the Year Award in 1988.

Humberto Cabañas (1947–)

Hotel Management

Born on September 3, 1947, in Havana, Cuba, Cabañas received a B.S. degree in hotel and restau-

rant management from Florida International University in 1974 and went on to rise through the ranks at Sheraton, Doral, and Stouffer hotels until becoming the founding president and CEO of the Benchmark Hospitality Group in Woodlands, Texas, in 1979. Benchmark properties include the Woodlands Executive Conference Center and resort, the Woodlands Country Club, the Exxon Conference Center, the Tournament Players Golf Course, and the San Luis Resort Hotel on Galveston Island. He has been a president of the International Association of Conference Centers from which he received a Distinguished Service Award in 1988. Cabañas serves on the industry advisory committee for the Conrad Hilton School of Hotel and Restaurant Management of the University of Houston and is a past president of the International Association of Conference Centers.

Gilbert Cuéllar, Jr.

Restaurant Chain Executive

Cuéllar is the chairman and CEO of the 50-year-old restaurant chain founded by his family. Formerly known as El Chico Corporation, the Dallas-based chain is now Southwest Cafes and has, under Cuéllar's direction, expanded to various states under

Gilbert Cuéllar, Jr.

such local names as Cantina Laredo, Cuéllar's Cafe, Casa Rose, and El Chico Restaurants. First becoming associated with the corporation in 1970, he has served in various capacities, including manager of quality control, product research and development, and director of marketing research. In 1977, Campbell Taggart acquired the restaurant chain and Cuéllar enrolled at North Texas State University and received an M.B.A. degree. After founding various restaurants of his own, he and his father were able to repurchase El Chico Corporation in 1982. In 1986, Cuéllar was named chairman of the corporation.

Remedios Díaz-Oliver (1938–)

The president and CEO of one of southern Florida's top companies, Díaz-Oliver was born on August 22, 1938, in Cuba, the daughter of a hotel owner. Her early experience in business was fostered by her father who often took his daughter along with him on business trips around the island and to the United States and Spain. She obtained a Master's degree from Havana Business University and a Ph.D. in Education from the university of Havana. After becoming a wife and mother, she was jailed by the Communist regime in Cuba in 1961 for her protesting government mail inspections; on her release later that year, she immigrated to the United States with her husband and daughter. Her first job in the United States was working as an accounting clerk in the Emmer Glass company of Miami for $55 a week. Within a year she founded an international division for Emmer and took charge of exporting glass containers. In 1976, Díaz-Oliver and her husband Fausto founded American International Container with Frank H. Wheaton Jr., one of the most respected names in U.S. glass manufacturing. By 1991, American International Container was grossing $90 million in revenues and was listed thirty-third on the list of top privately-owned companies in southern Florida by the *Florida Business Journal*. In 1991, she founded All American Container with her husband and two children, which distributes packaging products and materials, including plastic and glass bottles for such companies as Coca-Cola. Pepsi, McCormick and Kraft. Her sales offices are located throughout South America and in London and Sydney.

Roberto C. Goizueta (1931–)

Beverage Company Executive

Born on November 18, 1931, in Havana, Cuba, Goizueta received a B.S. degree in chemical engineering in 1953 from Yale University. He began at the Coca-Cola Company as an assistant vice president of research in 1964; by 1981, he had become the chairman of the board and CEO of Coca-Cola, one of the world's largest corporations. Goizueta has been active in service nationally and internationally. He is the founding director of the Points of Light Initiative and sits on the boards of the Ford Motor Company and Eastman Kodak, among others. Since 1980, he has been a trustee of Emory University. Among his many honors are being chosen a Gordon Grand fellow of Yale University in 1984, the 1984 Herbert Hoover Humanitarian Award of the Boys Clubs of America, and the 1986 Ellis Island Medal of Honor.

Fredrick J. González (1949–)

Design Engineering Executive

Born on June 28, 1949, in Detroit, Michigan, González received a B.S. degree in engineering and an M.S. degree in architecture and urban planning from Princeton University in 1971 and 1972, respectively. After working for three years as an architect for Smith Himchman Gryllis Associates, in 1975 he and his father founded their own firm, González Design Engineering in Madison Heights, Michigan, for which he has served as CEO since 1977, when his

Roberto C. Goizueta.

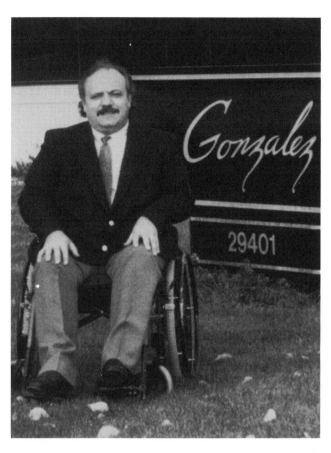

Fredrick J. González.

father died. In 1979, he also became the president of Semi-Kinetics, a printed circuit board assembly line in Laguna Hills, California. Since a 1968 automobile accident, González, who had been a high school football star, has been paralyzed from the waist down. Among his and his company's honors are being named by the White House as the National Minority Service Firm of the Year in 1975, selection as the 1989 Minority Businessman of the Year, and selection as the 1989 Minority Supplier of the Year by the National Minority Business Development Council. González participates on many boards, including the board of directors of the U.S. Hispanic Chamber of Commerce. González and his brother/partner, Gary, have been featured in full-page ads by General Motors as successful suppliers to the car company.

Frank A. Lorenzo (1940–)

Former Airline Company Executive

Born on May 19, 1940, in New York City, Lorenzo received a B.S. degree from Columbia University in 1961 and an M.B.A. degree from Harvard University in 1963. He began his career in air transportation as a financial analyst for Texas World Airlines from 1963 to 1965; and by 1966, he had founded and become chairman of his own company, Lorenzo Carney and Company. From 1972 to 1980 he served as president and chairman of Texas International Airlines, which eventually became a major national and international holding company for Continental Airlines, for which he served as president from 1980 to 1985, and then as chairman and CEO from 1986 to 1990. After developing the company into the world's largest carrier through the purchase of various other carriers, Lorenzo was embattled by strikes, rising costs, and competition, and the problems of deregulation, and he was eventually forced to resign.

Edgar J. Milán (1934–)

Controller

Born on November 23, 1934, in New York City, Mílan received a B.S. degree in accounting from Hunter College in 1957 and pursued additional courses toward an M.S. degree at the City College of New York. He rose through the ranks as a career accountant in oil companies, serving in the United States, Canada, England, Peru, and Nicaragua. After serving in a number of vice presidential positions in the financial divisions of Tenneco Oil, one of the

Edgar J. Milán.

largest U.S. corporations, Mílan was named vice president and controller in 1989. Mílan serves on a number of advisory boards, including those of Arte Público Press and the accounting programs for Texas Tech and Texas A & M Universities. Mílan was also an outstanding college basketball player; and in 1957, he was selected Hunter College Athlete of the Year; and in 1991, he was inducted into the Hunter College Athletic Hall of Fame.

Luis Nogales (1943-)

Known as one of the most outstanding Hispanic businessmen in the United States, Luis Nogales was born on October 17, 1943, in Madera, California, to migrant farm workers. His early years were spent picking crops in southern California, but he nevertheless was able to complete his education and go on to college and eventually graduate from Stanford Law School in 1969, whereupon he was hired by the university as an assistant to the president. He later went on to serve as a White House fellow and to travel to Europe and Asia in that capacity. Throughout his university education and his early career, Nogales was an advocate for Hispanic civil and educational rights. From 1973 to 1980, Nogales worked as vice president for Golden West Broadcasters and served on the board of directors of the Levi-Strauss corporation; he also served on the board of the Mexican American Legal Defense and Education Fund (MALDEF). In 1983, he assumed the position of executive vice president for United Press International (UPI), the second largest news agency in the world. Nogales resigned from UPI in 1985 and in 1987 became the president of the Univisión television network, a position which he kept for only one year. After that he continued his work in community projects and on the board of directors of Lucky Stores, Bank of California and Southern California Edison Company. In 1988, he became a member of the board of trustees of Stanford University.

Robert Ortega, Jr. (1947-)

Construction Company Executive

Born on February 1, 1947, in El Paso, Texas, Ortega received B.S. and M.S. degrees in civil engineering from the University of Texas at El Paso in 1970 and 1980, respectively. He worked as an engineer in the U.S. Public Health Service, the U.S. Bureau of Reclamation, and the El Paso Housing Department before founding Construction Management Associates in 1983. In 1988, his company was rated the fifth-fastest-growing Hispanic company in the United States by *Hispanic Business* magazine. In 1989, the company was named the Outstanding Small Business for the City of El Paso by the Small

Business Administration. In 1980, Ortega was named Young Engineer of the Year, and in 1989, Engineer of the Year by the Texas Society of Professional Engineers. He is a past president of the Texas Society of Civil Engineers and of the Associated Builders and Contractors.

Carlos D. Ramírez (1946-)

See Chapter 27.

Emyré Barrios Robinson (1926-)

See Chapter 10.

John Rodríguez (1958-)

Advertising and Public Relations

Born on August 9, 1958, in New York City, John Rodríguez is cofounder and president of AD One, an advertising and public relations firm in Rochester, New York. Rodríguez completed his bachelor's degree at the Rochester Institute of Technology, where he majored in advertising and photography. He continues his education by attending classes at local universities and is currently working toward a master's degree in communications. As a young entrepreneur, he has built his company, AD One, into a successful firm that specializes in international sales promotion, recruitment, and the Hispanic market. Their clients have included Eastman Kodak Company, Bausch and Lomb, Preferred Care, the University of Rochester, the Girl Scouts, Rochester City School District, and Mobil Chemical.

Oscar Rodríguez

Computers

Oscar Rodríguez was born and raised in San Antonio, Texas. He spent 17 years as a very successful entrepreneur in Boston, Massachusetts. He obtained his master's of business administration degree at Harvard University and then sold three successful computer-oriented companies. In 1985, after a highly successful business career, Rodríguez returned to San Antonio and, with Héctor Dávila, bought out a failing computer services company. The new company, Antares Development Corporation, assumed the computer support responsibility for 60 of San Antonio's most respected firms. By the end of 1988, the company had become one of the premier suppliers of computer services in San Antonio.

Eduardo G. Santiago (1949-)

Controller

Born on September 26, 1949, in Ponce, Puerto Rico, Santiago earned a B.S. degree in accounting from Baruch College in 1975 and a M.B.A. in finance from Pace University in 1979. He began his career as an accounting clerk for Guy Carpenter & Co. in 1969. He worked for American International Marine and for MacMillan until 1975, when he became the controller of Philip Morris International.

Lionel Sosa (1939-)

Advertising

Born on May 27, 1939, in San Antonio, Texas, Sosa became a graphic artist who developed a career in advertising, founding his own company, Sosart, in 1966. In 1974, he became a partner of Ed Yardang and Associates. In 1984, he founded Sosa and Associates, for which he serves as chairman and CEO. Sosa and Associates is the leading firm in handling national accounts targeted at Hispanic consumers. In 1990, *Adweek* magazine named Sosa and Associates the Agency of the Year and the Hottest Agency in the Southwest, with 1989 billings of $54.8 million. Sosa's clients include American Airlines, Anheuser-Busch, Burger King, Coca-Cola USA, Montgomery Ward, and Western Union. Among his many awards are the 1990 Entrepreneur of the Year, the 1989 Marketing Person of the Year Award, the 1989 Silver Award from the Public Relations Society of America, and the Gold ADDY from the American Advertising Foundation in 1988. Sosa is active in the community, participating on many local and national boards.

Jospeh A. Unanue (1926-)

Joseph A. Unanue took his father's company, Goya Foods Inc., and built it into the largest Hispanic-owned company in the United States. After his father's death in 1976, Unanue took over the chain that his father built from an importing business. Under his guidance, the company grew to sell more than 800 products. It's revenue rose to $453 million by 1992, a growth rate of some 12% annually. Unanue had refocused the company from principally serving Puerto Ricans and Cubans on the east coast of the United States to serving all Hispanics in the United States. The company then began importing and processing foods to cater specifically to Mexicans and Central Americans precisely at the time that these populations within the United States were experiencing their greatest growth. Despite this success, Goya has remained loyal to its initial customers and has been able to retain them even while faced with increasing competition from other Hispanic companies and mainstream corporations attempting to acquire a piece of the Hispanic market. While under Unanue the company has become one of the largest food pro-

Clifford Lane Whitehill.

cessors in the United States, Goya has remained a family-owned and operated; there are eight Unanues running the company across the U.S. today.

Clifford Lane Whitehill (1931-)

Corporate Attorney

Born on April 14, 1931, the son of Catalina Yarza and Clifford Whitehill, Whitehill earned a B.A. from Rice University in 1954, a LL.B. from the University of Texas, and a LL.M. from Harvard University in 1957 and 1958, respectively. He became a corporate attorney, working for various companies in Houston and New York until joining General Mills in Minneapolis as an attorney in 1962. He moved up the ranks to vice presidential positions and attained his present position of senior vice president, general counsel, and secretary in 1981. Among his honors is the 1988 Whitney North Seymour Sr. Award from the American Arbitration Society. Among the many boards and directorates on which Whitehill serves are the National Hispanic Scholarship Fund and the United Nations Association of the USA, both of which he directs.

References

Chipman, Donald E. *Spanish Texas, 1519–1821*. Austin: University of Texas Press, 1992.

Fontana, Bernard L. *Entrada: The Legacy of Spain and Mexico in the United States*. Albuquerque: University of New Mexico Press, 1994.

Henderson, Ann L., and Gary R. Mormino, eds. *Spanish Pathways in Florida*. Sarasota, FL: Pineapple Press, 1991.

Kanellos, Nicolás, with Cristelia Pérez. *Chronology of Hispanic American History*. Detroit: Gale Research, 1995.

Rosaldo, Renato, Robert A. Calvert, and Gustav L. Seligmann, *Chicano: The Evolution of a People*. Minneapolis: Winston Press, 1973.

Sheridan, Thomas E. *Los Tucsonenses: The Mexican Community in Tucson*. Tucson: University of Arizona Press, 1986.

Simmons, Helen, and Cathryn A. Hoyt, eds. *Hispanic Texas: A Historical Guide*. Austin: University of Texas Press, 1992.

Slatta, Richard W. *Cowboys of the Americas*. New Haven: Yale University Press, 1990.

"Special Report on Corporate America." *Hispanic Business* (January/February 1996).

Tardiff, Joseph C., and L. Mpho Mabunda, eds. *Dictionary of Hispanic Biography*. Detroit: Gale Research, 1996.

"The 100 Fastest Growing Hispanic Companies." *Hispanic Business* (August 1993).

"The Fastest Growing Hispanic-Owned Companies." *Hispanic Business* (January 1994).

Nicolás Kanellos

⑮

Labor and Employment

✳ Hispanics in Organized Labor ✳ Immigration and Migration ✳ Hispanic Employment in Industry
✳ Federal Employment Programs and Laws ✳ Youth Employment ✳ Women's Employment
✳ Government Programs ✳ Income, Poverty, and Unemployment

Hispanics are the fastest-growing major group in the labor force of the United States. Between 1980 and 1988, the number of Hispanics in the work force increased by 48 percent, representing 20 percent of U.S. employment growth. The employment of Hispanic women during this period increased by 56 percent, or more than two and one-half times the rate of other women.

Between 1980 and 1990, Hispanics increased from 6.1 percent to slightly more than 9 percent of the nation's work force. Their youth relative to other groups in the work force and continued high rates of immigration indicate that Hispanics will continue to increase their representation in the nation's work force in the foreseeable future.

Although the numbers have increased rapidly, conditions of employment for Hispanics have deteriorated during the 1980s. Many worker protections and benefits have been lost, incomes have declined in absolute terms, and the gap between Hispanics and whites has widened sharply.

In the final quarter of 1990, the median weekly earnings of Hispanic men were $331, compared with $370 for black men and $502 for white men. Hispanic women's weekly earnings were $283, compared with $313 for black women and $363 for white women. This means that white women and black men earned 74 percent, black women 62 percent, Hispanic men 66 percent, and Hispanic women 56 percent of that earned by white men. By March 1991, unemployment among Hispanics had reached 10.3 percent, roughly double the rate for whites.

Federal policy is partly responsible for the declining conditions, as the strategies of the Reagan-Bush era have resulted in the government's altering its priorities and shirking its earlier responsibilities. It has consciously adopted employment policies fa-

voring large employers and higher income groups at the expense of the poor, particularly blacks and Hispanics. Employer abuses have even extended to child labor. In the four-year period from 1986 to 1990, child labor violations increased by 128 percent.

Brief History of Hispanics in the Labor Force

Between the late 1500s and the incorporation of northern Mexico into the United States at the end of the Mexican-American War in 1848, workers of Mexican birth who resided in the present-day Southwest worked largely in agricultural tasks. Most of them held land on which they grew and raised most of their sustenance, which they often supplemented by working for others. As they lost their lands after the war, the majority of them became wage laborers. They were employed as field hands, cowboys, railroad maintenance workers, ditch-diggers, and miners.

The movement of Mexican American workers out of rural and agricultural tasks was relatively slow. As their numbers gradually increased in cities and towns, they found employment in service and manufacturing occupations. Yet, in contrast to the overall trend among whites, they experienced a marked downward mobility during the last half of the nineteenth century.

Another Hispanic group also appeared in the late nineteenth century. A small Cuban population migrated to Florida, partly in response to the independence movement against Spain, as exiles, revolutionaries, and workers. Applying skills they learned in Cuba, they were engaged largely in the tobacco industry, as field owners and workers, and in cigar factories of the State.

A new phase of the labor history of Hispanics in

César Chávez exhorting people to start a new grape boycott in 1986.

the United States began around the turn of the twentieth century, when employers in the Southwest, and soon afterward in the Midwest, began to recruit workers from the Mexican border. Their efforts set in motion a movement that has shaped migration patterns from Mexico throughout the twentieth century. Using labor contractors and other recruiters, they brought in workers from Mexico to perform largely unskilled, low-paying tasks. This planned labor migration quickly stimulated another pattern of individual migration that took on an independent character of its own and outpaced the rate of migration by labor recruitment. During the early twentieth century, the majority of Hispanic workers in the United States were Mexican immigrants and their children. In sheer numbers, the new arrivals soon overwhelmed the older Mexican-descent residents in most parts of the Southwest and Midwest, except New Mexico.

Mexico offered employers a reservoir of workers because of its high level of unemployment and very low incomes. The wage differential between Mexico and the United States throughout the century has always been very sharp. At present, an unskilled wage worker in the United States can earn approximately ten times as much as in Mexico, although the differences are largely offset by much higher prices for food, rent, and other living expenses in the United States.

In the early twentieth century, Mexicans were recruited largely for agricultural, railroad maintenance, and mining enterprises. Smaller numbers found employment in domestic and other service occupations, and in manufacturing. Mexican immigrant families often worked as a single unit in cotton, sugar beet, and fruit and vegetable planting, cultivation, and harvesting operations, especially in the Southwest. In other occupations, including mining, manufacturing, and most service occupations, adult workers were the rule, as child labor laws were harder to evade, restricting the employment of children.

As a result of the patterns of labor recruitment that evolved in the early twentieth century, cities and towns on and near the Mexican border, and eventually throughout the Southwest and in many Midwestern settings, developed large labor pools of Mexican workers who were available to perform un-

Mexican women working at a commercial tortilla factory in the 1930s.

A cotton picker in 1933. (Photograph by Dorothea Lange.)

skilled, low-paying jobs throughout the year. Characteristically, the Mexican workers found employment largely in seasonal tasks and experienced high rates of unemployment and frequent changes in employers. Although many of them brought skills from Mexico, few of the tasks they performed in the United States required high levels of training or English-language proficiency to perform.

The Spanish-American War in 1898 resulted in the incorporation of Puerto Ricans into the work force of the United States. As continental-based corporations quickly gained control of the best agricultural lands in Puerto Rico, they displaced many small landholders, offering them the alternatives of wage work in the fields or unemployment. By 1930, four U.S. corporations controlled about three-fifths of sugar production in Puerto Rico, and the sugar industry was responsible for more than two-thirds of all employment on the Island.

Because of World War I, Puerto Ricans were made citizens of the United States in 1917. The war also stimulated a modest migration from the island to New York City and environs, where the new arrivals worked in textiles and other low-wage industrial and service occupations.

Conditions of employment for all workers, but Mexicans in particular, deteriorated rapidly with the onset of the Great Depression in 1929. Immigration to the United States virtually ceased, and return migration to Mexico increased sharply. Mexican workers were singled out by employers and quickly fired or laid off, particularly in and near urban centers in both the Southwest and the Midwest.

In many cities, government agencies and employer groups collaborated to conduct organized repatriation drives that involved publicity and propaganda campaigns intent on convincing the English-speaking public that Mexicans were taking jobs away from U.S. citizens. Although the propagandists argued that repatriation would provide employment to unemployed citizens, most Mexicans had already lost their jobs. The underlying motive in the campaigns was to remove unemployed Mexicans from public welfare rolls. The intensity of the drives varied in different locations, but they were partly responsible for the reduction of the Mexican-descent population in the United States by about 25 percent during the early years of the Great Depression. Almost all the formal repatriation drives ended with the election victory of President Franklin D. Roosevelt and the ascendancy of the Democratic party in Congress in 1933. Unlike the Republicans, they did not consider Mexican workers a major cause of the depression.

In 1940 and 1941, the war in Europe stimulated production, and the demand for labor in the United States rose sharply. Employers wanted even more workers from Mexico, but the Mexican government opposed their efforts, concerned that another humiliating repatriation campaign might again occur at the time of the first economic downturn after the war. A compromise was reached in 1942 when employers convinced the U.S. government to make an agreement with the Mexican government to initiate a formal program of recruitment of contract laborers from Mexico for agricultural and railroad work. This new program included guaranteed minimum wages, worker protection, and an organized procedure for workers to return to Mexico on termination of the contract. The Mexican Labor Agreement was popularly called the Bracero Program. The war also stimulated labor migration from Mexico and the Caribbean to the United States via other formal programs and informal recruitment mechanisms.

World War II hastened changes in the employment profile of Hispanic workers in the United States. The agricultural industry, which was the major single employer prior to the Great Depression, had been declining in relative terms throughout the century. It peaked in absolute numbers shortly after

Mexican mine workers in the early 1900s.

the end of World War II. With the onset of the war, employment for Hispanics expanded more rapidly in several areas of manufacturing and in the services. Hispanic workers continued to concentrate in unskilled and semiskilled employment, largely in extractive agriculture, mining, and unskilled production tasks, especially as operatives, and in services.

The labor demands of World War II also stimulated a major wave of migration of Puerto Rican workers to the United States, largely through the auspices of Operation Bootstrap, a program initiated by the Puerto Rican government in 1944. Its major concern was to encourage industrialization in Puerto Rico and thereby diminish unemployment on the island. To further accomplish its goal of reducing the number of unemployed, it promoted a program of labor migration to the United States that involved arranging for labor recruiters to visit the island and also entailed working with airline companies to arrange for cheap flights from Puerto Rico to New York City. The labor migration program was aimed mostly at securing employment in urban locations, but as part of the plan the Puerto Rican Department of Labor also devised arrangements with agricultural employers to hire seasonal agricultural work-

ers under contract. Most of the agricultural workers went to eastern seaboard locations between Florida and New England to work in fruit and vegetable harvesting and canning operations. During the heyday of Operation Bootstrap, a net migration of at least 100,000 workers came to the United States from Puerto Rico each year, seeking permanent residence and employment principally in manufacturing and service industries.

A third phase of labor migration to the United States began in the 1960s, when the established patterns of movement from Mexico and Puerto Rico to the United States were modified, and migration from other countries increased. The Bracero Program ended in 1964, and after a brief decline in immigration, workers from Mexico increasingly arrived to work under the auspices of the H-2 Program of the Immigration and Nationality Act of 1952, as well as for family unification purposes or as undocumented workers. Workers from Puerto Rico continued to migrate to the United States, most often without promises of employment, but their migration at this time was increasingly offset by a massive return migration to Puerto Rico.

Another feature of this later labor migration has

Puerto Rican garment workers in New York City.

been the inclusion of people from a much wider range of countries in Latin America, and with a greater diversity of working backgrounds. Whereas Mexicans and Puerto Ricans continue to migrate for the most part as unskilled, semiskilled, or skilled workers, immigrants from other parts of the Caribbean and Central and South America have a wide range of backgrounds, including business and professional. This is particularly true of Cubans, the third most numerous Hispanic group in the United States. Their major wave of immigration occurred following the victory of the Cuban Revolution in 1959, and it included many prominent professionals and businesspeople. Later waves of Cuban immigrants were not as prosperous. The highly publicized Mariel boatlift in 1980 included many individuals from very poor, unskilled backgrounds, and with a lack of adequate job training. Many of them have had great difficulty becoming incorporated into the work regimen of the United States.

✳ HISPANICS IN ORGANIZED LABOR

As a predominantly working people, Hispanics have long been involved in efforts to organize as workers. One of their earliest groups, the Caballeros de Labor (Knights of Labor), was active in the Southwest in the late nineteenth century. Modeled after the American organization by the same name, Knights of Labor, its major stronghold was in New Mexico. It was never formally chartered, and it was more interested in land loss to recently arriving whites than labor issues. Other important cases of labor organizing in the late nineteenth century included Mexican cowboys in Texas and Cuban cigar workers in Florida.

During the late nineteenth and early twentieth centuries, a much greater number of Hispanic workers organized their own *mutualistas*, or mutual aid societies. These organizations engaged in social activities and provided for basic needs of workers, including insurance and death benefits for members. Mutualistas functioned largely as self-help organizations and did not threaten employers, which helps explain their greater success than unions. In the early twentieth century, a plethora of mutualistas appeared, especially among groups of recent immigrants, who were encouraged by the local Mexican consular officials. They continued to represent the most widespread form of worker organization.

Apart from the mutualistas, labor organizing among Hispanics in the late nineteenth and early twentieth centuries was hindered by several factors. Hispanics were concentrated geographically in largely antiunion settings in the South and Southwest. They also faced hostility and discrimination because of societal attitudes, which often portrayed them as taking jobs away from white workers. The major labor organization in the nation, the American Federation of Labor (AFL), tended to be craft-exclusive and structurally not interested in the participation of largely unskilled Hispanic workers. More important, the AFL itself could not resolve internally the nativism and racism pervasive in American society that often led it and its local unions to adopt exclusionary policies. These problems severely reduced Hispanic participation in organized labor and resulted in significant organizing efforts outside the mainstream labor federation.

In the early twentieth century, union organizing among Hispanic workers increased in many areas. The most notable efforts took place in agriculture, which was still the most important single occupation. Most organizing took place under the auspices of independent Mexican unions, while in some cases there were either independent interethnic unions or multiethnic organizations, often with support from the radical Industrial Workers of the World. Railroad and other urban workers joined together for brief periods under the leadership of independent or

Socialist organizations and, occasionally, the AFL. Many miners formed union organizations with the support and encouragement of the Western Federation of Miners in the early years of the twentieth century.

The most concentrated labor activity among the Spanish-speaking under the flag of the United States took place in Puerto Rico, led by the Federación Libre de los Trabajadores (Workers Labor Federation), or FLT, formed shortly before the turn of the century. In 1901, it affiliated with the American Federation of Labor, which broke from its more common policy of exclusivism toward non-whites. It accepted Puerto Rican workers because of its concern that they could enter freely into the United States and compete in the labor market and because of its fear of being overshadowed by rival organizations that also appeared in Puerto Rico. Important and widespread strikes in the sugar cane fields occurred in 1905 and 1906, and even larger ones took place in 1915 and 1916. After the early years of the century, however, the FLT organizing efforts turned more from the fields to the political arena.

Following a low point during the 1920s, labor organizing among Hispanic workers reached new peaks during the Great Depression. Independent organizations not affiliated with mainstream organized labor were most active and more typically composed of independent Mexican groups, Socialists, and members of the Communist party. In the later 1930s, leaders in the newly formed Congress of Industrial Organizations (CIO) also exhibited interest in organizing unskilled workers, and the CIO participated in the famous pecan shellers' strike in San Antonio in 1938, involving mostly young Mexican and Mexican American women. Organizers Emma Tennayuca and Manuela Solis Seger gained attention in Texas at that time and remained active in labor for many years afterward.

Organizing and strikes in the 1930s also occurred among mining, industrial, and agricultural workers throughout the country. Mexican farm workers in California were particularly active throughout the decade. Their efforts were highlighted by the Central Valley cotton strike of 1933, in which several groups of independent Mexican union organizers and radicals offered support. The AFL considered these activities a serious challenge to its dominance, and in many occupations it permitted the formation of local unions for the first time to attract Mexican workers into its fold.

In Puerto Rico, workers—upset with what they considered a sellout agreement between the FLT and U.S. owners—who belonged to the Association of Sugar Producers staged a massive but unsuccessful

Unemployed workers waiting in line at a relief office during the Depression.

spontaneous strike in 1933–34 to protest the arrangement. Their strike was the beginning of a long and protracted struggle against traditional FLT leadership that led to a sharp decline in the AFL-affiliated organization.

The turbulence of the 1930s reflected a sharp increase in expressions of sympathy toward unionism and unions among Hispanic workers. Much of the support had been latent but untapped until that time. Immigrants from Mexico frequently had strong union sympathies because of their earlier experiences before they arrived in the United States. Yet, traditional unions made only partial inroads into the Hispanic working population during the decade, hindered by continued employment discrimination, the success of employer efforts to pit workers against each other, and divisions within organized labor.

World War II served as a partial brake to direct labor organizing among Hispanic workers. But progressive elements within organized labor remained active, particularly in the struggle to eliminate many of the statutory forms of employment discrimination that Hispanics and other workers continually faced. Their efforts contributed to the formation of the Fair Employment Practices Committee (FEPC) in 1941. The FEPC investigated discrimination throughout the country by private companies with government contracts. Over a third of its cases in the Southwest involved Mexicans. Despite the efforts of President Truman, the FEPC was terminated at the end of World War II. It stands as an important predecessor to the corrective legislation and administrative bodies formed in the 1960s, particularly the Equal Employment Opportunity Commission.

Unionization among Hispanic workers increased rapidly in the 1940s and 1950s, as Hispanic workers and sympathizers within both the AFL and CIO struggled for reforms that permitted them equal access and fair treatment. In many local unions they formed their own caucuses to demand representation and changes in discriminatory procedures by the union hierarchy and to encourage the union to challenge discriminatory practices by employers. They demonstrated union loyalty, sympathy, and a class-consciousness reinforced by their work experiences and treatment in the workplace. During this period they participated in many notable strikes, perhaps the best known of which was the "salt of the earth" strike by miners in Silver City, New Mexico, led by the International Mine, Mill and Smelter Workers Union between 1950 and 1953. The efforts of the National Farm Labor Union, later called the National Agricultural Workers Union, to organize in California during the 1940s and 1950s were also noteworthy. Union leader Ernesto Galarza demonstrated keen insight as a union leader, scholar, and role model for a later generation of Chicano activists.

In Puerto Rico, the independent Confederación de Trabajadores Generales, or CGT, formed in 1940, but it quickly affiliated with the CIO. It soon replaced the Federación Libre de los Trabajadores (FLT) as the major labor organization on the island. Through its close links to the government, it attained its greatest influence and membership during the 1940s and 1950s.

Among Hispanics, a number of independent unions again began to form in both Puerto Rico and in the continental United States. The most notable was the National Farm Workers Association in California, led by César Chávez. It began as an independent organization in 1962 and became part of the AFL-CIO in 1966. It is now known as the United Farmworkers of America. During its numerous strikes and boycotts of table grapes, wines, and lettuce, it popularized many tactics involving ethnic alliances, community organizing, and a focus on protecting the environment that suggest alternative organizing strategies for organized labor in the future. Another creative venture, The East Los Angeles Community

Union (TELACU), was formed in 1971 as the result of cooperative efforts between the United Auto Workers and community organizers in East Los Angeles to build a "community" union.

Union-organizing activity in the United States peaked in the 1950s. From the early 1960s through the 1970s, the number of union members in the nation increased, though at a much slower rate than overall employment. The decrease in the rate of unionization during this period resulted from the reduction of jobs in highly unionized sectors, the growth of employment in traditionally nonunion occupations, the lack of vigilance of union leadership, increasingly sophisticated antiunion activities among employers and hostile government policy not enforcing protective labor legislation.

From the beginning of the Reagan Presidency in 1981 until 1985, union membership fell rapidly while total employment rose. Between 1985 and 1990, union membership declined more slowly, while total employment continued to rise. The decline in the 1980s is due to factors unfavorable to unions during the past generation, coupled with the most hostile federal government policy toward labor organizing and unions since the 1920s.

Unionization levels vary according to geography and occupation. Rates are highest in the Northeast and Midwest, and lowest in the South and Southwest, where Hispanic workers are most concentrated. In 1989, unionization in the public sector stood at 37 percent of workers, compared with 12 percent in private industry. It seems that private employers had a greater ability than the government to thwart worker organization despite the more rigid laws restricting labor organizing in the public sector. In the private arena, the more highly unionized sectors include transportation and public utilities at 32 percent, construction and manufacturing at 22 percent, and mining at 18 percent. In other major areas of private employment, union membership ranged from only 1 to 6 percent.

Union membership in 1990 was 16.1 percent of the working population over age 15, reflecting the continued decline over the past three decades. Unionization stood at 20 percent for men and 13 percent for women. By ethnicity, it was 22 percent among blacks, 16 among whites, and 15 percent among Hispanics. Among Hispanic men, 18 percent belonged to unions, compared to 20.8 percent of white men and 27.5 percent of black men. Among women, 14.2 percent of Hispanics, compared with 14 percent of whites and 21.2 percent of blacks, were union members.

Union benefits typically include better working conditions; a greater range of such benefits as health care, vacation, and leave policy; worker protection;

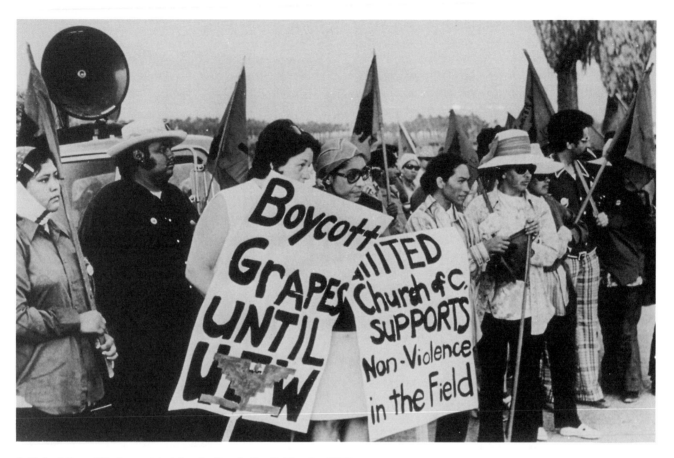

A United Farm Workers picket line in Coachella, California, 1973.

and higher wages. In 1990, union members earned an average of $420 per week, compared with $276 for nonunion members.

In 1991, there were approximately 1.3 million Hispanic union members. Although there are many union officers, vice presidents and directors, there are only two Hispanic presidents or directors among the 88 unions of the AFL-CIO: Arturo Rodríguez of the United Farm Workers (who succeeded César Chávez upon his death in 1993) and Dennis Rivera of the National Health and Human Services Employees Union, with 117,000 members. In 1973, the Labor Council of Latin American Advancement (LCLAA) formed to promote the interests of Hispanics within organized labor.

✳ IMMIGRATION AND MIGRATION

Since the late 1960s, two major factors affecting immigration to the United States have become clear: an increase in the rate of undocumented immigration and a shift from Europe to Asia as the predominant source of immigration. Despite annual fluctuations, Latin America, dominated by Mexico, has maintained its proportionate contribution, while it has increased its total contribution of immigrants to the United States substantially, both in legal and undocumented immigration.

In the period from 1955 to 1964, 50.2 percent of all legal immigrants to the United States were from Europe, with rates declining to 10.1 percent in 1988. Immigration from Asia, meanwhile, increased from 7.7 percent during 1955–64 to 41.1 percent in 1988. Immigration from the Americas during this period increased from 41.1 percent to 44.3 percent. In 1989, immigration from the Americas rose to 61.4 percent. Of the major countries, Mexico accounted for 37.1 percent of total documented immigration to the United States, the next highest number of immigrants being from El Salvador, 5.3 percent, the Philippines, 5.2 percent, Vietnam, 3.5 percent, Korea, 3.1 percent, and China, 3.0 percent.

Between 1985 and 1989, immigration accounted for 2.7 percent of the nation's net population growth, with rates varying from 1.8 percent of whites, 2.1 percent of blacks, 15.5 percent of Hispanics, and 29.7 percent of the increase for other races.

Several formal and informal programs have been established to encourage immigration of workers to the United States. The best-known forms of organized labor recruitment have involved agricultural workers from Mexico and Puerto Rico. These include the mechanisms in the Bracero Program and Operation Bootstrap. Labor recruitment by the U.S. Farm Placement Service to encourage labor migration for temporary seasonal employment has also influenced permanent settlement patterns. The H-2 Program within the Immigration and Nationality Act of 1952, as amended by the 1986 Immigration Reform and Control Act of 1986 (IRCA), continues to guide immigration patterns to the United States.

Immigration from Mexico, Central and South America, and the Caribbean has also been encouraged by labor recruiters and by informal networks that link individual families and communities in Latin America and the United States together.

Internal migration has greatly affected the population patterns of Hispanics within the United States. The most general patterns of migration include the dispersal of Mexicans from their historic concentrations in the Southwest to the Midwest, the Pacific Northwest, and recently to Florida and the East Coast; the spread of Puerto Ricans beyond New York to other areas of the country; and the relocation of Cubans to places other than Miami. Most of this migration has been through informal mechanisms, established at the level of individuals and families, and by word of mouth.

The major net flows of Hispanics within the United States are from the Northeast and Midwest to Florida, Texas, and California; from New York to neighboring states in the Northeast; and from California to neighboring states in the West. Cuban Americans are becoming increasingly concentrated at somewhat higher levels in Florida, while Central and South Americans are becoming more concentrated in California and New York. People of Mexican origin are tending to disperse from the Southwest, while Puerto Ricans are moving away from their center of concentration in New York City.

The total impact of migration and immigration in the 1970s and 1980s has been twofold. In absolute numbers, Hispanics have dispersed to a greater number of states and in wider areas within those states. In proportionate terms, they have concentrated at somewhat higher rates in the states already having large Hispanic populations. In 1970, 82 percent of the Hispanic population of the nation lived in nine states, with the proportion rising to 86 percent in 1990. The major recipients of Hispanic immigrants are California, Texas, and New York, and to a lesser degree Florida, Illinois, and New Jersey.

Hispanics born in the United States or residing in the country many years are more likely to migrate than are recent immigrants, who typically know less about the country, are less familiar with English, and generally of lower socioeconomic status. The recent immigrants are more likely to concentrate in ethnic enclaves for social and economic support.

Immigration remains an important factor accounting for the expansion of the labor force in the United States. The rates of immigration in the 1980s approached the levels of the early 1900s. Legal immigration during the first decade of the century reached 8.8 million, while during the 1980s 6.3 million immigrants were granted permanent residence. The immigrants are overwhelmingly young and in search of employment, and Hispanic immigrants continue to account for more than 40 percent of the total.

The Bracero Program

The term *bracero*, (from the Spanish *brazo*, meaning arm) applied to day laborers, generally; is sometimes used to refer to any Mexican worker in the United States under legal auspices. In this sense it includes workers entering the country under the H-2 Program of the Immigration and Nationality Act of 1952 and the H-2A Program of the Immigration Reform and Control Act of 1986, as well as to Mexican

A scene from the Bracero Program.

commuters often referred to as "green carders." "*Bracero*" is also occasionally used to refer to any unskilled Mexican workers brought into the United States.

The most popular use of "*bracero*" applies to the temporary Mexican agricultural and railroad workers first brought into the United States under contract in 1942 as an emergency measure to meet the temporary labor shortage of World War II. These braceros were an important part of the nation's agricultural labor force for almost a generation afterward. They dominated the harvest labor force in many parts of the Southwest and Midwest, particularly in sugar beets, cotton, pickles, tomatoes, and several other vegetable crops.

The Bracero Program, also referred to as the Mexican Farm Labor Supply Program and the Mexican Labor Agreement, began as a bilateral agreement between the governments of Mexico and the United States. It was given congressional sanction in 1943 as Public Law 45. Both governments considered it an important part of the Mexican contribution to the war effort.

The program was very popular among agricultural employers, who quickly organized and lobbied

A migrant work camp.

Congress to ensure its continuation beyond the end of the war. They were able to extend it temporarily several times, claiming a shortage of able and willing workers in the United States. Opponents of the Bracero Program, however, were able to reduce the scale of bracero employment in the late 1940s by demonstrating sufficient domestic worker availability. The outbreak of the Korean War in 1950, nevertheless, thwarted their efforts. In response to labor demands stemming from the war, agricultural employers convinced Congress in 1951 to pass Public Law 78, which renewed and expanded the program. On behalf of organized farm employers, the legislature passed several temporary extensions until 1964.

At the peak of the program in the late 1950s, the United States admitted more than 400,000 contract workers each season, almost twice as many as the number entering the country during the entire wartime emergency from 1942 to 1947.

The program was anathema to Mexican Americans and labor groups, who eventually gathered convincing evidence that, despite contract guarantees, braceros were not protected against abuses by employers and labor contractors, their working conditions were not adequate, and they frequently were not paid the wages guaranteed them by contract. The opposition also demonstrated the program had an adverse effect on wages and working conditions of domestic workers and stifled unionization efforts not only in agriculture, but also in southwestern industry. The struggle against the program in the 1950s focused largely on its adverse effects, seeking reforms requiring employer compliance with contract guarantees and permitting braceros joining unions. This effort, nevertheless, failed, convincing opposition later in the decade to conduct an all-out attack on the program. Ultimately a combined group of labor union representatives, Mexican American groups, religious and civic organizations, and their allies

A field worker in the Bracero Program.

The interior of a migrant labor shack.

gained the support of a more pro-labor Democratic administration and obtained Congressional termination of the temporary program in 1964.

Since 1964, employer groups in agriculture have initiated several efforts in Congress to pass new and modified versions of the Bracero Program by hiring temporary seasonal contract workers from Mexico. As of 1991, none of their efforts have succeeded.

Termination of Public Law 78 was an important victory for Mexican American and labor groups and helped pave the way for a flurry of labor organizing efforts in agriculture in the late 1960s.

The Maquiladoras

The abolition of the Bracero Program in 1964 demanded greater efforts by the Mexican government to relieve its own unemployment via industrialization. The most important element of its border industrialization program is the *maquiladora* (assembly plant) program, initiated in 1965. Mexico found industrialists and politicians in the United States very interested in the industrialization program. Mexico hoped that it could raise the standard of living in the northern border region, while both the

U.S. and Mexican governments were concerned about the possible negative political and economic consequences of leaving hundreds of thousands of Mexican workers stranded on the border without employment when the Bracero Program was ended. Industrialists were eager to reap the benefits offered by tax and tariff breaks and by the availability of unemployed and underemployed workers in Mexico.

The central feature of the plan established "twin plants" on both sides of the Mexico-U.S. border. It also set up a duty-free zone which permits industrialists in the United States to ship unfinished goods to Mexico under bond for partial assembly or completion. The goods are then returned duty free to the "twin plant" on the U.S. side, to complete the manufacturing process. In the early years of the program, about two-thirds of the products involved in the program were electric and electronic goods. As the program expanded in the 1970s and 1980s, the range of products expanded rapidly. By 1987, electric and electronic goods represented only about 35 percent of the total; textiles, clothing, and shoes, 18 percent; furniture, 10 percent; transportation equipment (including car motors), 9 percent; and a range of other goods, 28 percent.

The scale of production in the maquiladora industry also grew impressively. In 1966, it comprised 57 plants with about 4,000 workers. By 1979, it had about 540 plants hiring 120,000 workers, and by 1986 there were 844 plants employing 242,000 workers. By 1990, there were more than 1,000 plants employing about 450,000 workers. It is estimated that by 1995 there will be at least 1,500 plants with more than one million workers engaged in the program.

The maquiladora program in its actual operation is not at all as it was initially conceived. Its original intent was to alleviate the unemployment of male workers stranded at the end of the Bracero Program. Yet, the work force in the maquiladoras from the beginning has been approximately 85 percent female, mostly teenage women with very high rates of turnover. In sum, the program does not offer steady employment or work to unemployed men.

Another discrepancy is that the program was initially restricted to a 12.5-mile-wide strip along the Mexican-U.S. border. A 1972 amendment, however, permitted its expansion into the Mexican interior. As a result, plants are now located throughout northern and central Mexico.

Still yet another flaw in the original plan is that the "twin plant" concept never became operational. While the production phase was conducted in the Mexican plants, the "plants" on the U.S. side were essentially warehouses. Like their counterparts in Mexico, the operations in the United States offered low-wage, unskilled employment. The maquiladora program in effect, thus, became a runaway shop taking advantage of cheap Mexican labor and exemption from tariffs.

U.S. companies involved in maquiladora operations assert that the program enables them to produce in Mexico rather than transfer their operations to Asia. Yet, during the 1980s, Japanese industrialists took advantage of the maquiladoras to send greater amounts of raw materials to Mexico to have them finished, then shipped duty free into the United States. This led to a storm of protest in the United States, because, as Representative Duncan Hunter complained, "the Japanese can essentially use the program simply as a conduit into American markets without conferring benefits on American businessmen." In their discussion of the maquiladora program, very few politicians have considered the adverse impact on the much larger group of workers in the United States continuously displaced by the program.

The North American Free Trade Agreement (NAFTA) went into effect on January 1, 1994. Prior to its going into effect, various mechanisms were insisted upon by the U.S. Congress as well as trade unions and environmental groups to regulate the abuses that have characterized the maquiladoras to this date: the relocation of factories attempting to avoid unions in the U.S., abuses of workers and degradation of the environment under Mexico's more lax laws. Whether the new regulations and American observers as watchdogs will succeed in improving labor and environmental standards in Mexico is still being debated. What is certain is that with the economic downturn and crisis in the values of the peso in Mexico, following the NAFTA pact, the maquiladoras are experiencing an even greater boom.

Although supporters of the Free Trade Agreement maintain that it expands the size of markets in both Mexico and the United States, the sharp wage differential between Mexico and the United States makes it very difficult for Mexicans to afford to purchase the goods produced for export to the United States. In terms of worker protection, environmental damage, and the threat to the unity of Hispanic and Latin American workers on both sides of the border, the maquiladora program and the Free Trade Agreement pose even greater threats than the Bracero Program.

Migrant Farm Labor

A migrant worker is a person employed at a job temporarily or seasonally and who may or may not have a permanent residence in another community, state, or nation. It is a misconception to portray farm workers solely as migrants or Hispanics, or to portray all migrant workers as farm workers. Migrants comprise only a small portion of the total of the ethnically diverse farm labor force of the United States. Seasonal migrant workers are employed in a wide range of occupations, including mining, forestry, and fishing, in addition to agriculture, which is the best-known form of migrant labor in the United States.

Most people who work on farms are either families who own or rent them or residents of nearby farms and communities who travel to work and return home at the end of the workday. Migrant farm workers are concentrated in the harvest operations of fruit and vegetable crops in several locations throughout the United States. At other times of the year, they seek employment in agricultural or other occupations, often where they are permanently settled.

The number of agricultural migrant laborers has declined sharply since the late 1930s, when about four million people worked each season. Because of the problems of keeping track of them, it is very difficult to make an accurate estimate of their numbers. It is likely that about one million people were employed as migrant farm workers in the United States annually during the 1980s.

In the late nineteenth and early twentieth centuries, the size of the migrant labor force expanded rapidly owing to the introduction of large-scale commercial agriculture that was linked to the industrialization and urbanization of the nation's population. Millions of people left the farms and joined immigrants in the cities, augmenting the demand for foods they could not produce themselves.

Agricultural migrants at the turn of the century frequently were foreign immigrants who worked on farms temporarily while saving money to buy farms or seeking more permanent employment in nearby cities. On the West Coast, a large portion of the migrant farm workers at the end of the nineteenth and early twentieth centuries were Asians, while in other parts of the country most were Europeans and their children. With the expansion of the sugar beet, vegetable, and cotton industries in the early twentieth century, Mexican migrant workers increasingly took over seasonal farm labor, frequently returning to the Mexican border or nearby cities at the end of work in a crop or at the end of the season.

With the onset of the Great Depression, many Mexican migrant workers were displaced by southern whites and blacks, who dominated the migrant agricultural labor force in the 1930s and 1940s. In the 1950s and 1960s, black workers continued as the most numerous migrants along the eastern seaboard states, while Mexican and Mexican American workers soon dominated the migrant paths between Texas and the Great Lakes, the Rocky Mountain region, and the area from California to the Pacific Northwest. Some observers noted very rough patterns of movement referred to as "migrant streams" that went northward from Florida, Texas, and Southern California each season in the 1940s and 1950s; but these became increasingly blurred over time.

A very large portion of the migrant agricultural labor force that traveled long distances eventually settled permanently wherever they could find higher-paying and more steady employment, especially in nearby towns and cities. Sometimes they continued to work in agricultural or food-packing or food-processing activities, but more often they left agriculture entirely. As a result of this unstable movement, there was a very rapid movement into and out of agriculture. Migrant workers who left agriculture were constantly replaced by new workers.

Despite more sophisticated government programs on behalf of farm workers and governmental efforts to coordinate the needs of workers with the demands of employers since the 1950s, the movement of migrant workers between jobs remains very haphazard. Migrant and seasonal farm workers continue to experience long periods of unemployment, and are among the worst-paid and least-protected workers in the nation. They suffer high rates of illness, retain low levels of education, and they find few advocates within political circles. As outsiders to local communities, often separated by language and ethnic barriers, they seldom participate in decisions affecting the communities where they are employed.

In the 1960s and 1970s, the migrant agricultural work force changed rapidly. With the rise of the black power and Chicano movements, the appearance of modest protective legislation, and the increasingly successful unionization efforts of farm workers, employers increasingly sought to recruit and hire foreign workers to replace the citizens. Along the East Coast, they recruited increasingly from the Caribbean, and supplemented with workers from Mexico and Central America. In other parts of the country, they recruited mostly from Mexico and Central America. In the 1980s and 1990s, the vast majority of migrant farm workers in the United States have been foreign-born. Many of them migrate seasonally from Mexico and the Caribbean to the United States through the H-2 Program, which became an important mechanism of labor recruitment following the termination of the Bracero Program. In 1992 it still held that the majority of migrant workers were of Hispanic origin. Of these workers, the majority were of Mexican origin. In recent decades, undocumented workers from Latin America have become the most important part of the migrant labor force in many locations.

✳ HISPANIC EMPLOYMENT IN INDUSTRY

Service Industries

The employment profile of workers in the U.S. has changed sharply in recent decades. The major category of service is increasing, while that of manufacturing is declining.

The service industries include a wide range of activities, from private household work, restaurant, hotel, and food services, and health and personal service occupations. Employment in service industries, which nearly doubled between 1970 and 1990, is high among females in most areas. The rate of Hispanic employment in service occupations is about double that of the non-Hispanic population for males, and about 40 percent higher for females.

In March 1989, 17.7 percent of employed Hispanic men worked in service industries, compared with 9 percent for non-Hispanic men. The rates were 24.1

percent for Hispanic women and 17.1 percent for non-Hispanic women.

Manufacturing and Basic Industries

Manufacturing and basic industries, traditionally the mainstay of the U.S. economy and historically the indicator of the leading economic nations in the world, are declining rapidly. Manufacturing occupations include precision production workers, craft and repair people, as well as operators, fabricators, and laborers. Both Hispanic males and females are highly overrepresented in this category, males by almost 25 percent and females at rates roughly double those of non-Hispanic females.

In 1989, about 47.9 percent of Hispanic males were employed in the broad category of manufacturing, compared with 39.8 percent of non-Hispanic males. Among females, 21.3 percent of Hispanics worked in manufacturing, compared with 10.5 percent of non-Hispanics.

✳ FEDERAL EMPLOYMENT PROGRAMS AND LAWS

Title VII and the Equal Employment Opportunity Commission

The Economic Opportunity Act (EOA) of 1964 was the centerpiece of President Lyndon B. Johnson's War on Poverty. The philosophy behind the War on Poverty espoused private initiative and local efforts had not resolved longstanding problems of discrimination and poverty during the postwar boom in the United States. Furthermore, the government believed efforts to improve conditions were consistently thwarted by private interests, often in conjunction with local and state governmental authorities, where the poor, blacks and, Hispanics were seldom represented. The federal government, thus, decided to initiate a program to provide training for workers, to encourage recruitment, and to monitor hiring practices of public and private employers across the nation.

The EOA also created the Office of Economic Opportunity (OEO) to administer a number of programs on behalf of the nation's poor. These included the Job Corps, the Community Action Program (CAP), and the Volunteers in Service to America (VISTA).

The Job Corps is a job-training program whose goal seeks to help disadvantaged youths aged 16–21 find employment. In 1990, the typical Job Corps enrollee was 18 years old, 83.5 percent were high school dropouts, 75 percent were minorities, 75 percent had never had a prior full-time job, 67 percent were male,

and almost 40 percent came from families on public assistance.

VISTA, conceived as a domestic equivalent to the Peace Corps, worked with the poor in urban and rural locations. CAP was the primary OEO program, in which local groups combined the efforts of local government, business, labor, civic, and religious organizations and the poor to mobilize local resources to alleviate poverty.

Title VII of the Civil Rights Act of 1964 comprised the most important statute of the War on Poverty addressing employment discrimination. It prohibits discrimination on the basis of gender, creed, race, or ethnic background, "to achieve equality of employment opportunities and remove barriers that have operated in the past." Discrimination is prohibited in advertising, recruitment, hiring, job classification, promotion, discharge, wages and salaries, and other terms and conditions of employment.

Title VII also established the Equal Employment Opportunity Commission (EEOC) as a monitoring device to prevent job discrimination. In effect, it renewed and expanded the Fair Employment Practices Committee, which had been dismantled at the end of World War II. The EEOC works in conjunction with state agencies in investigating charges of discrimination.

The issue of employment discrimination has led to a great deal of litigation. Many important cases defined the scope of discrimination and employee protection under Title VII of the Civil Rights Act of 1964. In the key case of *Griggs v. Duke Power Company* (1971), Chief Justice Warren Burger, speaking for a unanimous Supreme Court, ruled that employers could not create screening devices in employment that operated as "built-in headwinds" for minority groups. The Court required employers to initiate practices that considered their impact on minorities. The ruling encouraged many employers in public and private sectors to devise programs encouraging the hiring of women and non-Euro-Americans.

Several of the important employment lawsuits directly involved Hispanics. *Espinoza v. Farah Manufacturing Company* (1973) held that Title VII does not protect discrimination against aliens. The Court also held, however, that Title VII prohibits practices that have "the purpose or effect of discriminating on the basis of national origin." In *Carino v. University of Oklahoma* (1984), the Court held that an employer cannot refuse to hire an individual "because the individual has the physical, cultural or linguistic characteristics of a particular national origin group," or discriminate "because of the individual's accent or manner of speaking."

In reaction to equal employment legislation and

the increasing presence of Hispanics and other non-English-speaking people in the workplace, some states in the past several years have enacted so-called English-only amendments to their constitutions. Collectively they imposed English as the official language of their state.

Following the spirit of this legislation, many employers attempted to restrict the use of foreign languages by imposing "English-only" rules in the workplace. Such actions are prohibited under Title VII, which prohibits discrimination on the basis of national origin. EEOC policy provides that rules "which require employees to speak English only at all times are presumptively unlawful because they unduly burden individuals whose primary language is one other than English, and tends to create a hostile or discriminatory environment based on national origin."

Language rights have thus become an important employment issue challenging Hispanic workers in the 1990s, particularly where their numbers are high. Public and private employers commonly engage in hiring Hispanic employees because of their special skills as translators, but seldom grant them compensation or consider such skills as important factors in job promotion. In *Pérez et al. v. Federal Bureau of Investigation* (1988), Hispanic FBI agents offered their special skills to the FBI more than Anglo Spanish-speakers and non-Spanish-speakers, but did not receive compensation. The federal district court held that by being concentrated in interpreting tasks, the Hispanic agents were treated differently from and denied promotional opportunities offered to Euro-American agents.

As a result of positive legislation and court interpretations, conditions of employment for Hispanics registered significant improvements in several areas during the 1960s and much of the 1970s.

The Office of Economic Opportunity (EEOC) and Comprehensive Employment and Training Administration (CETA) Under Nixon and Carter

During the Nixon presidency, the first efforts to dismantle the War on Poverty began. The Nixon administration did not overtly attack the concept of equal opportunity, nor did it challenge the theories or actual programs already established to deal with the chronically unemployed. Rather, its desire for changes focused on attempts to realign political relationships involving federal, state, and local governments and community organizations.

Its remedies were part of its "New Federalism" program. The Great Society programs in the Office of Economic Opportunity (OEO) were centralized, with training programs and a strong oversight mechanism headed by the federal government. Local involvement was conceived largely through participation in the organizations where citizens were directly involved, especially through the Community Action Program (CAP). The New Federalism sought to reduce federal involvement and place the programs in the hands of state and local governments.

While in theory local control should be superior in meeting local needs, the creators of the New Federalism conceived the change in political terms. The political problem they perceived was that under the War on Poverty programs, there was a modest shift in local power away from the old elites, particularly white politicians, in the direction of the poor, particularly Hispanics and blacks. They believed they could return power to the old elites by removing the presence of the federal government and eliminating the community organizations.

The poor were justifiably dubious of Nixon's argument that local officials were most responsive to those most in need, having recent memories of breaking down local barriers to education and employment, with the assistance of federal government intervention.

The Nixon administration placed all employment and training programs, previously in the OEO, into the new Comprehensive Employment and Training Administration (CETA), created in 1973. The major difference between the old and the new poverty efforts was that the earlier employment and training programs were clearly targeted to specific population groups and allocated as "categorical" grants, on the basis of national and local considerations. Under CETA, allocations were granted directly to local politicians in the form of "bloc" grants to state and local governments, which could then make decisions on the kinds of programs to establish. Another change was that the CETA plan reduced the power of the federal government's regulations, standards, and other monitoring mechanisms created to ensure the efficacy of the local programs. Furthermore, although the new plan intended to allow local people to determine needs locally, no affirmative action guidelines were established to ensure that the poor and, especially, women, blacks, and Hispanics—the people for whom the programs were intended—would be represented in the decision-making process. This was particularly evident as CAP was severely weakened. The success of CETA rested on the goodwill of federal and local authorities. During the Nixon administration, many of the community leaders were removed and CETA programs were made increasingly the province of local politicians.

During the Carter presidency, the federal government expressed an increased commitment to equal opportunity, and CETA was strengthened. It is no coincidence that at this time the economic well-being of Hispanics and other non-whites peaked and the gap with the white population narrowed.

Furthermore, CETA was considered a success by most of its Hispanic participants. In fiscal year 1978, 142,000 youths, or slightly more than one-tenth of those enrolled in CETA programs, were Hispanics. Overall, approximately 5 percent of the country's white youth, 19 percent of blacks, and 13 percent of Hispanic youth participated in CETA programs that year. Hispanic participation ranged from 23 percent of Puerto Ricans, 13 percent of Mexican Americans, and 7 percent of Cubans. Interviews conducted that year indicated that more than 87 percent were satisfied with the program, and more than 70 percent believed that it improved their job chances. Nevertheless, CETA and government training programs for the unemployed were being more strongly criticized than ever before by their nonparticipant detractors, who found their own opportunity when Reagan was elected president.

The Job Training Partnership Act

The Reagan administration philosophy led to a profound change in government policy on job training programs based on both political and economic thought. Politically, the Reagan administration adopted the position that although it must still provide a "safety net" to assist the needy poor, such assistance should be distinguished from support, and that support is not a federal government responsibility. It also carried the New Federalism concept much further politically and economically than Nixon by reducing the amount of federal assistance for job creation and other social service programs.

The federal government also reduced its direct involvement by operating more in "partnership" with private as well as state and local government bodies. The impact of government philosophy and policy is clearly evident in the Job Training Partnership Act (JTPA) of 1983, the central employment training program of the Reagan and Bush years. The JTPA, like its predecessor, CETA, delivers employment and training services to the economically disadvantaged in need. Compared with CETA, the JTPA depends much more on the private sector to deliver these services.

The new program departs sharply from earlier direct job creation strategies that were central to projects of the 1960s and the 1970s. Federally funded jobs created by the Public Service Employment, offering employment to both the cyclically and structurally unemployed, were eliminated under the JTPA. Part of the concept of less government support

for the poor, it represented a 60 percent reduction in subsidies for youth employment. It severely reduced employment prospects for many disadvantaged youth whose first full-time employment had come from CETA and its predecessors.

In effect, the JTPA is designed to serve the demands of employers rather than the needs of unemployed workers. It is performance-driven and is structured to reward programs with high placement rates and low costs. In practice however, its standards are ignored. Furthermore, government monitoring devices established by earlier programs have been virtually dismantled.

The JTPA, as an example of the New Federalism, has failed to meet its mandate of providing for the training needs of the unemployed. Its structure is flawed, does not meet the interests of society generally, and is riddled with corruption.

Several structural problems in the Job Training Partnership Act specifically hinder Hispanic participation. A high proportion of Hispanics are needy, in part because of a nearly 50 percent high school dropout rate and because over one-fourth are not fully proficient in English but they are vastly underserved. The JTPA penalizes these people more than any other among the poor by not including precisely those who are most disadvantaged and harder to place. In addition, the JTPA has income-based eligibility stipulations requiring that people must either be receiving food stamps or not have more than a specific level of income. Many Hispanics who are eligible for JTPA, however, are imbued with a work ethic and are unwilling to accept food stamps. Still others are not eligible because they are willing to accept jobs that place them in an income level slightly above the sharply increased level of eligibility requirements. Another problem is that the JTPA has increased requirements for documentation of eligibility beyond those of CETA—a policy that has been criticized as unduly burdensome. Furthermore, Mexican Americans, in particular, lack familiarity with government programs, and the means of informing them about JTPA programs are woefully lacking. Finally, Hispanics lack a presence in most JTPA policy-making forums, and thus lack consistent advocates to set policies.

Beyond their structural problems, the cutbacks in job training efforts caused by the JTPA program have even broader negative consequences for the society at large. The reduction in training has been criticized by proponents of human capital, who argue that the reduced investment in training workers will have a costly long-term impact by reducing federal revenues and entitlement expenditures in the future. The disinvestment will also contribute to high unemployment and an inadequately trained work force. Society benefits, such as income tax and revenues for programs like Social Security, will decline, while costs for public assistance will increase.

The impact of Reagan job training policy, continued under the Bush administration, is further evident in the case of the Job Corps, created under the EEOC, and presently part of the JTPA. The Job Corps has residential and nonresidential centers where enrollees take intensive programs in education, vocational training, work experience, and counseling. It is popular in both parties of Congress, and the U.S. Department of Labor (USDL) has acknowledged its success. A 1985 USDL study determined that the Job Corps returns $1.38 to the U.S. Treasury in only three years for each $1 invested by the federal government. The funds come from continuing taxes paid by former Job Corps trainees once they begin employment and from reduced welfare payments. The Job Corps, serving the most disadvantaged, nonetheless, was among the programs cut most sharply by the JTPA.

Even the inadequate funds for the program are not being utilized effectively. Congress established specific levels of spending to ensure sufficient funding establishing adequate programs for the needy; yet in many areas the funds are not being spent.

Congressional hearings in 1990 found that corruption abounds in the training process itself. Many private schools, so-called "proprietary schools," replaced government-trained OEO and CETA workers providing training. The proprietary schools are for-profit institutions set up specifically to receive government grants, and are paid to train workers. The recipients of the funds seldom have competent training in operating educational institutions. Many of the courses their schools teach lack rigor, are taught by untrained and uncertified teachers, prepare the workers for nonexistent jobs and are not placement driven.

The structural design of the incentives process created by the JTPA reveals severe difficulties in the program. Local JTPA offices are motivated by incentives based on the actual number of people hired by private employers. This has led to the process of "creaming" in client selection. Creaming selects the least-disadvantaged individuals because they are the easiest to place. The programs have targeted services primarily to in-school youth or high school graduates; thus, service to high school dropouts has declined sharply.

Furthermore, local employers are paid by JTPA funds to hire employees. This leads to widespread abuse, for it allows employers to receive government funds to "hire" individuals they would have other-wise hired without JTPA "incentives" of several weeks' or months' pay. The JTPA has become a major government subsidy for private employers, not a training program for those most in need.

The "New Federalism" originally was designed to transfer power from the federal government to local agencies and employers. In effect, it has taken away power from the poor and from community organizations, remaining largely pushed out of the decision-making process. In the past, community organizations worked in conjunction with federal government administrators. Under the JTPA, however, funding is granted directly to governmental agencies and private proprietors as rewards for their support. Because the monitoring system is so lax and community participation dismantled, efforts to expose the JTPA have been long delayed. As a result, the JTPA has shortchanged the needs of Hispanics, blacks, and others most in need of training, as well as society at large, while serving the narrow interests of employers in the private sector and their allies.

Employment Rights

During the 1980s, the Reagan and Bush administrations launched an attack on civil rights legislation as it extended to the workplace. The new Supreme Court justices appointed by Reagan and Bush helped change the direction of court protection of employees. In effect, its rulings have relaxed the duties of employers and have made it much more difficult for women and non-whites to convince the courts that violations of civil rights laws have taken place. The attack peaked in a series of 1989 Supreme Court decisions relating to employment law. In *Patterson v. McLean Credit Union* (1989), the Supreme Court ruled that an individual could no longer sue for racial harassment at work under a 1966 civil rights statute: "A practice of racial harassment adopted after an employee was hired does not by itself violate that employee's rights under the statute." In effect, it permitted the employer to hound Ms. Patterson out of her job because of race.

In *Wards Cove Packing Co. v. Antonio* (1989), the Court ruled that a group of employees who were able to demonstrate that an Alaska cannery that hired whites for well-paid and skilled jobs and minorities for low-paid, unskilled jobs, and even segregated employees by race in mess halls and dormitories, did not offer sufficient evidence of employment discrimination. It reversed 28 years of well-established law in its holding by imposing a heavier burden on employees in proving its employer did not have legitimate business reasons for engaging in such practices.

During the same period, other Supreme Court cases severely limited the filing of discrimination charges, and further ruled that a civil rights statute could not be used to sue local governments for damages for acts of discrimination. These and other cases successfully narrowed the coverage of civil rights statutes, making it extremely difficult for women and minorities to prove discrimination, simultaneously making it easier for those opposed to civil rights to post challenges.

The erosion of past civil rights legislation by the Supreme Court during the Reagan and Bush administrations resulted in efforts by representatives of civil rights, black, and Hispanic organizations to initiate a push for a new Civil Rights Act in 1990 to return to previous standards. The legislation sought to redress the discriminatory impact of recent Supreme Court decisions that in sum eliminated much of the thrust of equal employment opportunity law established in the previous generation. Although the 1990 bill had overwhelming support in both houses of Congress, the Bush administration vetoed the legislation on the grounds that it promoted quotas. A series of compromises produced a watered-down Civil Rights Act in 1991.

The Clinton administration was unable to improve the civil rights situation despite liberal appointments, such as that of Norma Cantú (the former director of MALDEF), to the position of Assistant Secretary for Civil Rights in the Department of Education, and Antonio Califa as Director of Civil Rights, Department of Transportation, among many other liberal civil rights and labor appointments. The very conservative Republic majority in Congress as of Clinton's second year in office curtailed all progressive legislation.

Affirmative Action

Affirmative action, centering on the Civil Rights Act of 1964, was a central concept of the Great Society programs of the Johnson administration. It accepted the premise that the high levels of unemployment and ongoing discrimination that women and many non-white groups encountered were impediments to the vision of the Great Society. The federal government accepted the responsibility to devise "affirmative action" programs to remedy such discriminatory practices and their consequences.

Affirmative action is designed to counter the effects of practices that exclude individuals from the workplace and other settings because of race, color, creed, gender, and national origin. It accepts the assumption that because of their background, many highly qualified people have been passed over in hiring and promotion practices and that steps should be taken to rectify exclusionary practices. The federal mandate was to encourage employers to voluntarily increase the presence of underrepresented minorities in the work force to levels commensurate with their presence in the local community. Compliance officers in the Equal Employment Opportunity Commission (EEOC) and the Department of Labor set goals, targets, and timetables for employers. For example, Executive Order 11246 in 1972 established two requirements: nondiscrimination, or "the elimination of all existing discriminatory conditions whether purposeful or inadvertent," and affirmative action, whereby employers are to take positive efforts "to recruit, employ and promote qualified members or groups formerly excluded." It also encourages individual employers to voluntarily adopt affirmative action programs.

Affirmative action programs were immediately criticized by some conservative elements in the country who argued that affirmative action favored minorities over more "qualified" whites. The struggle over affirmative action continued into the 1970s, when opponents coined the term "reverse discrimination," by which they suggested that white males were victims of discrimination as a result of affirmative action on behalf of women, blacks, Hispanics, and other underrepresented groups.

Within the federal government, the Reagan and Bush administrations in the 1980s intensified the attack and engaged in a systematic dismantling of affirmative action programs. The Reagan administration promoted the argument that affirmative action programs entailed quotas, constituting a form of reverse discrimination. The Justice Department under Reagan also spearheaded opposition to affirmative action, claiming that the administration "has profound doubts whether the Constitution permits governments to adopt remedies involving racial quotas to benefit persons who are not themselves the victims of discrimination." In essence it denied that broad discrimination against a group of people as a class could in theory exist. A highlight of the Reagan-Bush administration success was the Supreme Court decision in *City of Richmond v. Croson* (1989), which struck down an ordinance that set aside 30 percent of Richmond Virginia's construction contracts for minority businesses.

The attacks on affirmative action have had a profound impact on hiring policies in many sectors of private and public employment. They have contributed to the overall decline of the economic position of Hispanics and other ethnic minorities during the 1980s, both in absolute levels and in comparison with whites. It is most telling in top management positions in large corporations, where most surveys indicate that at least 95 percent of positions are still held by white males.

The federal government has failed not only to abide by its responsibility to serve as watchdog over affirmative action policies in the private sector but also to take affirmative steps itself. Although the Reagan administration could point to an increase in Hispanic representation in the federal work force from 4.3 percent to 4.8 percent between 1980 and 1988, the Hispanic population during that period increased from 6.4 percent to 8.1 percent. Thus, Hispanic underrepresentation in federal employment during the Reagan administration increased sharply, from 50 percent to 69 percent. The underrepresentation was most stark in the highest levels. At the top scale of government, senior executive service, Hispanics accounted for only 1 percent of the employees.

With the rise of conservatism in the 1990s, further empowered by a conservative take-over in 1994 of the U.S. Congress, affirmative action programs have been targeted for elimination. Politicians throughout the country, led by California Governor Pete Wilson, have made affirmative action an issue related to waste in government and economic recessions. Wilson and others have even linked the issue to the cost of serving immigrants, legal as well as undocumented. In 1995, empowered by various propositions on the California ballot, Wilson began tearing down the state's affirmative action structure, beginning with admissions and hiring at the University of California. Conservative governors in other states were soon announcing their following Wilson, while the House of Representatives utilized the budget negotiations to eliminate many affirmative action programs. President Clinton was forced to follow suit by announcing some the appointment of commissions to reform affirmative action. All of this came to a head in the election year of 1996, in which conservative candidates, such as Pat Buchanan and Robert Dole, demonized affirmative action and swore to eliminate it.

Undocumented Workers

Use of the term "undocumented" to refer to people who are in the United States without proper immigrant papers was established by the International Labor Organization in 1974. It was meant to be descriptive and neutral, in contrast to the term "illegal," which has negative connotations and implies criminality. The presence of undocumented aliens in the United States violates civil statutes but does not violate criminal laws. Some undocumented workers enter the country without legal authorization, while others enter under temporary permits but then extend their stay.

A Mexican worker being finger-printed for deportation.

Immigration and Naturalization Service

The number of undocumented aliens in the United States cannot be precisely determined, and is the subject of intense debate. In the 1970s, Immigration and Naturalization Service (INS) Commissioner Leonard Chapman, seeking to increase funding and expand the power of his organization, claimed that there were as many as 12 million undocumented workers in the country. Other observers most commonly place the number in the range of 3.5 million to five million people.

Popular perceptions and the press portray almost all undocumented workers as Mexicans. This is further bolstered by the policies of the INS, whose enforcement efforts are concentrated along the land border between Mexico and the United States, rather than at seaports and airports, or along the United States' northern border. About 95 percent of INS apprehensions are Mexicans, yet it is likely that only about half of all undocumented workers in the United States are Hispanics, the remainder being mostly natives of Europe and Asia.

In addition to their numerical importance, undocumented workers have been at the center of several political battles. On several occasions in recent decades, a national hysteria among citizens developed over their presence, typically during periods of economic recession and depression. Debates intensified during those periods over whether the undocumented take jobs away from U.S. citizens.

Operation Wetback, which occurred during a time of recession in 1954, involved a concerted campaign by the federal government that successfully apprehended more than one million undocumented Mexican workers. The frenzy subsided when the government and private employers expanded the scale of the bracero program, reducing the demand of agricultural employers for undocumented workers.

Following abolition of the bracero program in the mid-1960s, the number of undocumented workers again began to increase, and a new hysteria appeared in public circles, accompanied by increased activity by the border patrol. By 1977, the INS was again apprehending more than one million undocumented workers each year.

The hysteria over the undocumented intensified during the 1980s. Several ultraconservative and nativist groups attempted to stir up the nation. In 1986, for example, the Ku Klux Klan announced that the influx of "illegal aliens" was responsible for Texas' economic problems, including its high level of unemployment, and vowed to hunt down illegal aliens and turn them over to the border patrol.

The effect of undocumented workers on the economy has stirred a wide-ranging debate in the nation. One side of the argument is that they are a major drain on public services and that they displace U.S. citizens by accepting low-paying jobs. These arguments frequently are based on stereotypes and ethnic biases, and they seldom address the related issue of why employers are permitted to disregard protective labor statutes and immigration law.

An opposing position is that the undocumented pay taxes, and because they seldom use available social services, they make a very positive contribution to the nation's economy. Further, the jobs in which they are employed typically are those that others are unwilling to perform.

Undocumented workers enter the United States for various reasons. The most important are to escape political and social turmoil in their native country, to escape poverty and poor living conditions, and to achieve a better life in the United States. These are combined with active and aggressive recruitment by employers, often with the implied consent of the U.S. government.

Undocumented Hispanic immigrants are concentrated geographically in the South and Southwest and employed largely in service occupations, manufacturing, and agriculture. While their average earnings exceed the minimum wage, their wages are significantly lower than legal residents and citizens in the same occupations. Furthermore, they are commonly hired at wages below the legal minimum, working in unsafe conditions and facing inhumane and discriminatory treatment. Politically, they are vulnerable, and either unaware of their rights, or because of fear of deportation and loss of jobs, apprehensive about exerting the rights to which they are entitled under protective labor legislation.

Undocumented workers retain most employment rights of citizens, including those of minimum wage, joining and participating in union activities, the right to sue over contracts, and other protection under federal labor law. They are also deemed "employees" within the meaning of the National Labor Relations Act, and are protected under its provisions. Legal cases have also recognized the right to worker's compensation and protection under the Fair Labor Standards Act. Yet, employers frequently use the INS to escape their responsibilities under these laws and report for deportation workers who attempt to organize unions or assert other employment rights.

The anti-immigrant sentiments are often used by INS officials to increase their own power and that of the organization beyond its constituted civil authority. In its increasing exercise of violence, clearly in opposition to statutes that govern its operation, it is becoming a paramilitary organization. The tactic of INS workplace raids to apprehend undocumented workers has enabled the agency to violate workers' rights. In the 1984 INS Operation Jobs campaign, INS agents even raided businesses without valid search warrants or the consent of the employer.

In *Immigration and Naturalization Service v. Delgado* (1984), the Supreme Court ruled that workers were not subject to seizures as a result of INS raids on the workplace because the workers were "free to leave." Yet the raids occurred in the "presence of agents blocking each exit, armed with badges, walkie-talkies and guns and roving agents in open view questioning workers and taking some of them away." The INS has also intensified its border activities, increasing the use of force, intimidation, and other forms of violence.

Several observers, including the American Friends Service Committee, have reported widespread harassment and cases of assault by INS officers. They have documented "sexual abuse of undocumented immigrants, particularly refugee women," "beating undocumented immigrants, or those suspected of being undocumented immigrants," and the "deliberate destruction of immigrants' property or documents." Several tragedies occurred in the 1980s because of violent tactics of INS officials, including the deaths of at least 14 farm workers seeking to escape apprehension by the Border Patrol during field operations. Civil rights and other organizations have exposed cases of inhumane treatment, including strip searches, beatings, unprotected exposure to the direct sun for several hours, lack of medical attention, denial of visitation by family members, and denial of counsel. In defense of their tactics, INS officials have criticized individuals and groups seeking to educate undocumented immigrants about their rights as "incredible" and "against America."

Hostility directed against foreign workers, particularly the undocumented, surfaced again in the 1970s and 1980s in congressional circles, and demands for a change in the nation's immigration laws intensified.

The hostility came to a boil in 1994, 1995 and during the election year of 1996, when both legal and undocumented immigrants (especially Hispanics and Asians) were targeted for control. California passed various referenda to limit immigration, and the conservative Republican governors California and Florida filed suit against the federal government to recoup monies spent on providing services to immigrants. So intense was the immigrant bashing and increase of negative sentiments nationally toward immigration that President Bill Clinton named a commission, headed by Barbara Jordan, to study and revamp the policy on immigration, and Clinton changed the United States' 30-year policy of automatically accepting Cuban immigrants during the 1994–95 exodus of Cuban rafters—thousands of them were turned back to Cuba or placed in refugee camps in Guantanamo, Panama and neighboring Caribbean islands. Under Clinton's commission, as well, decades-old policies about re-uniting families through immigration was also threatened. The issue intensified in 1995 and 1996 during the campaign for the presidency, with Pat Buchanan, among other conservatives, bashing immigrants and swearing to close the borders.

The Immigration Reform and Control Act of 1986

Sensitive to the increased immigration that began in the 1960s and the economic uncertainty of the 1970s, the Ford administration appointed several task forces to address the issue of undocumented entry into the United States. It encouraged several congressional representatives to introduce new legislation to control immigration to the United States. After more than a decade of debate, Congress enacted the Immigration Reform and Control Act of 1986, popularly referred to as IRCA.

The proponents of IRCA argued that the legislation was necessary to reverse the perceived accelerated immigration of the undocumented, to "save jobs for Americans," and to halt the perceived drain on social services. Numerous careful studies produced since that time have demonstrated that none of the above perceptions was accurate.

IRCA contains three major provisions. First, it establishes civil and criminal penalties, referred to as employer sanctions, on employers who fail to verify the documentation of employees hired since 1986 whether they are eligible to work. This marks the first time in the history of the United States that employers have been prohibited by law from hiring undocumented workers. Second, IRCA provided a one-time provision to legalize undocumented workers in the United States. The legalization process included a separate program to legalize seasonal agricultural workers (SAWs) in the United States. Third, the law specifically prohibits several forms of employment discrimination. In response to the concerns of Hispanic and civil rights groups that the employer sanctions would result in discrimination, the law mandated that the General Accounting Office (GAO) conduct in an ongoing investigation of the impact of IRCA for three years. IRCA specifically provides Congress with the statutory authority to repeal employer sanctions if the GAO's final report were to conclude that widespread discrimination existed. To facilitate the provisions of the law, Congress also strengthened the power and personnel of the INS.

The GAO made its final report on IRCA to Congress on March 29, 1990. It observed that the implementation and enforcement of employer verification and sanctions provisions were not carried out satisfactorily, that they had caused a widespread pattern of discrimination against members of minority groups, and that they caused unnecessary regulatory burdens on employers. Many employers were confused about the law and its application and initiated illegal discriminatory hiring practices against Hispanics, Asians, and other people who appeared "foreign." Even white workers experienced discriminatory practices. The GAO concluded that there was a "widespread pattern" of discrimination based on national origin, practiced by 19 percent of the employers surveyed, that included not hiring foreign-appearing or foreign-sounding job applicants for fear of noncompliance with the law. In a "sting" operation involving pairs of Hispanic and Anglo "testers," it found that "Anglo testers received 52 percent more job offers than the Hispanic testers with whom they were paired."

The GAO investigation was narrow in its view of

what constituted "widespread discrimination" and did not support repealing employer sanctions. Other agencies and civil rights activists documented cases of discrimination, such as employers' firing applicants for legalization along with undocumented workers, depriving them of seniority and other benefits, imposing English-only rules, withholding paychecks, failing to pay overtime, harassing them sexually, assaulting them physically, and violating other civil and constitutional rights. In effect, IRCA pushed undocumented workers into even less regulated and more exploitative jobs.

Employers have also suffered the impact of employer sanctions. Estimates of total costs to businesses to perform record-keeping required by employer sanctions vary from $182 million to $675 million per year. Furthermore, businesses are paying millions of additional dollars in fines and otherwise suffering financially because of loss of workers and INS intrusions into the workplace.

In meeting one of its original goals, preventing the entry of undocumented workers into the United States, IRCA appears to have been successful in its first two years. Since that time, the entry of undocumented workers has increased sharply. In the early 1990s, it appears that the prohibitions of IRCA have not had a long-term impact on rates of undocumented entry into the country. They have proved to be a nuisance to employers and an additional burden to all workers—undocumented, legal residents, and citizens alike.

Thus, the GAO report and other evidence confirmed the fears of Hispanic groups before its enactment—that the law would intensify discrimination against Hispanics. On the basis of the GAO report and other evidence, employer sanctions are causing widespread discrimination. Hispanic activists are trying to convince Congress to comply with its own mandate and repeal employer sanctions.

✳ YOUTH EMPLOYMENT

The Hispanic work force is younger than other major work force groups, and in the future it will represent an even greater portion of the work force. Hispanics have lower levels of schooling than other groups. Among youths ages 16–21 not attending college, more than two-fifths of employed blacks and whites are high school graduates, compared with less than one-third of Hispanics. Because government job training programs are being cut back, the nation's future work force may be inadequate.

Hispanic youths are more likely to work full time and year round than either white or black youths. Employed Hispanic male youths are also more likely to be married than black and white males. As with other groups, Hispanic male youths are more likely to be employed than females.

Youths of all backgrounds tend to have much higher unemployment rates than older workers, and their rate of unemployment is more sensitive to business cycles. White youths have the lowest unemployment level, while blacks have the highest rate of unemployment, which tends to be less sensitive to changes in the economy than either the white or Hispanic rates. Unemployment rates for Hispanics fluctuate between the two others. During upturns in the economy, the rate of unemployment declines more sharply for Hispanic youths, while during downturns, it rises much more rapidly than for either whites or blacks.

In 1988, the unemployment rate for youths ages 16–19 was 12.7 percent for whites. For blacks it was 32.4 percent, and for Hispanics, 19.4 percent.

In the third quarter of 1990, the median weekly earnings for full-time male workers ages 16–24 were $283 for whites, $255 for blacks, and $238 for Hispanics. Among female youths, the earnings were $250 for whites and $225 for blacks and Hispanics.

✳ WOMEN'S EMPLOYMENT

During the past decade, the number of Hispanic women in the work force increased more rapidly than any other major population group, and by the end of the decade their rate of participation nearly equaled those of women in other groups. The distinctiveness of Hispanic women in employment has been largely erased. Between 1978 and 1988, Hispanic female participation in the work force more than doubled, from 1.7 million to 3.6 million. In 1988, 56.6 percent of Hispanic women were in the work force, compared with 66.2 percent of white women and 63.8 percent of blacks. The lower rate for Hispanic women can be attributed largely to their younger age and higher number of children than black and white women.

Hispanic women in 1988 formed 6.5 percent of the civilian labor force. Of the total of 3.6 million Hispanic women workers, 58.5 percent were of Mexican origin, 10.4 percent were Puerto Rican, 6.6 percent were of Cuban origin, and the other 24.5 percent were of other Hispanic backgrounds. By ethnicity, 53.9 percent of women of Mexican origin, compared with 54.9 percent of Cuban origin and 41.4 percent of Puerto Rican origin, were employed.

In March 1988, 41.1 percent of working Hispanic women were employed in technical, sales, and administrative support occupations, rates not much different from those of other women. At that same date, there were sharper differences in occupations of high and low pay and status. In the higher-status managerial and professional jobs, 15.7 percent of Hispanic women found employment, versus 25.3 percent of all women. Meanwhile, 16.6 percent of Hispanic women worked as lower-paid operators, fabricators, and laborers, compared with only 8.8 percent of all women. There were very few Hispanic women in extractive occupations, in mechanic and repairer jobs, or in most construction trades.

In the fourth quarter of 1990, the median weekly earnings of Hispanic women was $283, compared with $313 for black women and $361 for white women. Because of sharp increases in the work force, Hispanic women in the 1990s are about as likely to be employed in wage labor as other women. But their incomes remain substantially below those of women in the other major groups.

✳ GOVERNMENT PROGRAMS

The federal government committed itself to eliminating discrimination in employment when it passed the Fair Employment Practices Act in 1941. The act created a monitoring mechanism in the Fair Employment Practices Commission (FEPC), which went out of existence in 1945. Despite its ongoing commitment, the federal government made little systematic effort to address fair employment practices again until the Kennedy administration.

The Manpower Development and Training Act (MDTA), passed in 1962, initially offered vocational training for unemployed adult workers displaced by automation, and later it was expanded to include youth training programs. The government effort increased with the enactment of the Economic Opportunity Act (EOA) of 1964, the flagship of the War on Poverty. Among the programs included in the act aimed at the poor, including Hispanics, were the Neighborhood Youth Corp, the Job Corps, the Community Action Program, and VISTA. The EOA also had a section dealing specifically with migrant and seasonal farm workers.

The War on Poverty held a philosophical position that a culture of poverty existed. Leaders of the New Frontier and Great Society considered it the responsibility of the federal government to take steps to eradicate poverty through a centralized program of training and other forms of direct action. They were convinced that eliminating poverty and discrimination would not succeed if responsibilities remained in the hands of local authorities and employers, or if left to the individual efforts of the poor.

The New Frontier and Great Society were also responding to the needs of their own constituencies among labor, community, black, and Hispanic groups. Part of the EEOC thrust was directed toward Hispanics because of the efforts of the two most important Mexican American organizations in the country, the American G.I. Forum and the League of United Latin American Citizens (LULAC). Immediately after the EOA was passed, the two initiated an independent program, Jobs for Progress, commonly known as SER (service, employment, redevelopment; in Spanish *ser* means "to be"). SER began as a voluntary job placement center in Washington, D.C., and through its close ties to the government, soon expanded. By 1966, SER was receiving funds from the Office of Economic Opportunity, the Department of Health, Education and Welfare, the Department of Labor, and private sources to meet its goals of providing skills training and related services to the Hispanics of the Southwest. In 1970, SER became a categorical program under the Department of Labor. By 1972, it had expanded to 13 states in the Southwest and Midwest, plus the District of Columbia. SER is a nonprofit corporation whose principal objectives are to assist the disadvantaged, with a priority given to Hispanics and emphasis on manpower and related programs to upgrade educational and vocational skills and open career opportunities. It is the closest link between a Hispanic job training organization and the federal government.

The direction of government action and philosophy has undergone two major changes since the EOA was enacted in 1964. In 1973, the government created the Comprehensive Employment and Training Administration (CETA), an effort to alter the direction of government programs that it felt were gaining too much power. CETA, which was to be the major federal legislation governing employment and training programs for the next decade, offered a decentralized delivery system that gave state and local governments a greater degree of control over the programs, the original intent being to allow the poor, blacks, and Hispanics to have a direct voice in their own affairs.

The direction of CETA was sharply altered in 1983 when the Job Training Partnership Act (JTPA) was initiated. It became an employer-oriented organization in which the demands of local employers were given priority over the specific needs of the unemployed and poor.

Occupations

The occupational distribution of the Hispanic work force is highly overrepresented in manufacturing, operator, and service jobs, including semiskilled and clerical positions. Hispanics are highly underrepresented in managerial, sales, technical, and administrative areas. In 1989, 27 percent of Hispanic men were employed in managerial, sales, technical, and administrative positions, compared with 48 percent of non-Hispanic men. They were twice as likely to be employed in service occupations as non-Hispanics (18 percent versus 9 percent).

In 1989, Hispanic women were more likely than non-Hispanic women to be employed in service occupations (24 percent versus 17 percent), and less likely to work in managerial or professional occupations (15 percent versus 27 percent).

✳ INCOME, POVERTY, AND UNEMPLOYMENT

Median family income in 1989 for white families was $35,210; for blacks, $20,210; and for Hispanics, $23,450. Per capita income was $14,060 for whites, $8,750 for blacks, and $8,390 for Hispanics. Among Hispanics, family income was highest among Cuban and lowest among Mexican families. In 1988, non-Hispanics were twice as likely as Hispanics to earn more than $25,000 per year (42.7 percent versus 21.5 percent).

As individual workers, the incomes of Hispanic men and women in the late 1980s and early 1990s were lower than either blacks or whites. Between 1982 and 1988, the income gap between Hispanic and non-Hispanic families increased as median family income for Hispanic families fell from 68 percent to 57 percent of non-Hispanic family incomes.

Between 1978 and 1988, the proportion of Hispanic children living in poverty rose more than 45 percent, and by 1989, 38 percent of Hispanic children were living in poverty. Between 1978 and 1988, the rate of poverty for all whites rose from 8.7 percent to 10.1 percent; for blacks it rose from 30.6 percent to 31.6 percent; and for Hispanics it rose from 21.6 percent to 26.8 percent. During this same period, poverty rates for white children under age 18 rose from 11.3 percent to 14.6 percent; for black children from 41.5 percent to 44.2 percent; and for Hispanic children from 28 percent to 37.9 percent.

The poverty rates for married-couple Hispanic families are higher than for other major groups. Between 1978 and 1988, poverty rates for white families remained constant at 5 percent, fell for blacks from 13 percent to 11 percent, and for Hispanics increased from 13 percent to 16 percent. The median income of Hispanic families below the poverty level fell from $7,238 in 1978 to $6,557 in 1987, controlling for inflation.

In 1987, 70.1 percent of Hispanic female-headed households with children were living in poverty.

In 1988, the unemployment rate for whites was 4.5 percent, compared with 11.4 percent for blacks, and 8.0 percent for Hispanics. By December 1990, the rate for whites rose to 5.3 percent, for blacks to 12.2 percent, and for Hispanics to 9.3 percent. By January 1991, the highest rate of unemployment in the United States was in Puerto Rico, with a rate of 15.1 percent.

Hispanics are more than three times as likely as non-Hispanic Whites to be poor. In 1988, 26.7 percent of Hispanics, versus 10.1 percent of Whites and 31.3 percent of Blacks, lived below the poverty level. Between 1982 and 1988, the number of Hispanic families in poverty increased from 875,000 to 1.1 million. During the 1980s, the number of poor Hispanic families increased by 30 percent, while the number of poor White families declined by 10.3 percent.

Selected Labor Facts

Fact 1

Total Hispanic employment grew by 43 percent between 1980 and 1987. Rates of growth varied, from 48 percent for individuals of Mexican origin, to 24 percent for Puerto Ricans, 27 percent for Cubans, and 44 percent for other Hispanics. The rate of growth was almost three times the rate for other workers.

Fact 2

Hispanic men in the labor force is at 80 percent, compared with 74 percent for all other U.S. men.

Fact 3

Unemployment for Hispanics fell from 16.5 percent in March 1983 to 8.5 percent in March 1988. It then rose to 9.3 percent for whites and 12.2 percent for blacks.

Fact 4

Median weekly earnings in the third quarter of 1990 for white men were $492; for white women, $350; for black men, $438; for black women, $302; for Hispanic men, $317; and for Hispanic women, $302. In percentages, white women earned 71 percent of the amount earned by white men; black men earned 89 percent, Hispanic men 64 percent, and black and Hispanic women 61 percent of that amount. The earnings discrepancies between men and women of the same background were 71 percent for whites, 69 percent for blacks, and 95 percent for Hispanics. Of the three groups, income disparities between women and men were greatest among whites, and least among Hispanics.

Fact 5

In 1988, one-third of white and Hispanic union members were women, while 44 percent of black union members were women. Union membership among all women declined from 14.6 percent to 12.6 percent between 1983 and 1988.

Fact 6

In 1988, 6.5 percent of women in the labor force, or 3.6 million women, were of Hispanic origin. Of the total, 58.5 percent were of Mexican origin, 10.4 percent of Puerto Rican origin, 6.6 percent of Cuban origin, and 24.5 percent were of other Hispanic origin. Of all Hispanic women age 16 and over, 53.2 percent were in the labor force in 1988, compared with 36.6 percent for non-Hispanic women.

Fact 7

In 1988, labor force participation for all Hispanics was 67.4 percent, compared with 66.2 percent for whites and 63.8 percent for blacks.

Fact 8

In 1988, the mean family income for non-Hispanic families was $34,563; for those of Mexican origin it was $25,051; for those of Puerto Rican origin it was $21,963; for those of Cuban origin it was $33,350; and for those of Central and South American origin it was $30,641. On a per capita basis, income for non-Hispanics was $13,449; for Mexicans, $6,627; for Puerto Ricans, $7,652; for Cubans, $13,241; for Central and South Americans, $9,342; and for other Hispanics, $9,441.

Fact 9

In March 1989, 9.4 percent of non-Hispanic families were below the poverty line, compared with 23.7 percent of Hispanic families. Among specific groups, the rates were 24.9 percent for Mexicans, 30.8 percent for Puerto Ricans, 16.9 percent for Cubans, 16.6 percent for Central and South Americans, and 20.6 percent for other Hispanic families.

Fact 10

In March 1989 per capita earnings for individuals in non-Hispanic families was $12,701, compared with $7,287 for all individuals in Hispanic families. Among the different Hispanic groups, the amounts were $6,325 for Mexicans, $7,293 for Puerto Ricans, $12,855 for Cubans, $8,855 for Central and South Americans, and $8,925 for other Hispanics. The per capital earnings for Hispanics was 57.3 percent of that of non-Hispanics, 49.8 percent for Mexicans, 57.4 percent for Puerto Ricans, 101.2 percent for Cubans, 69.7 percent for Central and South Americans, and 70.2 for other Hispanics.

References

Acuña, Rodolfo. *Occupied America: A History of Chicanos,* third edition. New York: Harper and Row, 1988.

Bean, Frank D., and Marta Tienda. *The Hispanic Population of the United States.* New York: Russell Sage Foundation, 1988.

Cattan, Peter. "The Growing Presence of Hispanics in the U.S. Work Force." *Monthly Labor Review,* 111, No. 8, August 1988: 9–14.

McHugh, Kevin E. "Hispanic Migration and Population Redistribution in the United States." *Professional Geographer,* 41, No. 4, November 1989: 429–439.

Miranda, Leticia, and Julia Teresa Quiroz. *The Decade of the Hispanic: An Economic Retrospective.* Washington, D.C.: National Council of La Raza, 1990.

Portes, Alejandro, and Robert L. Bach. *Latin Journey: Cuban and Mexican Immigrants in the United States.* Berkeley: University of California Press, 1985.

Santos, Richard. *Hispanic Youth: Emerging Workers.* New York: Praeger, 1987.

U.S. Bureau of the Census. *Statistical Abstract of the United States: 1990,* 110th edition. Washington, D.C.: GPO, 1990.

U.S. Department of Labor. *Women of Hispanic Origin in the Labor Force.* Washington, D.C.: U.S. Department of Labor Women's Bureau.

Valdés, Dennis Nodín. *Al Norte: Agricultural Workers in the Great Lakes Region, 1917–1970.* Austin: University of Texas Press, 1991.

Dennis Valdez

16

Education

✳ Education of Hispanics in the Spanish Period, 1540–1821
✳ Education of Hispanics in the Mexican Period, 1821–1848
✳ Education of Hispanics: The American Period in the Nineteenth Century, 1850–1900
✳ Education of Hispanics in the Twentieth Century

The roots and patterns of contemporary Hispanic education can be found in the Spanish, Mexican, and Anglo conquests of North America. The original Spanish influence extended from the Carolinas and Florida on the East Coast, down through the Gulf Coast and on to the western part of the United States. By the end of the Spanish period in the early 1800s, the vast majority of Spanish subjects were concentrated in Indian-controlled lands of what we know today as the American Southwest: California, Arizona, New Mexico, and Texas. Informal rather than formal learning was the norm during the first 300 years of Spanish rule.

Formal learning, or schooling as it is more commonly known in today's world, began to emerge during the nineteenth century to meet the increasing needs of the Hispanic population for literacy and socialization. A variety of public, parochial, and private secular schools were established during this period. The schools provided, however, were limited in many respects. They were segregated, assimilationist, nonacademic in orientation, and inferior to those provided for other children. No higher education facilities were provided for Hispanic children. In the early twentieth century and until 1965, public education became the dominant form of learning in the Hispanic community. Private forms of schooling existed, but the community, augmented by an influx of Puerto Ricans from the island, began to increasingly support public education over other types of schooling. Due to their subordinate status in the society where they were concentrated, Mexican Americans and Puerto Ricans were provided with segregated and inferior forms of public education.

During the contemporary period, from 1965 to the present, public education continues to be the domi-

nant form of schooling for the Hispanic population. As a result of various pressures, the schools have become more sensitive to the academic, cultural, and linguistic needs of the Hispanic population during this period. However, the patterns of inequality have

Children during recess at the Guadalupe Aztlán alternative school in Houston, 1981. (Photograph by Curtis Dowell.)

391

continued. Unequal access to unequal schools contin-ues to characterize the schooling of Hispanics. Unlike the past, the Hispanic community is now more di-verse and includes a significant number of immi-grants from all areas of the Spanish-speaking world, including Mexico, Puerto Rico, the Caribbean, Cen-tral America, and the rest of Spanish America.

✳ EDUCATION OF HISPANICS IN THE SPANISH PERIOD, 1540–1821

During the years from 1540 to 1821, education in Spain's far northern frontier was a function of the Crown, the church, and, to some extent, the settlers. As in most agricultural societies, education was broadly conceived as an informal aspect of institu-tional life and included at least three elements: knowledge, skills, and behaviors needed in making a living, in maintaining a household, and in satisfying personal wants. Education, however, was not con-ducted in schools. Schools were available in the far northern region of the Spanish regime but they were rare. The missions at times established schools, but only sporadically. The missions in California and es-pecially in New Mexico made reference to formal instruction in them. There is no mention of schooling in any of the Texas missions. The primary reason given was that Texas Indians were more nomadic than those in other parts of the Southwest. Seden-tary groups such as those found in New Mexico were easier to teach than nomadic ones. Schooling in the missions was for the benefit of the Indians. Basic literacy skills were taught in them. Schools outside the mission were rarely found. The sons and daugh-ters of the Spanish settlers, including the military personnel, rarely received formal instruction on the frontier.

The diverse population that came to comprise the Hispanics, that is, the indigenous groups, the Span-iards, and the mestizos or other racially mixed groups, acquired basic literacy skills and knowledge or behaviors necessary for adult life not from schools per se but from other institutions. Education was an informal process that occurred in the three major institutions established in the far northern frontier: the missions, the settlements, and the presidios. The primary purposes of these institutions were to con-quer, civilize, and control the Indian population in this part of the Americas in order to exploit their resources for the benefit of Spain. These institutions, however, served an educational purpose. This is es-pecially the case with the missions. They provided informal instruction on political culture, moral, and religious values, and attitudes and skills needed for adult life in Spanish America.

Missions, presidios, and pueblos in the far north-ern frontiers were established decades after Span-iards in search of gold, glory, and new trade routes explored the area. Spaniards, for instance, explored Florida and the Atlantic coast from 1513 to the 1540s and both New Mexico and Arizona in the late 1530s. But after finding no gold or precious minerals, they left. Although Spain decided to withdraw from the area once it realized that there were no precious minerals to be found, the Jesuits and other religious orders stayed to convert the Indians. They made religious arguments for colonization, but their pleas went unheeded for nearly half a century.

Serious colonization of the far northern frontier began in the seventeenth century. These efforts were led by the missionaries who established a large num-ber of missions to convert the Indians to Christian-ity, that is, to a Spanish way of life. The missions were initially financed by the state, but eventually became self-supporting. Most missionaries were scholarly and literate "men of high calibre" who wrote many historical tracts, scientific documents, ethnographically rich reports and translations of In-dian languages. Unlike those in central Mexico, the missionaries in this far northern frontier, comprised of both Jesuit and Franciscans, requested the pres-ence of soldiers in their colonization efforts. Fear for their lives because of hostile Indians provided the rationale for such actions. Some of the soldiers as-signed to protect them, however, were a hindrance to their educational endeavors, since they mistreated the Indians.

Settlement efforts were first initiated in New Mexico during the 1590s. In 1595, a large force of missionaries, soldiers, and settlers set off to colonize New Mexico. The first permanent settlement was in 1598. However, by 1601 there was no missionary work done; it was mostly military. Missionary work and the construction of missions began in earnest between 1605 and 1608. By 1626, there were more than 25 missions, 43 churches, and more than 36,000 new converts.

Between 1659 and 1665, the new civil governors established a reign of tyranny and alienated all groups in the far northern frontier. They also did irreparable harm to the missions. Eventually these actions led to the 1680 Pueblo revolt and to the killing of the missionaries. The area was recon-quered by Spain between 1695 and 1698. Continuing conflict and tensions for the next decade, including a second rebellion involving at least 15 pueblos, slowed down but did not stop the Franciscans from doing their missionary work. However, the success of the past was not equaled. By 1774, some success in conversion, mission and church establishment, and in teaching the practical arts and education was made. The missions continued to decline after 1775 owing to insufficient number of missionaries and to friction between missionaries and local Spanish officials.

Arizona was the second area settled by the Spanish government. As in New Mexico, the missionaries led the way. Due to Indian resistance, this area was not settled until the late 1600s, although it had been explored in the 1630s. By 1680, there were six Franciscan missions in northeast Arizona. After the Pueblo revolt of 1680, these missions were abandoned and never rebuilt. In the south, the Jesuits founded several missions in 1700. During the next 67 years two missions and 11 visitas (substations) were founded. The Jesuits were expelled in 1767 and the missions were assigned to the Franciscans, but the hostility of Indians forced them to close five visitas. Two additional ones were established under them. Despite this activity, the missionaries were unable to establish more missions because of the Indian raids and the area's lack of strategic value. Few settlers went to Arizona. By the end of the colonial period, it contained a sparse Mexican population centered in the Santa Cruz Valley.

Defense against foreign powers rather than economic considerations was the major reason for settling California and Texas. Religious conversion, however, was still a primary goal of the missionaries. Successful missions were established in the El Paso region between 1659 and 1684. Missionaries explored east Texas in the 1670s but no missions were established until 1690, and then largely due to fears of French activity in that area. But Indian raids slowed the growth of a Spanish presence. For this reason missionary activity in Texas was more uneven and at times less successful than in New Mexico. By 1690, the missions were abandoned because of Indian resistance to missionary activity and agriculture. Some scholars have reported the founding of many more missions than originally suspected in other parts of the state. Sister Mary Stanislaus Van Well, in her *The Educational Aspects of the Missions of the Southwest* (1942), stated that as many as 50 of them were founded during the late 1600s and early 1700s. In San Antonio, more than five missions were founded. The first and longest-lasting one, San Antonio Mission, was founded in 1718.

Spain colonized California for defensive reasons, too, but missions came to dominate the life of the province. Fear of Russian traders in the north in 1769 encouraged Spanish authorities in Mexico to settle California. Between 1769 and 1823, for instance, 21 missions and a large number of presidios were constructed. Despite the large number of missions and the excellent climate, few individuals settled in California. Those who did settled in widely scattered pueblos throughout California. By 1821, the non-native population was located in pueblos scattered along the coast.

During this period, education occurred in the missions and in the pueblos. The mission community was considered a school of civilization. In a San Antonio mission founded in 1718, for instance, the missionaries taught Indian children and adults Catholic religious and moral instruction, adherence to Spanish custom and law, and training in agriculture and the domestic arts. All the Indians knew the Christian doctrine (prayers, beliefs, and so on) and spoke Spanish, and most played musical instruments or sang. They also dressed with "decency," assisted in making furniture, raised their own food, and went to school. The missionaries likewise taught the Indians family living, stock raising, European farming techniques, church construction, and furniture making.

Education also occurred in the Spanish settlements and to some extent in the presidios. As in most agricultural societies, the family and the community were the primary vehicles for teaching non-Indian youths in the pueblos and presidios the values and skills needed to survive. People also learned from other sources of nonformal education, including textbooks, folklore, oral history, drama, traveling puppet shows, and the Spanish mail service.

By the end of the Spanish period, several patterns of educational development were discernible. First, formal instruction was not an integral aspect of community development. If present, it was peripheral to other community institutions. Second, the primary goal of education in the mission was to assimilate, forcefully if need be. Education was for the purpose of teaching Indians the dominant political and religious values of Spanish culture. In the process of teaching Christianity and Spanish ways, the missionaries either showed contempt or else disregarded the population's native language and culture. Under the Spaniards, most of the indigenous institutions, including the educational traditions and native languages, were trampled and destroyed. The government's official policy toward language, for instance, called for the abolition of the native language in instruction and the sole use of Spanish in religious conversion. In 1793, King Carlos IV decreed that schools in the American empire should replace the Indian languages with Castilian. This did not occur because of the special linguistic circumstances faced by the missionaries. Third, the informal curriculum that was provided, especially in the mission, emphasized vocational or industrial education at the expense of academic instruction. Fourth, there was disagreement among the missionaries over the role that the native language would play in Christianization. Most of the Franciscans, for instance, strongly believed in Spanish and failed to learn the native languages of the Indians. The Jesuits, on the other hand, were supportive of native languages in conversion. They used Spanish whenever possible and learned the languages of those whom they sought to convert. But, the Jesuits, for the most part, were not in support of native language maintenance. They, like the Spanish Crown, believed that Spanish should replace the Indian languages. The use of the Indians' native language in instruction was a temporary measure aimed at more easily assimilating them into Spanish culture. Fifth, a distinct pattern of community distrust of educators and educational institutions emerged during this period. Owing to the foreign teachings and the mistreatment by soldiers and some missionaries, the Indian community began to distrust Spanish institutions and leaders. In New Mexico, especially, missionaries destroyed native religious objects, built the church away from the Indian community, utilized soldiers to ensure compliance with their rules, and imposed harsh discipline on Indians for failing to adhere to Spanish religious and work practices. These teachings and mistreatment were for the most part rejected or resisted by the native populations. These incipient patterns of educational development in the Spanish period were modified and eventually strengthened in the decades to come, especially with the emergence of schooling as an important socialization agency in the nineteenth and twentieth centuries.

✳ EDUCATION OF HISPANICS IN THE MEXICAN PERIOD, 1821–1848

During the latter part of the eighteenth and early nineteenth centuries, the family and the parish church replaced the missions as the key educational institutions in the northern provinces. The focus and objectives of instruction also shifted from teaching Indians to teaching non-Indian children, from propagating Spanish political, economic, and cultural values to preserving them, and from teaching religious values to teaching basic literacy skills. The decline in the number of missionaries and in the Indian population, as well as the increase in the non-Indian population (for instance, it nearly trebled in New Mexico from 1750 to 1800), led to increasing pressure to better serve the spiritual needs of the colonists who were concentrated in certain parts of the northern frontier. This period also led to the emergence of schools as important frontier institutions.

The Decline, Collapse, and Weakening of Frontier Institutions

The missions and pueblos of the American Southwest began to decline in significance in the late eighteenth century. Their complete collapse occurred under independent Mexico. The lack of federal funds, the shortage of priests, ideological opposition to missions, and various local conditions led to their eventual decline.

The order to secularize the missions led to their eventual demise. This order, issued originally in 1813 but resurrected in 1821 once Mexico gained its independence, was based on the notion that all men, including Indians, were equal before the law. These sentiments were embodied in the government's Plan of Iguala in 1821. It called for the elimination of all distinctions on the basis of race or class. The missions were antiquated institutions that oppressed Indians and had to be eliminated. The missions also aided the church in amassing immense wealth and property and in maintaining its influence in secular affairs. The need to undercut the church's power, both economic and political, thus served as a rationale for secularization.

Within a decade and a half after Mexico declared its independence, the missions of the far northern provinces fell to pieces. After secularization, Indians deserted the missions, the buildings began to decay, the fields lay bare, and the Franciscans disappeared from sight. With secularization, the colonizers became parishioners. This led to the emergence of the Catholic parish church as one of the most significant institutions involved in educating the population, composed now primarily of mestizo settlers.

The secularization of the missions brought an end to the influence of missionaries on the frontier and to the weakening of the Catholic church. The church remained strong in central Mexico, but weak in the frontier during the period of Mexican independence. It failed to fill the void created by the dismantling of the missions and the departing of the Franciscans for several reasons. First, its leadership decreased due to the expulsion of all Spaniards from Mexico during the 1830s. Second, there was a shortage of priests and funds. Mexico did not train its own priests and the Vatican forbade sending any new ones to Mexico. The church also abolished all tithes and service fees, for example for marriages, births, and deaths. The major result of the church's weakened leadership and lack of funds or priests was the neglect of the spiritual welfare of the mestizos and the decline in the morale and morality of frontier clerics.

In addition to the church's collapse, the military supremacy over the frontier also slipped away. In many areas of the frontier, the decades following independence saw relations worsen with the Indians, who rejected Christianity and much of Hispanic culture. The Indians increased their attacks on Mexican settlements for various reasons. According to David J. Weber, in *The Mexican Frontier, 1821–1846* (1982), missionaries had forcibly recruited Indian neophytes for missions or for slavery and settlers sought their land after secularization in 1830. But most important, Indian resistance to the Spanish/Mexican presence increased due to the influx of Anglos who upset the balance of power in the frontier, while the Mexican government failed to strengthen its military and economic posture. Anglo traders as well as some Mexican ones, in some cases, provided firepower to Indians in return for stolen goods and encouraged them to attack Mexican settlements and missions. Firepower upset the balance of power on the frontier. Anglo settlers also pushed Indians out of traditional areas in their westward expansion, especially in Texas.

The new resistance by Indians led to discussions of how best to deal with them. Mexicans for the most part were in disagreement whether Indians should be assimilated and provided with gifts to maintain the peace or whether they should be annihilated or removed, as in the United States. The former view prevailed, although it was perceived to be a failure.

The decline of these frontier institutions led to a disruption in the education of the population in the northern provinces. Other frontier institutions, especially the family, the Catholic parish church, and the state-sponsored public schools, began to replace the missions as key educational institutions. The emergence of these institutions accompanied the secularization of the missions and the growth of ranches and pueblos in the far northern provinces.

The Emergence of New Frontier Institutions and the Education of Hispanics in the Early Eighteenth Century

Ranches and pueblos emerged in California during the period of Spanish control. In addition to land provided for the establishment of the missions, the Spanish government also allotted land to private individuals. Independent Mexico confirmed these grants and distributed many more. The numbered ranches increased after the secularization of the missions in 1834. Similar to the early Spanish missions, the ranches provided most of the daily needs of their owners and workers. They raised sheep and hogs and cultivated grapes, fruit, wheat, and other grains.

Towns also were established during the Spanish period, but did not expand until the latter part of the 1700s, when Indian raids were halted and local economies began to expand. Pueblo life revolved around the plaza, a park-like square that formed the center of town. On one side of the plaza stood the church. Opposite the church was the town government building, known as the *cabildo,* and on the remaining two sides local ranchers built their town houses on lots referred to as *solares*.

In both the ranch and pueblo the extended family pattern was the norm. A typical household included parents, children, grandchildren, in-laws, other relatives, occasionally orphans, and Indian servants all living together. The children learned obedience, respect, political values, religious beliefs, and cultural traditions. The families in the ranches likewise taught routine household tasks such as cooking, washing, and the making of candles, soap, cloth, and wine. They also taught the planting of crops, the raising of cattle and sheep, and the making of clothing and other goods needed for survival on these ranches.

The church was another important institution that taught the knowledge, skills, and attitudes necessary for Christian living in these areas. It served an educational function through such activities as mass, religious rituals, weddings, christenings, wakes, and celebrations of town saints. The education of Indians decreased but learning among non-Indians increased.

In addition to the informal education provided by the church and the family residing in the ranches and pueblos, the state, especially in the form of the federal and provincial governments, began to express an interest in the formal instruction of the population. The declining influence of the church, as well as pressure from the settlers, encouraged the federal government late in the colonial period and in the Mexican era to support the establishment of public schools.

The Emergence of Schooling in the Far Northern Provinces

The initial interest for public education was expressed by the King of Spain in 1793 when he mandated the establishment of public schools in the colonies. High illiteracy among soldiers prompted the king to pass this mandate. However, nothing concrete was done to promote schooling in the far northern provinces until the early part of the 1800s. In 1802, for instance, Governor Juan Bautista Elguezábal of Texas issued a compulsory school attendance law for children up to age 12. This law however could not be enforced. As a result, no new schools were produced and existing ones were eradicated. Social and economic factors, compounded by political unrest, during these years ended the period of Spanish rule without a semblance of an educational system.

In California, two governors—Governor Diego de Borica and Pablo Vicente de Solá—promoted schooling in the latter part of the Spanish period. During Governor Borica's administration, from 1794 to 1800, approximately ten schools in five different cities were established. Under Governor Solá's administration, from 1815 to 1822, nine schools in two different cities were established. These schools, however, did not last long and had a negligible effect on the population. Public officials were unsuccessful in establishing a viable public school system in California during the Spanish period for many reasons, including the lack of public education tradition among the settlers, the isolation and sparseness of the population, general indifference, financial problems, shortage of funds, poor quality of teachers, external threats from foreign powers and rivalries, and internal bickering among state and local officials. No publicly sponsored schools were established in New Mexico during this same period.

Government leaders continued to support the establishment of public schools after Mexican independence. In Texas, for instance, state officials prodded local authorities and provided them with some financial assistance for the establishment of schools. In 1827, the state of Coahuila-Texas formulated a state constitution that required all municipalities to establish primary schools. Between 1828 and 1833, state officials issued several decrees attempting to encourage local authorities, usually known as *ayuntamientos,* to establish schools. Local officials, however, faced many obstacles in establishing schools, including individual and municipal poverty, lack of qualified teachers and lack of commitment to the importance of education among "ordinary" folks. In 1833, the state issued land grants for the support of local schools, but political unrest in central Mexico once again ended all efforts at establishing public schools. As in prior years, then a variety of social, political, and economic factors deflected government interest in formal education and prevented officials from establishing public schools.

In New Mexico, government officials were temporarily successful in establishing schools during the Mexican period. Between 1825 and 1827, for instance, 18 schools were established in New Mexico. Efforts by Mexican government officials to establish more schools were thwarted by indifference, political turmoil, and poverty.

Government officials were not the only ones interested in the establishment of schools in the far northern provinces of the Mexican nation. There was also a fluctuating interest in schooling on the part of religious leaders and private individuals. Anglo settlers in Texas, for instance, established some private schools. These private schools started by American settlers in Texas during the Mexican period fared better than public ones.

Formal education for the most part was not an important component of learning for the majority of the population during the latter part of the eighteenth and the first half of the nineteenth centuries. It nevertheless assumed an increasingly important part in the lives of Hispanics and other school children with the coming of Anglos and American rule after 1848.

✳ EDUCATION OF HISPANICS: THE AMERICAN PERIOD IN THE NINETEENTH CENTURY, 1850–1900

During the first half-century of American rule in the "Southwest," Hispanic traditions and institutions were trampled upon, modified to meet new needs, or gradually replaced by American ones. After the signing of the Treaty of Guadalupe Hidalgo in 1848, Americans introduced new political, economic, cultural, and social institutions and organized the society on the basis of certain Protestant, capitalist, republican, gender, and racial ideals. They sought to create a world in their own image, but encountered passive or active resistance by significant numbers of Hispanics. A few wealthy Hispanics initially supported these efforts, but by the turn of the century they had been dispossessed of their fortunes, had been relegated to wage earners in seasonal or low-paying jobs, and had lost any semblance of political influence and social status. Many of the Hispanic elite then joined the majority of the population as members of a cheap labor force, a politically powerless group, and the victims of social and cultural discrimination.

The family during this period continued to be the central agency for educating Hispanic children. The family assumed greater importance in many respects because of the rapid changes occurring in the society, for example, immigration and the transformation of the pueblos into barrios, the Americanization of the Catholic church, the emergence of Protestantism in the Southwest, and the decline of the ranches and the emergence of farming in the rural areas. Of primary importance to Hispanic education was the emergence of the institution of schooling. Schools were established during this period by private individuals, the Catholic church, Protestant groups, and public officials to meet the increasing needs of developing an American social order.

By the middle of the 1800s, schools had undergone

a significant transition from transmitter of basic literacy skills to the agency of socialization. This change was due to the desires of one group to assert control over others and to improve the lives of those viewed as racially or culturally inferior. The changed mission of the school touched off a debate between Hispanics and school-based reformers over who would decide the education of these children and what role would be assigned to the native languages and cultures.

Reformers believed that the school was to shape desirable behaviors for functioning in American society. More specifically, its purpose was to promote uniformity and eliminate all differences, including regional, class, and ethnic. Hispanics disagreed with this view and argued that the role of the schools was to teach these youngsters, but not at the expense of their cultural identity. Hispanics generally opposed school reforms if they were aimed at the elimination of their cultural and linguistic heritage.

During the first half-century of American rule, then, schools became increasingly important to Hispanics, but unlike in earlier decades, they were not viewed as supplementary to education or as part of community life. For most Hispanics, the schools became alien institutions aimed at controlling them. This was especially the case with public forms of schooling, which were vehement in their insistence on cultural assimilation. In many respects, the school became the setting for a struggle for the loyalties of the next generation as reflected in important controversies, such as English-language school laws and sectarian influences in public schools.

Schools established by individuals from the community and by the Catholic church were very much a part of Hispanic culture and continued in the United States after 1848. The number of Catholic schools expanded significantly during the second half of the nineteenth century. Ironically, increased Catholic education among Hispanics came to be associated with cultural tolerance at a time in which the Catholic church was undergoing its own transformation and becoming an instrument of Americanization. This apparent association of an Americanizing Catholic church with cultural tolerance was due to the large number of Spanish-speaking parishioners and the willingness by individual priests, nuns, and religious orders to accommodate to these differences. Demography and individual initiative rather than policy were the driving forces behind this apparent contradiction in church behavior. It is important to note that the Catholic church did not specifically create schools for Hispanic children. It founded schools that turned out to be attended primarily by Hispanics. Quite often it was residential segrega-

tion, not policy, that accounted for the development of "Hispanic" Catholic schools throughout the Southwest.

Reasons for the transformation of the Catholic church and for the expansion of its school system were varied. The emergence of secular institutions, especially public school systems, the growing educational needs of an increasing Catholic population, the anti-Catholic sentiments prevalent during the second quarter of the nineteenth century, and the proselytizing efforts made by various Protestant denominations acted as catalysts for the extension of Catholic parochial schooling in the Southwest. In response to these various forces, the Catholic church encouraged ecclesiastical authorities to promote the construction of additional parishes and schools by which an American Catholicism could be propagated.

Catholic education for Mexican children developed at uneven rates in the different states of the Southwest. In New Mexico, four religious orders came to dominate Catholic schooling during the period from 1851 to 1874: the Sisters of Loretto, the Christian Brothers, the Sisters of Charity, and the Jesuits. The Sisters of Loretto first came to the New Mexico territory in 1853. The Christian Brothers came from France to New Mexico in 1859. The other two religious orders, the Sisters of Charity and the Jesuits, arrived in New Mexico in 1865 and 1870, respectively. Together they established between 15 and 20 schools in as many cities.

In California, beginning in 1854 and continuing into 1889, ecclesiastical authorities encouraged the construction of additional parishes and schools by which an American Catholicism could be propagated. In order to staff these new parochial schools, at least nine religious orders were recruited. They established parochial schools for Catholic children in Santa Barbara, Ventura, Los Angeles, and throughout other parts of the state where the majority of the Mexican population was concentrated.

In Texas, religious orders also were requested to assist in the establishment of parochial schools. In some cases, Catholic parishes initially established these schools with the support of their parishioners. Carlos E. Castañeda, in his massive study of the Catholic heritage in Texas, identified more than 20 important religious orders that came to this state to establish missions, convents, and schools during the second half of the nineteenth century. The Catholic church, with the assistance of these religious orders, established some of the more well-known Catholic parochial schools attended by Mexican children in cities such as El Paso, Brownsville, Corpus Christi, and San Antonio.

Protestant denominations established schools for Hispanic children during the first half-century of American rule. Unlike the Catholic church, Protestant denominations acknowledged the presence of racially and ethnically distinct Hispanic children and took specific actions to encourage the establishment of schools for them.

Protestant schools varied tremendously within regions and across time, but they shared the common goals of Christianization and Americanization. The primary purpose of their elementary schools was, in the words of Melinda Rankin (1881), a prominent lay missionary of the 1850s, to "give them the Gospel, which is the antidote for all moral evils." In addition to these goals, the Protestant schools also promoted community leadership development. This task was assigned to the secondary schools established throughout the Southwest. One of the major goals of these schools was to train a Spanish-speaking Christian leadership that would propagate the Protestant faith and American ideals in their own communities. For this reason, some Protestant schools allowed for the use of the Spanish-language and Mexican cultural instruction in them. However, cultural and language diversity were viewed as means to an end, that is, as instruments for the more effective evangelization of the Mexican American population. Despite this end, ethnicity in education became one of the major distinguishing characteristics of Protestant secondary schooling.

Protestants have a long history of involvement with Spanish-speaking individuals in the Southwest. In the New Mexico territory, for instance, Protestant groups, including Presbyterians, Congregationalists, Baptists, and Methodists, all sponsored ambitious evangelization and educational programs during the second half of the nineteenth century. Presbyterian ministers began to conduct missionary work and organize schools in their missions in various cities as early as 1860. But they were unsuccessful in these early efforts because of lack of funds and support among the population. Despite these early setbacks, Presbyterian and other Protestant missionaries continued to evangelize and to establish schools. During the entire territorial period, from 1850 to 1912, they succeeded in establishing five major boarding schools and more than 40 mission day schools. The latter were commonly known as plaza schools. Most of this growth was spurred by favorable church policies and financial assistance from national lay and religious organizations, as well as by the determination of individual missionaries. Catholic opposition to Protestant schools, as well as Mexican American distrust of non-Catholic missionaries, acted as barriers to the establishment and growth of some of these schools.

While Presbyterians were the most active Protestant sect, important educational institutions were also founded by other denominations. The Baptists, for instance, preceded the Presbyterians and began to establish churches and schools as early as 1849. Several efforts were made to establish Baptist schools in Santa Fe during the 1850s and early 1860s. Other New Mexico Baptist schools operated briefly at Alcalde (1851), Albuquerque (1851, 1855), Peralta (1852), Cubero (1854), and Socorro (1857). Since few Anglos were located in the New Mexico territory, one can assume that all of these schools were for the conversion of Mexican children to Protestantism. These schools were vigorously opposed by the Catholic clergy and rapidly were forced to close their doors because of the lack of students.

Congregationalists in 1880 started several rural schools and academies. According to Jerry L. Williams, in *New Mexico in Maps* (1986), the Congregationalists opened more than a dozen schools between 1878 and 1891. Four of these were still in operation by 1911. The Methodists also conducted missionary work and educational development in New Mexico. They worked in New Mexico in the late 1840s and even established two mission schools in 1854. But these were not permanent ventures. In total, the Methodists opened approximately 11 schools during the second half of the nineteenth century. Three of them were still in operation by 1911.

In Texas, Presbyterians dominated, but occasionally a group such as the Methodists established lasting schools. During the period from 1845 to the early decades of the twentieth century, individual Protestant missionaries led the way in providing educational opportunities for native Mexican children. Of primary importance were the Presbyterians. In total, individual missionaries sponsored by Presbyterians established seven major schools.

Methodists also conducted "Spanish work" in Texas. Their major achievements were in the area of church development. Between 1874 and 1884, for instance, they organized four Mexican American districts in west Texas. To complement their ministry to Mexican Americans, the Methodists established several schools. Three major educational institutions for Mexican children were founded between 1880 and 1914: the Holding Institute, the Lydia Patterson Institute for Boys, and the Effie Eddington School for Girls. The former was founded in Laredo in 1880. The latter two were founded in El Paso in 1914. In addition, there was also a school called the Anglo-Mexican Mission Institute founded in El Paso in

1907. This school was built by the Baptists in the heart of "Mexican El Paso."

Probably owing to the presence of public schools at an early period and to the dominance of the Catholic church, few Protestant groups other than the Methodists established schools in California during the nineteenth century. The Methodists were the most prominent group in this state. They did not begin to minister to Spanish-speaking Catholics until 1879. In this year the Southern California Conference of the Methodist Episcopal Church appointed a committee to investigate the possibility of starting "Spanish work." This work began in Los Angeles in 1880 and had spread by 1900 to include missions in all three of the conference's districts. During this period of growth, the Methodist church established the Forsythe Presbyterian Memorial School in 1884. Several years later, in 1900, the Francis de Pauw Methodist School for Mexican Girls was founded. The Spanish American Institute for Boys was founded by the Presbyterians 11 years later.

Public officials began to establish schools in the second half of the nineteenth century. Unlike the religious groups or private individuals, public officials sought to develop a public school system that would eventually enroll all children residing in each state. Racial discrimination, ideological differences, and political tensions based on conflicts of heterogeneous values and different power relations, however, affected the development of Hispanic public education so much that by the end of the nineteenth century several distinct patterns had emerged. By 1900, Hispanic education was characterized by the following patterns: (1) denial of equal access to public schools, (2) the establishment of segregated facilities, (3) an absence of Hispanic individuals in decision-making positions, and (4) an assimilationist goal aimed at replacing Hispanic socioeconomic, political, moral, cultural, and linguistic ideologies with Anglo ones.

Denial of Equal Access to Public Schools

Local educators for the most part did not provide Mexican children with access to public school facilities until the post-Civil War period and usually years or decades after schools for white children had been established. During the period from 1836 to the late 1860s, they established a system of public education for the school-age population, but limited it only to white or Anglo students. Increasing financial ability and willingness, new state mandates, and local demands for education led to the establishment of public school facilities for the population. Political pressures from powerful economic interests and biased Anglo parents, local official indifference, and racial discrimination served to deny Hispanics full access to the emerging public school system. Some local communities, such as those in Santa Barbara and Los Angeles, California, did provide public school facilities for Hispanics during the 1850s and 1860s. But whenever enrollment occurred it was on Anglo terms. That is, access was based on the understanding that the Hispanic children's language and culture would be excluded from the schools.

Various means were used to deny Hispanics equal access to public schooling during these early years. Local officials either built public schools in Anglo communities and away from the Hispanic community or else allowed only members of the elite to enroll in the schools that were established. Once large numbers of working-class Hispanics were present and both the commitment and the resources were available, local officials began to provide Hispanics with their own school facilities.

The variety of conditions thus led to differential rates of public school access by Hispanics living in different parts of the Southwest. In California, Hispanics were allowed access to the public schools in the 1850s. Schools for Mexican children in Arizona were established in 1872, ten years after it became a territory. In Texas, public schools for Hispanic children in the urban areas were provided in the 1860s; rural school children were provided access to the schools in the 1880s. New Mexico officials failed to provide any significant access to public education until after 1872. The lack of finances, legal authority, and controversies over the issues of language, religion, and politics slowed educational developments in that territory.

Segregation

Although Hispanics were provided with increased access to public schools, the facilities provided in most cases were segregated owing to a combination of both race and residence. In most areas, residence played a large role in the establishment of segregated facilities. But in some districts race became a determining factor in the establishment of segregated schools for Mexican children. These segregated facilities were expanded over the years as the number of Hispanic children in the districts increased. Local officials expanded segregation through the use of containment and dispersal policies. In many cases, local officials prohibited the growing numbers of Hispanic children from enrolling in non-Mexican schools and kept assigning them to segregated facilities. If more Hispanic children enrolled, they usually added rooms to the existing school or purchased portables. Anglos on the other hand were provided with a greater number of school facilities that were dispersed throughout the local districts.

Absence of Hispanics in Decision-Making Positions

During the early years of American rule, Hispanics, especially members of the elite, were allowed to participate in the development of public education policy and in the establishment and operation of these schools. These individuals ran for political office and assumed important decision-making positions at various levels of government, including state or territorial legislatures, county boards of education, and local city councils and boards of education. In California, for instance, nine Hispanics were elected to the state senate and 12 to the state assembly during the years from 1849 to 1864. In the New Mexico territory, Hispanics were more fortunate, due to their numerical superiority and to the presence of a social and economic elite that was granted some political power. From 1850 to 1912, 177 Hispanics served in the territorial council and 531 served in the territorial house of representatives. Hispanics in the New Mexico territory also held other important legislative positions. Several of them were elected to the presidency of the upper chamber and nine were chosen to be Speaker of the House.

During the territorial period, from 1850 to 1912, Mexican Americans likewise assumed a few positions in the other branches of state government as well as in the federal government. Two Hispanics served as governor of the territory, one in the beginning of American rule and the other one at the turn of the century. Only one individual, Antonio José Otero, sat on the supreme court during the period from 1850 to 1912. Of the 18 individuals who were elected territorial delegates to the United States Congress from 1851 to 1908, 11 were Hispanics, including José M. Gallegos, Mariano A. Otero, Francisco Perea, J. Francisco Chávez, Mariano S. Otero, Tranquilino Luna, F. A. Manzanares, Antonio Joseph, and Pedro Perea.

Hispanics for a short period of time during the 1850s and 1860s also occupied on occasion a few important regional decision-making positions, including those of county superintendent and positions on county school boards and local boards of education. In California, for instance, approximately 6 out of 293 county superintendents serving between 1852 and 1865 were Hispanics. In New Mexico, the native Mexican population in the early decades of American rule made up a significant proportion of those elected to the office of county superintendent and county school boards. For example, in the 1873–74 school year, Mexican Americans comprised slightly over 75 percent of the total number of county superintendents in the territory. Out of 13 county superintendents, ten of these then were Hispanics.

By the latter part of the nineteenth century, Hispanics were relatively absent from the schools. Their involvement, for all intents and purposes, ceased to exist largely due to the relative increase of Anglo immigration, racial gerrymandering, vote-diluting policies and practices, structural changes in institutional life, and changing school policies and practices on governance and hiring. California legislators, for example, established citizenship and residency requirements for voting, used English-only ballots and voting procedures, and constantly changed registration procedures. They also enacted English literacy requirements for voting and holding office in the 1870s. This culminated in a constitutional amendment making English the official language of the state in 1890. Texas legislators voted to charge a poll tax for voting in the state beginning in the 1840s. They also established citizenship and literacy requirements for participation in the governmental process. Other forces, including the declining status of the Mexican population, the increasing proportions of non-Chicano immigrants to the areas, poverty, nonfamiliarity with the English language, and the legacy of distrust, acted to discourage any further participation and contributed to the decline of Mexican American officeholders.

The actions taken by school officials also played an important role in the decline in leadership positions by Hispanics. Local and state officials, for the most part, made no serious efforts to encourage the continuation of Hispanic participation in the shaping of public educational structures, policies, or practices. They did little to encourage the election, selection, or hiring of Hispanics to important positions of authority in the school structure. With one minor exception at the turn of the century, no Hispanics, for instance, were appointed to important statewide positions in education. Few if any Hispanics were hired to be administrators or teachers in the public schools during this period. In the case of New Mexico, where Hispanics played important roles in local and county government, their numbers decreased appreciably over time so that by 1912, when the territory became a state, the vast majority of the teachers, administrators, and school board members were Anglos. This was true even in areas that were predominantly Hispanic.

The decreasing political influence and voting power of Hispanics in general made it nearly impossible for them to elect their own members to important state positions, such as those of the superintendency or the board of education. No Hispanic, for instance, was elected to a state superintendent position during the second half of the nineteenth century in any of the southwestern states or territories. With the exception of New Mexico, no Hispanics served in the state boards of education either.

Assimilationism and School Content

The schools provided for Hispanics became rigidly assimilationist over the years and highly intolerant of cultural differences. They inculcated the dominant political, social, and moral ideologies through the use of English; they also devalued and excluded the Hispanic heritage from the curriculum. Between 1848 and 1900, three key aspects of Hispanic heritage were excluded from the schools—the Catholic heritage, the Hispanic cultural traditions, and the Spanish language.

Public policy toward Hispanic education was based on a developing and strengthening notion of the American national cultural identity that evaluated the religious, cultural, and linguistic heritage of Hispanics and rejected it from the schools. In its place, educators and political authorities proposed an "essentially American" identity that was comprised of Pan-Protestantism, republican values, and core British values, especially the ability to speak English. The schools were to embody and reproduce these ideological notions of American culture. Alternative forms of cultural identity, especially those based on Catholicism, non-English languages, Mexican cultural traditions, and racially distinct individuals who embraced these cultural traits, were to be replaced with American ideals, traditions, and individuals. Political leaders thus developed educational policies that promoted and transmitted the essential elements of an American cultural identity to the multitude of culturally diverse children, including Hispanics.

These assimilationist ideals, nevertheless, were internally inconsistent and at times in conflict with each other. Various groups of political authorities and educators in the Southwest supported different strands of these ideals with varying intensities. In the early decades of American rule, most Anglo rulers in the Southwest supported cultural pluralist policies and practices, primarily out of political expediency. But toward the latter part of the nineteenth century, officials began to support more assimilationist policies in the schools and to devalue cultural diversity in education. The stated purpose of these assimilationist policies was to facilitate the entry and success of Mexican immigrant children into mainstream society. However, the underlying reason was to structurally exclude them from participating in the society and to reproduce the dominant cultural ideology.

The process of cultural intolerance in the schools is reflected in the history of Catholic exclusion from the schools in the New Mexico territory and other areas, of cultural exclusion in the textbooks, and of school language policies in the Southwest.

School Language Policies

School officials at the state level at first tolerated Spanish in the schools, primarily out of political expediency. During the early years of American rule, political leaders enacted educational policies in the Southwest that were tolerant of language differences and accepted Spanish as an appropriate medium for conducting public affairs. For example, Texas legislators in the late 1830s tolerated Spanish and encouraged the printing of the republic's laws in that language. In California, legislators included in the 1849 constitution a provision requiring that all laws be printed both in English and Spanish. Prominent school leaders such as State Superintendent of Public Instruction John G. Marvin and San Francisco educator John Pelton also supported the teaching of Spanish and other modern languages in the public schools. Los Angeles city officials, as early as 1851, enacted a school ordinance supportive of bilingualism. It provided that "all the rudiments of the English and Spanish languages should be taught" in all the schools subsidized by public funds. In the Colorado territory, a school law of 1867 mandated the establishment of bilingual schools with at least 25 non-English-language children present.

The language policies developed during this early period of American rule were, in the words of H. Kloss in his *The Bilingual Tradition* (1977), "designed to serve certain ends of the government rather than the concerns of the minority." The use of Spanish in the conduct of local government agencies ensured their operation during a period in which many individuals lacked knowledge of English. It was in the interests of the state itself therefore to accommodate the first generation of non-English-speakers with respect to the language of public affairs. Publicly sponsored bilingualism also served to facilitate and accelerate the assimilation of culturally distinct groups.

The basis of this initial accommodation was power. Expediency-based language policies were based on the political balance of power between Anglos and Mexican Americans. Once Anglos consolidated their political control of state institutions, educational authorities began to enact subtractive school language policies (that is, policies that strengthened the use of English while weakening the use of Spanish). The primary purpose of these policies was to reproduce the dominant ideological and cultural order in the schools, not, as Arnold Leibowitz in his *Educational Policy and Political Acceptance* (1971) has argued, to deny Mexican children access to them or to their content. School language policies sought to reproduce the dominant cultural order by promoting English and simultaneously eliminating the use of Spanish in the schools. By the end of the century, nearly all the southwestern states that had at one time provided for the use of Spanish in public institutions, such as schools, had effectively converted to using English only. At the turn of the century, only New Mexico still formally recognized Spanish as a medium of communication in the schools and in other public institutions.

But within a decade after assuming political control of state institutions, educational authorities began to develop policies and practices that were subtractive. The policies strengthened the use of English by at first prescribing, then mandating it. They weakened Spanish by neglecting to use it in public life or by prohibiting its use in public and private institutions.

The establishment of subtractive policies and the shift to English in the Southwest began as early as 1841, when the Texas legislature adopted a resolution that suspended the printing of the laws in the Spanish language, and continued into the 1920s. During this period, policymakers eliminated Spanish-language use in the courts, the legislature, and the public schools and strengthened the use of English in public affairs. This is most apparent in the area of education, as school authorities enacted subtractive language policies that prescribed English as the language of instruction in education while simultaneously rejecting Spanish and other "foreign languages" in the schools. In some cases, Spanish and other non-English languages were rejected as academic subjects.

Policy decisions favoring the elimination rather than the preservation of the Spanish language in the Southwest were part of a larger national campaign against cultural and linguistic pluralism initiated at mid-century. The annexation of the Southwest in the late 1840s coincided with and probably facilitated the emergence of this campaign for conformity to American cultural and linguistic mores. This campaign deemphasized diversity of cultures and languages while it promoted the understanding of idealized American customs and the speaking of English. Strong assimilationist views motivated school leaders to seek the reduction or elimination of Spanish in public life. For the most part, Anglo officials and laypersons viewed non-English-language use among culturally different groups as a strong indicator of their "foreignness" and their unwillingness to adopt "American" ways over time. Elimination of non-English languages from all public institutions such as the schools was a sure way of encouraging the cultural incorporation of a group perceived to be "foreign" and unAmerican. It also served to maintain the cultural hegemony of white America while the diversity of this nation was increasing significantly during the second half of the nineteenth century.

These subtractive language policies, enacted in response to political pressure from groups with varying intensities of nationalist and racialist ideologies, did not go unchallenged. Hispanics and other groups supportive of cultural diversity sought to challenge, resist, and modify them over the years. At certain historical moments, changing political and economic circumstances created conditions that led to increasing degrees of tolerance and further modifications of these types of exclusionary policies. In most cases, however, these policies were ignored by the masses of Hispanics. The majority did not attend public or private schools during the nineteenth century and thus paid no attention to them. Those enrolled in the public schools also initially ignored the English-language policies and the culturally biased textbooks. They continued to speak their language in the schools, to overlook the demeaning comments made about their heritage in the curriculum, and to participate in the governance and administration of the public schools. Over the years, however, the exclusionary and assimilationist measures were strengthened. The increasing loss of wealth, political clout, and prestige made Hispanics unable to mount an effective challenge to them.

✳ EDUCATION OF HISPANICS IN THE TWENTIETH CENTURY

In the twentieth century, Hispanic education underwent many significant transformations. In many ways it reflected the tremendous social, economic, political, and cultural changes underway in American life and both affected and was affected by these developments. Despite these changes, the patterns of Hispanic education formed in the latter part of the nineteenth century did not change significantly. The schools continued to be exclusionary, discriminatory, and assimilationist.

During this century, Hispanics continued to be educated by a variety of formal and informal institutions. Parochial, Protestant, and private secular schools provided essential knowledge, values, and skills for Hispanic achievement. Hispanics also were

Mexican fourth-graders at Drachman School (circa 1913).

"taught" by new institutions, such as radio, TV, industry, the armed forces, the federal government, and their peers. Schooling, especially public education, assumed a new importance as it became the dominant form of education for all groups, including Hispanics. Increased state support for public schooling, as well as pressures from industry and from Hispanics, made this institution the dominant form of education in the twentieth century.

As did most institutions during the twentieth century, public education changed dramatically. So did the composition, status, and ideological orientation of the Hispanic population.

Between 1900 and 1980, the goals, structure, and content of public education were transformed as a result of pressures from various sources. Education was extended to individuals from all racial, national, gender, and age groups. Governance structures were altered to benefit middle-class individuals. New innovations in educational administration, such as standardized testing, were introduced. The curriculum was diversified to meet the varied needs of the heterogeneous student population. Educational programs were standardized. Instructional methodology was revolutionized through the introduction of a

new psychology and more sophisticated learning theories. One-room schools in rural areas were consolidated into larger units for efficiency, and schools became articulated from elementary to the postsecondary grades.

The Hispanic population changed and became more diversified during the twentieth century. Between 1900 and 1980, the composition, social class status, and ideological orientation of the Hispanic population underwent dramatic transformation. The Hispanic population became more heterogeneous and included multiple groups with a range of views and experiences with education.

Between 1848 and 1940, Mexican-descent individuals were the predominant and, in some areas, the only group of Hispanics in the United States. Most of these individuals were concentrated in the Southwest. During the 1920s, Mexican-descent individuals began to migrate to other parts of the United States, especially the Midwest. During the 1940s, the United States experienced a tremendous influx of Hispanics from Puerto Rico. Beginning in 1959, the United States again experienced another tremendous influx of Hispanics. This time it was from Cuba. Beginning in the mid-1960s and spurred by political conflict and economic instability in their homelands during the 1970s, there was a tremendous influx of immigrants from Central and South American countries, such as Guatemala, Nicaragua, and Peru. Despite the tremendous growth of this group in the last three decades, Mexicans, both citizen and noncitizen, continued to be the largest and oldest residing group of Hispanics in the United States.

The Hispanic population, with the exception of Cubans, is composed of a large poor and working-class sector and a small but increasing group of middle-class individuals. As a group, Hispanics are politically powerless, economically impoverished, and socially alienated. Most of them live in highly segregated communities, tend to speak Spanish as a group, and live in dismal housing conditions. Hispanics are predominantly a cheap source of labor for American industry.

Despite their "common lot," the Hispanic population has a range of views and experiences with education that has affected their schooling in this country. Some, such as the first wave of Cuban immigrants in 1959, were middle class in status and had benefited from education in their country. They embraced all forms of education and actively sought schooling in the United States. Others, such as Mexicans and Puerto Ricans, have more diverse experiences that range from no schooling of any sort to college degrees. They, unlike the Cubans, are more ambivalent about education in general and public schools in particular. A large proportion of those who migrated from poor rural areas in Mexico have no formal school traditions and tend to be indifferent or distrustful of education in this country. Still others, including the small but growing middle class and the more stable sectors of the working class, actively seek educational opportunities and take whatever measures are needed to obtain them.

The range of views and experiences with education, as well as the diversity of Hispanic groups, posed significant challenges for public schools over the decades. They, however, did not meet these challenges. For the most part, schools and those who shaped them ignored the special needs of the heterogeneous Hispanic student population or else interpreted them in such a way that the differences brought by these children had to be eliminated. In many cases, the schools responded not to the genuine needs of this diverse group of children but to those of other stronger political and economic interests. As a result of these contextual realities, the nineteenth-century pattern of inequitable, segregated, and inferior schooling was extended and strengthened over time. Hispanic students were provided with access to schools but it was inequitable.

The schools they were provided with also were segregated and inferior, discriminating, assimilationist, and academically weak.

School Access in the Twentieth Century, 1900–1990

In the twentieth century, Hispanics were provided with increasing albeit inequitable access to the elementary, secondary, and postsecondary grades of the public schools. In the first half of the century, Mexican American school-age children gained access to public education in large part owing to the increasing availability of school facilities, their migration to urban areas, greater economic stability, and, especially, their resolve and desire to educate their young.

Increased access to public education became apparent by 1930. In 1900, for example, slightly less than 50 percent of the Hispanic scholastics, that is, school-age children between five and 17 in New Mexico were enrolled in the public schools. By 1930, Hispanic enrollment in the public schools had increased to 74 percent in New Mexico. Data from other parts of the Southwest, although incomplete, show that

A poster encouraging Hispanics to register to vote, which shows education to be a top priority.

the proportion of Hispanic children enrolled in school also increased during these 30 years. In Texas at the turn of the century, for instance, less than 18 percent of the Hispanic scholastics were enrolled in any type of school, much less public ones. By 1930, close to 50 percent of Hispanic school-age children in Texas were enrolled. In that same year, the proportion of Hispanic scholastics enrolled in public schools of California stood at 58 percent.

Access to public education stemmed from a variety of forces, including increased district ability to finance the establishment of schools, local willingness to expand educational opportunities to all levels of society, and political support for the enactment and enforcement of child-labor and school-attendance laws. Community resolve was also an important factor in increased school enrollment. Hispanics had, as did most other groups, diverse views toward education. Some Hispanics, especially those from the poorer classes and recent immigrants from Mexico, were unaware of the importance of education as an instrument of mobility. They were distrustful of the assimilationist role of public education. They were unable to send their children to school for economic reasons. But there were other Hispanic individuals and groups within the community who were supportive of education and took whatever actions they could to enroll their children in the schools. Although the majority of those in support of education came from the wealthier sector of the community, there were also working-class individuals. The number of working-class Hispanic individuals and groups who, despite their dire circumstances, made great sacrifices to educate their children increased over time. During the latter part of the nineteenth and early twentieth centuries, a larger number of them began to send their children to the public schools. An increasing stability in employment, migration to urban areas within the Southwest, and a slight increase in their ability to send their children to school encouraged these trends.

Despite the increasing access to education, a large proportion of Hispanic students continued to be out of school, largely because of poverty, mobility associated with rural employment, and discrimination on the part of educational policymakers. Three major groups of students were denied full access to public education during the first half of the twentieth century: agricultural migrants, secondary school-age students, and postsecondary school-age students. School officials excluded these children from the public schools or else took little positive action to encourage their enrollment. In the 1920s and early 1930s, for instance, local officials refused migrant and rural children admission to the elementary grades. Although special laws were passed in areas such as California and New Mexico for the education of migrant children, no significant action was taken by public officials to ensure their enrollment. During the second quarter of the twentieth century, largely from 1925 to 1950, local officials also excluded older Hispanic students from gaining access to the secondary and postsecondary grades. Local officials refused to allow Hispanic students admission into Anglo high schools or failed to establish sufficient secondary schools for them. Higher-education officials also failed to recruit or allow Hispanics entry to postsecondary educational institutions.

After World War II, Hispanic access to the public schools increased so significantly that by the third quarter of the twentieth century this group gained parity in elementary and secondary school enrollment. Data from Texas, for instance, indicate that between 1942 and 1960 the proportion of Hispanic school-age children enrolled in public schools skyrocketed from 53 percent to 79 percent. Hispanic enrollment in the other states also became significant and ranged between 84 percent in Arizona to 91 percent in California.

Enrollment continued to increase so that by 1980 the overwhelming majority of Hispanic scholastics in the Southwest were enrolled in the elementary and secondary grades. By 1980, the proportion of Hispanic school-age children enrolled in the public schools increased to slightly over 91 percent.

Increased educational access during this period was spurred by a variety of forces, including the continued expansion and extension of public educational opportunities to all levels of society, the vigorous enforcement of child-labor and school-attendance laws, and the addition of new curricula aimed at working-class children. Added vigor in Hispanic resolve was also an important factor in increased school enrollment. The increased support by Hispanics for public education as well as their greater involvement in challenging the exclusionary and discriminatory character of public education likewise led to increased access.

Despite the increased access by Hispanics during the post-World War II period, there was still a significant proportion of these children who were not enrolled in the public schools. Two major groups of students continued to be excluded or denied full admission to the schools: noncitizens and college students. In the early 1970s, local officials, led by the state of Texas, excluded the children of undocumented workers from enrolling in public schools. Although this exclusionary practice was challenged and overturned by the courts, there were still thou-

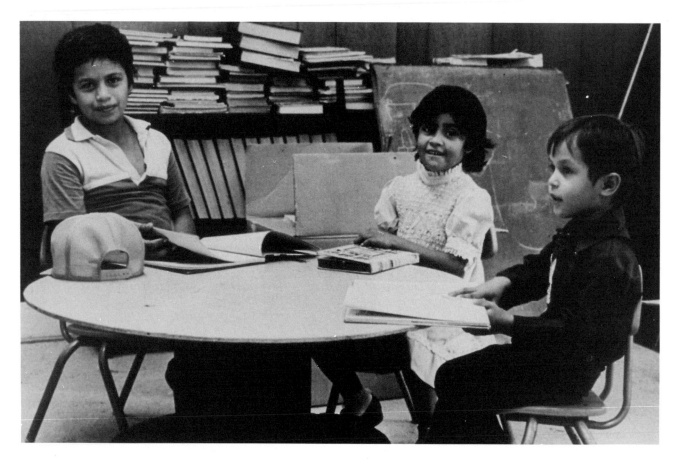

Children at the Guadalupe Aztlán alternative school in Houston in 1981, when public school education was denied to children of undocumented workers. (Photograph by Curtis Dowell.)

sands of children, both citizens and noncitizens, who were not allowed in the schools.

As noted earlier, by the 1970s, notwithstanding lingering inequities, Hispanics had reached parity with the total school-age population in the elementary and secondary grades, but not in postsecondary school enrollment. For this reason, the central issue by the 1970s was no longer access to the elementary and secondary grades but rather access to quality educational services within the public schools and access to higher education.

The Quality of School Facilities in the Twentieth Century: Separate and Unequal

Access to public schools for Hispanic children increased over time, but owing to their subordinate status, they were provided with segregated and unequal facilities. Although segregation originated in the mid-nineteenth century, it expanded significantly between 1890 and 1980. Segregation grew in existing communities in the Southwest in the first quarter of the twentieth century and expanded to the rest of the country by mid-century. Because of

the high withdrawal rates of Hispanic children from the public schools in the early decades of the twentieth century, segregation was confined to the elementary grades. But once Hispanic children began to seek access to secondary schooling, local officials established segregated facilities in these grades. The number of segregated secondary schools increased significantly after World War II. Today, Hispanics are now the largest single racial group in five of the 50 largest school districts in the country and more segregated than Afro-Americans.

Politics and prejudice were key in establishing segregated facilities, but culture and class became crucial in maintaining and extending this practice over time. State officials played an important role in the expansion of school segregation by sanctioning its presence and by funding local requests for increased Hispanic segregation. Residential segregation, demographic shifts in the population, and economic conditions likewise greatly affected the expansion of segregation in the twentieth century.

In addition to being separate, these schools were unequal in many respects to those provided for Anglo children. The facilities, for the most part, were older

A sixth-grade classroom in the Huelga School, an alternative school set up in St. Patrick's Chapel, Houston, when public education was denied children of undocumented workers. (Photograph by Curtis Dowell.)

and more dilapidated than those for Anglos. Recreation space was usually minimal and substandard in comparison to Anglo schools. The school equipment was generally less adequate for the students' needs. Per pupil expenditures in the Hispanic schools was extremely low. Finally, the staff of these schools were less appropriately trained, qualified, and experienced than those in Anglo schools. In many cases, the teachers were sent to the Mexican schools as a form of punishment or to introduce them to the teaching profession.

Discrimination in School Administration in the Twentieth Century

The third major pattern of Hispanic education was in school administration. Local officials developed administrative measures that were discriminatory toward these children. This can be seen in the evolution of assessment and placement practices and in the pattern of interaction between Hispanic students, their peers, and the teaching staff.

Hispanic children, similar to other working-class, immigrant, and racially different children, were consistently diagnosed as inferior, retarded, or learning-disabled, channeled into low-track classes, and deprived of opportunities for success. Their mental, emotional, and language abilities were assessed on the basis of biased instruments and used to classify Hispanic children as intellectually inferior, culturally backward, and linguistically deprived. These assessments were shaped by class and racial biases and economic imperatives. Once classified as inferior, Hispanic children were systematically placed in "developmentally appropriate" instructional groups, classes, or curricular tracks. At the elementary level, Hispanics were assigned to mostly slow-learning or nonacademic classes. At the secondary level, administrators assigned these culturally different children to vocational or general education courses (tracks) and discouraged them from taking academic classes. Tracking of Hispanics originated in the late 1920s and expanded after World War II. The policies, procedures, and practices utilized by school administrators to assess and classify students, place them in classes, or promote them through the grades served to stratify the student population according to various catego-

The
STATE DEPARTMENT
OF EDUCATION
believes in

equal opportunity

If you are interested in securing
employment information for
the Department of Education
call the . . .

AFFIRMATIVE ACTION OFFICE
721 Capitol Mall, Room 106, Sacramento, CA 95814.
Telephone (916) 322-4050. ATSS 8-492-4050.
Affirmative Action Program Manager, Robert G. Lee.
Wilson Riles · State Superintendent of Public Instruction · Sacramento

A poster encouraging affirmative action and equal opportunity in education in California.

ries and to reproduce the existing relations of social and economic domination in the classroom.

The discriminatory treatment of Hispanic children was also apparent in the interaction between them, the instructional staff, and their peers. Generally speaking, local educators provided Hispanic children with schools that were staffed by instructors who were insensitive or oblivious to the cultural and special educational needs of these children. Although some of these teachers were caring instructors, the majority had low expectations of the children's learning abilities, and they discouraged, at times unwittingly, Hispanics from achieving. They also ridiculed them for their culturally distinctive traits. Many a Hispanic child was punished simply for speaking Spanish at school or in the classroom. Teachers also interacted with Anglo students more and had less praise for Hispanic children.

The peers of Hispanic students likewise mistreated and ostracized them over time. Paul Taylor quoted, in *An American Mexican Frontier: Nueces County, Texas* (1934), Mexican students in the 1920s to illustrate what he called their severe "hazing" by Anglo children: "Some Americans don't like to talk to me," said one Hispanic youth in 1929. "I sat by one in high school auditorium and he moved away. Oh my god, it made me feel ashamed. I felt like walking out of school." Another student commented, "In grammar school they used to call us 'dirty Mexicans,' 'pelados' and greasers. A few times they moved away from me."

Curricular Policies

During the twentieth century, public officials continued to provide Hispanic children with a curriculum that was culturally partial toward Anglos and linguistically subtractive, despite minority efforts to reintroduce language and culture into the schools. Local educators also provided these children with a curriculum that was academically imbalanced.

The curriculum for Hispanic schoolchildren originally was comprised of the three Rs (reading, writing, and arithmetic) and some socialization, but in the early decades of the twentieth century it began to change. Sometime between 1880 and 1930, the Hispanic curriculum began to emphasize socialization and nonacademic concerns at the expense of academic ones. At the elementary level, it shifted its emphasis from the three Rs to the three Cs, that is, it focused more on the teaching of common cultural norms, civics instruction, and command of the English mother tongue. At the secondary grades, the emphasis was shifted to vocational and general education. Although composed of some elements of the three Rs, the curriculum for Hispanics in the secondary grades came to have larger doses of more practical instruction.

In addition to becoming academically imbalanced, the curriculum also was assimilationist. More particularly, it was linguistically and culturally intolerant. The latter was reflected in instructional materials and school textbooks, which, for the most part, either omitted or distorted the Hispanic cultural heritage. Linguistic intolerance was reflected in the English-only policies and anti-Spanish practices found in most public school systems throughout the country. Both cultural and language exclusion were opposed by Hispanics and other groups and at times challenged by them. The history of language policy in the United States illustrates this process of Hispanic challenges to assimilationism in the schools.

The curriculum for Hispanics was by the second decade of the twentieth century increasingly intolerant of diversity. It had negatively evaluated and rejected the Spanish language and the Hispanic cultural background of these children. This form of intolerance was reflected in curricular language policies and in the passage of English-only laws. English-language policies, however, were consistently questioned or challenged over the years by various groups, including Hispanics. The repeal of prescriptive laws by the Supreme Court in the 1920s, the modification of prescriptive English-only laws in the Southwest during the 1930s and 1940s, and the introduction of foreign languages into the elementary schools during the 1950s illustrate the result of these new pressures in support of language diversity in American public life. The most significant attempt to confront the ideology of assimilationism in the schools and in American life was initiated by various groups, especially Hispanics, during the period from 1965 to 1980. These groups viewed political empowerment and cultural resurgence as the key to academic and socioeconomic success. As a result of their resurgent awareness and their growing political strength, these new forces began to challenge the cultural and political hegemony of the dominant groups by promoting significant educational reforms and by supporting the reintroduction of language, culture, and community into the public schools. Specific language reforms were proposed by activists, including the elimination of the English-only laws and the enactment of federal and state legislation supporting the use of non-English languages in the conduct and operation of public institutions, especially the schools.

Hispanics and their allies were quite successful in accomplishing these goals and in promoting increased tolerance toward Spanish and other non-English languages in the schools, as well as in other aspects of government. Their efforts more particularly led to the repeal of subtractive language policies and to the enactment of more tolerant ones. Federal policies, for instance, began to recognize and urge the utilization of non-English languages in the schools. The United States Congress enacted bilingual education legislation, the Supreme Court forbade English-only instruction and sanctioned the use of native-language instruction in the schools, and the executive branch of government issued various documents supporting the use of non-English languages in educational services.

These actions served as catalysts for the increased support of bilingualism in the schools at the state and local levels. Between 1967 and 1980, for instance, more than 24 states passed some form of legislation either permitting or requiring the use of a language other than English in its public institutions, especially the public schools.

The increased use of non-English languages in the public schools led to much confusion over the goals of bilingual education and whether this program should be aimed at promoting bilingualism or English fluency. Although prominent educators and government officials argued that the ultimate goal of bilingual education was to promote bilingualism and biculturalism among schoolchildren, formal policy was geared toward the learning of English. The first piece of federal legislation, in 1968, for instance, said nothing about bilingualism. The reauthorized bills of 1974 and 1978 allowed for the use of two languages in instruction but underscored the importance of becoming proficient in English. The latter, especially, deemphasized the use of the primary language or of the minority culture in the instructional program. It also limited funding to accomplish this goal of English fluency. Even the Supreme Court decision *Lau v. Nichols,* as well as a variety of executive pronouncements, were aimed at promoting English fluency, not bilingualism.

In practice, English became the dominant language used in bilingual education programs. During the last two decades, various reports found empirical evidence of this fact. According to these reports, the vast majority of bilingual programs in the United States, usually over 80 percent of them, discouraged the use of minority children's native language and helped to facilitate language shift among them. Non-English languages then were rarely used in bilingual programs.

Manuel Pacheco, president of the University of Arizona.

Despite the dominance of English in bilingual policy and practice, even during its heyday in the 1970s, individuals and groups began to oppose the idea of non-English-language use in public life. In the 1980s, assimilationism once again, as in the 1920s, resurfaced with a vengeance, owing to, in many respects, the growing number of individuals and groups, such as the U.S. English and English First, who are opposed to pluralist and egalitarian ideologies. They have successfully led efforts to repeal bilingual policies and have enacted English-only laws. Although Hispanics continue to support bilingualism in American institutional life, the forces of assimilation have become once again dominant in today's world, including the public schools.

The Pattern of School Performance in the Twentieth Century

In the twentieth century, the major educational consequence of inferior schooling as well as unfavorable socioeconomic circumstances was the establishment of a pattern of skewed academic performance characterized by a dominant tradition of underachievement and a minor one of success.

The pattern of poor school performance has been documented over the decades by social scientists and scholars in general. The dimensions of the pattern of poor school performance can be documented by analyzing various measures, such as achievement test scores, withdrawal rates from school, and the median number of school years for the population age 25 years and older. For the most part, Hispanics have had lower test scores, higher withdrawal rates, and lower median number of school years than Anglos or the general population. Although there has been some improvement in these scores over the decades, the gap between these two groups has not changed significantly over time and continues into the contemporary period. Additionally, according to reports in 1991, the Hispanic dropout rate was significantly higher than that of other groups at 35.3 percent compared to 8.9 percent of whites and 13.6 percent of blacks.

The case of Hispanics in Texas illustrates this continuing pattern of poor school performance. In the 1920s, an overwhelming majority of Hispanics in Texas, approximately 75 percent of them, withdrew from school by the third grade. During the 1940s, half of the Hispanic student population withdrew from the public schools before reaching the secondary grades. Withdrawal rates were still abysmally high in the 1960s and 1970s, ranging anywhere from 40 percent to 80 percent, depending on local and state circumstances.

Not all Hispanic students have done poorly in school. Contrary to popular and scholarly opinion, a small proportion of them have done extremely well in achievement test scores, received a high school diploma, and continued into postsecondary education. This small group, of which we know little, experienced a pattern of school success, not academic failure. This group is composed of those individuals who completed secondary school during the interwar years, from 1917 to 1940, and of those who completed postsecondary education during the 1960s and 1970s. Considering that the overwhelming majority of Hispanic students dropped out between the third and sixth grades prior to the 1950s, completion of secondary school can be viewed as one aspect of academic achievement. The emergence of a professional and intellectual group of Hispanics likewise indicates scholastic achievement that has gone unrecorded. The existence of high school graduates in the past and college graduates in the contemporary period refutes the myth of unprecedented underachievement and suggests a more diverse pattern of school performance in the Hispanic community.

Hispanics, then, have had a checkered pattern of academic performance, not merely one of underachievement. The pattern of success should be explored further in order to better understand how these students overcame what were obviously tremendous odds.

References

Carter, Thomas P., and Roberto Segura. *Mexican Americans in the Public Schools: A History of Neglect.* Princeton, New Jersey: College Entrance Examination Board, 1979.

Castañeda, Carlos. *Our Catholic Heritage in Texas, 1519–1936.* New York: Arno Press, 1976.

Comptroller General of the United States. *Bilingual Education: An Unmet Need.* Washington, D.C.: GPO, 1978.

Crawford, James. *Bilingual Education: History, Policy, Theory and Practice.* Trenton, New Jersey: Crane Publishing, 1989.

De León, Arnoldo. *The Tejano Community.* Albuquerque: University of New Mexico Press, 1982.

"From a Dual to a Tri-partite School System." *Integrated Education,* 17, 1979: 27–38.

Gallegos, Bernardo P. *Literacy, Society and Education in New Mexico, 1693–1821.* Albuquerque: University of New Mexico Press, 1991.

Kloss, Heinz. *The Bilingual Tradition.* Rowley, Massachusetts: Newberry House, 1977.

Leibowitz, Arnold. *Education Policy and Political Acceptance.* Washington, D.C.: ERIC, 1971.

Manuel, Herschel T. *Spanish-Speaking Children of the Southwest.* Austin: University of Texas Press, 1965.

Meier, Kenneth J., and Joseph Stewart. *The Politics of Hispanic Education.* New York: Russell Sage Foundation, 1987.

Rankin, Melinda. *Twenty Years Among the Mexicans: A Narrative of Missionary Labor.* Cincinnati: Central Book Concerns, 1881.

San Miguel, Guadalupe, Jr. *Desegregation of Black and Hispanic Students from 1968 to 1980.* Washington, D.C.: Joint Center for Political Studies, 1981.

Schneider, Susan G. *Reform, Revolution, or Reaction.* New York: Las Americas Publishing Company, 1976.

Taylor, Paul S. *An American Mexican Frontier: Nueces County, Texas.* Chapel Hill: University of North Carolina Press, 1934.

Van Well, Sister Mary Stanislaus. *The Educational Aspects of the Missions of the Southwest.* Milwaukee: Marquette University Press, 1942.

Weber, David J. *The Mexican Frontier, 1821–1846: The American Southwest under Mexico.* Albuquerque: University of New Mexico Press, 1982.

Weinberg, Meyer. *A Chance to Learn.* New York: Cambridge University Press, 1977.

Williams, Jerry L., ed. *New Mexico in Maps.* Albuquerque: University of New Mexico, 1986.

Guadalupe San Miguel, Jr.

Scholarship

The biographies in this chapter are of scholars not covered in other chapters of this almanac, such as the ones on science, law and politics, and other chapters where scholars are studied or mentioned. Scholars that have become university presidents are included in the chapter on prominent Hispanics. Primarily, the scholars here have made their careers in the humanities and social sciences and have been pioneers in Hispanic studies, a field of scholarship that did not exist two decades ago. Many of them were involved in the civil rights movement of the late 1960s and were among the first scholars to research the history and culture of Hispanics in the United States. They were actively involved in creating the intellectual and structural bases for the creation of Mexican American, Puerto Rican, and Cuban studies departments and centers, as well as bilingual education programs at universities throughout the country. Many of them took as their models and mentors such early pioneer scholars as María Teresa Babín, Arthur León Campa, Carlos Castañeda, Luis Leal, Américo Paredes, and George I. Sánchez, who were among the extremely few Hispanic researches in academia during the 1940s, 1950s, and early 1960s. Today, most of them are tenured associate and full professors, continuing their efforts to broaden the curriculum so that Hispanic history and culture are not only taught but also attain their rightful place as a substantial part of the cultural identity of the United States as a whole. In addition, many of the social scientists are working toward alleviating many of the social and educational problems that continue to afflict Hispanics in American society. As a group, their research is contributing to the information about Hispanics that appears today in textbooks at every curricular level, from preschool to graduate school, and to the policies and practices of government at every level as well.

Edna Acosta-Belén (1948–)

Literature

Born on January 14, 1948, in Hormigueros, Puerto Rico, Acosta-Belén received her B.A. and M.A. degrees from the State University of New York, Albany, in 1969 and 1971, respectively, and her Ph.D. degree from Columbia University in 1977. She has been a National Endowment for the Humanities summer fellow at the University of Massachusetts (1982) and Princeton University (1978) and a visiting fellow at Yale University (1979–80). From 1972 to the present, she ascended the ranks from instructor to full professor with joint appointments in the Department of Latin American and Caribbean Studies and the Department of Women's Studies. From 1989 to the present, she has served as the director of the Center for Latin American and Caribbean Studies and, from 1983 to 1986 and again from 1988 to 1989, as chair of the Department for Latin American and Caribbean Studies. From 1987 to 1991, she was the cofounding associate director of the Institute for Research on Women. Acosta-Belén is one of the founders of the Puerto Rican Studies Association and has served as its president. She is also the recipient of numerous awards, including the New York State Chapter of the National Organization of Women's Making Waves Award (1991), the Chancellor's Award for Excellence in Teaching (1989), and the President's Award for Excellence in Teaching (1988). Her books include *In the Shadow of the Giant: Colonialism, Migration and Puerto Rican Culture* (1992), the co-edited *Integrating Latin American and Caribbean Women into the Curriculum and Research: Perspectives and Sources* (1991), *The Hispanic Experience in the United States* (1988), and *The Puerto Rican Woman: Perspectives on Culture, History and Society* (1979, 1986).

Rodolfo Acuña (1932–)

History

Born on May 18, 1932, in Los Angeles, California, Acuña received his B.A. and M.A. degrees from Los Angeles State College in 1957 and 1962, respectively, and his Ph.D. degree from the University of Southern California in 1968. He began his teaching career in 1962, at Mount St. Mary's as an instructor and has risen to the rank of full professor at California State University, Northridge. He is the founder of the Chicano studies department at Northridge and the author of the standard Chicano history textbook, *Occupied America: the Chicano's Struggle Toward Liberation* (1972, 1981, 1987). Acuña is a dynamic speaker and teacher as well as an assiduous researcher whose articles have been published far and wide.

Norma Alarcón (1948–)

Chicano Studies

Born in Mexico, Alarcón received her B.A., M.A., and Ph.D. degrees in Spanish from Indiana University in 1970, 1972, and 1983, respectively. From 1983 to 1987, she was an assistant professor at Purdue University. From 1987 to the present she has been a member of the Chicano studies department at the University of California, Berkeley. In 1991, she was promoted to associate professor with tenure. Alarcón has been an outstanding editor and promoter of Hispanic women's literature. From 1981 to the present, she has been the founding editor of Third Woman Press, and from 1975 to the present, a contributing editor of *The Americas Review*. She is the author of *La póetica feminista de Rosario Castellanos* (1992) and various articles on feminist literary theory, especially as it relates to women of color.

Fernando Alegría (1918–)

Literature

Born on September 26, 1918, in Santiago, Chile, Alegría received his early education in Chile, his M.A. degree from Bowling Green State University in 1941 and his Ph.D. degree in Spanish from the University of California, Berkeley in 1947. After receiving his doctorate, he made his entire career at Stanford University, where he ascended the ranks to full professor with a chair, and finally professor emeritus, which is his current status. Alegría has been a pioneer in the study of Hispanic American literature, in which his books have concentrated on narrative, and he has also been a novelist, essayist, and poet, recognized in both the Spanish- and English-speaking world. His book *Historia de la novela hispanoamericana* (*History of the Spanish American Novel*, 1965) has gone through

various editions and served as a standard text of Latin American literature.

Noted for his important critical works on Latin American literature, his poetry, and his novels, Alegría has been living in exile since a military junta overthrew Chilean President Salvador Allende's government on September 11, 1973. *The Chilean Spring,* is Alegría's fictionalized account of a young photographer's ordeal and death at the hands of the junta. Alegría has received a Guggenheim Fellowship and has won numerous other awards and distinctions. He was also one of the first and most influential scholars to acknowledge and promote Hispanic literature of the United States in academia.

Rodolfo Alvarez (1936–)

Sociology

Born on October 23, 1936, in San Antonio, Texas, Alvarez received his B.A. degree in 1961 from San Francisco State University and his M.A. and Ph.D. degrees from the University of Washington in 1964 and 1966, respectively. He served as an assistant professor at Yale University from 1966 to 1972, after which he moved to the University of California, Los Angeles, as an associate professor; in 1980 he became a full professor. From 1972 to 1974, he served as the director of the Chicano Studies Research Center at U.C.L.A., and from 1973 to 1975 he served as the founding director of the Spanish-Speaking Mental Health Research Center. Alvarez has been active in his profession and in the community, serving on numerous boards and committees, including the board of the Mexican American Legal Defense and Education Fund (1975 to 1979), the presidency of the ACLU of Southern California (1980 to 1981), and the presidency of the Society for the Study of Social Problems (1985–86). He has served as a management fellow at the University of California since 1994, and has coedited various books, including *Racism, Elitism, Professionalism: Barriers to Community Mental Health* (1976) and *Discrimination in Organizations* (1979).

María Teresa Babín (1910–)

Literature

Born in Ponce, Puerto Rico, in 1910, Babín received her early education in Ponce, her M.A. degree from the University of Puerto Rico in 1939, and her Ph.D. degree from Columbia University in 1951. She served for many years as the director of the Spanish-language program of the Puerto Rican Department of Public Instruction and the Hispanic Studies Program at the University of Puerto Rico at Mayagüez. During the 1970s, Babín finished her career as a pioneer in Puerto Rican studies at the City College of New York, where she taught some of the first courses in Puerto Rican literature and culture. Her best-known and most important book is her pioneering history and overview of Puerto Rican culture, *Panorama de la cultura puertorriqueña* (1958). Another pioneering work by Babín is the anthology that she cowrote with Stan Steiner, *Borinquen: An Anthology of Puerto Rican Literature* (1974), which is one of only two anthologies of Puerto Rican literature in the English language and which includes works by Puerto Rican (Nuyorican) writers of the United States. Babín's other books include *Introducción a la cultura hispánica* (*Introduction to Hispanic Culture,* 1949), *El mundo poético de García Lorca* (*The Poetic World of García Lorca,* 1954), and *García Lorca: Vida y obra* (*García Lorca: His Life and Works,* 1955). Babín is also a creative writer, the author of local-color essays, *Fantasía Boricua: Estampas de mi tierra* (*Puerto Rican Fantasy: Scenes from My Land,* 1956, 1957); a play, *La hora colmada* (*The Over-Filled Hour,* 1960); and a book of poems, *Las voces de tu voz* (*The Voices of Your Voice,* 1962).

Maxine Baca-Zinn (1942-)

Sociology

Born on June 11, 1942, in Santa Fe, New Mexico, Baca-Zinn received her B.A. degree from California State College in 1966, her M.A. degree from the University of New Mexico in 1970, and her Ph.D. degree from the University of Oregon in 1978. Since 1975 to the present, Zinn has taught at the University of Michigan, Flint. In 1988–89, she served as a visiting professor in the Women's Studies Program at the University of Delaware. She is the author of numerous articles on the Hispanic family. Baca-Zinn is currently the associate editor of the *Social Science Journal* and is acknowledged as an outstanding sociology scholar.

Frank Bonilla (1927-)

Political Science

Frank Bonilla received his B.B.A. from City College of New York in 1949, his M.A. in sociology from New York University in 1954, and his Ph.D. from the Department of Social Relations, Harvard University in 1959. From 1960 to 1963, Bonilla was a member of the American Universities Field Staff on a contract to be carried out on behalf of UNESCO, investigating the relations between social development and education in Argentina, Chile, Mexico, and Brazil. In 1963, he became an associate professor of political science at Massachusetts Institute of Technology; in 1967, he was promoted to full professor. In 1969, he be-

came a professor of political science at Stanford University. In 1973, he became a full professor of political science at the City University of New York, where he served as director of the Center for Puerto Rican Studies until 1993. He retired from teaching in 1994. Bonilla is a pioneer in Puerto Rican studies and is known for helping develop some of the most important scholars in the field and for administering the leading program in the field. His awards include the 1986 Ralph C. Guzmán Award from CUNY. He is the author of numerous articles, books, and monographs, including *The Failure of Elites,* (1970) and *Industry and Idleness,* (1986). He coauthored *Labor Migration under Capitalism* (1979).

Gloria Bonilla-Santiago (1954-)

Social Work

Bonilla-Santiago received her B.A. degree in political science from Glassboro State College in New Jersey in 1976, her M.S.W. degree from Rutgers University in 1978, her M.A. degree in philosophy from the City University of New York in 1986, and her Ph.D. degree in sociology from the City University of New York in 1986. In 1991, Bonilla-Santiago became a tenured professor in the Graduate School of Social Work at Rutgers University; she is also chairperson of the Hispanic Women's Task Force of New Jersey, and director of the Hispanic Women's Leadership Institute at the Graduate School of Social Work. In 1992, she received the Warren I. Sussman Excellence in Teaching Award at Rutgers. She is the author of numerous reports, articles, book chapters, monographs, and two books: *Hispanic Women Leaders Breaking Ground and Barriers* (1993) and *Organizing Puerto Rican Migrant Farmworkers: The Experience of Puerto Ricans in New Jersey* (1988). In addition to her academic career, Bonilla-Santiago has been instrumental in passing legislation for Hispanic women in New Jersey.

Juan David Bruce-Novoa (1944-)

Literature

Born on June 20, 1944, in San José, Costa Rica, Bruce-Novoa received his Ph.D. degree from the University of Colorado in 1974. He has taught Chicano literature at Yale University, Trinity University, and, since 1990, at the University of California, Irvine, as a full professor. In 1993, Bruce-Novoa became chairman of the Department of Spanish and Portuguese at U.C.-Irvine. In that department, he has coordinated the UC-Irvine Prize for Chicano Literature and sponsored numerous Chicano and Latin American literature conferences. In 1994, Bruce-Novoa began publishing commercial fiction, with his first novel in

English, *Only the Good Times,* being offered by Arte Público Press. Bruce-Novoa is a leading scholar in literary theory as applied to Chicano literature. His books include *Chicano Authors: Inquiry by Interview* (1980), *Chicano Poetry: A Response to Chaos* (1982), and *Retrospace* (1990). Bruce-Novoa has been particularly active in developing a following among European scholars for Hispanic literature of the United States by participating in the organization of conferences in Germany, France, and Spain.

Pastora San Juan Cafferty (1940–)

Social Work

Born on July 24, 1940, in Cienfuegos, Las Villas, Cuba, Cafferty received her B.A. degree in English from St. Bernard College and her M.A. and Ph.D. degrees in American literature and cultural history from George Washington University in 1966 and 1971, respectively. Cafferty served as assistant to the secretary of the U.S. Department of Transportation and the U.S. Department of Housing and Urban Development from 1967 to 1969 and from 1969 to 1970, respectively. Since 1971, Cafferty has been a professor in the School of Social Service Administration of the University of Chicago. Included among her honors are the following: Doctor in Humane Letters, Columbia College (1987), White House Fellow (1969), Smithsonian Research Fellow (1966), Woman of the Year, Operation PUSH(1975), and Award of Achievement, U.S. Girl Scouts (1987). Cafferty has cowritten various books: *Hispanics in the USA: A New Social Agenda,* with William Mc-Cready (1985); *The Dilemma of Immigration in America: Beyond the Golden Door,* with Barry Chiswick, et al. (1983); *The Politics of Language: The Dilemma of Bilingual Education for Puerto Ricans,* with Carmen Martínez (1981); and others.

Albert Michael Camarillo (1948–)

History

Born on February 9, 1948, in Compton, California, Camarillo received his B.A. and his Ph.D. degrees from the University of California, Los Angeles, in 1970 and 1975, respectively. Camarillo has taught at Stanford University, where he has risen in rank to full professor. From 1983 to 1988, he served as the executive director of the important Inter-University Program for Latino Research. From 1980 to 1985, Camarillo served as the director of the Stanford Center for Chicano Research. In 1988, he received the Lloyd W. Dinklespiel Award for Outstanding Service to Undergraduate Education at Stanford. He is the author of *Chicanos in a Changing Society* (1979), *Chicanos in California* (1984), and various coedited books.

Albert Michael Camarillo.

Arthur León Campa (1905–1978)

Folklore, Literature

Born on February 20, 1905, in Guaymas, Sonora, Mexico, of American parents (his father was a Methodist missionary killed by Francisco Villa during the revolution), Campa was raised in El Paso, Texas. He received his B.A. and M.A. degrees from the University of New Mexico in 1928 and 1930, respectively,

Arthur León Campa.

and his Ph.D. degree in Spanish from Columbia University in 1940. From 1933 to 1942 Campa rose from instructor to full professor at the University of New Mexico. From 1942 to 1945, he served in World War II as a combat intelligence officer, suffering a back injury and winning a Bronze Star. After the war, he returned to the University of New Mexico. During the postwar years he served as a State Department lecturer in Spain (1953) and as a cultural affairs officer at the U.S. embassy in Lima, Peru. During the 1960s he served as a language training coordinator for the Peace Corps and as a director of Peace Corps Training Projects in Peru, Ecuador, and Venezuela. Included among his many fellowships are the Guggenheim and the Rockefeller. He was named to the national academies of scholars in Argentina, Brazil, Chile, Mexico, Peru, and Spain. Campa also served as the regional editor for *Western Folklore* and on various other editorial boards. He won many awards for his numerous books, most of which were pioneering collections and analyses of Hispanic folklore of the Southwest. His last, all-embracing vision is represented by his book *Hispanic Culture in the Southwest* (1978).

Antonia I. Castañeda (1942–)

History

Born into a migrant labor family in Texas in 1942, Castañeda's family moved to the state of Washington while following the crops. In 1966, she received her B.A. degree in Spanish and in education from Western Washington State University; she received her M.A. degree in Latin American studies from the University of Washington in 1970 and her Ph.D. degree in American history from Stanford University in 1990. She has been the recipient of various fellowships, including the Ford (1976), the Whiting (1980), the American Association of University Women (1981), and the University of California, San Diego, chancellor's fellowship (1990). From 1971 to the present, she has taught Chicano, Latin American, and Women's history at various universities and colleges, including the University of Washington, Stanford University, Foothills Community College, University of California, Davis, Sacramento City College, and Pomona College. In 1991, she began as an assistant professor with a joint appointment in the Departments of Women's Studies and Chicano Studies at the University of California, Santa Barbara. In 1994, Castañeda relocated to the history department of the University of Texas at Austin. She is the author of numerous research articles and papers and the coeditor of the important historical anthology *Chicano Literature: Text and Context* (1972).

Carlos Eduardo Castañeda (1896–1958)

History

Born in 1896 in Ciudad Camargo, Chihuahua, Mexico, Castañeda moved with his family to Brownsville, Texas in 1906, where he received his early education, graduating valedictorian from Brownsville High School in 1916. After high school, his scholarship studies at the University of Texas were interrupted by his service in World War I. He received his B.A. and M.A. degrees from the University of Texas in 1921 and 1923, respectively. In 1923, he was appointed associate professor at William and Mary College in Virginia. He returned to the University of Texas in 1927 as a librarian and received his Ph.D. degree in history there in 1932. Castañeda is best known for his *Our Catholic Heritage in Texas,* a six-volume history of Texas from 1519 to 1836 and a history of the Catholic church in Texas from 1836. Castañeda worked on the voluminous history book from 1936 to 1950. It was in 1939 that he joined the faculty of the history department at the University of Texas, and in 1946 he became full professor. Over the course of his career, he served at various times as editor of the *Hispanic American Historical Review, The Americas Review,* and *The Handbook of Latin American Studies.* Over all, Castañeda produced 12 books and more than 80 articles on Mexican and Southwest history. He died on April 3, 1958.

Carlos E. Cortés (1934–)

History

Born on April 6, 1934, in Oakland, California, Cortés received his B.A. degree in communications and public policy from the University of California, Berkeley, in 1956, his M.S. degree in journalism from Columbia University in 1957, his M.A. degree in Portuguese and Spanish from the University of New Mexico in 1956, and his Ph.D. degree in history from the University of New Mexico in 1969. Since 1961, Cortés has developed his teaching and research career at the University of California, Riverside; since 1968, he has been a full professor there. Cortés has lectured widely throughout the United States, Latin America, Europe, and Asia. His honors include numerous fellowships and honors, including the 1980 Distinguished California Humanist Award, conferred by the California Council for the Humanities, and the 1974 Herring Award, conferred by the Pacific Coast Council on Latin American Studies. His books include *Three Perspectives on Ethnicity: Blacks, Chicanos and Native Americans; Understanding You and Them; Gaucho Politics in Brazil* (1974); *A Filmic Approach to the Study of Historical*

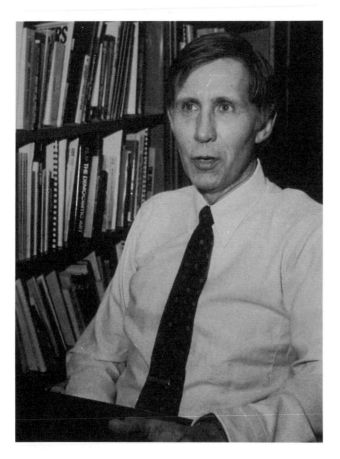

Carlos E. Cortés.

Dilemmas (1976); and *Images and Realities of Four World Religions* (1986).

Rodolfo J. Cortina (1946–)

Literature

Born on February 23, 1946, in Cuba, Cortina received his B.A. degree in Spanish and economics from Texas A & I University in 1966 and his M.A. and Ph.D. degrees from Case Western Reserve University in 1968 and 1972, respectively. In 1971, he began his career as an assistant professor of Spanish at the University of Wisconsin, Milwaukee, and was promoted to associate professor in 1977. In 1986, he moved to Florida International University as an associate professor and was promoted to full professor in 1989. At the University of Wisconsin, Milwaukee, he served in various administrative positions, including chair of the Department of Spanish, director of the Spanish-Speaking Outreach Institute, and chair of the Latin American Studies Program. At Florida International University from 1985 to 1989, he was the director of the Center for Multilingual and Multicultural Studies, and from 1989 to 1995, the director of Hispanic Research Programs. In 1995, Cortina relo-

cated to the University of Houston as a full professor and director of the bibliographic subproject for Recovering the Hispanic Literary Heritage, a national research program centered at the University of Houston. Cortina is the recipient of various awards, including the Jaycees Outstanding Young Man of America (1979), the Special Award of the Governor of Wisconsin (1980), and the Five Year Service Award at Florida International University (1991). He has coedited various anthologies of scholarly articles and is the editor of *Cuban American Theater* (1992). He is the author of *El lenguaje poético de Federico García Lorca* (*The Poetic Language of Federico García Lorca,* 1985) and *Blasco Ibáñez y la novela evocativa* (*Blasco Ibánez and the Evocative Novel,* 1973).

Rodolfo de la Garza (1942–)

Political Science

Born on August 17, 1942, in Tucson, Arizona, de la Garza received his B.S. and M.A. degrees in marketing from the University of Arizona in 1964 and 1967, respectively, and his Ph.D. degree in Latin American Studies from Arizona in 1972. He also studied foreign trade and political research at the American Institute of Foreign Trade and at the University of

Rodolfo J. Cortina.

Michigan Inter-University Consortium for Political Research in 1965 and 1971. From 1974 to 1980, he served as an assistant dean and, from 1978 to 1980, as director of the Southwest Studies Program at Colorado College. From 1981 to 1985 and again in 1987, he served as the director of the Center for Mexican American Studies at the University of Texas. Since 1983, he has been the codirector of the Inter-University Project of the Ford Foundation at the University of Texas, where he is a full professor. Among his many awards are the following: (University of Texas) Dean's Award for Outstanding Classroom Performance, 1987–88; University of Colorado Outstanding Faculty Award, 1980; Western Political Science Association Best Paper on Chicano Politics, 1979. De la Garza has also been a productive researcher and author on Hispanic political topics and has served on the editorial boards of the *Western Political Science Quarterly,* the *Social Science Quarterly,* the *Journal of Politics,* and the *Hispanic Journal of Behavioral Science.* He is the editor of two books: *The Mexican American Experience: An Interdisciplinary Anthology* (1985) and *Ignored Voices: Latinos and Public Opinion Poles in the United States* (1986). Since 1988, De la Garza has directed the National Latino Political National Survey.

Jorge I. Domínguez (1945–)

Government

Born on June 2, 1945, in Havana, Cuba, Domínguez received his B.A. degree from Yale University in 1967, and his M.A. and Ph.D. degrees from Harvard University in 1968 and 1972, respectively. From 1972 on, Domínguez developed his teaching career at Harvard University, becoming a full professor in 1979; in 1993, he became the Frank G. Thomson professor of government, and chair of the Latin American and Iberian studies department. Domínguez is a member of the editorial boards of *Political Science Quarterly, Mexican Studies, Journal of Inter-American Studies and World Affairs,* and *Cuban Studies,* for which he has served as coeditor since 1990. Domínguez's books include *To Make a World Safe for Revolution* (1989), *U.S. Interests in the Caribbean and in Central America* (1982), *Cuba: Internal and International Affairs* (1982), and *Insurrection or Loyalty: The Breakdown of the Spanish American Empire* (1980).

José B. Fernández (1948–)

History, Literature

Born on August 20, 1948, in Sagua la Grande, Cuba, Fernández received his B.A., M.A., and Ph.D. degrees in Spanish and history from Florida State University in Tallahassee in 1970, 1971, and 1973, respectively. From 1973 to 1976, he served as an assistant professor and, from 1976 to 1979, as associate professor at the University of Colorado at Colorado Springs, where he also served as chairman of the Department of Foreign Languages. From 1981 to the present, he has been a professor of history and foreign languages at the University of Central Florida in Orlando. Fernández has been a Fulbright Lecturer in Argentina (1984) and has received various other awards, including the University of Colorado (Colorado Springs) Outstanding Teaching Award (1977) and the Chancellor's Award (1979). Fernández is the author of numerous articles and books, including *Alvar Núñez Cabeza de Vaca: The Forgotten Chronicler* (1975), *Indice bibliográfico de autores cubanos* (*Bibliographic Index of Cuban Authors,* 1983), and (with Nasario García) *Nuevos Horizontes: Cuentos chicanos, puertorriqueños y cubanos* (*New Horizons: Chicano, Puerto Rican and Cuban Stories,* 1982).

Margarita Fernández Olmos (1949–)

Literature

Born in 1949 in New York City, Fernández Olmos received her B.A. degree from Montclair State Col-

Margarita Fernández Olmos.

lege in New Jersey in 1970 and her M.A. and Ph.D. degrees in Spanish from New York University in 1972 and 1979, respectively. Following her graduate studies, Fernández Olmos was able to develop her career at Brooklyn College of the City University of New York, where she rose to he present rank of full professor. Fernández Olmos has written extensively on Latin American and U.S. Hispanic literature, with a special interest in women's literature. Her books include *La cuéntistica de Juan Bosch* (*The Short Story Art of Juan Bosch*, 1982), *Sobre la literatura puertorriqueña de aquí y de allá: aproximaciones feministas* (*On Puerto Rican Literature from the Mainland and the Island: Feminist Approaches*, 1989), and two coedited anthologies of Latin American women's literature: (with Doris Meyer) *Contemporary Women Authors of Latin America: New Translations and Introductory Essays* (1983) and (with Lizabeth Paravisini-Gebert) *El placer de la palabra: literatura erótica femenina de América Latina* (*The Pleasure of the Word: Erotic Women's Literature of Latin America*, 1991).

Juan Flores

Literature, Sociology

Born in New York City, Flores received his B.A. degree in German from Queens College in 1964 and his M.A. and Ph.D. degrees in German from Yale University in 1966 and 1968, respectively. He began his career as an assistant professor of German at Stanford University in 1968, but in 1975 redirected his career toward Puerto Rican studies when he became the research director and consultant for the Center for Puerto Rican Studies at Hunter College, CUNY. From 1981 to 1989, he worked as an associate professor in the Department of Sociology of Queens College, CUNY; from 1990 to the present, he has been a member of the graduate faculty in the sociology program of the Graduate Center of CUNY. In 1994, Flores became the director of the Center for Puerto Rican Studies of the City University of New York. Flores is a distinguished researcher whose books have won important awards. His *Insularismo e ideología burguesa: Nueva lectura de Antonio S. Pedreira* (*Insularism and Bourgeois Ideology: A New Reading of Antonio S. Pedreira*, 1980) won the prestigious international Casa de las Americas prize. His other books include *Divided Borders: Essays on Puerto Rican Identity* (1992) and (with Jean Franco and George Yúdice) *On Edge: The Crisis in Contemporary Latin American Culture* (1992). His introduction and edition of Jesús Colón's *A Puerto Rican in New York* (1984) won the American Book Award.

Juan Gómez-Quiñones (1940–)

History

Born in 1940 in Parral, Chihuahua, Mexico, Gómez immigrated to the United States with his family as a young child and became a naturalized citizen. He received his B.A. degree in English, his M.A. degree in Latin American Studies, and his Ph.D. degree in history from the University of California, Los Angeles in 1962, 1974, and 1972, respectively. He is a full professor of history at the University of California, Los Angeles, where he has developed his entire career and served for many years as the director of the Chicano Research Center. He is a cofounder/codirector of the Mexican American Legal Defense and Education Fund and is a board member of the Los Angeles Urban Coalition. He is the author of numerous articles and books, including *Sembradores: Ricardo Flores Magón y El Partido Liberal: A Eulogy and a Critique* (1973), *Roots of Chicano Politics, 1600–1940* and *Chicano Politics: Reality and Promise, 1940–1990* (1995).

Deena J. González (1952–)

History

See Chapter 10.

Erlinda González-Berry (1942–)

Literature

The native New Mexican, born in 1942, received her B.A., M.A., and Ph.D. degrees from the University of New Mexico in 1964, 1971, and 1978, respectively. In 1974, she began as an assistant professor in Earlham College in Indiana, moved to New Mexico State University in 1978, and then to the University of New Mexico in 1979, where she has risen in rank to her present full professorship. González-Berry is an outstanding teacher and researcher. In 1984, she received the University of New Mexico President's Award as Outstanding Teacher of the Year and, in 1991, the Outstanding Teacher of the Year Award from the "Hispanics at UNM." González has published numerous articles on Chicano literature and is the editor of two books: *Pasó por Aquí: Four Centuries of New Mexican Hispanic Literature* (1989) and (with Tey Diana Rebolledo and Teresa Márquez) *Las mujeres hablan: An Anthology of Nuevomexicana Writings* (1988).

Richard A. Griswold del Castillo (1942–)

History

Born on October 26, 1942, in Los Angeles, California, Griswold received his B.A., M.A., and Ph.D. degrees from the University of California, Los Angeles, in 1968, 1969, and 1974, respectively. From 1974 to the present, he has taught at San Diego State University, where he is currently a full professor and chair of the Mexican American Studies. From 1985 through 1988, he was the recipient of the San Diego State Outstanding Faculty Award. Among his many publications are the following books: *The Treaty of Guadalupe Hidalgo* (1990), *La Familia Chicana: Chicano Families in the Urban Southwest, 1848 to the Present* (1984), and *The Los Angeles Barrio, 1850–1890: A Social History* (1980).

Ramón Gutiérrez (1951–)

History

Born on April 19, 1951, in Albuquerque, New Mexico, Gutiérrez obtained his B.A. degree from the University of New Mexico in 1973 and his M.A. and Ph.D. degrees from the University of Wisconsin in 1976 and 1980, respectively. Beginning in 1980, he served as an assistant professor at Pomona College; since 1982, he has taught at the University of California, San Diego, becoming a professor in 1988. His honors include a prestigious MacArthur Fellowship, 1983–88, as well as the Best Book Award for 1991

Erlinda González-Berry.

from the American Historical Association, Pacific Coast Branch, the Best Article Award from the AHA Conference on Latin American History in 1986, and the Hubert Herring Prize for the Best Dissertation in Latin American Studies in 1981. In 1994, President Clinton appointed Gutiérrez to the National Council on the Humanities. He has won numerous fellowships, including the Fulbright, Danforth, and National Defense Education Act. Gutiérrez is the author of numerous ground-breaking articles in Latin American and Chicano history and a book, *When Jesus Came the Corn Mothers Went Away: Marriage, Sexuality and Power in New Mexico, 1500–1846.*

José Hernández (1935–)

Puerto Rican Studies

Born on August 22, 1935, in Jersey City, New Jersey of Puerto Rican parents, José Hernández is one of the first Puerto Ricans to develop a career as a professor of Sociology in the United States. He received his B.A. and M.A. degrees from Fordham University in 1958 and 1960, respectively, and went on toe earn his Ph.D. at the University of Minnesota in 1966. After an initial position of assistant professor at the university of Arizona from 1970 to 1974, he served as the research director for the United States Civil Rights Commission for two years. Thereafter, he was an associate professor at the University of Wisconsin until 1983. He is currently a full professor in the Department of Black and Puerto Rican Studies at Hunter College in New York. His published research includes *Latinos in Metropolitan Chicago* (1983), *Hispanics in Higher Education: New Jersey* (1986) and numerous published articles and reports. From 1975 to 1980, Hernández served as the chair of the Spanish Origin Advisory Committee to the U.S. Census.

José Manuel Hernández (1925–)

History

Born on February 18, 1925, in Cuba, Hernández received his law degree from the University of Havana in 1947 and his M.A. and Ph.D. degrees in history from Georgetown University in 1969 and 1976, respectively. From 1973 to 1980, he served as assistant dean of the School of Languages and Linguistics at Georgetown University, and since 1980, as associate dean. From 1984 to 1987, he served as the director of the Latin American Studies Program at Georgetown. Included in his many honors is the Georgetown University Vicennial Medal. His published scholarship includes the book *ACU, los primeros cincuenta años* (*ACU, the First Fifty Years,* 1981).

María Herrera-Sobek

Literature

Born in Mexico, Herrera-Sobek received her B.A. degree in chemistry from California State University, Northridge, in 1974, her M.A. degree in Latin American studies from the University of California, Irvine, and her Ph.D. degree from the University of California, Los Angeles, in 1975. From 1975 to the present, she has developed her entire career at the University of California, Irvine, rising in rank from assistant to full professor as of 1987. Included among her honors are the Orange County Book of the Year Award (1980), the Hispanic Woman of the Year Award from the League of United Latin American Citizens, Orange County (1981), and the Educator of the Year Award given by the Mexican American Educators Association, Orange County chapter (1990). Herrera-Sobek has published numerous articles, edited various anthologies, and written the following books: *The Bracero Experience: Elitelore versus Folklore* (1979), *The Mexican Corrido: A Feminist Analysis* (1990), and *Northward Bound: The Mexican Immigrant Experience in Corridos and Canciones* (1993).

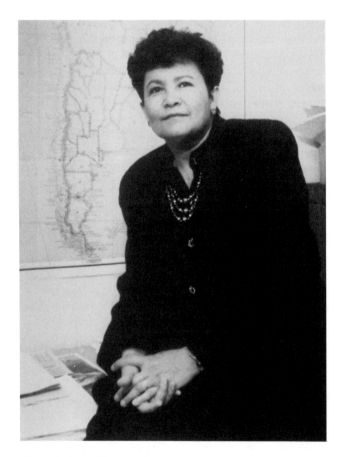

Olga Jiménez-Wagenheim.

Olga Jiménez-Wagenheim (1941–)

History

Born in Camuy, Puerto Rico, on September 24, 1941, Jiménez received her B.A. degree from the Inter-American University in Puerto Rico in 1970, her M.A. degree from the State University of New York at Buffalo in 1971, and her Ph.D. degree from Rutgers University in 1981. After achieving the Ph.D. degree, she has developed her university career at Rutgers University, where she has served as an associate professor since 1986. Her honors include the Hispanic Association for Higher Education Scholarly Achievement Award (1989), the Hispanic Women's Task Force of New Jersey Award (1988), and the Outstanding Teacher of the Year Award (1991) at Rutgers University-Newark. Jiménez's books include *Puerto Rico's Revolt for Independence: El Grito de Lares* (1985), *El grito de Lares: Sus causas y sus hombres* (*The Shout of Lares: Its Causes and Its Men*, 1984) and her coedited *The Puerto Ricans: A Documentary History* (1973).

Luis Leal (1907–)

Literature

Born on September 17, 1907, in Linares, Mexico, Leal received his B.A. degree from Northwestern University in 1940 and his A.M. and Ph.D. degrees from the University of Chicago in 1941 and 1951. Leal is one of the most productive, most respected, and most honored scholars of Latin American and Chicano literature, a true pioneer in both disciplines. In his long career, he has taught at the University of Chicago, the University of Mississippi, Emory University, the University of Illinois, where he has been professor emeritus since 1976, and the University of California, Santa Barbara, where he has served as a visiting professor and acting director of Chicano studies since 1980. He is the author of some 16 books, including his important *El cuento hispanoamericano* (*The Spanish American Short Story*, 1967) and his *Breve historia de la literatura hispanoamericana* (*Brief History of Spanish American Literature*, 1971). He has also edited some 21 anthologies and other books, besides publishing scores of articles. In 1978, a conference was held and a book published in his praise: *Homenaje a Luis Leal* (*Homage to Luis Leal*), edited by Donald W. Bleznick and Juan O. Valencia.

Francisco A. Lomelí (1947–)

Literature

Born on April 13, 1947, in Sombrerete, Zacatecas, Mexico, Lomelí received his B.A. and M.A. degrees from San Diego State University in 1971 and 1974,

Luis Leal.

respectively, and his Ph.D. degree from the University of New Mexico in 1978. Since 1978, he has ascended the ranks at the University of California, Santa Barbara, where he became a full professor in 1989. Lomelí has won numerous fellowships, including the Rotary International (1983), Fulbright (1969), Ford (1974), and Rockefeller (1989). He is the author of numerous articles of literary criticism and the editor of various reference works: *Dictionary of Literary Biography: Chicano Writers* (1989), *Chicano Literature: A Reference Guide* (1985), and *Aztlán: Essays on the Chicano Homeland* (1989). Lomelí also serves on the editorial board of various journals, including *The Americas Review, The Bilingual Review, Discurso Literario,* and *The Latino Studies Journal.*

Roberto Márquez (1942–)

Latin American Studies

Born on July 14, 1942, in New York City, Márquez received his B.A. in comparative literature from Brandeis University in 1964, and his M.A. and Ph.D. degrees in romance languages and literatures from Harvard University in 1970 and 1975, respectively.

From 1970 to 1986, he taught at Hampshire College in Hispanic American and Caribbean literatures, where in 1983 he was named the first incumbent of the Harold F. Johnson Professorial Chair. From 1986 to 1989, he was the Robinson Professor at George Mason University and, from 1989 to the present, the William F. Kenan Professor of Latin American studies at Mount Holyoke College. Márquez is the author of numerous articles, anthologies of Latin American poetry, which he also translates, and the book, *The Third World: The Dialectic of Culture* (1978). He is also the founder and editor of *Caliban: A Journal of New World Thought and Writing* (1975–1982).

Oscar Martínez (1943–)

History

Born in Mexico on March 4, 1943, Martínez received his B.A. degree from California State University in Los Angeles in 1969, his M.A. degree from Stanford in 1970, and his Ph.D. degree from the University of California, Los Angeles, in 1975. From 1975 to 1988, he ascended the ranks from assistant to full professor at the University of Texas at El Paso. From 1975 to 1988, he served as the director of the Institute for Oral History at U.T.E.P. In 1988, he became a full professor at the University of Arizona. He has served as president of the Association of Borderland Scholars and is a member of various editorial boards, including the *Journal of Borderland Studies,* the *Latin American Research Review,* and the *Journal of the Southwest.* He has won two book awards, 1978 and 1988, from the Border Region Library Association. His books include *Border Boom Town* (1978), *Fragments of the Mexican Revolution* (1983), *Across Boundaries* (1986), and *Troublesome Border* (1988).

Alfredo Matilla (1937–)

Puerto Rican Studies

Born in Valencia, Spain, on July 31, 1937, Matilla was raised in Puerto Rico. He received his B.A. from the University of Puerto Rico in 1959, his M.A. and Ph.D. from New York University in 1961 and 1967, respectively. From 1965 to 1968, he served as an assistant professor of Spanish at Goucher College; in 1968 he moved to Rutgers University as an associate professor, and then in 1980 to Brooklyn College. Since 1982, he has taught at the State University of New York, Buffalo, and was named full professor of Puerto Rican studies/American studies in 1988. Matilla is the author of various books and articles primarily on Puerto Rican and Nuyorican literature. With Iván Silén, he edited a ground-breaking anthology in bilingual format, *The Puerto Rican Poets/ Los poetas puertorriquenos,* 1972. He is also a respected poet, author of *Catálogo de locos (Catalog of Insane People,* 1977), and translations.

Carmelo Mesa-Lago (1934–)

Economics

Born on August 11, 1934, in Havana, Cuba, Mesa-Lago received his LL.M. degree in civil law from the University of Havana in 1965, his LL.D. degree from the University of Madrid in 1958, his M.A. degree in economics from the University of Miami in 1965, and his Ph.D. degree in labor economics from Cornell University in 1968. From 1967 on, Mesa-Lago developed his career at the University of Pittsburgh, beginning as an assistant professor in economics and rising to the rank of full professor in 1980. During his tenure there, he also served as the director of the Center for Latin American Studies (1974 to 1986). He has lectured and taught in Europe and Latin America as well and has held prestigious fellowships, including the Ford, Rockefeller, and Tinker. Mesa-Lago has also served as the president of the Latin American Studies Association (1980) and as regional advisor for the United Nations on Social Security and Development (1983–84). Included among his many honors is the Alexander von Humbolt Senior Research Award on Social Security (1990–92), the Bicentennial Medallion of the University of Pittsburgh (1987), and the Hoover Institution Prize for Best Article on Latin America (1986). Included among his many books are *Cuba after the Cold War* (1993), *Health Care for the Poor in Latin America and the Caribbean: Problems, Cases and Solutions* (1992), *Social Security and Prospects for Equity in Latin America* (1991), and *Portfolio Performance of Selected Social Security Institutes in Latin America* (1991), to name just some of the most recent.

Raúl Moncarraz

Economics

Born in Cuba, Moncarraz received his B.S. degree in business administration from Florida Atlantic University in 1965 and his M.B.A. and Ph.D. degrees in economics from Florida State University in 1966 and 1969, respectively. From 1969 to 1972, he rose from an assistant professorship to associate professor at Louisiana State University. From 1972 to the present, he has taught at Florida International University, where he became a full professor and chairman of the Department of Economics in 1988. Among his many honors is a Gold Medal from the Consulate of Venezuela in Miami (1984) and various scholarships and fellowships. Moncarraz is the au-

thor of numerous publications on development issues in Central America and the Caribbean and on labor market issues.

Sonia Nieto (1943–)

Children's Literature

Nieto received her B.S. degree in Education from St. John's University in 1965, her M.A. degree in Spanish from New York University in 1966, and her Ed.D. degree in curriculum with minors in bilingual and multicultural education from the University of Massachusetts, Amherst, in 1979. From 1972 to 1975, Nieto was and instructor and deputy chairperson of the Department of Puerto Rican Studies, Brooklyn College; from 1979 to 1980, the LAU Coordinator for the Massachusetts Department of Education; and in 1980, she began her career at the University of Massachusetts, rising to her present rank of associate professor and program director of Cultural Diversity and Curriculum Reform in 1988. Nieto received the Human and Civil Rights Award from the Massachusetts Teachers Association in 1988 and the Outstanding Accomplishment in Higher Education Award from the Hispanic Caucus of the American Association of Higher Education in

Raúl Moncarraz.

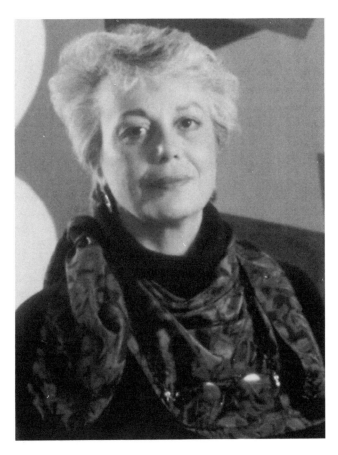

Sonia Nieto.

1991. Nieto is an expert on Hispanic and culturally diverse children's literature, which is reflected in her many articles, book chapters, lectures, and papers. She is the author of *Affirming Diversity: The Sociopolitical Context of Multicultural Education* (1992) and coauthor (with Roberto Márquez) of *Puerto Rican Literature and Society: A Curriculum for the Secondary School* (1986).

Julián Olivares (1940-)

Literature

Born on December 6, 1940, in San Antonio, Texas, Olivares received his B.A. degree from California State University at Los Angeles in 1968 and his M.A. and Ph.D. degrees from the University of Texas in 1974 and 1977, respectively. He served as an assistant professor at Bridgewater State College from 1978 to 1981, when he relocated to the University of Houston, becoming professor of Spanish in 1993. In 1994, Olivares became the chair of the Department of Modern and Classical Languages at the University of Houston, where he also served from 1981 to 1994 as the editor of the prestigious *The Americas Review* and senior editor of Arte Público Press. Ol-

ivares is a respected scholar in two fields: Golden Age Spanish literature and Chicano literature. He has won numerous fellowships, including the Ford (1975), National Endowment for the Humanities (1984), and National Research Council/Ford (1985). As editor of *The Americas Review,* he has won two unprecedented Citations of Achievement from the Council of Literary Magazines and Presses. His books include *Tras el espejo la musa escribe: Lírica femenina del Siglo de Oro* (Behind the Looking Glass the Muse Writes: Women's Lyrics of the Golden Age, 1992) and *The Love Poetry of Francisco de Quevedo* (1983). His edited books include *Hispanic Short Fiction* (1992), *International Studies in Honor of Tomás Rivera* (1985), and all of the works of Tomás Rivera (in four separate volumes).

Vilma Ortiz (1954-)

Social Psychology

Ortiz received her B.A. degree in psychology from the City College of New York in 1976 and her M.A. and Ph.D. degrees in social psychology from New York University in 1979 and 1981, respectively. From 1981 to 1985, she has had three postdoctoral fellowships at Fordham University, the University of Michigan, and

Julián Olivares.

the University of Wisconsin, respectively. From 1985 to 1987, she served as a visiting scholar at the Educational Testing Service in Princeton, New Jersey. She began her teaching career in 1988 as an assistant professor in the Department of Sociology, University of California, Los Angeles, where she has been an associate professor since 1990. Since 1990, Ortiz has been the director of the Interdepartmental Program in Chicana and Chicano Studies at U.C.L.A. Ortiz's specialties are urban poverty and social welfare policy, race and ethnicity, Puerto Rican migration, and Hispanic women, among other research interests that form the bases of her numerous articles and book chapters.

Harry Pachón (1945–)

Political Science

Born on June 4, 1945, in Miami, Florida, Pachón received his B.A. and his M.A. degrees from California State University in Los Angeles in 1967 and 1968, respectively, and his Ph.D. degree from the Claremont Graduate School in 1973. He served as an assistant professor at Michigan State University from 1974 to 1976 and as an administrative assistant at the United States House of Representatives from 1977 to 1981. From 1981 to 1986, he was an associate professor at the City University of New York, and since 1986, the Kenan Professor of Political Science at Pitzer College. Pachón is a founding board member of the National Association of Latino Elected and Appointed Officials (since 1981), and since 1983 he has served as its national director. Pachón has been a fellow of the National Endowment for the Humanities and has published research articles and two books: *Hispanics in the U.S.* (1985) and *Mexican Americans* (1975).

Amado Manuel Padilla (1942–)

Psychology

Born on October 14, 1942, in Albuquerque, New Mexico, Padilla received his B.A. degree in 1964 from New Mexico Highlands University, his M.S. degree in 1966 from Oklahoma State University, and his Ph.D. degree in 1969 from the University of New Mexico. He was an assistant professor at the State University of New York from 1967 to 1971 and at the University of California, Santa Barbara, from 1971 to 1974. He moved to the University of California, Los Angeles, in 1974, where he rose to the rank of full professor. From 1988 to the present, he has been a full professor at Stanford University. Padilla has been a Fulbright Scholar and is the recipient of the American Educational Research Association Distinguished Scholar Award (1987). His books include

Crossing Cultures in Therapy (1980), *Chicano Ethnicity* (1987), *Foreign Language Education: Issues and Strategies* (1990), and *Bilingual Education: Issues and Strategies* (1990).

Américo Paredes (1915–)

Folklore

Born on September 3, 1915, in Brownsville, Texas, Paredes received his B.A., M.A., and Ph.D. degrees from the University of Texas in 1951, 1953, and 1956, respectively. After working at a variety of jobs, including journalist, and serving in the armed forces, Paredes received an advanced education later in life and became one of the most distinguished Hispanic scholars in U.S. history. Paredes has taught at the University of Texas from 1951 on and is currently professor emeritus of English and anthropology there. He has been instrumental in the development of the field of folklore in academia as well as in the field of Mexican American studies. He has served as president of the American Folklore Society and been recognized for his leadership internationally. In the United States, he was awarded one of the nation's highest awards for a humanist, the Charles Frankel Prize given by the National Endowment for the Arts (1989), and in Mexico, the highest award given a foreigner by the Mexican government, the Aguila Azteca (the Aztec Eagle) medal (1991). Besides publishing numerous research articles, he is the author of *With a Pistol in His Hand: A Border Ballad and Its Hero* (1958), *Folktales of Mexico* (1970), *A Texas Mexican Cancionero* (1976), *Uncle Remus con chile* (title means "Uncle Remus with Chile," 1992), *Folklore and Culture on the Tex-Mex Border* (1993), and *The Hammon and the Beans and Other Stories* (1994). He is also the author of a novel, *George Washington Gomez* (1990) and a book of poems, *Between Two Worlds* (1991).

Gustavo Pérez-Firmat (1949–)

Literature

Born on March 7, 1949, in Havana, Cuba, Pérez-Firmat received his B.A. degree in English and M.A. degree in Spanish from the University of Miami in 1972 and 1973, respectively. He received his Ph.D. degree in comparative literature from the University of Michigan in 1979. Since 1979, he has developed his career at Duke University, where he has risen in rank from assistant to full professor in Spanish and in the Graduate Literature Program. Pérez-Firmat has created a dual career as a literary historian and critic and as a creative writer. His academic books include *Idle Fictions: The Hispanic Vanguard Novel, 1926–1934* (1982), *Literature and Liminality: Fes-*

tive Readings in the Hispanic Tradition (1986), *The Cuban Condition: Translation and Identity in Modern Cuban Literature* (1989), and *Life on the Hyphen: The Cuban American Way* (1994). His creative books include two collections of his poems: *Triple Crown: Chicano, Puerto Rican and Cuban American Poetry* (1987) and *Equivocaciones* (*Mistakes,* 1989). He is also the author of numerous articles and poems for journals and magazines.

Guadalupe C. Quintanilla (1937-)

Language

See Chapter 27.

Tey Diana Rebolledo (1937-)

Literature

See Chapter 10.

Eliana Rivero (1940-)

Literature

Born in Cuba in 1940, Rivero immigrated to the United States in 1961. She received her Ph.D. degree in Spanish from the University of Miami in 1968, and from that time on has developed her career at the University of Arizona, where she is currently a full professor in the Spanish department. Her specialties are Latin American and U.S. Hispanic literatures and women's literature and feminist criticism. Rivero is the author of *El gran amor de Pablo Neruda: estudio crítico de su poesía* (*The Great Love of Pablo Neruda: A Critical Study of His Poetry,* 1971), *Cuban American Women Writers: Breaking Boundaries,* (1989), *Isabel Allende's Storytelling: Splintering Darkness,* (1990), and numerous articles. She is also the coeditor (with Tey Diana Rebolledo) of *Infinite Divisions: An Anthology of Chicana Literature* (1993). Rivero is also a respected poet whose books include *De cal y arena* (*Of Lime and Sand,* 1975) and *Cuerpos breves* (*Brief Bodies,* 1977).

Sergio G. Roca

Economics

Born in Cuba, Roca received his B.A. degree in economics from Drew University in 1965 and his Ph.D. degree from Rutgers University in 1975. From 1971 to the present, he has developed his career at Adelphi University; he has been a full professor there since 1984. In 1988, he received the Adelphi University Merit Award for Scholarship. He is the author of numerous articles and two books: *Socialist Cuba: Past Interpretations and Future Challenges* (1988) and *Cuban Economic Policy and Ideology: The Ten Million Ton Sugar Harvest* (1976).

Clara Rodríguez (1944-)

Sociology

Born on March 29, 1944, Rodríguez received her B.A. degree in sociology from the City College of New York in 1965, her M.A. degree in Latin American studies from Cornell University in 1969, and her Ph.D. degree in sociology and urban and regional studies from Washington University in St. Louis in 1973. From 1974 to 1976, Rodríguez served as chair of the Department of Puerto Rican Studies at Lehman College, CUNY; beginning in 1976, she was dean of general studies at Fordham University, after which she took leaves of absence and visiting fellowships at the Massachusetts Institute of Technology and Yale University. From 1981 to the present, she has been a full professor at Fordham University. Rodríguez has presented numerous lectures and papers and published many articles on the sociology of race, ethnicity, and gender, especially as such subjects relate to Puerto Ricans. Her books include *Puerto Ricans: Born in the USA* (1989, 1991), *The Ethnic Queue in the United States: The Case of Puerto Ricans* (1974), and two coedited books: (with Virginia Sánchez Korrol and Oscar Alers) *The Puerto Rican Struggle: Essays on Survival in the U.S.* (1979) and (with Edwin Meléndez and Janice Barry-Figueroa) *Hispanics in the Labor Force: Issues and Policies* (1991).

Ricardo Romo (1943-)

History

Born on June 23, 1943, in San Antonio, Texas, Romo received his B.A. degree from the University of Texas in 1967, his M.A. degree from Loyola University of Los Angeles in 1970, and his Ph.D. degree from the University of California, Los Angeles, in 1975. From 1974 to 1980, he was an assistant professor at the University of California, San Diego, and from 1980 to the present, a full professor at the University of Texas at Austin. Since 1988, he has also been the director of the Tomás Rivera Center, a research institute in San Antonio. He has been a member of the board of editors of *Social Science Quarterly* since 1982 and has been the managing editor of the Mexican American Monograph Series at the University of Texas since 1981. Romo has received various fellowships during his career and he is the author of *East Los Angeles: A History of a Barrio* (1983) and coeditor of *The Mexican American Experience: An Interdisciplinary Anthology* (1985) and *New Directions in Chicano Scholarship* (1978).

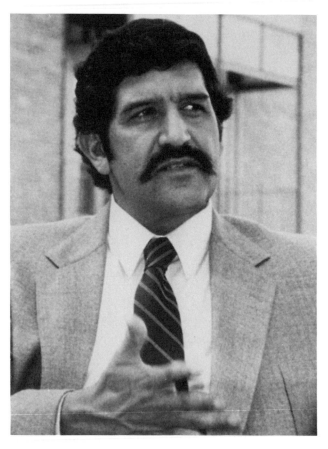

Ricardo Romo.

Ramón Eduardo Ruiz

History, Literature

Ruiz received his Ph.D. degree in history from the University of California, Berkeley, in 1954. He began his career as an assistant professor at the University of Oregon in 1956–57 and Southern Methodist University in 1957–58. He moved to Smith College in 1958 as an assistant professor and was promoted to associate professor in 1961 and to full professor of Latin American History in 1963. Since 1970, he has been a full professor at the University of California, San Diego. Among his many awards are the 1981 Hubert C. Herring Prize from the Pacific Coast Council on Latin American Studies for his *The Great Rebellion, Mexico, 1905–1924* (1980) and various fellowships, including the Fulbright. Included among his 13 books are *Triumphs and Tragedy: A History of the Mexican People* (1991), *The People of Sonora and Yankee Capitalists* (1988), and *Labor and Ambivalent Revolutionaries: Mexico, 1905–1924* (1976).

Vicki L. Ruiz (1955–)

History

See Chapter 10.

Julián Samora (1920–)

Sociology

Born on March 1, 1920, in Pagosa Springs, Colorado, Samora received his B.A. degree from Adams State College in 1942, his M.S. degree from Colorado State University in 1974, and his Ph.D. degree from Washington University in 1953. From 1955 to 1957, he was an assistant professor at the University of Colorado Medical School, associate professor at Michigan State University from 1957 to 1959, and a full professor at the University of Notre Dame from 1959 to 1985, when he became professor emeritus. Samora is one of the pioneer Hispanic sociologists and has trained a whole generation of important sociologists whose ranks include the noted Mexican sociologist Jorge Bustamante. Among his many awards is the White House Hispanic Heritage Award (1985) and the Mexican government's highest award given to a foreigner, the Aguila Azteca (Aztec Eagle) medal (1991). Included among his books are *A History of the Mexican-American People* (1977) and *Gunpowder Justice: A Reassessment of the Texas Rangers* (1979). In 1991, a research center at the Michigan State University was named in his honor.

Ramón Eduardo Ruiz.

George I. Sánchez (1906-1972)

Educational Administration

Born on October 4, 1906, in Albuquerque, New Mexico, to parents with long histories in the territory, Sánchez became a teacher while he was still a student at the University of New Mexico, which he attended only during the summer months. He graduated from the University of New Mexico in 1930 with a B.A. degree in Spanish. After that he received an M.S. degree in educational psychology at the University of Texas and then his Ed.D. in educational administration from the University of California, Berkeley, in 1934. During the next 35 years Sánchez became the foremost expert on the education of Hispanic children and a tireless and effective civil rights leader on their behalf. He also became an expert on Latin American education and a pioneer in bilingual, bicultural education. Since the early 1990s, Sánchez conducted research into Hispanic literary history, and, with Beatriz Pita, has prepared critical editions of two works by nineteenth-century California novelist María Amparo Ruiz de Burton: *The Squatter and the Don* (1992) and *Who Would Have Thought It?* (1994). Sánchez is also the editor of the journal *Crítica,* through which she has also published recovered nineteenth-century texts. Among his many writings are *Mexico: A Revolution by Education* (1936) and *Forgotten People* (1940), the latter a work that documents the educational neglect of Mexican American children in New Mexico during the 1930s. After working in the state of New Mexico educational administration, Sánchez joined the faculty of the University of Texas in 1940, and in 1941, became the president of the League of United Latin American Citizens. From then on, he used LULAC as a forum to struggle against the practices that were inhibiting the civil and educational rights of Hispanics. In 1951 he founded a national organization to bring together all of the civil rights-oriented Hispanic organizations and focus their efforts, the American Council of Spanish-Speaking People. It was this council that experienced early civil rights legal victories and prepared the way from many of the gains made during the 1960s and for the later emergence of the Mexican American Legal Defense and Education Fund. Because of his many pioneering studies, articles, and books, as well as the very important role he played in preparing the ground for the Hispanic civil rights and educational movements, George I. Sánchez has been the subject of numerous books, articles, and homages, and there is many a school named in his honor today.

Rosaura Sánchez (1941-)

Linguistics, Literature

Born on December 6, 1941, in San Angelo, Texas, Sánchez received her B.A. degree in Spanish and English in 1963, her M.A. degree in Spanish in 1969, and her Ph.D. degree in Romance Linguistics in 1974 from the University of Texas. Since 1972, Sánchez has developed her entire teaching career in the Literature Department at the University of California, San Diego, where she serves as a full professor. Sánchez is the author of *Chicano Discourse,* a fundamental book for the understanding of Mexican American Spanish and English patterns. She is also the author of numerous articles in linguistics and literature, as well as the author of short stories. Sánchez's work in linguistics has involved both the theoretical and the applied; she has been a pioneer in the teaching of Spanish to Spanish-speakers. In her literary studies, she has also concentrated on literary theory and feminist theory, as well as conducted critical studies of works by such writers as Gina Valdez, Arturo Islas, and Rolando Hinojosa.

José Sánchez-Boudy (1928-)

Literature

See Chapter 19.

Virginia Sánchez-Korrol (1936-)

History

See Chapter 10.

Saskia Sassen (1947-)

Economics, Sociology

Born on January 5, 1947, in The Hague, Netherlands, Sassen received first-year certificates from the University of Buenos Aires, Argentina, and the Universitá degli Studi in Rome in 1966 and 1968, respectively. She received her M.A. degree in sociology and her Ph.D. degree in economics and sociology from the University of Notre Dame in 1968 and 1971, respectively. From 1974 to 1975, she was a postdoctoral fellow at the Harvard Center for International Affairs, and she climbed the ranks at the City University of New York from assistant to full professor from 1976 to 1985. Since 1985, she has been a full professor of urban planning in the Department of Architecture at Columbia University. Sassen has been a consultant and member of policy groups on Hispanic social and political issues for the Ford Foundation, the Rockefeller Foundation, the Inter-University Group in Latino Research, the Russell Sage Foundation, and on women's and other issues for the United Nations. In 1986, Sassen was awarded the American Institute of Certified Planners National Award. She is the author of *The Mobility of Labor and Capital* (1988) and *The Global City: New York, London, Tokyo* (1990), as well as numerous research articles.

Adljiza Sosa-Riddell (1937–)

Political Science

See Chapter 10.

References

Martínez, Julio A. *Chicano Scholars and Writers. A Bio-Bibliographic Directory.* Metuchen, New Jersey: Scarecrow Press, 1979.

Meier, Matt S. and Feliciano Rivera. *Dictionary of Mexican American History.* Westport, Connecticut: Greenwood Press, 1981.

Unterberger, Amy L., ed. *Who's Who among Hispanic Americans 1991–92.* Detroit: Gale Research, 1991.

Nicolás Kanellos

18

Science

The story of Hispanics in the sciences is really a bittersweet tale of outstanding achievement, on the one hand, and underrepresentation of U.S. Hispanics in math and science careers, on the other. Hispanics have contributed to world scientific and classical learning since the Middle Ages in Spain, developed excellent medical schools in Spain and Spanish America, and founded the first universities in the New World. The American Indian tradition, which enriched the culture of the Spanish and Europeans that settled in the New World, was also one of achievement in such sciences as astronomy and horticulture. However, today the record of Hispanics born or raised in the United States shows high dropout rates, and low college admission and retention rates, with dismally few Hispanic students going into math and science. While there are many Hispanic scientists, engineers, and mathematicians, many of these were born and educated in Spain and Spanish America and have come to the United States to benefit from our excellent graduate schools or the excellent research institutions and industries here that can provide the intellectual communities, resources, and salaries that their own countries cannot. Many of these scientists remain in the United States, contribute greatly to world knowledge, become citizens here, and enrich all of our lives in and out of the Hispanic communities.

✸ A GENERAL OVERVIEW

Deeply ingrained in Spanish and Hispanic cultures are the attitudes about the natural world and the sciences that the Arabs brought to the Iberian Peninsula during their 800 years of living there, from the beginning of the eighth century until 1492. Arab civilization was a crucial link with the classical learning of the Greeks, whose work they translated, advanced, and began to introduce to medieval Europe. Furthermore, the Arabs established universities, academies, and seats of learning long before such institutions were established in Europe. In extending their commerce to the far reaches of Asia and Africa, they learned many things from the cultures that they encountered. The expansion and domination by Islam of lands and peoples far and wide during the Middle Ages was built on the bedrock of solid technological and scientific knowledge. In Spain, the Arab cities of Córdoba, Sevilla, and Toledo became centers of learning that drew students from the rest of western Europe. Arabs were the inventors of algebra, and they were able to apply the principles of mathematics to everything that they did, including architecture, design, and landscaping. Originating in arid climates, they became superb horticulturists and agronomers, and developed systems of water management and irrigation that still survive in many parts of the Americas today. Their advances in the medical sciences even extended to mastering delicate corneal operations. All of this and much more is part of the Arab contribution to Hispanic culture everywhere.

The native peoples of the Americas had also advanced scientific knowledge and its application long before the arrival of the Europeans. In particular, the Native Americans were outstanding horticulturists and agronomists. Over thousands of years, they took the wild plants of the Americas and developed them into foodstuffs that eventually would revolutionize the diet of the whole planet. The native Americans took a wild grass and a variety of tubers and developed them into foods that would become staples for millions upon millions of people around the world: corn and potatoes. In addition, they developed myriad varieties of other foods that are common parts of our diets today, including beans, tomatoes, squash, and many fruits. The native Americans were ecologists and land and game managers who respected the wildlife and all of the natural world in everything that they did. Only recently has modern man really begun to learn from them in this regard, now that we are suffering so much from the degradation of the natural environment that has come with wasteful industrial overdevelopment and pollution.

Native Americans throughout the hemisphere were attentive astronomers who arrived at complex calculations that even modern scientists cannot achieve by using the types of instruments that were available to these native peoples. Achievements by such cultures as the Mayan even included the construction of modern-looking observatories. The Mayan mathematicians even invented the concept of zero. Little is known of the medical advances and the medicines developed from plants of the Americas by these peoples, except what little has come down to us in the techniques and folk medicines of such healers as *curanderos* (folk healers). We cannot be sure today how many scientific and medical advances were achieved by the peoples of the Americas before the arrival of the Spaniards, for these Europeans burned the Mayan books and destroyed temples with hieroglyphs throughout Mesoamerica and the Andes, the seats of highest learning, in their fervor to convert the "Indians" to Christianity.

Of course, much of the exploration and colonization of the New World can be seen as a scientific adventure. The Spaniards, including Hispanicized Indians and Africans, who explored these lands became superb cartographers and geographers, leaving us a legacy of minutely detailed maps and descriptions not only of the topography, but also of the fauna and flora and of the human inhabitants. Besides being the first to chart all of the coasts of what became the United States, they were also the first to map ocean currents, islands, rivers and mountain ranges. One such discovery was that of the Gulf Stream on February 4, 1513, by pilot Antonio de Alaminos, during Juan Ponce de León's voyage to Florida. Antonio de Alaminos had served as the pilot on Columbus' fourth voyage (1502–1504). This discovery resulted in Havana becoming a major port of assembly and Florida becoming a strategic stopping place for voyages. The current runs from the Florida Strait into the Bahamas Channel, past the coast of the Carolinas into the open ocean, where it forks northward to Norway and east to the Azores. Spanish ships, thus, headed for the Azores, refitted, and returned to Spain. One of the most important maps was the one developed in 1562 by Diego Gutiérrez (b. 1485), a pilot, chart- and instrument-maker in Seville, who created the largest, most complete print map of the Americas, relying on the data collected by Spain during its explorations. The map included in-

formation on the people and settlements, fauna and flora from Tierra del Fuego all the way up to Labrador on the east coast of the Hemisphere and to California on the west coast. This was the largest printed map of the Hemisphere known up to that time.

Many of the explorers wrote reports, diaries and chronicles describing the life of the Native Americans, and in this they became the first ethnographers and anthropologists. The first social science and biological document for the study of the flora and fauna of the South and Southwest, particularly Texas and the Mariam, Avavar, Karankawa, and other Indians of the region, is the 1536 "Joint Report," which was written in 1536 in Mexico City by three shipwrecked Europeans and an Afro-European, including Álvar Núñez Cabeza de Vaca. No other region in today's United States was described so early with so much detail. In 1541, Rodrigo Rangel and a soldier known only as the Gentleman of Elvas were the first to describe the culture of the Caddo Indians, which they observed on the expedition of Hernando de Soto to southern Arkansas and east Texas.

Álvar Núñez Cabeza de Vaca (1490–1557) may be considered to have become the first anthropologist and ethnographer of the New World in studying the Indians of the South and Southwest of what would later become the United States. He documented his observations and experiences in his book, *The Account,* which was published in Spain in 1542 after his return from the New World. In the winter of 1528, Núñez Cabeza de Vaca was only one of 15 survivors from a shipwreck off the coast of Florida. The Indians, who were suffering from illness, forced the survivors to become "healers," and Cabeza de Vaca began his career as a renowned physician among the Indians. During the six years that he remained among the Indians along the Gulf Coast, as far west as Texas, Cabeza de Vaca also became a merchant, a translator. He recorded in great detail for the first time many observations about the Indians of the South and Southwest. In 1534, he and four other marooned survivors set out on a march west in search of New Spain. They marched on foot completely across Texas and into New Mexico, going from one tribe to the next as healers and traders. They finally encountered Spaniards in what is today northwestern Mexico in 1536. Cabeza de Vaca's ten-year journey from Florida to New Mexico ended when he set sail in April 1537, for Spain. His memoir, *La relación* ("The Account"), may be considered the first ethnographic study of the Americas, as well as a literary masterpiece, possibly the first book "American literature" written in a European language.

The first European to study and translate the languages of Indians residing in what is today the United States was Father Francisco Pareja who, from 1595 until his death sometime after 1626, became an expert in the Timicuan language and published four works on the language. These studies are the basic texts used by modern linguists to understand the now extinct language. Father Pareja was a missionary to the Timicuan Indians at the San Juan del Puerto Mission, founded in 1587, in what is now Georgia.

Much of the agricultural technology was developed and introduced to North America by the Spaniards, including the breeding and raising of the basic livestock, such as cattle, sheep, horses, hogs, and goats, on which much of the economy of the Southwest was once almost entirely based. The Spanish were the first to introduce the plow, systems of irrigation and farm-land distribution, but especially important was the heritage that they brought from the Arabs of farming in arid climates. The Spanish, Hispanicized Indian and mestizo colonizers were the first engineers to come to lands that would become the United States. By 1610, they had built the first irrigation canals and irrigation systems north of the Rio Grande, in Santa Fe, New Mexico. They dug two *acequias madres* (main ditches) on each side of the small river which passed through the center of the town they were establishing. The Spanish had strict codes and plans for the construction of irrigation systems for the towns they were founding in the arid Southwest; such systems were constructed often in advance of the building of the forts, houses and churches. The undertaking was quite often massive, calling for the digging, dredging, transportation of materials and feeding of humans and animals. This was the case in the founding of Albuquerque in 1706, that of San Antonio in 1731, and of Los Angeles in 1781. The canals of San Antonio were so well planned, lined with stone and masonry as they were, that many of them are still functioning today.

Other Hispanic engineers saw the feasibility of linking the two main coasts of North America. Around 1790, the idea for a transcontinental road first occurred to the Spanish governor of California, Pedro Fages, who wrote his viceroy for permission to contact George Washington about constructing a continental trail from Virginia to California, with the roads meeting in the Spanish fort at Saint Louis. The idea did not take hold until 1869 when the transcontinental railroad finally linked East and West.

As early as the nineteenth century, Hispanic engineers began to immigrate to the United States and left their mark on our society as it developed. In 1885, Spanish immigrant Rafael Guastavino (1842–1908) obtained the first of his 25 patents, this one for new mortars he developed for tiled floor and ceiling vaults, partitions and stairs. Over the years this architect and contractor developed fireproofing innovations and perfected traditional cohesive masonry for modern use; he was responsible for building the tiled vaults for such New York City monuments as Grand Central Station, Carnegie Hall, the old Penn Station, the Metropolitan Museum of Art, the Plaza and Biltmore hotels, the Cathedral of St. John the Divine, and many others. Born in Valencia, Spain, Guastavino studied architecture in Barcelona, where he built factories, houses, and theaters by using many of the traditional technologies of Mediterranean architecture. Guastavino immigrated to the United States in 1881 in search of broader markets and better mortars, and went on to become one of the most recognized designers and builders of vaults, domes and tiled surfaces, promoting their acoustics, elegance and economy. By 1891, Guastavino's company had offices in New York, Boston, Providence, Chicago and Milwaukee. In 1892, Guastavino documented his successful system of construction in his book, *Essay on the Theory and History of Cohesive Construction*. After his death, Guastavino's business was continued by his son Rafael II, who expanded the company and was responsible for numerous patents of his own. In all, the Guastavinos were responsible for domes built at state capitals, major universities, museums and railroad stations throughout the United States, including the United States Supreme Court building and the Natural History Museum in Washington, D.C.

Today there are many outstanding universities and research institutions in the Hispanic world, especially in Argentina, Chile, Cuba, Mexico, Puerto Rico, and Spain. But many of the countries in Spanish America suffer from economic and industrial underdevelopment as a result of at least four centuries of European and U.S. colonialism and exploitation of their natural resources, including the export and exploitation of their human resources, be they laborers or intellectuals. Many foreign students are drawn to the excellent graduate schools of the United States, quite often with scholarships and support from their home countries. After becoming scientists or doctors here, it is often quite difficult for them to return to their homelands because of the superior research facilities and resources here, and the greater opportunities for teaching and making a comfortable living within the relatively prosperous economy of the United States.

Also, the scientific and scholarly community of the United States is very rich, drawing on scientists and teachers from throughout the world and boasting the most advanced communications, publications, and conferences. Many other doctors and scientists from Spanish America and Spain, without having been trained in the United States, are drawn to these benefits and come to make their homes here. Then, too, political disruptions have also precipitated the immigration to the United States of many intellectuals and scientists from Spanish America and Spain: the Spanish Civil War, the Mexican and Cuban Revolutions, and periodic violent dictatorships in Argentina, Chile, Nicaragua, El Salvador, and elsewhere.

One of the most recent Nobel Prizes was authorized to a scientist born and educated in Mexico, but working in a U.S. institution. Mario Molina, a researcher and professor at the Massachusetts Institute of Technology, shared the Nobel Prize in Chemistry with two others for their work that led to the international ban on chemicals believed to be depleting the ozone protective layer of the earth. A native of Mexico with a B.S. in chemical engineering from the National Autonomous University of Mexico (1965) and a Ph.D. in physical chemistry from the University of California-Berkeley (1972), he has taught and conducted research at various universities in the United States.

What is certain is that the United States has benefited greatly from this "brain drain," often at the expense of the home countries that, as Third World nations, direly need physicians, scientists, and teachers. The Hispanic communities within the United States have always benefited as well from this continued source of renewal of creative and intellectual membership. The Hispanic medical and scientific community has always actively contributed to community life in the large urban areas of Hispanic concentration. In fact, it is precisely Hispanic community life that quite often draws these doctors and scientists to settle in such communities as Houston, Los Angeles, Miami, New York, or San Antonio. The Houston Medical Center, for example, is not only replete with doctors and researchers from throughout the Hispanic world, but it has also become one of the principal medical centers for all of Latin America.

While there are many doctors and researchers that have moved to the United States from Spain and Spanish America—thus proving that Hispanics can indeed become successful doctors and scientists—Hispanics raised and educated in the United States have had a dismal record of entering the medical and scientific professions. Hispanic students tend to have high dropout rates and low college admission and graduation rates. The rate of their going

on to and graduating from graduate and medical schools is far worse. All of the effects of poverty, discrimination, and culture clash, poor schools and educational tracking, as well as many other barriers have resulted in a serious lack of doctors and scientists coming out of the Hispanic communities of the United States.

There are programs and organizations today that aim to provide greater opportunities for Hispanics in these fields. And there are outstanding teachers, such as Jaime Escalante, who are proving that students—even from the poorest and most crime-ridden neighborhoods—can be outstanding achievers in math and science. Even the College Board has taken on as its number one priority equity in admissions and graduation rates for minorities by the year 2000.

Despite these problems, the scientists and doctors that Hispanic communities have produced, and the ones that have come from their homelands to make their careers in the United States, have achieved a record of outstanding success, working within the most respected hospitals, universities, laboratories, and research institutes we have to offer.

✱ PROMINENT HISPANIC SCIENTISTS

Carlos Alberto Abel (1930–)

Medicine

Born in Argentina on May 7, 1930, Abel graduated from the medical school of the University of Buenos Aires in 1957. He began his career at the Children's Hospital in Buenos Aires, but by 1959 had moved to Providence, Rhode Island, as an intern at St. Joseph's Hospital. Through years of residencies and further scientific study in Maryland, California, and England, Abel became a specialist in biophysics and genetics and became a noted immunologist. From 1970 to 1984, he taught at the University of Colorado Medical Center, rising to the rank of full professor. From 1984 until 1992, he was a senior scientist in immunology at the Institute for Cancer Research of the Medical Research Institute of San Francisco, where since 1993 he has served as chair of the research council. His research has centered on lymphocytes and the relationships of their components with various immunological functions. In particular, he has been researching the AIDS virus and how to combat it. He is a member of the University of California Task Force on AIDS.

Daniel Acosta, Jr. (1945–)

Pharmacology

Born on March 25, 1945, in El Paso, Texas, Acosta received his B.S. degree from the University of Texas in 1968 and his Ph.D. degree in pharmacology from the University of Kansas in 1974. He began as an assistant professor at the University of Kansas, and is currently a full professor at the University of Texas. He has been an Eli Lilly Centennial Fellow and a Ford Fellow. Acosta's research is in cell toxicology, particularly studying the effects of drugs and toxicants at the cellular and subcellular levels; he is particularly interested in heart cells and injury to them.

Francisco José Aisle (1934–)

Genetics

Born on March 12, 1934, in Madrid, Spain, Aisle received his B.S. degree from the University of Madrid in 1955 and his M.S. and Ph.D. degrees from Columbia University in 1963 and 1964, respectively. Since 1964, he has worked as a researcher and professor at various universities and institutes. Since 1974, he has been a professor of genetics at the University of California, Davis. He is the associate editor of *Molecular Evolution and Paleobiology,* a research journal. He also serves as the chairman of boards at the National Academy of Sciences and the National Research Council. His research concentrates on evolution, population genetics, and fitness of natural and experimental populations, among other subjects.

José Ramón Alcalá (1940–)

Anatomy, Biochemistry

Born in Ponce, Puerto Rico, on May 1, 1940, Alcalá began his high school education in Santurce, Puerto Rico, and finished it in Waynesville, Missouri, where he graduated in 1957. His stepfather, a career army man had been transferred to Fort Leonard Wood in 1956. Alcalá went on to receive his B.A. and M.A. degrees in Zoology from the University of Missouri in 1964 and 1966, respectively. He received his Ph.D. degree in anatomy from the University of Illinois Medical Center in 1972. Since 1972, he has taught and conducted research at the School of Medicine at Wayne State University, where he has been a full professor since 1987. Since 1990, he has been the director of the gross anatomy programs of the School of Medicine. Alcalá specializes in the anatomy of the eye, studying the biochemistry and immunochemistry of lens plasma membranes. This research has had great methodological and conceptual impact in the field of lens research for its first clear delineation of the protein composition of lens fiber plasma membranes. His continued work in this area has had impact on research on cataracts. In 1992, Alcalá returned to Puerto Rico to become chair of the anatomy department at the Ponce School of Medicine in Ponce, where he continued his studies of lens proteins. He is supervisor of the school's body donation program and a member of the state anatomy board of the Commonwealth of Puerto Rico.

Kenneth B. Alonso (1942–)

Pathology, Nuclear Medicine

Born in Tampa, Florida, on November 26, 1942, Alonso received his A.B. degree from Princeton University in 1964 and his M.D. degree from the University of Florida in 1968. He has worked as an intern, resident, and pathologist at various hospitals around the country from 1968 to 1976. In 1976, he became the director of laboratory procedures for Upjohn South Company in Georgia, and from 1978 to 1984, he worked as chief of staff and pathology for two hospitals. Since 1984, he has been the director of Lab Atlanta in Riverdale, Georgia. His research interests include immunological disorders, especially receptors, membrane transport, human tumor stem cell assay, and monoclonal antibodies.

Anne Maino Alvarez (1941–)

Plant Pathology

Born on April 14, 1941, in Rochester, Minnesota, Alvarez received her B.S. degree from Stanford University in 1963 and her M.S. and Ph.D. degrees from the University of California, Berkeley, in 1966 and 1972, respectively. Since that time she has worked at the University of Argentina in Nequen, from 1969 to 1970, and at the University of Hawaii, where she is currently a researcher and educator in plant pathology. Alvarez has done field research in Argentina, Costa Rica, and Mexico on bacterial diseases in fruits and crops and on epidemiology and disease control. She has particularly studied the orchard and postharvest diseases of the papaya.

Luis Walter Alvarez (1911–1988)

Experimental Physics

Born in San Francisco, California, on June 13, 1911, Luis Alvarez was one of this country's most distinguished and respected physicists. In addition to B.S. (1932) and Ph.D. (1936) degrees from the University of Chicago, Alvarez received a number of honorary degrees from universities in the United States and abroad. He developed most of his work at the University of California, Berkeley, beginning in 1936. From 1954 to 1959 and from 1976 to 1978, he served as associate director of the prestigious Lawrence Berkeley Lab. In 1986, Alvarez was awarded the Nobel Prize in physics; he also received the Collier Trophy (1946), the Scott Medal (1953), the Einstein

Medal (1961), the National Medal of Science (1964), and many other awards. Alvarez was a pioneer in particle physics, astrophysics, ophthalmic and television optics, geophysics, and air navigation. He died on September 1, 1988, in Berkeley, California.

Angeles Alvariño de Leira (1916–)

Marine Biology

Born on October 3, 1916, in El Ferrol, Spain, Alvariño received her master's (1941) and doctorate degrees in chemistry and sciences in 1951 and 1967, respectively, from the University of Madrid. From 1941 to 1957, she worked at universities and institutes in Spain as a biological oceanographer. In 1957, she began her career in the United States as a biologist at the Scripps Institute of Oceanography of the University of California, La Jolla. In 1970, she assumed her current position of fishery research biologist at the National Marine Fisheries Service in La Jolla. Alvariño has held concurrent positions at universities in England, Mexico, and Venezuela, and she has been a Fulbright scholar and a National Science Foundation fellow a number of times. Alvariño has been the discoverer of 11 new species of chaetognatha and three new species of syphono-

Angeles Alvariño de Leira.

phorae, which are her specialty, along with zooplankton and medusae. Although Alvariño officially retired in 1987, she continues to conduct research on zooplankton. In 1993, she was awarded the Great Silver Medal of Galicia by King Juan Carlos I.

Ralph Amado (1932–)

Theoretical Physics

Born in Los Angeles on November 13, 1932, Amado received his B.S. degree from Stanford University in 1954 and his Ph.D. degree from Oxford University, England, in 1957. After graduating, he began his career as a research associate at the University of Pennsylvania and has remained at that institution; his current title is professor of physics. Besides research and teaching duties at Penn, Amado has worked as a consultant to the Arms Control and Disarmament Agency. His specialties are theoretical nuclear physics, many-body problems, particle physics and scattering theory.

Elías Amador (1932–)

Medicine, Pathology

Born in Mexico City, Mexico, on June 8, 1932, and educated at the Central Mexico University (B.S. degree, 1959) and the National University of Mexico (M.D. degree, 1956), immediately after becoming a doctor, Amador relocated to the United States and developed his career here at various hospitals and universities. Since 1972, he has served as professor and chairman of the Department of pathology of the Charles R. Drew Postgraduate Medical School, professor at the University of Southern California, and chief of pathology of the Martin Luther King, Jr., General Hospital, all three positions held concurrently. He has been a teaching fellow at Harvard Medical School (1957–58) and at the Boston University School of Medicine (1959–60). His research concerns the development of accurate and sensitive methods for diagnosis and detection of disease.

Alberto Vinicio Baez (1912–)

Physics

Born in Puebla, Mexico, on November 15, 1912, Baez received his B.S. degree from Drew University in 1933, his M.A. degree from Syracuse University in 1935, and his Ph.D. degree from Stanford University in 1950. Over his long career he has taught and conducted research at various universities, including Cornell, Drew, Stanford, Wagner (New York), and Redlands and Harvey Mudd (both in California). Between 1961 and 1974, he worked for UNESCO in New York and Paris in science education. He has also held various international board and committee

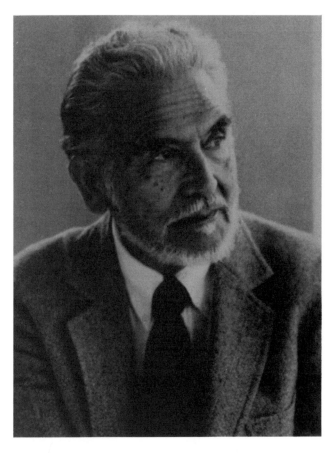

Alberto Vinicio Baez.

positions, and from 1974 to 1978, served as the chairman of the Committee on Teaching Sciences of the International Council of Science Unions. Since 1984, he has been chairman emeritus of Community Education, International Union for the Conservation of Nature and Natural Resources, Glantz, Switzerland. In 1991, the S.P.I.E. conferred the Dennis Gabor Award on Baez and his coresearcher, Paul Kirkpatrick, in recognition of their pioneering contributions to the development of X-ray imaging microscopes and telescopes. The Kirkpatrick-Baez Lamar X-ray telescope was approved for use on the Freedom Space Station. In his research, Baez specialized in x-ray radiation, optics, and microscopy, as well as in science and environmental education.

Teresa Bernárdez (1931–)

Medicine, Psychiatry

See Chapter 10.

Caridad Borras (1942–)

Radiological Physics

Born in Spain on February 18, 1942, Borras received her M.S. and Ph.D. degrees from the Univer-

sity of Barcelona in 1964 and 1974, respectively. Until 1966, she worked in Barcelona in hospitals; in 1967, she relocated to Thomas Jefferson University in Philadelphia as an assistant physicist. Since 1974, she has served as a radiological physicist at the West Coast Cancer Foundation. Since 1982, she has also been a clinical assistant professor at the University of California. Borras studies the radioembryopathological effects of high LET nuclides, as well as the physics of diagnostic radiology and radiation therapy.

César A. Cáceres (1927–)

Medicine, Computer Science

Born on April 9, 1927, in Puerto Cortés, Honduras, Cáceres received his B.S. and M.D. degrees from Georgetown University in 1949 and 1953, respectively. He then served as an intern and resident in Boston hospitals, but returned as a fellow in cardiology to George Washington University from 1956 to 1960, and from 1960 to 1971 he moved up the ranks there from assistant professor of medicine to full professor and department chairman. From 1960 to 1969, he was also chief of the Medical Systems Development Lab for the United States Public Health Service. In 1971, he founded his own company, Clinical Systems Associates, for which he still serves as president to date; he also worked concurrently as a professor of electrical engineering at the University of Maryland from 1971 to 1976. Cáceres specializes in electrocardiography, cardiology, medical diagnosis, and computers in medicine.

Marta Cancio (1928–)

Biochemistry

Born in San Sebastián, Puerto Rico, on December 8, 1928, Cancio received her B.S. degree from the University of Puerto Rico in 1949 and her M.S. and Ph.D. degrees from the University of Missouri in 1952 and 1954, respectively. In 1954, she began as an associate biochemist at the University of Puerto Rico School of Medicine and moved up the ranks. Since 1966, she has served as the supervisory research chemist for the Veterans Administration Hospital, and since 1971, as associate professor of biochemistry and nutrition at the University of Puerto Rico Medical School. Her research concerns lipid and protein chemistry, malabsorption, and immunochemistry.

Graciela Candelas (1922–)

Molecular Biology

Born in Puerto Rico in 1922, Candelas received her B.S. degree from the University of Puerto Rico in

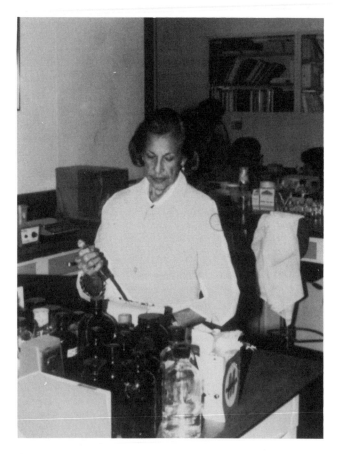

Graciela Candelas.

1944, her M.S. degree from Duke University in 1959, and her Ph.D. degree from the University of Miami in 1966. Since 1966, she has moved up the ranks at the University of Puerto Rico; since 1971, she has been a full professor of cell and molecular biology there. She has also held visiting and concurrent positions at the University of Syracuse, Rockefeller University, City University of New York, and the Medical College of Georgia. She was given the Special Science Award by the Puerto Rican Institute in New York in 1985 and the Distinguished Alumnus Award by the Alumni Organization of the University of Puerto Rico in 1988. One of her research interests is fibroin synthesis and its regulation using a pair of glands from the spider *Nephila clavipes*.

Oscar A. Candia (1935–)

Physicology, Biophysics

Born in Buenos Aires, Argentina, on April 30, 1935, Candia received his M.D. degree from the University of Buenos Aires in 1959. After working as a researcher in Buenos Aires, he relocated to the University of Louisville in 1964 as a research associate and moved up the ranks there to full professorship.

Since 1984, he has been professor of opthalmology and physiology at Mt. Sinai School of Medicine in New York. He received career development awards from 1966 to 1971 from the National Institutes of Health. He is an associate editor of *Investigations in Opthalmology and Visual Science,* a research journal. In 1985, he won the Alcon award. His principal research concern is ion transport in biological membranes.

Fernando Caracena (1936–)

Atmospheric Physics, Physics

Born on March 13, 1936, in El Paso, Texas, Caracena received his B.S. degree from the University of Texas at El Paso in 1958 and his M.S. and Ph.D. degrees from Case Western Reserve in 1966 and 1968, respectively. From 1958 to 1961, he worked as an atmospheric physicist for the Department of Defense at White Sands Missile Range, and from 1969 to 1976, he worked as an assistant professor at Metropolitan State College, Denver, Colorado. Since 1976, he has been working as an atmospheric physicist at the Environmental Research Labs of the National Oceanic and Atmospheric Administration. His research concerns air safety, especially clear air turbulence, low altitude wind shear, and the meteorology of wind-shear-related aircraft accidents.

Mary Janet M. Cárdenas (1942–)

Biochemistry

Born in Miami, Oklahoma, on January 31, 1942, Cárdenas received her B.A. degree from Oklahoma State University in 1963 and her M.S. and Ph.D. degrees from the University of Illinois in 1965 and 1967, respectively. From 1967 through 1981, she taught at various universities, achieving the rank of associate professor of chemistry at the University of North Carolina. Since 1981, she has been health science administrator at the National Eye Institute of the National Institutes of Health. Her research concerns the sensorimotor aspects of vision, especially culomotor disorders.

Manuel Cardona (1934–)

Physics

Born in Barcelona, Spain, on September 7, 1934, Manuel Cardona received his B.S. degree in physics from the University of Barcelona in 1955 and his Ph.D. degree in applied physics from Harvard University in 1959. After graduation, he worked until 1964 at RCA Laboratories in Switzerland and in Princeton, New Jersey. Since then he has been a researcher associated with various universities and institutes, most notably as professor of physics at

Manuel Cardona.

Baylor University College of Medicine as a professor and researcher in cardiology and rehabilitation. He moved up the ranks to his present positions: professor of physiology, professor of rehabilitation, head of the cardiopulmonary lab, and director of biomath. Among his many awards are a Gold Medal from the Sixth International Congress on Physical Medicine in 1972, a Licht Award for Excellence in Science Writing in 1980, and the Narcis Monturiol Medal from Catalunya, Spain, in 1984. In 1993, Cardús was elected president of the International Society for Gravitational Physiology. He has researched experimental exercise and respiratory physiology, mathematical and computer applications to the study of physiological systems, and rehabilitation medicine.

Alberto Castro (1933–)

Biochemistry, Endocrinology

Born on November 15, 1933, in San Salvador, El Salvador, Castro received his B.S. degree from the University of Houston in 1958 and his Ph.D. degree in biological chemistry from the University of El Salvador in 1962. He moved up the ranks from assistant to full professor at the University of El Salvador from 1958 to 1966. From 1966 to 1970, he was an

Brown from 1964 to 1971, and, since 1971, as the director of the Max-Planck-Institut for Solid State Research in Stuttgart, Germany. In 1967, Cardona became a naturalized citizen of the United States. He is the author of some 700 scientific publications in journals and nine monographs on solid-state physics. Among his many awards are the Frank Isakson Prize from the American Physical Society (1984), the Grand Cross of Alfonso el Sabio from Spain (1987), the Príncipe de Asturias Prize from Spain (1988), the Kronland Medal from Czechoslovakia (1988), and the Excellence in Superconductivity Award of the World Congress on Superconductivity (1992). He is a member of both the American and European Academies of Science.

David Cardús (1922–)

Cardiology, Biomathematics

Born on August 6, 1922, in Barcelona, Spain, Cardús received his M.D. degree from the University of Barcelona in 1949. He did his internship and residency in Barcelona and postgraduate work in cardiology and physiology there. In 1960, Cardús relocated to Texas and embarked on a career at the

David Cardús.

NIH fellow at the University of Oregon, and from 1970 to 1973, he was a lab director at the United Medical Lab. From 1973 to 1977, he once again moved up the ranks to full professor of medicine, pathology and microbiology at the University of Miami Medical School. Since 1973, he has been the director of the Hormone Research Lab there. His primary work is in carbohydrate biochemistry, metabolism, and modes of action, and hormone mechanisms and their interrelationship to hypertension.

George Castro (1939–)

Physical Chemistry

Born February 23, 1939, in Los Angeles, California, Castro received his B.S. degree in chemistry from the University of California, Los Angeles, in 1960 and his Ph.D. degree in physical chemistry from the University of California, Riverside, in 1965. He has been a postdoctoral fellow at the University of Pennsylvania, Cal Tech, and Dartmouth, but has worked as a researcher for IBM since 1968. Since 1986, he has been the manager of Synchrotron Studies for IBM at the Almaden Research Center. In 1978, he received the Outstanding Innovation Award from IBM, and in 1990, he was elected a fellow of the American Physical

George Castro.

Society. Castro is the discoverer of the mechanism of the intrinsic charge carrier of organic photoconductors. Years later, such materials in the form of organic polymeric films became the basis for flexible photoconductors that are used in photocopying machines and high-speed printers. Castro assumed the leadership of the physical sciences of the IBM San Jose Research Lab in 1975, three years after its formation. He has built the organization into one that is world-famous for its scientific discoveries. These include the discovery of the first superconducting polymer, novel organic metals and superconductors, high-resolution laser techniques, and new methods of investigating magnetic materials.

Peter Castro (1943–)

Zoology, Parasitology

Born on July 20, 1943, in Mayagüez, Puerto Rico, Castro received his B.S. degree from the University of Puerto Rico at Mayaguez in 1964, and his M.S. and Ph.D. degrees in zoology from the University of Hawaii in 1966 and 1969, respectively. From 1970 to 1975, he worked as a teacher and researcher in the biology department of the University of Puerto Rico at Mayaguez. Since 1975, he has been an associate professor of Biological Sciences at California State Polytechnical Institute in Pomona. Castro has been a fellow and visiting researcher at Stanford, the Smithsonian Institute, and Moss Landing Marine Labs. Castro's research concerns ecological, physiological, and behavioral aspects of marine symbiosis.

Asunción Elena Charola (1942–)

Analytical Chemistry, Physical Chemistry

Born in Argentina on February 23, 1942, Charola received her Ph.D. degree in analytical chemistry from the National University of La Plata in 1974. After receiving a fellowship to New York University from 1974 to 1976, Charola remained in the United States as an assistant professor of chemistry at Manhattan College from 1978 to 1981 and at the Metropolitan Museum of Art from 1981 to 1985. Since 1985, she has been an associate scientist at the ICCROM in Rome, Italy. Her research concerns solid-state chemistry, polymorphism, and x-ray crystallography, among other subjects.

Guillermo B. Cintrón (1942–)

Medicine

Born on March 28, 1942, in San Juan, Puerto Rico, Cintrón received his B.S. degree from the University of Puerto Rico in 1963 and his M.D. degree from Loyola-Stritch School of Medicine in Chicago in 1967. After residencies in Washington, D.C., Cintrón

Guillermo B. Cintrón.

cal School. His research interests include the biochemistry and metabolism of steroid hormones; he has published more than 80 research articles.

Julio Cordero (1923-)

Fluid Engineering

Born on January 10, 1923, in San José, Costa Rica, Cordero received his B.S. degree from Wayne State University in 1948 and his M.S. degree from the University of Minnesota in 1951. From 1951 to 1976, he worked as a research scientist at a number of universities and industries. Since 1976, he has been chief engineer at the Magnetohydrodynamics Research Facility of the Massachusetts Institute of Technology. His principal research concerns shock wave phenomena and supersonic and hypersonic aerodynamics.

Francisco Dallmeier (1953-)

Wildlife Biology

Born on February 15, 1953, in Caracas, Venezuela, Francisco Dallmeier received his licentiate in biology from the Central University of Venezuela in 1979 and his M.S. and Ph.D. degrees in wildlife biology from the

returned to Puerto Rico, where from 1975 to 1983, he taught and conducted cardiac research at the University of Puerto Rico Medical School. Since 1983, he has been an associate professor at the University of Southern Florida School of Medicine. Since 1987, he has been the associate director of cardiology there. His principal research concerns heart disease and its causes and prevention.

Antonio E. Colás (1928-)

Biochemistry

Born on June 22, 1928, in Muel, Spain, Colás received his B.S. degree from the University of Zaragoza in 1951 and his M.D. degree from the University of Madrid in 1953. In 1955, he received his Ph.D. degree in biochemistry from the University of Edinburgh in Scotland. Following his studies at Edinburgh, Colás took various teaching and research positions in Spain, Colombia, and finally, in 1960, in the United States at the University of Oregon Medical School, where he served as professor of obstetrics and gynecology until 1968. Since then, he has been professor of obstetrics and gynecology and physiological chemistry at the University of Wisconsin Medi-

Antonio E. Colás.

Francisco Dallmeier.

University of Colorado in 1984 and 1986, respectively. From 1973 to 1977, he was the director of the La Salle Museum of Natural History and a member of the ecology team of the Institute of Tropical Zoology of the Central University of Venezuela. From 1977 to 1986, he worked as a biologist and researcher in various positions in Venezuela and the United States. Since 1986, he has worked for the Smithsonian Institute in Washington, D.C., for which he has served as director of the Man and the Biosphere Biological Diversity Program since 1989. In that capacity, he coordinates field biodiversity research and training in Bolivia, Brazil, Peru, Ecuador, Guatemala, Panama, Puerto Rico, the Virgin Islands, Tennessee, and Washington, D.C. His major research focuses on the integration of biological diversity and natural resources and conservation and management programs. His latest studies concern neotropical waterfowl and wetlands ecology and management.

Henry Frank Díaz (1948–)

Atmospheric Sciences

Born in Cuba on July 15, 1948, Díaz received his B.S. degree from Florida State University in 1971,

his M.S. degree from the University of Miami in 1974, and his Ph.D. degree in geology and climatology from the University of Colorado in 1985. From 1974 through 1985, Díaz worked as a meteorologist at the Environmental Data Service, the National Climate Center, and the Environmental Research Lab. Since 1985, he has been acting director of the Climate Research Program of the National Oceanic and Atmospheric Administration. In 1977 and 1983, he received awards for outstanding achievement at the Environmental Research Lab. Díaz researches climatology and climatic variation, developing long-term historical climatic data bases. He is especially recognized for his 1992 study *El Niño: Historical and Paleoclimatic Aspects of the Southern Oscillation.*

Javier I. Escobar (1943–)

Psychiatry, Psychopharmacology

Born on July 26, 1943, in Medellín, Colombia, Escobar received his M.D. degree from the University of Antioquia in Colombia in 1967; in 1969, he became a resident at the University of Minnesota Hospitals, and by 1976, had attained the rank of associate professor of psychiatry there. From 1976 to 1979, he worked at the University of Tennessee, and in 1979, he became an associate professor of psychiatry at the University of California, Los Angeles. Today he is a full professor at that institution. Escobar has worked with many hospitals and numerous research projects on a regional and national level. His research concerns clinical projects in schizophrenia and affective disorders, including testing for new treatments. He is also a specialist in cross-cultural psychiatry as it concerns somatization traits across different cultures.

José Alberto Fernández-Pol (1943–)

Medicine

Born on March 17, 1943, in Buenos Aires, José Alberto Fernández-Pol received his M.D. degree from the University of Buenos Aires in 1969. From then until 1971, he was affiliated with various hospitals in Buenos Aires; in 1971, he became a resident physician at the State University of New York, Buffalo. After that he worked at various microbiology and cancer research labs in the United States, notably at the National Cancer Institute of the National Institutes of Health from 1975 to 1977. In 1977, he began as an assistant professor of medicine at St. Louis University; since 1985, he has been a full professor there. Fernández's research concerns growth control mechanisms in normal and cancerous cells, oncogenies.

Jorge Fischbarg (1935–)

Opthalmology

Born on August 14, 1935, in Buenos Aires, Argentina, Jorge Fischbarg received his early education there and graduated with a B.S. degree from the Colegio Nacional de Buenos Aires in 1953. He received his M.D. degree from the University of Buenos Aires in 1962 and his Ph.D. degree in physiology from the University of Chicago in 1971. From 1961 to 1969, he held various postdoctoral fellowships and traineeships in Buenos Aires, Louisville, Kentucky, and Chicago. Since 1970 he has pursued a career in physiology (ophthalmology) research and teaching at Columbia University. In 1984 he became head of the Membrane Biology Laboratory (Eye Research Division) at Columbia. He has received research awards from and worked closely with the National Institute of Health, and has been a visiting scientist in France (1974 and 1978) and England (1976–1977). In 1986, he was awarded the Alcon Recognition Award from the Alcon Research Institute. Fischbarg has been a member of the editorial board of *Experimental Eye Research* since 1986. His research interests include the transport of fluid and electrolytes across epithelial membranes, corneal physiology, and molecular biophysics of water channels in cell membranes.

José Alberto Fernández-Pol.

Alfredo Mariano García (1927–)

Biology, Anatomy

Born on September 12, 1927, in Itati-Corrientes, Argentina, García received his M.D. degree from the University of Buenos Aires in 1953 and a Ph.D. degree in zoology from Columbia University in 1962. Since 1957, he has worked in the United States at various hospitals and research institutes. Since 1964, he has been a professor of anatomy at the State University of New York Upstate Medical Center in Syracuse; he achieved full professorship status in 1974. His research concerns quantitative cytochemistry and fine structure and nucleic acid metabolism of mammalian blood cells.

Carlos Ernesto García (1936–)

Mechanical Engineering

Born on May 14, 1936, in Las Vegas, New Mexico, García received his three degrees from New Mexico State University: B.S. (1958), M.S. (1962), and D.Sc. (1966). He has worked as a research engineer at a variety of government institutions and private industries, including the Atomic Energy Commission, from 1971 to 1973, as a weapons development engineer. Since 1984, he has been the director of the environmental safety and health division of the U.S. Department of Energy. His specialty is hydromechanical missile control systems and shock wave phenomena, including the study of underground nuclear explosions.

Celso Ramón García (1921–)

Obstetrics and Gynecology

Born on October 31, 1921, in New York City, García received his B.S. degree from Queens College in 1942 and his M.D. degree from the State University of New York in 1945. He has worked as a professor and researcher at various hospitals and universities, including Harvard and the University of Puerto Rico. He held the William Shippen Jr. Chair in Human Reproduction at the School of Medicine at the University of Pennsylvania until 1992, when he became professor emeritus. From 1973 to 1978, he was the vice chairman of the Department of Obstetrics and Gynecology and the director of the Division of Human Reproduction. Since 1978, he has been the director of reproductive surgery. Included among his many awards are the Carl Harman Award from the Human Fertility Society (1961), Extraordinary Professor, University of San Luis Potosí, Mexico (1974), and the Pincus Lecturer, School of Medicine, Wayne

Celso Ramón García.

State University (1974). His specialty is reproductive physiology and infertility.

José D. García (1936–)
Physics

Born in Santa Fe, New Mexico, on January 3, 1936, García received his B.S. degree from New Mexico State University in 1957, his M.A. degree from the University of California, Berkeley, in 1959, and his Ph.D. degree from the University of Wisconsin, Madison, in 1966. In 1967, he joined the faculty of the University of Arizona; since 1975, he has been a full professor of physics at Arizona. He has a been a Fulbright fellow (1957), a NASA postdoctoral fellow (1963), a NORDITA visiting fellow in Stockholm (1972), and an elected fellow of the American Physical Society since 1979. His principal research concerns quantum theory and ion-atom and ion-surface interactions.

Elma González (1942–)
Cell Biology

Born in the United States on June 6, 1942, González received her B.S. degree from Texas

Woman's University in 1965 and her Ph.D. degree in cell biology from Rutgers University in 1972. After working with a fellowship in plant physiology at the University of California, Santa Cruz, from 1972 to 1974, González became an assistant professor of cell biology at the University of California, Los Angeles in 1974. Since 1981, she has been an associate professor there. Her research concerns the mechanisms and regulation of the formation of microbodies and other metabolic compartments.

Paula González (1932–)
Environmental Science, Bioethics

Born on October 25, 1932, in Albuquerque, New Mexico, González received her A.B. degree from the College of Mt. St. Joseph in 1952, her M.S. degree from the Catholic University of America in 1962, and her Ph.D. degree in cell physiology from there in 1966. González has taught at high schools, schools of nursing, and at the university level. From 1965 to 1982, she moved up the ranks from assistant professor to full professor at the College of Mt. St. Joseph; from 1968 to 1973, she served as the chairman of the Department of Biology. Her research concerns nucleolar changes during the cell cycle, energy and environment, and biomedical advances and their human implications.

Richard Rafael González (1942–)
Physiology

Born on September 15, 1942, in El Paso, Texas, González received his B.S. degree from the University of Texas in 1962, his M.S. degree from the University of San Francisco in 1966, and his Ph.D. degree in Physiology and Biophysics from the University of California-Davis in 1970. After spending two years as a U.S. Public Health Service fellow at Yale University, during the next four years he went from assistant professor to associate professor of environmental physiology at Yale University. Since 1976, he has worked in ergonomics and environmental medicine at the U.S. Army Research Institute. His research concerns thermal physiology, peripheral circulation, and environmental physiology.

Enrique Hernández (1951–)
Medicine

Born on October 25, 1951, in Vega Baja, Puerto Rico, Hernández received his B.S. and M.D. degrees from the University of Puerto Rico in 1973 and 1977, respectively. From then until 1981, he was a fellow, intern, and resident at the Johns Hopkins Hospital. After academic appointments at the Johns Hopkins

University School of Medicine and the College of Osteopathic Medicine of the Pacific, he joined the faculty of the Medical College of Philadelphia, where he has been a full professor since 1989. In 1987, Hernández became the director of the Division of Gynecological Oncology at the college. He has had a number of hospital appointments in Philadelphia and Hawaii, as well as numerous consulting positions. In 1985, he became a fellow of the American College of Obstetricians and Gynecologists, and in 1986, a fellow of the American College of Surgeons. One of his main research interests is cancer of the female reproductive tract; he is the coauthor of the *Manual of Gynecological Oncology,* as well as of many other studies published in medical journals. Among his numerous awards are the 1994 Award for Excellence in Teaching at the Medical College of Pennsylvania. He was also named "Top Doctor" by *Philadelphia Magazine* in 1991 and 1994.

Gonzalo J. Hernández (1936–)

Optics, Atmospheric Physics

Born in San José, Costa Rica, in 1936, Hernández received his B.S. degree from the University of Notre Dame in 1958 and his Ph.D. in physical chemistry from the University of Rochester in 1962. From 1961 to 1969, he worked as a physicist at the Cambridge Research Lab of the air force, and from 1970 to 1985, he was the director of the Fritz Peak Observatory. From 1985 to 1987, he was a research scientist at the Space Physics Research Lab of the University of Michigan. He has been professor in the graduate program in geophysics at the University of Washington since 1988. Hernández has been a physicist for the Environmental Research Labs of the National Oceanic and Atmospheric Administration since 1969. He is a specialist in upper atmosphere physics and high-resolution spectroscopy.

Michael Louis Ibáñez (1916–)

Pathology

Born on November 9, 1916, in Havana, Cuba, Ibáñez received his M.D. degree from the University of Havana in 1948. He became an intern at Hermann Hospital in Houston in 1949–50 and developed a career in pathology there and at other hospitals. Since 1975, he has been professor of pathology, and since 1974, pathologist for the Cancer Center of the M. D. Anderson Hospital and Tumor Institute in Houston. Ibáñez has researched the pathologic anatomy of cancer and the pathology of the thyroid gland.

Vicente José Llamas (1944–)

Solid-State Physics

Born on February 15, 1944, in Los Angeles, California, Llamas received his B.S. degree from Loyola University of Los Angeles in 1966 and his M.S. and Ph.D. degrees from the University of Missouri, Rolla, in 1968 and 1970, respectively. From 1970 to 1984, he went from assistant to full professor of physics at New Mexico Highlands University. Since 1984, he has been chairman of the Department of Physics and Math. His research concerns surface studies of alkali halides in the infrared, as well as the atmospheric study of air pollutants.

Joseph Llauradó (1927–)

Nuclear Medicine, Biomedical Engineering

Born on February 6, 1927, in Barcelona, Spain, Llauradó received both M.D. (1950) and Ph.D. (1960) degrees from the University of Barcelona. After teaching and researching in countries around the world, including England, Italy, Holland, New Zealand, and Venezuela, he became a senior endocrinologist for Pfizer and Co. in Connecticut from 1959 to 1961. From 1963 to the present, he has been a researcher and professor at universities in the United States. Since 1983, he has been professor of radiation science at the Loma Linda School of Medicine and chief of nuclear medical services of the Veterans Administration Hospital in Loma Linda. Llauradó researches radionuclides in cardiology and radionuclide treatment of pulmonary cancer.

Rodolfo Llinas (1934–)

Neurobiology, Electrophysiology

Born on December 16, 1934, in Bogotá, Colombia, Llinas received his M.D. degree from the Pontificial Universidad Javierana in Bogotá in 1959 and a Ph.D. degree in neurophysiology from the Australian National University in 1965. He has worked at the National University of Colombia, the University of Minnesota, the American Medical Association, and the University of Iowa. Since 1976, he has been professor and chairman of physiology and biophysiology at New York University Medical Center. Since 1975, he has been the editor-in-chief of *Neuroscience Journal.* He conducts structural and functional studies of neuronal systems and also studies the evolution and development of the central nervous system.

Diana Montes de Oca López (1937–)

Microbiology, Immunology

Born on August 26, 1937, in Havana, Cuba, López received her B.S. degree from the University of Havana in 1960 and her M.S. and Ph.D. degrees in microbiology from the University of Miami in 1968 and 1970, respectively. From 1970 to 1983, she went from research associate to full professor of microbiology at the University of Miami School of Medicine, where she continues to pursue her career. Since 1980, she has been the section leader in tumor virology and immunology for the state of Florida Comprehensive Cancer Center. Her research concerns tumor immunology, viral oncogenesis, and cell kinetics.

Cynthia Luz Marcelo (1945–)

Cell Physiology

Born on August 13, 1945, in New York City, Marcelo received her B.S. degree from Mt. St. Vincent College in 1967 and her M.S. and Ph.D. degrees in cell physiology from the State University of New York at Buffalo in 1969 and 1973, respectively. From 1975 to 1983, she went from assistant to associate professor of physiology in dermatology at the University of Michigan; since 1983, she has been the director of the research division of dermatology there. Her research concerns the control of epidermal cell function and the use of tissue culture technology to study growth factors and the effects of hormones and vitamin A on growth and function.

Michael Allen Mares (1945–)

Mammalian Biogeography

Born on March 11, 1945, in Albuquerque, New Mexico, Mares received his B.S. degree from the University of New Mexico in 1968, his M.S. degree from Kansas State University in 1969, and his Ph.D. degree in zoology from the University of Texas in 1973. He went from assistant to associate professor of ecology at the University of Pittsburgh from 1973 to 1981. In 1981, he went to the University of Oklahoma; he is currently a professor of zoology there and director of the Stovall Museum. Mares has been a fellow and fieldworker in Argentina as well as in the Southwest of the United States. In his research, he examines convergent evolution, adaptation and community organization of desert rodents of the world, as well as ecology, conservation, evolution, and systematics of South American mammals.

Richard Isaac Martínez (1944–)

Physical Chemistry

Born on August 16, 1944, in Havana, Cuba, Martínez received his B.S. degree from McGill University in 1964 and his Ph.D. degree in chemistry from the University of California, Los Angeles, in 1976. Martínez has worked as a research chemist at

San Diego State University, Shell Oil, and UCLA. Since 1976, he has been a research chemist for the National Bureau of Standards of the U.S. Department of Commerce. In 1981, he was the recipient of the Bronze Medal Award from the Department of Commerce, and in 1983, he received the Independent Research 100 Award. He has worked on the development and application of tandem mass spectrometry MS/MS to the study of kinetics of complex organic reaction systems relevant to oxidation and atmospheric chemistry.

José Méndez (1921–)

Physiology, Nutrition

Born on August 17, 1921, in Tapachula, Mexico, Méndez received his B.S. degree from the Universidad de San Carlos in Guatemala City in 1947, his M.S. degree from the University of Illinois in 1948 and his Ph.D. degree in physiology from the University of Minnesota in 1957. From 1965 to 1966, he was associate professor of nutrition at the Massachusetts Institute of Technology; since 1966, he has been professor of health and applied physiology at Penn State University. He is a specialist in nutrition studies and nutrition training in developing countries and the adaptation of man to different environmental stresses.

Manuel Gaspar Meléndez (1935–)

Atomic Physics, Molecular Physics

Born in New York City on June 15, 1935, Meléndez received his B.Ch.E. and his Ph.D. degrees in chemical physics from the University of Florida in 1958 and 1963, respectively. From 1965 to 1966, he worked as an atomic physicist at the National Bureau of Standards and as a staff scientist at Martin Marietta from 1966 to 1969, when he relocated to the University of Georgia. He is currently professor of physics at Georgia. His research concerns ionization mechanisms at intermediate and low energies.

Teresa Mendoza

Engineering

Teresa Mendoza was born in Oakland, California, and brought up in a bilingual environment. She received her primary education there and later her B.S. in Civil Engineering from San Jose State University in 1979. Subsequently, she received training in Environmental Studies and Program Management with the state of California Department of Transportation. In 1980, Mendoza joined the U.S. Army Corps of Engineers' Rotational Engineering Program, and by 1986 became the chief of the Emergency Management Branch, supervising the Emergency Management Center, which deals with such natural disasters as earthquakes and floods. She is a founder and serves as the Chief of the Earthquake Preparedness Center for the U.S. Army Corps of Engineers. Among her many honors is the 1988 Emergency Manager of the Year Award from the U.S. Army Corps of Engineers and the 1993 Hispanic Engineer Award for Professional Achievement.

Teresa Mercado (1921–)

Histochemistry, Cytochemical Pathology

Born on October 15, 1921, in Ponce, Puerto Rico, Mercado received her B.S. degree from the College of Mt. St. Vincent in 1947 and her M.S. and Ph.D. degrees in biological physiology from the Catholic University of America in 1947 and 1950, respectively. Since 1949, she has been a research physiologist at the National Institute for Allergy and Infectious Diseases of the National Institutes of Health. Her research is in pathologic physiology, histochemistry, biochemistry, and cytochemistry of parasitic diseases, especially experimental malaria and trypanosomiases.

Mario Molina. (Photograph by Donna Coveney.)

Mario Molina (1943–)

Chemistry

Mario Molina was born in Mexico City on March 19, 1943. In 1995, as a researcher and professor at the Massachusetts Institute of Technology, Molina shared the Nobel Prize in Chemistry with two others for their work that led to the international ban on chemicals believed to be depleting the ozone protective layer of the earth. The native of Mexico earned his B.S. degree in Chemical Engineering from the National Autonomous University of Mexico in 1965 and his Ph.D. in Physical Chemistry from the University of California-Berkeley in 1972. Molina has taught and conducted research at various universities in the United States. From 1982 until 1989, Molina was a Senior Research Scientist at the Caltech Jet Propulsion Laboratory. In 1989, he was appointed Professor in the Department of Earth, Atmospheric and Planetary Sciences at the Massachusetts Institute of Technology. In 1992, he became the Lee and Geraldine Martin Professor of Environmental Sciences at MIT. Molina has been a world leader in developing scientific understanding of the chemistry of the stratospheric ozone layer and its suscepti-

Teresa Mercado.

bility to man-made perturbations. He has explained through his laboratory experiments new reaction sequences that enable the catalytic processes which account for most of the observed ozone destruction in the Antarctic stratosphere. Dr. Mario J. Molina became the first Hispanic scientist to receive the NASA Medal for Exceptional Scientific Achievement. That same year he was also the first Hispanic to receive the United Nations Environmental Programme Global 500 Award. His other awards include the United Nations Environment Programme Global 500 Award (1989) and the Pew Scholar on Conservation, the Environment (1990–92) and the Hispanic Engineer National Achievement Award (1992).

Héctor Rolando Nava-Villarreal (1943–)

Medicine, Oncology

Born in Nuevo Laredo, Tamaulipas, Mexico, on May 23, 1943, Nava received all of his education in Mexico, including his M.D. degree from the Universidad de Nuevo León in 1967. He did his internship in Corpus Christi and his residency at the Roswell Park Cancer Institute in Buffalo, New York, where he also served as a fellow in surgical oncology from 1974 to 1976. From 1968 to 1970, he served in active duty in the U.S. Army, spending time from 1969 to 1970 as a battalion surgeon in Vietnam. From 1976 to the present, he has been a cancer researcher at the Roswell Park Cancer Institute. From 1991 to the present, he has been the vice chairman of the surgical oncology program there. Nava has been a pioneer in the use of lasers to treat cancer.

Isabel Cristina Pérez-Farfante (1916–)

Zoology

Born on July 24, 1916, in Havana, Cuba, Pérez received her B.S. degree from the University of Havana in 1938 and her M.S. and Ph.D. degrees in biology from Radcliffe College in 1944 and 1948, respectively. From 1948 to 1960, she was a professor of invertebrate biology at the University of Havana. Since 1966, she has worked as a systematics zoologist at the National Marine Fisheries Service. Her research interests include systematics, morphology, and distribution of decapod crustacea, with special reference to western Atlantic and eastern Pacific regions.

Víctor Pérez-Méndez (1923–)

Physics

Born on August 8, 1923, in Guatemala City, Guatemala, Pérez received his B.S. degree in 1947 from the Hebrew University in Jerusalem and his Ph.D. degree in physics from Columbia University in 1951.

He became a research scientist at the Lawrence Berkeley Lab in 1953 and has remained there until this date. Since 1969, he has been a professor of physics (radiology) at the University of California, San Francisco; from 1969 to 1977, he was the head of that department. Pérez has published more than 300 papers on his research in the fields of nuclear and high-energy physics, radiation detectors, and medical imaging.

David Pimentel (1925–)

Ecology, Entomology

Born on May 24, 1925, in Fresno, California, Pimentel received his B.S. degree from the University of Massachusetts in 1948 and his Ph.D. degree in entomology from Cornell University in 1951. From 1951 to 1953, he was chief of the Tropical Research Lab at the U.S. Public Health Service in San Juan, Puerto Rico. From 1955 to 1976, he moved up the ranks from assistant to full professor of insect ecology at Cornell University, which is his current position. He has had a number of prestigious fellowships in the United States and Europe, and from 1964 to 1966, he was a member of the President's Science Advisory Council; he has also worked extensively

Isabel Cristina Pérez-Farfante.

with the United Nations, UNESCO, the National Academies of Science, HEW, USAID, the Environmental Protection Agency, and the Department of Energy. He has also been a lecturer and keynote speaker at the principal biological and entomological societies in Africa, Europe, Canada, and the United States. His research concerns ecology and genetics of insect-plant, parasite-host, and predator-prey population systems. In 1992, Pimentel received the Award for Distinguished Service to rural Life from the rural Sociological Society Council. In addition, he has been selected to present numerous keynote speeches prestigious scientific organizations in the United States and abroad. In addition to his more than 400 scientific publications, of which 17 are books, Pimentel has served on the editorial boards of such journals as *Ecological Economic, Journal of Sustainable Agriculture,* and *Crop Protection.*

Fausto Ramírez (1923–)

Organic Chemistry

Born on June 15, 1923, in Zulueta, Cuba, Ramírez received his B.S., M.S., and Ph.D. degrees from the University of Michigan in 1946, 1947, and 1949, respectively. He made his career at the University of Virginia, Columbia University, the Illinois Institute of Technology, and the State University of New York at Stoney Brook, where he was professor from 1959 to 1985; today he is professor emeritus there. Ramírez developed a record of lectures, fellowships, and honors around the world. In 1969, he was awarded the Silver Medal of the City of Paris, and in 1968, the Cresy-Morrison Award from the New York Academy of Sciences. His research concerns the theoretical and practical aspects of the chemistry of phosphorus and sulfur compounds, organic synthesis, and molecular biology.

Mario E. Ramírez (1926–)

Medicine

Mario Ramírez was born in Roma, Texas, on April 3, 1926. He received his early education there and went on to graduate from the University of Texas with a B.A. in 1945; after that he received his M.D. degree from the University of Tennessee College of Medicine in 1948. Since that time he has led a distinguished career in family practice and in medical education, rising to the governing boards of medical institutions in the state of Texas and to membership on the Coordinating Board of Texas Colleges and Universities (1979–85) and the Board of Regents of the University of Texas System (1988–95). Throughout his career he has won numerous awards, including the American Academy of Family Physicians and the *Good Housekeeping* magazine Family Doctor of the Year Award (1978) and the Bicentennial Dr. Benjamin Rush Award of the American Medical Association (1985).

Marian Lucy Rivas (1943–)

Medical Genetics, Computer Systems

Born on May 6, 1943, in New York City, Rivas received her B.S. degree from Marian College in 1964 and her M.S. and Ph.D. degrees in medical genetics from Indiana University in 1967 and 1969, respectively. After serving with a fellowship at Johns Hopkins University from 1969 to 1971, Rivas worked as an assistant professor of biology at Douglas College of Rutgers University from 1971 to 1975; thereafter, she was an associate professor from 1975 to 1982 at the Hemophilia Center of the Oregon Health Science University. Since 1982, she has been a full professor there, and since 1978, an associate scientist at the Neurological Science Institute of Good Samaritan Hospital. She has served in genetics committees at the National Institutes of Health and in adjunct positions at universities in the United States and in Venezuela. Her research concerns human gene mapping, genetic aspects of epilepsy, computer applications in clinical genetics, and genetic counseling.

Evelyn Margaret Rivera (1929–)

Endocrinology, Cancer

Born on November 10, 1929, in Holister, California, Rivera received her A.B., M.A., and Ph.D. degrees in zoology from the University of California, Berkeley, in 1952, 1960, and 1963, respectively. She was a fellow of the American Cancer Society in England from 1963 to 1965. From 1965 to 1972, she went from assistant to associate professor of zoology at Michigan State University; from 1972 on, she has been a full professor. In her research she has worked for the National Cancer Institute and held fellowships for her work on cancer and endocrinology from a number of institutions. In 1965, Rivera was given the UNESCO Award from the International Cell Research Organization. Rivera's research interests include cell transformation and the biology of tumors.

Eloy Rodríguez (1947–)

Biology

Born in Edinburg, Texas, on January 7, 1947, Rodríguez is the founder of the discipline of zoopharmacognosy, or self-medication by primates and is a world-renown expert on natural products chemistry and biology. He received his B.A. in Biology and his Ph.D. in phytochemistry and plant biology in

Eloy Rodríguez.

1969 and 1975, respectively, from the university of Texas at Austin. He followed these degrees with post-graduate work at the University of British Columbia in Vancouver, Canada. From 1976 to 1995, he served as a professor with a joint appointment in the Toxicology Program and the Department of community and Environmental Medicine at the University of California-Irvine. In 1995, Rodríguez was selected for the Jane Perkins Chair of Environmental Studies at Cornell University. Rodríguez has conducted research and served as a consultant all over the world. He is the discoverer of numerous important organic chemicals from tropical and desert plants, which are being tested as drugs in the fight against cancer and other diseases. Included among his many awards are the *Los Angeles Times* Professional Research Accomplishment Recognition (1989) and the First Hispanic Educator Award from the League of United Latin American Citizens (1984). Rodríguez has raised millions of dollars in grants to fund his extensive research projects. Among his professional activities, he has served as the chair of a special study section for the National Cancer Institute, Director of the National Chicano Council on Higher Education and Vice President of the Society

for Advancement of Chicanos and Native Americans in Science. Rodríguez is has also the been the editor of various newsletters and served on the editorial boards of scientific journals, such as *Phytochemical Analysis* (1989–1992).

Juan Guadalupe Rodríguez (1920–)

Entomology

Born on December 23, 1920, in Española, New Mexico, Rodríguez received a B.S. degree from New Mexico State University in 1943 and M.S. and Ph.D. degrees from the University of Ohio in 1946 and 1949, respectively. From 1949 to 1961, he went from associate entomologist to full professor of Entomology at the University of Kentucky, where he still does research and teaches in the College of Agriculture. He has been awarded the Thomas Poe Cooper Award for Distinguished Research by the University of Kentucky. Rodríguez's research concerns axenic culture of arthropods, insect and mite nutrition, and insect pest management.

Juan Carlos Romero (1937–)

Animal Physiology, Computer Science

Born on September 15, 1937, in Mendoza, Argentina, Romero received his B.S. degree from San José College in Argentina in 1955 and his M.D. degree from the University of Mendoza in 1964. From 1968 to 1973, Romero worked as a research associate physiologist at the University of Michigan. From 1973 to 1980, he ascended the ranks to become a professor of physiology at the Mayo School of Medicine of the Mayo Foundation, a position he still holds today. Since 1982, he has also served as the director of the Hypertension Research Lab. He has been associated with and served on numerous committees that deal with heart disease and hypertension, including the Pan American Council on High Blood Pressure, the National Heart, Lung and Blood Institute of the NIH, the American Heart Association, and NASA. In his research, Romero studies mechanisms by which the kidney can produce high blood pressure; he identifies hormones that control renal circulation and excretion of salt. Among Romero's numerous awards are the Teacher of the Year Award from the Mayo School of Medicine in 1981. In 1991, he was elected by the Council on High Blood Pressure Research to give the Lewis K. Dahl Memorial Lecture in the American Heart Association's 464th scientific session.

Albert William Saenz (1923–)

Theoretical Physics

Born in Medellín, Colombia, on August 27, 1923, Saenz received his B.S., M.S., and Ph.D. degrees in physics from the University of Michigan in 1944, 1945, and 1949, respectively. He then worked at the Naval Research Laboratory, where he later became head of the theory consulting staff in the condensed matter and radiation science division. He has been a visiting scientist at the Oak Ridge National Lab, the Massachusetts Institute of Technology, Johns Hopkins University, Princeton University, and elsewhere. In 1969, he was the recipient of the Pure Science Award at the Naval Research Lab. His research interests include special and general relativity, symmetry and degeneracy in quantum mechanics, and quantum scattering theory.

Pedro Antonio Sánchez (1940–)

Agronomy, Soil Fertility

Born on October 7, 1940, in Havana, Cuba, Sánchez received his B.S., M.S., and Ph.D. degrees in soil science from Cornell University in 1962, 1964, and 1968, respectively. From 1968 to the present, he has been associated with North Carolina State University, where he has been a professor of soil science and leader of the Tropical Soils Program since 1979.

Pedro Antonio Sánchez.

His research and consultancies have taken him abroad, most frequently to Latin America. For his outstanding service, the government of Peru awarded him the Orden de Mérito Agrícola Medal. Currently, Sánchez is professor emeritus from North Carolina State and director of the International Centre for Research in Agroforestry (ICRAF), Nairobi, Kenya. ICRAF is devoted to alleviating poverty, tropical deforestation, and land degradation, through improved agroforestry systems. He also serves as chairman of the board of the worldwide Tropical Soil Biology and Fertility Program and as chairman of the National Academy of Sciences panel on sustainable agriculture and the environment in the humid tropics. Sánchez's research concerns the fertility and management of tropical soils, especially rice soils and tropical pastures.

Alberto Serrano (1931–)

Psychiatry

Born on April 7, 1931, in Buenos Aires, Argentina, Serrano was raised and educated in Argentina, where he became a medical doctor after graduating from the Buenos Aires School of Medicine in 1956. He did his internship at the Clínica Córdoba and at the National Institute of Mental Health, both in Buenos Aires. In 1957, he immigrated to the United States and began developing his career in is psychiatry as a resident in the Department of Neurology and Psychiatry at the University of Texas Medical Branch in Galveston, Texas. Since that time he has grown to become one of the finest psychiatrists and professors of psychiatry, specializing in child psychiatry in the United States. He rose the ranks at the University of Texas, first in Galveston, then in San Antonio, where he became the director of child and adolescent psychiatry. From 1986 to the present, he has served as professor of psychiatry and pediatrics and director of the Division of Child and Adolescent Psychiatry at the University of Pennsylvania School of Medicine. In the communities that he has lived, Serrano has been a director of various mental health clinics; since 1986, he has been the medical director of the Philadelphia Child Guidance Clinic and the psychiatrist-in-chief and director of the psychiatry division of the Children's Hospital of Philadelphia. In 1991, he became associate chairman of the Department of Psychiatry of he University of Pennsylvania School of Medicine. Among his various international recognitions, the American Family Therapy Association recognized him in 1986 for his "Pioneering Contribution to Family Therapy."

Margarita Silva-Hunter (1915-)

Mycology, Microbiology

Born on November 28, 1915, in Río Piedras, Puerto Rico, Silva received her B.A. degree from the University of Puerto Rico in 1936 and her M.S. and Ph.D. degrees from Harvard University in 1945 and 1952, respectively. From 1945 to the present, she has worked in the College of Physicians and Surgeons of Columbia University, where she has been an associate professor of dermatology since 1963. She has worked as a consulting mycologist and researcher at a number of hospitals and institutes, including the U.S. Public Health Service, the Squibb Institute for Medical Research, and the American Board of Medical Microbiology. Her research concerns the morphology, taxonomy, and biology of pathogenic fungi.

Aída R. Soto (1931-)

Organic Chemistry, Biochemistry

Born on December 3, 1931, in Havana, Cuba, Soto received her B.S. degree from the University of Havana in 1953 and her M.S. and Ph.D. degrees in chemistry from the University of Miami in 1962 and 1966, respectively. After serving as an instructor in the Department of Pharmacology and the School of Medicine of the University of Miami, in 1969 Soto became a researcher for the Dade division of the American Hospital Supply Company, where she has been a section head since 1984. Among her research interests are clinical enzymology, radioimmunoassays, and the use of immunologic techniques in clinical chemistry.

John Taboada (1943-)

Physical Optics, Applied Physics

Born on September 8, 1943, in Tampico, Mexico, Taboada received his B.A. degree from Trinity University (San Antonio) in 1966 and his M.S. and Ph.D. degrees in physics from Texas A & M University in 1968 and 1973, respectively. Since 1966, he has worked for the U.S. Air Force, first in the radiation science division, and since 1968 in the data Science division. In 1915, he received the Outstanding Technical Achievement Award, and in 1975, the Outstanding Science Achievement Award from the air force. Taboada's research concerns the biophysics of ultrashort pulsed lasers, laser spectroscopy, nonlinear optics, and applied optics.

Frank Talamantes (1943-)

Biology

Frank Talamantes was born on July 8, 1943 and raised in El Paso, Texas. He received his B.A. in biology from the University of St. Thomas in Houston, his M.A. in Biology from Sam Houston State University in 1970 and his Ph.D. in Endocrinology from the University of California-Berkeley in 1974. From 1974 on, Talamantes developed his research and teaching career at the University of California-Santa Cruz, where he became a full professor in 1984. Talamantes' research concerns the endocrine function of the placenta and the structure and regulation of various hormones, including the growth hormone. His work in reproductive endocrinology is internationally recognized. In recognition of his achievement, in 1991 he was selected to give the Transatlantic Medal Lecture by the Society for Endocrinology of the United Kingdom. In 1993, he also received the Research award from the Society for the Study of Reproduction. From 1986 to 1988, Talamantes served as the associate editor of the journal *Endocrinology*.

Gladys Torres-Blasini

Microbiology

Born in Ponce, Puerto Rico, Torres received a B.S. degree from the University of (San Antonio) Puerto Rico in 1948 and M.S. and Ph.D. degrees in bacteriology from the University of Michigan in 1952 and 1953, respectively. From 1952 on, she made her career at the Medical School of the University of Puerto Rico, where she has been head of the Department of Microbiology and Medical Zoology since 1977. She has held grants from the U.S. Public Health Service, Hoffman-LaRoche, the National Institutes of Health, and Veterans Administration hospitals. Her research in bacteriology includes the comparison of the phagocytosis of various candid species.

Pedro Ramón Urquilla (1939-)

Clinical Pharmacology

Born on July 18, 1939, in San Miguel, El Salvador, Urquilla received his M.D. degree from the University of El Salvador in 1965. From 1966 to 1969, he held fellowships from the Pan American Health Organization and from the National Institutes of Health. From 1969 to 1979, he developed a career as a professor of pharmacology at the University of Madrid. Since 1979, he has worked in private industry in the United States; since 1981, he has been the associate director of clinical research for Pfizer, Inc. His research concerns the analysis of the pharmacological receptors of the cerebral arteries.

James J. Valdés (1951-)

Biotechnology

Born on April 25, 1951 in San Antonio, Texas, Valdés received his B.S. degree in psychology and biological sciences from Loyola University in Chicago in 1973. He received an M.S. degree in physiological psychology from Trinity University in San Antonio in 1976 and a Ph.D. degree in neuroscience from Texas Christian University in 1979. From 1979 to 1982, he did postgraduate work in toxicology and environmental health sciences at Johns Hopkins University. In 1982 he began working as a researcher for the Department of the United States Army in Maryland. Valdés has won many awards from the army for his achievements as a researcher. His research interests include biosensors, receptor and ion channel response to toxic commands, and mechanisms of neurotransmission.

Gaspar Rodolfo Valenzuela (1933-)

Electronic Engineering

Born on January 6, 1933, in Coelemu, Chile, Valenzuela received his B.S. and M.S. degrees in electrical engineering from the University of Florida in 1954 and 1955, respectively; he received his Dr. Eng. degree from Johns Hopkins University in 1965. Between 1957 and 1968, he worked as a research engineer at Johns Hopkins. Since 1968, he has been a research electronic engineer for the Naval Research Lab in Washington, D.C. His research concerns electromagnetic theory, rough surface scattering theory, and the interaction of electromagnetic waves with the ocean.

Carlos Vallbona (1927-)

Community Medicine

Born on July 29, 1927, in Granollers, Barcelona, Spain, Vallbona received all of his primary education there, and his B.S. and M.D. degrees from the University of Barcelona in 1944 and 1955, respectively. He did postgraduate work in Barcelona, Paris, and Louisville, Kentucky. Vallbona began at the Baylor College of Medicine in Houston, Texas, as a pediatric resident in 1955 and has remained with that institution throughout his career. There he has served as service professor and chairman of the Department of Community Medicine at Baylor and chief of staff of the Community Health Program of the Harris County Hospital District. He has received numerous awards for his contributions to academic medicine and to community health. Moreover, Vallbona has done extensive research on the applications of computers in medicine, cardiorespiratory problems of disabled persons, community medicine, and the control of hypertension and diabetes in the community.

Lydia Villa-Komaroff (1947-)

Biology

Biologist Lydia Villa-Komaroff was born in 1947 in Las Vegas, New Mexico, the oldest of six children. While still in high school, she began studying biology in a Texas college program sponsored by the National Science Foundation during summers. Villa-Komaroff received her B.A. degree from Goucher College in Maryland in 1970 and her Ph.D. in cell biology from M.I.T. in 1975. Following her studies, she became an assistant professor at the University of Massachusetts and, since 1986, has been an associate professor at the Harvard Medical School. Villa-Komaroff's research in molecular biology focuses on cloning and on how bacteria can produce insulin brought her national attention. Her current research deals with the development of the brain. Villa-Komaroff has been selected to give major lectures at scientific conferences and, in 1992, she received the Hispanic Engineer National Achievement Award. She serves on the editorial boards of *Journal of molecular Evolution, BioTechniques* and *Journal of Women's Health*.

References

Jaques Catell Press, eds. *American Men and Women of Science,* 16th edition. New York: R. R. Bowker, 1986.

Amy L. Unterburger, ed. *Who's Who among Hispanic Americans.* Detroit: Gale Research, 1991.

Nicolás Kanellos

Literature

* The Colonial Period * The Nineteenth Century * The Early Twentieth Century
* World War II to the Present * Outstanding Hispanic Literary Figures

Hispanic literature of the United States is the literature written by Americans of Hispanic descent. It includes the Spanish-language literature of what became the U.S. Southwest before this territory was incorporated through war and annexation. It thus incorporates a broad geographic and historical space, and even includes the writings of early explorers of the North American continent as well as Spanish-speaking immigrants and exiles who made the United States their home. It is a literature that reflects the diverse ethnic and national origins of Hispanics in the United States, and thus includes writers of South and Central American, Caribbean, and Spanish descent, as well as writers of Afro-Hispanic and Indo-Hispanic literatures; it may also include writers of Sephardic (exiled Spanish Jews) origins who identified themselves as Hispanic, should their works be brought to light in the future. Finally, Hispanic literature of the United States is a literature that also reflects the linguistic diversity of the people and has been written and published in both Spanish and English and even bilingually.

* THE COLONIAL PERIOD

The roots of Hispanic literature were planted north of the Rio Grande long before the landing of the Mayflower at Plymouth Rock. Juan de Oñate's 1598 colonizing expedition up from central Mexico into what is today New Mexico is doubly important as the beginning of a written and oral literary tradition in a European language, Spanish. The written tradition is represented by the landmark epic poem *La conquista de la Nueva México* (*The Conquest of the New Mexico*), by one of the soldiers on the expedition, Gaspar Pérez de Villagrá. The oral Spanish literary tradition was introduced with the improvised dramas, songs, ballads, and poetic recitations

of the soldiers, colonists, and missionaries, some of which have survived in New Mexico and the Southwest to this date.

The Northeast of what is today the United States, on the other hand, can point to its earliest written and oral expression in Spanish with the founding of the colony of Sephardic Jews in New Amsterdam in 1654. Both the Northeast and Southwest can boast an unbroken literary tradition in Spanish that predates the American Revolutionary War. Much of this early literary patrimony from the colonial period has been lost or has not been collected and studied; the same can be said of all periods of literature except for contemporary Hispanic literature in the United States. A missionary and colonial literature of historical chronicles, diaries, and letters and an oral literature developed in the Southwest until the Mexican-American War of 1846–48.

* THE NINETEENTH CENTURY

Following the Mexican-American War and up to 1910, the foundation was really laid for the creation of a true Mexican American literature, a U.S. Hispanic literature, with the resident population of the Southwest adapting to the new U.S. political and social framework. It was the period when many Spanish-language newspapers begin publishing throughout the Southwest and when they and the creative literature they contained became an alternative to Anglo-American information and cultural flow. During this period the important commercial centers of San Francisco and Los Angeles supported numerous newspapers, which, besides fulfilling their commercial and informational functions, also published short stories, poetry, essays, and even serialized novels, such *Las aventuras de Joaquín Murieta* (*The Adventures of Joaquín Murieta*), a novel of the legendary California social bandit, published in 1881 by the Santa Barbara newspaper *La gaceta*. Among the more important newspapers in California were Los Angeles' *El clamor público* (*The Public Clamor*) and *La estrella de Los Angeles* (*The Los Angeles Star*), issued in the 1850s, and *La crónica* (*The Chronicle*), from the 1870s to the 1890s, and San Francisco's *La voz del Nuevo Mundo* (*The Voice of the New World*), *La sociedad* (*Society*), *La cronista* (*The Chronicles*), and *La República* (*The Republic*), issued during the last four decades of the century. In New Mexico, *El clarín mexicano* (*The Mexican Clarion*) and *El fronterizo* (*The Frontier*), in the 1870s, *El nuevomexicano* (*The New Mexican*), from the 1850s to the turn of the century, and *El defensor del pueblo* (*The People's Defender*), in the 1890s, were important. Among Texas' contributions during this period were San Antonio's *El bejareño* (*The Bejar County*) during the 1850s, El Paso's *Las dos Américas* (*The Two Americas*) in the 1890s, and *El clarín del norte* (*The Northern Clarion*) in the 1900s. These were but a few of the literally hundreds of newspapers that provided for the cultural enrichment and entertainment of the Mexican American communities while they provided information, helped to solidify the community, and defended the rights of Mexican Americans in the face of the growing influence of Anglo-American culture.

During the latter part of the nineteenth century various literary authors were published in book form. In southern California, María Amparo Ruiz de Burton was one of the first writers to contribute important novels in the English language. Writing under the pseudonym C. Loyal, she published *The Squatter and the Don* in 1881, a novel that effectively exploits the genre of the romance to document the loss of family lands by many Californios to squatters and other interests supported by the railroads, corrupt bankers and politicians in the newly acquired American territory and later the new state of California. From a wealthy California family herself, she underwrote the cost of publication of *The Squatter* and of her other novel, *Who Would Have Thought It?* (1872), which satirizes Yankee attitudes toward Indians, Mexicans and blacks during and after the Civil War.

Also in 1881, New Mexican Manuel M. Salazar published a novel of romantic adventure, *La historia de un caminante, o Gervacio y Aurora* (*The History of a Traveler on Foot, or Gervacio and Aurora*), which creates a colorful picture of the pastoral life in New Mexico at this time. Another New Mexican, Eusebio Chacón (1869–1948) published two short novels in 1892 that are celebrated today: *El hijo de la tempestad* (*Child of the Storm*) and *Tras la tormenta*

Miguel A. Otero.

la calma (*The Calm after the Storm*). New Mexican Miguel A. Otero (1859–1944) issued a three-volume autobiography, *My Life on the Frontier* (1935), in English, in which he covers his life from age five until just after his term as governor of New Mexico ended in 1906.

During the late 1870s, California bookseller and historian Hubert H. Bancroft had numerous autobiographies transcribed from oral dictation in his research for writing the history of California. In the process, some 15 Hispanic women of early California were able to dictate their autobiographies, some of which are literary documents that reveal women's perspectives on life, culture, politics and gender roles. Notable among these autobiographies are those of María Inocenta Avila's *Cosas de California* (*Things of California*), Josefa Carrillo de Fotch's *Narración de una californiana* (*Narration by a California Woman*), Apolinaria Lorenzana's *Memorias de una beata* (*Memories of a Pious Woman*), Eulalia Pérez's *Una vieja y sus recuerdos* (*An Old Woman and Her Memories*) and Felipa Osuna de Marrón's *Recuerdos del pasado* (*Memories of the Past*).

During the nineteenth century, poetry was primarily lyric, amorous, and pastoral and appeared regularly in the newspapers, with very few authors ever collecting their works in books. Among the most frequently appearing poets were the Texan E. Montalván in *El bejareño,* Felipe Maximiliano Chacón and Julio Flores in New Mexico papers, and Dantés in Santa Barbara's *La gaceta* (*The Gazette*). One of the most interesting poets of the turn of the century was Sara Estela Ramírez, who published her poems and some speeches in Laredo's *La crónica* (*The Chronicle*) and *El demócrata* (*The Democrat*) and in her own literary periodicals, *La corregidora* (*The Corrector*) and *Aurora,* between the years 1904 and 1910. In her life and in her literary works, Ramírez was an activist for the Mexican Liberal Party in its movement to overthrow dictator Porfirio Díaz, and for workers' and women's rights. But much work needs to be done in collecting and analyzing Ramírez's works and the thousands upon thousands of other poems that were published throughout the Southwest during the nineteenth century.

On the other hand, the late nineteenth century is the period when the Mexican *corrido,* (a folk ballad related to the *romance* introduced by the Spanish colonists and missionaries) came into maturity and proliferated throughout the Southwest. In particu-

Title page of *El hijo de la tempestad* by Eusebio Chacón.

lar, the border ballad, which chronicled the adventures of social bandits, like Joaquín Murieta, Aniceto Pizaña, and even Billy the Kid, became a popular anvil on which was forged a Mexican American identity. The corrido increased its popularity in the twentieth century and became a living historical and poetic document that records the history of the great Mexican immigrations and labor struggles between the two world wars.

During the nineteenth century, the New York area sustained various Hispanic literary activities and cultural institutions. The newspapers came to play a key role in providing a forum for literary creation for a community that at that time was made up principally of Spaniards and Cubans. Such newspapers as *El menasajero semanal* (*The Weekly Messenger*) and the weekly *El mercurio de Nueva York* (*The New York Mercury*), during the late 1820s and the 1830s published news of the homeland, political commentary and poetry, short stories, essays, and even excerpts of plays. One of the first novels to be written and published in the United States by an Hispanic was also the very first historical novel written in the Spanish language: *Jicoténcal,* written by Father Félix Varela, the Cuban religious philoso-

Eusebio Chacón.

pher and publisher of Philadelphia's newspaper, *El habanero*. A promoter of Cuban independence from Spain, Varela details the treachery of Spanish conquistadors in Mexico during the early colonial period, probably as an ideological basis for Cuban separation from Spain. Two other early newspapers were *La crónica* (*The Chronicle*) and *La voz de América* (*The Voice of America*), appearing in the 1850s and 1860s, respectively. Among the poets publishing at this time were Miguel Teurbe Tolón (1820–1858), who was born in the United States, educated in Cuba, and became a conspirator for Cuban independence from Spain. One of the few books of poetry in Spanish was published in 1828: *Poesías de un mexicano* (*Poems by a Mexican*), by Anastacio Ochoa y Acuña.

But it was not until the late nineteenth century that newspaper, magazine, and book publishing really began to expand, because of increased immigration and the political and cultural activity related to the Cuban, Puerto Rican, and Dominican independence movements and the Spanish-American War. In this regard, the most noteworthy institution was the Cuban newspaper *La patria,* in whose pages could be found essays by the leading Cuban and Puerto Rican patriots. Furthermore, numerous essays, letters, diaries, poems, short stories, and literary creations by some of Puerto Rico's most important literary and patriotic figures were written in New York while they worked for the revolution. Included among these were Eugenio María de Hostos, Ramón Emeterio Betances, Lola Rodríguez de Tió, and Sotero Figueroa. Active as well in literature and political organizing were the revolutionary leaders Francisco González "Pachín" Marín, a Puerto Rican, and the Cuban José Martí. Marín, a typesetter by trade and an important figure in Puerto Rican poetry for his break with romanticism, left us an important essay, "Nueva York por dentro; una faz de su vida bohemia" ("New York on the Inside; One Side of Its Bohemian Life"), in which he sketches New York from the perspective of a disillusioned immigrant; this is perhaps the earliest document in Spanish that takes this point of view and can be perhaps considered the beginning of Hispanic immigrant literature. Martí was an international literary figure in his own right, and his writings are still studied today in Latin American literature classes throughout the world; he has left us a legacy of many essays and other writings that relate directly to his life in New York and elsewhere in the United States.

Also of importance as the most widely circulated weekly was *Las novedades* (1893–1918, *The News*), whose theater, music, and literary critic was the famed Dominican writer Pedro Henríquez Ureña.

Cuban literary and patriotic figure, José Martí.

An early Puerto Rican contribution was *La gaceta ilustrada* (*The Illustrated Gazette*), edited in the 1890s by writer Francisco Amy. Many of the Spanish-language literary books published in New York were also related to the Cuban independence struggle, such as Luis García Pérez's *El grito de Yara* (1879, *The Shout at Yara*) and Desiderio Fajardo Ortiz's *La fuga de Evangelina* (1898, *The Escape of Evangelina*), the story of Cuban heroine Evangelina Cossío's escape from incarceration by the Spaniards and her trip to freedom and the organizing effort in New York.

✳ THE EARLY TWENTIETH CENTURY

The Southwest

The turn of the century brought record immigration from Mexico to the Southwest and Midwest because of the Mexican Revolution of 1910. During the period from 1910 until World War II, immigrant workers and upper-class and educated professionals from Mexico interacted with the Mexican-origin residents of the Southwest, who had been somewhat cut off from the evolution of Mexican culture inside Mexico. During this period Hispanic newspaper and book publishing flourished throughout the Southwest. Both San Antonio and Los Angeles supported Spanish-language daily newspapers that served diverse readerships made up of regional groups from the Southwest, immigrant laborers, and political refugees from the revolution. The educated, political refugees played a key role in publishing, and in light of their upper social class, they created an ideology of a Mexican community in exile, or "México de afuera" [Mexico on the outside].

In the offices of San Antonio's *La prensa* (*The Press*) and Los Angeles' *La opinión* (*The Opinion*) and *El heraldo de México* (*The Mexican Herald*), some of the most talented writers from Mexico, Spain, and Latin America, such as Miguel Arce, Esteban Escalante, Gabriel Navarro, Teodoro Torres, and Daniel Venegas, earned their living as reporters, columnists and critics. These and many others wrote hundreds of books of poetry, essays, and novels, many of which were published in book form and marketed by the newspapers themselves via mail and in their own bookstores. Besides the publishing houses related to these large dailies, there were many other smaller companies, such as Laredo Publishing Company, Los Angeles' Spanish American Printing, and San Diego's Imprenta Bolaños Cacho Hnos.

The largest and most productive publishers resided in San Antonio. Leading the list was the publishing house founded by the owner, of *La prensa* and Los Angeles' *La opinión,* Ignacio Lozano. The Casa Editorial Lozano was by far the largest publishing establishment ever owned by a Hispanic in the United States. Among the San Antonio publishers were the Viola Novelty Company, probably a subsidiary of P. Viola, publisher of the satiric newspapers *El vacilón* (*The Joker*) and *El fandango* (*The Fandango*), active from 1916 until at least 1927; the Whitt Company; and the Librería Española, which still exists today as a bookstore. Many of the novels produced by these houses were part of the genre known as "novels of the Mexican Revolution"; the stories were set within the context of the revolution and often commented on historical events and personalities. In the United States, the refugees who wrote these novels were very conservative and quite often attacked the revolution and Mexican politicians, which they saw as the reason for their exile. Included among these were Miguel Bolaños Cacho's *Sembradores de viento* (1928, *Sewers of the Wind*), Brígido Caro's *Plutarco Elías Calles: dictador volchevique de México* (1924, *Plutarco Elías Calles: Bolshevik Dictator of Mexico*), and Lázaro Gutiérrez de Lara's *Los bribones rebeldes* (1932, *The Rebel Rogues*). Many were the authors of this very popular genre, including Miguel Arce, Conrado Espinosa, Alfredo González, Esteban Maqueo Castellanos, Manuel Mateos, Ramón Puente, and Teodoro Torres. The most famous has become Mariano Azuela, author of the masterpiece that is one of the foundations of modern Mexican literature, *Los de abajo* (*The Underdogs*), which was first published in 1915 in a serialized version in *El Paso's* newspaper El paso del norte (*The Northern Pass*) and was issued later by the same newspaper in book form.

Although most of the novels published during these years gravitated toward the political and counterrevolutionary, there were others of a more sentimental nature and even some titles that can be considered forerunners of the Chicano novel of the 1960s in their identification with the working-class Mexicans of the Southwest, their use of popular dialects, and their political stance in regard to U.S. government and society. The prime example of this new sensibility is newspaperman Daniel Venegas' *Las aventuras de Don Chipote o Cuando los pericos mamen* (1928, *The Adventures of Don Chipote or When Parakeets May Suckle Their Young*), a humorous picaresque account of a Mexican immigrant, Don Chipote, who travels through the Southwest working here and there at menial tasks and running into one misadventure after the other, suffering at the hands of rogues, the authorities, and his bosses while in search of the mythic streets of gold that the United States is supposed to offer immigrants. *Don Chipote* is a novel of immigration, a picaresque novel, and a novel of protest all wrapped into one, and furthermore, it is the one clear forerunner of today's Chicano literature.

One of the most important literary genres that developed in the newspapers at this time was *la crónica,* (chronicle). It was a short satirical column that was full of local color, current topics, and observation of social habits. It owed its origins to Addison and Steele in England and José Mariano de Lara in Spain, but was cultivated extensively throughout Mexico and Latin America. In the Southwest it came to function and serve purposes never before thought of in Mexico or Spain. From Los Angeles to San Antonio, Mexican moralists satirized the customs and behavior of the colony whose very existence was seen as threatened by the dominant Anglo-Saxon culture. It was the *cronista's* (cronicler's) job to enforce the ideology of "México de afuera" and battle the influence of Anglo-American culture and the erosion of the Spanish language caused by the influence of speaking English. The cronistas, using such pseudonyms as El Malcriado (The Spoiled Brat—Daniel Venegas), Kaskabel (Rattler—Benjamín Padilla),

Az.T.K. (Aztec), and Chicote (The Whip), were literally whipping and stinging the community into conformity, commenting on or simply poking fun at the common folks' mixing of Spanish and English and Mexican women's adapting American dress and more liberalized customs, such as cutting their hair short, raising the hemlines, and smoking.

First and foremost behind the ideology of the crónica writers and the owners of the newspapers was the goal of returning to the homeland; as soon as the hostilities of the revolution ended, the immigrants were supposed to return to Mexico with their culture intact. Quite often the target of their humorous attacks were stereotyped country bumpkins, like Don Chipote, who were having a hard time getting around in the modern American city. They also poked fun at the Mexican immigrants to the United States who became impressed with the wealth, modern technology, efficiency, and informality of American culture, to the extent that they considered everything American superior and everything Mexican inferior. In some of his chronicles, Jorge Ulica satirized women who made much to do about throwing American-style surprise parties and celebrating

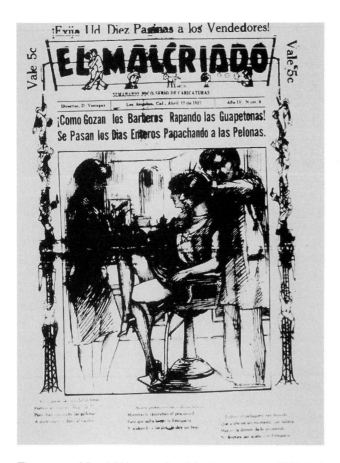

The cover of Daniel Venegas' satirical newspaper, *El Malcriado*.

Thanksgiving, and criticized their taking advantage of greater independence and power at the expense of men's machismo. The cronistas quite often drew from popular jokes, anecdotes, and oral tradition to create these tales. Two of the most popular cronistas, who saw their columns syndicated throughout the Southwest, were the aforementioned Benjamín Padilla, an expatriate newspaperman from Guadalajara, and Julio Arce, who was also a political refugee from Guadalajara and used the pseudonym Jorge Ulica for his "Crónicas Diabólicas" (Diabolical Chronicles). So popular was this type of satire that entire weekly newspapers, usually of no more than eight pages in length, were dedicated to it. Daniel Venegas' weekly *El Malcriado* (*The Brat*) and P. Viola's *El vacilón* (*The Joker*) are prime examples of these.

Clustered around the publication of newspapers in the Southwest were communities of women intellectuals who not only aimed their journalism at the service of the Mexican Revolution and women's empowerment, but also penned and published some of the most eloquent editorials, speeches and poems in support of their liberal causes. Most noteworthy were Sara Estela Ramírez's newspapers and magazines, mentioned above; Andrea and Teresa Villarreal's *El obrero* (*The Worker*), founded in San Antonio in 1910; Isidra T. de Cárdenas' *La voz de la mujer* (*The Woman's Voice*), founded in El Paso in 1907; and *Pluma roja* (*Red Pen*), edited and directed by Blanca de Moncaleano from 1913 to 1915 in Los Angeles. In the anarchist *Pluma roja,* there was a consistent editorial articulation of reconfiguring the role of women in society as central to the struggle for social, political and economic freedom; it was presented as an integral part of the ideal of anarchism. Blanca de Moncaleano addressed both men and women, urging them to free women of their enslavement and to encourage their education and politicization. In a February 1, 1914, editorial entitled "Hombre, educad a la mujer" ("Man, Educate Woman"), she pled for men to let women obtain an education.

One of these women activists, Leonor Villegas de Magnón (1876–1955), was born and raised in Mexico, but emigrated to Laredo, Texas. She provided one of the very few autobiographies of the Mexican Revolution to be written by a woman: *The Rebel*, which was finally published posthumously in 1994 after the author was unsuccessful in having it published in her Spanish and/or English versions during her lifetime. Villegas de Magnón was associated with the ideological precursors of the Mexican Revolution, the Brothers Flores Magón, and in fact spent her inherited fortune in support of the revolutionary forces. Villegas was the founder of a women's nursing corps, made up mostly by women from the Texas side of the border, which tended to the wounded in Venustiano Carranza's army. As such, she worked side-by-side with the future victor of the Revolution and president of the republic. Upon seeing how fast official sources had ignored the women's contribution, she specifically created her two autobiographies to document the role of women in Mexico's cataclysmic insurgency. Villegas was both an heroic figure and a dramatic writer, one who wrote with documentary care, but with literary style and flair.

Much of this literary activity in the Mexican American Southwest came to an abrupt halt with the Great Depression and the repatriation, forced or voluntary, of a large segment of that society back to Mexico. Some writers during the depression, like Américo Paredes, began to write in both Spanish and English and to express a very pronounced and politicized Mexican American sensibility. His English novel *George Washington Gómez* was written from 1936 to 1940 (but not published until 1990), and during the 1930s and 1940s he was a frequent contributor of poetry in Spanish, English, and bilingual format to newspapers in Texas, including *La prensa*. In 1937, he published a collection of poems, *Cantos de adolescencia* (*Songs of Adolescence*), at age 22, but it was not until 1991 that his collected poems were issued, under the title *Between Two Worlds,* a collection containing works selected from his writings from the late 1930s to the 1950s.

Another very important literary figure who emerged during the depression and began to publish poetry and tales based on New Mexican folklore was Fray Angelico Chávez. A Franciscan monk, Chávez's poetry books are principally made up of poems to Christ and the Virgin Mary: *Clothed with the Sun* (1939), *New Mexico Triptych* (1940), *Eleven Lady Lyrics and Other Poems* (1945), *The Single Rose* (1948), and *Selected Poems with an Apologia* (1969). From the 1930s to the 1950s there appeared a number of short story writers who succeeded in publishing their works in mainstream English-language magazines. Most of these, such as Texas' Josefina Escajeda and Jovita González, based their works on folktales, oral tradition, and the picturesque customs of Mexicans in the Southwest. Robert Hernán Torres, who published some of his stories in *Esquire* magazine, focused his works on the cruelty and senselessness of the revolution in Mexico. Another prose writer in English who experienced relative success was Josephina Niggli; she focused many of her novels and short stories on life in Mexico after the revolution. Despite the significance of Chávez, Paredes, Niggli, and the others, it

Fray Angelico Chávez.

was not until the 1960s that there was a significant resurgence of Mexican American literary activity, except that by the end of that decade it was called Chicano literature.

Josephina Niggli was successful in having a number of her works published by general market presses in the United States. While writing as an adult, Niggli was able to vividly recreate the small-town settings of her rural upbringing in Mexico. Although born in 1910, she was somewhat of a nineteenth-century regionalist in her descriptions and evocations. Her *Mexican Village* (1945), for example, portrays the power of land and locale over individuals and community, in this case a fictional town on the northern border of Mexico. Like many of the New Mexico writers, Niggli was also concerned with tradition and the passage of customs and worldview from one generation to the other.

Emerging in the English-language literary world at the same time as Angélico Chávez was a group of New Mexican women writers who sought to examine the colonial and territorial past and preserve the folkways and customs that were fast passing away. Their contributions ranged from fiction and literary folklore to personal narrative and social history. Included among their works are: Nina Otero Warren's *Old Spain in Our Southwest* (1936); Cleofas Jaramillo's *The Genuine New Mexico Tasty Recipes: Old and Quaint Formulas for the Preparation of Seventy-five Delicious Spanish Dishes* (1939), a kind of culinary autobiography; Aurora Lucero White Lea's *Literary Folklore of the Hispanic Southwest* (1953); Fabiola Cabeza de Vaca's *The Good Life: New Mexico Traditions and Food* (1949) and *We Fed Them Cactus* (1954). Many of the personal reminiscences in these books are framed within the traditional practices of telling stories within the family, of passing recipes down from mother to daughter and relating them to life experiences and family history, of preserving the songs and other oral lore of the family and the region. In these women, we find a somewhat nostalgic recreation of the past that is an embryonic resistance to the Anglo-American ways that were eroding traditional New Mexican culture.

An English-language short fiction writer, María Cristina Mena (1893–1965), was also born and raised in Mexico and moved to the United States at age 14. In New York from 1913 to 1916, Mena published a series of short stories in *The Century Illustrated Monthly Magazine*. In 1927, many of these stories, along with new ones, were published in a collection under her husband's name, Henry K. Chambers, a dramatist and journalist. In the 1940s, she developed into a prolific novelist: *The Water Carrier's Secret* (1942), *The Two Eagles* (1942), *The Bullfighter's Son* (1944), *The Three Kings* (1946), and *Boy Heroes of Chapultepec: A Story of the Mexican War* (1953). Behind all of her writing was her desire to inform the public in the United States of the history and culture of Mexico, proposing to correct the negative image that Mexico has held in the popular media.

The Northeast

In New York, the period from the turn of the century up into the Great Depression was one of increased immigration and interaction of various Hispanic groups. It was a period of increased Puerto Rican migration, facilitated by the Jones Act, which declared Puerto Ricans to be citizens of the United States, and later of immigration of Spanish workers and refugees from the Spanish Civil War. Artistic and literary creation in the Hispanic community quite often supported the Puerto Rican nationalist movement and the movement to reestablish the Spanish republic.

At the turn of the century, Cuban and Spanish writers and newspapers still dominated the scene. The first decade of the century witnessed the founding of *La prensa* (*The Press*), whose heritage continues today in *El diario-La prensa* (*The Daily-The Press*), born of a merger in 1963. Also published during the decade were *Sangre latina* (*Latin Blood*), out of Columbia University, *Revista Pan-Americana* (*Pan American Review*), and *La paz y el trabajo* (*Peace and Work*), a monthly review of commerce, literature, science, and the arts. Even places as far away as Buffalo began to support their own publications, such as *La hacienda* (*The State*), founded in 1906.

Spanish-language literary publishing did not begin to expand until the late teens and early twenties. By far the most interesting volume that has come down to us from the teens is an early example of the immigrant novel. Somewhat similar in theme to *Don Chipote*, Venezuelan author Alirio Díaz Guerra's *Lucas Guevara* (1917) is the story of a young man who comes to the city seeking his fortune, but is ultimately disillusioned. While *Lucas Guevara* was probably self-published at the New York Printing Company, there were several Spanish-language publishing houses functioning during the teens in New York. One of the most important and long-lived houses, Spanish American Publishing Company, began issuing titles at this time and continued well into the 1950s. It too was an early publisher of books on the theme of Hispanics in New York, such as Puerto Rican playwright Javier Lara's *En la metrópoli del dólar* (*In the Metropolis of the Dollar*), circa 1919. *Las novedades* newspaper also published books, including Pedro Henríquez Ureña's *El nacimiento de Dionisos* (1916, *The Birth of Dionysus*).

Although during the 1920s the Spanish American Publishing Company, Carlos López Press, The Phos Press, and others were issuing occasional literary titles, it was not until the late twenties and early thirties that there was an intensification of activity. To begin with, various specialized newspapers began to appear. Probably as an outgrowth of the very active theatrical movement that was taking place in Manhattan and Brooklyn, *Gráfico* (*Graphic*) began publishing in 1927 as a theater and entertainment weekly newspaper under the editorship of the prolific writer Alberto O'Farrill, who was also a playwright and a leading comic actor in Cuban blackface farces (*teatro bufo cubano*). As was also the custom in the Southwest, *Gráfico* and the other newspapers and magazines published numerous poems, short stories, literary essays, and crónicas by the leading New York Hispanic writers. Among the most notable cronistas were those unknown writers using the pseudonyms Maquiavelo (Machiavelli) and Samurai; O'Farrill himself was an important contributor to the tradition, signing his columns "Ofa." As in the Southwest, these cronistas labored in their writings

Cover of the first issue of *Gráfico* newspaper.

to solidify the Hispanic community, which in New York was even more diverse than in the Southwest, drawing from many ethnic and national backgrounds. They too were protecting the purity of Hispanic culture against the dangers of assimilation, as they voiced the political and social concerns of the community and corrected and satirized current habits. While in the Southwest the cronistas promoted a "México de afuera," York they often attempted to create a "Trópico en Manhattan" (A Tropical [or Caribbean] Culture in Manhattan).

Unlike in the Southwest, there were no massive repatriations and deportations disrupting the cultural life in the Hispanic community during the Great Depression. In fact, New York continued to receive large waves of Hispanics during the depression and World War II: refugees from the Spanish Civil War, workers for the service and manufacturing industries flown in from Puerto Rico during World War II in the largest airborne migration in history, and Hispanics from the Southwest. Newspapers were founded that reflected this renewed interest in Spanish, Puerto Rican, and working-class culture: *Vida obrera* (1930, *Worker's Life*), *Alma boricua* (1934–35, *Puerto Rican Soul*), *España libre* (1943,

Free Spain), and *Cultura proletaria* (1943, *Proletariat Culture*). The pages of these newspapers are valuable sources of an important body of testimonial literature that reflected the life of the immigrant. They frequently took the form of autobiographical sketches, anecdotes, and stories, quite often in a homey, straightforward language that was also replete with pathos and artistic sensibility. Despite the many sources available in print, a large part of Puerto Rican, Cuban, Dominican, and Spanish literature in New York is an oral literature, a folk literature, completely consistent with and emerging from the working-class nature of the immigrants. For the Caribbean peoples there is an immense repository of lyric and narrative poetry that is to be found in their songs, such as the *décimas, plenas,* and *sones,* and in the popular recorded music of such lyrical geniuses as Rafael Hernández, Pedro Flores, and Ramito, whose compositions began appearing on recordings in the 1930s and continue to influence Puerto Rican culture on the island and in New York to the present. Of course, the compositions of Hernández and Flores have influenced Hispanic popular music around the world.

As the Puerto Rican community grew in the late 1920s and into World War II, Puerto Rican literature began to gain a larger profile in New York, but within a decidedly political context. It also seems that the literature with the most impact for the Puerto Rican community was dramatic literature, if published books are a measure. Poet Gonzalo O'Neill (1867–1942) was a businessman who, during the 1920s and 1930s, was at the hub of Puerto Rican and Hispanic cultural life, not only as a writer, but as a cultural entrepreneur, investing his money in the theater and protecting and offering support to other writers. O'Neill began his literary training and career in Puerto Rico as a teenager in association with a magazine, *El palenque de la juventud* (*The Young People's Arena*), which featured the works of some of the most important writers in Puerto Rico, such as Luis Muñoz Rivera, Lola Rodríguez de Tió, Vicente Palés, and many other notables. O'Neill's first published book was a dramatic dialogue in verse, more appropriate for reading aloud than staging: *La indiana borinqueña* (1922, *The Puerto Rican Indians*). Here O'Neill revealed himself to be intensely patriotic and interested in Puerto Rican independence from the United States. His second published book was the three-act play *Moncho Reyes,* named after the central character, issued by Spanish American Publishing in 1923. In 1924, O'Neill published a book of nationalistic poetry, *Sonoras bagatelas o sicilianas* (*Sonorous Bagatelles or Sicilian Verses*), of which Manuel Quevedo Baez stated in the prologue

Lola Rodríguez de Tió.

that "Gonzalo is a spontaneous and ingenuous poet. . . . He is a poet of creole stock, passionate, tender, and as melancholic as Gautier Benítez" (Gautier Benítez was Puerto Rico's greatest poet to date). Although all of his plays, even *La indiana borinqueña,* enjoyed stage productions, it was his third play, *Bajo una sola bandera* (1928, *Under Only One Flag*), that won critical acclaim and was produced on stages in New York as well as in Puerto Rico. *Bajo una sola bandera* examines the political options facing Puerto Rico, as personified by down-to-earth flesh-and-blood characters. A glowing review in San Juan's *La democracia (Democracy)* on April 16, 1929, marveled at O'Neill's conserving perfect Spanish and his Puerto Rican identity, despite having lived in the United States for 40 years. O'Neill certainly continued to write, although the remainder of his work is unknown or has been lost. Newspapers report that another play of his, *Amoríos borincanos (Puerto Rican Loves)*, was produced for the stage in 1938.

Following the example of Gonzalo O'Neill, there were many other Puerto Ricans who wrote for the stage and even published some of their works from the late 1920s to the 1940s, such as Alberto M. González, Juan Nadal de Santa Coloma, José Enamorado Cuesta, Frank Martínez, and Erasmo Vando. But one poet-playwright stands out among the rest as a politically committed woman, although the major portion of her work has been lost: Franca de Armiño (probably a pseudonym). Franca de Armiño wrote three works that have been lost and are inaccessible today: *Luz de tienieblas (Light of Darkness)*, a book of poems on various themes; *Aspectos de la vida (Aspects of Life)*, philosophical essays; and *Tragedia puertorriqueña (Puerto Rican Tragedy)*, a comedy of social criticism. Her one published and available play, *Los hipócritas: comedia dramática social (The Hypocrits: A Social Drama)*, self-published in 1937 at the Modernistic Editorial Company, is a major work that demands critical attention. Dedicated to "the oppressed and all those who work for ideas of social renovation," the work is set in Spain during the time of the republic and is openly anti-Fascist and revolutionary, calling for a rebellion of workers. *Los hipócritas,* which begins with the 1929 stock market crash, deals with a daughter's refusal to marry her father's choice, the son of a duke. Rather, she is romantically involved with a man of the working class, Gerónimo, whom her father calls a Communist and who has led her into atheism. The plot is complicated, with Gerónimo organizing workers for a strike, a Fascist dictatorship developing in Spain, and a corrupt priest trying to arrange for Gloria to become a nun so that the church will receive her dowry. The play ends with Gloria and Gerónimo together, the traitors unmasked, and the workers' strike prevailing over police, who attack them brutally. While full of propaganda and stereotyped characters, *Los hipócritas* is a gripping and entertaining play that reflects the tenor of the times, as far as the Great Depression, labor organizing, and the Spanish Civil War are concerned.

A cigar roller who settled in New York in 1916, Bernardo Vega reconstructed life in the Puerto Rican community during the period between the two great wars. Written in 1940, his *Memorias de Bernardo Vega* was published in 1977, and its translation was published in English as *The Memoirs of Bernardo Vega* in 1984. Valuable as both a literary and a historical document, Vega's memoirs make mention of numerous literary figures, such as poet Alfonso Dieppa, whose works were either not published or are lost to us. Vega is an important forerunner of the Nuyorican writers of the 1960s because he wrote about New York as a person who was there to stay, with no intention to return to live in Puerto Rico.

A figure similar to the women activists of the Hispanic Southwest was Luisa Capetillo, who came to New York from Puerto Rico in 1912 and wrote for various labor publications. In *Cultura obrera* (*Worker Culture*), she consistently built a case for women's emancipation. She re-emerged in the cigar factories of Tampa and Ybor City and continued her intellectual as well as her activist life there, and later in Puerto Rico. In Tampa, she published the second edition of her book, *Mi opinión* (*My Opinion*) in 1913, and published a new book of essays, *Influencia de las ideas modernas* (*The Influence of Modern Ideas*) in 1916.

The literature of this period is also represented by a newspaper columnist who wrote in English and was very active in the Communist Party: Jesús Colón, author of columns for the *Daily Worker.* Colón's was a heroic intellectual battle against the oppression of workers and racial discrimination; he nevertheless wrote about and supported Puerto Rican culture and literature, even to the extent of founding a small publishing company that has the distinction of issuing some of the first works of the great Puerto Rican novelist and short story writer José Luis González. In 1961, Colón selected some of the autobiographical sketches that had appeared in newspapers and published them in book form in *A Puerto Rican in New York,* which was perhaps the one literary and historical document that was accessible to young Nuyorican writers and helped to form their literary and social awareness, as well as stimulate their production of literature. Colón, a black Puerto Rican, had created a document that, tempered with his political ideology, presented insight into Puerto Rican minority status in the United States, rather than just immigrant or ethnic status. In this it was quite different from all that had preceded it.

✳ WORLD WAR II TO THE PRESENT

Chicano Literature

Scholars consider the year 1943 as the beginning of a new period in Mexican American history and culture. This is the year when the so-called Zoot Suit Riots occurred in the Los Angeles area; they mark a stage in the cultural development of the Mexican American in which there was a consciousness of not belonging to either Mexico or the United States. Rather, Mexican Americans began to assert a separate independent identity, just as the zoot-suiters in their own subculture were doing by adopting their style of dress, speech, and music (zoot-suiters were Mexican American youth who used baggy pants and long, feathered, wide-brimmed hats—elements that

made up a zoot suit—as symbols of their subculture.) Then, too, Mexican American veterans serving in and returning from World War II, where they proportionately suffered more casualties and won more medals for valor than any other group in U.S. society, now felt that they had earned their rights as citizens of the United States and were prepared to assert that citizenship and to reform the political and economic system so that they could participate equitably. Thus, the quest for identity in modern American society was initiated, and by the 1960s, a younger generation made up of children of veterans, not only took up this pursuit of democracy and equity in the civil rights movements but also explored the question of identity in all of the arts, paramount of which was literature.

Because of the interruption caused by the depression, repatriation, and World War II, and the decreased production of literature that ensued during the 1940s and 1950s, the renewed literary and artistic productivity that occurred during the 1960s has often been considered a Chicano renaissance. In reality, it was an awakening that accompanied the younger generation's greater access to college and its participation in the civil rights movements as well as the farm-worker labor struggle and the protest movement against the Vietnam War. For Chicano literature the decade of the 1960s was characterized by a questioning of all the commonly accepted truths in society, foremost of which was the question of equality. The first writers of Chicano literature in the 1960s committed their literary voices to political, economic, and educational struggles. Their works were frequently used to inspire social and political action, quite often with poets reading their verses at organizing meetings, at boycotts, and before and after protest marches. Many of the first writers to gain prominence in the movement were the poets who could tap into an oral tradition of recitation and declamation, such as Abelardo Delgado, Ricardo Sánchez, and Alurista (Alberto Urista), and create works to be performed orally before groups of students and workers, in order to inspire them and raise their level of consciousness.

The most important literary work in this period that was used at the grass roots level as well as by university students to provide a sense of history, mission, and Chicano identity was an epic poem written by an ex-boxer in Denver, Colorado: Rodolfo "Corky" González's *I Am Joaquín/Yo Soy Joaquín* (1964). The short, bilingual pamphlet edition of the poem was literally passed from hand to hand in the communities, read from at rallies, dramatized by street theaters, and even produced as a slide show on film with a dramatic reading by none other than Luis

Valdez, the leading Chicano director and playwright. The influence and social impact of *I Am Joaquín* and poems such as "Stupid America," by Abelardo Delgado, which was published and reprinted in community and movement newspapers throughout the Southwest, and later cut out of those papers and passed hand to hand, is inestimable. "Stupid America" was included as well in Abelardo's landmark collection, *Chicano: 25 Pieces of a Chicano Mind* (1969). This period was one of euphoria, power, and influence for the Chicano poet, who was sought after, almost as a priest, to give his blessings in the form of readings at all cultural and Chicano movement events.

The 1960s was an era of intense grass roots organizing and cultural fermentation, and along with this occurred a renewed interest in publishing small community and workers' newspapers and magazines, such as the California farm workers' *El Malcriado* (*The Brat*) and Houston's *Papel Chicano* (*Chicano Newspaper*), which were now quite often published bilingually. During the late 1960s and early 1970s, literary magazines proliferated, from the academic, such as Berkeley's *El grito* (*The Shout* [for independence]), to the grass roots type printed on newsprint and available for 25 cents, such as San Antonio's *Caracol* (*Shell*), to the artsy, streetwise, avant-garde, and irreverent, such as Los Angeles' *Con Safos* (*Safety Zone*).

In 1967 appeared the most influential Chicano literary magazine, *El grito,* which initiated the careers of some of the most prominent names in Chicano literature and, along with the publishing house Editorial Quinto Sol, which it established in 1968, began to delineate the canon that is the official identity of Chicano literature by publishing those works that best exemplified Chicano culture, language, themes, and styles. The very name of the publishing house emphasized its Mexican/Aztec identity, as well as the Spanish language; the "quinto sol" (fifth sun), referred to Aztec belief in a period of cultural flowering that would take place some time in the future, in a fifth age that conveniently coincided with the rise of Chicano culture. In 1968 Quinto Sol published an anthology, *El espejo/The Mirror,* edited by the owners of Quinto Sol, Octavio Romano and Herminio Ríos. It included works by such writers as Alurista, Tomás Rivera, and Miguel Méndez, who are still

(Left to right) Albelardo Delgado, Ron Arias, and Rolando Hinojosa at the Second National Latino Book Fair and Writers Festival, Houston, Texas, 1980.

models of Chicano literature today. *El espejo* recognized the linguistic diversity and the erosion of Spanish literacy among the young by accompanying works originally written in Spanish with an English translation; it even included Miguel Méndez's original Yaqui-language version of his short story "Tata Casehue." In *El espejo* and in later books that Quinto Sol published, there was a definite insistence on working-class and rural culture and language, as exemplified in the works of Tomás Rivera, Rolando Hinojosa, and most of the other authors published in book form. Also, there was not only a tolerance but a promotion of works written bilingually and in—the code of street culture that switches between both English and Spanish in the same literary piece—as in the poems of Alurista and the plays of Carlos Morton.

In 1970, Quinto Sol, a Chicano publishing house founded in 1968 by Octavio Romano and Herminio Ríos, reinforced its leadership in creating the concept of Chicano literature by instituting the national award for Chicano literature, Premio Quinto Sol (Fifth Sun Award), which carried with it a $1,000 prize and publication of the winning manuscript. The first three years of prizes went to books that today are still seen as exemplary Chicano novels and, in fact, are still among the best-selling Chicano literary texts: Tomás Rivera's *. . . y no se lo tragó la tierra/ . . . And the Earth Did Not Part* (1971), Rudolfo Anaya's *Bless Me, Ultima* (1972), and Rolando Hinojosa's *Estampas del valle y otras obras/ Sketches of the Valley and Other Works*. Rivera's outwardly simple but inwardly complex novel is much in the line of experimental Latin American fiction, demanding that the reader take part in unraveling the story and in coming to his own conclusions about the identity and relationships of the characters, as well as the meaning. Drawing upon his own life as a migrant worker from Texas, Rivera constructed a novel in the straightforward but poetic language of migrant workers in which a nameless central character attempts to find himself by reconstructing the over-heard conversations and stories as well as events that took place during a metaphorical year, which really represents his whole life. It is the story of a sensitive boy who is trying to understand the hardship that surrounds his family and community of migrant workers; his path is first one of rejection of them only to embrace them and their culture dearly as his own at the end of the book. In many ways, *. . . y no se lo tragó la tierra* came to be the most influential book in the Chicano search for identity.

Rivera, who became a very successful university professor and administrator—he rose to the position of chancellor of the University of California, Riverside, before his death in 1984—wrote and published other stories, essays, and poems. Through such essays as "Chicano Literature: Fiesta of the Living" (1979) and "Into the Labyrinth: The Chicano in Literature" (1971) and his personal and scholarly activities, he was one of the prime movers in the promotion of Chicano authors, in the creation of the concept of Chicano literature, and in the establishment of Chicano literature and culture as legitimate

The original manuscript of the Tomás Rivera poem, "When love to be?"

Evangelina Vigil-Piñón, reciting at the Third National Hispanic Book Fair, Houston, 1987. (Photograph by Julián Olivaries.)

his attempts to understand good and evil and his role in life by the folk healer, Ultima, who passes on many of her secrets and insights about life to Antonio. Anaya puts to good use his knowledge of the countryside of New Mexico in fashioning this novel full of mystery and symbolic references to American Indian, Asian, and Spanish culture.

Anaya went on to become celebrated in his home state and to head the creative writing program at the University of New Mexico. His subsequent novels, all dealing with Chicano/Indian culture in New Mexico, have not been as well received by the critics: *Heart of Aztlán* (1976), *Tortuga* (1979, *Tortoise*), *The Silence of the Llano* (1982), and *Lord of the Dawn: The Legend of Quetzalcoatl* (1987). As can be seen from these titles, Anaya is a promoter of the concept of Aztlán, the mythical place of origin of the Aztec, supposedly located in what has become the five states of the Southwest. He and numerous other Chicano writers have derived both poetic inspiration and a sense of mission in reviving the cultural glories of Mexico's indigenous past. For Anaya and especially for poets and playwrights such as Alurista and Luis Valdez, the Aztec and Mayan past has been a

academic areas in college curriculum. In 1989, his stories were collected and published under the title *The Harvest,* and in 1990 his poems were collected and published under the title *The Searchers,* both by Arte Público Press, which has also kept his first novel in print and has recently published *Tomás Rivera: The Complete Works* (1990). In 1987, *. . . y no se lo tragó la tierra* was given a liberal translation into Texan dialect under the title *This Migrant Earth* (1987) by Rolando Hinojosa; the translation that accompanies the Arte Público bilingual edition was done by poet Evangelina Vigil-Piñón. By any accounts, Tomás Rivera remains the most outstanding and influential figure in the literature of Mexican peoples in the United States.

Rudolfo Anaya's *Bless Me, Ultima* is a straightforward novel about a boy's coming of age. Written in a poetic and clear English, it has reached more readers, especially non-Chicano readers, than any other Chicano literary work. In *Bless Me, Ultima,* again we have the search for identity, but this time the central character, Antonio, must decide between the Spanish heritage of the plainsman-rancher or the Indian heritage of the farmer; he is guided and inspired in

The cover of Rudolfo Anaya's best-selling novel, *Bless Me, Ultima.*

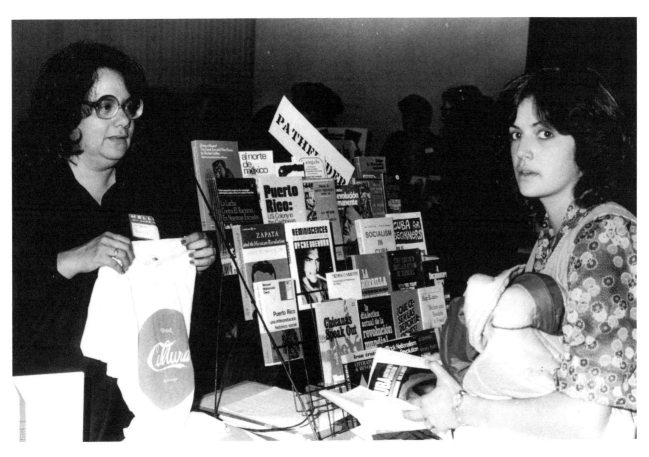

A vendor at the First National Latino Book Fair in Chicago, 1979.

source of imagery, symbols, and myths that have enriched their works.

Rolando Hinojosa is the most prolific and probably the most bilingually talented of the Chicano novelists, with original creations in both English and Spanish, published in the United States and abroad. His Quinto Sol Award-winning *Estampas del valle y otras obras / Sketches of the Valley and Other Works* is a mosaic of the picturesque character types, folk customs, and speech of the bilingual community in the small towns along Texas' Rio Grande valley. His sketches and insights, at times reminiscent of the local color of the crónicas of the 1920s, are considered among the most sophisticated contributions to Chicano literature.

Estampas consists of the first portion of a continuing novel that has become a broad epic of the history and culture of the Mexican Americans and Anglos of the valley. It takes place in the fictitious Belken County and centers on two fictitious characters and a narrator—Rafa Buenrostro, Jehú Malacara, and P. Galindo—all of whom may be partial alter egos of Hinojosa himself. What is especially intriguing about Hinojosa's continuing novel, which he calls the Klail City Death Trip Series, is his experimentation

with various forms of narration—derived from Spanish, Mexican, English, and American literary history—in respective installments of the novel. *Klail City y sus alrededores* (1976, *Klail City and Surroundings*) owes much to the picaresque novel, *Korean Love Songs* (1980) is narrative poetry, *Mi querido Rafa* (1981, *Dear Rafe*) is part epistolary novel and part reportage, *Rites and Witnesses* (1982) is mainly a novel in dialogue, *Partners in Crime* (1985) is a detective novel, *Claros varones de Belken* (1986, *Fair Gentlemen of Belken*) is a composite, and *Becky and Her Friends* (1990) continues the novel in the style of reportage, but with a new unnamed narrator, P. Galindo having died.

While there have been translations by others of his works, Hinojosa has penned and published recreations in English and Spanish of all of these books, except for the English titles *Korean Love Songs, Rites and Witnesses,* and *Partners in Crime. Mi querido Rafa* is especially important because it represents the first novel to experiment with bilingual narration and demands of the reader a good knowledge of both English and Spanish and their south Texas dialects.

Because of his many awards—including the inter-

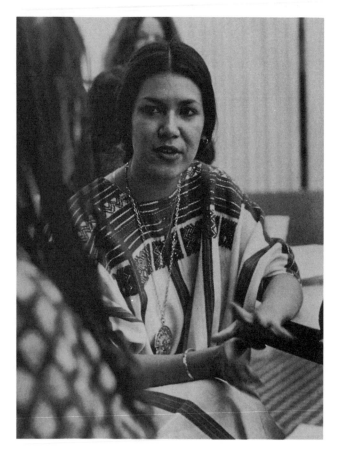

Ana Castillo, 1979.

1980s. In nine finely crafted stories and a novella, Portillo Trambley presents a series of female characters who draw from an inner strength and impose their personalities on the world around them. In the novella that gives title to the collection, a fat and unattractive central character overcomes her own dreams of beauty and social acceptance to prevail as a woman capable of controling and determining the action around her. She has chosen her life and how to live it, refusing to be imposed upon by others. In the most feminist of the short stories, "If It Weren't for the Honeysuckle," the eldest of three women being oppressed and enslaved by a drunk and irrational male succeeds in poisoning him and in freeing the women. In this, as in the other stories, as well as in her books to follow—*The Day of the Swallows* (1971), the collection of plays *Sor Juana* (1983, *Sister Juana*), and the novel *Trini* (1986)—Portillo Trambley has created strong women who prevail in a male-dominated world. Her work, *Trini,* is the story of a Tarahumara woman who leaves her Indian life behind and, after numerous tragedies and betrayals, crosses the border to give birth to her child in the United States, where she is able to control her life for

national award for Latin American fiction given in Cuba, Premio Casa de las Americas, 1976—his academic background and doctorate in Spanish, and the positive response to his sophisticated art from critics and university professors, in particular, Hinojosa is one of the few Hispanic writers in the country to teach in creative writing programs at a high level. In holding the distinguished title Ellen Clayton Garwood Professor of English and Creative Writing at the University of Texas, Hinojosa is the most recognized and highest-ranking Chicano/Hispanic author in academia.

It was not until 1975 that the Quinto Sol Award—an annual award given by Editorial Quinto Sol for outstanding Chicano literature—was given to a woman, Estela Portillo Trambley, for her short story collection *Rain of Scorpions,* and it marked the ascendancy of women's voices in Chicano literature, which had previously been dominated by males. Portillo Trambley's strong feminist and irreverent stories did much both to sensitize the publishing powers in Chicano literature and to encourage a new generation of women writers to persevere in getting their works published; their works were soon to change the character of Chicano literature in the

Helena María Viramontes, 1986. (Photograph by Georgia McInnis.)

herself and even become a landowner. In all of her work Portillo Trambley has demonstrated an uncompromising pursuit for equality and liberation for women.

By the end of the 1970s most of the literary magazines and Chicano literary presses had disappeared, including Editorial Quinto Sol and *El grito*. Fortunately, since 1973 a new Hispanic magazine, *Revista Chicano-Riqueña (Chicano-Rican Review)*, edited by Nicolás Kanellos and Luis Dávila in Gary, Indiana, had been operating and making greater incursions into academia than any other Hispanic literary publication. In 1979, Kanellos founded Arte Público Press as an outgrowth of the magazine and relocated both to Houston, Texas, just in time to carry on where Quinto Sol had left off and to assume the leadership in publishing the works of a blossoming Hispanic women's literary movement. During the 1980s, Arte Público published books of poetry by San Antonio poets Evangelina Vigil and Angela de Hoyos, Chicago poets and prose writers Ana Castillo and Sandra Cisneros, San Francisco Bay Area novelist and poet Lucha Corpi, Los Angeles short story writer and former editor of the magazine

ChismeArte, and New Mexico novelist and playwright Denise Chávez, who were to produce some of the best-selling and most highly reviewed Chicano books of the decade.

Along with Arte Público and *Revista Chicano-Riqueña*, which in 1987 became *The Americas Review* and was edited by Julián Olivares and Evangelina Vigil, *Third Woman*, the magazine/book publisher directed by Norma Alarcón, was founded in Indiana in 1980 and relocated to the University of California, Berkeley, in 1985. Around the same time, another Hispanic book publisher with an academic base, *Bilingual Review Press*, also relocated, from Binghamton, New York to Arizona State University in Tempe. Supported by these three establishments and various other presses that were occasionally issuing women's titles, this first full-blown generation of Chicana writers flourished, finding a welcome space for their books in the academic curriculum, not only in Chicano literature courses but also in women's studies programs and American literature courses. The majority of the women were more educated than the 1960s and 1970s writers; most of them were college graduates—two of its representa-

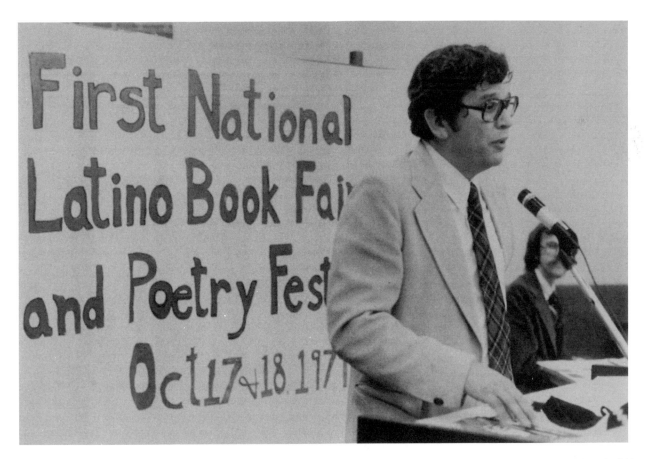

Luis Dávilla, co-editor of *Revista Chicano-Riquería,* at the First National Latino Book Fair, University of Illinois-Chicago Circle, 1979.

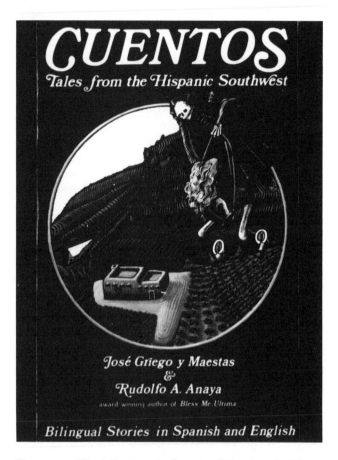

The cover of Rudolfo Anaya's *Cuentos: Tales from the Hispanic Southwest.*

ful writers in being chosen for the general American literature textbooks and for such canonizing texts as *The Norton Anthology of American Literature* include Pat Mora and Denise Chávez. Mora is the author of three books of poetry, her first two winning the Southwest Book Award: *Chants* (1984), *Borders* (1986), and *Communion* (1991). Drawing upon the desert landscape and a Mexican Indian sensibility, *Chants* is a richly textured exploration, in beautiful whispered tones, of the desert as a woman and of women as holders of the strength and endurance of the desert. In *Borders,* Mora, an El Paso native, continues in the same vein, drawing upon folk customs and the insight of healers as she explores all types of borders: the political and cultural ones between the United States and Mexico, the borders between the sexes, and so forth. Her latest book, *Communion,* is about communion with other women and other peoples of the earth, as she expands her vision to Asia and Africa.

Denise Chávez is a talented actress and a prolific playwright, but it is as a novelist that she has gained a deserved place in Chicano and American literature as a whole. For Chávez, as for Rolando Hinojosa, literature is very much the art of writing about lives,

tives, Denise Chavez and Sandra Cisneros, had even obtained master's degrees in creative writing—and they were mostly dominant in English, thus the Spanish language was no barrier to their works' entering literature courses and becoming accessible to broader circles of the reading public. As a whole, they were thoroughly versed in the mainstream feminist movement while preserving their own Chicana identities and culture and developing their literature from it.

At the close of the decade, mainstream textbook publishers began responding to the reform movements occurring in academia and also to the new demographic statistics relating to the public school markets in the most populous states, which demonstrated overwhelming Hispanic enrollments. As a result, most of the textbook publishers have begun to desperately search out and include Hispanic writers. In 1990, the nation's largest textbook publisher, Harcourt Brace Jovanovich, in fact, even went so far as to issue a high school English anthology titled *Mexican American Literature,* which includes selections of works from the colonial period to the present in its more than 700 pages. Some of the success-

Pat Mora, 1986.

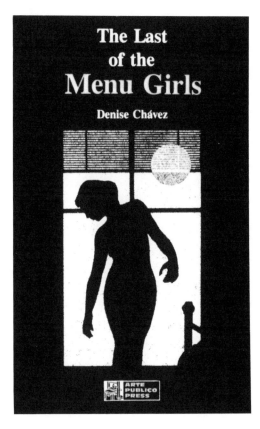

The cover of Denise Chávez's *The Last of the Menu Girls*.

about individuals, and about the stories they have to tell. Both of her novels, *The Last of the Menu Girls* (1986) and *Face of an Angel* (1993), present series of lives and characters talking for themselves within a loose biographic structure. In the case of her first novel, the unifying structure is the life of Rocío Esquivel, who, through a series of interconnected stories gains maturity by rebelling against the social roles created for her. *Face of an Angel,* on the other hand, centers on the life of a waitress and the unfortunate and tragicomic amorous relationships that she has with men; in the midst of the narration are brought in various types of unlikely elements, such as a manual on how to become a good waitress that the protagonist is writing. Both Mora and Chávez have won attention from the world that was previously off-limits to Chicano writers: the pages of the *New York Times Book Review* and the Norton anthologies, important fellowships, and awards.

While women were ascending in the world of Chicano literature, so was a younger generation of male writers who were the products of creative writing programs at universities, through which they gained access to opportunities for study, travel, and publishing never before had by Chicanos (nor Chicanas).

To date, theirs is the only Chicano poetry that has begun to become part of the American literary establishment. Of this new cadre of American poets who no longer speak or write in Spanish and no longer derive sustenance from the oral tradition, recitation, and political action, the most famous and prolific is Gary Soto, currently a tenured associate professor in creative writing and ethnic studies at the University of California, Berkeley. He is the winner of numerous prestigious awards, including the Academy of American Poets Prize (1975), the *Discovery-Nation* Award (1975), a Guggenheim fellowship (1979), an American Book Award, and many other prizes. His poetry is finely crafted, down-to-earth, and rigorous, mostly inspired by the life of the common working man in the fields and factories.

Quite often, as in his book *The Elements of San Joaquin,* published, as are most of his other poetry books, by the prestigious University of Pittsburgh Press poetry series, his work is a recollection of growing up in Fresno. While dealing with very real and concrete pictures of life in a particular time and setting, such as his youth in the agricultural San Joaquin Valley, Soto frequently approaches his subject from a classical frame of reference. For instance, in the second section of the book, the Valley is envisioned according to the four universal elements of the Greek philosophers: earth, air, water, and fire. He takes these elements and transforms them into the particular sights, smells, and labors of the Valley.

Among Soto's other books of poetry are *The Tale of Sunlight* (1978), *Where Sparrows Work Hard* (1981), *Black Hair* (1985), and *Who Will Know?* (1990). In 1985, Soto also began publishing autobiographical prose essays, which have met with a great deal of success, his first three books winning an American Book Award: *Living Up the Street* (1985), *Small Faces* (1986), and *Lesser Evils: Ten Quartets* (1988).

Among other writers who have made it into university creative writing programs as professors are Arizonan Alberto Rios and Californians Ernesto Trejo and Lorna Dee Cervantes. Cervantes did not follow the usual trek through master of fine arts programs in creative writing for entrance into her career. She was very much a product of the 1970s and the Chicano literary movement, during which she began reading her poetry in public at a theater festival in 1974, published her first works in *Revista Chicano-Riqueña* in 1975, and shortly thereafter founded and edited a literary magazine, *Mango,* which was free-form and experimental and not limited to publishing Chicanos. By 1981, her first book of poems, *Emplumada (Plumed),* was published by the University of Pittsburgh Press. Despite her many publications in magazines and success as a

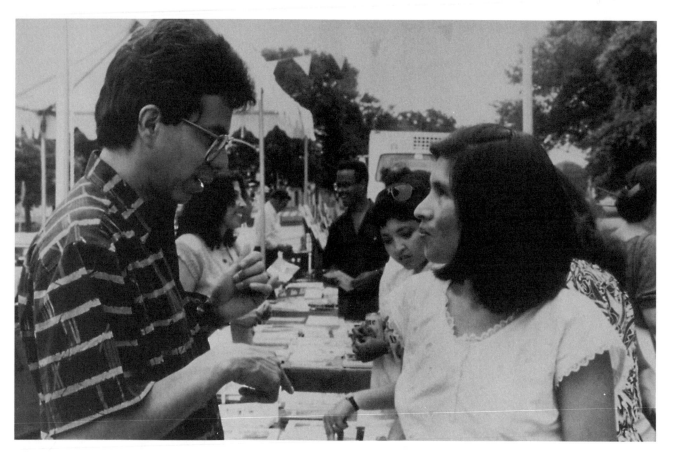

Gary Soto and Evangelina Vigil-Piñón at the Third National Hispanic Book Fair and Writers Festival in Houston, Texas, 1987.

performer of poetry, it was not until 1986 that she finished her B.A. degree. In 1990, she earned a Ph.D. in the history of consciousness at the University of California, Santa Cruz. She currently teaches creative writing at the University of Colorado.

Perhaps better than anyone yet, Lorna Dee Cervantes has described the pain of separation from family in such poems as "Refugee Ship" and "Oaxaca, 1974." Her work also deals with the dehumanizing landscape and the dehumanization that is caused by racism and sexism. Today she is still very much a hard-driving poet who takes risks and is not afraid to deal with taboo topics and violence, whether it be racist, sexist, or psychological, as can be seen in her book *From the Cables of Genocide* (1991).

Today, as greater opportunities in academia have opened up for both Hispanic students and writers, the larger commercial world of publishing is beginning to open its doors to a few more Chicano writers.

The 1990s have seen the "discovery" by large commercial presses of Chicano literature as represented by a generation of Chicano authors who are the product of creative writing departments at universities. During this decade, such publishers as Random

House and simon and Schuster have published their the most recent works of handful of these newer writers, such as those of Sandra Cisneros, Ana Castillo, Denise Chávez, Gary Soto and others. More importantly, these publishers also re-issued some of their earlier works. After this incursion by the younger generation, some of the publishers began to take notice of the older pioneers and re-issued the works of Oscar Zeta Acosta, Rudolfo Anaya and others. The mainstream publishing houses also began publishing works by similarly educated Puerto Ricans, Dominicans and Cubans, such as Esmeralda Santiago, Julia Alvarez, Oscar Hijuelos and Virgil Suárez. They also reissued works by such pioneers as Piri Thomas and Nicholasa Mohr. Then, too, the Hispanic publishers were also growing, with Arte Público Press not only capable of creating bestsellers such as Victor Villaseñor's *Rain of Gold* but also of selling the lucrative paperback rights to such giants as Bantam Doubleday Dell. In fact, after Arte Público registered the success with *Rain of Gold*, Bantam Doubleday Dell made the unprecedented move of buying back rights from Arte Público to Villaseñor's book, *Macho,* which Dell had originally published only to let go out-of-print. Today, Chicano authors have greater alternatives for publication through both the commercial and non-commercial presses.

Nuyorican Literature

In 1898, Puerto Rico became a colony of the United States and in 1917, Puerto Ricans became citizens of the United States. Since that time, Puerto Ricans have never really been immigrants to the United States, but migrants. Puerto Ricans on the island and those on the continent, despite geographic separation, hold in common their ethnicity, history, and their religious and cultural traits and practices. They also both deal with the confrontation of two languages and cultures. Thus, whether they reside in the continental United States or on the island of Puerto Rico, Puerto Ricans are one people. That is true whether they prefer the Spanish language or English, whether they were born on the island or not. Thus, most attempted divisions of the people are for vested interests, whether political or prejudicial.

Puerto Rican culture today is the product of powerful political, economic, and social forces who descended upon the small native population and at-tempted to evangelize, assimilate, decimate, or otherwise transform them. Christopher Columbus first initiated this process when he discovered the island in 1493. It was this act of "discovery" that resulted in Puerto Rico's becoming a colony in the Spanish Empire until 1898, when it passed into the possession of the United States. Puerto Rico is therefore a land that has been and still is subject to overseas rule—politically and economically, as well as artistically.

Despite being an island geographically cut off from the rest of Latin America and despite being ruled as a colony and not enjoying complete self-determination, Puerto Rican literature has been rich, for it has developed out of the many cultures and experiences that make up its peoples. In the middle of the nineteenth century, it assumed a creole, Hispanic American identity, emphasizing the new speech, customs, and history of people in this hemisphere as opposed to the Spanish in Europe— Puerto Rico and Cuba were among the very last remnants of Spain's colonial empire, the rest of Spanish America having gained its independence at the beginning of the nineteenth century. After 1898,

(Central figures) Ricardo Sánchez, Alejandro Morales, critic Salvador Rodríguez del Pino, and Victor Villaseñor at a book fair in Mexico City in 1979.

Puerto Ricans began emphasizing their Latin American, Spanish-speaking identity as separate from the Anglo-American United States. Therefore, while Puerto Rican artists initially sought to create a nationalism or an ethnic identity based on *mestizaje,* a blending of the cultures and the values of the New World, but due to the presence of the United States, Puerto Ricans have since insisted on the use of the Spanish language and on maintaining their relationship with Latin America, its cultures and arts.

At the turn of the century, the island's literature began developing along the lines of Latin American modernism, which was heavily influenced by French, peninsular Spanish, and Latin American models. As was the case in Mexico, Peru, Argentina, and Cuba, Puerto Rican artists and writers turned to the indigenous people of the island, their folklore, and national models in an effort to define the true identity of their national culture.

Although he was one of Puerto Rico's master poets, Luis Llorens Torres (1878–1944) was a European-educated intellectual who adapted the verse forms of the plaintive mountain songs (*décimas*) and folk speech of the jíbaros, or highlanders, in poems that took pride in rural life and its values rather than in the sophistication and modern advances of the city. His jíbaros were always skeptical and unmoved by the bragging and showing off of Americanized Puerto Ricans who believed in Yankee ingenuity and progress. Puerto Rico's greatest and most universally studied poet, Luis Palés Matos (1898–1959), was the first Puerto Rican literary figure to achieve a lasting impact on the evolution of Latin American literature, principally through the development of a poetic style that was inspired by the rhythms and language of Africa and the black Caribbean. His landmark book, *Tun tun de pasa y grifería* (1937), whose onomatopoic title has no translation, openly claimed a black African heritage and presence for the cultural makeup of Puerto Rico. Like Torres, the primitivism, vigor, and freedom of his black verses represent his critical stance toward Europe and the United States. In Palés Matos' master poem, "La plena de menéalo" ("The Dance of Shake It"), Puerto Rico is personified by a seductive *mulata* who sweats rum as she erotically dances close to, but just out of reach of, a drooling Uncle Sam.

Two figures are essential in recognition of the transition of Puerto Rican literature from the island to the continent: Julia de Burgos (1914–1953) and René Marqués (1919–1979). The former cultivated beautiful, sensuous verses, odes to her beloved countryside, only to die tragically on the streets of New York. Her lyricism served the parallel desires for personal as well as national liberation. René Marqués, the most widely known Puerto Rican playwright, spent time in New York as well, and was able to capture the true meaning of the dislocation of the native populations from Puerto Rico and their relocation to foreign lands and values. Even more moving than John Steinbeck's *Grapes of Wrath* is the plight of the family of displaced mountain folk in Marqués' *La carreta (The Oxcart),* which was first produced on stage in New York in 1953 and then published in Spanish in 1961 and in English in 1969. *La carreta,* which dramatizes the tragic life of this family as they are forced to move from their farm to a San Juan slum and then to New York, ends with an appeal to Puerto Ricans not to leave their homeland and to return to the island and the values of the countryside.

To a great extent, today's major Puerto Rican writers on the island still draw upon Marqués' spirit, style, and message in their attempt to preserve the integrity of the Puerto Rican culture and in their call for the political independence of the island. Prose writers like José Luis González, Pedro Juan Soto, Luis Rafael Sánchez, and Jaime Carrero satirize the complacency of the Americanized middle class, which would like Puerto Rico to become a U.S. state.

Julia de Burgos.

José Luis González.

enced by roving bards, reciters, storytellers, salsa music composers, and the popular culture and commercial environment of New York City.

Thus Nuyoricans are typically the children of working-class Puerto Rican migrants to the city; they are generally bilingual and bicultural, and so is their literature. During the search for ethnic roots and the civil rights movements of the 1960s, young Puerto Rican writers and intellectuals began using the term *Nuyorican* as a point of departure in affirming their own cultural existence and history as divergent from that of the island of Puerto Rico and that of mainstream America, much as the Chicanos were doing. A literary and artistic flowering in the New York Puerto Rican community ensued in the late 1960s and early 1970s as a result of greater access to education for Puerto Ricans raised in the United States and as a result of the ethnic consciousness movement. Although the term "Nuyorican" was first applied to literature by playwright-novelist Jaime Carrero in his poem "Neo-Rican Jetliner/Jet neorriqueño" in the late 1960s when he resided in New York, and the term finds some stylistic and thematic development in his plays *Noo Jall* (a blending of the Spanish pronunciation of "New York" and

They also develop the themes of Puerto Rico's past as Edenic and the jíbaro as a child of nature, with his intense code of honor and decency. Most of today's island novelists, while romanticizing the island's past, have, however, also created a one-dimensional image of Puerto Ricans in New York, only focusing on the tragedy of the rootlessness, poverty, and oppression of the second-class citizens who seem to by lost in the labyrinth of the monster city.

Puerto Rican writing in New York dates back to the end of the nineteenth century, and writing in English begins about the time that Jesús Colón was writing his columns for the *Daily Worker*. This seems to be a rather appropriate beginning, given that most of the Puerto Rican writers in English that followed identify with the working class. Unlike the writers of the island, who largely are members of an elite, educated class and many of whom are employed as university professors, the New York writers, who came to be known as Nuyoricans, are products of parents transplanted to the metropolis to work in the service and manufacturing industries. These writers are predominantly bilingual in their poetry and English-dominant in their prose; they hail from a folk and popular tradition heavily influ-

Luis Rafael Sánchez.

Pedro Juan Soto.

the word "jail") and "Pipo Subway no sabe reír" (Pipo Subway Doesn't Know How to Laugh), it was a group of poet-playwrights associated with the Nuyorican Poets' Café in the lower East Side of New York who later defined and exemplified Nuyorican literature in their works. Included in the group were Miguel Alagarín, Lucky Cienfuegos, Tato Laviera, and Miguel Piñero. Two members of the group, Cienfuegos and Piñero, were ex-convicts who had begun their writing careers while incarcerated and associating with Afro-American convict-writers; they chose to concentrate on prison life, street life, and the culture of poverty and to protest the oppression of their peoples through their poetry and dramas. Algarín, a university professor, owner, and operator of the Nuyorican Poets' Café, contributed a spirit of the avant-garde for the collective and managed to draw into the circle such well-known poets as Alan Ginsberg. Tato Laviera, a virtuoso bilingual poet and performer of poetry (declamador), contributed a lyrical, folk, and popular culture tradition that derived from the island experience and the Afro-Caribbean culture but was cultivated specifically in and for New York City.

It was Miguel Piñero's work (and life), however, that became most celebrated, his prison drama, Short Eyes, having won an Obie and the New York Drama Critics Award for Best American Play in the 1973–74 season. His success, coupled with that of the autobiography of fellow Nuyorican writer and ex-convict Piri Thomas and that of poet Pedro Pietri, who developed the image of a street urchin always high on marijuana, resulted in Nuyorican literature and theater's often being associated with crime, drugs, abnormal sexuality, and generally negative behavior. Thus, many writers who in fact were affirming Puerto Rican working-class culture did not want to become identified with the movement. Still others wanted to hold onto their ties with the island and saw no reason to emphasize differences, but, rather, wanted to stress similarities.

What exacerbated the situation was that the commercial publishing establishment in the early 1970s was quick to take advantage of the literary fervor in the Puerto Rican community by issuing a series of ethnic autobiographies that insisted on the criminality, abnormality, and drug culture of New York Puerto Ricans. Included in this array of mostly paperbacks was, of course, Piri Thomas' Down These Mean Streets (1967, issued in paper in 1974),

Thomas' *Seven Long Times* (1974), Thomas' *Stories from El Barrio* (1978, issued in paper in 1980), Lefty Barreto's *Nobody's Hero* (1976), and a religious variation on the theme: Nicky Cruz's *Run Nicky Run.* So well worn was this type of supposed autobiography that it generated a satire by another Nuyorican writer, Ed Vega, who comments in the introduction to his novel *The Comeback* (1985) as follows:

> I started thinking about writing a book, a novel. And then it hit me. I was going to be expected to write one of those great American immigrant stories, like *Studs Lonigan, Call It Sleep,* or *Father.* . . . Or maybe I'd have to write something like *Manchild in the Promised Land* or a Piri Thomas' *Down These Mean Streets.* . . . I never shot dope nor had sexual relations with men, didn't for that matter, have sexual relations of any significant importance with women until I was about nineteen. . . . And I never stole anything. . . . Aside from fist fights, I've never shot anyone, although I've felt like it. It seems pretty far-fetched to me that I would ever want to do permanent physical harm to anyone. It is equally repulsive for me to write an autobio-

Bernardo Vega, 1948.

graphical novel about being an immigrant. In fact, I don't like ethnic literature, except when the language is so good that you forget about the ethnic writing it.

The Comeback is the story of a confused college professor who creates for himself the identity of a Puerto Rican-Eskimo ice hockey player; he suffers a nervous breakdown and is treated for the classical symptoms of an identity crisis. Throughout the novel, Vega satirized all types of characters that populate the barrio as well as popular culture, such as Puerto Rican revolutionaries, psychiatrists, and a Howard Cosell-type sportscaster. In his interrelated collection of stories told by fictitious narrator Ernesto Mendoza, *Mendoza's Dreams* (1987), Vega surveys the human comedy of everyday barrio life and relates tales of success in small ways in reaching for the American Dream. In his collection *Casualty Report* (1991), he shows us the inverse: the physical, psychological, and moral death of many who live within the poverty and deprivation of the Puerto Rican barrio, as well as in the larger ghetto of a racist society.

More than anything else, the first generation of

Jesús Colón, circa 1950s.

Nuyorican writers was one that was dominated by poets, many of whom had come out of an oral tradition and had honed their art through public readings; thus the creation of the Nuyorican Poets' Café was a natural outcome of the need to create a specific space for the performance of poetry. Among the consummate performers of Nuyorican poetry were Victor Hernández Cruz, Tato Laviera, Miguel Piñero, and Miguel Algarín. Like his fellow poets, Cruz's initiation into poetry was through popular music and street culture; his first poems have often been considered to be jazz poetry in a bilingual mode, except that English dominated in the bilingualism and thus opened the way for his first book to be published by a mainstream publishing house: *Snaps: Poems* (Random House, 1969). It was quite a feat for a 20-year-old from an impoverished background. In *Snaps* were the themes and styles that would dominate and flourish in his subsequent books; in all of Hernández Cruz's poetry sound, music, and performance are central. He also experiments with bilingualism as oral poetry [and written symbols of oral speech], and he searches for identity through these sounds and symbols. His next two books were odysseys that take the reader back to Puerto Rico and primordial Indian and African music and poetry (*Mainland,* 1973) and across the United States and back to New York, where the poet finds the city transformed by its Caribbean peoples into their very own cultural home (*Tropicalization,* 1976). *By Lingual Wholes* (1982) is a consuming and total exploration of the various linguistic possibilities in the repertoire of a bilingual poet, and *Rhythm, Content and Flavor* (1989) is a summary of his entire career.

Tato Laviera's bilingualism and linguistic inventiveness have risen to the level of virtuosity. Laviera is the inheritor of the Spanish oral tradition, with all of its classical formulas, and the African oral tradition, which stresses music and spirituality; in his works he brings both the Spanish and English languages together as well as those of the islands of Puerto Rico and Manhattan—a constant duality that is always in the background. His first book, *La Carreta Made a U-Turn* (1979) was published by Arte Público Press, which has become the leading publisher of Nuyorican literature, despite its location in Houston. *La Carreta Made a U-Turn* uses René Marqués' *Oxcart* as a point of departure but redirects back to the heart of New York, instead of back to the island, as Marqués had desired; Laviera believes that Puerto Rico can be found here too. His second book, *Enclave* (1981) is a celebration of diverse heroic personalities, both real and imagined: Luis Palés Matos and salsa composers, the neighborhood gossip and John Lennon, Miriam Makeba and

Tito Madera Smith, the latter being a fictional, hip offspring of a jíbara and a southern American black. *AmeRícan* (1986) and *Mainstream Ethics* (1988) are surveys of the lives of the poor and marginalized in the United States and a challenge for the country to live up to its promises of equality and democracy.

One of the few women's voices to be heard in this generation is a very strong and well-defined one, that of Sandra María Esteves, who from her teen years has been very active in the women's struggle, Afro-American liberation, the Puerto Rican independence movement, and, foremost, the performance of poetry. In 1973, she joined El Grupo, a New York-based touring collective of musicians, performing artists, and poets associated with the cultural wing of the Puerto Rican Socialist party. By 1980, she had published her first collection of poetry, *Yerba Buena,* which involves the search for identity of a colonized Hispanic woman of color in the United States, the daughter of immigrants from the Caribbean. All three of her books, *Yerba Buena, Tropical Rains: A Bilingual Downpour* (1984), and *Mockingbird Bluestown Mambo* (1990), affirm that womanhood is what gives unity to all of the diverse characterizations of her life.

Sandra María Esteves, 1979.

(Left to right) Nicholasa Mohr, Publisher Nicolás Kanellos, and Ed Vega on the occasion of their reading at the Bookstop in Houston, Texas, 1985.

The most productive and recognized Nuyorican novelist is Nicholasa Mohr. Her works, *Nilda* (1973), *El Bronx Remembered* (1975), *In Nueva York* (1986), were all published in hardback and paperback editions by major commercial publishing houses and are still in print, three of them having been reissued by Arte Público Press. Her books have entered the mainstream as have no other books by Hispanic authors of the United States. They have won such awards as the *New York Times* Outstanding Book of the Year, the *School Library Journal* Best Children's Book, and many others, including a decree honoring her by the state legislature of New York. Her best-loved novel, *Nilda,* traces the coming of age of a young Puerto Rican girl in the Bronx during World War II. Unlike many other such novels of development, Nilda gains awareness of the plight of her people and her own individual problems by examining the racial and economic oppression that surrounds her and her family, in a manner that can be compared to Tomás Rivera's central character in . . . *y no se lo tragó la tierra.*

In two of her other books, *In Nueva York* and *El Bronx Remembered,* Mohr examines through a series of stories and novellas various Puerto Rican neighborhoods and draws sustenance from the common folks' power to survive and still produce art, folklore, and strong families in the face of oppression and marginalization. *Rituals of Survival: A Woman's Portfolio* (1985), in five stories and a novella, portrays six strong women who take control of their lives, most of them by liberating themselves from husbands, fathers, or families that attempt to keep them confined in narrowly defined female roles. *Rituals* is the book that the mainstream houses would not publish, wanting to keep Mohr confined to what they saw as immigrant literature and children's literature, as in her *Felita* and *Going Home.*

While not banding together with groups and collectives, Mohr has been one of the most influential of the Nuyorican writers out of sheer productivity and accomplishment. She has also led the way to greater acceptance of Nuyorican and Hispanic writers in creative writing workshops, such as the Millay Colony, in Poets, Editors and Novelists (PEN), and on the funding panels of the National Endowment for the Arts and the New York State Council on the Arts.

Another Nuyorican writer who has not participated in nor benefitted from collective work is Judith Ortiz Cofer, who grew up in Paterson, New Jersey, and has lived much of her adult life in Georgia and Florida. Cofer is one of the few Nuyorican products of the creative writing programs, and much of her early poetry was disseminated through establishment small presses in the South that may have been intrigued by the exoticism of her Puerto Rican subjects, packaged in finely crafted verses, with a magic and mystery that is similar to that of Pat Mora's poetry.

Her first book of poems, *Reaching for the Mainland* (1987), is a chronicle of the displaced person's struggle to find a goal, a home, a language, and a history. In *Terms of Survival* (1987), she explores the psychology and social attitudes of the Puerto Rican dialect and how it controls male and female roles; in particular she carries on a dialogue with her father throughout the poems of the book. In 1989, Cofer published a highly reviewed novel of immigration, *Line of the Sun,* through the University of Georgia Press and in 1990 an even more highly reviewed book, made up of a collection of autobiographical essays, in the style of Virginia Wolf, *Silent Dancing: A Remembrance of Growing Up Puerto Rican,* through Arte Público Press.

In 1988, Cofer and five other writers—Nicholasa Mohr, Tato Laviera, Rolando Hinojosa, Alberto Ríos, and Lorna Dee Cervantes—were featured reading and performing their works in a historic documentary, *Growing Up Hispanic,* directed by Jesús Treviño, presented on national television by the Corporation for Public Broadcasting. The future of Hispanic literature in the United States promises to be very fruitful, and more and more segments of the population are getting the message.

Cuban American Literature

Cuban culture and literature in the United States dates back to the nineteenth century when writer-philosopher José Martí and other patriots plotted from the U.S. mainland for Cuban independence from Spain. During the first half of the twentieth century, Cubans and Spaniards dominated Hispanic arts and media in New York. While Cuban culture was on the ascendancy in New York, its island literature had already joined that of Mexico and Argentina in the leadership of Spanish American letters since the nineteenth century, with such internationally acknowledged masters as Gertrudis Gómez de Avellaneda, José Echeverría, Julián del Casal, and José Martí, and in the twentieth century with such leaders as patriarch Nicolás Guillén, who has taken Spanish American poetry from a markedly Afro-Caribbean to a Pan Hispanic vision in support of universal socialist revolution. Cuban writers who have contributed to the Latin American literary boom include Alejo Carpentier, José Lezama Lima, and Gabriel Cabrera Infante.

It is no wonder then that the inheritors of such a rich and dynamic tradition would contribute so greatly to Hispanic culture in the United States, especially given the fact that their mass immigration took place so recently, beginning in 1959 as refugees from the Cuban Revolution. In contrast, whereas Puerto Rican mass migration really had begun during World War II, when the American economy drew heavily on its island territory for workers, the Cubans came as political refugees from a land that had never been a colony of the United States, although it had been a protectorate and an economic dependent since the Spanish-American War. Most of the Puerto Ricans had come as workers and generally did not have the level of education nor the financial resources and relocation services that the Cubans did. This first mass of Cubans came with an outstanding written tradition well intact. And the Cuban literary aesthetic, unlike the Puerto Rican one, had never been so obsessed with protecting the

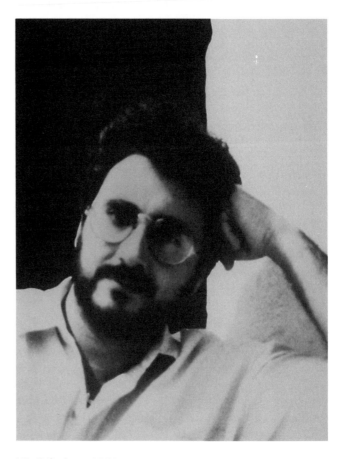

Virgil Suárez, 1991.

Spanish language and Hispanic culture while defending itself against Anglo-American culture and language. Numerous writers and intellectuals immigrated to the United States as refugees; many of them were able to adapt to and become part of the U.S. Hispanic and mainstream cultural institutions.

Today, after three decades of new Cuban culture in New York, New Jersey, Miami, and dispersed throughout the United States—in contrast to the older Cuban communities in New York City and Tampa—a Cuban American literary and artistic presence has developed. Younger writers are no longer preoccupied with exile, with eyes cast only on the island past; instead they are looking forward to participating in the English-language mainstream or serving the intellectual and cultural needs of the U.S. Cuban and Hispanic communities. Thus, there has developed a definite separation of purpose and aesthetics between the younger writers—Roberto Fernández, Iván Acosta, Virgil Suárez, and Oscar Hijuelos, for instance—and the older writers of exile—Lydia Cabrera, Matías Montes Huidobro, José Sánchez Boudy, and so on. Also, there continues to be an influx of exiled writers, disaffected with Cuban communism, like Heberto Padilla, who must be viewed differently from the earlier generation of exiles who have already created for themselves a solid niche within Hispanic and mainstream institutions such as publishing houses and universities.

What we have seen during the last decades is a literature that almost exclusively attacked the Cuban Revolution and Marxism. The novel of exile became another weapon in the struggle. Following the first antirevolutionary novel, *Enterrado vivo* (*Buried Alive*), published in Mexico in 1960 by Andrés Rivero Collado, were a host of others published in the United States and abroad by minor writers, such as Emilio Fernández Camus, Orlando Núñez, Manuel Cobo Souza, Raúl A. Fowler, Luis Ricardo Alonso, and many others. When they were not openly propagandistic and rhetorical, they were nostalgic for the homeland to the point of idealization. Poetry and drama followed the same course, for the most part. Later, political verse would come to form a special genre of its own, what has been called by critic Hortensia Ruiz del Viso "poesía del presidio político" (political prisoner poetry), as in the works of Angel Cuadra, Heberto Padilla, and Armando Valladares, who resides in Spain but is quite active in the United States.

A key figure in providing a new direction for Cuban literature in the United States has been Celedonio González, who, beginning with *Los primos* (1971, *The Cousins*), changed ssiofocus to concentrate on Cuban life and culture in the United States.

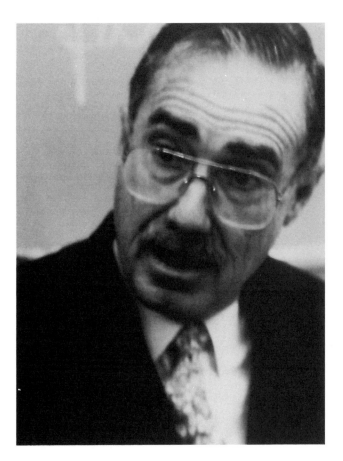

José Sánchez Boudy.

Later, in *Los cuatro embajadores* (1973, *The Four Ambassadors*) and *El espesor del pellejo de un gato ya cadáver* (1978, *The Thickness of the Skin on a Cat Already a Corpse*), he not only examined culture shock and conflict between Cubans and Americans, but he also treated a very taboo topic: criticism of the economic system of the United States, especially in its exploitation of Cuban workers. González presents us with Cubans who do not yet see themselves as Americans but who are also conscious that Cuba is no longer theirs.

Ironically, one of the most important writers in forging a Cuban American literature and in breaking new ground in his use of the English language is a professor of Spanish, Roberto Fernández. Through his novels, Fernández not only touches upon all the taboo subjects in the Cuban community of Miami—the counterrevolutionary movement in the United States, racism, acculturation, and assimilation—but also helps the community to take them in a less serious vein and to laugh at itself. In his two open-form mosaiclike novels, *La vida es un special* (1982, *Life Is on Special*) and *La montaña rusa* (1985, *The Roller Coaster*), Fernández presents a biting but loving satire of a community transformed by the materialism and popular culture of the United States, but somewhat paralyzed by the nostalgia and political obsession with a Communist Cuba. In 1988, Fernández continued the community saga in English, with the publication of *Raining Backwards,* which has become his best known and most regarded novel. Here as in his other works, the hilarious parade of characters, language styles—with quite a bit of bilingual humor—and diverse social events are aimed at encouraging the community to take stock of its present circumstances and reckon with a future here in the United States.

One of the most influential literary magazines of Cuban literature in the United States has been *Linden Lane,* which is published in Spanish. Published by writer Heberto Padilla and edited by poet Belkis Cuza Malé, who is a professor at Princeton University, the magazine has created a forum for the whole Cuban writing community, both the generation of exile and the new Cuban American generation. In 1990, the magazine formally announced the advent of a Cuban American literature with its publication of an anthology containing works in both English and Spanish and entitled *Los atrevidos: Cuban American Literature,* edited by Miami poet Carolina Hospital, also an editor of *Linden Lane.* In 1991, Arte Público Press published an anthology that also proclaimed a Cuban American identity, *Cuban American Theater,* edited by critic Rodolfo Cortina. Both collections draw upon writers dispersed throughout the United States, not just from the Miami and New York communities.

Among the new generation of Cuban American writers growing up in the United States, there are a few who have gone through creative writing programs at universities and who thus have had access to mainstream publishing opportunities. A graduate of the important writing program at Louisiana State University, Virgil Suárez has had two novels published, *Latin Jazz* (1989) by Morrow and *The Cutter* (1991) by Ballantine Books. His third book, a very fine collection of short stories, *Welcome to the Oasis,* was not accepted by commercial publishers who prefer novels; it was published in 1991 by Arte Público Press. *Latin Jazz* is a somewhat different type of ethnic biographical novel, portraying a whole Cuban family, instead of just one individual; in alternate chapters devoted to each of the family members, Suárez provides their respective histories, hopes, and desires as they wait for a missing family member to arrive in Miami with the Mariel boat-lift.

Probably the most important of the Cuban American writers to come out of the creative writing schools is Oscar Hijuelos, who is not the son of refugees from the Cuban Revolution, but of earlier immigrants to New York. Nevertheless, Hijuelos' first offering, *Our House in the Last World* (1983), is a typical ethnic autobiography and may be seen as a symbol of Cuban assimilation in that it is one of the few novels that negatively portrays the island culture, as personified by an alcoholic and machistic father, while developing the common theme of the American dream. His novel *The Mambo Kings Play Songs of Love* (1990) made history; it is the first novel by a Hispanic writer of the United States to win the Pulitzer Prize. It is also the first time that a major publishing house, Simon and Shuster, has ever invested heavily in a novel by a Hispanic writer, bringing it out at the top of its list and promoting the book very heavily. *The Mambo Kings* is the story of two musician brothers during the prime of mambo music in the 1950s. The novel thus has a historical background that lends it a rich texture; it allows us to see a portion of American popular culture history through the eyes of two performers very wrapped up in the euphoria of the times and then the waning of interest in things Latin in the United States. The story of the tragic ending of the duo is very touching, but offers hope for the potential of Hispanic culture to influence the mainstream. In fact, Hijuelo's book and the recognition that it has won may open the door to mainstream publishing for other U.S. Hispanic writers.

✴ OUTSTANDING HISPANIC LITERARY FIGURES

Iván Acosta

See Chapter 21.

Miguel Algarín (1941–)

A native of Santurce, Puerto Rico, Algarín grew up in a hardworking family that loved music and the arts. His parents passed on to their children an appreciation of opera and classical music; Miguel's father taught him to play the violin. The Algaríns moved to New York City in the early 1950s; they settled in Spanish Harlem for a while, and then moved to Queens. Miguel Algarín began his higher education at City College and finished his B.A. degree at the University of Wisconsin in 1963; in 1965, he graduated with a master's degree in English from the Pennsylvania State University. After teaching English literature at Brooklyn College and New York University for a time, Algarín went on to teach at Rutgers, where he is an associate professor in the English department.

Algarín is the founder and proprietor of the

Miguel Algarín reciting his poetry at the First National Latino Book Fair, Chicago, 1979.

Algarín published translations of the poetry of Chilean Nobel Prize winner Pablo Neruda, under the title *Canción de gesta / A Song of Protest.*

Alurista (Alberto Baltazar Urista) (1947–)

Alurista is considered one of the pioneers of Chicano literature. He was one of the first poets to support the Chicano movement through his poetry, a writer and signer of important manifestoes of the movement, a founder of the Moviemiento Estudiantil de Aztlán (MECHA, Chicano Student Movement of Aztlán) in 1967, and one of the first to establish the concept of Aztlán in literature, which forecasts a return to the glories of Aztec civilization by the Chicanos in the mythic homeland of the Aztec, what is today roughly the five states of the Southwest.

Born in Mexico City on August 8, 1947, Alberto Baltazar Urista spent his early years in the states of Morelos and Guerrero. At age 13 he immigrated to the United States with his family, which settled in San Diego, California. He began writing poetry at an early age and was a restless and widely-read student. He began Chapman College in 1965 and transferred to and graduated from San Diego State Uni-

Puerto Rican Poets' Café, which is dedicated to the support of writers performing their art orally. It was especially important as a gathering place of young writers during the early 1970s when Nuyorican literature was being defined. Algarín played an important leadership role in the definition of that literature by compiling, with Miguel Piñero, an important anthology, *Nuyorican Poetry: An Anthology of Puerto Rican Words and Feelings* (1975). He also founded a short-lived publishing house, the Nuyroican Press, which only issued one book, his own *Mongo Affair* (1978). One year later, he took part in the launching of Arte Público Press, which became the leading publisher of Nuyorican literature.

Algarín has written plays, screenplays, and short stories, but is principally known as a poet. His books include *Mongo Affair, On Call* (1980), *Body Bee Calling from the 21st Century* (1982), and *Time's Now / Ya es tiempo* (1985). Algarín's poetry runs the gamut from jazz-salsa poetry to the mystical and avantgarde. He is one of the foremost experimenters with English-Spanish bilingualism and has even penned trilingual works that incorporate French. In 1976,

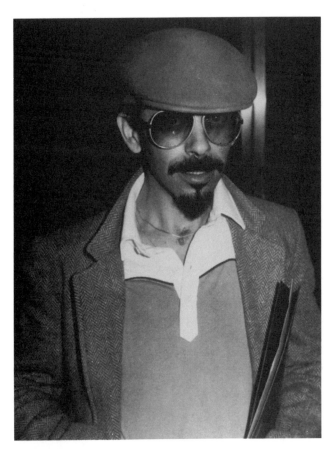

Alurista, 1980.

versity in 1970 with a B.A. degree in psychology. He later obtained an M.A. degree from that institution and a Ph.D. degree in literature from the University of California, San Diego, in 1983. Around 1966, he began writing poetry seriously for publication and assumed the pen name Alurista, which is virtually the only name he uses now.

Alurista is a consummate reader and performer of his poetry, which has led to many travels to fulfill invitations nationally and internationally to read his works. He was the founder and coeditor, with his wife, Xelina, of the literary magazine *Maize* and the publishing house associated with it; both ceased to exist after he became an associate professor of Spanish at California State Polytechnic, San Luis Obispo, in 1986. In 1992, he became a professor of Chicano Studies at the University of California, Santa Barbara. Alurista is a prolific and talented poet, a pioneer of bilingualism in Chicano poetry. Throughout his career, his study of the Nahuatl and Mayan languages and mythology have enriched his poetic works and inspired his promotion of the ideology of Aztlán. But it is his bilingualism that has opened new frontiers in poetry, with his free experimentation in combining the sounds, meanings, and graphic representations of Spanish and English in the same poem, quite often achieving surprising and beautiful effects.

Alurista has published the following books of poetry: *Floricanto en Aztlán* (1971), *Nationchild Plumaroja, 1967–1972* (1972), *Timespace Huracán: Poems, 1972–1975* (1976), *A'nque* (1979), *Spik in Glyph?* (1981), and *Return: Poems Collected and New* (1982).

Julia Alvarez

Novelist and poet Julia Alvarez was born to Dominican parents in New York City. She received her early education in the Dominican Republic, but returned with her family to the United States when she was ten years old. Alvarez's narratives are loosely based on her growing up between the two cultures of the United States and the Dominican Republic, although her perspective has always been one of growing up in privilege as the daughter of a successful medical doctor with political connections both in the United States and in her parents' homeland. However, when her father became involved in a plot to overthrow dictator Rafael Trujillo, the failed coup led to her father's exile in the United States and Julia Alvarez's permanent residence here. She thus finished her education in the United States, earning college degrees in literature and writing. She went on to become an English professor at Middlebury College and receive grants from the National En-

dowment for the Arts and the Ingram Merrill Foundation. After publishing stories and poems in literary magazines, she published a book of verse, *Homecoming* in 1984 and, in 1991, the novel that brought her to a national audience: *How the García Girls Lost Their Accents*. She thus joined the wave of Hispanic writers with creative writing degrees that were making their way into mainstream presses. These were followed in 1994 with her second novel, *In the Time of the Butterflies* and, in 1995 with another collection of poems, *The Other Side/El Otro Lado*. The largely favorable reviews in the press have tended to cast her works as immigrant literature, and her second novel reinforces this judgment, as it engages a theme of political assassination back in the Dominican Republic.

Rudolfo A. Anaya (1937–)

Rudolfo A. Anaya was born on October 30, 1937, in the village of Pastura, New Mexico, in surroundings similar to those celebrated in his famous novel about growing up in the rural culture of New Mexico: *Bless Me, Ultima*. He attended public schools in Santa Rosa and Albuquerque and earned both his B.A. (1963) and his M.A. (1968) degrees in English from the University of New Mexico. In 1972, he also earned an M.A. degree in guidance and counseling from the same university. From 1963 to 1970, he taught in the public schools, but in 1974 he became a member of the English department of the University of New Mexico; in 1993, he became professor emeritus. With the success of his writing career, Anaya has risen to become the head of the creative writing program at the University of New Mexico. Included among his many awards are the following: an honorary doctorate from the University of Albuquerque, the New Mexico Governor's Award for Excellence, the President's National Salute to American Poets and Writers in 1980, and the Premio Quinto Sol in 1972 for his novel *Bless Me Ultima*. Since 1989, Anaya has been the founding editor of *Blue Mesa Review*. Anaya is also a fellow of the National Endowment for the Arts and the Kellogg Foundation through whose auspices he has been able to travel to China and other countries for study.

Anaya is very much a believer and promoter of a return to pre-Columbian literature and thought through the reflowering of Aztec civilization in Aztlán, the mythic homeland of the Aztec, which corresponds to the five states of today's Southwest. He sees his role in literature as that of the shaman; his task as a storyteller is to heal and reestablish balance and harmony. These ideas are present throughout his works, but are most successfully represented in his prize-winning novel *Bless Me, Ul-*

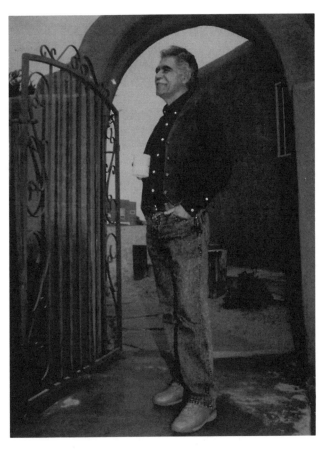

Rudolfo A. Anaya.

tima, in which the folk healer Ultima works to reestablish harmony and social order in the life of the Mares family and to bring psychological well-being to Antonio, the protagonist, who is struggling to understand the roles of good and evil in life. Anaya's other books are *Heart of Aztlán* (1976), *Tortuga* (1979), *The Silence of the Llano* (1982), *The Legend of La Llorona* (1984), *The Adventures of Juan Chicaspatas* (1985), *A Chicano in China* (1986), *The Farolitas of Christmas* (1987), *Lord of the Dawn: The Legend of Quetzalcoatl* (1987), *Alburquerque* (1992), *Zia Summer* (1995), and *Jalamanta: A Message from the Desert* (1996). He is also the author of plays and screenplays and has coedited three literary anthologies: with Simon Ortiz, *Ceremony of Brotherhood, 1680–1980* (1980); with José Griego y Maestas, *Cuentos: Tales from the Hispanic Southwest* (1980), and with Antonio Márquez, *Cuentos Chicanos* (1980, *Chicano Stories*).

In 1995, Anaya signed a multi-book contract with giant Warner Books to reissue all of his novels as well as to publish his new works. This is the first time that such financial and marketing commitment has been extended to an Hispanic creative writer.

The first new title of Anay's issued by Warner was a detective novel, *Zia Summer,* in 1996.

Jimmy Santiago Baca (1952–)

Jimmy Santiago Baca is one of the most successful Chicano poets to come out of the oral tradition, tempered by prison experiences and the Chicano Movement; in this and other aspects, his background is similar to that of Ricardo Sánchez. Baca was born in Santa Fe, New Mexico, in 1952 to Mexican and Apache-Yaqui parents who abandoned him to be raised by his Indian grandparents; he was later raised in an orphanage. In 1973, Baca was sentenced to five years imprisonment for narcotics possession. In the a maximum security prison in Arizona, Baca taught himself to read and write and he passed his G.E.D. exam. In prison, Baca discovered poetry and began penning his first compositions. While still serving time, *Mother Jones* magazine published his first poems. By the time of his release in 1978, his first book of poems, *Immigrants in Our Own Land* had been accepted for publication by the prestigious Louisiana State University Press, which issued the book in 1979. Baca's poems were highly polished, but naturalistic, and met with immediate critical approval; the accolades from mainstream critics expanded with his next books: *What's Happening* (1982), *Martin and Meditations on the South Valley* (1987) and *Black Mesa Poems* (1989), the latter two published by one of the most important literary houses in the United States: New Directions. In 1993, Baca also published a book of autobiographical essays, *Working in the Dark: Reflections of a Poet in the Barrio* and, in 1993, wrote a screenplay for a film, *Bound by Honor,* which was released by Disney's Hollywood Pictures. For *Black Mesa Poems,* Baca became the first Hispanic poet to win the important Wallace Stevens Poetry Award. Baca has served as a poet in residence at Yale University and the University of California-Berkeley.

Lorna Dee Cervantes (1954–)

Lorna Dee Cervantes was born into an economically deprived family of Mexican and American heritage, on August 6, 1954, in the Mission District of San Francisco. At age five she moved with her mother and brother to San Jose to live with her grandmother when her parents separated. Cervantes began writing poetry when she was six years old; poems written when she was 14 were eventually published in a magazine after Cervantes had established her career as a writer. She later attended college, but did not finish her B.A. degree from California State University until after she had initiated her writing career; in 1990 she obtained a Ph.D.

degree from the University of California, Santa Cruz, where she studied philosophy and aesthetics. She then went on to teach creative writing at the University of Colorado in Denver.

Emplumada (1981, *Plumed*), Cervantes' first collection of poems, is made up of works published in literary magazines throughout the Southwest. The book's popularity has made it the best-selling title in the University of Pittsburgh's prestigious poetry series. *Emplumada* presents a young woman coming of age, discovering the gap that exists in life between one's hopes and desires and what life eventually offers in reality. The predominant themes include culture conflict, oppression of women and minorities, and alienation from one's roots. Cervantes' poetry is very well crafted and has the distinction of using highly lyrical language while at the same time being direct and powerful. The same can be said of her second book, *From the Cables of Genocide,* which is very much the work of a mature poet dealing with the great themes of life, death, social conflict, and poverty. *From the Cables of Genocide* won the Paterson Poetry Prize and the national Hispanic Poetry

Lorna Dee Cervantes, 1990. (Photograph by Georgia McInnis.)

Prize given by New York's *La Brújula / The Compass* magazine.

Angélico Chávez (1910–)

Fray Angélico Chávez is one of the most renowned religious poets in the United States. The author of some 19 books, Chávez is also a historian of his order, the Franciscan brothers, and of the Catholic church in New Mexico. Born on April 10, 1910, in Wagon Mound, New Mexico, he was named Manuel Chávez by his parents. Chávez was raised in Mora and attended St. Francis Seminary in Cincinnati, Ohio, and colleges in the Midwest. In 1937, he became the first New Mexican to become a Franciscan friar. From the time of his ordination at age 27, until age 62, he served as a pastor in several towns and Indian pueblos of New Mexico.

What unifies Chávez's large output as a poet and historian is his interest in New Mexico's past, the work of his order in New Mexico, and his own Catholicism. Beginning as essentially a religious poet, he later took an interest in historical fiction and, finally, in the history of the region itself, as in his most famous historical essay, *My Penitente Land: Reflections on Spanish New Mexico* (1974). Other historical writings by Chávez were intended to provide an accurate understanding of Hispanic New Mexico; these include *Our Lady of the Conquest* (1948), *Origins of New Mexico Families in the Spanish Colonial Period* (1954), *Coronado's Friars* (1968), *But Time and Chance: The Story of Padre Martínez of Taos, 1793–1867* (1981), and other edited books.

His works of historical fiction include *New Mexico Triptych: Being Three Panels and Three Accounts: 1. The Angel's New Wing, 2. The Penitente Thief, 3. Hunchback Madonna* (1940), *La Conquistadora: The Autobiography of an Ancient Statue* (1954), *From an Altar Screen / El retablo: Tales from New Mexico* (1957), and *The Lady from Toledo* (1960).

Chávez's reputation as a creative writer rests upon an important body of poetic works that include *Clothed with the Sun* (1939), *Eleven Lady Lyrics, and Other Poems* (1945), *The Single Rose; the Rose Unica and Commentary of Fray Manuel de Santa Clara* (1948), and *The Virgin of Port Lligat* (1959). Although Chávez's poetry and all of his works are grounded in New Mexico Catholicism, his poems are not local-color pieces celebrating New Mexico's picturesque landscape; instead they depict Chávez's inner life. In *The Single Rose,* Chávez was so intent on communicating the poems' inner religious meaning that he included commentary in the book, which studies the rose as an allegorical figure for human and divine love. Chávez's last poetry collection was *Selected Poems, With an Apologia* (1969), which brought together some of his most successful poems along with an apologia that announced that he would no longer publish poetry, due to changing fashions in poetry and his loss of excitement in writing verse.

Denise Chávez (1948–)

Denise Chávez is a novelist, playwright, and poet who, through her writings, has brought to life entire populations of memorable characters of the Southwest, both Mexican American and Anglo-American. Born on August 15, 1948, in Las Cruces, New Mexico, Chávez was raised principally by her mother Delfina, a teacher; her father had abandoned the family while she was still young. After attending schools and colleges in Las Cruces, Chávez obtained a master's degree in theater arts from Trinity University in San Antonio, Texas, in 1974, and a master's degree in creative writing from the University of New Mexico in Albuquerque in 1984. During her career she has taught and been a writer in residence at numerous institutions in New Mexico and elsewhere. She taught in the drama department of the University of Houston from 1988 to 1993, when she

Denise Chávez.

became a visiting professor of creative writing at New Mexico State University.

Denise Chávez has won numerous awards and fellowships, including Best Play award for *The Wait* from New Mexico State University in 1970, the Steele Jones Fiction Award in 1986 for her story "The Last of the Menu Girls," two fellowships from the National Endowment for the Arts (in 1981 and 1982), a Rockefeller Foundation fellowship in 1984, and the Creative Writing Arts fellowship from the Cultural Arts Council of Houston in 1990.

As a playwright, Chávez has written numerous plays, many of which have been produced on the stage but not published. Her writings include *Novitiates* (1971), *Elevators* (1972), *The Mask of November* (1977), *Nacimiento* (1979, *Birth*), *Santa Fe Charm* (1980), *Sí, Hay Posada* (1980, *Yes, There Is Room*), *El Santero de Córdova* (1981, *The Saintmaker of Córdova*), *Hecho en México* (1982, *Made in Mexico*) (with Nita Luna), *The Green Madonna* (1982), *La Morenita* (1983, *The Little Brown Girl*), *Francis!* (1983), *How Junior Got Throwed in the Joint* (1981), *Plaza* (1984), *Novena Narrativa* (1986, *A Narrative Novena*), *The Step* (1987), *Language of Vision* (1987), and *The Last of the Menu Girls* (1990).

She has also had three of her children's plays produced on stage: *The Adobe Rabbit* (1979), *El Más Pequeño de Mis Hijos* (1983, *The Smallest of My Children*), and *The Flying Tortilla Man* (1975), which was also published in a high school textbook, *Mexican American Literature,* edited by Charles Tatum (1990). Chávez has also edited an anthology of plays, *Plays by Hispanic Women of the United States* (1991).

Despite Chávez's high productivity as a playwright, it is her published works of fiction that have contributed most to her national reputation. Chávez has published short stories in magazines and has two novels in print, *The Last of the Menu Girls* (1986) and *Face of an Angel* (1993). The first of these is a series of stories, centering on the coming of age of Rocío Esquivel, that come together to form a novel. As Rocío compares her own life to that of her mother and as she encounters a wide range of characters in her neighborhood and at work, she begins to formulate her own identity. By the end of the book, we realize that we have been participating in the making of a novelist, and that what we have been reading is the product of Rocío's creative and psychological exploration.

While still centering on the life of a female central character and her development, *Face of an Angel* is completely different from Chavez's first novel. It is an unrestrained, bawdy, irreverent, and hilariously funny novel that explores some of the major themes of the women's liberation movement as represented in the life of a waitress, Soveida Dosamantes, who is an author in her own right (of a manual on waitressing that is included in the novel). Dosamantes is depicted as someone who repeatedly gets involved with the wrong men. The novel consists of her experiences with a number of lazy, good-for-nothing men who are irresistible to her. *Face of an Angel* is populated with a host of humorous and tragic figures that represent a cross section of life in the Southwest.

Sandra Cisneros (1954–)

Sandra Cisneros was born in Chicago, the daughter of a Mexican immigrant father and a Mexican American mother. A graduate of Loyola University in Chicago and of the prestigious University of Iowa Writers' Work with an M.F.A., Cisneros began publishing her poems while she was working at an alternative high school in Chicago, teaching English and creative writing to barrio children. From those days almost to the present, she has developed a creative persona of a young girl and has maintained a youthful reader as her ideal audience. Not only do such essays as her "Notes to a Young Writer" cultivate this relationship, but her most important book, *The House on Mango Street,* casts a teenager, Esperanza, as the narrator and protagonist coming of age with the desire to become a writer. *The House on Mango Street,* published in 1984 by what eventually became the leading Hispanic press, Arte Público Press, became an underground best seller, principally among college and high school students and won the Before Columbus Foundation American Book Award, despite the book having received very few reviews. Today, the loosely framed, novelistic collection of poetic stories is a mainstay on college English and ethnic studies curricula. More importantly, the book became Cisneros' calling card for entrance into mainstream presses. Her next prose venture was a highly regarded collection of essays and stories, *Woman Hollering Creek,* published in 1991 by Random House, which had also bought the rights for and re-issued *The House on Mango Street.* Cisneros published her first full-length collection of poems, *My Wicked Wicked Ways* in 1987 with a Hispanic feminist press, Third Woman Press, of Berkeley, California. In 1995, Cisneros became the first Hispanic writer to win the highly funded and prestigious MacArthur fellowship.

Judith Ortiz Cofer (1952–)

Judith Ortiz Cofer was born in Hormigueros, Puerto Rico, on February 24, 1952, into a family that was destined to move back and forth between Puerto Rico and Paterson, New Jersey. Her father, Jesús Ortiz Lugo, was in the navy, first assigned to the Brooklyn Navy Yard and then other points around the world. In Puertro Rico, the young Judith attended San José Catholic School in San Germán, and in Paterson she went to public schools at first and then to Saint Joseph's Catholic School. In 1968, after her father had retired from the navy with a nervous breakdown, the family moved to Augusta, Georgia, where she attended high school and Augusta College. She met John Cofer at the college and they were married. After graduation and the birth of her daughter, they moved to West Palm Beach, Florida, and she earned an M.A. degree at Florida Alantic University. She was also awarded a scholarship to do graduate work at Oxford University by the English-Speaking Union of America. Included among many other awards were fellowships from the Florida Arts Council (1980), the Bread Loaf Writers Conference (1981), and the National Endowment for the Arts (1989).

While teaching English in south Florida colleges, Cofer began writing poetry, and her works were soon appearing in such magazines as the *New Mexico Humanities Review, Kansas Quarterly, Prairie Schooner, Revista Chicano-Riqueña, Southern Hum-*

Judith Ortiz Cofer.

anities Review, Southern Poetry Review, and elsewhere. Her collections of poetry include four chapbooks—*Latin Women Pray* (1980), *Among the Ancestors* (1981), *The Native Dancer* (1981), *Peregrina* (1986)—and two full-length books—*Reaching for the Mainland* (1987) and *Terms of Survival* (1987). Her well-crafted poetry reflects her struggle as a writer to create a history for herself out of the cultural ambiguity of a childhood spent traveling back and forth between the United States and Puerto Rico. Through her poetry she also explores from a feminist perspective her relationship with her father, mother, and grandmother, while also considering the different expectations for the males and females in Anglo-American and Hispanic cultures. In particular, her book of autobiographical essays, *Silent Dancing: A Remembrance of a Puerto Rican Childhood* (1990), pursues this question. Her novel *The Line of the Sun* (1990) is based on her family's gradual immigration to the United States and chronicles the years from the Great Depression to the 1960s. Since 1992, she has been writing and teaching full-time at the University of Georgia.

Jesús Colón (1901–1974)

Jesús Colón's writings are considered to be landmarks in the development of Puerto Rican literature in the continental United States because he is one of the first writers to become well known through his use of English, because of his identification with the working class, and because of his ideas on race. These three factors in the essays that he was already writing in the 1940s and 1950s make him a clear forerunner of the Nuyorican writers who began to appear two decades later.

Colón was born in 1901 into a working-class family in Cayey, Puerto Rico. At age 16, he stowed away on a ship that landed in Brooklyn. In New York, he worked in a series of jobs that exposed him to the exploitation and abuse of lower-class and unskilled workers. He became involved in literary and journalistic endeavors while working as a laborer, trying to establish a newspaper and writing translations of English-language poetry. As he strived to develop his literary and journalistic career, he encountered racial prejudice, mainly because of his skin color, for Colón was of Afro-Puerto Rican heritage. Despite discrimination, Colón became active in community and political activities. He became a columnist for the *Daily Worker,* the publication of the national office of the Communist party, as an outgrowth of these activities and his literary interests. Colón also founded and operated a publishing house, Hispanic Publishers (Editorial Hispánica), which published history and literary books, as well as political infor-

mation in Spanish. In 1952 and 1969, he ran for public office on the Communist party ticket, but was unsuccessful.

A selection of Colón's newspaper columns and essays was collected and published in 1961 in book form under the title *A Puerto Rican in New York and Other Sketches.* In this work, Colón's major themes are (1) the creation and development of a political consciousness, (2) his own literary development and worth, (3) advocacy for the working-class poor, and (4) the injustices of capitalist society in which racial and class discrimination is all too frequent and individual worth does not seem to exist. The collection as a whole is richly expressive of a socially conscious and humanistic point of view. He died in 1974. In 1994, a second collection of his journalistic columns was published: *The Way It Was and Other Writings.*

Victor Hernández Cruz (1949–)

Victor Hernández Cruz is the Nuyorican poet most recognized and acclaimed by the mainstream. Born on February 6, 1949, in Aguas Buenas, Puerto Rico, he moved with his family to New York's Span-

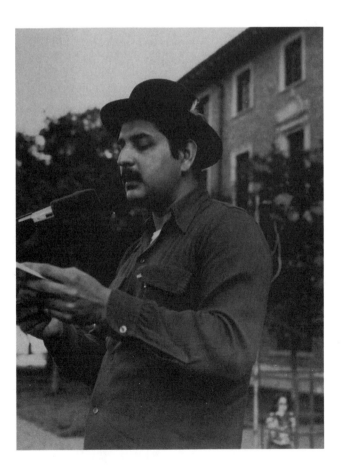

Victor Hernández Cruz.

ish Harlem at age 5. Cruz attended Benjamin Franklin High School, where he began writing poetry. In the years following graduation, his poetry began to appear in *Evergreen Review, New York Review of Books, Ramparts, Down Here,* and in small magazines. In 1973, Cruz left New York and took up residence in San Francisco, where he worked for the U.S. Postal Service. In 1989, he moved back to Puerto Rico, where he currently resides.

Cruz's poetry books include *Papa Got His Gun* (1966), *Snaps* (1969), *Mainland* (1973), *Tropicalization* (1976), *By Lingual Wholes* (1982), and *Rhythm, Content and Flavor* (1989). Classifying his poetry as Afro-Latin, Cruz has developed as a consummate bilingual poet and experimenter who consistently explores the relationship of music to poetry in a multiracial, multicultural context. Cruz has often been considered a jazz poet or an African American poet. The April 1981 issue of *Life* magazine included Cruz among a handful of outstanding American poets.

Abelardo Delgado (19311–)

Abelardo "Lalo" Delgado is one of the most renowned and prolific Chicano poets, a pioneer of bilingualism in Hispanic poetry and a consummate oral performer of his works. Delgado was born in the small town of La Boquilla de Conchos in northern Mexico on November 27, 1931. At age 12 he and his mother immigrated to El Paso, Texas. In El Paso, he lived in a poor Mexican barrio until 1969. Despite early problems in school with the English language, Delgado excelled as a student, and by graduation in 1950 from Bowie High School, he had become vice president of the National Honor Society chapter there. He went on to college while working at a variety of jobs and graduated from the University of Texas, El Paso, in 1962. Since that time he has earned his living as a counselor for migrant workers and as a teacher in Texas and later in Colorado. During the late 1960s and throughout most of the 1970s, Delgado was also one of the most popular speakers and poetry readers in the Southwest, which translated into a life of frequent tours and engagements. This was the height of the Chicano movement, and Delgado was one of its most celebrated animators and poet laureates.

Besides writing numerous poems, essays, and stories that have been published in literary magazines and anthologies nationwide, Delgado is the author of some 14 books and chapbooks; many of these were published through his own small printing operation known as Barrio Press. Delgado's first book, *Chicano: 25 Pieces of a Chicano Mind* (1969), is his best known, containing many of the poems that were

Abelardo Delgado.

performed personally in the heat of the protest movement and that subsequently received widespread distribution through small community newspapers and hand-to-hand circulation throughout the Southwest. Poems such as his "Stupid America" not only embodied the values of life in the barrio but also called for the types of social reform that became anthems for the Chicano movement. Other noteworthy titles include *It's Cold: 52 Cold-Thought Poems of Abelardo* (1974), *Here Lies Lalo: 25 Deaths of Abelardo* (1979), and his book of essays, *Letters to Louise* (1982), which ponder the feminist movement and the social roles of women and men and was awarded the Premio Quinto Sol, the national award for Chicano literature. In all, Delgado is a remarkably agile bilingual poet, an outstanding satirist and humorist, an undaunted and militant protester and pacifist, and a warmhearted and loving narrator and chronicler of the life and tradition of his people.

Roberto Fernández (1951–)

Roberto Fernández is in the vanguard of Cuban American literature, having made the transition from a literature of exile to a literature very much a part of the culture and social conditions of Cubans in the United States, and having made the transition from producing works in Spanish to writing in English. Born in Sagua la Grande, Cuba, on September 24, 1951, just eight years before the Cuban Revolution, he went into exile with his family at age 11. His family settled in southern Florida, not in the Cuban community of Miami but in areas where Anglo-American culture was dominant. This required adjustment to an apparently hostile environment, which accounts for some of the culture conflict that is depicted in his writings. The Fernández family did maintain close ties with the Miami community, and this too became subject matter for the writer. Fernández became interested in writing as an adolescent, and this interest led him to college and graduate school. In 1978, he completed a Ph.D. degree in linguistics at Florida State University; by that time he had already published two collections of stories, *Cuentos sin rumbo* (1975, *Directionless Tales*) and *El jardín de la luna* (1976, *The Garden of the Moon*). At this point he also began his career as an academic, teaching linguistics and Hispanic literature at Florida State University in Tallahassee.

Fernández is the author of three novels that have created for him the reputation of being a satirist and humorist of the Miami Cuban community. In all three, he is a master at capturing the nuances of Cuban dialect in Spanish and English. *La vida es un special* (1982, *Life Is on Special*), *La montaña rusa* (1985, *The Roller Coaster*), *Raining Backwards* (1988), and *Holy Radishes!* (1995) are all mosaics made up of monologues, dialogues, letters, phone conversations, speeches, and other types of oral performance that, in the composite, make up a continuing tale of the development of the exile community and its younger generations of increasingly acculturated Cuban Americans. Through the pages of these books the author charts the goings-on at social clubs and coming-out parties, follows counterrevolutionary guerrilla movements in the Florida swamps and the emergence of a Cuban pope, plots a mystery novel, discusses a poetry and art contest, and gives many other episodic bits and pieces that create a broad spectrum of a dynamic community caught between two cultures, two sets of values, two languages, and two political systems. *Raining Backwards,* Fernández's first book to be published in English, became something of a small press hit, receiving outstanding reviews from coast to coast in major newspapers and magazines (including *The New York Times, USA Today, San Francisco Chronicle*), and was optioned to become a feature film.

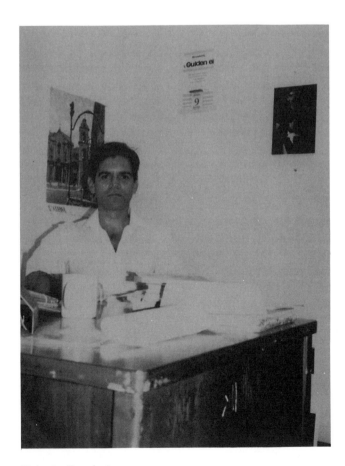

Roberto Fernández.

Lionel G. García (1935–)

Lionel G. García is a novelist who has created some of the most memorable characters in Chicano literature in a style that is steeped in the traditions of Texas tall-tales and Mexican American folk narratives. Born in San Diego, Texas in 1935, García grew up in an environment in which Mexican Americans were the majority population in his small town and on the ranches where he worked and played. García grew up in a middle-class family; his father was an auto body worker and his mother was a teacher. He excelled in school and became one of the few Mexican Americans admitted to Texas A & M University. He majored in biology, but was encouraged by one of his English professors to write. After graduating he attempted to become a full-time writer but was unsuccessful in getting his works published. He served in the army, and after being discharged honorably, he returned to Texas A & M and graduated from that institution in 1969 as a doctor of veterinary science. Since then he has developed a successful career as a veterinarian.

Throughout this time he continued to write. In the early 1980s, he once again attempted to publish, and he found that there were many more opportunities. In 1983, he won the PEN Southwest Discovery

Lionel G. García.

attention most to the trials, tribulations, and successes of the Cuban refugees and their children in the United States. Born on September 9, 1923, in the small town of La Esperanza in central Cuba, González began his education in the neighboring city of Santa Clara at a Catholic school and later graduated from a Protestant high school in the city of Cárdenas. Upon returning to La Esperanza he began working in his family's farming enterprises, which he eventually came to manage. He was a supporter of progressive causes and of Castro's revolution, but by 1960 he had become disillusioned with the revolution and was imprisoned for two months as a counter-revolutionary. Upon release, he immigrated to the United States with his wife and children. In Miami he eked out a living at a number of odd jobs. In 1965, he and his family resettled in Chicago in search of a better living.

It was there that he began writing, but it was not until his return to Miami at age 41 that he wrote his first successful novel, *Los primos* (1971, *The Cousins*), a mirror of Cuban life in Miami during the 1960s. The same year, his short stories depicting the loneliness of Cuban exile life in the United States, *La soledad es una amiga que vendrá* (*Solitude Is a Friend Who Will Come*), were published in book form. His novel *Los cuatro embajadores* (1973, *The Four Ambassadors*) criticizes American capitalism and the dehumanization in American life. His greatest work to date is his *El espesor del pellejo de un gato ya cadáver* (1978, *The Thickness of Skin of a Dead Cat*), a call for Cubans to give up their dreams of returning to the island of their birth and to make the best of life in the United States. González's short stories also deal with American life from the vantage point, quite often, of the Cuban laboring classes and small-scale shopkeepers.

Award for his novel in progress, *Leaving Home,* which was published in 1985. This and his second novel, *A Shroud in the Family* (1987), draw heavily on his family experiences and small-town background. In part, *A Shroud in the Family* also demythologizes the "great" Texas heroes, such as Sam Houston and Jim Bowie, who have become symbols of Anglo-Texans' defeat of and superiority over Mexicans; this was García's contribution to the Texas sesquicentennial celebrations. His novel *Hardscrub* (1989) is a departure from his former works; it is a realistically drawn chronicle of the life of an Anglo child in an abusive family relationship. García has also published short stories in magazines, newspapers, and anthologies. Lionel García's latest works are a novel, *To a Widow with Children* (1994) and a collection of short stories, *I Can Hear the Cowbells Ring* (1994).

Celedonio González (1923–)

Celedonio Gonzalez has been known as "el cronista de la diáspora" (the chronicler of the Cuban diaspora or flight from Cuba). Of all of the Cuban exile novelists, he is the one who has turned his

Oscar Hijuelos (1951–)

Born on August 24, 1951, to Cuban American working-class parents in New York City, Hijuelos was educated in public schools and obtained a B.A. degree in 1975 and an M.A. degree in 1976, both in English, from City College of the City University of New York. While at City College he studied creative writing with the noted novelist Donald Barthelme. Hijuelos is one of the few Hispanic writers to have formally studied creative writing and to have broken into the Anglo-dominated creative writing circles, participating in prestigious workshops such as the Breadloaf Writers Conference, and benefiting from highly competitive fellowships, such as the American Academy in Rome fellowship from the American Academy and the Institute for Arts and Letters

(1985), the National Endowment for the Arts fellowship (1985), and the Guggenheim fellowship (1990).

Hijuelos is the author of numerous short stories and four novels, *Our House in the Last World* (1983), *The Mambo Kings Play Songs of Love* (1989), *The Fourteen Sisters of Emilio Montez O'Brien* (1993), and *Mr. Ives' Christmas* (1995). His first novel follows in the tradition of ethnic autobiography as it chronicles the life and maladjustment of a Cuban immigrant family in the United States during the 1940s. *The Mambo Kings Play Songs of Love* examines a time period in which Hispanic culture was highly visible in the United States and was able to influence American popular culture: it takes place during the 1950s at the height of the mambo craze and the overwhelming success of Desi Arnaz's television show, "I Love Lucy." Written in a poetic but almost documentary style, the novel follows two brothers who are musicians trying to ride the crest of the Latin music wave. While providing a picture of one segment of American life never seen before in English-language fiction, the novel also indicts, as does *Our House in the Last World,* womanizing and alcoholism as particularly Cuban flaws.

Rolando Hinojosa (1929–)

Rolando Hinojosa is the most prolific and well-respected Hispanic novelists in the United States. Not only has he created memorable Mexican American and Anglo characters, but he has completely populated a fictional county in the lower Rio Grande Valley of Texas through his continuing generational narrative that he calls the Klail City Death Trip Series.

Born in Mercedes, Texas, on January 21, 1929, to a Mexican American father and an Anglo-American mother, his paternal ancestors arrived in the lower Rio Grande Valley in 1749 as part of the José Escandón expedition. Hinojosa received his early education in Mexican schools in Mercedes and later in the segregated public schools of the area where all his classmates were Mexican Americans. His classes were not integrated until his junior high years. It was in high school that Hinojosa began to write, publishing his first English pieces in an annual literary magazine entitled *Creative Bits*. Hinojosa left the valley in 1946 when he graduated from college, but the language, culture, and history of the area form the substance of all his novels. The ensuing years saw a stretch in the army, studies at the University of Texas, reactivation into the army to fight in the Korean War (an experience that informs his poetic narrative *Korean Love Songs*), graduation form the University of Texas in 1954 with a degree in Spanish, and back to Brownsville as a teacher,

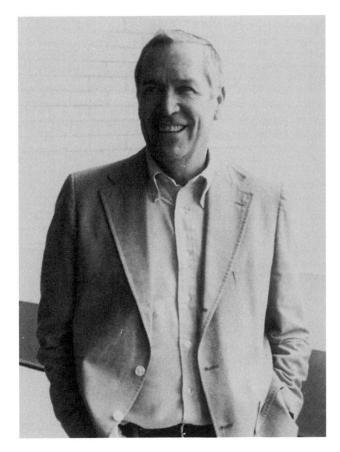

Rolando Hinojosa.

among a variety of other jobs, and finally, on to graduate school. In 1969 he obtained his Ph.D. degree in Spanish from the University of Illinois and returned to teach at Texas colleges. Hinojosa has remained in academia in a variety of positions at several universities; today he serves as Ellen Clayton Garwood Professor of English and Creative Writing at the University of Texas.

Although he has written throughout his life, Hinojosa did not begin publishing until 1973, his first work being *Estampas del Valle y otras obras,* which he recreated in English and published as *The Valley* in 1983. The book won the national award for Chicano literature, Premio Quinto Sol. Since then, he has become one of the most prolific Chicano novelists, publishing one novel after another in his generational narrative that centers on the lives of two of his alter egos, Rafa Buenrostro and Jehú Malacara, in individual installments that vary in form from poetry and dialogue to the picaresque novel and the detective novel. His titles in English alone include *Korean Love Songs* (1980), *Rites and Witnesses* (1982), *Dear Rafe* (1985), *Partners in Crime: A Rafe Buenrostro Mystery* (1985), *Claros varones de*

Belken/Fair Gentlemen of Belken County (1986, bilingual edition), *Klail City* (1987), *Becky and Her Friends* (1989), and *The Useless Servants* (1993). His original Spanish version of *Klail City,* entitled *Klail City y sus alrededores* (1976), won an international award for fiction, Premio Casa de las Américas, from Cuba in 1976; it was issued there under this title and one year later, a version was published in the United States under the title *Generaciones y semblanzas.* The book was also published in German two years later. In addition, Hinojosa has published several short stories and essays, as well as installments of a satirical running commentary on life and current events in the United States, known as "The Mexican American Devil's Dictionary," supposedly created by another of his alter egos who is also one of the narrators of the Klail City Death Trip Series: P. Galindo (meaning "right on target" in Spanish).

Hinojosa has been hailed as a master satirist, an acute observer of the human comedy, a Chicano William Faulkner for his creation of the history and people of Belken County, and a faithful recorder of the customs and dialects in Spanish and English of both Anglos and Mexicans in the lower Rio Grande Valley. One of the best-loved and most highly regarded Hispanic writers, Hinojosa is universally lauded for his commitment to and realistic portrayal of Mexican American life.

Jesús Abraham "Tato" Laviera (1951–)

Jesús Abraham "Tato" Laviera is the best-selling Hispanic poet of the United States, and he bears the distinction of still having all his books in print. Born in Santurce, Puerto Rico, on May 9, 1951, he migrated to New York at age ten with his family, which settled in a poor area of the lower East Side. After finding himself in an alien society and with practically no English, Laviera was able to adjust and eventually graduate high school as an honor student. Despite having no other degrees, his intelligence, aggressiveness, and thorough knowledge of his community led to his developing a career in the administration of social service agencies. After the publication of his first book *La Carreta Made a U-Turn* (1979), Laviera gave up administrative work to dedicate his time to writing. Since 1980, his career has included not only writing but touring nationally as a performer of his poetry, directing plays, and producing cultural events. In 1980, he was received by President Jimmy Carter at the White House gathering of American poets. In 1981, his second book, *Enclave,* was the recipient of the American Book Award of the Before Columbus Foundation.

All Tato Laviera's books have been well received by critics, most of whom place him within the context of Afro-Caribbean poetry and U.S. Hispanic bilingualism. *La Carreta Made a U-Turn* is bilingual, jazz- or salsa-poetry that presents the reader with a slice of life drawn from the Puerto Rican community of the lower East Side. As such, it examines both oppression of the migrant community and its alienation through such popular culture forms as soap operas; it probes crime and drug addiction while affirming the spiritual and social values of the community and the place of art, poetry, and music in what many may consider to be the unlikeliest of social environments. Laviera, here as in the rest of his books, acknowledges and supports the existence of a true Puerto and Latino culture within the heart of the metropolis and within the very belly of the United States. He further affirms that there is no need to return to a homeland on an island or south of the border, for Latinos have made their home here and are transforming not only mainstream culture in the United States, but throughout the hemisphere.

In *Enclave,* Laviera celebrates such cultural heroes, both real and imagined, as Alicia Alonso, Suni Paz, John Lennon, Miriam Makeba, the fictitious

Tato Laviera, 1990. (Photograph by Georgia McInnis.)

half-southern black, half-Puerto Rican Tito Madera Smith, the barrio gossip Juana Bochisme, and the neighborhood tough Esquina Dude. As in *La Carreta Made a U-Turn,* Laviera acknowledges his debt to Afro-Caribbean music and poetry in his eulogies of salsa composer Rafael Cortijo, the famed poetry reciter Juan Boria, and master poets Luis Palés Matos and Nicolás Guillén. *AmeRícan* (1986), published on the occasion of the centennial celebration of the Statue of Liberty, is a poetic reconsideration of immigrant life in New York City and the United States. *Mainstream Ethics* (1988) proposes transforming the United States from a Eurocentric culture to one that is ethnically and racially pluralistic in its official identity. *Continental* (1992), published during the Columbus quincentenary, extends these themes and imperatives to the whole hemisphere.

Despite Laviera's outstanding publishing record, the sophistication of his vision, and his artistic bilingualism, he is an oral poet, a consummate performer of his poetry, which slowly but surely is constituting a living epic of the Hispanic peoples of the United States. Even Laviera's written and published poems have been created out of a process that attempts to re-create as much as possible the oral performance. For Laviera, part of that oral tradition and performance are the structures, spirit, and rhythms of popular and folk music, especially those drawn from Afro-Puerto Rican music.

Nicholasa Mohr, 1990.

Julio Matas

See Chapter 21.

Nicholasa Mohr (1935–)

To date, Nicholasa Mohr is the only Hispanic American woman to have developed a long career as a creative writer for the major publishing houses. Since 1973, her books for such publishers as Dell/Dial, Harper & Row, and Bantam Books, in both the adult and children's literature categories, have won numerous awards and outstanding reviews. Part and parcel of her work is the experience of growing up a female, a Hispanic, and a minority in New York City.

Born on November 1, 1935, in New York City, Nicholasa Mohr was raised in Spanish Harlem. Educated in New York City schools, she finally escaped poverty after graduating from the Pratt Center for Contemporary Printmaking in 1969. From that date until the publication of her first book, *Nilda* (1973), Mohr developed a successful career as a graphic artist. *Nilda,* a novel that traces the life of a young Puerto Rican girl confronting prejudice and coming of age during World War II, won the Jane Addams Children's Book Award and was selected by *School*

Library Journal as a Best Book of the Year. After *Nilda*'s success, Mohr was able to produce numerous stories, scripts, and the following titles: *El Bronx Remembered* (1975), *In Nueva York* (1977), *Felita* (1979), *Rituals of Survival: A Woman's Portfolio* (1985), *Going Home* (1986), *All for the Better* (1992), *Isabel's New Mom* (1993), *Jaime and His Conch Shell* (1994), and *Old Letivia and the Mountain of Sorrows* (1994). Selections from all these story collections have been reprinted widely in a variety of anthologies and textbooks.

Mohr's works have been praised for depicting the life of Puerto Ricans in New York with empathy, realism, and humor. In her stories for children, Mohr has been able to deal with the most serious and tragic of subjects, from the death of a loved one to incest, in a sensitive and humane way. Mohr has been able to contribute to the world of commercial publishing—where stereotypes have reigned supreme—some of the most honest and memorable depictions of Puerto Ricans in the United States. In this and in her crusade to open the doors of publishing and the literary world to Hispanics, Nicholasa Mohr is a true pioneer.

Matías Montes Huidobro

See Chapter 21.

Cherríe Moraga (1952–)

The works of Cherríe Moraga have opened up the world of Chicano literature to the life and aesthetics of feminism and gay women. Moraga's works are well known in both feminist and Hispanic circles for their battles against sexism, classism, and racism. Born in Whittier, California, on September 25, 1952, to a Mexican American mother and an Anglo father, Moraga was educated in public schools in the Los Angeles area, after which she graduated from college with a B.A. degree in English in 1974. While working as a teacher she discovered her interest in writing, and in 1977 moved to the San Francisco Bay Area, where she became acquainted with the Anglo lesbian literary movement. In part to fulfill the requirements for a master's degree at San Francisco State University, Moraga collaborated with Gloria Anzaldúa in compiling the first anthology of writings by women of color, *This Bridge Called My Back: Writings by Radical Women of Color* (1981), which has become the most famous and best-selling anthology of its kind and has inspired a movement of Hispanic feminist and lesbian writers. In her writings here and in other books, Moraga explains that her understanding of racial and class oppression suffered by Chicanas only came as she experienced the prejudice against lesbians. In 1983, Moraga edited another ground-breaking anthology with Alma Gómez and Mariana Romo-Carmona, *Cuentos: Stories by Latinas. Cuentos* attempts to establish a poetics or a canon of Hispanic feminist creativity, a canon where there is room for, and indeed, respect for, the insights of lesbianism. In 1983, Moraga published a collection of her own essays and poems dating back to 1976, *Loving in the War Years: (lo que nunca pasó por sus labios),* in which she explores the dialectical relationship between sexuality and cultural identity. Her conclusion here, as elsewhere, is that women must be put first. Moraga is also a playwright whose work *Giving Up the Ghost* was produced in 1984 and published in 1986. Her latest produced play, *The Shadow of a Man,* was published in 1991. To date, Moraga remains one of the most militant and controversial of the Hispanic literary figures.

Alejandro Morales (1944–)

Alejandro Morales is one of the leading Chicano novelists, having published substantial novels in both Spanish and English in the United States and Mexico and having created through them a better understanding of Mexican American history, at least as seen from the vantage point of working-class cul-

ture. Born in Montebello, California, on October 14, 1944, Morales grew up in East Los Angeles and received his B.A. degree from California State University, Los Angeles. He went on to complete an M.A. degree (1973) and a Ph.D. degree (1975) in Spanish at Rutgers University in New Jersey. Today Morales is a full professor in the Spanish and Portuguese department at the University of California, Irvine.

Morales is at once a recorder of the Chicano experience, basing many of his narratives on historical research, and he is also an imaginative interpreter of that experience by creating memorable and dynamic characters and language. His first books were written in Spanish and published in Mexico, due to the lack of opportunity here in the United States. *Caras viejas y vino nuevo* (1975, translated as *Old Faces and New Wine,* 1981), examines the conflict of generations in a barrio family. *La verdad sin voz* (1979, translated as *Death of an Anglo,* 1988) is a continuation of the earlier novel, but is created against the backdrop of actual occurrences of Chicano-Anglo conflict in the town of Mathis, Texas. The novel also includes autobiographical elements in the form of a section that deals with racism in academia, which

Alejandro Morales.

comes to a head when a Chicano professor goes up for tenure. *Reto en el paraíso* (1983, *Challenge in Paradise*) is based on more than 100 years of Mexican American history and myth, as it centers on a basic comparison of the decline of the famed Coronel family of Californios and the rise of the Irish immigrant Lifford family. The novel charts the transfer of power and wealth from the native inhabitants of California to the gold-and land-hungry immigrants empowered by Manifest Destiny. *The Brick People* (1988) traces the development of two families connected with the Simons Brick Factory, one of the largest enterprises of its type in the country. Again, Morales uses the technique of comparing the lives of two families, those of the owners of the factory and those of an immigrant laborer's family. Morales' novel *The Rag Doll Plagues* (1991), while still incorporating a historical structure, follows the development of a plague and a Spanish Mexican doctor who is forever caught in mortal battle with this plague in three time periods and locations: colonial Mexico, contemporary Southern California, and the future in a country made up of Mexico and California united together.

In all, Morales is a meticulous researcher and a creator of novelistic circumstances that are symbolic of Mexican American history and cultural development. His novels have an epic sweep that are cinematic and highly literary.

Alberto O'Farrill

See Chapter 21.

Josephina Niggli (1910-1983)

Josephina Niggli demonstrated many of the sensibilities that would develop into a full-blown literary movement in the 1960s and 1970s. Born on July 13, 1910, in Monterrey, Mexico, she came to the United States with her parents in 1913 during the Mexican Revolution. Educated in American schools, she attended a Catholic high school in San Antonio, received her B.A. degree from Incarnate Word College (1931), and an M.A. degree from the University of North Carolina (1937). During her adolescence she began her writing career, publishing short stories and poems in such magazines as *Ladies' Home Journal* and *Mexican Life*. By age 18, she had published her first collection of poetry, *Mexican Silhouettes* (1928). She later received training in playwriting and had various plays produced and some screenplays made into Hollywood films. The following plays have been published in anthologies: *Soldadera* (1938), *This Is Villa* (1939), *Red Velvet Goat* (1938), *Sunday Costs Five Pesos* (1939), *Miracle at Blaise* (1942), *The Ring of General Macías* (1943), and *This Bull Ate Nutmeg* (1945). In 1945, the University of North Carolina Press published her novel *Mexican Village*. The press had already published her collection of *Mexican Folk Plays* in 1938; from 1942 on, Niggli embarked upon a career as an instructor and later, a professor of radio, television, theater arts, and speech at the University of North Carolina. While working as a professor at the University of North Carolina, Niggli also published another novel, *Step Down, Elder Brother* (1947), which was so successful that it was distributed by the Book-of-the-Month Club. In 1964, she published a young adult book, *A Miracle for Mexico*. Niggli died in 1983.

Niggli's writings reveal a thorough knowledge of Mexican customs, traditions, and history. Some of her works also analyze the role of women in Mexican life, especially from her bicultural perspective. All of her work set in Mexico can been seen as a mosaic of Mexican life and character types; her depiction of the Mexican Revolution is realistic and epic in nature, acquainting her readers with the struggles that would bring about the birth of modern Mexico.

Gustavo O'Neill

See Chapter 21.

Américo Paredes

See Chapter 17.

Pedro Pietri (1943-)

Pedro Pietri is famous for the literary persona of street urchin or skid-row bum that he has created for himself. His works are characterized by the consistent perspective of the underclass in language, philosophy, and creative and psychological freedom. Pietri was born in Ponce, Puerto Rico, on March 21, 1943, just two years before his family migrated to New York. He was orphaned of both parents while still a child and raised by his grandmother. Pietri attended public schools in New York City and served in the army from 1966 to 1968. Other than his having taught writing occasionally and participated in workshops, very little else is known about this intentionally mysterious and unconventional figure.

Pietri has published collections of poems and poetry chapbooks: *The Blue and the Gray* (1975), *Invisible Poetry* (1979), *Out of Order* (1980), *Uptown Train* (1980), *An Alternate* (1980), and *Traffic Violations* (1983). Nevertheless, it was his first book of poetry, *Puerto Rican Obituary* (1971), that brought him his greatest fame and a host of imitators. In 1973, a live performance by him of poems from this book was recorded and distributed by Folkways Records. In 1980, Pietri's short story *Lost in the Museum of Natural History* was published in bilingual format in Puerto Rico. Pietri has also had numerous unpublished, but produced, plays and one published collection, *The Masses Are Asses* (1984). Always a master of the incongruous and surprising, Pietri has created unlikely but humorous narrative situations in both his poetry and plays, such as that in his poem "Suicide Note from a Cockroach in a Low Income Housing Project" and in a dialogue between a character and her own feces in his play *Appearing in Person Tonight—Your Mother*. Pietri's work is one of a total break with conventions, both literary and social, and it is subversive in its open rejection of established society and its hypocrisies.

Miguel Piñero

See Chapter 21.

Dolores Prida

See Chapter 21.

Tomás Rivera

See Chapter 17.

Richard Rodríguez (1944–)

Essayist Richard Rodríguez was born on July 31, 1944, in San Francisco, the son of Mexican immigrants. Having begun school as a Spanish-speaker, he had to make the difficult transition to English in order to progress in school. As he recalled in his autobiographical book-length essay, *Hunger of Memory,* he came to believe that English was the language of U.S. school and society and that the Spanish language and Hispanic culture were private matters, for the home. Rodríguez went on to have outstanding success in school and eventually received a B.A. in English from Stanford University in 1967, and M.A. from Columbia University in 1969 and doctoral work at the University of California, which he never terminated because his writing career had begun and he had not submitted his dissertation. In 1981, Rodríguez published the above mentioned autobiography which received praise from mainstream critics across the nation for its elegant and passionate prose as well as for its rejection of bilingual education and affirmative action programs. Rodríguez immediately was seen by Hispanics as an Uncle Tom or Tío Taco for having bought success at the price of attacking Hispanic language, culture and programs aimed to assist Hispanics in education and employment. To this date, despite a successful career as an essayist, television commentator and opinion writer for newspapers, Rodríguez is not embraced by Hispanic critics as an authentic or valuable voice. His second book, *Days of Obliga-*

tion: An Argument with My Mexican Father (1992), which does not have the political content of *Hunger of Memory,* received fewer, but generally good reviews and passed with very little criticism by from Hispanic quarters.

Ricardo Sánchez (1941–1995)

Ricardo Sánchez was one of the most prolific Chicano poets, one of the first creators of a bilingual literary style, and one of the first to be identified with the Chicano movement. Born the youngest of 13 children on March 21, 1941, he was raised in the notorious Barrio del Diablo (Devil's Neighborhood) in his hometown of El Paso, Texas. He was a high school dropout, an army enlistee, and later a repeat offender sentenced to several prison terms in both Soledad Prison in California and Ramsey Prison Farm Number One in Texas; at these prisons he began his literary career, shortly before his last parole in 1969. Much of his early life experience, which includes oppressive poverty, overwhelming racism, suffering in prisons, and his self-education and rise to a level of political and social consciousness, is chronicled in his poetry, which although very lyrical, is considered the most autobiographical of all the Hispanic poets. Once his writing career was established and Sánchez began to publish his works with both mainstream and alternative literary presses, he assumed a number of visiting appointments as a professor or writer in residence at various universities. He was a founder of the short-lived Mictla Publications in El Paso, editor of various special issues of literary magazines, such as *De Colores* and *Wood/Ibis,* a columnist for the *San Antonio Express,* a bookseller, a migrant worker counselor, and remains an active performer of his poetry on tours in the United States and abroad.

Sánchez's poetry is characterized by an unbridled linguistic inventiveness that not only calls upon both English and Spanish lexicon but is also a source of neologisms and surprising combinations of the sounds and symbols of both languages in single works. His work can be virile and violent at one moment and delicate and sentimental at the next, as he follows the formulas and dictates of a poetry written for oral performance. His is often the exaggerated gesture and emotion of the *declamador* (poetic orator), whose works are performed to inspire a protest rally, inaugurate a mural, celebrate a patriotic holiday, or eulogize the dead. Most of all, Sánchez was an autobiographical poet who cast himself as a Chicano Everyman participating in the epic history of his people through his poetry. His bilingual facility and immense vocabulary and inventiveness were legendary in Chicano literature.

Ricardo Sánchez.

Besides publishing hundreds of poems in magazines and anthologies, Sánchez was the author of the following collections: *Canto y grito mi liberación (y lloro mis desmadrazgos) (I Sing and Shout for My Liberation [and Cry for My Insults]*, 1971), *Hechizospells: Poetry / Stories / Vignettes / Articles / Notes on the Human Condition of Chicanos & Pícaros, Words and Hopes within Soulmind* (1976), *Milhuas Blues and Gritos Norteños* (1980), *Amsterdam cantos y poemas pistos* (1983), *Selected Poems* (1985), and *American Journeys* (1995).

Gustavo Solano

See Chapter 21.

Gary Soto (1952–)

In academic and creative writing circles, Soto is considered the most outstanding Chicano poet; he is certainly the most widely known Hispanic poet in the Anglo-American poetry establishment, as represented by creative writing departments, magazines, and workshops. Born to Mexican American parents in Fresno, California, on April 12, 1952, Soto was raised in the environs of the San Joaquin Valley and attended Fresno City College and California State University in Fresno, where he came under the guidance of poet Philip Levine and his creative writing career was born. Soto graduated magna cum laude from California State University in 1975, and in 1976 he earned an M.F.A. degree in creative writing from the University of California, Irvine. From 1977 until 1993, when he began writing full-time, he taught at the University of California, Berkeley, in the English and ethnic studies departments.

Soto has more prestigious awards than any other Hispanic poet in the United States, including the Academy of American Poets Prize in 1975, the

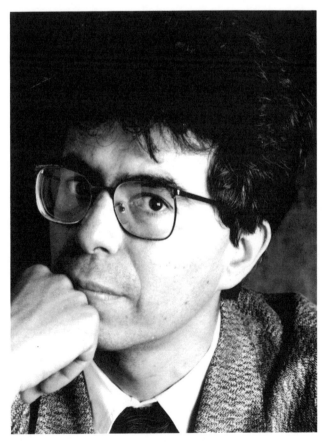

Gary Soto, 1991. (Photograph by M. L. Marinelli.)

Discovery-Nation Award in 1975, the United States Award of the International Poetry Forum in 1976, the Bess Hopkins Prize from *Poetry* magazine in 1977, a Guggenheim fellowship in 1979, a National Association fellowship in 1981, the Levinson Award from *Poetry* magazine in 1984, and the American Book Award from the Before Columbus Foundation in 1984.

Soto's books of poetry include the following: *The Elements of San Joaquin* (1977), *Father Is a Pillow Tied to a Broom* (1980), *Where Sparrows Work Hard* (1981), *Black Hair* (1985), *Who Will Know Us?* (1990), *Home Course in Religion: New Poems* (1991), and *New and Selected Poems* (1995). Soto has also published three collections of autobiographical essays and stories: *Living Up the Street: Narrative Recollections* (1985), *Small Faces* (1986), *Lesser Evils: Ten Quartets* (1988), *A Summer Life* (1990), and *The Bike* (1991). During the 1990s, Gary Soto launched a new career as a prolific writer for young adults and children, largely through commercial houses that were seeking to serve the burgeoning Hispanic school-age population. From 1990 to 1995 along, he published 12 such titles, including the highly regarded *Baseball in April and Other Stories* (1990), *The Pool Party* (1993), *Too Many Tamales* (1993), *Jesse* (1994), and *Chato's Kitchen* (1995). He has also produced two short films: *The Pool Party,* based on his book of the same title (1993), and *Novio Boy* (1994).

All of Soto's works are highly autobiographical and characterized by a highly polished craft. In his poetry and prose, there is also a great attention paid to narration and characterization; whether he is writing a poem or an essay, Soto is always cognizant of telling a story. Critics have always stated that Soto has something important and human to say, and it is poignantly said in well-crafted writing. While writing from his particular ethnic stance and worldview, he also maintains that there are certain values, experiences, and feelings that are universal.

Piri Thomas (1928–)

Piri Thomas is one of the most widely known cultivators of ethnic autobiography; his *Down These Mean Streets* (1976) was so successful as a powerful chronicle of growing up in the barrio that it spawned a host of Puerto Rican imitators. Piri (John Peter) Thomas was born on September 30, 1928, in New York City, to a Puerto Rican mother and a Cuban father. Thomas grew up during the Great Depression, facing both poverty and racism in New York's East Harlem. American society perceived Thomas as black, while his family perceived him as Puerto Rican and encouraged his identification with the

island that he had never seen. However, out on the streets and later in prison, he began to see himself as an African American, and to take pride in that identity, even becoming a Black Muslim for a while.

Thomas entered a life of theft, gang violence, and criminality in adolescence, and he eventually landed in prison. After serving seven years of a 15-year term, he was paroled at age 28. While in prison he had obtained his high school equivalency diploma and also had begun to learn to express himself in writing; he also developed a sense of dignity and self-respect. After returning to his old neighborhood and then to his family, who now lived in Long Island, he worked at a variety of jobs, but eventually developed his career as a writer.

All of Thomas' literary works are highly autobiographical, dealing mostly with his upbringing in the atmosphere of poverty, racism, and culture conflict in the barrio. In addition to his well-known *Down These Mean Streets,* Thomas also wrote a sequel, *Saviour, Saviour Hold My Hand* (1972), and a book on his seven-year imprisonment, *Seven Long Times* (1974). He has also published a collection of stories, *Stories from el Barrio* (1978). In addition, Thomas has written numerous articles and essays and has written plays that have been produced on stage. Thomas' works are important for having entered the mainstream, with all of his books issued by major publishers, and *Down These Mean Streets* was so highly reviewed that it projected Thomas into the television talk-show circuit and instant celebrity. A powerful and charming speaker, Thomas became an important spokesperson for the Puerto Rican community. In his books and in his public presentations he became identified with the search for identity, and to many readers and critics of the time this became the most important characteristic of Hispanic literature in the United States.

Omar Torres

See Chapter 21.

Estela Portillo Trambley (1936–)

Estela Portillo Trambley is one of the first women writers to successfully publish prose in the early male-dominated stages of the Chicano literary movement. Born in El Paso, Texas, on January 16, 1936, she was raised and educated in El Paso, where she attended high school and the University of Texas, El Paso, for her B.A. degree (1957) and her M.A. degree (1977). After graduation from college, she became a high school English teacher and administrator. Since 1979, she has been affiliated with the Department of Special Services of the El Paso Public

Schools. From 1970 to 1975, she served as dramatist in residence at El Paso Community College.

Trambley was the first woman to win the national award for Chicano literature, Premio Quinto Sol, in 1973, for her collection of short stories and novela *Rain of Scorpions and Other Writings,* which was published in 1975. Besides stories and plays published in magazines and anthologies, Portillo Trambley has written a collection of plays, *Sor Juana and Other Plays* (1981), and a novel, *Trini* (1983). In both her prose and drama, Portillo Trambley develops strong women who resist the social roles that have been predetermined for them because of their sex. In her fiction, women command center stage and achieve a level of self-determination and control over social and cultural circumstances. The culmination of her pursuit of strong women is represented in her exploration of the life of the eighteenth-century poet and essayist Sor Juan Inés de la Cruz in her play *Sor Juana.* The protagonist of her novel, *Trini,* is a fictional character who struggles against poverty and adversity to make her way in life; she eventually leaves Mexico and crosses the border illegally to find the power over her own life for which she has been searching.

Sabine Ulibarrí (1919–)

Short story writer, poet, and essayist Sabine Ulibarrí has had one of the longest and most productive literary careers in Chicano literature. He is a well-known and highly respected chronicler of the way things once were in his beloved New Mexico. Born on September 21, 1919, in the small village of Tierra Amarilla, New Mexico, he was raised on a ranch by his parents, both of whom were college graduates. Besides learning the ways of rural life and the rugged countryside, Ulibarrí also experienced firsthand the folk culture of the area, which included not only the full repository of oral literature but also a strong connection to the language and oral literature of Spain and the Spanish-speaking Americas. His early love for the Spanish language and Hispanic literature took Ulibarrí to college and eventually to a Ph.D. degree in Spanish. Over the years he taught at every level, from elementary school to graduate school, except during World War II, when he flew 35 combat missions as an air force gunner. Today he is a professor emeritus of the University of New Mexico, where he spent most of his academic career as a student and professor.

Among Ulibarrí's awards are the following: Governor's Award for Excellence in Literature (1988), Distinguished Alumni Award and Regents' Medal of Merit, University of New Mexico (1989), and the White House Hispanic Heritage Award (1989). Uli-

Sabine Ulibarrí.

barrí has had published two books of poems, *Al cielo se sube a pie* (1966, *You Reach Heaven on Foot*) and *Amor y Ecuador* (1966, *Love and Ecuador*), and the following collections of short stories in bilingual format: *Tierra Amarilla: Stories of New Mexico/Tierra Amarilla: Cuentos de Nuevo México* (1971), *Mi abuela fumaba puros y otros cuentos de Tierra Amarilla/My Grandma Smoked Cigars and Other Stories of Tierra Amarilla* (1977), *Primeros encuentros/First Encounters* (1982), *El gobernador Glu Glu* (1988, *Governor Glu Glu*), and *El Cóndor and Other Stories* (1989).

In all of his work, Ulibarrí preserves a style, narrative technique, and language that owes much to the oral folk tradition. Through his works he has been able to capture the ethos and the spirit of rural New Mexico before the coming of the Anglo. His works memorialize myths and legends and such distinctive characters of the past as cowboys, sheriffs, folk healers, penitents, and just the common everyday folk. Quite often writing two versions of the same story, in English and Spanish, in all of modern Chicano literature his works are among the most direct and accessible to broad audiences.

Luis Valdez

See Chapter 21.

Ed Vega (1936–)

Ed Vega is a Puerto Rican fiction writer who bases many of his works on life in New York City's Spanish Harlem. Edgardo Vega Yunqué was born in Ponce, Puerto Rico, on May 20, 1936, where he lived with his family until they moved to the Bronx, New York, in 1949. He was raised in a devout Baptist home, his father having been a minister of that faith; today, Vega and his wife and children have adopted the Buddhist faith. As a child, books were very accessible at home, and he began both his education and writing at an early age in Spanish in Puerto Rico. After moving to New York and going through the public education system of the city, he served in the air force and studied at Santa Monica College in California under the G.I. Bill. In 1963, Vega almost graduated as a Phi Beta Kappa from New York University with a major in political science; he was short three hours of credit and did not actually graduate until 1969. He did not return to finish until that date because he had become disillusioned after personally experiencing racism at the university. After leaving

Ed Vega.

there in 1963, he worked in a variety of social service programs. In 1969, he returned to academic life as a lecturer for Hunter College and thereafter assumed various other lecturing and assistant professor positions at other colleges. From 1977 to 1982, he worked at such community-based education programs as ASPIRA of New Jersey. From 1982 to the present, he has been a full-time writer.

Vega is one of the most prolific Hispanic prose writers, although much of his work remains unpublished. In 1977, his short stories began to be published by Hispanic magazines, such as *Nuestro, Maize* and *Revista Chicano-Riqueña*. In 1985, his novel *The Comeback,* a rollicking satire of ethnic autobiography and the identity crisis, as personified by a half-Puerto Rican, half-Eskimo ice hockey player who becomes involved in an underground revolutionary movement for Puerto Rican independence, was published. In 1987, a collection of interconnected short stories, *Mendoza's Dreams,* narrated by a warmhearted observer of the human comedy, Alberto Mendoza, was published. An additional common thread holding these barrio stories together is their charting of various Puerto Ricans on the road to success in the United States; thus, once again we have a Puerto Rican interpretation of the American dream. Vega's third book, *Casualty Report* (1991), is just the opposite; for the most part the collection of stories included here chronicle the death of dreams, as characters faced with racism, poverty, and crime succumb to despair in many forms: violence, alcohol and drug abuse, withdrawal, and resignation.

Daniel Venegas

Daniel Venegas was a harbinger of today's Chicano writers not only in openly proclaiming a Chicano identity and pursuing working-class language but also in generating a style and a literary attitude that would come to typify the Chicano novels of the late 1960s and the 1970s. Very little is known of his life. Born and raised in Mexico, his level of formal education is uncertain. In Los Angeles, he maintained an active life in the world of Mexican journalism and the theater during the 1920s and 1930s. There he founded and edited a weekly satirical newspaper, *El malcriado (The Brat)*, from 1924 into the 1930s. He was the director of a popular vaudeville theatrical company and the author of numerous plays, short stories, and one novel that relates to the language, customs, and values of working-class Mexican immigrants, who at that time were known as *chicanos.*

All of his theatrical works have been lost, only one issue of *El malcriado* has been located (this containing two short stories by Venegas). His novel, *Las aventuras de Don Chipote o Cuando los pericos mamen* (1928, *The Adventures of Don Chipote or When Parakeets Suckle Their Young*), was rediscovered and reissued in 1985. *Don Chipote* is the humorous tale of the trials and tribulations of one Don Chipote, who immigrates to the United States from Mexico believing naively that he can shovel up the gold from the streets and send it back to his family. The novel becomes a picaresque story of Chipote's struggle to survive in the alien environment while facing oppression and exploitation from foremen and representatives of industry and the legal authorities. In the course of the novel Chipote also serves as a target for con men and other underworld characters bent on fleecing him. The satirical tale ends with a moral that warns Mexicans not to come to the United States in search of riches. What is important about *Don Chipote* is the identification of the author-narrator with Chicanos and his having as ideal readers the Chicanos themselves. Not only does it imply that a good portion of those workers knew how to read, but also that those workers, like the author himself, were capable of producing literature and art.

Víctor E. Villaseñor (1940–)

Víctor Villaseñor is a novelist and screenwriter who has brought Chicano literature to mainstream audiences through his novel of immigration, *Macho!*, issued in 1973 by the world's largest paperback publisher, Bantam Books; through the epic saga of his own family in *Rain of Gold* (1991); and through the television screenplay *The Ballad of Gregorio Cortez*, the miniseries *Rain of Gold,* and the feature film, *Macho.* Born on May 11, 1940, in Carlsbad, California, the son of Mexican immigrants, Villaseñor was raised on a ranch in Oceanside and experienced great difficulty with the educational system, having started school as a Spanish-speaker and dyslexic. He dropped out of high school and worked on the ranch and in the fields and as a construction worker. After attempting college at the University of San Diego for a brief period, he again dropped out and went to live in Mexico, where he discovered the world of books and learned to take pride in his identity and cultural heritage. From then on he read extensively and taught himself the art of writing fiction. During years of work in California as a construction worker, he completed nine novels and 65 short stories, all of which were rejected for publication, except for *Macho!*, which launched his professional writing career. His second publishing venture was the nonfiction narrative of the life and trial of a serial killer, *Jury: The People versus Juan Corona* (1977). Negative experiences with stereotyping and discrimina-

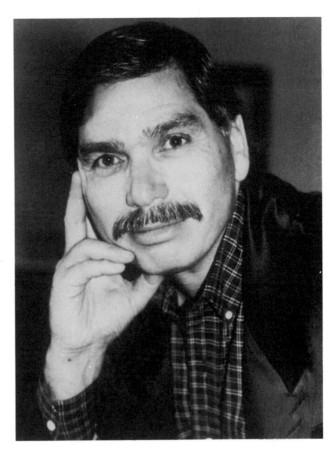

Víctor E. Villaseñor.

tion of Hispanics in the commercial publishing world led Villaseñor to publish his most important literary effort with a small, not-for-profit Hispanic press, Arte Público Press of Houston.

Macho! tells the tale of a young Mexican Indian's illegal entry into the United States to find work; it is in many ways a classic novel of immigration, though it departs from the model in that, upon return to his hometown in central Mexico, the protagonist has been forever changed. He is unable to accept the traditional social code, especially as it concerns *machismo. Rain of Gold* is the nonfiction saga of various generations of Villaseñor's own family, their experiences during the Mexican Revolution, and their eventual immigration to California. The saga is narrated in a style full of spiritualism and respect for myths and oral tradition, derived not only from Villaseñor's own childhood but also from the years of interviews and research that he did in preparing the book. The popularity of *Rain of Gold* has brought to millions of Americans one family's stories of the social, economic, and political struggles in Mexico that have resulted in widespread Mexican immigration to the United States, a place where new stories of racism, discrimination, and the triumph over these barriers continue to develop in the epic of Mexican American life. In 1994 and 1996, respectively, Villaseñor published two sequels to *Rain of Gold* featuring his parents and grandparents in Mexico—*Walking Stars and Other Stories* and *Wild Steps of Heaven*—the former to glowing reviews and the latter to very mixed commentary.

Jose Yglesias (1919–1995)

Jose Yglesias was born in the Ybor City section of Tampa, Florida, and grew up within the tradition of Cuban cigar rollers. As a young man he moved to Grenwich village, New York City, to become a writer. From his early twenties on, he became politically engaged; his politics would initiate him in the groups of writers and artists who militated against fascism in Spain under Franco, who promoted Socialism in the United States and who were the first supporters of Fidel Castro in Cuba. His early journalistic writing, in the *Daily Worker* and elsewhere, during the late 1940s and early 1950s eventually led to his opening several journalistic books on Spain and Cuba, such as *The Goodbye Land* in 1967, *In the Fist of the Revolution: Life in a Cuban Country Town* in 1968, *Down There* in 1970 and *The Franco Years* in 1977. But it is Yglesias' work as a novelist that is most enduring, with his very humane narrators, eloquent prose and sly humor as noteworthy. Moreover, Yglesias is one of the very first U.S. Hispanic writers to be published by mainstream presses in the United States. His first novel, *A Death in Ybor City* is considered to be a classic of U.S. Hispanic literature. His other novels include *The Kill Price* (1976) and *Tristan and the Hispanics*. Yglesias was a working writer until his death from cancer in 1995. Two important new and highly received novels were published posthumously: *Break-in* (1996), set in Tampa and exploring the theme of race relations, and *The Old Gent* (1996), set in New York and dealing with the final days of an aging novelist. Jose Yglesias is the father of novelist and screen writer Rafael Yglesias.

Jose Yglesias.

References

Kanellos, Nicolás. *Biographical Dictionary of Hispanic Literature in the United States.* Westport, Connecticut: Greenwood Press, 1989.

Lomelí, Francisco, and Julio A. Martínez, eds. *Chicano Literature: A Reference Guide.* Westport, Connecticut: Greenwood Press, 1985.

——, and Carl F. Shirley, eds. *Chicano Writers: First Series.* Detroit: Gale Research, 1989.

Tatum, Charles M. *Chicano Literature.* Boston: Twayne, 1982.

Nicolás Kanellos

Illustrations

A Historical Overview:

p. 4: Isabella of Castile (reproduced by permission of Archive Photos); p. 5: Major paths of early European penetration of the United States (courtesy of U.S. Department of the Interior and the National Park Service); p. 14: A vaquero in early California (reproduced by permission of the Bancroft Library, University of California); p. 15: Viceroy Francisco Fernández de la Cueva Enríques, Duke of Albuquerque; p. 15: Rules that were issued by the King of Spain regarding the founding and governance of presidios on the frontier; p. 17: European claims in the United States to 1763 (courtesy of U.S. Department of the Interior and the National Park Service); p. 18: Presidio and pueblo of Santa Barbara in 1829 (from a lithograph by G. & W. Endicott; reproduced by permission of the Bancroft Library, University of California); p. 19: Soldier at the Monterey presidio in 1786 (reproduced by permission of the Bancroft Library, University of California); p. 20: Wife of a presidio soldier in Monterey, 1786 (reproduced by permission of the Bancroft Library, Univesity of California); p. 20: A patrón in early California (reproduced by permission of the Bancroft Library, University of California); p. 21: General Manuel Mier y Terán, Laredo; p. 23: Pío Pico (1801–1894) was the last governor of California under Mexican rule (reproduced by permission of the California Historical Society); p. 29: Confederate officers from Laredo, Texas: Refugio Benavides, Atanacio Vidaurri, Cristóbal Benavides, and John Z. Leyendecker (courtesy of the Laredo Public Library); p. 29: Albizu Campos, leader of the Puerto Rican independence movement, at a press conference on December 16, 1947; p. 30: Luis Muños-Rivera, patriot of Puerto Rican independence; p. 43: Luis Muñoz Marín, architect of the present commonwealth status of Puerto Rico; p. 47: Fidel Castro; p. 48: The first flight of American citizens repatriated from Cuba on December 19, 1966; p. 50: Cubans arriving in Miami during the Mariel boat-lift; p. 51: A legally immigrating Cuban woman is reunited with her granddaughter in Miami in 1980 (reproduced by permission of the Texas Catholic Herald).

Spanish Explorers and Colonizers:

p. 58: Frontispiece from the original 1493 edition of Cristóbal Colón's letter to the Catholic Kings describing his discoveries (reproduced by permission of Arte Público Press); p. 59: Juan Ponce de León; p. 64: Title page of Cabeza de Vaca's account of his trip, La relación, 1542 (reproduced by permission of Arte Público Press); p. 67: A portrayal of Hernando de Soto by an unknown eighteenth-century artist (courtesy of U.S. Department of the Interior and the National Park Service); p. 68: Pedro Menéndez de Avilés (reproduced by permission of Arte Público Press); p. 69: Drawing of the type of free black militia that were stationed in Spanish colonies in Florida and elsewhere, 1795 (reproduced by permission of Arte Público Press).

Historic Landmarks:

p. 134: Carmel Mission (reproduced by permission of Bettmann Archives); p. 136: Royal Presidio Chapel, Monterey (courtesy of U.S. Department of the Interior and the National Park Service); p. 137: San Francisco de Asís Mission (Mission Dolores) (Archive Photos); *p. 138:* San Luis Rey de Francia Mission, Oceanside (photograph by Henry F. Whitey, 1936, W.P.A); *p. 139:* Santa Barbara Mission (photograph by Henry F. Whitey, 1936, W.P.A); *p. 139:* General Vallejo House (photograph by Roger Sturtevant, 1934); *p. 141:* The Cabildo in New Orleans (courtesy of U.S. Department of the Interior and the National Park Service); *p. 142:* Palace of the Governors, Santa Fe (reproduced by permission of Associated Press/Wide World); *p. 142:* San Miguel Mission, Santa Fe (courtesy of U.S. Department of the Interior and the National Park Service); *p. 143:* Convent of Porta Coeli, San Germán; *p. 143:* The Alamo, San Antonio (courtesy of U.S. Department of the Interior and the National Park Service); *p. 145:* Monument honoring the fallen at the Alamo, San Antonio (courtesy of U.S. Department of the Interior and the National Park Service); *p. 146:* San Francisco de la Espada Mission, San Antonio; *p. 146:* San José y San Miguel de Aguayo Mission, (photograph by Arthur W. Stewart, 1936, W.P.A).

Relations with Spain and Spanish America:

p. 152: An early rally in East Lower Harlem (El Barrio) in Manhattan in support of the independence of Puerto Rico (reproduced by permission of The Jesús Colón Papers. Center for Puerto Rican Studies, Hunter College, CUNY; Benigno Giboyeaux for the Estate of Jesús Colón; and the Communist Party of the United States of America); *p. 170:* Archbishop Oscar Romero of El Salvador (reproduced by permission of *Texas Catholic Herald*); *p. 170:* Guerrillas of El Frente Farabundo Martí por Liberación Nacional (FMLN) in El Salvador; *p. 171:* Demonstrators on the U.S. capitol steps opposing U.S. military aid to El Salvador in 1980 (reproduced by permission of *Texas Catholic Herald*).

Population Growth and Distribution:

p. 186: Senior citizens at the Domino Park in Little Havana, Miami (reproduced by permission of *Texas Catholic Herald*); *p. 187:* Undocumented workers entering the United States at El Paso, Texas, 1990 (reproduced by permission of *Texas Catholic Herald*); *p. 188:* A group of Hispanics have just been issued their temporary residence cards, 1991 (photograph by Les Fetchko, *Texas Catholic Herald*); *p. 189:* The drive to legalize undocumented workers in Houston, Texas (photograph by Curtis Dowell, reproduced by permission of *Texas Catholic Herald*); *p. 190:* Mexican Independence Day Parade, Houston, Texas, 1982 (photograph by Curtis Dowell, reproduced by permission of *Texas Catholic Herald*); *p. 192:* A mass citizenship swearing-in ceremony at Hoffheinz Pavilion, University of Houston, 1987 (photograph by Curtis

Dowell, reproduced by permission of *Texas Catholic Herald*).

Language:

p. 196: The Teatro Puerto Rico in October 1960 (reproduced by permission of Justo A. Martí Collection, Center for Puerto Rican Studies Library, Hunter College, CUNY); *p. 202:* Downtown El Paso, Texas (reproduced by permission of *Texas Catholic Herald*); *p. 204:* Two scenes from the "Villa Alegre" television series; *p. 205:* A customer buying *La prensa,* the Spanish-language daily newspaper (reproduced by permission of Justo A. Martí Collection, Center for Puerto Rican Studies Library, Hunter College, CUNY); *p. 206:* A typical Hispanic grocery store in New York City (reproduced by permission of Justo A. Martí Collection, Center for Puerto Rican Studies Library, Hunter College, CUNY); *p. 208:* A voter-registration drive in New York City (reproduced by permission of Justo A. Martí Collection, Center for Puerto Rican Studies Library, Hunter College, CUNY); *p. 209:* Our Lady of Guadalupe Church in Queen Creek, Arizona (reproduced by permission of *Texas Catholic Herald*).

The Family:

p. 214: The Lugo Family at Bell Gardens, California, circa 1888 (Los Angeles County Museum of Natural History); *p. 215:* A child's birthday party in New York City (reproduced by permission of Justo A. Martí Collection, Center for Puerto Rican Studies Library, Hunter College, CUNY); *p. 216:* Community action through family and parent power: United Bronx Parents, Inc. (reproduced by permission of Records of the United Brox Parents, Inc., Center for Puerto Rican Studies Library, Hunter College, CUNY); *p. 217:* A Puerto Rican mine worker in Bingham Canyon, Utah (reproduced by permission of Historical Archive, Departamento de Asuntos de la Comunidad Puertorriqueña, Center for Puerto Rican Studies Library, Hunter College, CUNY); *p. 221:* Mexican Mother of the Year, 1969: Dolores Venegas and her husband, Miguel, Houston, Texas (reproduced by permission of *Texas Catholic Herald*).

Women:

p. 237: A beauty queen for the Fiestas Patrias celebration, Houston, Texas (photograph by Curtis Dowell, reproduced by permission of *Texas Catholic Herald*); *p. 237:* Poster advertising a Hispanic women's conference in Texas in 1987 (reproduced by permission of Arte Público Press); *p. 239:* A workshop at the Chicana Issues Conference, California, 1980; *p. 245:* Polly Baca-Barragán; *p. 246:* Teresa Bernárdez; *p. 249:* Emyré Barrios Robinson (reproduced by permission of Arte Público Press); *p. 250:* Carmen Delgado Votaw.

Religion:

p. 255: The Franciscan method of teaching the Indians by pictures (from an engraving based on Fray Diego Valdés, O.F.M., in his *Rhetorica Christiana,* Rome, 1579); *p. 255:* Bartolemé de las Casas (1474–1566); *p. 256:* San Juan Capistrano Mission in San Antonio, Texas (photograph by Silvia Novo Pena, reproduced by permission of *Texas Catholic Herald*); *p. 257:* The image of Our Lady of Guadalupe on tour from Mexico at Our Lady of Guadalupe Church in Houston, Texas, 1992 (photograph by Curtis Dowell, reproduced by permission of *Texas Catholic Herald*); *p. 266:* Feast of the Crowning of Mary, Sacred Heart Cathedral, Houston, 1987 (photograph by Curtis Dowell, reproduced by permission of *Texas Catholic Herald*); *p. 267:* Annual mass on the feast day of Our Lady of Guadalupe, Houston, Texas (reproduced by permission of *Texas Catholic Herald*); *p. 268:* The celebration of the feast day of Our Lady of Caridad del Cobre, in Houston, 1986 (photograph by Curtis Dowell, reproduced by permission of *Texas Catholic Herald*); *p. 269:* A Christmas *posada* sponsored by the Club Sembradores de la Amistad in Houston, 1988 (photograph by Curtis Dowell, reproduced by permission of *Texas Catholic Herald*); *p. 270:* Diversity in Hispanic evangelism (photograph by Curtis Dowell, reproduced by permission of *Texas Catholic Herald*); *p. 271:* A Catholic charismatic prayer meeting (reproduced by permission of *Texas Catholic Herald*).

Military:

p. 277: Santos Benavides; *p. 277:* Robert Léon Cárdenas; *p. 278:* Richard E. Cavazos; *p. 279:* Francisco de Miranda; *p. 279:* Luis R. Esteves; *p. 280:* David G. Farragut; *p. 280:* Diego E. Hernández; *p. 281:* Edward Hidalgo; *p. 281:* Benjamin F. Montoya; *p. 282:* Horacio Rivera; *p. 282:* Carmelita Schemmenti; *p. 283:* Juan N. Seguín.

Law and Politics:

p. 296: Four charts on law school enrollment (*Consultant's Digest,* May 1991); *p. 298:* Michael J. Aguirre (reproduced by permission of Arte Público Press); *p. 298:* Wilfredo Caraballo; *p. 299:* Antonia Hernández; *p. 300:* Mario G. Obledo; *p. 305:* Raymond L. Acosta; *p. 305:* Arthur L. Alarcón; *p. 307:* Ferdinand Francis Fernández; *p. 308:* Ricardo H. Hinojosa; *p. 309:* Harold R. Medina, Sr.; *p. 311:* Cruz Reynoso; *p. 311:* Dorothy Comstock Riley; *p. 315:* Henry Barbosa González; *p. 316:* Matthew G. Martínez (reproduced by permission of AP/Wide World); *p. 317:* Solomon P. Ortiz; *p. 317:* William B. Richardson (reproduced by permission of AP/Wide World); *p. 318:* Ileana Ros-Lehtinen; *p. 318:* José E. Serrano; *p. 319:* Frank Tejeda; *p. 319:* Esteban Edward Torres; *p. 321:* Herman Badillo (reproduced by permission of AP/Wide World); *p. 322:* Dennis Chávez; *p. 323:* Joseph M. Montoya; *p. 325:* Edward R. Roybal (reproduced by permission of AP/Wide World); *p. 326:* Henry G. Cisneros; *p. 327:* Antonia Coello Novello (reproduced by permission of AP/Wide World); *p. 328:* Federico Fabian Peña; *p. 329:* Everett Alvarez, Jr.; *p. 330:* Romana Acosta Bañuelos; *p. 331:* Lauro F. Cavazos; *p. 332:* Katherine Davalos Ortega; *p. 333:* Toney Anaya; *p. 333:* Jerry Apodaca; *p. 334:* Art Torres; *p. 335:* Ygnacio D. Garza; *p. 336:* Gloria Molina (reproduced by permission of AP/Wide World); *p. 336:* Louis E. Saavedra; *p. 337:* Xavier L. Suárez.

Business:

p. 343: Poster for the 1985 U.S. Hispanic Chamber of Commerce convention (reproduced by permission of Arte Público Press); *p. 358:* Gabriel Eloy Aguirre; *p. 359:* Carlos José Arboleya; *p. 359:* Gilbert Cuéllar, Jr.; *p. 360:* Roberto C. Goizueta (reproduced by permission of Arte Público Press); *p. 361:* Fredrick J. González (reproduced by permission of Arte Público Press); *p. 361:* Edgar J. Milán; *p. 353:* Clifford Lane Whitehill.

Labor and Employment:

p. 366: César Chávez exhorting people to start a new grape boycott in 1986 (reproduced by permission of *Texas Catholic Herald*); *p. 366:* Mexican women working at a commercial tortilla factory in the 1930s (courtesy of Library of Congress); *p. 367:* A cotton picker in 1933 (photograph by Dorothea Lange, courtesy of Library of Congress); *p. 368:* Mexican mine workers in the early 1900s (reproduced by permission of Arizona Historical Society); *p. 369:* Puerto Rican garment workers in New York City (reproduced by permission of Arte Público Press); *p. 370:* Unemployed workers waiting in line at a relief office during the Depression (courtesy of Library of Congress); *p. 372:* A United Farm Workers picket line in Coachella, California, 1973 (reproduced by permission of *Texas Catholic Herald*); *p. 373:* A scene from the Bracero Program (courtesy of Library of Congress); *p. 374:* A field worker in the Bracero Program (courtesy of Library of Congress); *p. 374:* A migrant work camp (courtesy of Library of Congress); *p. 375:* The interior of a migrant labor shack (reproduced by permission of *Texas Catholic Herald*); *p. 383:* A Mexican worker being finger-printed for deportation (courtesy of Library of Congress).

Education:

p. 391: Children during recess at the Guadalupe Aztlán alternative school in Houston, 1981 (photograph by Curtis Dowell, reproduced by permission of *Texas Catholic Herald*); *p. 403:* Mexican fourth-graders at

Drachman School, circa 1913 (reproduced by permission of Arizona Historical Society); *p. 404:* A poster encouraging Hispanics to register to vote; *p. 406:* Children at the Guadalupe Aztlán alternative school in Houston in 1981, when public school education was denied to children of undocumented workers (photograph by Curtis Dowell, reproduced by permission of *Texas Catholic Herald*); *p. 407:* A sixth-grade classromm in the Huelga School, an alternative school set up in St. Patrick's Chapel, Houston (photograph by Curtis Dowell, reproduced by permission of *Texas Catholic Herald*); *p. 408:* A poster encouraging affirmative action and equal opportunity in education in California; *p. 409:* Manuel Pacheco.

Scholarship:

p. 416: Albert Michael Camarillo; *p. 416:* Arthur León Campa (reproduced by permission of Arte Público Press); *p. 418:* Carlos E. Cortés (reproduced by permission of Arte Público Press); *p. 418:* Rodolfo J. Cortina (reproduced by permission of Arte Público Press); *p. 419:* Margarita Fernández Olmos (reproduced by permission of Arte Público Press); *p. 421:* Erlinda González-Berry (reproduced by permission of Arte Público Press); *p. 422:* Olga Jiménez-Wagenheim (reproduced by permission of Arte Público Press); *p. 423:* Luis Leal (reproduced by permission of Arte Público Press); *p. 424:* Raúl Moncarraz (reproduced by permission of Arte Público Press); *p. 425:* Sonia Nieto (reproduced by permission of Arte Público Press); *p. 425:* Julián Olivares (reproduced by permission of Arte Público Press); *p. 428:* Ricardo Romo (reproduced by permission of Arte Público Press); *p. 428:* Ramón Eduardo Ruiz (reproduced by permission of Arte Público Press).

Science:

p. 436: Angeles Alvariño de Leira; *p. 437:* Alberto Vinicio Baez (reproduced by permission of Arte Público Press); *p. 438:* Graciela Candelas (reproduced by permission of Arte Público Press); *p. 439:* Manuel Cardona (reproduced by permission of Arte Público Press); *p. 439:* David Cardús (reproduced by permission of Arte Público Press); *p. 440:* George Castro (reproduced by permission of Arte Público Press); *p. 441:* Guillermo B. Cintrón (reproduced by permission of Arte Público Press); *p. 441:* Antonio E. Colás (reproduced by permission of Arte Público Press); *p. 442:* Francisco Dallmeier (reproduced by permission of Arte Público Press); *p. 443:* José Alberto Fernández-Pol (reproduced by permission of Arte Público Press); *p. 444:* Celso Ramón García; *p. 447:* Teresa Mercado; *p. 448:* Isabel Cristina Pérez-Farfante; *p. 450:* Eloy Rodríguez; *p. 451:* Pedro Antonio Sánchez.

Literature:

p. 456: Miguel A. Otero (reproduced by permission of Miguel A. Otero Collection, University of New Mexico Library); *p. 457:* Eusebio Chacón (reproduced by permission of Miguel A. Otero Collection, University of New Mexico Library); *p. 457:* Title page of *El hijo de la tempestad* by Eusebio Chacón (reproduced by permission of Special Collections, University of New Mexico Library); *p. 458:* Cuban literary and patriotic figure, José Martí; *p. 460:* The cover of Daniel Venegas' satirical newspaper, *El Malcriado* (reproduced by permission of Arte Público Press); *p. 461:* Fray Angelico Chávez (reproduced by permission of Special Collections, University of New Mexico Library); *p. 463:* Cover of the first issue of *Gráfico* newspaper (reproduced by permission of Arte Público Press); *p. 464:* Lola Rodríguez de Tió (reproduced by permission of Arte Público Press); *p. 466:* Albelardo Delgado, Ron Arias, and Rolando Hinojosa, Houston, Texas, 1980; *p. 467:* The original manuscript of the Tomás Rivera poem, "When love to be?"; *p. 468:* Evangelina Vigil-Piñón, Houston, 1987 (photograph by Julián Olivaries, reproduced by permission of Arte Público Press); *p. 468:* The cover of Rudolfo Anaya's best-selling novel, *Bless Me, Ultima*; *p. 469:* A vendor at the First National Latino Book Fair in Chicago, 1979 (reproduced by permission of Arte Público Press); *p. 470:* Ana Castillo, 1979 (reproduced by permission of Arte Público Press); *p. 470:* Helena María Viramontes, 1986 (photograph by Georgia McInnis, reproduced by permission of Arte Público Press); *p. 471:* Luis Dávilla, 1979 (reproduced by permission of Arte Público Press); *p. 472:* The cover of Rudolfo Anaya's *Cuentos: Tales from the Hispanic Southwest*; *p. 472:* Pat Mora, 1986 (reproduced by permission of Arte Público Press); *p. 473:* The cover of Denise Chávez's *The Last of the Menu Girls*; *p. 474:* Gary Soto and Evangelina Vigil-Piñón, Houston, Texas, 1987 (reproduced by permission of Arte Público Press); *p. 475:* Ricardo Sánchez, Alejandro Morales, critic Salvador Rodríguez del Pino, and Victor Villaseñor, Mexico City, 1979 (reproduced by permission of Arte Público Press); *p. 476:* Julia de Burgos (reproduced by permission of Arte Público Press); *p. 477:* José Luis González; *p. 477:* Luis Rafael Sánchez (reproduced by permission of Arte Público Press); *p. 478:* Pedro Juan Soto; *p. 479:* Jesús Colón, circa 1950s (reproduced by permission of Centro de Estudios Puertorriqueños, Hunter College, CUNY); *p. 479:* Bernardo Vega, 1948 (reproduced by permission of Centro de Estudios Puertorriqueños, Hunter College, CUNY); *p. 480:* Sandra María Esteves, 1979 (reproduced by permission of Arte Público Press); *p. 481:* Nicholasa Mohr, Publisher Nicolás Kanellos, and Ed Vega, Houston, Texas, 1985; *p. 482:* Virgil Suárez, 1991 (reproduced by permission of Arte Público Press); *p. 483:* José Sánchez Boudy (reproduced by permission of Arte Público Press); *p.*

485: Miguel Algarín, Chicago, 1979 (reproduced by permission of Arte Público Press); *p. 485:* Alurista, 1980 (reproduced by permission of Arte Público Press); *p. 487:* Rudolfo A. Anaya; *p. 488:* Lorna Dee Cervantes, 1990 (photograph by Georgia McInnis, reproduced by permission of Arte Público Press); *p. 489:* Denise Chávez; *p. 490:* Judith Ortiz Cofer; *p. 491:* Victor Hernández Cruz; *p. 492:* Abelardo Delgado (reproduced by permission of Arte Público Press); *p. 493:* Roberto Fernández (reproduced by permission of Arte Público Press); *p. 494:* Lionel G. García (reproduced by permission of Arte Público Press); *p. 495:* Rolando Hinojosa (reproduced by permission of Arte Público Press); *p. 496:* Tato Laviera, 1990 (photograph by Georgia McInnis, reproduced by permission of Arte Público Press); *p. 497:* Nicholasa Mohr, 1990 (reproduced by permission of Arte Público Press); *p. 498:* Alejandro Morales (reproduced by permission of Arte Público Press); *p. 501:* Ricardo Sánchez; *p. 501:* Gary Soto, 1991 (photograph by M. L. Marinelli); *p. 503:* Sabine Ulibarrí (reproduced by permission of Arte Público Press); *p. 504:* Ed Vega (reproduced by permission of Arte Público Press); *p. 505:* Víctor E. Villaseñor (reproduced by permission of Arte Público Press); *p. 506:* Jose Yglesias.

Art:

p. 509: Bell wall, San Juan Capistrano Mission, 1760–87, San Antonio, Texas (photograph by Jacinto Quirarte); *p. 510:* Facade, San José y San Miguel de Aguayo Mission, 1768–82, San Antonio, Texas (photograph by Kathy Vargas); *p. 510: Saint Joachim* portal sculpture, 1768–82, San José y San Miguel de Aguayo Mission, San Antonio, Texas (photograph by Kathy Vargas); *p. 511: Saint Anne* portal sculpture, 1768–82, San José y San Miguel de Aguayo Mission, San Antonio, Texas (photograph by Kathy Vargas); *p. 511:* Facade, 1783–97, San Xavier del Bac Mission. Tuscon, Arizona (photograph by Jacinto Quirarte); *p. 512: Saint Lucy,* Portal sculpture, 1783–97, San Xavier del Bac Mission, Tucson, Arizona (photograph by Jacinto Quirarte); *p. 513:* Main portal, 1755, Nuestra Señora de la Purisma Concepción de Acúna Mission, San Antonio, Texas (photograph by Kathy Vargas); *p. 513:* Polychromy (reconstruction, 1948), south tower, 1768–82, San José y San Miguel de Aguayo Mission, San Antonio, Texas (photograph by Kathy Vargas); *p. 516:* José Benito Ortega, *Saint Isidore the Farmer,* 1880s–1907 (reproduced by permission of Denver Art Museum); *p. 517:* José Dolores López, *Expulsion from the Garden of Eden* (reproduced by permission of Museum of International Folk Art, Santa Fe, New Mexico); *p. 519:* Theodora Sánchez, *Nicho* (Yard Shrine), 1957, Tucson, Arizona (photograph by Jacinto Quirarte); *p. 521:* Octavio Medellín, *Xtol* print (photograph courtesy of the artist); *p. 522:* Edward Chávez, *Indians of the Plains,* 1943, Service Club, Fort

Warren, Wyoming (photograph courtesy of the artist); *p. 526:* Ralph Ortiz, *Piano Destruction Concert Duncan Terrace,* Destruction in Art Symposium, September 1966, London (photograph courtesy of the artist); *p. 529:* Judy Baca, *The Great Wall of Los Angeles,* "350 Mexicans Deported and Dustbowl Refugees" (photograph by Jacinto Quirarte); *p. 530:* Carmen Lomas Garza, *Lotería—Table Llena,* 1974 (photograph courtesy of the artist); *p. 531:* Victor Ochoa, *Gerónimo,* 1981, Centro Cultural de la Raza, Balboa Park, San Diego, California (photograph by Jacinto Quirarte); *p. 532:* Victor Ochoa, *Chicano Park,* 1981, Centro Cultural de la Raza, Balboa Park, San Diego, California (photograph by Jacinto Quirarte); *p. 533:* Cesar Martínez, *La Pareja,* 1979 (photograph courtesy of the artist); *p. 534:* Jesse Treviño, *Panadería,* late 1970s (photograph courtesy of the artist); *p. 535:* José González, *Barrio Murals,* 1976, cover design for *Revista Chicano-Riquería* (photograph courtesy of the artist); *p. 536:* Marcos Raya, *Stop World War III.* Mural, Chicago, Illinois (photograph courtesy of the artist); *p. 540:* Willie Herrón and Gronk, *Black and White Mural,* 1973 and 1978, Estrada Courts, Los Angeles, California (photograph by Jacinto Quirarte); *p. 541:* Willie Herrón and Gronk, *Black and White Mural,* (diagram by Jacinto Quirarte); *p. 542:* Raymond Patlán and others, *History of the Mexican American Worker,* 1974–75, Blue Island, Illinois (photograph by Jose Gonzales); *p. 542:* Raymond Patlán and others, *History of the Mexican American Worker* (diagram by Jacinto Quirarte); *p. 544:* Raúl Valdez and others, *La Raza Cósmica,* 1977, Austin, Texas (photograph by Jacinto Quirarte); *p. 544:* Raúl Valdez and others, *La Raza Cósmica,* 1977 (diagram by Jacinto Quirarte); *p. 544:* Raúl Valdez and others, *La Raza Cósmica,* 1977 (diagram by Jacinto Quirarte); *p. 545:* Raúl Valdez and others, *La Raza Cósmica,* 1977 (diagram by Jacinto Quirarte); *p. 545:* Raúl Valdez and others, *La Raza Cósmica* (diagram by Jacinto Quirarte); *p. 546:* Rogelio Cárdenas, *En la lucha ... ponte trucha,* by Rogelio Cárdenas, 1978, Hayward, California (photograph by Jacinto Quirarte); *p. 546:* Rogelio Cárdenas, *En la lucha ... ponte trucha,* by Rogelio Cárdenas, 1978 (diagram by Jacinto Quirarte); *p. 547:* Gilberto Garduño and others, *Multicultural Mural,* 1980, Santa Fe, New Mexico (photograph by Jacinto Quirarte); *p. 548:* Gilberto Garduño and others, *Multicultural Mural,* 1980 (diagram by Jacinto Quirarte).

Theater:

p. 551: Los Angeles' California Theater (reproduced by permission of Arte Público Press); *p. 552:* The Mason Theater, Los Angeles (reproduced by permission of Arte Público Press); *p. 554:* Rosalinda Meléndez (reproduced by permission of Arte Público Press); *p. 556:* The García girls chorus line from the Carpa García tent show (reproduced by permission of Arte Público Press); *p. 557:* Don Fito, the Carpa García tent show (reproduced by permission of Arte Público Press); *p. 561:* The cover of a program for the performance of an operetta at the Centro Español in 1919; *p. 562:* A full house at the Centro Asturiano in 1937 (reproduced by permission of Dorothea Lynch Collection, George Mason University Library); *p. 563:* A scene from *El niño judio* at the Centro Asturiano (reproduced by permission of Dorothea Lynch Collection, George Mason University Library); *p. 564:* Manuel Aparicio, at center, directing a rehearsal of Sinclair Lewis' *It Can't Happen Here* in Spanish at the Centro Asturiano (reproduced by permission of Dorothea Lynch Collection, George Mason University); *p. 565:* Manuel Aparicio in Jacinto Benavente's *La Malquerida* (reproduced by permission of Dorothea Lynch Collection, George Mason University Library); *p. 566:* A scene from El Teatro Urbano's *Anti-Bicentennial Special* in 1976 (reproduced by permission of Arte Público Press); *p. 567:* A scene from El Teatro de la Esperanza's production of Rodrigo Duarte Clark's *Brujerías* (reproduced by permission of Arte Público Press); *p. 569:* Poster from La Farándula Panamericana theater group's 1954 production of *Los árboles mueren de pie,* starring Marita Reid (reproduced by permission of Arte Público Press); *p. 570:* Postcard photograph of the Bronx's Pregones theater company in 1985 (reproduced by permission of Arte Público Press); *p. 571:* The elaborate costuming of a Miami production of José Zorilla's *Don Juan Tenorio* (reproduced by permission of Arte Público Press); *p. 573: Romeo and Juliet* being performed in Spanish in Miami (reproduced by permission of Arte Público Press); *p. 581:* A scene from the Los Angeles production of Dolores Prida's *Beautiful Señoritas* (reproduced by permission of Arte Público Press); *p. 583:* Luis Valdez (reproduced by permission of Arte Público Press); *p. 584:* Carmen Zapata in the Bilingual Foundation for the Arts' production of *Moments to Be Remembered* (reproduced by permission of Arte Público Press).

Film:

p. 595: Henry Darrow as Zorro; *p. 605:* Carmen Miranda; *p. 605:* Freddie Prinze, star of "Chico and the Man" (reproduced by permission of Arte Público Press); *p. 606:* Erik Estrada, star of "CHiPs" (reproduced by permission of Arte Público Press); *p. 607:* The Sharks face off with the Jets in *West Side Story* (reproduced by permission of Arte Público Press); *p. 608:* A scene from *Boulevard Nights* (reproduced by permission of Arte Público Press); *p. 611:* The poster for *El norte; p. 613:* Jesús Salvador Treviño, 1978 (reproduced by permission of Arte Público Press); *p. 624:* Néstor Almendros; *p. 625:* Desi Arnaz; *p. 625:* Rubén Blades; *p. 626:* Lynda Córdoba Carter (reproduced by permission of Arte Público Press); *p.*

627: Linda Cristal; *p. 627:* Dolores del Río; *p. 628:* Emilio Estévez; *p. 629:* Emilio "El Indio" Fernández; *p. 630:* Fernando Lamas; *p. 631:* Adele Mara; *p. 631:* Margo; *p. 632:* Richad "Cheech" Marín; *p. 632:* Mona Maris; *p. 633:* Cris-Pin Martin; *p. 633:* Ricardo Montalbán (reproduced by permission of Archive Photos); *p. 634:* María Montez; *p. 634:* Silvia Morales (reproduced by permission of Arte Público Press); *p. 635:* Rita Moreno; *p. 635:* Barry Norton; *p. 636:* Ramón Novarro; *p. 636:* Edward James Olmos; *p. 637:* Anthony Quinn; *p. 637:* Gilbert Roland; *p. 638:* César Romero; *p. 639:* Lupe Vélez; *p. 639:* Raoul Walsh; *p. 640:* Raquel Welch.

Music:

p. 643: Mexican musicians in the 1890s in California (reproduced by permission of Huntington Library, San Marino, California); *p. 644:* Xavier Cugat and his orchestra in the 1940s (reproduced by permission of Arte Público Press); *p. 645:* Augusto Coen and his Golden Orchestra, circa 1930s–1940s (reproduced by permission of José Martí Collection. Center for Puerto Rican Studies Library, Hunter College, CUNY); *p. 647:* Lidia Mendoza with Marcelo, comic Tin Tan, and Juanita Mendoza in Chicago in the 1950s (reproduced by permission of Arte Público Press); *p. 648:* A working-class *orquesta,* circa 1930 (courtesy of Thomas Kreneck); *p. 654:* An *orquesta tipica* in Houston (courtesy of Thomas Kreneck); *p. 657:* Beto Villa y su Orquesta, circa 1946 (courtesy of Chris Strachwitz); *p. 658:* Alonzo y su Orquesta, a typical orchestra, circa 1950 (courtesy of Thomas Kreneck); *p. 659:* Octavo García y sus GGs, circa 1952 (courtesy of Octavio García); *p. 660:* An outdoor *salsa* concert in Houston, Texas; *p. 661:* Celia Cruz at the Hollywood Palladium; *p. 663:* The Joe Cuba Sextet; *p. 663:* A Machito album cover; *p. 664:* A Tito Puente album cover; *p. 665:* Eddie Palmieri (reproduced by permission of Berkeley Agency).

Media:

p. 681: Ignacio E. Lozano, Jr.; *p. 682:* Mónica Lozano-Centanino; *p. 682:* José I. Lozano; *p. 683:* Marti Buscaglia; *p. 683:* Peter W. Davidson; *p. 684:* Carlos D. Ramírez; *p. 685:* Phillip V. Sánchez; *p. 689:* Charlie Erikson; *p. 692:* Pedro J. González, pioneer of Spanish-language radio in California (reproduced by permission of Arte Público Press); *p. 692:* Pedro J. González's singing group, Los Madrugadores; *p. 693:* Banner headlines in *La Opinión* newspaper announcing the guilty verdict in the Pedro J. González case; *p. 695:* McHenry Tichenor; *p. 696:* Amancio V. Suárez; *p. 702:* Gustavo Godoy; *p. 704:* Henry R. Silverman; *p. 704:* Saul P. Steinberg; *p. 706:* Joaquín F. Blaya; *p. 707:* Rosita Perú; *p. 708:* Univisión news studio; *p. 709:* Jorge Ramos and María Elena Salinas of

"Noticiero Univisión"; *p. 709:* Cristina Saralegui, host of Univisión's "El Show de Cristina"; *p. 712:* Enrique Gratas, host of Telemundo's "Occurió Así"; *p. 712:* Andrés García and Rudy Rodríguez, stars of Telemundo's soap opera "El Magnate".

Sports:

p. 722: Ramón Ahumada (reproduced by permission of Arizona Historical Society); *p. 723:* A baseball team of Mexicans and Anglos in Los Angeles in the 1870s (reproduced by permission of Huntington Library, San Marino, California); *p. 727:* Luis Aparicio; *p. 728:* Rod Carew (reproduced by permission of Bettmann Archive/Newsphotos, Inc.); *p. 728:* Rosemary Casals; *p. 729:* Orlando Cepeda; *p. 730:* Roberto Clemente (reproduced by permission of Bettmann Archive/Newsphotos, Inc.); *p. 730:* Dave Concepción (reproduced by permission of Bettmann Archive/Newsphotos, Inc.); *p. 732:* Roberto Durán (reproduced by permission of Bettmann Archive/Newsphotos, Inc.); *p. 732:* Sixto Escobar (reproduced by permission of Arte Público Press); *p. 732:* Tony Fernández; *p. 734:* Tom Flores (reproduced by permission of AP/Wide World); *p. 734:* Lefty Gómez; *p. 735:* Pancho González (reproduced by permission of Bettmann Archive/Newsphotos, Inc.); *p. 735:* Keith Hernández (reproduced by permission of AP/Wide World); *p. 736:* Al López; *p. 736:* Nancy López (reproduced by permission of Bettmann Archive/Newsphotos, Inc.); *p. 737:* Juan "Manito" Marichal; *p. 738:* Orestes "Minnie" Miñoso; *p. 738:* Amleto Monacelli (reproduced by permission of Arte Público Press); *p. 739:* Anthony Muñoz (reproduced by permission of Arte Público Press); *p. 739:* Tony Oliva; *p. 740:* Carlos Ortiz; *p. 741:* Manuel Ortiz; *p. 741:* Jim Plunkett (reproduced by permission of Bettmann Archive/Newsphotos, Inc.); *p. 742:* Chi Chi Rodríguez; *p. 743:* Alberto Bauduy Salazar (reproduced by permission of Bettmann Archive/Newsphotos, Inc.); *p. 743:* Vicente Saldívar; *p. 744:* Luis Tiant; *p. 744:* José Luis "Chegui" Torres (reproduced by permission of José A. Martí Collection, Center for Puerto Rican Studies Library, Hunter College, CUNY); *p. 745:* Lee Treviño (reproduced by permission of Bettmann Archive/Newsphotos, Inc.); *p. 745:* Fernando Valenzuela.

Organizations:

p. 747: A march by the Council of Puerto Rican Organizations from the Lower East Side of New York City over the Brooklyn Bridge to protest the poor conditions of public schools in the Puerto Rican community (reproduced by permission of Historic Archive of the Department of Puerto Rican Community Affairs in the United States, Center for Puerto Rican Studies Library and Archives, Hunter College, CUNY); *p. 748:* A celebration of the Three Kings sponsored by the Puerto Rican Workers Mutual Aid Society, New York City (reproduced by permission of Jesús Colón Papers, Center for Puerto Rican Studies Library and Archives, Hunter College, CUNY); *p. 748:* A parade organized by Tucson's Alianza Hispano-Americana (reproduced by permission of Arizona Historical Society); *p. 750:* President Ronald Reagan presents the Medal of Freedom to Dr. Héctor García, founder of the American G. I. Forum.

Prominent Hispanics:

p. 757: Tomás A. Arciniega (reproduced by permission of Arte Público Press); *p. 758:* Philip Arreola; *p. 758:* Tony Bonilla (reproduced by permission of Arte Público Press); *p. 759:* Rubén Bonilla, Jr; *p. 759:* Harry Caicedo (reproduced by permission of Arte Público Press); *p. 760:* Vikki Carr (reproduced by permission of AP/Wide World); *p. 760:* César Chávez; *p. 761:* Bert Corona; *p. 761:* José R. Coronado (reproduced by permission of Arte Público Press); *p. 762:* Jaime Escalante; *p. 763:* Joseph A. Fernández (reproduced by permission of Arte Público Press); *p. 764:* Archbishop Patrick F. Flores (reproduced by permission of AP/Wide World); *p. 764:* Ernesto Galarza; *p. 765:* Elsa Gómez (reproduced by permission of Arte Público Press); *p. 766:* Carolina Herrera (reproduced by permission of Arte Público Press); *p. 766:* Dolores Fernández Huerta (reproduced by permission of AP/Wide World); *p. 767:* Tania J. León; *p. 767:* Modesto A. Maidique; *p. 768:* Eduardo Mata (reproduced by permission of AP/Wide World); *p. 769:* Julián Nava (reproduced by permission of Arte Público Press); *p. 770:* Manuel Pacheco (photograph by Julieta González, reproduced by permission of Arte Público Press); *p. 771:* Guadalupe C. Quintanilla; *p. 771:* Geraldo Rivera; *p. 772:* Paul Rodríguez (reproduced by permission of Arte Público Press); *p. 773:* Luis Santeiro (reproduced by permission of Arte Público Press); *p. 773:* Cristina Saralegui (reproduced by permission of Arte Público Press); *p. 774:* Roberto Suárez (reproduced by permission of Arte Público Press).

Glossary

A

acto – a one-act Chicano theater piece developed out of collective improvisation.

adelantado – the commander of an expedition who would receive, in advance, the title to any lands that he would discover.

audiencia – a tribunal that ruled over territories.

agringado – literally "Gringo-ized" or Americanized.

Aztlán – originally the mythological land of origin of the Mechica nations, to which the Toltecs and the Aztecs belong. Chicanos identify this land of origin as the geographic region of the American Southwest, figuratively their homeland.

B

babalao – a spiritual healer, witch, or advisor, especially in *santería*.

barrio – neighborhood.

batos locos – See *pachuco(s)*.

behareque – thatched huts used by Indians of the Caribbean.

bodega – a small general store.

bohíos – thatched-roofed huts used by the Caribbean Indians.

botánica – a shop that specializes in herbs and folk potions and medicines.

bracero – from *brazo,* arm, someone who works with their arms or performs manual labor; originally applied to temporary Mexican agricultural and railroad workers, it is also occasionally used to refer to any unskilled Mexican worker.

bulto – a wooden sculpture in the image of a Catholic saint.

C

cacique – the American Indian village chieftain.

caló – a Mexican-American dialect, often associated with *pachucos.*

canción – song.

capilla – chapel.

carpa – from the Quechua word meaning an "awning of branches;" in Spanish it has come to mean a tent; circuses and tent theaters have come to be known as *carpas* by extension.

carreta – cart.

caudillo – chief, leader, originally of the rural poor, but today quite often used to refer to any grass-roots political leader.

charrerías – contests of the Mexican cowboys.

charro – a Mexican cowboy of the Jalisco region, maintaining the dress and customs often associated with *mariachis.*

Glossary

Chicano – derivative of *Mechicano,* the same Nahuatl word that gave origin to the name of Mexico. The term originally meant Mexican immigrant worker in the early twentieth century, but became the name adopted by Mexican Americans, especially during the days of the civil rights and student movements.

chinampa – a man-made island or floating garden, developed by Meso-American Indians as an agricultural technique.

cimarrones – runaway slaves.

colonia – literally a "colony," it refers to the enclave of Hispanic population within a city, much as the term *barrio* is used today.

compadrazgo – godparenthood, usually through the baptism of a child. *Compadrazgo* is the extension of kinship to non-relatives and the strengthening of responsibilities among kin.

compadres – co-parents; godparents.

confianza – trust, the basis of the relationships between individuals in many spheres of social activity, but especially among kin.

conjunto – said of a Texas, northern-Mexico musical style as well as of the ensemble that plays it, usually made up of a guitar, a base guitar, a drum, and a button accordion.

corrido – a Mexican ballad.

criollo – a Creole, that is, someone of Spanish (European) origin born in the New World.

crónica – a local-color newspaper column often satirizing contemporary customs.

cronista – the writer of a *crónica.*

curandero – a folk healer who combines the practices of the Mexican Indians and Spanish folk-healing.

E

encomendero – the owner of the *encomienda.*

encomienda – the system by which a Spaniard held in high esteem by the King and Queen was given ownership of land in the New World and authorized to "protect" the Indians who had occupied the land in exchange for their free labor. This failed attempt at establishing feudal baronies was marked by the exploitation of the Indians.

ex-voto – a gift presented to a saint as a show of gratitude for a favor conceded.

F

familia, la – the greater family, which includes the immediate nuclear household and relatives that are traced on the female and male sides.

finca – farm, ranch.

G

gallego – in Cuban farce, the stock Galician Spaniard, known for his hard head and frugality.

H

hacendado – the owner of a *hacienda.*

hacienda – a large ranch derivative of the *latifundia* system.

hermandad – brotherhood.

I

indigenismo – an emphasis on American Indian and Pre-Columbian origins and identity.

ingenios – plantations, especially of sugar.

Isleños – descendants of the Canary Island settlers in southern Louisiana.

J

jíbaro – originally an American Indian world for "highlander," it is what Puerto Ricans call the rural mountain folk, but has also come to be symbolic of the national identity of Puerto Ricans.

K

kiva – a secret underground ceremonial chamber, especially as used in Pueblo culture for ceremonies and meetings.

L

latifundia – a large estate or ranch originating in ancient Roman civilization.

lectores – professional (hired) readers who would read books, magazines, and newspapers to cigar-rollers as they performed their laborious tasks.

M

macana – a wooden war club.

manda – a sacrificial offering to a saint in order to receive some favor.

maquiladora – a factory on the Mexican side of the border that performs part of the manual assembly of products at the comparatively lower wages offered by the Mexican economy. These products would then be shipped back to the United States for finishing and marketing by the partner company.

Marielito – a Cuban refugee who arrived in the United States as a result of the Mariel boatlift in the 1980s.

mestizo – an individual of mixed Spanish (or European) and American Indian heritage.

milagro – a charm made of tin, gold, or silver, and shaped in the form of an arm, a leg, a baby, or a house, representing the favor (usually of healing) that is desired from a saint.

morada – the meeting house of the *Penitente* lay brotherhood.

mulata – the stock female Mulatto character in Cuban farce.

música norteña – *conjunto* music from the northern region of Mexico (also includes Texas).

mutualista – mutual aid society, an organization that engaged in social activities and provided basic needs for immigrant workers and their families, including insurance and death benefits for members.

N

nacimiento – a nativity.

Nañiguismo – membership in the secret society of Abakúa, which combines elements of the Efik culture of the southern coast of Nigeria and Freemasonry.

negrito – in Cuban farce, the stock character in black face.

nitainos – principal advisors among the Arawak Indians, quite often in charge of the labor force.

nopal – the prickly pear cactus.

norteño – of northern Mexican origin.

Nuyorican – literally "New York-Rican," a term developed colloquially by Puerto Ricans born or raised in New York to distinguish themselves from those identifying solely with the island.

O

orishas – the African deities of *santería.*

orquesta – a Mexican American musical ensemble that develops its style around the violin.

P

pachuco/batos locos – member of a Mexican-American urban youth subculture, known as the pachucos or batos locos, which characteristically developed its own style of dress (zoot suit), its own dialect (*caló*), and its own bilingual-bicultural ideology during the 1940s and 1950s.

padrinos – godparents.

parentesco – kinship sentiment.

parientes – blood relatives.

pastorela – the shepherds play; a folk drama reenacted during the Christmas season.

patria – fatherland.

patria chica – the home region within the fatherland.

pelado – literally the "skinned one" or shirtless one, he was the stock underdog, sharp-witted picaresque character of Mexican vaudeville and tent shows.

Penitente – literally "penitent;" it is the name of a religious brotherhood in New Mexico.

piraguas – a narrow, high-prowed canoe used by the Caribbean Indians.

posada – a community Christmas pageant where carolers go door to door asking for shelter in reenactment of Joseph and Mary's search for lodging.

presidio – a fort, especially characteristic of frontier settlements.

promesa – literally a "promise," it is a sacrificial offering to a saint in order to receive some favor.

R

renegado/a – a renegade, someone who denies his or her Mexican identity.

repartimiento – a form of the *encomienda,* which vested the rights over the Indians in the civil authorities.

reredo – altar screen.

retablos – paintings on panels behind the altar in a Catholic church.

revista – a vaudeville musical review.

S

salsa – literally "sauce," it refers to Afro-Caribbean music.

santería/santerismo – a synchretic religious sect growing out of the original African religion and the Catholicism of slaves.

santero – in the Southwest, a sculptor of wooden saints; in the Caribbean, a devotee of an *orisha* in *santería.*

santos – the sculpted figures representing saints of the Catholic church; used in worship and prayer.

T

Taino/Nitaino – a group of sedentary tribes native to the Caribbean.

V

vaquero – cowboy.

vegas – plantations, especially of coffee.

Y

yerberías – shops specializing in medicinal plants, herbs, and potions.

yerberos – folk healers and spiritualists who use herbs in their practices.

yuca – manioc root.

Z

zarzuela – a type of Spanish operetta.

zemíes – gods of the Arawak Indians, also the small Taino religious figure made of clay that represented these gods.

General Bibliography

A

Acosta-Belén, Edna, ed. *The Puerto Rican Woman,* New York: Praeger, 1986.

Acuña, Rodolfo. *Occupied America: A History of Chicanos.* New York: Harper and Row, 1981.

Alvarez, Robert R. *Familia: Migration and Adaptation in Alta and Baja California 1850-1975.* Berkeley: University of California Press, 1987.

B

Barrera, Mario. *Race and Class in the Southwest: A Theory of Radical Inequality.* Notre Dame, Indiana: University of Notre Dame Press, 1979.

Bean, Frank D., and Marta Tienda. *The Hispanic Population of the United States.* New York: Russell Sage Foundation, 1988.

Beardsley, John, and Jane Livingston. *Hispanic Art in the United States: Thirty Painters and Sculptors.* New York: Abbeville Press, 1987.

Boswell, T. D., and J. R. Curtis. *The Cuban American Experience.* Totawa, New Jersey: Rowan and Allenheld, 1984.

C

Camarillo, Albert. *Chicanos in a Changing Society.* Cambridge, Massachusetts: Harvard University Press, 1979.

Cotera, Marta P. *Latina Sourcebook: Bibliography of Mexican American, Cuban, Puerto Rican and Other Hispanic Women Materials in the U.S.A.* Austin, Texas: Information Systems Development, 1982.

E

Elias Oliveres, Lucia, ed. *Spanish in the U.S. Setting: Beyond the Southwest.* Rosalyn, Virginia: National Clearinghouse for Bilingual Education, 1983.

F

Fitzpatrick, Joseph P. *Puerto Rican Americans: The Meaning of Migration to the Mainland.* Englewood Cliffs, New Jersey: Prentice Hall, 1987.

Furtaw, Julia C., ed. *Hispanic American Information Directory, 1992–1993.* Detroit, Michigan: Gale Research, 1992.

G

García, Mario T. *Mexican Americans.* New Haven, Connecticut: Yale University Press, 1989.

Garza, Hedda. *Latinas: Hispanic Women in the United States.* Chicago: Franklin Watts, 1994.

H

Hendricks, G. L. *The Dominican Diaspora: From the Dominican Republic to New York City.* New York: Teacher's College Press of Columbia University, 1974.

Hispanics in U.S. History, two volumes. Englewood Cliffs, New Jersey: Globe Book Company, 1989.

History Task Force of the Centro de Estudios Puertorriqueños. *Labor Migration under Capitalism: The Puerto Rican Experience.* New York: Monthly Review Press, 1979.

Horseman, Reginald. *Race and Manifest Destiny. The Origins of American Racial Anglo-Saxonism.* Cambridge: Harvard University Press, 1981.

K

Kanellos, Nicolás. *A History of Hispanic Theater in the United States: Origins to 1940.* Austin: University of Texas Press, 1990.

Kanellos, Nicolás, ed. *Biographical Dictionary of Hispanic Literature.* Westport, Connecticut: Greenwood Press, 1985.

Kanellos, Nicolás. *Hispanic Firsts.* Detroit: Gale Research, forthcoming.

Kanellos, Nicolás, and Claudio Esteva-Fabregat, general editors. *Handbook of Hispanic Cultures in the United States,* four volumes. Houston: Arte Público Press, 1994–95.

Kanellos, Nicolás, with Cristelia Pérez. *Chronology of Hispanic American History.* Detroit: Gale Research, 1995.

Knight, Franklin W. *The Caribbean.* New York: Oxford University Press, 1990.

L

Llanes, J. Cuban Americans, Masters of Survival. Cambridge, Massachusetts: Harvard University Press, 1982.

Lomeli, Francisco, and Julio A. Martínez. *Chicano Literature: A Reference Guide.* Westport, Connecticut: Greenwood Press, 1985.

M

McKenna, Teresa Flora, and Ida Ortiz, eds. *The Broken Web: The Educational Experience of Hispanic American Women.* Berkeley, California: Floricanto Press and the Tomás Rivera Center, 1988.

Meier, Kenneth J., and Joseph Stewart. *The Politics of Hispanic Education.* New York: Russell Sage Foundation, 1987.

Meier, Matt S., and Feliciano Rivera. *Dictionary of Mexican American History.* Westport, Connecticut: Greenwood Press, 1981.

Melville, Margarita, ed. *Twice a Minority: Mexican American Women.* St. Louis: Mosby, 1980.

Mirandé, Alfredo, and Evangelina Enríquez. *La Chicana: The Mexican American Woman.* Chicago: University of Chicago Press, 1979.

Moore, Joan, and Harry Pachón. *Hispanics in the United States.* Englewood Cliffs, New Jersey: Prentice Hall, 1985.

Morales, Julio. *Puerto Rican Poverty and Migration: We Just Had to Try Elsewhere.* New York: Praeger, 1986.

O

Office of the Secretary of Defense, *Hispanics in America's Defense.* Washington, DC: U.S. Printing Office, 1990.

P

Pedraza-Bailey, S. *Political and Economic Migrants in America.* Austin: University of Texas Press, 1985.

Portes, Alejandro, and Robert L. Bach. *Latin Journey: Cuban and Mexican Immigrants in the United States.* Berkeley: University of California Press, 1985.

Powell, Philip Wayne, *Tree of Hate. Propaganda and Prejudices Affecting United States Relations with the Hispanic World.* New York: Basic Books, 1971.

R

Rodríguez, Clara. *Born in the U.S.A.* Boston, Massachusetts: Unwin Hyman, 1989.

Ryan, Bryan, ed. *Hispanic Writers.* Detroit, Michigan: Gale Research, 1991.

S

Sánchez-Korrol, Virginia. *From Colonia to Community.* Westport, Connecticut: Greenwood Press, 1983.

Sandoval, Moisés. *On the Move: A History of the Hispanic Church in the United States.* Maryknoll, New York: Orbis Books, 1990.

Schorr, Edward Allen. *Hispanic Resource Directory.* Juneau, Alaska: Denali Press, 1988.

Shirley, Carl F., ed. *Chicano Writers: First Series.* Detroit, Michigan: Gale Research, 1989.

Smedley, Audrey. *Race in North America: Origin and Evolution of a Worldview.* Boulder, Colorado: Westview Press, 1993.

Suchliki, Jaime. *Cuba: From Columbus to Castro.* Washington, D.C.: Pergammon Press, 1986.

U

United States Commission on Civil Rights. *Puerto Ricans in the Continental United States: An Uncertain Future.* Washington, D.C.: U.S. Commission on Civil Rights, 1976.

Unterburger, Amy L., ed. *Who's Who among Hispanic Americans, 1992–1993.* Detroit, Michigan: Gale Research, 1992.

V

Veciana-Suárez, Ana. *Hispanic Media: Impact and Influence.* Washington, D.C.: The Media Institute, 1990.

Vivó, Paquita, ed. *The Puerto Ricans: An Annotated Bibliography.* New York: R. R. Bowker, 1973.

W

Wagenheim, Kal. *A Survey of Puerto Ricans in the U.S. Mainland in the 1970s.* New York: Praeger, 1975.

Weber, David. *The Mexican Frontier, 1821–1846: The American Southwest Under Mexico.* Albuquerque: University of New Mexico Press, 1982.

Index

A

Abel, Carlos Alberto: 434

Abelardo. *See* Delgado, Abelardo

Abreu, Virgilio: 556–557

Academy Award: 574, 600, 614–615, 624, 635, 637, 675

Acevedo, Mario: 538

Aceves, José: 520–521

Acheson, Dean: 165

Acoma Pueblo: 71–72, 142, 509, 514

Acosta, Daniel, Jr.: 434

Acosta, Raymond L.: 305

Acosta-Belén, Edna: 413

Acquired Immune Deficiency Syndrome (AIDS): 244, 434, 616, 634, 714

Acuña, Rodolfo: 414, 650

Acuña y Rossetti, Elisa: 238

Adams, John: 287

Adams, John Quincy: 151, 153, 157

Adams-Onís Treaty: 150

adelantado: 60, 63, 72

AFL. *See* American Federation of Labor

AFL-CIO. *See* American Federation of Labor and Congress of Industrial Organizations (AFL-CIO)

Agency for International Development (AID): 168, 301, 449

Aguayo, Marquis of: 73

Agueibana: 58

Aguila, Guz. *See* Aguilera, Antonio Guzmán

Aguilar, Robert P.: 305

Aguilera, Antonio Guzmán: 553–554, 576

Aguirre, Gabriel Eloy: 358

Aguirre, Michael J.: 297–298

Ahumada, Ramón: 722

Ai Indians: 55

AIDS. *See* Acquired Immune Deficiency Syndrome (AIDS)

Aiken, Susan: 622

Aisle, Francisco José: 435

Ajo, Arizona: 133

Alabau, Magaly: 242

Alam, Juan Shamsul: 572

Alaminos, Antón de: 60–62

Alamo, El: 13, 16, 22, 135, 143, 145–146, 153, 180, 261, 283, 555–556, 604, 608, 619, 626, 638, 667

Alarcón, Arthur L.: 302, 305

Alarcón, Hernando de: 12

Alarcón, Norma: 244, 414, 471

Albizú, Olga: 243

Aleandro, Norma: 610, 624

Alegría, Fernando: 414

Alexander VI, Pope: 4, 60

Alfonso, Carlos: 537

Algarín, Miguel: 480, 484–485, 572, 580

Alianza Hispano Americana: 39

Alicia, Juana: 243

Alien Act: 287

All American Container: 360

Allen v. State Board of Elections: 293, 313

Allende, Salvador: 168, 414, 610

Alliance for Progress: 167

Almaraz, Carlos: 527–528

Almeida, Rafael: 724

Almendros, Nestor: 624

Alonso, Kenneth B.: 435

Alonso, María Conchita: 612

Altamira, José: 137

Alurista: 465–468, 485–486

Alvarado Construction Inc.: 358

Alvarado, Elvia M.: 243, 618

Alvarado, Linda: 358

Alvarez, Anne Maino: 435

Alvarez, Everett, Jr.: 276, 329

Alvarez, Julia: 474, 486

Alvarez, Luis Walter: 435

Alvarez, Marina: 616

Alvarez, Rodolfo: 414

Alvarez de Pineda, Alonzo: 62

Alvariño de Leira, Angeles: 436

Alverio, Rosita Dolores. *See* Moreno, Rita

Amado, Ralph: 436

Amador, Elías: 436

American Airlines: 349, 363

American Dream: 276, 348, 479, 484, 504, 525, 675, 710

American Federation of Labor (AFL): 369–371, 765

American Federation of Labor and Congress of Industrial Organizations (AFL-CIO): 371–372, 760
American G.I. Forum: 39, 276, 280, 387, 749, 755, 765
American Hispanic-Owned Radio Association (AHORA): 697
American International Container: 360
American Lodge: 278
American Revolution: 16, 150, 274, 278–279, 285, 287, 455, 576
Americanization. (see also assimilation): 38–39, 265, 396–398
Americas Review, The: 242, 414, 417, 423, 425, 471, 473, 490, 504, 535, 691
Amlin, Patricia: 617
Amy, Francisco: 458
anarchists: 244, 460
Anaya, Rudolfo A.: 467–468, 472, 474, 486–487, 616, 628
Anaya, Toney: 333
Anderson, Richard C.: 151
Angeles Negros, Los: 666
Anglicisms: 204–205, 209–210
Anglo-Mexican Mission Institute: 398
Anglo-Saxon: 176, 179–181, 183, 211, 459, 591–592, 594
Anguiano, Lupe: 245
Anheuser-Bush: 349, 357
Anselmo, Reynold (René): 701–702, 717
Antonio Maceo Brigade: 49
Antush, John: 572
Anza, Juan Bautista de. See Bautista de Anza, Juan
Anzaldúa, Gloria: 241, 498
Apache Indians: 18–19, 134, 142, 259, 261, 329
Apalachee Indians: 55, 65–66
Apalachicola Fort: 133
Aparicio, Carlos: 622
Aparicio, Manuel: 561–562, 564–565, 573
Apodaca, Jerry: 333, 689
Apollo Theater: 559
Aragón, José Rafael: 514, 517
Aranda, Guillermo: 538–539
Arawak Indians: 4–6, 56–57, 59, 74, 191
Arbenz, Jacobo: 165
Arboleya, Carlos José: 357–359
Arcano y sus Maravillas: 663–664
Arce, Julio: 460
Arce, Miguel: 459
architecture: 54, 261
Archuleta, Diego: 274, 329
Arciniega, Tomás A.: 757

Arellano, Tristán de: 70
ARENA Party: 173
Arévalo, Juan José: 165
Arias Sánchez, Oscar: 172
Arizona Association of Chicanos for Higher Education: 340
Armas, Castillo: 166
Armendáriz, Pedro: 600, 624
Armida: 625
Armiño, Franca de: 244, 464, 559–560
Army Appropriation Act: 160
Arnaz, Desi: 495, 601, 605, 625, 676
Arnaz y de Acha, Desiderio Alberto III. See Arnaz, Desi
Arreola, Philip: 757–758
Arte Público Press: 242, 248, 362, 416, 425, 468, 471, 474, 480–482, 484–485, 490, 505, 568
Artenstein, Isaac: 614, 617–619, 676, 679, 692
Asamblea Mexicana: 37
Asociación Nacional Pro Personas Mayores: 749
ASPIRA of America: 612
assimilation: 38, 40, 178, 203, 391, 397, 399, 401–402, 404–405, 408–410, 463, 483–484, 553, 556, 593, 609, 655–656
Astol, Lalo. See Astol, Leonardo García
Astol, Leonardo García: 555–556, 565, 575, 692
Ateneo Hispano: 748
audiencia: 12, 62, 64
Austin, Moses: 21
Ausubel, Ken: 614
Avalos, David: 532
Avila, Francisco: 135
Avila House: 135
Ayala, Ramón: 653, 667
Azcárraga Milmo, Emilio: 701
Azcárraga Vidaurreta, Emilio: 701
Aztec Indians: 9–12, 14, 40, 53–55, 62, 64, 72–73, 248, 257–258, 485–486, 530, 545
Aztlán: 9, 40, 54, 201, 243, 468, 485–487, 529, 532, 538, 542, 547, 566, 616, 650, 691
Azuela, Mariano: 459, 582

B

babalao: 271–272
Babenco, Hector: 610
Babín, María Teresa: 413–414
Baca, Jimmy Santiago: 487
Baca, Joseph Francis: 306
Baca, Judith: 243, 529–530, 539
Baca-Barragán, Polly: 245, 334
Baca-Zinn, Maxine: 216, 250, 415

Badillo, Herman: 320–321
Baez, Alberto Vinicio: 436–437
Báez, Myrna: 243
Balaguer, Joaquín: 168, 223
Ballad of Gregorio Cortez, The: 505, 619, 628, 636, 649, 675
Ballesteros, Jack: 614
Bamba, La: 568, 584, 609, 618–619, 623, 675, 717
banana industry: 198
banda: 667–669
Banderas, Antonio: 619
Bank of California: 362
Bañuelos, Romana Acosta: 329–330
Baptists: 265, 398–399, 504
Barajas, Salvador: 538–539
Barela, Casimiro: 334
Barela, Patrocino: 518
Barnum and Bailey Circus: 556
Barrera, Mario: 615
Barrera, Rolando: 568
Barreto, Lefty: 479
Barrio Boyzz: 667–668
Barrio de Analco Historic District: 141
Barro, Mary Helen: 758
Batista, Fulgencio: 46, 166, 191, 225, 731
Battle of Puebla: 40
Bautista Alvarado, Juan: 135
Bautista de Anza, Juan: 19, 74, 135, 344
Bay of Pigs: 48, 167, 508
Bazaar, Philip: 275
Beato, Alfonso: 621
Beauchamp, Eduvigis: 239
Becerra, Xavier: 314, 320
Bedoya, Alfonso: 600, 604, 625
Belén, Edna Acosta. See Acosta-Belén, Edna
Bélen Gutiérrez de Mendoza, Juana: 238
Belgrano, Manuel: 151
Bellán, Esteban: 723
Beltrán, Bernardino: 71
Benavides, Fortunato P.: 302
Benavides, Roy: 277
Benavides, Santos: 274, 277
Benchmark Hospitality Group: 357, 359
Berbers (see also Germanic tribes): 3
Bernal, Paulino: 653–654
Berrio: 62
Betances, Ramón Emeterio: 29, 458
Beveridge, Albert C.: 156
biculturalism: 409, 659
Bidlack, Benjamin: 154
Bilingual Review Press: 471
Bilingual Review: 242, 423

bilingualism: 46, 202, 206–207, 209–211, 238, 240, 292, 326, 328, 401, 409–410, 413, 480, 485–486, 492, 496–497, 500, 566, 609, 616, 763, 765, 771
Birabén, Alfedo. *See* Norton, Barry
biracial: 183–184, 186
Bishop, Maurice: 171
Black and White Mural: 537, 540–541
Black Panthers: 45
blacks: 178–180, 182, 184, 188, 190, 196, 200, 214, 257, 273, 365, 371–372, 377–382, 386–389, 410, 456, 588–589, 593, 597, 602–603, 606, 612, 623, 662, 724–725
Blackton, Stuart: 588
Blades, Rubén: 610, 617, 622, 625, 664
Blaine, James G.: 155–156
Blaz, Ben: 320
Bobadilla, Francisco de: 58
Bobo, Willie: 665
Boland Amendment: 172
Bolaños Cacho, Miguel: 459
Bolívar, Simón: 151, 279
Bonilla, Bobby: 726
Bonilla, Frank: 415
Bonilla, Henry: 314, 320
Bonilla, Rubén: 759
Bonilla, Tony: 758–759
Bonilla-Santiago, Gloria: 415
Borica, Diego de: 396
Borinquen: 7, 42–45, 58, 415, 536, 559
Born in East L.A.: 609–611, 618, 632, 675, 772
Borras, Caridad: 437
Borras, Edelmiro: 559
Bosch, Juan: 168, 420
Botero, Fernando: 524
Boulevard Nights: 606, 608
Bowie, Jim: 22, 494
Box, John C.: 38
Bracero Program: 39, 43, 201, 207, 230, 286, 315, 367–368, 373–377, 384
Bracetti, Mariana: 239
Brackenridge, Henry M.: 151
Bradley, Tom: 299
Braga, Sonia: 611
brain drain: 434
Bravo, Edgar Michael: 616
Bravos del Norte, Los: 653
Briceño, Carlos: 727
Brito-Avellano, María: 243
brotherhoods: 42, 52, 262–263, 272, 515, 536, 542, 601, 748
Brown Berets: 40, 45, 539
Bruni, Toni: 614

Bryan-Chamorro Treaty: 160, 162
Bucareli, Antonio María: 74
Buchanan, Pat: 383, 385
Buenos Aires Inter-American Conferences: 163
Bugarín, Pedro: 656
Bukis, Los: 666–667
Bull of Demarcation: 60
Bunau-Varilla, Philippe: 159
Burger King: 349, 363
Burger, Warren: 378
Burgos, Julia de: 244, 476, 621
Bush, George: 304, 331–333, 762, 774
Bustamante, Albert G.: 320
Bustamante, Anastasio: 22

C

Caballeros de Labor: 369
Caballeros de San Juan: 44
Cabán, Roger: 242, 581
Cabañas, Humberto: 357, 359
Cabeza de Vaca, Álvar Núñez. *See* Núñez Cabeza de Vaca, Álvar
Cabildo, The: 140–141
Cabot, Sebastian: 60
Cabral, Reid: 168
Cabranés, José A.: 306
Cabrera Infante, Gabriel: 482
Cabrera Infante, Saba: 244
Cabrera, Lydia: 242, 483
Cáceres, César A.: 437
Cáceres, Ramón: 161
Cacho, Miguel Bolaños. *See* Bolaños Cacho, Miguel
Caddo Indians: 73, 146, 432
Cadena Radio Centro: 699
Café de California: 340
Cafferty, Pastora San Juan: 416
Caicedo, Harry: 690, 759
Calderón Sol, Armando: 173
Califa, Antonio: 382
California Land Act: 25
California Theater: 551
Calpe Americano: 748
Calusa Indians: 55
Camacho, Joe: 616
Camargo, Diego de: 62
Camargo, Velia: 565
Camarillo, Albert Michael: 416
Camino Real: 144, 262
Campeche Show: 667
Camplis, F. X.: 615
Campos, Albizu: 29, 621
Campos, Santiago E.: 306
Campubrí, José: 683
Cana Brava: 668
Canales, Nemesio: 620
Cancio, Marta: 437
canción: 579, 645–647, 652, 656

Candelas, Graciela: 437–438
Candia, Oscar A.: 438
Cannella, John M.: 307
Canseco, José: 727
Cansino, Margarita Carmen. *See* Hayworth, Rita
Cantinflas. *See* Moreno, Mario
Cantú, Norma: 382
Capdevielle, María. *See* Maris, Mona
Capella, Antonio: 620
Caperton, William B.: 161
Capetillo, Luisa: 240, 244, 465
Capó, Bobby: 568
Capote, Ernesto: 572
Caraballo, Wilfredo: 298
Caracena, Fernando: 438
Carbajal, Jesús: 615
Cárdenas, Isidra T. de: 244, 460
Cárdenas, López de: 70
Cárdenas, Mary Janet M.: 438
Cárdenas, Raúl de: 572
Cárdenas, Robert Léon: 277
Cárdenas, Rogelio: 537, 545–546
Cardinali, José: 685
Cardona, Florencia Bisenta de Casillas Martínez. *See* Carr, Vikki
Cardona, Manuel: 438–439
Cardús, David: 439
Carew, Rod: 727–728
Carib Indians: 4–6, 56–57, 63, 191
Caridad del Cobre, La: 268, 271
Carino v. University of Oklahoma: 378
Carioca, José: 596
CARISSMA: 612
Carlos IV: 393
Carlos López Press: 462
Carmel Mission: 134
Carmen, Julie: 611
Carnegie, Andrew: 156
Caro, Brígido: 459
carpa: 37, 556, 567, 584, 613
Carpa Cubana: 556–557
Carpa García: 556–557
Carpentier, Alejo: 482
Carr, Vikki: 667, 759–760
Carranza, Venustiano: 162, 461, 539
Carrera, José Miguel: 151
carriage industry: 347
Carrillo, Eduardo: 552
Carrillo, Leo: 592, 596, 602, 626
Carrillo, Leopoldo: 347
Carrillo, Sean: 617
Cart War: 347
Carter, Jimmy: 49, 169, 247–248, 289, 304–306, 308, 319, 330–331, 496, 702, 742, 759
Carter, Lynda Córdoba: 605, 626

Carthaginians: 2
Casa Alvarado: 135
Casa Aztlán: 542
Casa Cubana: 240
Casa Editorial Lozano: 459
Casa Galicia: 748
Casals, Rosemary: 728
Casanova de Villaverde, Emilia: 240
Casas, Bartolomé de las: 64, 179,
    182, 255
Casas, Juan Bautista: 274
Casas, Melesio: 524–525
Casiano, Domingo: 620
Casso, Henry: 264
Castañeda, Antonia I.: 417
Castañeda, Carlos E.: 397, 413
Castañeda, Tomás: 538
Castaño de Sosa, Gaspar: 71
caste system: 20, 177–178, 183
Castejón, Blanca de: 620
Castellanos, Leonard: 539
Castelló, Hugo M.: 728
Castile: 2, 4, 57
Castilian. See Spanish language
Castilians: 3–4, 594
Castilla y O'Donnell, Marie
    Marguerita Guadalupe Teresa
    Estela Bolado. See Margo
Castillo, Alonso del: 66
Castillo, El: 135
Castillo, Leonel J.: 330
Castillo, Mario: 542
Castillo, Sylvia: 244
Castro, Alberto: 439
Castro, Fidel: 46–49, 166, 169, 191,
    225, 287, 289, 292, 506, 508, 606
Castro, George: 440
Castro, José: 134
Castro, Peter: 440
Castro (José) House: 137
Catholic church: 2, 4, 11, 20, 22, 37,
    42, 47, 54, 153, 209, 221, 238,
    240, 258, 264–265, 270–271, 273,
    343, 394, 396–399, 417, 488, 515,
    634, 764
Catholic Kings: 4, 11, 58, 176
Catholic schools: 397, 494
Catholicism: 2, 11, 28, 42, 73, 177,
    179, 253–254, 257–258, 263, 265,
    271, 397, 401, 488, 518, 567, 660
cattle ranching: 15, 134, 222, 262,
    344–346, 648, 677, 725
caudillo: 162
Cavazos, Lauro F.: 330–331
Cavazos, Richard E.: 276, 278
Celts (see also Iberian-Celtic culture
    and Gaelic culture): 2, 176
Central American Common Market:
    287

Central American Court of Justice:
    160
Central American Union: 197
Central Bank of Mexico: 174
Central Intelligence Agency (CIA):
    166–168
Centro Asturiano: 560–564, 572,
    748
Centro Cultural de la Raza: 529,
    531–532, 537
Centro Español de West Tampa:
    560
Centro Obrero: 560, 563–564
Cepeda, Orlando: 729
Cerezo, Carmen C.: 307
Cerón, Juan: 59
Cervantes, Lorna Dee: 473–474,
    482, 487–488
Cervantes, Pedro: 522
Cervántez, Yreina: 243
Chacón, Eusebio: 456–457
Chacón, Felipe Maximiliano: 457
Chacón, Iris: 621
Chamizal National Monument: 144
Chamorro, Violeta: 172
Chaplin, Charles: 588
Chapultepec, Act of: 164
Charles III: 75, 262
Charles IX: 69
Charola, Asunción Elena: 440
Chata Noloesca, La. See Escalona,
    Beatriz
Chatfield, Frederick: 155
Chávez, Angélico: 461, 488
Chávez, César: 366, 371–372, 539,
    542–543, 565, 583, 613, 760, 767
Chávez, Denise: 241, 471–474, 489
Chávez, Dennis: 314, 320, 322
Chávez, Manuel. See Fray Chávez,
    Angélico
Chicago Working Woman's Union:
    238
Chicanas: 236–237, 239, 243, 421,
    426–427, 471–473, 498, 529, 601,
    603, 613, 618, 634, 750
Chicano Advocates for Employment.
    See Café de California
Chicano films: 609, 612
Chicano identity: 465, 504, 533, 539,
    546
Chicano literature: 241
Chicano Moratorium: 539, 541, 638,
    650
Chicano Movement: 242, 487, 615,
    657
Chicano theater: 565–569, 583
Chicanos: 40, 45, 184, 186, 200, 213,
    215–216, 219, 230, 232, 244, 247,
    250, 266, 298, 328, 371, 377, 400,
    414, 416, 420–422, 450, 459,

465–474, 477, 485–487, 492,
    495–496, 498–502, 504–505, 507,
    516, 523–525, 527–535, 537–545,
    547, 565–568, 583–584, 587,
    597–603, 606–610, 612–620, 628,
    634, 636, 638, 650, 653, 656–657,
    659, 662, 665, 667, 674–677, 680,
    688, 693, 753
Chichimecas: 9, 12
child labor laws: 238, 366
chinampa: 8–9, 54
Chinese Exclusion Act: 286, 288
Chiquita Banana: 605
Chong, Thomas: 611
Christian Brothers: 397
Christian Castilians: 3
Christianity: 2–3, 61, 177, 253–254,
    258–260, 262, 265, 392–393, 395,
    432
Chua Ranch, La: 344
Chumacero, Olivia: 243
Ciboney Indians: 5, 56–57
Ciccone, Oscar: 569
Cid Pérez, José: 572
Cienfuegos, Lucky: 478, 572
cigar industry: 45–46, 182, 207
Cintrón, Guillermo B.: 440–441
Circo Cubano. See Carpa Cubana
Circo Escalante: 37
Círculo Cubano: 560, 748
Círculo Valenciano: 748
Cisco Kid: 568, 584, 594, 605, 626,
    632–633, 637–638, 676
Cisneros, Henry G.: 326, 616
Cisneros, Sandra: 241, 471–472,
    474, 490
citizenship: 30, 40–41, 43, 119, 153,
    180–181, 183–184, 191–192, 207,
    219, 263, 276, 285–288, 290–294,
    400, 465, 562, 675, 701, 753
Civil Rights Act: 291–292, 294–295,
    303, 378, 382
civil rights legislation: 184, 295,
    312, 338, 381–382, 602
civil rights movement: 276, 413,
    535, 587, 600–602, 604, 612
civil rights organizations: 276, 280,
    615, 748
Civil War, United States: 155, 157,
    236
civil wars: 28, 32, 36, 53–54, 155,
    161, 165, 172, 181, 198, 241,
    274–275, 277, 279, 287, 301, 310,
    321, 323–325, 329, 336, 345, 348,
    399, 456
Claretians: 263
Clavijo, Uva: 242
Clay, Henry: 150, 153, 156
Clayton, John M.: 155
Clemente, Roberto: 730

Cleveland, Grover: 325
Cleveland, Richard J.: 346
Clifton and Morenci, Arizona: 133
Clinton, Bill: 245, 327–328, 334, 385, 761
Club Sembradores de la Amistad: 269
Cobo Souza, Manuel: 483
Coca-Cola Inc.: 349, 357–358, 360, 363
code-switching: 204, 210–211
Codina, Armando: 357
Codina Group: 357
Cody, W. F. "Buffalo Bill": 725
Coen, Augusto: 645
Cofer, Judith Ortiz. *See* Ortiz Cofer, Judith
coffee industry: 27, 29, 41, 149, 156, 163, 207, 219, 222
Cold War: 173, 424
Collazo, Julito: 662
Colmenares, Margarita Hortensia: 246
Colón, Jesús: 420, 465, 477, 479, 491, 570
Colón, Miriam: 569–570, 574, 576, 620–621
Colón, Willie: 622, 664
Colón-Morales, Rafael: 536
colonia: 33, 35–38, 42–44, 231
Colonialism: 413
colonization: 1–2, 4, 11, 13–14, 16, 18, 21, 57, 59, 68, 73, 75, 80, 82, 98, 103–104, 153, 176–177, 180, 254, 256, 268, 273, 285, 343–344, 346, 392, 394, 432–433, 549
Colorado Institute for Hispanic Education and Economic Development: 340
Colorado Rockies baseball team: 358
Columbus, Christopher: 4–7, 57, 147, 253, 285, 475
Columbus, Diego: 59, 63
Comanche Indians: 14–16, 21, 73, 181
Comisión Femenil Mexicana Nacional: 750
comisiones honoríficas: 38
Common market: 173, 287
communism: 27, 47, 51, 165–166, 168, 170, 172–173, 483, 572, 727
Community Action Program (CAP): 378–379, 387, 767
compadrazgo: 216–219, 223, 227, 231–232
Compañia, La: 616
Comprehensive Employment and Training Administration: 379, 387
Compromise of 1850: 180
Concepción, Dave: 730

Concepción Mission: 144
Confederación de Trabajadores Generales: 371
Confederación de Trabajadores Generales (CGT): 371
Confederacy: 273–274, 277, 324
Conference of Puerto Rican Women: 250, 339, 753–754
confianza: 216, 218–219, 221, 223–224, 231
Congregationalists: 398
Congreso de Artistas Chicanos en Aztlán: 537–538, 540
Congreso Mexicanista: 37
Congress of Mexican American Unity: 605
Congressional Hispanic Caucus: 314–316, 318–320, 326, 750, 769
Conjunto Bernal, El: 653
conjunto: 644–645, 652–656, 658, 662, 666, 668
Connecticut Association for United Spanish Action: 340
conquistadors: 10–11, 58, 63–64, 66–67, 70, 72, 144, 254–255, 258, 270, 458
Consortium of National Hispanic Organizations: 751
Contadora Group: 172
Continental Airlines: 357, 361
Contras: 172
Convent of Porta Coeli: 143
conventos: 509
Cordero, Angel: 730
Cordero, Julio: 441
Cordero y Bustamante, Antonio: 146
Córdova, Pedro de: 627
Córdova House: 133
Corea, Chick: 665
Corona, Bert: 761
Coronado, Francisco. *See* Vasquez de Coronado, Francisco
Coronado, José R.: 761
Coronado National Memorial: 133
Coronel, Antonio F.: 550
Corpi, Lucha: 471
Corporation for Public Broadcasting: 482, 679, 763
Corpus Christi de la Ysleta Mission: 144
Corral, Edward A.: 762
corrido: 457, 538, 566–567, 583, 614, 645–651
Cortés, Carlos E.: 417–418
Cortés, Hernán: 6–7, 9, 14, 54–55, 62, 64, 73, 254, 257
Cortez, Gregorio: 619, 649
Cortez, Raúl: 693, 700
Cortina, Juan Nepomuceno: 649
Cortina, Rodolfo J.: 418, 484, 572

Cosío y Cisneros, Evangelina: 236
Cossío, Evangelina: 458
Costello, Diana: 615
Cotera, Manuel: 555
cotton industry: 32, 34, 55, 153, 263, 291, 347, 366–367, 370, 374, 377, 523, 652
Council of the Indies: 12, 60, 65, 72
cowboy diplomacy: 159
cowboys: 34, 344–346, 365, 369, 503, 556, 589, 595, 603, 614, 649, 655, 676, 721–722, 725–726
Creek Indians: 133, 344
Cremata, Ernesto: 572
Creoles: 97–98
Crespi, Juan: 135
criollo: 13–14, 29, 41, 177–178, 242
Cristal, Linda: 605, 626–627, 677
Cristo Negro de Esquipulas: 267
Crockett, Davey: 22
crónica: 456–460, 462, 469, 577
Crusades: 3, 549
Cruz Azaceta, Luis: 536
Cruz Blanca, La : 241
Cruz, Celia: 660–661, 664
Cruz, Nicky: 479
Cruz-Romo, Gilda: 762
Cuadra, Angel: 483
Cuauhtemoc: 10
Cuba, Joe: 663
Cuban American Foundation: 359
Cuban American Legal Defense and Education Fund: 337, 750
Cuban American National Council: 751
Cuban Film Institute: 621
Cuban folklore: 242
Cuban Revolution: 30, 41, 208, 240, 369, 434, 482–484, 493, 573, 575, 723–724, 731
Cuban Revolution of 1959: 28, 45, 225, 358, 572
Cuban Women's Club: 240
Cuéllar, Gilbert, Jr.: 359
Cuervo y Valdés, Francisco: 141
Cuesta, José Enamorado: 464, 559–560
Cugat, Xavier: 631, 644
Cuitlahuac: 10
curandero: 270–271, 432, 621
Customs House (Monterey, California): 135
Cuza Malé, Belkis: 242, 484

D

Dallmeier, Francisco: 441–442
Dana, Bill: 605
Dantés: 457
Darrow, Henry: 595, 621, 626, 638
Darwinism: 180

Davidson, Peter W.: 683–684
Dávila, Luis: 471
Dawson, Thomas C.: 160
de Alaminos, Antón. *See* Alaminos, Antón de
de Alániz, Jerónimo. *See* Alániz, Jerónimo de
de Alarcón, Hernando. *See* Alarcón, Hernando de
de Alonso, Luis Antonio Dámaso. *See* Roland, Gilbert
de Alvardo, Pedro. *See* Alvardo, Pedro de
de Armiño, Franca. *See* Armiño, Franca de
de Bobadilla, Francisco. *See* Bobadilla, Francisco de
de Borica, Diego. *See* Borica, Diego de
de Burgos, Julia. *See* Burgos, Julia de
De Córdova, Arturo: 600, 620, 627
de Gali, Francisco. *See* Gali, Francisco de
de la Garza, E. (Kika): 314, 320
de la Garza, Rodolfo: 418
de la Hoya, Oscar. *See* Hoya, Oscar de la
de la Riva-Baza, Sandra Lynn: 731
de Leira, Angeles Alvariño. *See* Alvariño de Leira, Angeles
de Lugo, Ron: 320
de Pineda, Alonzo Alvarez. *See* Alvarez de Pineda, Alonzo
de Santo Silas, María Africa Vidal. *See* Montez, María
De Soto Caverns: 133
De Soto Falls: 133
de Soto, Hernando. *See* Soto, Hernando de
de Varona, Donna: 731
de Villalobos, María Guadalupe Vélez. *See* Vélez, Lupe
DeAnda, James: 307
Decade of the Hispanic: 349
del Río, Dolores: 596, 600, 612, 619, 627
del Valle, Pedro A.: 278
Delano, Jack: 620
Delgado, Abelardo: 465–466, 492
Delgado, Adelaida. *See* Mara, Adele
Delgado, Ana Albertina: 243
Delgado, Lalo. *See* Delgado, Abelardo
DeLome, Dupuy: 157
democracy: 46, 121, 156, 165–168, 278, 464–465, 480, 589, 599
Democratic National Committee Hispanic Caucus: 339
Democratic Party: 280

deportation: 230, 286, 339, 383–384, 463, 553, 580, 610, 628, 672, 675
Depression: 28, 38–39, 43, 163, 230, 286, 326, 329, 367, 370, 377, 461–464, 491, 502, 552–556, 561, 564, 574–575, 578, 580–582, 587, 596, 598, 600–601, 610, 614, 655
Devine, John: 346
Diario-La Prensa, El: 683–684
Díaz Castro, Tania: 242
Díaz del Castillo, Bernal: 9, 62, 254
Díaz Guerra, Alirio: 462
Díaz, Henry Frank: 442
Díaz, Patricia: 618
Díaz, Porfirio: 33–34, 41, 160–161, 230, 238, 244, 286, 457, 599, 747
Díaz Valcárcel, Emilio: 620
Díaz Vara Calderón, Gabriel: 258
Díaz-Balart, Lincoln: 314–315
Díaz-Oliver, Remedios: 360
dictators: 46, 153, 165–166, 173, 191, 222–223, 225, 230, 244, 286, 289, 292, 434, 457, 459, 464, 486, 535, 582, 610–611, 685, 731, 747
Diego, Juan: 257, 514, 546
Dillon, C. Douglas: 167
dime novels: 594, 674
diplomacy: 41, 159, 317, 765, 768, 770
discrimination: 33, 37, 39, 44, 119, 133, 179, 184, 214, 231, 264, 275–276, 286, 291–295, 297, 304, 313–314, 327, 339, 369–371, 378–379, 381–382, 385–387, 396, 399, 405, 407, 434, 465, 491, 505, 531, 556, 616, 618, 621, 628, 650–651, 656, 659, 714, 755
Disney, Walt: 487, 596, 609, 674, 676, 699
District of Columbia Commission on Latino Community Development: 340
Dole, Robert: 383
dollar diplomacy: 161, 183
Domenicci, Porfirio: 683
domestic workers: 374
Domínguez, Cari M.: 327
Domínguez, Jorge I.: 419
Don Catarino. *See* Pirrín, Eusebio
Don Francisco (Mario Kreutzberger): 712
Don Lalo. *See* Astol, Lalo
Donciano Vigil House: 141
Dorantes, Andrés: 66
Down These Mean Streets: 478–479, 502
Draft Act on Peace and Cooperation: 172
Drake, Francis: 73, 181
drugs: 173, 332, 572, 580, 714, 736

Duke of Albuquerque: 15
Dulles, John Foster: 161, 165
Durán, Roberto: 731–732
Duvalier, Jean Claude: 289

E

Echeverría, Diego: 622
Echeverría, José: 482
Economic Opportunity Act (EOA): 378, 387
Editorial Quinto Sol: 241, 466–467, 469–471, 486, 492, 495, 503
educational attainment: 192, 226
Edwards, Philip: 346
Effie Eddington School for Girls: 398
Eisenhower, Dwight D.: 47, 165
Eisenhower, Milton: 165
El Alamo. *See* Alamo, El
El Conde Gris. *See* Solano, Gustavo
El Norte: 248, 611, 618–619, 675, 679
El Super: 610
Elizondo, Hector: 607
Elizondo, Virgilio: 254, 264, 268, 270
Elliot, Alejandro: 568
Elvas, Gentleman of: 432
Elysian Park: 135
embargo: 162–164, 167, 724
Emergency Relief Administration Act (ERA Act): 562, 574
Emplumada (Plumed): 473, 488
En la lucha . . . ponte trucha (mural): 537, 545–546
encomienda: 6–7, 11–12, 14, 59, 64–66, 254–255, 260
Encuentros: 264
Endara, Guillermo: 173
engineering: 246
Engle, Margarita: 242
Enrique, Luis: 668
Enríquez, E.: 236
entertainment industry: 456, 462, 550, 553, 555–556, 565, 568, 593, 653, 662, 671, 679–680, 683–685, 688–691, 699–700, 706–707, 712, 717, 719, 747, 771–772
entrada: 16, 259
environmental groups: 376
Equal Employment Opportunity Commission (EEOC): 236, 311, 371, 378–379, 381–382, 387, 612
Erickson, Charles A.: 672–673, 690
Escajeda, Josefina: 461
Escalante, Esteban: 459
Escalante, Jaime: 434, 675, 762
Escalante Fontaneda, Hernando de: 238

Escalona, Beatriz (La Chata Noloesca): 559, 565, 568, 574
Escandón, José: 345, 495
Escobar, Javier I.: 442
Escobar, Marisol: 524
Escobar, Sixto: 726, 732, 740
Espada Aqueduct: 144
Esparza, Moctezuma: 243, 608–609, 614, 619, 675, 679
Espejo, Antonio de: 14, 71
Espinosa, Conrado: 459
Espinosa, Paul: 614–615, 628, 692
Espinoza v. Farah Manufacturing Company: 294, 378
Espíritu Santo de la Bahía Mission: 145
Esquivel, Antonio: 725
Essex Theater: 572
Estefan, Gloria: 668
Estevanico: 66, 70
Esteves, Luis R.: 279
Esteves, Sandra María: 241, 480
Estévez, Emilio: 608, 612, 623, 628, 638
Estévez, Ramón. *See* Sheen, Martin
Estrada, Erik (Enrique): 606
Estrada, Fred: 689–690
Estrada, Juan B.: 160
Estrada Cabrera, Manuel: 161
Estrada Palma, Tomás: 30
Estrella del Castillo, Amalia: 550
Estudillo, José Antonio: 135
Estudillo House (San Diego, California): 135
ethnicity: 45, 51, 186, 188, 203, 210, 371, 386, 398, 426–427, 475, 587–588, 594, 604, 659, 673, 747
evangelization: 254–255, 258–259, 261–262, 398
extended family: 216–219, 221–222, 224, 227–228, 231–232, 266, 395

F

Fábregas, Virginia: 37, 551
Fages, Pedro: 433
Fair Employment Practices Committee (FEPC): 371, 378, 387
Fajardo Ortiz, Desiderio: 458
Falcon Records: 653
Familia de Hoy, La: 689
familia, la: 215–217, 219, 231, 567
family life: 222, 233, 752
Farabundo Martí National Liberation Front (FMLN): 169–170, 172–173
Farándula Panamericana, La: 568–569
farm workers: 37, 201, 238, 286, 291, 338, 362, 370, 376–377, 385, 387, 466, 543, 565, 583, 613–615, 697, 733, 756, 760–761, 772
farming: 41, 53, 55–56, 255, 393, 396, 433, 494, 654
Farmworkers Organizing Committee: 760
Farragut, David G.: 274, 279–280
Federación Libre de los Trabajadores: 244, 370–371
Federal Art Project: 518
Federal Theater Project: 560–561, 574
Feliciano, José: 665
Feliciano Canyon: 135
Félix, Charles: 539–540
Ferdinand, King: 11
Ferdinand VII: 151
Fernández Camus, Emilio: 483
Fernández, Emilio (El Indio): 628–629
Fernández, Ferdinand Francis: 302, 307
Fernández, Gigi: 732–733
Fernández, José B.: 419
Fernández, Joseph A.: 763
Fernández, Manuel José Manny: 721, 726
Fernández, Mary Joe: 733
Fernández, Ricardo R.: 763
Fernández, Roberta: 241
Fernández, Roberto: 483, 492–493, 577
Fernández, Tony: 733
Fernández-Rundle, Katherine: 240
Ferra, Max: 571
Ferrer, José: 574, 621
Ferrer, Mel: 629
Ferrer, Rafael: 524, 526
Festival Latino: 568–569
feudalism: 3
field workers: 237, 374
Figueres, José: 165
Figueroa, Gabriel: 629
Figueroa, Pablo: 617
Figueroa, Sotero: 458
Fillmore, Millard: 288
First Battalion of Native Cavalry: 274
First Congress of Women Workers: 244
Fischbarg, Jorge: 443
Fish, Hamilton: 157
Fish & Company: 347
Flores, José: 135
Flores, Juan: 420
Flores, Julio: 457
Flores, Patrick F.: 264, 764
Flores, Pedro: 463
Flores, Roy: 617
Flores, Thomas Raymond: 733
Flores House (South Pasadena, California): 135
Flores Magón brothers: 747
Florida Commission on Hispanic Affairs: 340
folklore: 1, 242, 275, 393, 416–417, 426, 461–462, 476, 481, 553, 565–567, 574, 596, 649, 655, 662
Font, Rosa María de: 239
Fontánez, Angela: 243
Food Assistance Act: 169
food processing: 349
Foraker Act: 41
Ford Foundation: 250, 419, 429, 568
Ford, Gerald R.: 168, 304
Foreign Assistance Act: 169
Fornés, María Irene: 571, 575
Fort Caroline: 68–69, 258
Fort Mose: 273
Fort Point National Historic Site: 135
Fort San Carlos de Barrancas: 138
Fort San Lorenzo: 143
Fortaleza, La: 143, 526
Forumeer, The: 749
Fougá, Bernardo: 555
Fountain of Youth: 60
Fraguada, Federico: 572
Franciscans: 16, 19, 72, 74–75, 134, 143, 258, 260–262, 392–394
Fray Chávez, Angélico: 488
free men: 65, 179, 346
Free Trade Agreement: 376
freed slaves: 178
freight industry: 346–347
Frito Bandito: 605, 680
Fuentes, Carlos: 258, 602, 610
Fuera de Liga: 668
Fundación Puertorriqueña de las Humanidades: 622
Fuste, José Antonio: 307
Fuster, Jaime B.: 250, 320
Futurismo: 568

G

G.I. Bill: 276, 504, 768, 772
Gabaldón, Guy: 275
Gaelic culture: 2
Gage, Thomas: 179
Gagemi, Renate: 618
Gaitán, Fernando J.: 307
Galán, Héctor: 615, 628, 679
Galan Productions: 615
Galarza, Ernesto: 371, 764
Galavisión: 702, 707, 716
Gali, Francisco de: 73
Galindo, Rudy: 734
Gallardo, Edward: 568, 570, 572
Gallegos, Celso: 517
Gallegos, José Manuel: 322, 400

Galtieri, Leopoldo: 172
Gálvez, Bernardo de: 274, 278
Gálvez, José de: 19, 74, 262
Gamboa, Harry: 527, 541
gangs: 34, 44, 331, 502, 580, 599,
    604, 606–607, 612, 617, 619, 621,
    623, 649, 675, 677
Garay, Francisco de: 62
Garcés, Pedro de: 19
García, Alfredo Mariano: 443, 602,
    629
García, Ana María: 622
García, Andrés: 714
García, Andy: 608–609, 629
García, Antonio: 520, 522
García, Arturo. *See* De Córdova,
    Arturo
García, Carlos Ernesto: 443
García, Celso Ramón: 443–444
García, Cristina: 242
García, Daniel P.: 299
García, David: 613
García, Edward J.: 307
García, Héctor Pérez: 765
García, José D.: 444, 621
García, Juan: 133
García, Lionel G.: 493–494
García, Manuel V.: 556
García, María Cristina Jurado. *See*
    Jurado, Katy
García, Octavo, y sus GGs: 659
García, Rifino: 133
García, Rupert: 528, 531
García Astol, Leonardo (*see also*
    Astol, Lalo): 575
García Torres, José: 621
Garci-Menéndez, Andrés Arturo. *See*
    García, Andy
Garduño, Gilberto: 537, 547–548
Garza, Emilio M.: 302, 308
Garza, Juan: 617
Garza, Reynaldo G.: 302, 308, 313,
    335
Garza, Sabino: 616
Garza Falcón, Blas María de la: 345
Geada, Rita: 242
gender: 238, 240–241, 295, 378,
    382, 396, 403, 427, 456, 680, 752
General Treaty: 160
genízaros: 14
genocide: 4, 176, 603
Germanic peoples: 2–3, 176, 179
Gierbolini, Gilberto: 308
Gil, Lourdes: 242
Ginorio, Beatriz Angela: 246
Ginsberg, Alan: 478
Girone, Maria Elena: 246
glass ceiling: 356
Glazer, Nathan: 235
Godoy, Gustavo: 703, 706

Goizueta, Roberto C.: 356–357, 360
gold: 6–7, 11, 14, 24–25, 31–32,
    57–59, 61–67, 69–71, 90, 110,
    114, 133, 135, 155, 285, 392, 459,
    499, 505, 518, 594, 602–603, 610,
    672
Golden West Broadcasters: 362
Gómez, Elsa: 765
Gómez, Lefty: 734
Gómez, Vernon Louis. *See* Gómez,
    Lefty
Gómez de Avellaneda, Gertrudis:
    482
Gómez Peña, Guillermo: 617
Gómez-Quiñones, Juan: 420
Gonzales, Stephanie: 334
González, Adalberto Elías: 552–553,
    575
González, Alberto M.: 464
González, Alfredo: 459
González, Balde: 656
González, Celedonio: 483, 494, 572
González, Deena J.: 247
González, Elma: 444
González, Henry B.: 320
González, José Luis: 465, 476–477,
    570
González, Jovita: 461
González, Justo: 265, 267
González, Lucía Eldine: 238
González, Lucía Parsons: 247
González, Miguel: 724
González, Pancho: 735
González, Paula: 444
González, Pedro J.: 614, 679,
    692–693
González, Raymond Emmanuel: 765
González, Richard Alonzo. *See*
    González, Pancho
González, Richard Rafael: 444
González, Rodolfo "Corky": 465, 542
González, Speedy: 596
González, Xavier: 520, 523
González-Alvarez House: 139
González Amezcua, Chelo: 522
González-Berry, Erlinda: 420–421
González González, Pedro: 556
González-Irizarry, Aníbal: 700
González Pando, Miguel: 572
González Parson, Lucy. *See*
    González, Lucía Eldine
Gordillo, Francisco: 63
Gorras Blancas, Las: 25
Goya Foods Inc.: 349, 352, 363
Graham v. Richardson: 293
Gran Chichimeca, El: 12
Gran Colombia: 152
Grand Opera House: 550
Grant, Ulysses S.: 158
Gratas, Enrique: 714

Grattan, Alejandro: 618
grazing rights: 344
greaser laws: 24
Great Society: 379, 382, 387
Greeks: 2–3, 431
green card: 374
Griffith, David Wark: 590
Griggs v. Duke Power Company: 378
Grijalva, Juan de: 6
Griswold del Castillo, Richard A.:
    420
Grito de Lares: 29, 41, 239, 422, 559
Grito, El: 244
Group of Eight: 172
Grupo, El: 480
Grupo Lluvia: 667
Grupo Wao: 668
grupos: 645, 666–667
Guadalupe Theater: 567
Guajardo Lepicier, Rita: 616
Guastavino, Rafael: 433
Guastella, Marino: 621
Guerra, Juan Luis: 668
Guerrero, Lalo: 650, 656
Guerrero, María: 551, 561
Guerrero, Vicente: 21, 550
Guevavi Mission: 133
Guillén, Nicolás: 482, 497
Gulf Stream: 432
gunboat diplomacy: 166, 170, 183
Gurulé, Jimmy: 331
Gutiérrez, Ana Sol: 335
Gutiérrez, Diego: 432
Gutiérrez, Efraín: 616–618
Gutiérrez, Jusepe: 72
Gutiérrez, Luis: 315
Gutiérrez, Marina: 243
Gutiérrez, Ramón: 421
Gutiérrez Alea, Tomás: 577, 624
Gutiérrez de Humaña, Antonio: 71
Gutiérrez de Lara, Bernardo: 274
Gutiérrez de Lara, Lázaro: 459
Gutiérrez de Mendoza, Juana: 244
Guzmán Aguilera, Antonio (Guz
    Aguila). *See* Aguilera, Antonio
    Guzmán
Guzmán, Nuño de: 11–12
Guzmán, Suzanna: 766
gypsies: 176

H

H-2 Program: 368, 373, 377
hacienda: 2, 15–16, 18, 26–27, 31,
    33–34, 135–136, 462, 725
Haig, Alexander: 172
Hall of Famers: 248, 250, 331, 362,
    574, 722, 724, 726, 728–731,
    735–737, 740, 766, 771
Hancock, John: 151
Harding, William: 159

hardware industry: 347
Harrison, Benjamin: 325
Hart, William S.: 588
Hasinai Indians: 260–261
Hatuey: 59
Havana Cubans: 722
Havana Ten Thousand: 49
Hawikuh: 66, 70, 141
Hawley-Smoot Tariff Act: 163
Hay, John: 105, 158
Hay-Pauncefote Treaty: 158
Haya, Ignacio: 348
Hayek, Salma: 619
Haymarket Riot: 238
Hayworth, Rita: 592, 595, 612, 626, 630–631
Hearst, William Randolph: 157, 161, 182
Helms, Jesse: 173
Henríquez Ureña, Pedro: 458, 462
Henry, Guy V.: 41
Henry, O.: 594
Hermanas, Las: 264, 751
hermandades. (*see also* brotherhoods): 42, 44
Hernández, Antonia: 299, 338
Hernández, Enrique: 444
Hernández, Ester: 529, 531
Hernández, Gonzalo J.: 445
Hernández, José Manuel: 421
Hernández, Keith: 735
Hernández, Leopoldo: 572
Hernández, Oscar: 653, 664
Hernández, Pete: 184, 293
Hernández, Rafael: 43, 463, 621
Hernández Cruz, Victor: 480, 491
Hernández de Córdoba, Francisco: 6
Hernández Martínez, Maximiliano: 163
Hernández v. New York: 294
Hernández v. Texas: 184, 291, 293
Herrera, Carolina: 766
Herrera, Miguel: 515, 520
Herrera-Sobek, María: 422
Herrón, Willie: 527, 540–541
Hidalgo, Edward: 276, 281, 331
Hidalgo, Miguel: 274, 285
Hidalgo de la Riva, Osa: 243
Hidalgo y Costilla, Miguel: 20, 539, 542, 545
Hijuelos, Oscar: 474, 483–484, 494
Hinojosa, Alejandro: 617
Hinojosa, María de Lourdes: 244
Hinojosa, Ricardo H.: 308
Hinojosa, Rolando: 212, 429, 466–469, 472, 482, 495
Hipócritas, Los: 244
hiring practices: 295, 378, 385
Hise, Elijah: 155
Hispania: 2, 716

Hispanic Academy of Media Arts and Sciences: 751
Hispanic American Broadcasting Corporation: 703–704, 706, 713
Hispanic Association of Colleges and Universities: 751
Hispanic Business magazine: 349–353, 355–357, 362, 689, 709, 756, 770
Hispanic Elected Local Officials Caucus: 339
Hispanic films: 600, 605, 609, 623
Hispanic identity: 177, 203, 592
Hispanic Link: 672–673, 689–690
Hispanic market: 51, 349, 362–363, 517, 604, 609–610, 684, 689, 691, 693, 695–697, 706, 716–718
Hispanic National Bar Association: 298, 300, 303, 331, 337, 689
Hispanic Political Action Committee: 339
Hispanic studies: 413, 771
Hispanic Women's Council of California: 340
Hispanism: 177
Hispano U.S.A.: 699
History and Heroes (mural): 537–538
History of the Mexican American Worker (mural): 537, 542–543
Holding Institute: 398
Hollywood formula: 593
Homar, Lorenzo: 243
home altars: 266, 516, 519–520, 531
homemakers: 238, 244
Homestead Act: 25, 346
homesteading: 25, 344, 346, 588
Hoover, Herbert: 162–163, 360
horsemanship: 274, 725
hospitality industry: 357
Hostos, Eugenio María de: 458
House of Representatives: 121–124, 131, 158, 245, 312, 314–315, 319–320, 322–323, 325, 332, 334, 383, 426
housing: 37, 44, 48, 126, 167, 183, 214, 221, 224, 231, 236, 240, 245, 297, 311, 334, 337–339, 404, 539–540, 552, 561, 750, 755
Houston, Sam: 22, 146, 153, 494
Hoya, Oscar de la: 730
Huerta, Dolores Fernández: 766
Huerta, Jorge: 568
Huerta, Victoriano: 36, 161
Hughes, Charles Evans: 162
Huidobro, Matías Montes: 483, 572, 577–578
Huitzilopochtli: 9–10, 54
Hull, Cordell: 163
human rights: 118–119, 121, 255

Hunter, Duncan: 376
Hunter, Pancho: 547

I

I Am Joaquín: 465–466, 584, 613
Ibáñez, Michael Louis: 445
Ibarra Reyes, Conchita: 618
Iberian Peninsula: 1–3, 10, 70, 176, 253, 273, 431, 549
Iberian-Celtic culture: 1–2
identity: 1, 12–13, 36–38, 40, 42, 44–45, 50, 99, 152, 176, 178, 184, 196, 201, 203, 210, 223–224, 226, 230, 232, 241–243, 265, 275, 348, 397, 401, 413, 464–468, 475–476, 479–480, 484, 489, 497–498, 502, 504–505, 522, 528–530, 533, 566, 570, 595, 609, 614, 617, 643, 651, 661–662, 664, 666, 690, 697, 753
illegal aliens. *See* undocumented immigrants/workers
immigration: 213–214, 219, 223, 225–231, 239, 264, 286–293, 297, 299, 302, 310–311, 338–339, 347–349, 365, 367–369, 372–373, 384–385, 396, 400, 434, 457–459, 462, 482, 491, 505, 508, 516, 520, 557, 560, 564, 666, 669, 672, 676, 679, 682, 690, 697–698, 726, 752
Immigration Act of 1990: 289, 293
Immigration and Nationality Act: 288, 292, 368, 373
Immigration and Naturalization Service (INS): 290, 293, 330, 339, 383–386
Immigration Reform and Control Act: 290–291, 293–294, 326, 373, 385
Impacto de Montemorelos: 667
import duties: 560
Inca Indians: 53, 63, 97
Ince, Thomas H.: 588
Inclán, Cristino R.: 561
independence movements: 365, 458, 480, 557, 622
Independence War: 182
Independent School District: 294
Indias, Las: 6
Indies: 6, 75, 337
indigenismo: 36–37
Industria del Amor: 667
Industrial Workers of the World: 247, 369
industrialization: 27, 167, 219, 368, 375, 377
Inquisition: 177
Institute for Higher Education Law and Governance: 300
Institutional Revolutionary Party (PRI): 174

Instituto Arte Teatral (IATE): 570
Instituto Cubano de Artes Cinematográficas: 244
Instituto del Arte e Industria Cinematográfica: 624
Instituto San Carlos: 240
Inter-American Conference. *See* Buenos Aires Inter-American Conferences.
Inter-American Defense Board: 164
intermarriage: 177, 179, 219, 236, 579
International Association of Conference Centers: 357, 359
International Broadcasting Company: 693
International Company of Mexico: 230
International Court of Justice: 172
International Labor Defense: 238, 247
International Mine, Mill and Smelter Workers Union: 371
International Monetary Fund: 174
international trade: 343
International Workers of the World: 238
Iowa Spanish-Speaking Peoples Commission: 340
iron forging: 347
irrigation: 55, 144, 322, 431, 433, 523
Isabel, Queen: 11
Isabella, Queen of Castile: 3–4, 11, 57–58, 74, 253–254
Islam: 3, 176–177, 431
Isleños: 195
Iturbide, Augustine: 21
Iturralde, Iraida: 242

J

Jackson, Andrew: 139, 150, 153, 286
Jackson Square: 140
Jacobo, Daniel: 617
Janer, Edwin: 568
Jaramillo, Don Pedrito: 270
Jarri, Jean: 72
Jarrico, Paul: 598
Jeaga Indians: 55
Jefferson, Thomas: 21, 150, 157, 182, 287, 750
Jeronymite Fathers: 74
Jesuits: 16, 75, 255, 258, 262, 325, 392–394, 397
Jesús, María de: 260
Jews: 3–4, 176–177, 179, 253–254, 455
jíbaro: 27–28, 197, 476–477, 620
Jimenez, Flaco: 666, 668
Jiménez, Lillian: 243, 524–525

Jiménez, Orlando: 244
Jiménez-Wagenheim, Olga: 422
Jiménez y Muro, Dolores: 238
Job Corps: 378, 381, 387
John Blair & Company: 704
Johnson, Lyndon Baines: 48, 168, 171, 245, 276, 301, 304, 334, 378, 524, 650, 769
Jones Act: 40–41, 43, 183, 207, 219, 287–288, 292, 462
Jones v. City of Lubbock: 313
Jordan, Barbara: 385
Joseph Papp's New York Shakespeare Festival: 569, 571
journalism: 205, 244, 460, 504, 559, 578, 588, 673, 691, 701, 703, 753, 759, 770–771, 773
Juana la Loca, Queen of Spain: 11
Juárez, Mexico: 37, 539, 543, 577, 599–600, 617, 627, 638, 687, 701, 713
Juchereau de St. Denis: 260
Juliá, Raúl: 569, 576, 608, 610–611, 621, 623, 630
Jumano Indians: 72, 260
Junco, Tirso del: 327, 702
Junta Patriótica Mexicana: 550, 747
Jurado, Katy: 598, 600–601, 630
JUSTICIA: 612

K

Kamehameha III: 346
Kanellos, Nicolás: 471, 481, 535, 568, 692
Kansas Advisory Committee on Hispanic Affairs: 340
Karankawa Indians: 144, 259, 261
Kardec, Alan: 270
Kaskabel. *See* Padilla, Benjamin
KCOR-AM (San Antonio): 693, 695, 700
KCOR-TV (San Antonio): 699–700
Kearny, Stephen Watts: 23, 137, 141, 329
Kennedy, John F.: 48, 167, 245, 281, 329, 334, 337, 520, 533
Kennedy, Robert F.: 245, 334
Khrushchev, Nikita: 167
Kid Chocolate. *See* Sardiñas, Elgio
King Ranch: 330, 345
Kino, Father Eusebio: 18, 75, 133–134, 261–262, 344
kinship: 31, 216–218, 224, 228, 232
KLVE-FM (Los Angeles): 691, 696
KMPC (Los Angeles): 692
Knights of America: 749
Knights of Labor: 238, 369
Korean War: 308, 315, 319, 374, 495
KWKW-AM (Los Angeles): 691, 696

L

La carreta (The Oxcart): 207, 476, 569, 577, 621
La Plata, George: 309
La Raza Cósmica (mural): 544–545
Labor Council of Latin American Advancement (LCLAA): 372
labor force: 56, 189–190, 192–193, 201, 220, 222–223, 227–228, 240, 365, 373–374, 376–377, 386, 388–389, 396, 673
labor organizers: 239–240, 244
labor unions: 42, 173, 204, 583, 749
Laffitte, Héctor M.: 309
Laguna Santero: 514
Lamas, Fernando: 612, 630–631, 674
Lamy, Jean Baptiste: 263
land grants: 14, 16, 21, 135, 230, 266, 286, 343–346, 396
land-use: 344
Landeta, Matilde: 618
landlords: 41, 347, 594
language usage: 204, 212, 556
Lara, Javier: 462
Laria, María: 714
Larkin, Thomas O.: 154
Las Trampas Historic District: 141
Las Vegas Old Town Plaza: 141
Lasansky, Mauricio: 524
latifundia See hacienda.
Latin American Group (ADAL): 571
Latin American League: 151
Latin American Theater Ensemble (LATE): 570
Latin Empire: 622
Latin jazz: 622, 645, 665
Latin rock: 645, 665, 669
Latino: 51, 184, 188, 193, 213, 219, 228, 232, 235, 248–249, 299, 312, 317, 336, 339, 416, 419, 423, 426, 429, 466, 469, 471, 485, 496, 568, 582, 604, 606–607, 610, 614, 616–618, 628, 634, 643–645, 651, 662, 664–666, 668–669, 671, 673, 675–676, 678–681, 687, 691–692, 695–696, 698, 704, 716–717, 753
Lau v. Nichols: 294, 409
Laviera, Jesús Abraham Tato. *See* Laviera, Tato
Laviera, Tato: 478, 480, 482, 496, 572
Lavoe, Héctor: 664
Laws of Burgos: 11
Laws of the Indies: 254–255
League of Nations: 162
League of United Latin American Citizens (LULAC): 38–39, 44, 239, 294, 300, 314–315, 339, 387,

422, 429, 450, 612, 678, 680, 749, 751–752, 755, 758–759, 765
Leal, Luis: 413, 422–423
Lear, Norman: 677, 702, 706
Lecuona, Ernesto: 663
legal education: 294–295, 337–338, 752
Legal Services Corporation: 297, 337–338
Lend-Lease Act: 164
León, Alonso de: 15, 260, 345
León, Antonio de: 72
Lesseps, Ferdinand de: 158
Lewis and Clark: 21
Leyba, Albert: 547
Leyva de Bonilla, Francisco: 71
Lezama Lima, José: 482
Liga de Béisbol Profesional Cubana: 722
Liga de Hijas de Cuba: 240
Liga Femenil Mexicanista, La: 239
Liga Protectora Mexicana, La: 37
Lima Conference: 164
Lima Group: 172
Limite: 668
Limón, José: 654
Lincoln, Abraham: 23, 155, 275, 329, 336, 543, 599
Linden Lane magazine: 242, 484
Lindsay, Walter O.: 551
literacy: 35, 152, 167, 288, 292, 313, 391–392, 394–395, 397, 400, 467
Little Joe and the Latinaires. (*see also* Little Joe y La Familia): 656
Little Joe y la Familia: 616, 656–657, 659, 666
livestock industry: 344–346
Llamas, Vicente José: 445
Llauradó, Joseph: 445
Llinas, Rodolfo: 445
Llunas, Marcos: 667
Lobato, Rogelio A.: 617
Lodge, Henry Cabot: 156
Lomas Garza, Carmen: 243, 530–531
Lomelí, Francisco A.: 422
Longhorn cattle: 345
Longoria, Félix: 276, 650
Longoria, Valerio: 652
López, Al: 736
López, Carlos: 520, 523
López, Efraín: 621
López, Félix A.: 534
López, Francisco: 71, 135, 622
López, George: 518
López, Isidro: 656
López, José Dolores: 516–518
López, Nancy: 736
López, Yolanda: 243, 528, 531

López de Santa Anna, Antonio: 22–24, 283, 619
López del Castillo, Gerardo: 550, 576
López Portillo, José: 315
Lorenzo, Frank A.: 357, 361
Los Alamos Ranch House: 135
Los Angeles Negros. *See* Angeles Negros, Los
Los Fantasmas del Caribe: 667
Los Flamers: 667
Los Four: 527–528, 539
Los Lobos: 616, 634, 668
Los Mier: 667
Los Nogales: 144
Los primos (*The Cousins*): 483, 494
Lotus Communications Corporation: 696
Louisiana Purchase: 200
Lozano, Ignacio: 348, 459
Lozano, José I.: 682
Lozano, Rudolpho: 309
Lozano-Centanino, Mónica: 682
Lucayo Indians: 56
Lucero, Carlos: 302
Lucey, Robert E.: 264
Lucky Stores: 362
Lugo Family: 214
Luján, Manuel, Jr.: 320, 331
Luna, James: 617
Luna, Tranquilino: 400
Luna, Tristán de: 68
Lupe, La: 660
Lusitania: 2
Luz, La: 688
Lydia Patterson Institute for Boys: 398

M

Maceo, Antonio: 178
machismo: 216, 243, 460, 505, 601, 603
Machito: 622, 663–664
Madero, Francisco I.: 34, 36, 161
Madison, James: 150
Mafia, La: 666–668
magazines: 51, 204, 242, 244, 249, 291, 350, 356, 358, 362–363, 458, 460–463, 466, 471, 473, 484, 486–490, 492–495, 499–504, 524, 552, 577–579, 592, 595, 608–609, 636, 671, 680, 682, 688–691, 697–698, 708, 710, 712, 714, 716, 753, 757, 759, 766, 770, 773
Mahan, Alfred T.: 156
Maidique, Modesto A.: 767
Maize: 9, 486, 504
Malcriado, El. *See* Venegas, Daniel
Maldonado, Alicia: 614
Maldonado, Diego de: 67

Maldonado, Tony: 620
Malváez, Inés: 238
Mambo Kings Play Songs of Love, The: 484, 495
Mandret, Luis: 568
mango: 271, 473
Manifest Destiny: 21–22, 154, 179–182, 285, 499, 621, 672
Mann, Thomas C.: 168
Manuel de Céspedes, Carlos: 28, 46
manumission: 178
Manzanares, F. A.: 400
Mapula, Olga: 247
Maqueo Castellanos, Esteban: 459
Maquiavelo: 462
maquiladora: 173, 375–376, 638
Mar, Marcia del: 242
Mara, Adele: 631
Mares, Michael Allen: 446
Margil de Jesús, Antonio: 261
Margo: 631
Mariel boat-lift: 50, 484
marielito: 197
Marín, Richard "Cheech": 568, 584, 610–611, 623, 632, 675
Maris, Mona: 632
Marqués, René: 207, 476, 480, 569–570, 576–577, 620–621
Marshall, George C.: 165
Martí, José: 28, 30, 96, 176, 240, 263, 458, 482, 557, 582
Martí Theater: 572
Martin, Cris-Pin: 632
Martín, Manuel: 571
Martin, Ysabel Ponciana Chris-Pin. *See* Martin, Cris-Pin
Martínez, A.: 678
Martínez, Agueda: 243, 614
Mártinez, Betita: 244
Martínez, César: 532
Martínez, Chela: 562
Martínez, Frank: 464
Martínez, Matthew G.: 316, 320
Martínez, Narciso: 652
Martínez, Oscar: 423
Martínez, Robert: 332
Martínez, Velia: 561, 564
Martínez, Vilma S.: 313
Martínez Asunsolo López Negrete, Lolita Dolores. *See* del Río, Dolores
Martínez Ybor, Vicente: 45–46, 244, 347–348, 465, 560
Marvin, John G.: 401
Maryland Commission on Hispanic Affairs: 340
Más: 489, 688–689, 708, 710
Mason Theater: 552
Mata, Eduardo: 768
Matas, Julio: 572, 577

Mateos, Manuel: 459
Matilla, Alfredo: 423
matriarchal patterns: 222
Matta, Daniel: 616
Matthews v. Díaz: 294
Mayan Indians: 9, 53–54, 173–174, 197–199, 530
Mayo Indians: 16, 36, 70, 162, 272, 288, 299, 316, 321, 326, 335–337
Mazz: 666–667
McCarthy, Joseph: 165
McCarthyism: 597
McKinley, William: 30, 157, 182
McKinley Tariff: 157, 182
McLish, Rachel Elizondo: 737
McWilliams, Carey: 257
Mechicano Art Center: 539
Medal of Honor: 275, 277, 331, 360, 600, 764
Medellín, Octavio: 520–522
media. (*see also* magazines; newspapers; periodicals; radio; television): 39, 155, 179, 181, 195, 203–204, 212, 244, 462, 482, 526, 528–529, 568, 588, 604–606, 609, 612, 723, 726, 753, 759, 761, 770–771, 774
medicine: 17, 56, 65–66, 167, 432, 543, 614
Medina, Harold R.: 309
Meléndez, Manuel Gaspar: 446
Meléndez, Rosalinda: 554
melting pot: 203, 593
Melville, Margarita: 236
Méndez, José: 446, 724–725, 737
Méndez, Miguel: 466–467
Méndez Caratini, Héctor: 622
Méndez-Longoria, Miguel Angel: 300
Mendieta, Ana: 243
Mendoza, Antonio de: 12, 66, 70, 73
Mendoza, Lydia: 556
Mendoza, Teresa: 446
Mendoza, Tomás: 557
Mendoza, Vicente: 537, 543
Menéndez, Francisco: 273
Menéndez, Ramón: 618–619, 675
Menéndez, Robert: 316
Menéndez Avilés, Pedro: 68, 258
Menéndez Márquez, Tomás: 344
Mercado, Teresa: 447
mercantile business: 347
merengue: 28, 668, 691
Merry, William L.: 158
Mesa-Baines, Amalia: 528, 531
Mesa-Lago, Carmelo: 424
Mesilla Plaza: 141
mestizos: 6, 11–14, 17, 19, 28, 136, 177–179, 186, 191, 200, 214, 254, 256–258, 262, 270, 273, 343, 346,

392, 394, 433, 539, 549, 594, 596, 616, 725
Mestre, Ricardo: 608–609
Methodists: 265, 398–399
Mexican American Bar Association: 298–299
Mexican American Democrats of Texas: 314, 339
Mexican American Generation: 655–656, 658–659
Mexican American Legal Defense and Education Fund (MALDEF): 299–300, 304, 312–313, 338, 362, 382, 414, 420, 429, 752
Mexican American Political Association: 339, 749
Mexican American Women's National Association: 246, 339
Mexican border: 32, 60, 145, 155, 201, 204, 223, 228, 289, 314, 346, 366, 377, 611, 617–618, 653, 668, 701
Mexican Farm Labor Supply Program: 374
Mexican Labor Agreement: 367, 374
Mexican League: 723, 731, 744
Mexican Liberal Party: 238, 457
Mexican Revolution: 34, 36, 162, 191, 214, 230, 237, 241, 286, 348, 459–460, 499, 505, 521, 539, 551, 553, 575, 579, 582, 594, 600, 602, 616, 628, 764, 768
Mexican Revolution of 1910: 28, 33, 236, 458, 508, 516, 539, 545, 602, 610
Mexican Spitfire: 595, 639
Mexican War: 31, 34, 135, 144–145, 157, 179–180, 200, 236, 274, 279, 283, 285, 462
Mexican-American War: 25, 154, 199–201, 228–229, 275, 336, 365, 455, 552, 619, 648, 725
Mexico Border: 249
México de afuera: 459, 463
México Lindo: 36, 38, 40, 42
Mexico-US: 375
Michigan Commission on Spanish-Speaking Affairs: 340
Mier y Terán, Manuel: 21–22
Migrant Legal Action Program: 297, 338
migrant workers: 238, 264, 309, 376–377, 458, 467, 492, 500, 615, 747, 767
milagro: 518–520, 620
Milán, Edgar J.: 357, 361
Miles, Nelson: 41
military academies: 276
Military Assistance Program: 167
Miller, Edward G.: 165

Mina, Xavier de: 151
Minnesota Spanish-Speaking Affairs Council: 340
Minority Telecommunications Development Program: 694–695
Miranda, Francisco de: 151, 278–279
Miruelo, Diego: 61–62
Misisipí, El: 681
Miskito Indians: 198
misogynism: 241
Missionary Catechists of Divine Providence: 264
Mobile Act: 150
Moctezuma II: 10
Modernistic Editorial Company: 464
Mohr, Nicholasa: 241, 474, 481–482, 497
Molina, Gloria: 335–336
Molina, Mario J.: 434, 447–448
Mollá, Angel: 551
Monacelli, Amleto Andrés: 738
Moncaleano, Blanca de: 244, 460
Moncarraz, Raúl: 424
Monroe, James: 77, 79–80, 82, 151, 167
Monroe Doctrine: 80, 82–86, 151–152, 154, 156, 160–161, 163, 171, 183
Montalbán, Ricardo: 598, 611–612, 618, 633, 674, 677
Montalván, E.: 457
Monteagudo, Antonio Garride. *See* Moreno, Antonio
Monterey Old Town Historic District: 135
Montes, Matías. *See* Huidobro, Matías Montes
Montes de Oca López, Diana: 445
Montevideo Conference: 163
Montez, María: 633–634, 674
Montoya, Benjamin F.: 281
Montoya, José: 616
Montoya, Joseph Manuel: 314, 320, 323, 333
Montoya, Malaquías: 529, 531
Montoya, Nestor: 320, 324
Moore, James: 344
Moors: 3–4, 57–58, 176–177, 253–254, 549
Mora, Francisco Luis: 520, 522
Mora, Pat: 241, 472, 482
moradas: 269, 515
Moraga, Cherríe: 241, 498
Moraga, José: 135
Moraga House (Orinda, California): 135
Morales, Alejandro: 475, 498
Morales, Esai: 612
Morales, Sylvia: 243, 616, 618, 634

Morales Carrión, Arturo: 329
Moreno, Antonio: 634
Moreno, Federico A., Sr.: 310
Moreno, Mario: 554
Moreno, Rita: 606, 616, 635, 677
Morgan, J. P.: 161
Morín, Raúl: 276
Morlete, Juan: 71
Morley, Sylvanus: 54
Morton, Carlos: 467, 568, 578, 616
Moscoso, Luis de: 67
Moslems: 177, 267, 725
movie industry: 39, 291, 348, 552,
    554–555, 558–559, 565, 567–568,
    573, 575–576, 578, 582, 584, 588,
    590–596, 600–604, 606–607,
    609–610, 619–621, 623–624, 626,
    631, 636, 656, 660, 674, 676, 684,
    691, 700–701, 706–707, 709,
    717–718, 735, 772
Movimiento Artístico Chicano
    (MARCH): 535, 542
Movimiento Familiar Cristiano: 752
Movimiento Femenino Anti-
    comunista de Cuba: 240
Moya del Pino, José: 520, 523
Mujeres Activas en Letras y Cambio
    Social: 752
Mujeres Muralistas: 529
mulattoes: 49, 177–178, 257, 273,
    346, 588, 591, 597
Multicultural Mural: 537, 547–548
multiracial: 184, 186, 492
Muñoz, Anthony: 721, 726, 739
Muñoz, Susana: 617
Muñoz Marín, Luis: 43, 117–118
Munras, Esteban: 137
Murieta, Joaquín: 455, 457
música norteña: 644, 646, 651, 666
música tropical: 645, 665–666
Muslims: 3, 6, 70, 253, 502
mutual aid societies: 36, 348, 369,
    560, 563–564, 747–748
Mutual Security Act: 164

N

Nadal de Santa Coloma, Juan: 464,
    578
NAFTA. *See* North American Free
    Trade Argeement (NAFTA)
Nafus, Chale: 616
Náñez, Alfredo: 265
Nañiguismo: 272
Napoleon: 20, 211, 270
Napoleonic Code: 2
Napoleonic Wars: 150
Nario, José: 537, 543
Narváez, Pánfilo de: 64–65
National Association for Bilingual
    Education: 749, 763

National Association for Chicano
    Studies: 749, 752
National Association of Cuban
    American Women: 339, 673–674,
    753
National Association of Hispanic
    Publications: 674, 753
National Caucus of Hispanic School
    Board Members: 753
National Coalition of Hispanic
    Health and Human Services: 753
National Congress for Puerto Rican
    Rights: 754
National Congress of Puerto Rican
    Veterans: 754
National Council of Hispanic
    Women: 250, 754
National Council of La Raza: 317,
    584, 612, 688, 749, 754
National Farm Labor Union: 371,
    765
National Farm Workers Association:
    371
National Health and Human Ser-
    vices Employees Union: 372
National Hispanic Chamber of Com-
    merce: 749
National Hispanic Corporate Coun-
    cil: 754
National Hispanic Council on
    Aging: 754
National Hispanic Democrats: 339
National Hispanic Leadership Con-
    ference: 339, 758
National Hispanic Media Coalition:
    674
National Immigration Law Center:
    297, 338
National Latinas Caucus: 339
National Latino Communications
    Consortium: 615
National Origins Quota Act: 38
National Public Radio: 244
National Puerto Rican Coalition:
    247, 250, 339, 764
National Puerto Rican Forum:
    44–45, 339, 755
National Rainbow Coalition: 300
National Women's History Project:
    618
nationalism: 4, 29, 36, 40, 42, 153,
    163, 348, 476, 554, 560, 566, 592,
    655
Native Americans. (*see also* specific
    tribes): 4, 6–8, 10–19, 25, 27,
    31–32, 37, 53–57, 59–64, 67, 70,
    72–73, 78, 90, 96–99, 133–134,
    137, 142–144, 146–147, 149,
    177–181, 183–184, 191, 198, 214,
    238, 244, 254–262, 267, 270, 273,

275, 285, 313, 321, 329, 343–347,
    353, 358, 391–395, 431–433, 450,
    456, 463, 468, 470–472, 480,
    487–488, 505, 507–509, 519,
    521–523, 525, 528, 537, 539,
    546–549, 560, 579, 588–589,
    591–594, 596–597, 603, 617,
    628–629, 672, 675, 679, 697, 721,
    725
Naturalization Act: 287
Nava, Gregory: 618–620, 675, 679
Nava, Julián: 768–769
Nava-Villarreal, Héctor Rolando:
    448
Navaira, Emilio: 666–667, 669
Navajo Indians: 344
Navarro, Gabriel: 459, 552–553, 578
Navarro (José Antonio) House: 144
Navas, Manuel R.: 620
Nazario, Zydnia: 243, 622
Nebraska Mexican American Com-
    mission: 340
Negro leagues: 722–725, 731, 738
Neri, Manuel: 524–525
Neuku, Cathe: 622
Nevada Association of Latin Ameri-
    cans: 340
Nevada Hispanic Services: 340
Nevárez, Miguel A.: 769
New Almadén: 135
New Deal: 39, 322
New Federalism: 379–381
New Jersey Office of Hispanic Af-
    fairs: 341
New York State Governor's Office
    for Hispanic Affairs: 341
Newman, Philip: 310
newspapers: 23, 30, 42, 97, 134,
    150, 198, 204–205, 238, 244, 263,
    324, 348, 455–466, 491–494, 500,
    504, 539, 550, 552–554, 557–559,
    561, 564, 575–576, 578–580, 599,
    651, 671–674, 681–687, 690, 693,
    695, 697, 753, 774
Nicandro, Glugio Gronk: 527, 537,
    540–541, 617
Nieto, Sonia: 424–425
Niggli, Josephina: 241, 461, 499
Nilda: 241, 481, 497
Niño Fidencio: 270
Niño Perdido, El: 267
Nixon, Richard M.: 166, 168, 304
Niza, Marcos de: 66, 69–70
Nobel Prize: 172, 434–435, 447,
    485, 610, 622
Nogales, Luis: 362
Noloesca, La Chata. *See* Escalona,
    Beatriz
Noriega, Manuel: 173, 558, 579

norteño: 32–34, 200, 643, 652–653, 655, 662, 665, 667–668
North American Free Trade Argeement (NAFTA): 131, 173–174, 376
Norton, Barry: 635
NOSOTROS: 605, 612
Noticias del Mundo: 684–685
Noticiero Latino: 697–698
Novarro, Ramón: 635–636
Novello, Antonia Coello: 327
Nuestra Señora de la Luz Mission: 144
Nuestra Señora de los Dolores: 75, 261, 344
Nuestra Señora del Rosario Mission: 144
Nueva Sangre: 242, 581
Nuevo Círculo Dramático: 569
Nuevo Herald, El: 685–686, 774
Nuevo Teatro Pobre de las Américas, El: 569
Núñez, Ana Rosa: 242
Núñez Cabeza de Vaca, Álvar: 64–66, 72, 238, 259, 419, 432
Núñez, Orlando: 483
Nuyorican: 221, 235, 415, 464–465, 475, 477–482, 485, 491, 570–572, 580
Nuyorican literature: 423, 478, 480, 485, 572, 580
Nuyorican theater: 571–572

O

Obejas, Achy: 242
Oblates of Mary Immaculate: 263
Obledo, Mario G.: 300
Ocampo, Sebastián de: 6, 59
Ochoa, Ellen: 769
Ochoa, Estevan: 347
Ochoa, Victor: 531–532
Ochoa y Acuña, Anastacio: 458
Ofa. *See* O'Farrill, Alberto Ofa
O'Farrill, Alberto Ofa: 462, 559, 579
Office for Coordination of Inter-American Affairs: 596
Office of Economic Opportunity (OEO): 378–379, 381, 387
Ohio Commission on Spanish-Speaking Affairs: 341
oil industry: 357
Ojeda, Manuel: 675
Olcott, Sidney: 588
Old El Paso: 349
Oliva, Pedro. *See* Oliva, Tony
Oliva, Tony: 739
Olivares, Antonio de: 261
Olivares, Julián: 425, 471
Olmecs: 8–9, 539

Olmos, Edward James: 608–609, 616, 619–620, 623, 636, 638, 675, 677
Olney, Richard: 156
Oms, Alejandro: 725, 740
Oñate, Juan de: 14, 72, 141–142, 200, 259, 344, 455, 549
Once in a Lifetime: 609, 618, 628, 632
Onda Chicana, La: 656–658, 660, 666
O'Neill, Gonzalo: 463–464, 560, 579
Operation Bootstrap: 43, 236, 368, 373, 622
Operation Wetback: 286, 384
Opinión, La: 552, 582, 672, 681–683, 693
Order of the Sons of America: 749
Oregon Commission on Hispanic Affairs: 341
Oregon Council for Hispanic Advancement: 341
Organización Editorial Mexicana: 687
Organization of American States: 156, 166–168, 171–172, 250, 330
Oropeza, Vicente: 726, 740
Orozco, José Clemente: 528, 539, 545
Orozco, Raymond E.: 769
orquesta: 644–646, 648, 653–660, 664–666, 768
Orquesta Aragón: 664
Ortega, Robert, Jr.: 362
Ortego, Katherine D.: 357
Ortiz, Francis V.: 770
Ortiz, Juan: 66
Ortiz, Manuel: 741
Ortiz, Ralph: 524, 526
Ortiz, Solomon P.: 316–317, 320
Ortiz, Susana: 618
Ortiz, Vilma: 425
Ortiz Cofer, Judith: 241, 482, 490
Ortiz del Rivero, Ramón: 620
Ostend Manifesto: 157, 181
Otero, Mariano S.: 324, 400
Otero, Miguel A.: 324, 456
Otero, Sabino: 320, 346
Otero, Toribio: 346
"Our America": 96, 98–100
Our Lady of Guadalupe: 37, 44, 209, 257–258, 266–268, 270–271, 510, 513–514, 516, 519–520, 528–529, 531, 533, 539, 543, 546, 549
Our Lady of Providencia: 266
Our Lady of San Juan de los Lagos: 266, 268, 519
Our Lady of Sorrows: 266
Our Lady of Talpa: 514–515
Oviedo, Gonzalo Fernández de: 59

P

Pacheco, Johnny: 664
Pacheco, Manuel Trinidad: 409, 770
Pacheco, Romualdo: 320
Pachón, Harry: 225, 426
Pact of El Zajón: 28
Padilla, Amado Manuel: 426
Padilla, Benjamin: 459
Padilla, Heberto: 483–484
padrino: 217, 232
Palace of the Governors: 142–143
Palacio, Adolfo: 133
Palés, Vicente: 463
Palés Matos, Luis: 476, 480, 497, 620
Palmieri, Charlie: 664
Palmieri, Eddie: 664–665
Palo Alto Battlefield: 144
Palomino, Ernesto: 524–525
Pan American Union: 156, 764
Panchito: 596
Papago Indians: 18, 134
Papp, Joseph: 568, 572
Paredes, Américo: 413, 426, 461, 648–649, 675
Pareja, Francisco: 433
parentesco: 216–219, 221, 223–224, 231
Parra, Richard: 618
Parsons, Albert: 238, 247
Partido Liberal Mexicano: 747
Pastor, Ed: 320
pastorela: 549, 568
Patlán, Raymond: 537, 542–543
patria potestad: 13
patriarchy: 216, 221, 675
patrón: 20
Payeras, Mariano: 345
Peace Corps: 276, 329–330, 378, 417
pecan shellers: 370
Pedroso, Paulina: 240
pelado: 408, 553–554, 556, 583
Pellón, Pedro C. de: 551
Pelton, John: 401
Peña, Elizabeth: 676
Peña, Juan: 135
Peña House (San José, California): 135
Penichet, Carlos: 616
Penichet, Jeff: 614, 618
penitente: 269–270, 611
Pennsylvania Governor's Advisory Commission on Latino Affairs: 341
Pentecostalism: 265–266
peonage: 29, 161
Peralta, Pedro de: 72, 143, 259
Perea, Francisco: 320, 325, 400
Perea, Pedro: 320, 325, 400

Perea, Pedro de: 16

Perenchio, A. Jerrold: 702, 705–706

Perera, Hilda: 242

Pérez, Ignacio: 134

Pérez, Severo: 568, 613, 616, 628

Pérez Balladares, Ernesto: 173

Pérez de Almazán, Fernando: 73

Pérez de Villagrá, Gaspar: 238, 455

Pérez-Farfante, Isabel Cristina: 448

Pérez-Firmat, Gustavo: 426

Pérez-Giménez, Juan M.: 310

periodicals: 42, 150, 457, 574, 681, 687, 691

Perón, Juan: 164

Pershing, John J.: 162

Perú, Rosita: 708

Petaluma Adobe State Historic Park: 136

pharmaceuticals industry: 357

Philip IV: 260

Phillip, Prince of Austria: 11

Phoenicians: 2

Phos Press: 462

pianolo: 346

Pico, Andrés: 137

Pico, Pío: 23, 136, 178

Pico Hotel (Los Angeles, California): 136

Pico House(s) (Mission Hills and Whittier, California): 136

Pierce, Franklin: 157, 181

Pietri, Pedro: 478, 499, 570, 572

Pike, Zebulon: 21

Pima Indians: 16, 18, 262, 309, 344

Pimentel, David: 448

Pinckney Treaty: 150

Piñero, Miguel: 478, 480, 485, 572, 580

Pinochet, Augusto: 169

pioneers: 14, 181, 215, 218, 220, 231, 258, 309, 347, 413–415, 417, 422, 428–429, 436–437, 448, 451, 474, 485–486, 492, 497, 521, 525, 530, 532, 565, 570, 574, 614, 681, 692, 699–700, 718

pirates: 7, 73, 143, 181

Pirrín, Eusebio (Don Catarino): 553, 555, 580

Pita, Juana Rosa: 242

Pizaña, Aniceto: 457

Plan de San Luis Potosí: 34

Plan of Iguala: 394

plantations: 2, 4, 7, 26–27, 41, 45, 153, 178, 182, 198, 207, 219, 226, 346

Platt, Orville: 160

Platt Amendment: 30, 47, 160, 183

Plaza Ferdinand VII: 139

Plunkett, Jim: 726, 741

pocho: 201, 209, 211, 556

Poinsett, Joel: 151

police brutality: 37, 44–45, 328

political organizations: 276, 749, 755, 761

political participation: 24, 292, 300, 313, 339, 755

Polk, James K.: 22, 153

poll taxes: 400

Ponce, Mary Helen: 241

Ponce de León, Juan: 12, 58–59, 63, 65, 258, 286, 432

Ponce de León, Michael: 524

Popé: 14, 72, 260

Popol-Vuh: 54

Porter, Edwin S.: 588

Porterfield, L. B.: 161

Portillo, Elsie: 616

Portillo, Lourdes: 243, 616–617

Portillo-Trambley, Estela: 470, 502

Porto Rico Photoplays: 620

Pórtola, Gaspar de: 135, 137

posada: 269, 549, 596

poverty: 33, 37, 44–45, 161, 169, 173, 190, 193, 214, 220–221, 228, 233, 237, 286–287, 294, 297, 314, 322, 378–379, 384, 387–389, 396, 400, 405, 426, 434, 451, 477–479, 488, 497, 500, 502–504, 554, 558, 563, 614, 673, 726, 744

Pozo, Señor del: 558

Prado, Edward C.: 310

Prado, Miguel de: 151

Pre-Columbian Period: 8, 11, 37, 40, 53, 55–56, 486, 507, 520, 525, 527–528, 533, 538–540, 542–543, 546, 565, 613, 618, 634

Preferida, La: 349

Pregones: 570

prejudice: 24, 35, 39, 51–52, 124, 178–179, 207, 209, 253, 264, 406, 491, 497–498, 530, 563, 590, 593, 598, 616, 653, 675

Presbyterians: 265–266, 398–399

President's Council on Educational Excellence: 331

Presidio de Santa Cruz de Terrenato: 134

Presidio Nuestra Señora de Loreto de la Bahía: 144

Presidio Saint Louis: 145

presidios: 15, 18–20, 73–74, 134–138, 144, 146–147, 261, 273, 343, 392–393, 483

Prida, Dolores: 242, 568, 570–571, 580–581

Priests Associated for Religious, Educational and Social Rights (P.A.D.R.E.S.): 264, 752

Prieto, Francisco: 258

Primer Congreso Mexicanista, El: 239

Principal, Victoria: 605

Prinze, Freddie: 604–605, 676

Pro Arte Gratelli: 572

Producciones Borinquen: 621

production code: 587

property rights: 25, 131–132, 286

Protestantism: 153, 179, 253–254, 258, 264–265, 267, 273, 348, 396–399, 401–402, 494, 515, 550, 589

Public Law: 128, 374–375

public relations: 333, 349, 362, 598, 745, 774

publishing: 246, 348, 415, 422, 426, 455, 458–459, 461–463, 465–467, 470–471, 473–474, 478, 480–481, 483–486, 490–491, 495, 497, 501, 505, 577, 583, 674, 681–682, 684–686, 689–690, 773

Pueblo Indians: 13–14, 55, 71–72, 142–143, 229, 259–260

Pueblo Revolt: 143, 260

Puente, Ramón: 459

Puente, Tito: 664

Puenzo, Luis: 610

Puerto Rican Family Institute: 247, 755

Puerto Rican Forum. *See* National Puerto Rican Forum

Puerto Rican Legal Defense and Education Fund: 297–298, 339, 755, 763

Puerto Rican Traveling Theater: 570–571, 574

Puerto Rican Workers Mutual Aid Society: 748

Puerto Rico Animation Workshop: 622

Puerto Rico Conservation Trust: 622

Puig, Manuel: 576, 610, 630

Pulitzer: 182, 484

Purísima Concepción Mission, La: 345

Purísima Concepción Mission State Historic Park: 136

Q

Quesada, Eugenio: 524–525

Quetzalcoatl: 9–10, 55, 468, 487

Quevedo, Abraham: 538

Quexos, Pedro de: 63

Quiburi, Arizona: 134

Quinn, Anthony: 600, 603–604, 616, 637

Quintanilla, Guadalupe C.: 770–771

Quinto Sol. *See* Editorial Quinto Sol

Quirarte, Jacinto: 509, 511–512, 519, 529, 540–542, 544–548, 616

Quiroga, Joaquín: 347
Quivera: 12, 70–72

R

Rabell, Arnaldo Roche: 537
racial diversity: 27, 46, 59, 99–100, 176, 179–183, 238, 260, 269, 372, 481, 497, 499, 588, 591, 593, 601
racism: 28, 33, 161, 176, 241, 369, 474, 483, 498, 500, 502, 504–505, 531, 558, 563, 590, 597, 599, 622, 634, 672, 675, 680, 748
radio: 51, 198, 203–204, 207, 244, 248, 348, 403, 499, 529, 559, 565, 575–577, 582–583, 614, 619, 666–668, 671, 676, 679, 683, 691–703, 706, 708, 717–718, 758, 773
Radio América: 696
Radio Bilingüe: 697–698
Radio Noticias: 698
railroads: 25, 27, 32–34, 39, 95, 105–107, 109–110, 112–113, 115, 155, 160, 173, 229–231, 286, 324, 345, 347–348, 365–367, 369, 374, 433, 456, 515, 543, 604
Rain of Gold: 474, 505–506
Rain of Scorpions: 470, 503
Raining Backwards: 484, 493
Ramírez, Arnaldo: 653
Ramírez, Carlos D.: 683–684
Ramírez, Fausto: 449
Ramírez, Mario E.: 449
Ramírez, Ramiro: 725
Ramírez, Sara Estela: 239, 244, 457, 460
Ramírez, Yvette: 572
Ramito: 463
Ramón, Domingo: 16, 261
Ramos, Armando: 742
Ramos, Jorge: 710
Ramos, Rudy: 612
Ramos Otero, Manuel: 570
Rancho de las Cabras: 145
Rancho el Encino (California): 136
Rancho Real de Santa Petronila: 345
Rancho Santa Margarita (California): 136
Rangel, María: 678
Rangel, Rodrigo: 432
Rankin, Melinda: 398
Raya, Marcos: 535–536
Raza, La: 40, 201, 337, 537, 566, 616, 638, 680, 688
Reagan, Ronald: 170, 276, 304, 306, 333, 750, 762, 769, 774
Real, Manuel L.: 310
Rebolledo, Tey Diana: 248, 420, 427

Reciprocal Trade Agreements Act: 163
Reclamation Act: 286, 292
Reconquest: 3–4, 6, 10, 143, 176–177, 254, 267
record industry: 39
Redón, Juan: 346
REFORMA: The National Association to Promote Library Services to the Spanish Speaking: 756
Refugee Act: 289, 292–293
regionalism: 218, 522, 748
Reid, Marita: 568–569, 581
Reies Tijerina: 266
Relámpagos del Norte, Los: 653
Reliance Capital Group: 704, 706
repartimiento: 13, 59, 254–255, 262
repatriation: 38, 230, 367, 461, 463, 465, 553–556
Réplica: 688
Republic of Texas: 23, 273, 282, 285
Republic of the Rio Grande: 144
Republican Party: 774
Requena, Manuel: 336
Resaca de la Palma Battlefield: 145
respeto: 216
restaurant industry: 228, 310, 332, 348–349, 359–360, 377, 685–687
Restrepo, José Manuel: 152
retail trade: 27, 350
Retinto cattle: 345
Revista Chicano-Riqueña. See Americas Review, The
revolutionary movements: 36, 182, 244, 483, 504, 557
Reyes, Luis: 614, 676–677
Reyna, Cornelio: 653
Reynoso, Cruz: 310–311
Ribault, Jean: 68
Richardson, Bill: 312
Richter, Hans: 624
Riley, Dorothy Comstock: 311
Ringling Brothers: 557
Rio Treaty: 166
Ríos, Alberto: 482
Ríos, Herminio: 466–467
Ríos, Lalo: 601, 675
Ríos Bustamante, Antonio: 615
Rivas, Bimbo: 621
Rivas, Marian Lucy: 449
Rivera, Dennis: 372
Rivera, Evelyn Margaret: 449
Rivera, Geraldo Miguel: 678, 771
Rivera, Horacio: 282
Rivera, Jerry: 667
Rivera, Juan C.: 559
Rivera, Pedro: 622
Rivera, Tomás: 425, 427, 466–468, 481, 628
Rivera Moncada, Fernando: 74

Rivero, Eliana: 242, 427
Rivero, Isel: 242
Rivero, Jorge: 603
Robinson, John: 557
Robles, Belén: 239
Robles, Bernabé: 346
Robles, Mireya: 242
Roca, Sergio G.: 427
Rocafuerte, Vicente: 151
Rocha, Ramiro: 519
Roche Rabell, Arnaldo. *See* Rabell, Arnaldo Roche
Rockefeller, Nelson D.: 596
Rodarte, Los: 667
rodeos: 614, 667–668, 721, 725–726, 734, 740
Rodrigo, Rosita: 559
Rodrigues, R.: 133
Rodrigues Cermenho, Sebastiao: 73
Rodríguez, Adalberto: 621
Rodríguez, Antonio: 559
Rodríguez, Arsenio: 663
Rodriguez, Chi Chi: 262, 742
Rodríguez, Clara: 236, 427
Rodríguez, Elizabeth: 248
Rodríguez, Eloy: 449–450
Rodríguez, Gloria G.: 771
Rodríguez, John: 362
Rodríguez, Joseph H.: 311
Rodriguez, Juan. *See* Rodriguez, Chi Chi
Rodríguez, Oscar: 362
Rodríguez, Patricia: 243, 529, 531
Rodríguez, Paul: 609, 623, 676–677, 712, 772
Rodríguez, Pedro: 545
Rodríguez, Peter: 524
Rodríguez, Richard: 500
Rodríguez, Robert: 619
Rodríguez, Roberto: 569
Rodríguez, Rudy: 714
Rodríguez, Slowpoke: 596
Rodríguez, Tito: 664
Rodríguez de Cabrillo, Juan: 73
Rodríguez de Tió, Lola: 239, 458, 463–464
Rodríguez del Pino, Salvador: 475
Roja, Zona: 668
Rojas, Tito: 668
Roland, Gilbert: 595, 600, 637
Román, Arturo: 538–539
Roman Empire: 2–3
Romans: 2–3, 176
Romero, Carlos Humberto: 169, 320
Romero, César: 595, 638
Romero, Frank: 527–528
Romero, Juan Carlos: 450
Romero, Leo M.: 301
Romero, Oscar: 170
Romo, Ricardo: 427–428

Ronstadt, Federico: 347
Roosevelt Corollary: 82, 163, 183
Roosevelt, Franklin D.: 162–163, 323, 367, 599
Roosevelt, Theodore: 82–86, 156, 159, 161, 183, 274
Ros-Lehtinen, Ileana: 240, 314, 317–318, 320
Rosado Rousseau, Leoncia: 240
Rosete, Guillermo: 538–539
Rosetti, Julio: 618
Rough Riders: 274
Rovirá, Luis D.: 312
Roxie y Los Frijolitos: 667
Royal Presidio Chapel (Monterey, California): 136–137
Roybal, Edward R.: 320, 325
Roybal-Allard, Lucille: 318, 320, 326
Ruíz, José Luis: 613–614, 616
Ruiz, Ramón Eduardo: 428
Ruiz, Rey: 667
Ruiz, Vicki L.: 249
Ruiz de Burton, María Amparo: 237, 241, 429, 456
Ruiz del Viso, Hortensia: 483
rum industry: 149, 344
Ruthsdotter, Mary: 618

S

Saavedra, Louis E.: 336–337
Sabez, Jorge: 616
Sacred Heart of Jesus: 267, 271
Saenz, Albert William: 450
Salas, Lauro: 742
Salazar, Alberto Bauduy: 742–743
Salazar, Daniel: 614
Salazar, Rubén: 539, 584, 613, 650–651
Salcedo, Manuel de: 274
Saldívar, Vicente: 743
Salinas, María Elena: 710
Salinas, Porfirio: 522
Salinas de Gortari, Carlos: 174
salsa: 28, 477, 480, 485, 496–497, 610–611, 622, 626, 643–645, 656, 660–668, 675, 691
Salt of the Earth: 598–599, 674
Saludos Hispanos: 690
Samaniegos, Ramón. *See* Novarro, Ramón
Samora, Julián: 428
Samurai: 462
San Antonio and San Xavier del Bac: 510
San Antonio Cine Festival: 614–618
San Antonio de Bexar Mission. *See* Alamo, El.
San Antonio Independent School District v. Rodríguez: 294
San Bernardino Ranch: 134

San Carlos Borromeo Mission. *See* Carmel Mission
San Carlos School: 240
San Diego de Alcalá Mission: 136
San Diego Presidio: 136
San Estevan del Rey Mission Church: 142
San Felipe de Neri Church: 142
San Fernando Cathedral: 145
San Fernando Rey de España Mission: 136
San Francisco Acatepec: 512
San Francisco Bay Discovery Site: 136
San Francisco de Asís Mission: 138
San Francisco de Asís Mission Church: 142
San Francisco de la Espada Mission: 144–146
San Francisco de los Tejas: 73, 260, 345
San Francisco de los Tejas Mission: 146
San Francisco de Solano Mission: 137
San Gabriel Arcángel Mission: 137
San Gabriel del Yungue-Ouige: 142
San José de Gracia Church: 142
San José de los Jémez Mission: 142
San José de Palafox: 146
San José de Tumacacori Mission: 133–134, 261–262
San José Mission: 137
San José y San Miguel de Aguayo Mission: 146–147, 510–511, 513
San Juan Bautista Mission: 137
San Juan Bautista Plaza Historic District: 137
San Juan Capistrano Mission (Texas): 137, 146, 256, 509
San Juan del Puerto Mission: 433
San Luis de Apalache: 139
San Luis de las Amarillas Presidio: 146
San Luis Rey de Francia Mission: 137, 139
San Miguel Arcángel Mission: 137
San Miguel Church: 143
San Miguel de Aguayo, Marquis: 345
San Miguel del Vado Historic District: 143
San Pasqual: 137
San Xavier del Bac Mission: 511–512
Sánchez, George I.: 413, 429
Sánchez, Luis Rafael: 476–477
Sánchez, Oscar Arias. *See* Arias Sánchez, Oscar
Sánchez, Pedro Antonio: 451

Sánchez, Phillip V.: 685
Sánchez, Ricardo: 465, 475, 487, 500–501, 616
Sánchez, Theodora: 519
Sánchez, Tomás: 144
Sánchez, Virginia Korrol: 249, 427
Sánchez Boudy, José: 483, 572
Sánchez Chamuscado, Francisco: 71
Sánchez-Padilla, Beverly: 243, 616
Sánchez-Scott, Milcha: 568
Sanctuary of Chimayo: 269
Sandinista National Liberation Front: 169
Sandinista Revolution: 208
Sandinistas: 169–170, 172
Sandino, César Augusto: 163
Sandoval, Jorge: 617
Sandoval, Moisés: 253, 263
Santa Anna. *See* López de Santa Anna, Antonio
Santa Barbara Mission: 137, 140
Santa Barbara Presidio: 138
Santa Fe Expedition: 283
Santa Fe Plaza: 143
Santa Fe Ring: 25, 321
Santa Fe Trail: 141, 143, 154
Santa Rosa, Gilberto: 668
Santamaría, Mongo: 665
Santeiro, Luis: 772–773
santería: 28, 242, 268, 271–272, 611, 660–662, 664
santerismo. See santería
santeros: 271, 513–518, 534–535
Santiago, Eduardo G.: 362
Santo Niño de Atocha, El: 267
Santuario de Chimayó: 143
Saralegui, Cristina: 699, 710, 773
Sardiñas, Elgio: 579, 726, 743
Sassen, Saskia: 429
Schemmenti, Carmelita: 282
Scott, Winfield: 23, 154
Secada, Jon: 668
Second Vatican Council: 264
Secretariat for Hispanic Affairs: 264, 755
Secretary of the Navy: 276, 281, 331
secularization: 136, 146, 394–395
Security Assistance: 169
Segarra, Antonio: 622
segregation: 37, 39, 44, 183, 229, 231, 236, 276, 315, 397, 399, 406, 563, 723–724, 763
Seguín, Erasmo: 21
Seguín, Juan N.: 24, 144, 274, 282–283
Selecciones en Español: 717–718
Selective Service Act: 35
Selena: 667, 669
Sennett, Mack: 588
Sephardic Jews: 455

SER-Jobs for Progress: 387, 749, 755
Sergeant, John: 151
Serna, Marcelino: 275
Serra, Fray (Father) Junípero: 19, 74–76, 134, 136–137, 146, 262, 344
Serrano, Alberto: 451
Serrano, José E.: 318, 320
service industry: 368, 377, 653
settlers: 2, 6–7, 14, 16, 18–19, 21, 31, 58, 68, 72–74, 141, 195, 200–201, 213–214, 217, 219, 227, 229, 235, 258–260, 262, 267, 285–286, 292, 343–346, 392–396, 522, 651, 654, 672, 725
Seven Cities of Cíbola: 12, 70, 133
Seven Cities of Gold: 259
Seven Years' War: 16, 20
sexual abuse: 243, 384
sexual appetite: 11
Shaler, William: 151
Sheen, Charlie: 612, 628, 638
Sheen, Martin: 608, 611, 623, 628, 638
sheep ranching: 15, 325, 343–345, 347, 395, 433
shipping industry: 32, 107, 113, 149, 336, 344–346
Short Eyes: 478, 572, 580
Silva, Rufino: 524
Silva, Trinidad: 612
Silva de Cintrón, Josefina: 244
Silva-Hunter, Margarita: 452
silver: 7, 12–14, 16–18, 32, 59, 67, 69–70, 90, 96, 259, 344, 363, 518, 705
Siqueiros, David Alfaro: 528, 538, 543, 545
Sisters of Charity: 397
Sisters of Loretto: 397
slave states: 157
slave trade: 26–27, 346, 662
slavery: 21, 26–29, 120, 151–153, 178–181, 183, 191, 259, 272–273, 324, 346, 395
Slidell, John: 23
Smits, Jimmy: 568, 584, 610–611, 620, 677
smuggling: 35, 41, 182, 344–345, 729
Social and Public Art Resource Center: 530, 539
social classes: 233, 235, 403, 459, 678, 721–722, 747–748
social clubs: 240, 493
Social Progress Trust Fund: 167
socialists: 171, 370, 480
Sociedad Abakúa: 272
Sociedad Benito Juárez: 36, 748

Sociedad Cuauhtemoc: 36
Sociedad Hidalgo: 748
Sociedad Hispana La Amistad: 748
Sociedad Industrial Cine Puerto Rico: 620
Sociedad Martí-Maceo: 748
Sociedad Pro Arte: 570
Socorro Mission: 144, 146
Solano, Gustavo: 581
sole proprietorships: 355
Solís, Carlos, Jr.: 617
Sombra, La : 667
Somoza, Anastasio: 163, 169
Sonics, Los: 666
sonorense: 16
Sosa and Associates: 349, 358, 363
Sosa, Lionel: 358, 363
Soto, Gary: 473–474, 501–502
Soto, Hernando de: 12, 66–68, 133, 432
Soto, Jorge: 536
Soto, Pedro Juan: 207, 476, 478, 570
Soto, Ricardo (Richard): 613, 615
South Sea Company: 182
Southern California Edison Company: 362
Southwest territories: 291
Southwest Voter Registration Education Project: 340, 755
Soviet Bloc: 173
Soviet Union: 47–48, 53, 165, 170, 172, 211
"Spanglish": 209, 211
Spanish America: 2, 96, 98, 151, 172, 177–180, 182–183, 193, 235, 266, 278, 344, 392, 431, 433–434, 507–508, 515, 520
Spanish American Institute for Boys: 399
Spanish American Publishing Company: 462
Spanish Black Legend: 179–181
Spanish Broadcasting System: 696
Spanish Civil War: 434, 462–464, 557, 559, 564, 749
Spanish Colonial Arts Society: 516–517
Spanish Empire: 16, 19, 28, 59, 74–76, 253, 475, 508
Spanish Governor's Palace: 147
Spanish Information Systems: 698
Spanish International Communications Corporation (SICC): 701–702, 704, 707
Spanish International Network (SIN): 700–704, 706–707, 709
Spanish language: 1–3, 7, 21, 28, 36, 42, 74, 117, 130, 185, 199, 204, 208, 212

Spanish-American War: 40–41, 158–159, 207, 219, 225, 236, 265, 274–275, 286, 292, 367, 458, 482, 557
Spanish-Speaking Community of Maryland: 340
Special Agricultural Workers: 290
spirituality: 37, 54, 253–254, 256, 258, 261–264, 266, 270–271, 394, 480, 496, 505, 528, 530, 565, 567, 761
Spiro, Ellen: 616
Spooner Amendment: 159
squatters: 25–26, 32, 198, 237, 241, 456
Squier, Ephraim G.: 155
St. Francis of Assisi: 271
Stand and Deliver: 609–610, 618–619, 623, 630, 636, 639, 675
statehood: 180–181, 200, 347
Steinberg, Saul P.: 704–705
stereotypes: 52, 181, 196, 216, 297, 384, 460, 464, 497, 556, 560, 566, 568, 587, 589, 592–593, 595–596, 598–601, 604–607, 611, 617, 623, 671–677, 679
Stockton, Robert: 135
Su Teatro: 567
Suárez, Amancio V.: 696–697, 706
Suárez, Roberto: 773–774
Suárez, Virgil: 474, 482–484
Suárez, Xavier L.: 337
suffrage: 24, 119, 240, 244
sugar industry: 4, 7, 26–27, 29, 34, 41–43, 85, 149, 156–157, 160, 163, 166, 182, 191, 207, 219–220, 222–223, 225–226, 366–367, 370, 374, 377, 662
Sun Trust Banks: 357
Sundance Film Festival: 619, 623
Super Bowl: 699, 733, 739, 741
Supreme Revolutionary Congress: 145
Sylvester, Edwin E.: 265

T

Taboada, John: 452
Taft, William Howard: 159–160
Taino Indians. (see also Arawak Indians): 5–7, 56, 537
Talamantes, Frank: 452
Taller Boricua: 243, 536
tallow: 32, 343–346
Tano Indians: 55, 146
Tanon, Olga: 668
Tapia, Luis: 534
Tarascans: 11
tariffs: 29, 91–92, 131–132, 153, 157, 163, 173, 182, 375–376
Taylor, Paul Schuster: 36, 408

Taylor, Zachary: 23, 144–145, 154–155
teamsters: 24, 347
Teatro Alarcón: 550
Teatro Americano: 551
Teatro Arena: 569
Teatro Bellas Artes: 572
teatro bufo cubano: 462, 572–573
Teatro Campesino, El: 565–568, 583–584, 613–614, 618
Teatro Campoamor: 558
Teatro Capitol: 552
Teatro Cervantes: 551, 558
Teatro Cuatro: 569
Teatro de la Esperanza, El: 566–568, 616
Teatro de la Gente, El: 566
Teatro de la Merced: 550
Teatro Español, El: 558, 579
Teatro Guazabara: 569
Teatro Hidalgo: 552, 554, 576
Teatro Hispano, El: 43, 558
Teatro Intimo: 565
Teatro Jurutungo: 569
Teatro La Danza: 572
Teatro Las Máscaras: 572
Teatro México: 552
Teatro Miami: 572
Teatro Nacional: 552, 574–575
Teatro Nacional de Aztlán (TENAZ): 567, 569
Teatro Orilla: 569
Teatro Recreo: 551
Teatro Repertorio Español: 570–571
Teatro Urbano: 566
Teatro Zaragoza: 575
Teatro Zendejas: 552
Tejada, Raquel. See Welch, Raquel
Tejada-Flores, Rick: 613, 617
Tejano: 283, 615, 617, 667–669
Tejeda, Frank: 318–320
telecommunications industry: 173, 357, 681, 694–695
Telemundo: 704–707, 711–716, 718
TeleMúsica: 707, 717
Telesistema Mexicano: 701
Televisa: 701–702, 704, 707, 716
television: 39, 51, 203–204, 207, 244, 248, 266, 348, 362, 436, 482, 495, 499–500, 502, 505, 526, 532, 565, 567–568, 572, 574–577, 580–582, 584, 593, 595–596, 602, 604–605, 607–609, 612–615, 618–619, 621, 623–626, 629, 633, 636, 640, 650, 668, 671, 676–680, 682–683, 689, 691, 693, 696, 699–713, 716–718, 731, 739, 751, 758, 763, 770–773
Teller Amendment: 159
Téllez, Ray: 614, 617

Temas: 688, 703, 710
Temerarios, Los: 666–667
Temple's Theater: 550
Ten Years' War: 28, 46, 182
Tennayuca, Emma: 370
Tenneco Inc.: 357
tent shows: 556–557
Tequesta Indians: 55
Terán, Domingo de: 73
Terrícolas, Los: 666
Teurbe Tolón, Miguel: 458
Tex-Mex: 209, 656–657, 659, 667–668, 691
Texas Association of Mexican American Chambers of Commerce: 341
Texas Rangers: 277, 291, 347, 637, 675, 727
textile industry: 153, 173, 344, 367, 375
Thalia: 570, 573
Third Woman: 242, 244, 414, 471, 490
This Bridge Called My Back: 498
Thomas, John Peter. See Thomas, Piri
Thomas, Piri: 474, 478–479, 502, 570, 572
Three Points Ranch: 346
Tiant, Luis, Sr.: 725, 744
Tiant Vega, Luis Clemente. See Tiant, Luis, Sr.
Tichenor, McHenry Taylor: 695–696
Tichenor Media System: 695–696
Tienda, José de la: 345
Tigres, Los: 667
Tigua Indians: 144
Tiguex: 70–71
Timicuan Indians: 433
Timicuan language: 433
Tin Tan: 647
tinieblas: 269
Tinoco, Federico: 161
Tió, Salvador: 620
Tirado, Cándido: 572
Tirado, Romualdo: 554, 558–559, 582
Title VI of the Civil Rights Act: 294, 378–379
Tlaxcalans: 10, 14, 257
tobacco industry. (see also cigar industry): 27, 41, 45, 149, 157, 160, 182, 207, 219–220, 225–226, 244, 365, 523, 560, 620, 622
Tocobaga Indians: 55
Toddman, Terence A.: 169
Tohono O'odom. See Papago Indians
Tolosa, Juan de: 12
Toltecas en Aztlán: 532, 537–538
Toltecs: 9, 54–55, 520
Torero, Mario: 540

Torres, Art: 334
Torres, Ernest C.: 312
Torres, Esteban Edward: 319–320
Torres, Francisco: 616
Torres, Gerald: 301
Torres, Luis: 614, 744
Torres, Omar: 571, 582
Torres, Salvador Roberto: 523, 532, 538
Torres, Teodoro: 459
Torres-Blasini, Gladys: 452
Torriente, Cristóbal: 725
Torruella, Juan R.: 312
trade routes: 229, 346, 392
trading posts: 6, 346
Trambley, Estela Portillo. See Portillo-Trambley, Estela
transcontinental railroad: 229, 324, 433
Transcontinental Treaty. See Adams-Onís Treaty
transportation industry: 156, 166, 328, 330, 346–347, 350, 361, 371, 375, 382, 433, 446, 523, 551
Treaty of Guadalupe Hidalgo: 23–25, 94–95, 154–155, 180, 183, 229, 236, 262, 286, 292, 322, 396, 421
Treaty of Madrid: 182
Treaty of Paris: 30, 103–104, 149, 158, 182, 259, 286–287
Treaty of San Ildefonso: 150
Trejo, Ernesto: 473
Treviño, Jesse: 532–534, 617
Treviño, Jesús Salvador: 482, 612–615, 617–619, 638, 679
Treviño, Lee: 721, 745
Treviño, Rudy: 532–533
Tribune Broadcasting Company: 718
Triplets, Las: 668
Trist, Nicholas: 154
Tropical Film Company: 620
Tropical/Salsa: 667–668
Troyano, Ela: 622
Trúan, George: 533
Trucco, Orestes: 622
Truchas Master: 514
Truffaut, Francois: 624
Trujillato: 222
Trujillo, Molina: 222
Trujillo, Rafael: 163, 168, 486, 583
Trujillo, Richard: 614
Trujillo-Herrera, Rafael: 565
Truman, Harry S: 288
Tubac, Arizona: 74, 134
Tubac Presidio: 134
Tucson, Arizona: 134, 309, 632, 668
Tufiño, Nitza: 243
Tufiño, Rafael: 620

Tully, Ochoa & Company: 347
Tully, Pickney Randolph: 347
Tumacacori. *See* San José de Tumacacori Mission
Tun tun de pasa y griferia: 476
Turco, El: 70
Turn Verein Hall: 550
26th of July Movement: 47
Tyler, John: 153

U

U.S. Army Corps of Engineers: 446–447
U.S. Bureau of the Census: 236
U.S. Customs Service: 239
U.S. Department of Housing and Urban Development: 416
U.S. Department of Transportation: 335, 416
Ubico, Jorge: 163, 165
Ugarte, Salvador: 572
Ulibarrí, Sabine: 503
Ulica, Jorge. *See* Arce, Julio
Unanue, Joseph A.: 349, 352, 363
underemployment: 42, 236
undocumented immigrants: 185–188, 286, 289–290, 384–385
undocumented workers: 189, 244, 293, 368, 377, 383–386, 405–407, 615, 673
Unión Benéfica Mexicana: 748
Unión de Mujeres: 240
Unión Martí-Maceo: 560, 563
Union Theater: 550
United Auto Workers: 319, 371
United Bronx Parents: 216
United Farm Workers: 40, 372, 525, 615, 756, 760, 767
United Farmworkers of America: 371
United Fruit Company: 161, 165
United Nations: 164, 166, 171–172, 280, 363, 424, 429, 448–449, 765, 771
United Press International (UPI): 362, 683, 685, 687, 698, 704, 731
United Provinces of Central America: 152
United States Commission on Civil Rights: 280
United States Information Agency (USIA): 168, 719
Univisa: 702, 707, 716
Univisión: 362, 689, 696, 702–704, 706–710, 712, 714, 716–718
Uranga, Lauro D.: 553
urbanization: 377
Urdaneta, María-Luisa: 249
Uribe, Juan A.: 617

Urista, Alberto Baltazar. *See* Alurista
Urquilla, Pedro Ramón: 452
USS *Maine*: 30, 135, 157–158, 225
Utah Governor's Office on Hispanic Affairs: 341
Ute Indians: 329

V

Vaca, Juan Manuel: 135
Valadez, John: 527
Valdés, James J.: 453
Valdez, Abelardo López: 301
Valdez, Daniel: 613
Valdez, Luis: 466, 468, 565–568, 583–584, 607–608, 617–619, 625, 628, 636, 656, 675, 679
Valdez, Patssi: 527
Valdez, Raúl: 537, 544–545
Valenzuela, Fernando: 745–746
Valenzuela, Gaspar Rodolfo: 453
Valenzuela, José: 616
Valenzuela, Ritchie: 609
Valladares, Armando: 483
Vallbona, Carlos: 453
Vallejo, Guadalupe Mariano: 136
Vallejo, José de Jesús: 138
Vallejo, Salvador: 274
Vallejo Adobe (Fremont, California): 138
Vallejo House (Sonoma, California): 138, 140
Valles, Andrew: 614
Vancouver, George: 346
vandals. *See* Germanic tribes
Vanderbilt, Cornelius: 155
Vando, Gloria: 242
vaqueros. (*see also* cowboys): 14, 345–346, 600, 604, 614, 637–638, 649, 721, 725
Varela, Félix: 263, 457
Vargas, Adolfo: 616
Vargas, Diego de: 260
Vásquez, Esperanza: 243
Vásquez, Joseph B.: 618, 622
Vásquez, Joseph P.: 609, 619
Vásquez Borrego, José: 144
Vásquez de Coronado, Francisco: 12–13, 70, 133
Vásquez Villalpando, Catalina: 332, 774
Vatican: 263–264, 394
vaudeville: 37, 196, 348, 504, 552–553, 555, 558, 562, 565, 568, 572, 574–575, 580, 583, 588–589, 617, 626, 635
Vázquez de Ayllón, Lucas: 62–64
Vega, Bernardo: 464, 479
Vega, Cecilia: 569
Vega, Ed: 479, 481, 504

Velasco, Carlos Ygnacio: 134
Velasco, Luis de: 68, 71–73
Velasco House (Tucson, Arizona): 134
Velásquez, Nydia Margarita: 319
Velásquez v. City of Abilene: 313
Velásquez de Cuéllar, Diego: 6–7
Velázquez, Janeta Loreta: 236
Vélez, Lupe: 592, 595, 638–639
Venegas, Daniel El Malcriado: 459–460, 466, 504, 756
Venema, Paul: 616
Vera, Eduardo: 620
Verdugo, Elena: 677
Vergelín, José: 616
Vespucci, Amerigo: 6, 60
Veterans Administration: 276, 329, 437, 445, 452
Viacom Latino Americano: 706
Vietnam War: 277, 289, 329–330, 465, 539, 566
Vigil-Piñón, Evangelina: 241, 468, 474
Viguié Cajas, Juan Emilio: 620
Viguié Film Productions: 620
Villa, Beto: 656–657, 659
Villa, Francisco (Pancho): 35, 162, 270, 416, 539, 553, 575, 583, 602, 606, 610, 615–616, 629, 639
Villa-Komaroff, Lydia: 453
Villafañe, Angel de: 68
Villalobos, Reynaldo: 620
Villalongín, Carlos: 555
Villalongín, María: 555
Villar, Arturo: 690
Villarini, Pedro: 524, 526
Villarreal, Homer A.: 614
Villarreal, Teresa: 244, 460
Villaseñor, Victor: 474–475, 619, 675
Villegas de Magnón, Leonor: 237, 241, 460
Villita, La: 147
Viola Novelty Company: 459
Viola, P.: 459–460
Viramontes, Helena María: 241, 470
Visigoths. (*see also* Germanic tribes): 3, 176
Vissepó, Mario: 621–622
Vitoria, Francisco: 254
Viva Kennedy Clubs: 280
Vivó, Paquita: 250
Vizcaíno, Sebastián: 73
Volunteers in Service to America (VISTA): 378, 387
voodoo: 271–272
Votaw, Carmen Delgado: 250
Voting Rights Act Amendments of 1982: 293, 313

Voting Rights Act of 1965: 292, 303, 312–313
Voting Rights Act of 1970: 292

W

Walker, William: 155, 181
Walker Commission: 158
Walsh, Raoul: 639
War of Spanish Succession: 259
War on Poverty: 378–379, 387
Warren, Earl: 293
Washington, George: 151, 280, 433, 533
Washington Commission on Hispanic Affairs: 341
weaving: 53, 55, 256
Welch, Raquel: 592, 595, 603, 639–640
West Side Story: 44, 607, 635
Westcott, James D.: 180
Western Federation of Miners: 370
Weyler, Valeriano: 30, 157
Wheaton, Frank H., Jr.: 360
Whitt Company: 459
Wild West Show: 725, 740
Wilson, Pete: 383
Wilson, William: 35
Wilson, Woodrow: 36, 86, 159, 161–162, 171, 288
Wisconsin Governor's Council on Hispanic Affairs: 341

Women's Research and Education Institute: 731
Women's Sports Foundation: 731
wool industry: 32, 259, 344, 347
working-class: 44, 50, 141, 185–186, 192, 208, 222, 227, 319, 348, 399, 404–405, 407, 459, 463, 467, 477, 491, 494, 504, 553–556, 559, 565, 568–569, 571–573, 575, 645, 648, 652–653, 656, 658, 666, 677, 749
working-class culture: 463, 478, 498, 572, 653
World Cup of Soccer: 726
World Series: 699, 724, 727, 729–730, 734–735, 744
World War I: 34–35, 38, 42, 162, 225, 230, 275, 278–279, 286, 367, 417, 516, 520, 526, 620, 674, 749
World War II: 40, 43–44, 163, 165, 168, 191, 207, 225, 230, 232, 241, 275–276, 278, 280, 282, 286, 288, 305–310, 322–323, 326, 331, 348, 367–368, 370–371, 374, 378, 405–407, 417, 458, 463, 465, 481–482, 497, 503, 524, 535–536, 556, 561, 564, 580–581, 587, 593, 596–597, 601, 607, 611, 618, 645, 649–653, 655–656, 674, 693, 749, 760, 765, 768

Y

Yamassee Indians: 273

Yaqui Indians: 16, 36
Ybor. *See* Martínez Ybor, Vicente
yellow journalism: 30, 157, 180, 182
Yonics, Los: 666
Yoruba slaves: 271
Young, Robert: 619–620
Young Lords: 45
Yuma Indians: 74, 347

Z

Zabludovsky, Jacobo: 704
Zaldívar, Gladys: 242
Zaldívar, Vicente de: 72
Zambrana, Ruth: 237
Zamora, Francisco de: 259
Zamora Casas, David: 617
Zapata, Carmen: 582, 584
Zapata, Emiliano: 34, 173, 533, 539, 542
Zapatista National Liberation Army: 173
Zapotecs: 9
Zavala, Lorenzo de: 274
Zelaya, José Santos: 155, 160
Zoot Suit: 567, 584, 609, 618–619, 636, 675
Zoot Suit Riots: 465, 616
Zorro: 594–595, 626–627, 633, 637, 676
Zumárraga, Juan de: 12, 256
Zuni Indians: 55, 72, 141, 259